THE DEVIL'S MILK

In the Rubber Coils
Punch, 1906

THE DEVIL'S MILK
A Social History of Rubber

by JOHN TULLY

MONTHLY REVIEW PRESS
New York

Library of Congress Cataloging-in-Publication Data

Tully, John A. (John Andrew)

  The devil's milk : a social history of rubber / John Tully.

     p. cm.

  Includes bibliographical references and index.

  ISBN 978-1-58367-231-0 (pbk.) — ISBN 978-1-58367-232-7 (cloth)

  1. Rubber industry and trade. I. Title.

  HD9161.A2.T85 2010

  338.4'7678209—dc22

                        2010042687

Monthly Review Press

146 West 29th Street, Suite 6W

New York, NY 10001

5 4 3 2 1

Contents

Dedicated to Roger Casement, Walt Hardenburg, Edmund Morel, Benjamin Saldaña Rocca, Wilmer Tate, Tran Tu Binh, Emile Vandervelde, and Chico Mendes for making a difference; to Steve Miletich, Akron rubber worker who died at Belchite in Spain fighting Franco (who was backed by Harvey Firestone); to Primo Levi, who bore eloquent witness; and to Maria Szaglai and her baby—murdered at Auschwitz-Birkenau—so that we do not forget.

Acknowledgments

Thanks to Goodyear Tyre & Rubber for the experience of taking apart the Banbury mixer at their Melbourne plant back in 1979 and 1985: it was pretty filthy work, but it provided the original impetus for this book. Years later, when I was writing it, my repeated polite requests for a tour of the firm's Melbourne factories did not rate a reply, for reasons about which I can only speculate. The plant is now closed.

Librarians and archivists were much more helpful. Research and writing meant visits to libraries and archives on four continents. Many people helped and among these I must mention Michele Losse, Anne Marshall, Fiona Ainsworth and other members of the archives and library staff at the Royal Botanic Gardens at Kew in London. Piotr Setkiewicz and his staff at the archives of the State Museum of Auschwitz in Poland provided me with invaluable assistance. Dr. Setkiewicz kindly provided me with an English translation of a chapter from a book he recently published on Monowitz.

While on the subject of Oświęcim—the Polish name for Auschwitz— I should thank the staff of the Interfaith Center for Dialogue and Prayer, where I stayed during my visit. After I read about horrible things all day, they provided me with a warm refuge and restored my faith in humanity.

John Miller, Vic Fleischer, Craig Holbert and their colleagues at the University of Akron Archives patiently dealt with my requests for yet more boxes of files, and John kindly loaned me his bicycle so that I could ride down the beautiful Cuyahoga River valley to see the beavers. Thanks to Jeff Franks of the University of Akron's Bierce Library for his help in locating books on his city and for providing me with a temporary library card and email access. Judy James and Mike Elliot of the Akron-Summit County Public Library went out of their way to acquaint me with the library's holdings, including some archival material. Norma Hill at the *Akron Beacon Journal* library kindly assisted me and made me welcome during a visit in 2008. Thanks, too, to Cara Gilgenbach at the Kent State University special collections and archives.

I owe much appreciation to the staff of the Ohio Historical Center in Columbus, Ohio, and to those at the Center for Archival Research, Bowling Green State University, Bowling Green, Ohio. Thanks are also due to the staff of the British Library in London, the Bodleian Library in Oxford, the National Library of Australia in Canberra and the National Archives in London, where I mined much of the material for this book. I also spent some productive days in the Australian Archives at Canberra, made pleasant by the attentive staff and, incredibly in these "user-pays" days, by the near-utopian free tea and coffee! Much of my original spade-work was done in the State Library of Victoria and various university libraries in Melbourne, and many staff offered me their kind assistance. If I do not know their names, it does not mean that I do not appreciate their help. One librarian I must not forget is my colleague Mark Armstrong-Roper at Victoria University. Mark was unfailingly helpful in tracking down and obtaining books and theses from around the world. Nor should I forget the staff of the archives of the Belgian Ministry of Foreign Affairs in Brussels, who allowed me access even though I turned up one cold winter's morning at what, after all, is a busy civil service department, seeking material on what remains a touchy subject for many Belgians. The staff of the French overseas archives at Aix-en-Provence bravely suffered my accent and catered to my needs. I should also thank Peter Arfanis and his staff at the National Archives of Cambodia in Phnom Penh. I particularly appreciated Peter's valiant efforts to keep the lights and computers on when the privatized power company kept turning off the electricity. Nor should I neglect my faculty at Victoria University, which allowed me extended research leave in Europe in December 2005–January 2006 on full pay, and also granted me a half-time faculty research fellowship in 2005, a fully funded trip to Akron in 2006, and gave me leave of absence to return to the city in 2008. Thanks, too, to Dr. Julia Kindt from the Classics Department at Sydney University for sharing her knowledge of Herodotus.

My friends Tony Dewberry and Mike Frost also read chapters and were friendly and supportive, although not uncritically so. Thanks too to

Gabrielle Thomson for reading some chapters and letting me know that they were accessible for an intelligent young person. I should not neglect my colleagues at Victoria University for their suggestions. In particular, thanks to Professor Phillip Deery, who has always been positive about the project and has read portions of the manuscript, and to Dr. Julie Stephens and Professor Rob Pascoe for standing in for me when I was absent overseas. I must also express my gratitude to Professor Michael Yates, editor at Monthly Review Press, for his support and encouragement in guiding this book to publication. My friend and old teacher, Professor David Chandler, also read portions of the manuscript closely and made invaluable suggestions about style and content; in particular he reminded me to avoid adjectival excess. Thanks also to the voluntary staff of the Jewish Holocaust Centre in Melbourne for their efforts to track down survivors of the Buna and finding other material.

Next, I cannot forget my family, including my eldest son Sean and my daughter-in-law Vicky, who welcomed me into their home during my visits to London. Sean's mother, Anna, and her husband, Phillip Turner—as ever—also provided me with hospitality in London, for which I cannot thank them enough. I owe a debt of gratitude to my two younger sons, Alex and Ciaran, for putting up with my absences and being interested even to the extent of always looking out for stories about rubber. I am deeply indebted to my wife, Professor Dorothy Bruck, for her constant support and encouragement and for her intelligent suggestions about the writing and content of this work. It goes without saying that responsibility for any errors is mine alone and my gratitude does not imply that all who helped me necessarily share my interpretations and opinions. All translations, too, are mine unless indicated.

Why a Book on Rubber?

"A book on *what?*" scoffed an acquaintance. "Why rubber?" another demanded incredulously. These were fair questions. The beginning of the answer lies back over twenty years ago when I worked as a rigger in heavy industry and construction. One job involved the overhaul of the Banbury mixer in the Goodyear tire factory in suburban Melbourne: in fact, I worked on it twice in half a decade. Wrestling the machine with chain-block and winch was a filthy job and it took numerous showers and a sauna to get rid of the grime. To this day, my rigger's ticket is stained black. We hoisted ten-ton gearboxes and drive shafts dripping with oil, grease, rubber, and carbon black from a crepuscular basement up towards the sun. My workmates and I were like surgeons suddenly able to walk inside the body of a patient on the operating table, cutting, rejoining, and replacing bits to restore his health. When functioning, our patient—this colossal machine named after a Cornish engineer[1]—gobbled up masticated rubber, carbon black, and sundry other chemicals and vomited it out as the raw material for tires. Working there was a temporary purgatory for us in the engineering crew, but it was everyday life for the ill-paid immigrant machine minders.

Emerging into the daylight thickly coated in muck, a "king of infinity" under the blue sky after the claustrophobic cellars and vats, I wondered if passing motorists had any idea of where the rubber for their tires came from. Upon reflection, the situation bore out what Marx meant when he wrote: "At the first glance, a commodity seems a commonplace sort of thing, one easily understood [but that] analysis shows, that it is a very queer thing indeed, full of metaphysical subtleties and theological whimsies."[2] Beneath the surface impressions of this banal commodity we call rubber is a whole buried world of social relations. Although motorists rarely give their tires a second thought, life as we know it is impossible without rubber.

Decades later, I did postgraduate and postdoctoral research on French colonialism in Indochina. In 1999, delving into the Cambodian and French National Archives for my book *France on the Mekong*,[3] I came across a wealth of documents on the country's rubber plantations. This material formed the basis for a chapter of that book entitled "King Rubber." Further reflection led me to consider writing an entire book on the social aspects of rubber, for while many books have told rubber's story, most have focused on the aspects of invention and technological progress. I do not neglect these aspects of the commodity in this work, but take up the novelist Vicki Baum's point that "what people did to rubber . . . is fascinating," but "more interesting yet . . . [is] what rubber did to people."[4] Janus-faced, rubber has been—as we shall see—both a blessing and a curse.

Marx analyzed capitalism in an earlier period of its development, and while he was remarkably prescient in his forecasts, he did not live to see the era of monopoly capitalism: the economic domination of the globe by giant transnational corporations. Along with the oil business, the rubber industry is perhaps the best illustration of this development. Rubber firms such as Michelin, Goodyear, Dunlop, and Firestone were among the first of the giant corporations to emerge at the beginning of the twentieth century. Given that rubber is crucial for the modern economy, it is little wonder that at certain junctures the industry formed synergic bonds with the state. This was the case in the Third Reich in Germany between 1933 and 1945 when the chemicals giant IG Farben worked in tandem with the Nazi party and the SS to produce synthetic rubber for Hitler's war machine. During the same period, this was also the case in the Western democracies, when the dogmas of free-market capitalism were weighed upon the scales of war and found wanting. U.S. rubber corporations played a key role in the resulting state-directed capitalism.

While the *raison d'être* of capitalism is the accumulation of capital via the production of commodities, all commodities are not the same in their relative economic and social importance. Some, including rubber, are truly indispensable: hence the marriage of the Nazis and IG Farben and the union of Goodyear, Firestone, and BF Goodrich with the U.S. government and military during the Second World War.

It has also been a cruel industry. The monstrous oppression of the rubber slaves at the IG Farben plant at Auschwitz illustrates the depths to which men will sink in pursuit of profits and power. Fifty years or more before the IG Farben rubber plant rose from the Silesian plains, rubber companies were exterminating Indians in the valley of the Putumayo in Peru and King Leopold's rubber men were butchering the people of the Congo basin on a colossal scale.

This book is written from a socialist humanist and ecological perspective, although I hope to have avoided adjectival excess, sectarianism, and intrusive didacticism. Where possible, I have preferred to record the facts and let the reader judge. For me, the story of rubber highlights the problems at the heart of human society and humanity's relationship with nature. As Jack Mundey, the legendary Australian trade unionist and urban ecologist, wrote in his book *Green Bans and Beyond*, "Ecologists with a socialist perspective and socialists with an ecological perspective must form a coalition to tackle the wide-ranging problems relating to human survival. . . . My dream and that . . . of millions . . . of others might then come true: a socialist world with a human face, an ecological heart and an egalitarian body."[5] I second that.

The Muscles and Sinews
of Industrial Society

Think of our industrial structure as a living thing, the skeleton of which is composed of metal and cement, the arterial system of which carries a life stream of oil, and the flexing muscles and sinews of which are of rubber.

—PAUL W. LITCHFIELD
president of Goodyear Tire & Rubber, 1939[1]

Rubber's special characteristics make it what Paul Litchfield called "one of a handful of indispensable industrial commodities." He was speaking to an audience of industrial chemists shortly after the start of the Second World War. War sharpens our wits in many ways, makes us realize what is essential and what isn't. Modern mechanized warfare is absolutely dependent upon a handful of commodities, among them steel, petroleum, and rubber. Rubber has extraordinary qualities found nowhere else in nature. It is elastic: both when stretched and when squeezed it will return to its original shape and size. Its cousin gutta-percha provides a natural plastic, and was once much in demand for electrical and telegraphic insulation. Rubber is flexible, watertight, and airtight, and has a far higher resistance to abrasion than steel and other metals. For this reason, a particularly tough type of vulcanized rubber is sold under the trade name of Linotex and used to line steel bins, chutes, and storage hoppers in mines.[2] Its robust nature is further illustrated by the survival of naturally vulcanized rubber found in 55 million-year-old lignite deposits in Germany. This fossil rubber was still elastic when dug from the ground.[3] Rubber is useful to paleontologists, as Richard Fortey found on a trip to Newfoundland where the rocks containing fossils were so "desperately hard" that specimens could not be removed and taken back to the laboratory. Instead, "pots of latex solution were lugged over the cliffs, and painted on [the fossils] to solidify in the wind." After several coats had congealed, the casts could be peeled off to give perfect replicas of the fossils.[4] In late 2008, NASA found another intriguing use for rubber. The agency dropped ninety yellow rubber ducks into moulins—tubular holes—in the Jakobshavn glacier on Greenland's west coast. The bathtub toys were part of an experiment to ascertain how quickly Arctic ice is melting. Although low-tech, the rubber ducks were chosen for their affordability, buoyancy, and for their ability to withstand low temperatures and physical buffeting. The ducks will drift into the ocean sooner or later, and NASA is offering a reward of $100 to the first person who finds a duck.

The qualities prized by Fortey and NASA hint at the endless industrial and domestic possibilities of rubber. Rubber is resistant to many acids and alkalis, and it can be bonded to wood and a variety of textiles and metals. It can also be blended with common textiles such as nylon, rayon, polyester, and glass fiber into a resilient fabric.[5] It can even be flavored and chewed—chewing gum is made from sapodilla, which is a member of the rubber family. Gum was first patented in the United States in 1869, but it seems that the Mesoamericans chewed sapodilla gum hundreds of years before. By the late 1930s, motorcars contained over 200 rubber parts, apart from the tires. These components, which included radiator hose, fan belts, engine mountings, floor mats, and seat cushions, weighed almost as much as the tires. In 1934, an Akron rubber company boasted that it manufactured 32,000 different products.[6] Many people have heard of the "Ho Chi Minh sandals" worn by Indochinese peasant guerrillas, but few today know that they were once worn by peasants in Mexico and in Greek Macedonia and Thrace. Called *tchariks* in Greece, they were in such demand during the 1920s that 50,000 old tire casings were imported annually into the port of Salonika.[7] On a more whimsical level, an English "cat and dog outfitter" today proudly advertises a set of three mint-scented rubber tennis balls for £20, presumably for sale to wealthy Chelsea dowagers. These uses testify to rubber's versatility. By 1939, crude rubber was, in dollar value, the largest single import into the United States.[8]

India Rubber World, 1930

Its ubiquity is illustrated in the many everyday phrases and expressions we use. Dubious statistics are said to be "rubbery," and decisions endorsed by political puppets are said to be "rubber-stamped" (after J. Leighton's invention of 1862).[9] People who retrain for different jobs are sometimes called "retreads." Naïve gawkers are called "rubbernecks," presumably because their heads swivel about as if on elastic necks. Because it is so commonplace, rubber is as taken for granted by most of us as the air we breathe. We denizens of Western modernity have lost much of the capacity for wonder, yet rubber is a commodity like no other as far as its chemical and physical properties go, and doubly mysterious to most of us in the circumstances of its production. Commodities might generally be nothing more than "ordinary, palpable thing[s]," as Marx put it,[10] but rubber is truly an *extraordinary* substance. To its physical strangeness we should add the enigma that Marx wrote of: "the mystery of the commodity form is simply this, that it mirrors for men the social character of their own labour, mirrors it as an objective character attaching to the labour products themselves, mirrors it as a social natural property of these things."[11] It is with this social character of the commodity of rubber that this book is primarily concerned, although we shall not lose sight of it as a veritable nonpareil among commodity forms.

Origins of the Name "Rubber"

The widespread misinformation about the origins of rubber is mirrored in misconceptions over the history of the word itself. Originally, rubber seems to have gone in the English-speaking world by its French name of *caoutchouc*, itself probably a corruption of the evocative Amerindian word *cauchu* meaning "weeping wood."[12] The tale that the eighteenth-century London savant Dr. Joseph Priestley invented the word "rubber" and its use as an eraser is patently false.[13] Priestley himself made no claims to have invented the use or the name.[14] It was already known as India rubber because of its origin in the West Indies, but it is unlikely that we will ever know who named it. Rubber industry historian B. D. Porritt claims that it was first used as an eraser in France in 1752 and was taken from there to Priestley in London.[15] The Americans seem to have forgotten this usage, as strangers who have walked into a U.S. stationery shop and asked for a "rubber" can attest. If the blushing shop assistant has enough sangfroid, the customer might be directed to a drug store in search of another rubber product—the condom! The origins of the word "latex," which describes the milky secretions of rubber-bearing plants,[16] are more straightforward. The first recorded use of the word "latex" was in 1835 and the word itself is borrowed from the Latin word for liquid. The word was first used for synthetic rubber emulsion in 1937.[17]

The Natural Distribution of Rubber

Rubber is a naturally occurring hydrocarbon, a polymer of the monomer isoprene, described by the chemical formula of CH_2: $C(CH_3)CH:CH_2$.[18] It draws its remarkable elasticity from its molecular structure of "long, crinkled chains,"[19] the structure of which is modified by high heat and the application of sulfur to create a uniquely manmade product by the process of vulcanization. Today, roughly half of the world's rubber comes from natural sources and half is made synthetically. Whether this ratio will or should continue stirs ecological debate. We must consider on the one hand the invasive nature of plantation agriculture on tropical ecosystems and, on the other, the nature of the synthetic industrial process, which relies on polluting raw materials and large inputs of energy and water.[20] The overwhelming bulk of the natural product is grown on plantations in tropical countries and most of this is in turn obtained from the *Hevea brasiliensis* tree, which is native to South America. A smaller amount of rubber is obtained from the *Castilloa elastica* tree, which grows widely in Central and South America. In addition, a variety of native African, Asian, and Oceanic vines were harvested during the rubber boom of the late nineteenth and early twentieth centuries and again during the Second World War. Rubber plants also have a close cousin in the gutta-percha tree (*taban*), which grows wild in Sumatra, Kalimantan, and Malaya, and which was later cultivated on plantations. The coagulated latex of this tree can be formed into a natural plastic, pliable in hot water, but inelastic in ordinary conditions and once prized for electrical insulation, especially for submarine cables. As we shall see in chapter eight, gutta-percha was essential for the electric telegraph, which consolidated the grip of the European powers on their colonial empires.

Such exploited trees and vines, however, form only a fraction of the world's rubber-bearing plants. There are thousands of such plants scattered across the globe, in habitats ranging from tropical rainforests and temperate meadows to the arid mountain slopes of Central Asia. There are some 268 native rubber-bearing plants in India alone, around 137 in Africa, and many potential sources in northern Australia.[21] Of this vast array of plants, however, "few contain enough [rubber] to make extraction worthwhile."[22] A prime example of this is the common European dandelion, the *Taraxacum officinale*, whose leaves are eaten in salads and whose feathery ball-like head figures in games of "she loves me/she loves me not." Although the European countryside contains a vast amount of rubber in the milky secretions of this plant, to collect it, wrote one scientific expert, would be "about as practical as sweeping the highways with a view to collecting and reclaiming rubber dust from abraded tire treads."[23] A better bet is the *Kok-Saghyz*, or "Russian dandelion," which contains about 10 percent rubber. The plant was harvested for high-quality rubber during the Second World War, along with native American shrubs such as goldenrod or milkweed and *guayule* (also known as *Parthenium argentatum*). Thomas Edison became obsessed with the idea of producing commercial quantities of rubber from guayule and other American plants.[24] Just before his death in 1931, he ridiculed the claim that the Soviet Union had produced synthetic rubber from petroleum and advised the United States to stick to guayule "if they would hope to supplant or supplement plantation hevea."[25] As we shall see in part five, such beliefs were to imperil the United States and its allies during the Second World War.

Voracious Demand

The Industrial Revolution eventually created such a demand for raw rubber that the wild rubber producers of the tropical world could not meet it. As early as 1838, the caoutchouc manufacturer Thomas Hancock forecast that there would be a need to plant rubber trees outside of South America to guarantee the supply of raw rubber.[26] Almost forty years later Henry Wickham smuggled thousands of Brazilian hevea seeds to London's Kew Gardens, from whence they were exported to set up plantations elsewhere in the tropical world. These matters are dealt with in part four of this book.

For better or worse, rubber revolutionized land transport and tipped the balance against that other great communications marvel of the nineteenth century, the railroad.[27] The pneumatic tire was to cause U.S. industrial cities, such as Akron, Ohio, to expand at breakneck speed to house the workers required in the gigantic rubber factories. In the process, as we shall see, it was to trigger savage confrontations between Capital and Labor.

Far to the south, the Brazilian metropolis of Manáus emerged, seemingly miraculously, nine hundred miles from the sea in the middle of the trackless Amazonian jungle, its tramways, docks, bordellos, churches, and gin palaces paid for by the soaring profits from the wild rubber industry. The demand for rubber was to see men carve out huge plantations from tropical forests around the world. Roads and railways would be built, along with docks, power stations, and reticulated water supplies. In the process, whole populations would be transplanted to provide the labor power, and the ethnic composition of whole countries would be changed forever, as in Singapore and Malaysia. The demand was to lead to barbarism, as in the Belgian Congo and on the remote banks of the Putumayo River in Peru. It was to render whole technologies obsolete or push them into second place. It is often assumed that the world's multinational corporations postdate the Second World War, but in fact many of them sprang up in the rubber industry in the early twentieth century.[28] In 1848, Marx and Engels had forecast such phenomenal growth—what we call globalization today[29]—arguing that: "the need of a constantly expanding market . . . chases the bourgeoisie over the entire surface of the globe."[30] This is the logic of expansion typically practiced by the giants of the rubber industry.

Household Words

Over the course of the twentieth century, industrial rubber barons became household names; few people have not heard of Firestone, Bridgestone, Pirelli, Goodyear, Michelin, Dunlop, or BF Goodrich. Partly this was due to the aggressive advertising campaigns used to market their products. Rubber manufacturers searched for superlatives and memorable symbols with which to brand their wares. In the early twentieth century, Goodyear's Frank Seiberling adopted the "Wingfoot" symbol for his firm and ceaselessly promoted the company under the slogan of "protect our good name."[31] France's Michelin chose the comically grotesque figure of Bibendum as the company symbol. Found in newspapers and magazines the world over after his birth in 1898, the fat man became one of the most instantly recognizable advertising symbols in history.[32] Bibendum also adorned the splendid stained glass windows of Michelin's art deco offices on London's Fulham Road[33]—and still does, although the premises currently house a restaurant. The English manufacturer Henry A. Cole compared the reliability of his industrial rubber belting to Britannia, who appeared in his advertisements replete with helmet, trident, and Union Jack shield, perched atop a roll of the company's product.[34]

Married to the Rubber Company

For those in managerial and supervisory positions, rubber was an all-embracing way of life, often generating a loyalty to the company that was nearly fanatical. The Australian writer Robert Drewe recalls his father's proud boast: "I'm a Dunlop man."[35] The Pennsylvania Dutchman Walter Klippert was indignant that he didn't immediately get a white collar job in Akron despite his college degree, but he was to spend forty years with the company, most of them in a supervisory role on Goodyear's plantations in the Dutch East Indies.[36] Robert Drewe's father surrounded his family with an extraordinary array of rubber objects:

> We wore, played with, slept on, walked on, sat on, floated on, swam in, sheltered under, showered behind, warmed our feet on, and kept our bathwater from going down the plughole with Dunlop products. . . . We were a one-hundred percent Dunlop family.[37]

Tom Coyne, the "gum-dipped" American-Irish superintendent of Firestone's Xylos plant at Akron, would "belt out safety slogans in the shower" at home and proudly show off his employer's giant factories to his children.[38] Coyne and his wife were as married to Firestone as Robert Drewe's father and mother were to Dunlop, but there was a painful ending for the Coyne family. Demoted to janitor to make way for college-educated men after thirty-seven years of loyal service, Coyne's heart was broken and he contemplated suicide—all too aptly with a rubber tube attached to his car's exhaust pipe in a scene that mirrors Willy Loman's despair in Arthur Miller's *Death of a Salesman*.[39]

Economic Jiu-Jitsu in Finished Form

Industrial society's rubber dependency was highlighted during the two world wars of the last century. During the First World War, a British blockade on the high seas starved Germany and its allies of rubber and contributed in no small way to their defeat. Twenty-odd years later, the Japanese invasion of Southeast Asia cut off the bulk of the Allies' supply of natural rubber: "economic jiu-jitsu in finished form" according to testimony in the U.S. Congress for an economy that had "for more than 100 years . . . accepted rubber as a matter of course" and used it in some 35,000 products.[40] War created an insatiable demand for rubber: every battleship, for example, gobbled hundreds of tons; a medium tank demanded 826 lbs.; a 75 mm gun carriage required 409 lbs.; a fighter plane needed only 146 lbs., not including the tires.[41] The crisis hastened the scientific development and mass production of synthetic rubber and caused the belligerents to scour the globe for alternative sources of the natural product. Their laboratories worked overtime to develop substitutes. Scientists at BF Goodrich's Brecksville, Ohio, laboratories even extracted latex from mushrooms and concluded that although it was "perfectly suited to make heavy high speed truck and aircraft tires," the low rubber yield per plant prevented commercial production.[42] As discussed in chapter 18, slave laborers toiled in a curious greenhouse complex in the village of Rajsko near Auschwitz. Here, the SS *Landwirtschaft* worked on one of Heinrich Himmler's pet projects: the commercial production of the Russian dandelion. Close by at Monowitz, other slaves and "free" workers were building a giant synthetic rubber plant for IG Farben. Thousands of miles away across the Atlantic, a new generation of tappers reopened Brazil's wild rubber industry, which had been ruined by competition from plantation hevea.

In our prosaic and utilitarian industrial societies, we forget rubber's truly remarkable qualities. Rubber, as Austin Coates notes, "can be stretched repeatedly to many times its length, and after each stretching return to the same dimensions." "Nothing else in nature," he concludes, "possesses such elasticity."[43] Indeed, as Jean-Baptiste Serier reminds us in his history of rubber, rubber has "two almost metaphysical characteristics" and seems to exist outside of time and space: because of its elasticity, it will not break, even in the most violent falls, and unlike other heavy solids thrown on the ground it will rebound, rising up with "magical force" almost to the level from which it was dropped.[44] If, as Karl Marx held, commodities are deceptive things, "full of metaphysical subtleties and theological whimsies," then the doubly metaphysical rubber is an incredible commodity indeed.

PART ONE

From the Sacred Essence of Life
to the Muscles and Sinews
of Industrial Society

CHAPTER ONE

Rubber in Mesoamerican Civilizations

The Balls made thereof tho' hard and heavy to the Hand, did bound and fly as well as our Footballs, there being no need to blow them.

—ANTONIO DE HERRARA, 17th century Spanish traveler[1]

Rubber was unknown to most of humanity until Post-Columbian times. Like tobacco, tomatoes, chili, maize, and potatoes, it was a New World product that gradually became available to the rest of the world following the Iberian conquest of the Americas. Before 1492, the peoples of Mexico and Central America had used rubber for recreational, religious, and utilitarian purposes for many centuries, but claims that it was used in Europe in ancient times are dubious. The assertion that King Croesus's Lydian subjects in ancient Asia Minor played with rubber balls, for example, rests upon a faulty reading of Herodotus. The ancient historian does indeed mention that the Greeks inherited ball games from the Lydians[2] and there are extant bas-reliefs depicting such games,[3] but there is no evidence to suggest that the balls were made of rubber. The claim that the Lydians were introduced to rubber balls by the Egyptians, who in turn were introduced to them by the Ethiopians, is embroidery on an already fanciful tale.[4] The contention that a Cairo museum housed a 5,000-year-old Egyptian chariot whose wheels were fitted with rubber tires[5] is also false, although the tale still reemerges from time to time in pulp fiction.

Rubber came into its own with the growth of modern industrial society, but it was important for industrial, religious, trading, medicinal, and recreational purposes in the pre-Columbian civilizations of Mesoamerica.[6] Rubber trees do not grow on the high plateaux of the Mexican interior[7]—and highlanders such as the Aztecs had to import rubber as trade, plunder or tribute from the Gulf coast where the *Castilloa elastica* tree grows wild.[8] Often transported for thousands of miles, the rubber was exchanged for commodities such as jade. It had a variety of domestic applications: the Maya of Yucatan used it for hafting weapons; it was burnt as incense; and the Aztecs and Maya used it to waterproof clothing.[9] While Aztec rubber raincoats shed water, they tended to melt in sunlight,[10] a problem that was unsolved until the nineteenth century. Howard and Ralph Wolf, in their monumental 1936 study of rubber, claim that the Mexicans also used rubber to make shoes and breastplates, and to reinforce arrow quivers.

The earliest European accounts of rubber date from the period of the Spanish conquest, but some of what is reported as "fact" by modern writers using secondary sources is dubious and there are many conflicting claims. A number of writers assert that Christopher Columbus observed the Arawak people playing ball games on his second voyage to Hispaniola in 1493–94[11] and that his crewmate Michele de Cuneo noted latex-bearing trees on the island.[12] Whether this is true is difficult to say. According to T. R. Dawson, the first reference to rubber in print was made by the Spaniard P. M. d'Anghiera in 1530,[13] but we know that Peter Martyr published an earlier account of rubber in 1511.[14] A number of sixteenth and seventeenth century Spanish missionaries observed its use by the Mexicans for medicinal purposes and in religious rites. F. J. de Torquemada, for example, refers to "oil extracted from 'Ulli' [i.e., latex] used to soothe colds in the chest," adding that "it is [also] drunk mixed with cocoa" to ward off dysentery.[15] A modern British writer claims that the Aztecs used rubber for syringes, "which had definite physiological applications."[16]

The Ball Games

Antonio de Herrara y Tordesillas, writing nearly a century after Martyr,[17] has left detailed descriptions of rubber's use in the ball games of the Aztecs. The games have also been described in some detail by modern authors specializing in pre-Columbian history and the period of the Spanish conquest,[18] and echoes of the game of *batey* survive among indigenous people in Mexico today.[19] In an account published in 1915, the English writer Joseph Woodroffe claimed to have observed Indians on the remote Putumayo River of the upper Amazon basin playing a game with a rough rubber ball.[20] Variations on the ball game appear to have been played by Mesoamerican civilizations stretching from Yucatan to Arizona, the latter thousands of miles north of the rubber growing areas.[21] The balls, Herrara wrote, were solid and "made of the Gum of a Tree that grows in hot Countries, which having Holes made in it distils great white Drops, that soon harden and being work'd and moulded together turn as black as pitch" and he marveled at their combination of weight, hardness, and bounce.[22] Some of these ancient, pre-Columbian balls still exist: one dating from tenth-century Chichen Itza in Yucatan resides in the Peabody Museum at Harvard University,[23] and another can be seen in the Musée de Nîmes in France.[24]

Herrara claims that Aztec emperor Montezuma introduced the Spaniards to the ball game, which was played in large stone "tennis courts."[25] Contemporary observers agree that it was an astounding spectacle. The solid balls flew at tremendous speeds, and the players wore thick leather belts and pads to protect themselves from injury, much as the Indians of Sinaloa do today. Even so, writes the Australian Aztec specialist Inga Clendinnen, "the terrible impact of the hard-driven ball . . . was still sometimes sufficiently bruising to lead to internal bleeding and death."[26] The players were celebrities in much the same way as today's sports heroes, although the games they played were infinitely more dangerous than football. Another major difference is that the Mesoamerican games had great religious significance whereas our sporting arenas are populist and secular. "Every Tennis-court was like a Temple," writes Herrara. Priests officiated over proceedings and each court contained two religious idols: one to the god of gaming and the other to the god of the game itself.[27]

In 1552, another traveler, Francisco López de Gómara, published a detailed description of the games, noting that the winner who managed the difficult feat of hitting the heavy ball through a kind of "goal" placed side-on in the walls of the court was "obliged to sacrifice to the gods of the game and the stone."[28] Herrara does not repeat this ambiguous claim, although he writes that "the spectators seeing the Ball so drove through the Hole, which they look'd upon as miraculous, tho' it was only an accident, were wont to affirm, that the Man who did it was certainly a Thief, or an Adulterer, or would dye very soon, since he was so fortunate, and this Success was talk'd of for a long time, till the like hapning again it was forgot."[29] Clendinnen, on the other hand, cites the friar Diego Durán to the effect that such a player "was honoured like a man who had vanquished many warriors in single combat." Apart from such accidental goals, scoring was normally by the slower accumulation of points.[30] The original game appears to have been prohibited by the Spanish, "because of the Mischief that often hapned [sic] at it."[31] However, it is likely that the ban stemmed from the more general suppression of Indian culture and religion. Claims that the conquistador Hernán Cortés took balls and players to the Spanish court in 1528 cannot be verified[32] and appear doubtful given that the Spanish banned the game. Gómara—who appears to be the putative source of the claims—only records that Cortés took back "eight tumblers, several very white Indian men and women, and dwarfs and monsters."[33] Thereafter the game died out rapidly. Fifty years after the conquest and the arrival of Christianity, Durán had difficulty coaxing a group of Aztec elders into staging an unsatisfactory simulacrum of the game.[34]

Blood, rubber, and metaphysics

In our contemporary world, rubber is primarily a utilitarian substance. Yet it also had important ritual/religious uses for the Mesoamerican peoples; unlike us "moderns" living in a globalized age, they seem to have regarded it with awe and veneration. As American academic Susan Toby Evans[35] has observed, rubber symbolized the "sacred essence" of life: the flow of latex from the rubber tree was associated with the flow of blood and "the rubber ball in motion expressed the vitality common to all things that move." In common with many other preindustrial peoples, the Mesoamericans believed that they dwelt in a "living landscape" in which spiritual forces inhabited all things: trees, water, even rocks. In particular, "they revered things that showed signs of life—reflecting mirrors, featherwork, banners that ruffled in the breeze, shining metal that cast hints of brilliance."[36] Rubber, with its unique physical properties, "represented a potent life force" and it was used liberally in the rituals of human sacrifice that cast so dark a pall over these people's lives. The French historian Jean-Baptiste Serier notes that the victims of human sacrifice were painted with stripes of rubber prior to their dispatch at the hands of the priests: "Rubber, the blood of the tree, was the symbol and the substitute for human blood, the substance the most worthy of being offered in sacrifice to the gods."[37] This is gloomy stuff indeed, but as we shall see in later chapters, the Europeans' secular quest for rubber was to cast an even more somber shadow over the lives of the Amerindians and other indigenous peoples.

CHAPTER TWO

Rubber in the Industrial Revolution

Life should not be estimated exclusively by the standard of dollars and cents.
I am not disposed to complain that I have planted and others have gathered
the fruits. A man has cause for regrets only if he sows and no one reaps.
—CHARLES GOODYEAR, inventor of vulcanization[1]

Europeans long regarded rubber as a curiosity. Rolls of *caoutchouc* and balls of rubber—known as "niggerheads" from their alleged resemblance to the skulls of black people—arrived in Europe aboard returning slave ships engaged in the Triangular Trade,[2] and were marveled at for their properties of stretch and bounce. There were some practical uses: the early Spanish troops in Mexico were said to have adopted the local custom of using latex to waterproof their clothing,[3] but it was some time before rubber was considered suitable for such purposes in Europe itself. Consideration of the commercial and industrial possibilities of rubber date from the Enlightenment, and it was not until the nineteenth century's Industrial Revolution that rubber's potential began to be realized.

The Enlightenment

During the eighteenth-century Enlightenment, a number of scientific expeditions left Europe to study the geography and plants and animals of South America. The French savant Charles Marie de la Condamine, who

sailed to Guayaquil on the west coast of South America in 1734, led one
of the most important of these expeditions. In an epic journey,
Condamine crossed the Andes and paddled by canoe down the Amazon
River to the port of Pará (Belém). Two native Amazonian plants in particular caught his attention: the cinchona bush, from which quinine is
derived, and the mighty tree he named the "heve," which under the name
of hevea (*Hevea brasiliensis*) was to become the world's most prolific
source of natural rubber.[4] Quinine, it should be noted, was to prove
essential to ward off malaria for rubber workers and planters when the
hevea was later transplanted from Amazonia to Asia and Africa.
Condamine took samples of hevea latex to Paris in 1736 and his writings
caught the attention of the educated public. He had observed the Omagua
people of the Solimões reaches of the Amazon using rubber to make bottles, shoes, hollow balls, and drinking syringes,[5] and he experimented
with his samples upon his return to Paris, using them to waterproof a coat
and make a case for his quadrant.[6]

Condamine's contemporary, the French military engineer François
Fresneau, further stimulated public curiosity. Fresneau had spent fourteen years working on the fortifications at Cayenne and used his spare
time to make a close study of the hevea tree, which grew wild in the nearby forests. He used the latex to make tarpaulins and airtight bags to preserve food, and in a paper written in 1747 he foresaw rubber's use in an
even wider variety of products, including "waterproof cloth, fire-fighting
pumps, awnings, diving suits, pot handles, ammunition cases, boots and
carriage harnesses."[7] Shortly afterwards, Parisian draftsmen used rubber
as an eraser, it was used to make surgical catheters, and French boys
played games with rubber balls.[8] According to the American writer Mark
Kurlansky, the Basques introduced the balls to Europe shortly after the
conquest of the New World.[9]

Rubber Balloons and Manned Flight

Within a few decades, rubber was being employed for purposes that
Fresneau may not have imagined. Man's yearning to fly was encapsulated
in the legend of Icarus, who soared into the sky only to have his waxen
wings melt in the sunlight. According to a well-known poem by Bertolt
Brecht,[10] in 1592 a tailor crashed to the cobblestones after leaping from a
German cathedral spire flapping a pair of artificial wings. In fact, the tai-

lor, Albrecht Berblinger, lived much later, and in 1811 he was dragged from the freezing waters of the Danube after an abortive flight from Ulm's Adler Bastion. In Brecht's version, the city's bishop had sneered that man was not a bird and could never fly. Rubber, however, was to help prove the bishop wrong on the second count.

On September 19, 1783, King Louis XVI of France witnessed a remarkable spectacle unfold on the grounds of his palace at Versailles when paper manufacturers Joseph and Jacques Montgolfier managed to launch a sheep, a rooster, and a duck in a basket suspended from a hot air balloon powered by the updraft from burning paper. The following year Pélâtre de Rosier and the Marquis d'Arlandes flew six miles across Paris at a height of 300 feet in a similar device. A few years later, the physicist Jacques Charles ascended to a height of 9,000 feet in a balloon from the Tuileries gardens and traveled twenty-seven miles in a little over two hours, an astoundingly short time compared with the terrestrial travel of the day. Significantly for our story and for future aviation, Charles had made his balloon leakproof by painting the cloth with rubber dissolved in turpentine.[11] Two years later, French aeronaut Jean Pierre Blanchard and American physician John Jeffries crossed the English Channel in a similar machine. In 1797, the intrepid A. J. Garnerin jumped from a balloon above Revolutionary Paris, suspended by a silk parachute coated in rubber, and landed safely.[12] For the times, these flights were as momentous as the launch of Sputnik in 1957 and Yuri Gagarin's trip into space in 1960 aboard a spacecraft that also depended on a myriad of rubber parts. They were also precursors of the giant Zeppelins of Germany and Akron—huge lighter-than-air dirigibles—that were once regarded as the alternative to airplanes.[13] Although given a bad name following disasters involving hydrogen-filled craft, it is possible that Zeppelins filled with the inert gas helium might yet make a comeback as the cost of aviation fuel for conventional aircraft becomes prohibitively expensive and oil reserves continue to decline.

Technical Problems of Caoutchouc

There were, however, serious drawbacks with India rubber, or *caoutchouc*, as it was still widely known. It was sticky and smelly in temperate conditions, melted in heat, and when cold or aged, it became brittle, so that cloth treated with the rubber and turpentine mixture could not be folded without cracking. It was many years before chemists solved these problems, but even by the 1790s there were some improvements; M. Fabroni substituted "rectified petrol" or light oil for turpentine to render rubber fluid and M. Gassart discovered that rubber could be bonded to itself or other substances if dissolved in ether, a finding that was later to have great practical consequences. Another Frenchman named Foucroy discovered that alkalis could check the natural coagulation of latex,[14] and although this seemed of little practical use then, there would come a time when large volumes of liquid latex were shipped across the oceans and stored in vats in the industrial cities of America and Europe. Some 130 years later, Dunlop scientists created foam rubber by processing liquid latex with domestic electric whisks. The outcome was the "Dunlopillo" mattress, which came on the market in 1929.[15] The work of Fabroni and Jacques Charles had more immediate commercial consequences: a number of manufacturers began production of rubberized garments in the late eighteenth century. Samuel Peel of London patented waterproofed cloth in 1790, and George Angus and Co. manufactured rubberized hose and belting at their St. John's Works in Newcastle-upon-Tyne and at Bentham in Yorkshire the same year.[16] In 1803, an Austrian entrepreneur opened a rubber factory at St. Denis in Paris, producing elastic (rubber) bands, garters, and braces.[17] Three years earlier, the Brazilian Francisco Xavier d'Oliveira advertised his rubber goods in the *Gazete de Lisboa*; these included "fine rubber probes, rubber candles, and little bags to hold the urine of incontinent persons or even 'gonorrheal' materials . . ."[18] D'Oliveira's products were rudimentary, but they presaged the rubber medical goods that are indispensable today.

The Industrial Revolution

The efforts of a small number of industrial innovators and entrepreneurs established rubber as one of the Industrial Revolution's foremost indispensable commodities. One of these innovators was the self-taught engineer, canny entrepreneur, and notable eccentric Thomas Hancock, a Wiltshire coachmaker who came to London in 1815 to make his fortune. He became interested in rubber—possibly because he was interested in keeping his coach passengers dry—and set his mind to improving the machinery to process it at his factory on the Goswell Road in Stoke Newington. In 1821, he built his first "masticator," a machine to chew up raw rubber for easier conversion into finished products.[19] Shrewdly, he kept its workings secret for a dozen years—calling it his "pickling machine"—before his competitors discovered how it worked (although by then he had patented it).[20] He also invented elastic rubber thread, but this was not really a viable product until after the invention of the vulcanization process. After his Stoke Newington factory burned down in 1834, Hancock shifted his enterprise to Manchester, where he went into partnership with another of the great rubber entrepreneur-inventors of the Victorian era, the Glaswegian chemist Charles Macintosh.[21]

In 1823, Macintosh radically improved the quality of rubberized fabric by sandwiching a layer of naphtha-treated rubber between two layers of cloth. Naphtha was a cheap and plentiful byproduct of coal gas production and of little economic value until Macintosh used it to treat rubber. The following year he moved his business to Manchester, partly because he was unable to raise sufficient capital in Glasgow for his new venture and partly because of the easy availability of cloth and coal in smoky "Cottonopolis." Both he and Manchester became synonymous with rubberized raincoats. Later, he joined forces with the formidable Thomas Hancock, who turned out high-quality rubber sheeting and other products in his new Manchester factory. By the end of the century, two-thirds of the world's eponymous "Mackintoshes" (or "macs" as the British call them) were made in Manchester and Salford and Britain supplied 90 percent of the world's demand.[22] Macintosh's reputation was made in 1827, when a bag of cocoa fell into the sea on Captain W. E. Parry's epic voyage to the North Pole. Parry attested that "This bag, being made of Macintoshes [sic] waterproof canvas, did not suffer the slightest injury . . . I know of no other material with an equal weight as equally durable and watertight—in the latter quality it is altogether perfect."[23] In view of his work, Macintosh was made a Fellow of the Royal Society.[24] In time, the Mackintosh [sic] Company faced strong competition from rivals such as Joseph Mandleburg and Isidore Frankenburg, Jewish immigrants from Kraków, Poland, and Russia. Frankenburg even became mayor of Salford in 1905;[25] this was no mean feat in a pervasively anti-Semitic era. The industry Macintosh founded remained a mainstay of the Manchester economy until the 1950s, when cheaper chemically waterproofed clothing and synthetic materials such as Terylene and plastic supplanted it. Today, the original macs survive in the United Kingdom as a niche market product.[26]

The Discovery of Vulcanization

When Macintosh and Hancock were setting up, rubber goods still had
many unpleasant characteristics. They were smelly and while they maintained pliability if warmed by body heat, they would become hard and
brittle at low temperatures. A solution to the problem was discovered
across the Atlantic. The United States had been importing finished rubber goods for some time from Brazil, but in 1832 Edwin M. Chaffee
decided to try his luck and launch a rubber factory in New England.
Chaffee was a brilliant engineer in his own right: in 1836 he built what
was probably the first mill and calendar for mixing and sheeting rubber.
Named "the Mammoth," it was sold at auction seven years later when his
business folded under the impact of recession.[27] The Roxbury Company
also secured commercial rights for patent leather made from rubber, but
technical difficulties plagued its production.[28] One of the unlucky Chaffee
employees was a young chemist from Connecticut named Charles
Goodyear. If any scientist-inventor in history fits the stereotype of the gifted but unworldly boffin it is this man. His is the archetypal tale of the
genius in a garret, scoffed at and considered mad, but for once the hyperbole is slight. Goodyear often lived hand to mouth and died bankrupt,
leaving others to capitalize on his great invention, which he called "vulcanization" after Vulcan, the ancient Roman god of fire.

In 1839, working in his improvised laboratory, Goodyear found that if
rubber was mixed with sulfur at high temperatures it was radically meta-
morphosed and could stand extremes of heat and cold without melting or
cracking. The process also did away with the atrocious odor, which had
deterred potential customers from purchasing rubber goods. In effect,
Goodyear had created a new substance from raw rubber and in 1843 he
took out a patent on the process. He unlocked what one author considered "the greatest industrial secret of the ninetheenth century"[29] and the
road was clear for a rubber revolution. By the 1850s, a thriving rubber
industry had grown in New York State and Salem, Massachusetts.[30] In
1844, across the Atlantic, perhaps independently of Goodyear, Thomas
Hancock also succeeded in vulcanizing a batch of rubber, but he does not
appear to have claimed the invention as his own.

The Great Transformation

By Thomas Hancock's death in 1865, Victorian industrial and domestic life was transformed by vulcanized rubber. The industry was producing a huge range of products including "hose and belting, flooring and footwear, sports goods, waterproof garments, anesthetic equipment, catheters, airbeds, hot water bottles, railway buffers, piston rings, electric insulation, dental plates, washers, gaskets, grommets, seals"[31] and much more. Housewives and manufacturers used rubber seals on preservative jars for foodstuffs, which was essential before refrigeration. Costermongers, many of them children, hawked rubber garters in the streets of London.[32] Macintosh's "Pocket Siphonia" appeared: a lightweight raincoat weighing only 10 ounces that could be rolled up and stuffed into a pocket when not in use.[33] Rubber bands (patented by the English inventor Stephen Perry in 1845) were used for a myriad of purposes in the home, shops, offices, and industries—leading to the well-known engineers' joke about machines held together by rubber bands. In 1858, the American inventor Hyman Lipman was granted a patent for the first pencil with an eraser attached, only to have it withdrawn when the authorities decided that it was merely a combination of two existing products.[34] Rubber was indispensable in pumps and steam engines. Hancock's elastic thread—viable after vulcanization—was widely used in elastic-sided boots, surgical bandages, belts, braces, and the like. Rubber and gutta-percha replaced leather drive belting in factories and firemen doused blazes with water pumped through solid rubber hoses covered in proofed canvas.[35]

Most rubber is soft and pliable, but in 1843 Thomas Hancock made a hard rubber he called ebonite or vulcanite by heating rubber for two hours with molten sulfur at temperatures of over 300° Fahrenheit. The resulting substance was almost black in color and resembled horn in appearance and texture. By the 1860s, vulcanized rubber was widely used for a variety of goods including combs, corset stays, electrical insulators, and parts for telegraph equipment, battery cases, jewelry, buttons, brooches, fountain pens, flutes, revolver hand grips, and cigarette lighters.[36] Hancock's multifarious rubber wares are described and illustrated in a book he published in 1857, and this remains a valuable historical record.[37] His products included buffer and bearing springs, cylinders, foot and valve pumps for ocean steamers, solid rubber tires, engine packing, forcing pumps, teagles or hoist strops for lifting in lieu of manila rope slings, gas bags, rollers for letterpress printing, sewer and sink valves, hydrostatic beds, chemical aprons, sleeves and gloves, injection bottles, breast bottles, exhausting bells, enemas, urinals, earpads, truss pads, corn protectors, finger stalls, chest expanders, sponging baths, gum rings, nipples, nursing aprons, bathing caps, tobacco pouches, dress dilators, decanter stoppers, footballs, cricket gloves and bat covers, capes, chesterfield wrappers, webbing for gussets, braces, ladies' paletots, sou'westers, deck boots, life belts, and curious items of Victorian apparel called diving dresses.[38] In 1845, a firm in Cincinnati, Ohio, began the manufacture of billiard tables with rubber cushions, thus improving a game dating back through Elizabethan England to the ancient Greeks.[39] The carriages used on the first line of the London Underground railway, opened on January 10, 1863, were gas-lit, the coal gas being stored in "long India rubber bags within wooden boxes . . . and piped through to the lights."[40] The method was used until the introduction of electric lighting in 1890,[41] and even then, rubber and gutta-percha were employed as electrical insulators on the wires and fittings.

In 1850, there was an unsuccessful attempt to lay a rubber-insulated submarine cable from Dover to Calais. The second attempt one year later succeeded, and in 1858 the first transatlantic cable was laid between Ireland and Newfoundland by civil engineer Isambard Kingdom Brunel's colossal steamship, *The Great Eastern*.[42] The cable, the brainchild of an American financier named Cyrus Field, weighed well over 2,000 tons, over one-eighth of which was gutta-percha insulation, made of latex from trees in Malaya and Sumatra. Although the cable was protected by layers of tarred hemp and wound iron wire, the gutta-percha was essential protection and insulation from the seawater. By the 1880s, there were some 200,000 nautical miles of deep-sea telegraph cables crisscrossing the ocean floors—an unprecedented communications revolution and a *sine qua non* of the far-flung European empires. More prosaically, British citizens were able to remain dry-footed when rubber replaced leather for their Wellington boots (gumboots or rubber galoshes) from the early 1850s, and by this time the Americans were importing over half a million pairs of rubber shoes each year from Pará in Brazil, where they were made by Indians in primitive workshops.[43] Some of these "shoes" were made by allowing latex to coagulate on the makers' bare feet.[44]

Rubber was prominent at the opening of the Crystal Palace in West London in 1851, when millions of people attended the trade fair. There, in that "palace built of iron and glass" as the American newspaperman

Horace Greeley observed, "India rubber was everywhere," with almost a dozen manufacturers displaying their wares to the "rubbernecking" multitudes. One of these exhibitors was Charles Goodyear.[45]

In the 1850s, a now forgotten but inventive Frenchman named Lavater went into the rubber business, manufacturing a range of goods including rubber urinals, pessaries, and surgical goods. He also appears to have invented the rubber suction bracket (circa 1859), by which shelving and other objects could be affixed to walls, and the colored rubber toy balloon, which became an instant success. Fifty years later, a man called Ambrose Foster recalled his experiences working in northern England as Lavater's balloon salesman:

> Most of the goods being comparative novelties, I had very little trouble disposing of them . . . we had for customers for these balloons all the vagabonds, street hawkers and costermongers for miles around waiting a long time before the place was open. They actually fought for them, there was such a quick sale. They all had to be inflated by a bellows, coloured powder being blown into them and tied at the end before being ready for sale. . . .[46]

By the 1880s, the uses of rubber seemed limitless. A rubber manufacturer coyly advertised his "Ladies' Bust Improver" in the pages of the *India Rubber Journal*,[47] rubber chest expanders had come into vogue, the alarmingly named Sphincter Grip Armoured Hose Company was warning competitors against patent breaches,[48] and a German engineer called Busse had used rubber for pavement in Hanover, Berlin, and Basle.[49] By 1888, U.S. lawmen were taking advantage of silent rubber soles to creep up on criminals. This innovation was introduced by the London police in their vain attempt to apprehend the serial killer Jack the Ripper, who was terrorizing Whitechapel in 1888. The police speculated that the killer was able to surprise his victims by wearing noiseless rubber-soled boots.[50]

Curiously, there is little inkling of any of this great transformation in the works of Charles Dickens, one of the century's greatest writers and social critics. As George Orwell observed, "Dickens shows no interest either in the details of machinery or in the things machinery can do. . . . Several of the inventions and discoveries which have made the modern world possible (the electric telegraph, the breech-loading gun, India-rubber, coal gas, wood-pulp paper) first appeared in Dickens' lifetime, but he scarcely notes them in his books."[51] Rubbish tips (also known as landfills), Orwell might have added, are archaeological treasure troves, but the reader of Dickens' *Our Mutual Friend* is given little inkling of what the tip that gave wealth to Mr. Boffin, "the Golden Dustman," might have contained.

The Vulcanized Rubber Condom

Hancock and other Victorian chroniclers are too prudish to mention it, but another balloon-like product to benefit from vulcanization was the humble condom. As authors Susan Zimet and Victor Goodman[52] note in their book *The Great Cover Up: A Condom Compendium*, prior to the vulcanized rubber version, which first appeared in 1843, people had tried all kinds of bizarre methods and materials for contraception.[53] Vulcanized rubber condoms, owing to their unrivalled efficacy, became the almost universal form of birth control and were obtainable in barbershops. Rubber pessaries were also available. Some English condoms were sold in packets bearing a picture of Queen Victoria, who may not have been amused, particularly had she lived to hear the Beatles sing of her portrait on such a packet in a man's pocket in the song "Penny Lane." Other packets bore a likeness of her Prime Minister, William Ewart Gladstone,[54] who may have dispensed them during his social work endeavors with "fallen women."

Prudishness and religious dogma would seem to have impeded advertisements for the devices and in some cases prevented their manufacture. Robert Drewe records how his father, a Dunlop executive in Australia, contemplated going back into condom production fifty years after the product had been scrapped by a Catholic company chairman,[55] although historian Geoffrey Blainey considers the tale to be of dubious authenticity.[56] The first instance of an advertisement for condoms may have appeared in *The New York Times* in 1861, when a firm touted "Dr. Powers' French Preservatives," but a Goodyear catalog advertised vaginal pessaries in 1843.[57] Twelve years after the Powers advertisement, the Comstock Act made such advertisements illegal and also allowed the confiscation of condoms sold through the mail.[58]

Condom users were often jittery for other reasons. A proportion of condoms were defective, and official prudishness impeded quality control. A BBC journalist noted that, "one rumor in the early days of condom manufacture was that the law required every tenth condom to be faulty, and another said that Catholic workers in condom factories would stick holes in condoms with pins."[59] Intriguingly, the early rubber condoms needed to be laundered, although this became unnecessary with the introduction of latex models in the 1930s. More recent innovations include biodegradable condoms, sheaths that glow in the dark, flavored condoms, and even Japanese musical prophylactics implanted with a microchip that play the Beatles' song "Love Me Do" during coitus. Most bizarre of all, perhaps, were the camouflaged condoms once issued by the Swedish army.[60]

The latex condom has always played a part in the prevention of sexually transmitted diseases (STDs), and this use has skyrocketed in recent decades with the spread of HIV-AIDS and new strains of the hepatitis virus. Indeed, it might be argued that without the humble condom, society as we know it might perish in parts of the world. Figures from nine sub-Saharan African countries indicate that on average the citizens of those countries used almost 200 million condoms per year between 1989 and 2000, which produced encouraging results in combating AIDS as a result.[61] The urban legend of Catholic workers being instructed by the clergy to pierce holes in condoms is fanciful, but in the face of the HIV pandemic, the Church still persists in its folly of banning condom use and urging people to practice abstinence. The Church's ignorance is matched by that of the former President of South Africa, Thabo Mbeki, who denied any connection between HIV and AIDS.

Mr. and Mrs. Blowup and Friends

The boundaries between fashion and fetish have often been indistinct. Rubber fetishism is a persistent phenomenon, but could not have existed before the invention of vulcanized rubber clothing. Steele writes of an advertisement in a London newspaper in 1870 for a "gentleman's night-shirt" made of rubber, with a "night cap in macintosh cloth"[62] completing what must have been a sweatily constricting ensemble clearly not aimed at the mainstream sleeper. One of the oldest English fetishists' clubs is the Mackintosh Society, the members of which are a primary market for the old macs, which were sidelined during the 1950s by garments made of new synthetic waterproof fabrics. Although the substance is harmless in itself, it would seem that *Vogue*'s Candice Bushnell is correct in saying, "[t]o put it bluntly, rubber is power and sex." Rubber is the preferred garb for many dominatrixes; the sight of a woman dressed in a tight-fitting rubber corset and shiny high-heeled boots screams domination. Many rubber fetishists are obsessed with the gothic fantasies and weird apparel of such U.S. super-heroes as Batman and Robin. Homosexual rubber fetishists—who can be seen in Gay Mardi Gras parades in many cities today—call themselves "rubbermen." Thus, the rubber and latex fetishists are one group who most decidedly do not view rubber as mundane. As Janet Bloor and John D. Sinclair have written, "The hardest thing to get across in a book is the tactile nature of rubber—its supple capacity to change and deform constantly during use. Rubber must be touched to be fully appreciated. Rubber fetishists know this—to them it's the ultimate sensual experience."[63] Bloor and Sinclair's book, in fact, is bound in a rubber cover. Manifestations of this fetish are amusing, bizarre, or attractive, depending on one's predilections, and include "wet look" latex, rubber gas masks, brassières and underpants, and "gimps" or full rubber head masks with zips. In a recent search, one online catalogue offers products such as latex masks, bondage helmets, gags, inflatables, deflatables, bags, uniforms, TV clothing, underwear, corsets, capes, latex polish, dresses, skirts and tops, leotards, and male and female catsuits. The curious Londoner can visit the monthly London Fetish Fair, which features a stall run by the rubber enthusiasts Mr. and Mrs. Blowup, who have appeared on television wearing rubber outfits to "pad around the house."[64] I was disturbed to find that long ago a fetishist, perhaps, had torn out the pages corresponding to an article entitled "Style for bathing accessories" in a 1930 edition of *India Rubber World* in the State Library of Victoria.[65] Even more desperate, perhaps, was the twenty-three-year-old man recently charged with breaking into the Laneway Adult Shop in Cairns, Australia. The *Cairns Post* reported that the man smashed his way into the shop, had sex with the rubber blow-up dolls, and discarded them in a nearby alley.[66]

Rubber Alligators, Dy-Dee Dolls, and Other Toys

In 1928, the *India Rubber Journal* carried an article describing the "Blud-Rub," a rubber "scalp massage device" with an electric motor attached which "gently but firmly grips the scalp and gives a deep and thorough manipulation." As a result, the article continued, "[c]irculation is quickened, toxic poisons and waste matter carried away, fresh nourishment is brought to the entire scalp, and the dry, shriveled hair cells begin to take on new life."[67] Despite this claim, the device vanished without a trace. Rubber was also indispensable for early Hollywood movie props. By the 1930s, a number of Akron rubber workers had moved to California to make rubber rifles, pistols, hand grenades, handcuffs, and other "g-men paraphernalia," along with more prosaic items such as rubber fish and roast chickens. The film *Murder in the Zoo* demanded the appearance of an alligator, so a plaster cast was made of a live saurian manipulated "in a dormant state." Artists rendered the rubber reptile lifelike with paint and it was mounted on small trucks, which were moved around below the water line. *The Country Doctor* called for rubber babies, and when a director complained that the wooden decks used in *Mutiny on the Bounty* were too noisy underfoot, they were replaced with sponge rubber. The creation of cinematic monsters posed few problems for inventive rubber propmakers.[68]

In 1937, Akron journalist Pres Bergin reported that the city's rubber industry was "helping to teach the world's young ladies between toddling age and the teens and up the duties of motherhood." By Christmas, she estimated, three quarters of a million American girls would be the proud owners of the new rubber "Dy-Dee dolls," who wet their diapers.[69] In the same year, a toymaker of Volga German and Dutch ancestry called Dietrich G. Rempel started work for the Sun Rubber Company at Barberton on the outskirts of Akron. Although the company later switched to hot water bottles and moved to California, in its heyday Rempel gained some fame as a mold designer for an array of once well-known rubber toys such as Frisky the Horse, Milky the Cow, and Balky the Mule.[70]

"Bulletproof" rubber

While rubber is an amazing substance, some people attributed to it miraculous qualities that the most dedicated fetishist would find farfetched. In the mid-nineteenth century, the British War Office decided that rubber was bulletproof. They believed this because someone had fired a live round through a piece of rubber sheeting covered with paper and upon inspection the paper was seen to have a hole in it, whereas the rubber did not. Thomas Hancock warned that the hole in the rubber had simply closed up, but the mandarins did not believe him. Worried that British soldiers would be clad in rubber vests and sent to certain death, Hancock staged a more rigorous experiment to deter the bureaucrats from their folly: he fixed a side of mutton to a wall, covered it with rubber sheeting, took aim and shot it. As James McMillan recounts, the rifle ball not only penetrated both rubber and mutton, but also embedded itself halfway into the bricks behind.[71] Almost a century later, the ability of rubber sheeting to "heal" itself after being punctured was to lead to the development of self-sealing fuel cells for military aircraft. Also, in an irony that Hancock did not anticipate, rubber was used to make the so-called "Belfast dildo" used by the British army during the "Troubles" in the North of Ireland from the late 1960s. These were long blunt-nosed black rubber bullets of "about the same weight and hardness as a cricket ball," that sped from the muzzle of a squaddie's rifle at double the speed of a ball hurled by the fastest baseball pitcher. Used as a supposedly non-lethal alternative to regular bullets, they killed a number of civilians, including children, and caused facial disfigurement, blindness, and anosmia in others.[72] Some decades earlier, at the outset of the Second World War, the Mayo Clinic in the United States had pioneered the use of rubber for prosthetic noses and ears for war-wounded soldiers. Made of almost translucent, unvulcanized rubber, these flesh-like artificial appendages could even be given wrinkles and other blemishes.[73]

At the same time as the British War Office "wallahs" were appalling Hancock, chemists were laying the basis for the development of synthetic rubber. As early as 1833, scientists in England and Germany were attempting to break down rubber into its constituents. In 1860, the Englishman Greville Williams succeeded in isolating isoprene and then "polymerizing" it back into rubber. Other scientists discovered that it was relatively easy to convert isoprene back into rubber by treating it with hydrochloric acid. The problem, however, was that the raw material for the "synthetic" rubber was natural rubber: it was an interesting academic exercise, but not yet of practical value. In 1882, however, William Tilden made the first "true" synthetic rubber in his laboratory by deriving isoprene from turpentine. Unfortunately, turpentine, which is extracted from certain types of pine tree, was "expensive, relatively scarce and just as subject to market manipulation as rubber."[74] The production of synthetic rubber on a commercial basis had to wait until, under the stimulus of natural rubber shortages during the First World War, large chemical corporations were able to devote large amounts of capital and know-how to its manufacture.

Tire builder in the Goodyear plant, Akron, OH, early 20th century.

The Pneumatic Tire

Today, rubber is virtually synonymous with pneumatic tires. The wheel is rightly reckoned as one of the most significant inventions in human history, but it took the addition of compressed air-filled rubber tires to bring it to perfection. The Scottish engineer Robert William Thomson took out the first patent on a pneumatic tire in 1845. It was not very successful or reliable and was regarded as something of a novelty, even by Thomson himself, who lost interest in the idea.[75] Solid rubber tires seemed assured of a long future even though the influential Thomas Hancock suggested some eleven years after Thomson that a serviceable pneumatic tire was possible.[76] Hancock, after all, was manufacturing a number of other successful inflatable rubber products, including pontoons and boats.[77] The bicycle itself had been invented in 1839 by another Scotsman, Kirkpatrick Macmillan, a few years after smooth road surfaces had been developed by his countryman, civil engineer Thomas McAdam. Cruelly, Thomson has been forgotten, and the tire is almost universally associated with the Ulster Scot John Boyd Dunlop. Dunlop was a Belfast veterinarian, a "big, shambling, black-bearded fellow," whose son was a keen cyclist. The bicycles of the day were known, very aptly, as bone-shakers. Even if equipped with solid rubber tires over their steel rims, they bruised the cyclist's nether regions. In 1888, Dunlop took his son's bicycle into his workshop and equipped it with primitive pneumatic tires made of cloth wrappings and inflated lengths of rubber sheeting. The other children laughed at the bulbous wheels, but their derision soon turned to admiration when Dunlop Junior was able to comfortably navigate rough surfaces with a greater turn of speed than they had imagined possible. The new tires were soon afterwards used in cycle races with the same effect and the guffaws of spectators subsided into respectful murmurs.

Dunlop moved to Dublin in 1889 when he entered a partnership with the du Cros family and set up the Dunlop Rubber Company. Alas, Dunlop's business acumen did not match his technical ingenuity and his wily Huguenot partners soon took control of the firm. The firm struck a major hitch when it was disclosed that Robert Thomson's original patent was still valid. This was offset when the firm bought the rights to detachable tires and valves, although Dunlop himself resigned from the company in 1895. According to James McMillan's history of the firm, John Dunlop never really gave a reason for this, and was seemingly content to retire on the £100,000 he received for his share of the business. Shortly afterwards, the company moved the center of its operations to Coventry in England, some said because of complaints by Dubliners about the stink of naphtha, although the du Cros family joked that it was because they could not stand the stench of the Liffey. Afterwards they sold the firm for a large profit, and it eventually mushroomed into the globe-spanning multinational corporation that is a household word today.[78] Meanwhile, cycling, already popular before Dunlop, claimed many millions of new enthusiasts around the world. One of these was King Norodom, the nominal ruler of the remote French protectorate of Cambodia. On a number of occasions, French bystanders laughed as the king wobbled by over the pot-holed streets of Phnom Penh, followed by a clutch of cycling courtiers. Inevitably, the king would fall off, whereupon in order that he might save face, his faithful retinue would deliberately follow suit.[79] More competent cyclists thought nothing of cycling fifty miles in a day, and the du Cros family cheerfully pedaled the 103 miles from Dublin to Belfast and back between sunrise and sunset.[80] Another keen cyclist was a Frenchman named Michelin, who tried the new pneumatic tires on a trip from Paris to Rouen.[81] Afterwards, he was to become famous as part owner of a great rival of the Dunlop's. It was only a matter of time before the pneumatic tire was adapted for the new motor vehicles, thus creating the greatest single market for raw rubber.

CHAPTER THREE

The Dark Side of the Rubber Revolution

[I saw] three of the very dirtiest men I have ever laid eyes on lying . . . just
outside the factory mill room. . . . They were quite evidently sick as well as
dirty . . . for we . . . saw that not only were they covered with carbon black,
but they were choking out blue-colored froth from their mouths.
—FERNLEY H. BANBURY, after a visit
to the Pennsylvania Rubber Company, 1916[1]

No capitalist concern is in business for the love of it. The motivating force is
dollars, dollars, and more dollars.
—SHERMAN H. DALRYMPLE, International President United Rubber
Workers of America, radio broadcast, Akron, Ohio, February 1936[2]

By the 1890s, rubber had come to stay: mass industrial society could not
function without it. Indubitably, rubber was a boon for humanity, yet the
growth of the industry contained a massive contradiction for it brought
with it industrial drudgery, in which men and women spent their lives in
factories and workshops that remained Dickensian until well into the
twentieth century (and beyond in the case of the Third World). It was also
accompanied by profound ecological degradation. We have already mentioned Mayhew's child costermongers, who hawked garters on London
streets or balloons in Leeds or Manchester, but many thousands of other
children were slaves to the machines in the stench and gloom of the rub-

ber factories. Details of working lives in the early rubber factories are scanty, although as the writer F. I. Tuckwell has speculated, we can assume that "they were as bad as in other industries at that time" and that "the workers were probably 'sweated'; their hours long and their wages at subsistence level." No rubber worker has left his or her memoirs, and those captains of the industry who did write focused on invention and commerce, not the lives of the laborers. Thomas Hancock writes of waterproofing between 3,000 and 4,000 yards of fabric in a day, but as Tuckwell notes, "it would be interesting to know the length of the day." These early factories were often set up in "'adapted buildings' in which space was cramped; lighting was poor; ventilation and heating were scarcely considered; whilst noise from the machinery and the dirt and smell from the rubber must have been almost intolerable."[3] Unguarded machinery was widespread and often led to appalling accidents. In one instance at the India Rubber Company's works at College Point, Long Island, in 1888, a laborer named William Smith bent to blow dust from the gears of a machine. Unfortunately, "[h]is long beard caught in the [unguarded] gears, and pulled the flesh entirely off his chin, and partly from his cheeks."[4]

Deskilling

Some early rubber workers seem to have had levels of skill far above the norm for later operatives in the industry. Skilled weavers were employed to make elastic thread into webbing for elastic-sided boots and surgical bandages. Other operatives made the whole of a rubber boot themselves, "for Hancock mentions the fact that a man could make 12 pairs of shoes a day."[5] Mass production brought with it deskilling and what Harry Braverman called the division of labor at the enterprise level: one worker would make the heels, another would fashion the soles, another cut out the sides of the boot, and yet another assembled the pieces and glued them together. Although production was streamlined, perhaps more importantly, the bargaining power and control of the skilled craftsmen over their work was vastly diminished. As will be shown in later chapters, a similar process of deskilling occurs in the mass production sectors of the rubber industry, particularly with the manufacture of automobile tires.

Fire was a constant hazard in all sections of the industry. As already noted, Thomas Hancock shifted his premises from London to

Manchester in 1834 after his Stoke Newington works burned down. Almost seventy years later, another fire partly destroyed the St Mungo Golf Ball Company's factory in Glasgow.[6] Such incidents were common; textile historian Sarah Levitt records that the press cuttings section of the Manchester Central Library is "peppered with accounts of 'conflagrations'" in the city's rubberized garment industry. Five workers died at Charles Macintosh's works in 1838 when a large vat of highly inflammable naphtha caught fire on the top floor, causing several stories to collapse. The more enlightened David Moseley, Macintosh's keen rival in Manchester, kept his naphtha tanks in separate buildings, and it seems that he deliberately sited his factory in a bend in the River Medlock in order to have ready access to water for firefighting.[7] Nevertheless, fires continued to be a major hazard in rubber plants; there was, for instance, a serious naphtha fire at a Hackney factory in 1891.[8] It also would seem that minor fires were a constant threat to those employed in glueing pieces of raincoat together: "it is no unusual thing," according to the *India Rubber Journal* in the 1880s, "to see a whole piece of cemented cloth suddenly burst into flame from the heat of the drying table."[9]

Workers Trying to Fly

Many of the chemicals used in the industry were highly toxic. The naphtha used as a rubber solvent had a strongly disagreeable odor, and one journalist noted after a visit to the Macintosh works in 1890 that it irritated the lungs. Worse still, those who worked with it would sometimes develop excruciating headaches and would act as if they were drunk. A worker informed the journalist "that after a busy day in his part of the factory, he no sooner emerged into the fresh air than he has commenced staggering and reeling as if under the influence of strong spirits." American workers would later call the condition "naphtha jag" and worry about its long-term effects. Another widely used chemical was carbon bisulfide, which caused workers to hallucinate and even run around "flapping their arms and trying to fly."[10]

Conditions in the Manchester mackintosh trade were no better than in such London and American death traps. Although there were some progressive employers who provided fire escapes, decent lighting, and fresh air and water for their employees, many workers slaved in primitive conditions for long hours. In 1889, the House of Lords set up a select committee under Lord Dunraven to probe conditions in the industry, and found that long hours, poor ventilation, and low wages were the norm. An employee called Kate Hughes testified to receiving breadline wages of five shillings and sixpence a week, with seasonal variations, and Joseph Gronnowksi, an employer, gave evidence of employees working up to twenty hours straight.[11] The Jewish rubberized garment workers might have smiled wryly at Morris Rosenfeldt's Yiddish poem, "In the Sweat Shop," had they the time to read it:

> There are times when the clock
> Seems to scorn and to mock,
> And I will understand
> What is meant by each hand;
> What the dull ticking sound
> Says to drive and to hound
> And to goad me so sore,
> As it cries ever more:
> "Get to work! Get to work!
> Never pause, never shirk
> For thou art a machine!"[12]

Maisie Mosco's novel *Almonds and Raisins*,[13] published in 1979, tells of the lives of Manchester's Jewish mackintosh workers in an earlier age when much of the trade was dominated by small businessmen who operated on the very edge of profitability by cutting corners on safety and paying well below the official union rates in their sweatshops. The working day often extended from six or seven a.m. until midnight[14] and the workers were crammed into every conceivable bit of space in converted houses: as late as 1947, Board of Trade inspectors found "sewing machines under the stairs."[15] Mosco describes her fictional hero's first impressions of such a den:

Abraham caught his breath at the foetid atmosphere which came at him in a sickening wave. At first he thought the room was windowless. Harsh gaslight hollowed the workers' faces as they bent over sewing machines crammed into every inch of available space . . . [However] this room was not windowless he saw now, but the grime-blackened glass was like a shutter between the people who toiled here and the sky, denying the existence of any other world but this . . .[16]

A little later, Abraham's companion informs him:

"Here they make waterproofs, I can tell by the stink. It makes me want to
throw up. . . . It's the varnish they glue the hems down with," Shloime told
him when they reached the workroom. "Judah's a *shmearer*, that's what they
call those who do that job." Abraham got a glimpse of the *shmearer*'s fingers
swooping birdlike into cans of the malodorous substance, then flying lightning fast along the edges of garments. . . . [17]

When Abraham shudders that he wouldn't do that job even "for a fortune." Shloime tells him, "For that job they don't pay no fortune," but
adds that "Me, I'd do anything," because "[a]nything is better than nothing."[18] Such attitudes, Mosco comments, perpetuated poor wages and
conditions: "the main reason for continued exploitation was the trump
card held by the employers; the majority of Jewish garment workers still
thought they were lucky to be employed and feared they would lose their
jobs if they joined a union."[19] Yet there were attempts to unionize the
mainly Jewish immigrant workforce in the 1880s and there were a number of strikes in the 1890s. One of these, in September 1890, was led by
trade unionist Mr. I. Sugar. The workers demanded an end to cuts in
piecework rates, a fifty-nine-hour week, and a ten-hour cap on weekly
overtime.[20] The most effective workers' organization seems to have been
the Waterproof Garments and Machinists Trade Union, set up in 1907.
Despite its existence, as late as 1935 the union journal *The Waterproofer*
wrote of the "sheer horror" of the working conditions in the sweatshops
and wondered how the workers could stand it.[21]

Chemicals, Dust, Heat, and Noise

If the working conditions in this earlier, laissez-faire period of capitalist
production were poor, monopoly capitalism proved only marginally better. The conditions of workers in the rubberized garment trades were
duplicated in some respects in the huge tire factories that sprang up with
the mass production of motor cars. In the mills at Akron, Ohio, workers
routinely endured "dust and flying soapstone" or nodded "drunkenly in
the benzine vapors above concrete tanks," state the Wolf brothers.[22]
Soapstone or steatite is a naturally occurring soft rock comprised mainly
of talc. It is widely used in tire manufacture and in garages to keep inner

tubes and other components elastic and prevent them from cracking under heat. As *The New York Times* advised its readers, "A liberal use of talc or soapstone on the inside of the tire before the tube is put in will help to overcome the bad effects of heat. . . ."[23] The effect of talc dust on workers' respiratory systems is another question.

The veteran union organizer John D. House recalled the pressures of work on the tire builders at Akron in the 1920s. Coaxed, cajoled, and threatened by foremen and company pacesetters to ever greater outputs, House and his fellow tire builders had to toughen their hands with formaldehyde and tallow. Even then, they would finish each shift with their fingers rubbed raw and bleeding.[24]

Among the worst places to work were "the hot, black, stinking environment called the mill room" and the enervating heat of the tire curing floor, dubbed "the Pit,"[25] where men worked stripped to the waist in a lather of sweat with the stench of sulfuretted hydrogen in the air. In 1926, Dan Goodenberger, a Firestone supervisor, told a journalist that the Pit got its name "because of the terrible conditions. The heat was so intense in summer and the ventilation was poor." An old-timer named William Moore, who had come to Akron from Montreal to work for the Diamond Rubber Company in 1908, told the reporter that "[d]ue to the intense heat, congested condition of the Pit, the suffocating steam and wet floors, it was very often necessary to slow down work during the summer months as men on every hand were prostrated."[26] When he spoke to the reporter in 1926, Moore was sixty-three years old and had worked in the Pit for almost twenty years. He was pleased to say that during that time some of the worst aspects of the place had been improved, with better ventilation and "cleverly designed machines" that made the work lighter.[27] Yet the Pit maintained its grim reputation, and the new technology also had the effect of eliminating jobs.

Workers complained of "rubber poisoning." In 1913, Belle Myers, a female rubber worker in an Akron plant, complained of soapstone dust on her clothing, and of the oppressively acid atmosphere and the lack of ventilation in the mill. Others routinely experienced headaches, dizziness, and nosebleeds.[28] The heat and chemicals that were used combined with the insufficient ventilation also caused dermatitis, chronic rashes, and even unconsciousness. The company doctors declared there was no such thing, yet there was no doubt about the potential harm of the aromatic solvents commonly used in the mills,[29] which included benzene, toluene, xylene, and naphtha. Experts have attested that "any odor [of aromatics] means that concentrations are above safe levels." Furthermore, exposure to high concentrations of aromatic hydrocarbons can destroy bone marrow, induce leukemia and other cancers, and damage chromosomes and genetic material. Ominously, "people who work with aromatics gradually lose their ability to smell them."[30]

The effects of exposure to the reek of impure carbon bisulfide,[31] which was widely used in the process of cold vulcanization, had been known for decades. A worker who showed a journalist around a British rubber plant in the 1880s testified that once in the open air after a busy day in the factory working with the chemical, he would commence "staggering and reeling" as if under the influence of strong drink. After inhaling carbon bisulfide, he claimed, men and boys would run round flapping their arms, as if trying to fly.[32] Afterwards, those who were affected would inevitably develop a splitting headache. In 1898, a London rubber manufacturer had been prosecuted for illegally employing a child of thirteen years of age to use the chemical in his work. Revealingly, the defense attorney justified his client's actions by arguing that "it would be impossible to carry on the business at a profit if men had to be employed to do the work." The company was fined twenty shillings with twenty-five shillings costs.[33]

The atmosphere in the Akron mills was thick with toxins such as hydrogen sulfide and sulfur dioxide, gases that irritate the eyes and upper respiratory tract and can cause pulmonary edema, a condition causing its victim's lungs to fill with fluid. Prolonged exposure to these gases can also cause brain damage. Another culprit widely used in the rubber factories was lead, which builds up in the brain, liver, kidneys, aorta, bones, and muscles, and can cause permanent damage to the central and peripheral nervous systems.[34] Decades after the effects of such toxins were validated in medical journals, the Akron companies could not claim ignorance as an excuse. And yet in 1941 three claims for death and twenty-two for disability from benzene poisoning in the Ohio rubber factories were filed in the Ohio Industrial Committee.[35] The Firestone company still denies ever using benzene at Akron, despite evidence that tire builders routinely used "benny" to add "tack" to rubber.[36]

The Blue Men

Perhaps most bizarre of all was the condition in which men's skin literally turned blue from cyanosis[37] following exposure to aniline dye, a chem-

ical that BF Goodrich scientist Dr. George Oenslager had discovered
would strengthen rubber products and speed up the vulcanization
process. After trials with unwitting human guinea pigs, Dr. Oenslager
found that although most workers could tolerate only limited exposure to
the chemical without falling sick, a select few "blue men" were apparently immune to its deleterious effects. These same men were also unaffect-
ed by the great 1919 influenza epidemic that killed millions around the
world, he observed,[38] although what the connection is remains a mystery.
Aniline dyes were in use in the Akron mills as late as 1930[39]; despite the
industry admitting that they were a serious health hazard they were much
too profitable to discard.[40]

Decades later, despite company safety campaigns and union scrutiny,
the rubber mills remained dangerous places. The Akron memoirist Joyce
Dyer describes the Xylos recycling plant in South Akron where her father,
Tom Coyne, worked for thirty-seven years as superintendent of
Firestone's most dangerous factory. Not only was there a witch's brew of
caustic chemicals at Xylos, but there were hog mills with rotating rolls and
giant mechanical scissors and tottering piles of tires stacked everywhere
under a three-storey digester plant that "belched . . . sour air into South
Akron twenty-four hours a day."[41] Roger Shuy, a linguistic researcher,
recorded the difficulties he encountered talking with Firestone workers
because of the high levels of noise inside the plant.[42] Frances Golliday, a
Goodyear employee during the Second World War, told of how she
worked rolling glue onto the seams of rubber barrage balloons and how
"You'd get drunk in there—from the fumes."[43] Dorothy Chevin, who
worked in the company's dope room at the same time, wondered how
long workers lived after exposure to the poisonous fumes.[44]

Rubber factories are hot places, and it has since been recognized that
continual exposure to high temperatures can be injurious to health.
Working in the hot and ill-ventilated parts of the rubber factories such as
the mill room and curing pits, particularly during the summer months,
was taxing as there was little understanding of the necessity to gradually
accustom workers to high heat and to constantly rehydrate, given that the
sensation of thirst lags behind the actual need for replenishment of flu-
ids.[45] It is unlikely that pausing to drink water was factored into the calculations of the management, who regarded their "subjects" as machines.

Sometimes the occupational health issues have extended far beyond
the rubber industry itself. In the late twentieth century, for example, there
was an epidemic of disabling dermatitis and asthma among medical work-

ers who had worn cheap latex gloves and were affected by the low-quality powdered latex on them. In the worst cases, the condition led to anaphylactic shock and death. In 2001, the British Trades Union Congress (TUC)[46] estimated that at least 100,000 National Health Service staff had developed latex allergies, along with between 500,000 and three million people in the British population as a whole. In Germany, according to the same source, one third of all occupational asthma cases resulted from exposure to latex. Although use of the gloves was promoted to protect healthcare workers from blood-borne diseases, the TUC argued, the cheap gloves perhaps caused more problems than the illnesses they were designed to prevent.[47]

Rubber workers fought back. The *India Rubber Journal* reported a number of strikes in the English elastic webbing trade in the 1880s and 1890s. In 1888, the Bruce & Wykes works at Leicester was strikebound for five months after repeated cuts to the men's wages had reduced their earnings to between 40 and 50 percent of what they had made fourteen years previously. Such wages, the workers complained, were "impossible to live on,"[48] but just enough not to die on, as the old saying goes. In the same year, female sole and heel workers at the Myer Rubber Company put their tools down when the company closed the factory windows on a hot summer day, claiming that the goods were affected by "prickly heat." The women only returned to work "when they were promised plenty of fresh air."[49]

The Great Silvertown Strike

In 1889, a bitter strike broke out at the huge works of the India Rubber, Gutta-Percha and Telegraph Company's works at Silvertown in London's East End. The company claimed that a majority of employees were opposed to the strike but were "intimidated into leaving their work" by large crowds of picketers. The union claimed that the dispute was a lockout, engineered after the company reneged on an agreement to increase pay, despite making a clear profit of £166,000 per year from its lucrative cable manufacturing and intercontinental laying operations. The union accused the company of "slave driving" and a large proportion of the population of Silvertown and West Ham agreed. Mass meetings and parades of strikers and their supporters turned out despite "bitterly cold weather" to hear union heavyweights such as Ben Tillett and Tom Mann urge them to stick together for victory. The dispute wore on amidst rumors of the imminent arrival of strikebreakers, and there were serious clashes between picketers and police. The London Trades Council urged the strikers to stay out, but the cold winter, uncertainty about the outcome, and company intransigence saw first a trickle, and then a flood of strikers returning to work. In the end, twelve weeks after the dispute began, the last of the strikers slunk back through the factory gates.[50] It was later revealed that the company had been able to comfortably maintain production at their other factory in France,[51] especially as there was a growing shortage of gutta-percha. As we shall see in subsequent chapters, the rubber industry in the United States witnessed industrial battles of enormous proportions.

. . .

THE RUBBER MANUFACTURING INDUSTRY of Europe and North America was established during the early, laissez-faire period of capitalism in the nineteenth century and was characterized by relatively small-scale production, constantly evolving technology, and fierce competition between large numbers of small producers. During this chaotic and uneven period of growth what Karl Polanyi called the "self-regulating market"[1] was given its head by compliant governments. It was an experiment—a gigantic leap of faith into the future—that had profound consequences for humanity and even the ecology of the planet. The "experimental" and unfinished nature of the new rubber industry was reflected in the ad hoc way the raw material for its mass production was obtained. The manufacturing industry was essentially supplied by a primitive pre-capitalist "mode of extraction" that resembled feudalism and contained elements of slavery. It is extraordinary how such a primitive extractive industry was able to service a modern manufacturing industry. Perhaps most extraordinary of all was the fact that gutta-percha, the indispensable natural plastic used to insulate the hundreds of thousands of miles of undersea telegraph cable on which the colonial empires depended, was extracted by similar means.

PART TWO

Wild Rubber:
A Primitive "Mode of Extraction"

CHAPTER FOUR

The Amazon Rubber Boom

The Brazilians can see nothing here but. . . the damnable commodity which
is . . . [Amazonia's] ruin. . . . The passengers on the river boats are rubber
men, and the cargoes are rubber. All the talk is of rubber. There are no manufactures, no agriculture, no fisheries, and no saw-mills, in a region that could
feed, clothe, and shelter the population of a continent.

—H. M. TOMLINSON, 1912[1]

The Amazon basin is an immensity of tropical lowland which contains
some 30,000 miles of waterways and comprises an area two-thirds the
size of Europe. Much of it is blanketed by *selvas* (dense rainforests) which
shelter the most biodiverse environment on earth.[2] Although there is evidence that intensive agriculture in Pre-Columbian times supported a fairly large population,[3] since the arrival of the Portuguese the basin has
relied economically on the extraction of products from wild plants and
animals, including spices such as cloves and vanilla, brazil nuts, animal
skins, vegetable oils and saps, tropical timbers, turtle eggs, and *cinchona*
bark (or quinine). During the nineteenth and early twentieth centuries,
the foremost of these exports was rubber from the basin's many species of
wild rubber trees, such as the *Castilloa elastica* and the *Hevea brasiliensis*.[4] Between 1890 and 1920 the basin was gripped by rubber fever, a
speculative boom that went bust when cheaper and more reliable supplies
of plantation hevea became available. Although the production of
Amazonian rubber did not immediately cease—and the volume initially

increased after 1910—there was a steep decline in profit rates, and the region steadily lost ground to the plantation product. The local economy never recovered from the blow.

The Rubber Barons

"At Manaos," wrote an observer in 1887, "there is enough India rubber to coat the civilised world."[5] The Amazon rubber barons employed thousands of men to extract the rubber and get it to the market. The Bolivian government granted huge concessions to local and overseas businessmen, who were entitled to purchase land at four centavos per acre and to enjoy tax-free profits for sixty years. The foreign concessionaires included the American Vanderbilt family, a cousin of U.S. President Teddy Roosevelt, and the Briton Sir Martin Conway. One of the prominent local barons was Vaca Diaz, a Bolivian who settled at the confluence of the Orton and Beni rivers in 1881, granted himself the title of "doctor," and lived the life of a *grand seigneur* in a great villa. Like other barons, Diaz was a ruthless monopolist who forced out competitors on a lawless frontier.[6] His greatest competitor, the "king" of the Javary region in Brazil, Colonel Resendo da Silva, ruled over an estate bigger than Long Island and his splendid house was erected atop sixteen-foot poles.[7] Diaz's Bolivian rivals were Nicolas and Francisco Suarez, who ran a business so large that the French rubber writer Jean-Baptiste Serier dubbed it an empire.[8] In all, the brothers had rubber concessions of over five million hectares and employed some 10,000 workers,[9] including British mechanics and German clerks at their Esperanza headquarters.[10] The "Rockefellers of Rubber" also controlled portage around the cataracts on the Bolivian rivers, extorting a large percentage of the value of all cargoes.[11] Another competitor was the tyrant Tomás Funes, who became Governor of Venezuela's Amazonas province, and whose death by firing squad is recorded in José Eustasio Rivera's novel *La Voragine* (The Vortex).[12] Nor can we forget the sinister Peruvian, Julio César Arana, whose activities are the subject of a following chapter.

The Cities on the Amazon

The Brazilian city of Manáus lay at the center of the rubber lands, nine hundred miles upstream from the Atlantic and six miles up the broad and

dark Rio Negro from its confluence with the Amazon. Near the mouth of
the Amazon sits the old port of Belém, or Pará as it was then known. A further 1,000 miles upstream from Manáus, at the highest navigable point for
ocean-going shipping, is the Peruvian river port of Iquitos. These three
ports, and to a lesser extent the town of Santarém, which lies between
Manáus and Pará where the Tapajós River meets the Amazon, were the
hubs of a vast trade in wild rubber. Between 1860 and 1910, Amazonia
supplied around 60 percent of the world's needs.[13] J. Orton Kerbey,
Pará's U.S. consul at the turn of the nineteenth century, considered the
city to be the "New Orleans of the Amazon."[14] In 1852, rubber made up
almost half of Para's exports, but unsustainable rates of tapping largely
destroyed the hevea stands in the lower Amazon basin.[15]

Iquitos was a frontier slum compared to Pará: perhaps the Amazon's
Dodge City. Originally built to house workers in the government's
machine shops and foundries, which serviced the Peruvian navy's gunboats, the town had also spawned a fringe population of ne'er-do-wells
and speculators who lived by their wits. Some of these were to make a
name—and a fortune—for themselves in the rubber trade. Paramount
among them was Julio César Arana, the town's uncrowned king. After
Callaō on the Pacific coast, this was Peru's second seaport, and its primary export was rubber.[16]

The St. Louis of the Amazon

Manáus, which Consul Kerbey regarded as "the St. Louis" of the
Amazon,[17] was salubrious and cultured in comparison to Iquitos, and certainly far larger: in 1910 it boasted around 50,000 inhabitants. The
American historian E. Bradford Burns[18] has left us a finely drawn, if sanitized, portrait of the town at the zenith of the rubber trade: a city in which
flâneurs could stroll past fashionable shops with French names and, if they
had sufficient funds, could dine in French restaurants. The city boasted a
museum, a spacious public library, public gardens, a zoo, and a meteoro-
logical observatory.[19] Capping it all off was the Opera House, built
between 1891 and 1896 at a cost of around $2,000,000 (not much short
of $50 million in 2007 values).[20] Roofed in blue and gold tiles, it vied for
attention with the city's "massive customs building—modeled on that of
New Delhi, prefabricated in England and shipped out in pieces"[21]—and
with a soaring cathedral and some luxury hotels. The city also housed a

variety of gambling joints, speakeasies, bars, and taverns. An army of prostitutes catered to the city's carnal appetites, for single women were scarce in the city and the authorities winked at the brothels. These contrasts mirrored the sharp social divisions of the boom city, for although "per capita incomes in the Brazilian Amazon climbed by 800 percent" during the fifty years before 1910,[22] they were unevenly distributed. The slums on the edge of town had pools of stagnant water that provided a breeding ground for yellow fever and malaria, and vultures swarmed around the city's garbage dumps.[23] A British Foreign Office report of 1900 noted that only the central city had a proper drainage system.[24]

The Port of Manáus

Steam navigation had begun in the 1850s, but the Amazon was not opened up to foreign competition until 1867.[25] The British-owned Booth Line, which ran a regular service from Liverpool via Portugal across the Atlantic to Pará and up as far as Iquitos, enjoyed a near monopoly of the river's traffic. Originally possessing only a poor river basin, subject to wildly fluctuating water levels, the British-owned Manáus Harbor Ltd. had built an impressive floating dock.[26] In the holds of the foreign-owned ships came the cargoes that kept the city alive, and back into them went wooden boxes packed with raw rubber. In 1910, some 1,675 vessels called at the port, which became so congested that ships would drop anchor midstream to wait for a berth.[27] Despite the bustle, the volume of imported goods and the foreign ownership of shipping and wharf facilities highlighted major problems of economic dependence for the city and Amazonia as a whole.

The Rubber Frenzy

American historian Lewis Tambs dates the start of the Amazonian rubber boom from 1820.[28] More prudently, Barbara Weinstein dates the start of the boom to 1850,[29] with the demand for raw rubber accelerating following the discovery of vulcanization in 1839. Another writer believes that until 1889 "the rubber trade was characterized by a steady and reasonable growth." After that, with the mass production of pneumatic tires for bicycles and cars, the demand for rubber became insatiable in "a succession

of waves which took prices to new levels." Finally, in 1910 came the dizzy-
ing final surge, which took the price of raw rubber to around three dollars
a pound, followed by a sudden and catastrophic crash.[30] By 1919, the
price had fallen to about fifty cents a pound[31] and the boom was over for
good.

The industrialized world's appetite for rubber was enormous and fed
a rollercoaster of boom and bust. Brazilian production rose from 26,750
long tons in 1900 to 42,000 in 1909, but even this was insufficient to feed
industry's hungry maw.[32] The United States consumed two-thirds of
Amazonian rubber, and steamships leaving Pará were said to carry cargoes worth over $500,000.[33] In the mad rush for profit, all sense of pro-
portion was abandoned. By 1907 in Madagascar, the wild rubber plant
known locally as *voehena* had been virtually wiped out by twenty years of
unsustainable harvesting.[34] In 1904, the authorities in British Papua
declared a moratorium on tapping the native *Ficus Rigo* because rubber
companies had been "ruthlessly tapping the trees and cutting up the
vines."[35] Orton Kerbey deplored the profligate methods of rubber collection in Peru, where the *Castilloa elastica* trees were chopped down for the
sake of an immediate fifty cents' worth of latex apiece[36] in what was later
known as "slaughter tapping." The Englishman Percy Fawcett noted that
the rubber industry in Bolivia was being ruined by reckless over-tapping,
with tens of thousands of pounds' worth sitting on the docks waiting shipment to Manáus.[37] Rubber from "God's Tree"[38] accounted for one-third
of Nicaragua's foreign exchange in the 1870s[39] but by the early 1890s
there was scarcely a *Castilloa* left standing on the Mosquito Coast.[40]

This was not the first time the Amazonian basin had been seized by
rubber hysteria. In 1853 the English botanist Richard Spruce had
observed people casting aside their regular occupations to tap rubber:
"Mechanics threw aside their tools, sugar-makers deserted their mills,
and Indians their *roças* [farm clearings], so that sugar, rum, and even *farinha* [manioc flour] were not produced in sufficient quantity."[41] In 1910,
the Pará tram system ground to a halt because the drivers and conductors
had run away to tap rubber.[42]

The "Toff's Riot" in London

In the same year as the Pará fraças, the *Daily Mirror* reported a veritable
"toff's riot" in London over rubber. A crowd of "city men and their

clerks, most of whom were wearing frock coats and silk hats" laid siege to the Chartered Bank of India, China, and Australia in Bishopsgate Street. The disturbance was triggered by people anxious to grab shares in the newly floated Rubana Rubber Estates, managed by the Ramsden group in Malaya. Peace was only restored by the bank's rugby team, which saved the premises from "a dangerous rush."[43]

Meanwhile, in nearby Mincing Lane the rubber trade was booming. In 1910 the ancient lane was a commercial rookery, but in the words of the *India Rubber Journal* "the volume of business and the resources of the firms concentrated . . . [here] are greater than the wealth represented by some of the longest and most imposing West End shopping thorough-fares." Should the visitor have penetrated "the dim interiors of [the] old-fashioned buildings," he would have seen samples of rubber from around the world spread on long tables.[44] The better grades of rubber were said to smell like "fine old Virginia ham"[45] but the worst stank so badly that those working with it were shunned while the lowest quality grades from the Congo were infested with maggots.[46] Although most wild rubber imported into Europe and North America came from Amazonia, a bro-kers' report records smaller amounts from Africa, Assam, Rangoon, Borneo, Madagascar, Java, Mozambique, Central America, the West Indies, Colombia, Carthagena, and Guayaquil.[47] The Akron rubber mogul Harvey Firestone, Jr. told his listeners in a 1932 broadcast how "[a]t the height of the boom, whenever a new rubber company's shares were floated in the morning, they were invariably over-subscribed by night. One morning in January 1910, the Madagascar Company offered its shares for sale, and by evening the shares had been subscribed twenty times over. In the same year a Belgian company declared a dividend of 520 percent or a rate of 10 percent per week. During one period of eight years, net profits totaled more than $6 million from an original capital investment of $200,000."[48]

The Devil's Railway

The rivers were the natural routes of communication in the jungles but the shipment of Bolivian rubber was impeded by a 380-kilometer-long series of cataracts on the Madeira River, a major tributary of the Amazon. Boatmen were frequently drowned in the boiling waters and over one-third of all cargoes were lost in accidents.[49] Therefore, most goods were transported around the cataracts by the Suarez brothers at an exorbitant cost. In 1867, a German engineer named Franz Keller investigated various options for the rapids, including a haulage way, a road, a railroad, and a canal with locks. Three years later, the Massachusetts-born Colonel George E. Church began construction of the rail link, but by 1873 the project was plagued by financial difficulties and he had to abandon what had become known as "the devil's railway."

The project itself had become a tropical "charnel house" in which Spanish, Irish, and Italian navvies died in droves.[50] In places the jungle along the line was so thick that three expert axemen could cut a trail only three feet wide and two hundred yards long in a day, compared with 1,450 yards in the United States. The workers also had to combat hostile Indians and plagues of fire ants, jaguars, deadly snakes, wild pigs, and the deadly piranha fish in the streams. There were also the "sweat flies," a kind of bee that clogged a man's face, nose, and eyes. Quinine was in short supply and half the workforce succumbed to malaria. Yellow fever, blackwater fever, beriberi, and dysentery struck many more workers.[51]

Church resumed his railway project in 1879, this time with an American, Bolivian, and Brazilian workforce, although he was to admit final defeat three years later.[52] With the political support of the Brazilian government and under pressure from the Bolivians, the final successful push for the railroad began in 1907, under the supervision of Percival Farquhar, a Yale-trained engineer who had electrified Havana's tramways.[53] Again, the construction cost human lives. Although the popular claim that each railroad tie represented a human life was hyperbole, the truth was sobering enough: when the line was completed in 1912, out of a total of over 13,000 workers, 1,238 had died, mainly of malaria.[54] Nor did the Bolivians get their sea link, for the rail line was never extended into Bolivian territory.[55] The final irony is that that construction wasn't completed until after the zenith of the rubber boom. Today, one train a week trundles along at thirty miles per hour over a short section of the line:[56] a curious piece of industrial archaeology and a reminder of the dashed hopes of the Amazon rubber boom.

The Collapse of the Boom

U.S. Consul Kerbey sounded like a "booster" when he forecast that "[j]ust as the Amazon is the greatest river in the world, its valleys will

some day be the seat of the greatest empire of the world."[57] His prediction was never fulfilled. As the economic historians Barham and Coomes
have observed, "By the early 1920s . . . per capita income levels had
shrunk to pre-boom levels. Today, nearly a century later, such incomes
(in real terms) have yet to return to boom levels in many areas despite
massive state investment in Amazonia."[58] The world recession following
the First World War pushed rubber prices down to around or even below
the cost of production: in 1918 they fell to sixteen pence a pound;[59] by
1922, the price had plummeted to seven pence a pound and even in well-
organized plantations in the colonial world, tapping virtually ceased.[60] In
comparison to these new plantations, the Amazonian wild rubber industry was backward and it was doomed as a result. "How can Brazil ever
expect to compete against the East as regards costs," complained Joseph
Woodroffe in 1915, "so long as she continues to put out her rubber
amidst such costly, wasteful, and generally undesirable conditions?"[61]
The year 1913 was an important milestone in the history of the rubber
industry, for in that year the output of the Asian plantations exceeded
that of Amazonia by 25 percent.[62] Moreover, Asian rubber was cheaper:
in the same year, the average production cost of Asian rubber was one
shilling and ten pence a pound whereas Amazon rubber cost two
shillings and four pence per pound to produce.[63]

The Ecological School

Economic historians still debate the reasons for the decline of the Amazon
industry and the broader question of blocked economic development. In
1876, English planter and adventurer Henry Wickham transported
70,000 Brazilian hevea seeds to Liverpool and then to the Royal Botanic
Gardens at Kew. The seeds were the stock for the cultivation of plantation
hevea in Asia on a massive scale. By the First World War, the new industry was to supplant Amazonia as the major provider of raw natural rubber.
By cruel ecological irony, belated attempts to farm hevea on a commercial
basis in Brazil were doomed to failure. While *Hevea brasiliensis* grows
happily interspersed with other trees in the Amazon forests, attempts to
cultivate it on plantations fell victim to leaf blight, a fate that all the wealth
of the U.S. tycoon Henry Ford could not change.[64] There is some evidence of formal plantations in the Brazilian Amazon as early as 1865,[65]
and there were certainly castilloa plantations in Belize, Nicaragua, and the

Chiapas region of southern Mexico in the 1890s,[66] but such agribusiness was the exception rather than the rule. C. E. Akers claims that only about 20 percent of two million heveas planted in Brazil before the First World War survived.[67] The English traveler Percy Fawcett considered that the difficulties might have been overcome, had the rubber men not been consumed by "the general desire to get rich quick."[68] It is possible, as Barham and Coomes argue, that the fungus leaf blight only appeared *after* the end of the boom.[69] If this is the case, it reinforces Fawcett's opinion about the get-rich-quick mentality of the rubber barons. Revealingly, the elder of Bolivia's Suarez brothers told the American geographer Earl Hanson in 1931 that he had no need for plantation rubber as heveas flourished in the wild. When pressed on this statement, Suarez said, "Nobody in the Amazon basin had patience enough to care for the young trees during the years that must elapse before they bear fruit."[70]

Dependency Theory

Dependency theorists argue that the Amazon basin was dominated by predatory foreign and domestic capital, which had little interest in balanced economic development. The profits of the boom years, these theorists argue, were simply sucked out of the region.[71] There is a great deal of truth in this: one simply has to ask the question of what happened to the massive profits generated by the rubber trade during the boom years. The shipping industry the basin depended on was foreign-owned, the only bank in Manáus was British, and foreign consortiums were prominent in the rubber industry. Prices were dictated by the buyers in metropolitan countries and Amazonia acted as a huge sponge for a flow of manufactured goods from Europe and North America. The dependency hypothesis has been challenged by Barbara Weinstein, who argued that internal social and economic factors such as class formation and the transition from pre-capitalist modes of production were as important as the external capitalist market in blocking development.[72] In the Amazon, writes Weinstein, industry was dominated by "collecting expeditions" rather than mining or plantations[73]; Michael Stanfield calls this "a mode of extraction" rather than a "mode of production."[74] In the wilder reaches of the basin, rubber entrepreneurs enslaved local Indian tribes in an inefficient, wasteful, and morally indefensible system. In short, Weinstein argues, the industry was organized along primitive, pre-capitalist lines and "a more fragile foundation for a major manufacturing industry is difficult to imagine."[75] It should be added, however, that these systems existed within the mesh of the world imperialist order.

The labor force consisted largely of *seringueiros* (subcontract tappers) who had little interest in wage labor. Together with the rubber bosses (*patrãos*) they were bound into an inefficient and costly "mode of extraction" that enriched parasitic middlemen, turned the *seringueiros* into debt slaves, and acted as a brake on development. The state and federal governments—who controlled import and export taxes respectively—and the Manáus city council were content to milk the trade. Much of the economic windfall of the boom was sucked away by corruption or expended in what were basically "pharaoh projects"—the Manáus Opera House being a case in point—rather than being invested in sustainable economic development. The authorities' profligate habits are best illustrated by Governor Ribeiro's boast that he would have the Opera House pulled down and replaced with an even more opulent building as the city continued to expand. In the same spirit, his successor dynamited the half-built gubernatorial palace and replaced it with a more luxurious residence, all at public expense.[76] This reckless, wasteful public spending was matched by the squandering of the private sector. Much of the domestic profit from the rubber industry was frittered away on imported luxury goods: the tales of Manáus rubber barons watering their favorite horses with buckets of champagne and swells lighting cigars with 500-milreis notes[77] (the equivalent of £30) might be exaggerated, but they bear witness to the dissipation of the boom years.

Import Frenzy

Almost every item sold in Manáus and across the region as a whole was imported. Tinned butter came from Scandinavia, condensed milk provided by Fussell, gramophones were made by Victor, whisky was White Label and Black and White, gin was Booths or Gilbeys; there were French wines and perfumes, European shoes, German machinery, Omega watches, Smith and Wesson revolvers, and Winchester rifles. Even the machetes were imported, along with American typewriters and the German Deutz cars that were confined to the city limits by the jungle.[78] The citizens dined on Portuguese potatoes and salted cauliflower from Belgium,[79] washing them down with imported stout and India Pale Ale from

Seringueiro, native of Ceara,
in Amazon basin,
Brazil, c. 1942

England.[80] The staples of life for the laboring poor were rice from
Rangoon via Liverpool and beans from Argentina, supplemented with
imported tinned fish and fruit,[81] all imported at vastly inflated prices
despite the bounty of nearby tropical forests and rivers teeming with fish
and fruit. Farinha, the staple bread substitute of the poor, was imported
from Marahaõ. Jerked beef was brought from Rio Grande do Sul and
Argentina. Dried codfish was imported from Europe via Hamburg. Flour
was from the United States. The British Foreign Office recorded that
"fancy goods" and jewelry came from Germany and France: hardware,
clocks, earthenware jars, building materials (including sawn timber—a
feat akin to selling ice to Eskimos or carrying coals to Newcastle given the
region's immense forests) were all imported. Bricks and tiles were imported from Marseilles; cement, lime, house fittings, iron girders, and pillars
from Britain; locks, kerosene, and electrical fittings from the United
States; matches from Britain and Sweden via Germany; and furniture and
firearms from Belgium, Germany, and Great Britain.[82] Only after the end
of the rubber boom was there any attempt to broaden the local industrial
base, a program of import substitution made necessary because the population could no longer afford to buy imported goods.[83]

The Curse of the Boom

Looked at in this way, the rubber boom was a curse: economic and social development in the unrestricted free market conditions was dangerously unbalanced by windfall profits and wildcat speculation. What economists call the "Dutch disease"[84] might just as well be called the Brazilian disease. The fortunes generated by the rubber boom evaporated or were sucked away overseas. The entire economy of the Amazon basin was distorted in the process and the social effects of the collapse were grim. When American geographer Earl Hanson traveled through from the Orinoco via the Rio Négro and the Amazon to the Madeira in 1931 and 1932, he saw numerous abandoned towns and villages, some of them with churches and substantial plazas moldering in the heat and damp:

> Outward physical effects of regression were plentifully visible, especially on the lower river [Rio Négro], in the form of numerous ruined stone houses two and sometimes three stories high, grandly and expensively built by the rubber barons, and a number of small villages and trading posts that had obviously been well populated in the rubber days but now were either completely or almost completely abandoned.[85]

Hanson concluded: "It is probable that the present regression of the region is the most complete in its history since the first advent of the Spaniards."[86] The only positive effect was that the Indians who had been forced to gather rubber were now left in peace.[87]

CHAPTER FIVE

The Lives of the *Seringueiros*

The human cattle market was open as long as there was hunger, and there was no lack of buyers. Rare was the steamer in which large numbers of Ceará people were not shipped out.

—Eyewitness cited by Eduardo Galeano[1]

The development of the pneumatic tire in the late nineteenth century sent demand for raw rubber soaring. Profits spiraled dizzily, yet the system that supplied the raw material was wasteful, inefficient, and ultimately unsustainable. In contrast, as the nineteenth century unfolded, most essential raw materials were being extracted by ever more sophisticated machinery. Mines and quarries, for example, were increasingly mechanized and required disciplined armies of workers. Tropical regions saw the expansion of industrial methods of farming that mirrored the mass production industries of the industrial heartlands. Large-scale plantations supplied commodities such as coffee, sugar, cotton, and tea grown and harvested by regimented workforces. It is extraordinary that Latin America's rubber manufacturing industry was dependent upon fickle wild rubber supplies extracted in remote areas by the most primitive of tools and techniques, and without a proletarian labor force. It was as if the iron and steel industry were dependent on minerals grubbed from shallow pits in the ground by lone individuals equipped with no more than a shovel, pickaxe, and wheelbarrow—and then ferried by rowboat many hundreds of miles to the nearest steamship![2]

Although there were some small-scale hevea, castilloa and ficus plantations in Latin America and India from the 1870s, the overwhelming bulk of the world's rubber and gutta-percha was collected from the wilderness. Modern manufacturing was kept afloat by what in some respects resembled a cottage industry in which *seringueiros* carried out much of the work. As demand soared, the rubber-rich Amazon and Congo basins saw the resurgence of slavery to compete, however unsuccessfully, with the new Asian plantations. Whereas the plantations provided a largely standardized product, the quality of Amazon wild rubber varied: it might be not properly cured, or the balls might contain stones and other impurities deliberately concealed within them to defraud the buyer, or a cargo of allegedly fine hard pará might be found to contain low-grade scrap or "sernamby" as it was known in the trade. Yet, as Joseph Woodroffe observed in 1915, it was the system itself, "built up entirely on slavery and peonage," which was "the cause of the crisis in the rubber industry."[3]

"The Most Miserable Life Imaginable"

Over 90 percent of the "free" *seringueiros* were employed under a peculiar and exploitative "sub-contractor" system. Englishman Kenneth Grubb, who traveled through the *selvas* in the early 1930s, said, "The life of the *seringueiro* is the most miserable that can be imagined."[4] Robert Cross, who undertook several expeditions in the basin on behalf of the Royal Botanic Gardens at Kew, told the *Gardener's Chronicle*, "The life of the balsam [i.e., latex] collector . . . is of the most wretched description."[5] The work was seasonal, in part because the torrential rains of the wet season washed the latex from the collection cups and floods made the rivers impassable. The tappers were plagued with swarms of insects, including malarial mosquitoes. Lizzie Hessell, who was married to a plantation manager at Orton, claimed to have killed thirty of the insects in the time it took to write a few brief lines to a friend.[6] For the *seringueiros*, quinine was always in short supply; a sad irony given that the cinchona plant is native to the same forests they worked in. Reptilian terror slithered in the jungle, particularly the savage bushmasters that grow to fourteen feet in length and are best countered with a scythe.[7] Even if the claim of boa constrictors measuring fifty-six feet long is a gross inflation,[8] the truth was frightening enough. Percy Fawcett wrote

that on the day he arrived at the Suarez brothers' settlement of Santa
Rosa on the Abuna River, three rubber tappers died of snakebite.[9] Black
caimans and flesh-eating piranha fish infested the rivers, with crocodiles
in the Orinoco basin. The moist heat coupled with poor sanitation and
diet meant that disease was a constant threat.[10] Hessell recorded that
many tappers succumbed to consumption,[11] and she herself died of a
fever after less than three years in the jungle. The forests also bred ennui;
immured in that endless expanse of massive "broccoli" even the hardiest
of souls could go stir-crazy, mocked by the cries of the black howler monkeys, the crackle and hiss of convectional thunder and rain, and the
ceaseless gurgling of the rivers.

Upon entering those green wastes, there was little chance of the
seringueiro ever seeing home again. A director of the London-based
Eastern Rubber and Produce Trust believed that "[o]f every three laborers
that go into the [Brazilian] forest each season only two return alive . . .
according to published Government figures . . . [and] only desperate men
will go into the forest to do such work and supervise it."[12] In an atypical
account, Percy Fawcett considered that the Brazilian *seringueiros* in the
disputed territory of Acre had a pleasant enough life at the height of the
rubber boom. They were, he claimed, "free from any form of constraint
beyond a contract, and every one of them was making between £500 and
£1,500 a year. They were well-fed, clothed and armed, and lived in *cen-
tros*, huts erected on the river bank close to their *estradas.* . . . Some were
educated men, and most possessed photographs."[13] However, one sus-
pects that these men were a kind of Brazilian elite in Bolivia and not representative of the tappers as a whole.

Housing generally consisted of whatever the *seringueiros* could
improvise. They would clear a patch of jungle with their machetes, taking
care to leave the stumps a yard or so high off the ground. One observer in
the 1880s wrote:

> The *mestizo*,[14] with a genius for saving himself trouble, allows some of the
> harder trees to remain, in order to serve as supports for the roof. The floor of
> the projected dwelling must be raised above the reach of the water, and
> accordingly the felled trees are placed upon the stumps for that purpose.
> Small strips of the murati palm are laid down as flooring. To form the frame-
> work of the roof thin trunks are fixed to the stems that have been left stand-
> ing, and over this are placed immense palm leaves, sheltering a space proba-
> bly sufficient to accommodate a company of twenty persons.[15]

Mats strung from the roof served as walls. Rubbish and excrement was simply hurled from the platform into the jungle or watercourse, with predictable results for the health of the tappers and their families.

The seringueiro's *work*

The working day lasted ten hours. Each *seringueiro* was normally allotted two *estradas* or paths winding between the hevea trees, usually numbering between 130 and 150, but up to 200. This was not an orderly plantation. The wild heveas, majestic trees rising seventy-five or one hundred feet into the upper canopy of the rainforest,[16] were spaced well apart where nature planted them,[17] one quarter of a mile apart on the Orton Rubber Company's concession for instance.[18] In order to let the trees rest, *seringueiros* usually tapped a different *estrada* on alternate days,[19] although sustainable extraction might be abandoned at times of soaring demand and profit. Traveling between the trees took time, and once at the base of a hevea, the *seringueiro* sometimes had to climb as high as forty feet up, using the slashes cut for latex collection as hand and foot holds, to a makeshift platform to tap the tree with his sharp *machadinho* knife.[20] This was dangerous work. An 1873 Indian Government report noted the "fearful risk" to tappers, many of whom were "killed outright" climbing wild rubber trees in Assam.[21] Next, the tapper had to pour the new latex that had drained into tin cups from earlier slashes in the bark into a larger receptacle and lug the buckets through the forest, stopping for more latex at the other trees of the *estrada*, before he returned to his clearing many hours later. The worst, however, was the squalid hut the *seringueiro* called his *defumador.* There, in the humid gloom, he would build a fire, heaping onto it piles of the indigenous inedible nuts known as *ucurury*, or ucururi. Hevea latex, being 60 percent water, rapidly rots if not cured. The ucururi nuts gave off fumes of carbonic acid, essential for the rubber curing process in which the tapper would twirl sticks coated in latex, alternately re-dipping and rotating the growing lump of hardened rubber for up to three hours a day. At the conclusion of his labors, the *seringueiro* would have fashioned a ball of up to 50 lbs. of smoked solidified rubber, the rule of thumb having been that the interiors of the larger balls could not be properly cured. He would then step outside into the cool of evening, his eyes smarting from the smoke, coughing from his lungs the poison of the nuts.[22] Despite the primitive nature of the work, the wild rubber trade provided vast quantities of rubber. The first Transatlantic telegraph cable, laid in 1858, required over 260 tons of gutta-percha to protect the copper wires from seawater. That weight would be the equivalent of over 11,000 50-pound balls of rubber, the manufacture and collection of which would take a single tapper a lifetime to complete. Brazilian scholar Roberto Santos estimates that by 1912 there were some 190,000 rubber workers in the Amazon basin.[23]

The tapper's evening meal—prepared by his wife should he have one in a region cursed with a shortage of women—was frugal and monotonous. The staples were rice and beans, washed down with black coffee or rum (or water in leaner times). He could supplement this fare with meat from a turtle, fish, tapir, monkey, or peccary, generally cut into strips and dried in the sun. There was fruit in the forest, but the cultivation of kitchen plants was discouraged in order to bolster the profits of the *patrão*. On the tapper's table, it was typical to find canned fruit and vegetables from across the oceans obtained at exorbitant prices. John Hemming claims that *aviadores* even employed men to pierce ancient cans of beef in order to let out the putrescent gases before re-soldering them for sale to the tappers.[24]

When the sun set, there would be little else for the tapper to do but to retire to his makeshift bed or hammock and await the dawn and another identical day. The rainy season between late January and late May brought with it a long period of enforced idleness. The tapper and his family would shiver in their little hut in the wilderness in the torrents of rain that fell for weeks on end. The river levels steadily rose as much as thirty feet above their dry season level and the higher ground turned to mud. Partly owing to the weather, school was out of the question for the children and they grew up illiterate with little inkling of what lay beyond their green prison. Other basic needs were affected by the rain and humidity: leather was prone to rapidly mildewing and powder and shot were rendered useless by the damp, as was the staple manioc flour, imported from the southern provinces and called *farinha* by the Brazilians. Summing up her views on the tappers' lives, Lizzie Hessell lamented the inflated prices they paid for shoddy goods and concluded, "alone in the forest for months, I should go mad."[25]

"A Man Working to Enslave Himself"

The tappers, strictly speaking, were not proletarians. Their days were not
punctuated by alarm clocks, gongs, or factory whistles or by the roar of an
angry foreman's voice. They were subcontractors, paid a percentage of
the price paid to the *patrão* for the rubber they tapped. Theoretically,
they could take days off when they chose, and could work what hours
they wanted so long as they delivered their quota of rubber. It is possible
that in the early days of the boom, some of the men were reasonably content with their lot, as Fawcett claims. In the early nineteenth century, some
tappers probably even worked for themselves, getting full market price for
their rubber, or were at least able to haggle with a middleman. This
changed as the century wore on. John Hemming considers that the
seringueiro was a "gigantic contradiction [for] he is a man working to
enslave himself."[26] From the moment that he accepted a ticket for the long
boat trip up the Amazon, he was in debt to the *patrão*. Richard Collier
estimates that when a newly enlisted Ceará man arrived in the forests near
Iquitos, he was already £30 in debt to his employer[27]: the cost of the ticket had been subtracted from his earnings with interest. Likewise, the exorbitant price of the rotten foodstuffs he was forced to consume would be
deducted from his earnings. The cost of his tapper's knife, hammocks,
latex cups and buckets, and whatever other modest domestic utensils he
required, would also be deducted from the price paid for his rubber.
Should he wish for a Yankee Winchester rifle and ammunition, he would
be forced to pay the boss or the trader many times what the gun would
cost in Europe or the United States. For most goods, he could expect to
pay 300–400 percent more than the cost of the product when it was landed on the Manáus docks. In short, this was a truck system—a variation of
the company store—calculated to keep the *seringueiro* in perpetual debt
so that he was chained to his *estrada* until the constantly receding date
when he could pay off what he owed. It was also likely that many of the
patrãos were themselves indebted to even more powerful men. All in all,
the *seringueiro* was, despite his appearance as a free man, a slave. Brazilian
law did not prohibit a man from leaving an employer to whom he was in
debt, but the rubber barons made their own law on the remote frontiers
and the consequences of absconding could be savage. In Bolivia, the
barons also had the law on their side, and deserters could be punished
with fines or imprisonment. The remoteness and the impenetrability of
the forests served as prison bars.

Poverty, the Best Recruiting Agent

Such conditions beg the question: why would anyone be willing to bury themselves indefinitely in the remote jungles to tap rubber? Perhaps some came for the adventure, others because they had heard stories of the fabulous wealth created by the rubber boom. Undoubtedly those who fled the Pará tramways to tap rubber fell into the latter category. So too, perhaps, did those whom Akers describes as "flotsam and jetsam from gangs employed on contract work, various trades, deserters from ships, or discharged sailors and others who have drifted to the Amazon valley."[28] Escaped jailbirds and runaway husbands, too, might consider the *estrada* preferable to a cell or kitchen in Belém or São Paulo. The promise of steady work and income was a magnet for the dirt-poor *cablocos* of the drought-stricken province of Ceará in Brazil's northeast. In 1877–78, a particularly severe drought there coincided with an epidemic of smallpox, which carried off half a million people.[29] For these chronically malnourished and often landless mixed-blood peasants, any work at all was better than none. Whenever there was drought—the dreaded *seca*—there would be a fresh supply of recruits desperate to make their marks on the recruiters' contract forms and undertake the long journey up the Amazon, crammed on the afterdecks of river steamers along with cattle, horses, and sheep.[30] As the Uruguayan writer Eduardo Galeano observed:

> Peasants with no nutritional reserves went from the dry lands to the swampy jungle, where fevers lay in wait for them. Packed into ships' holds for the long journey, many anticipated their fate by dying en route. Others did not even reach the ships. In 1878, 120,000 of Ceará's 800,000 population headed for the Amazon, and less than half got there; the rest collapsed from hunger or disease on the *sertão* trails or in the suburbs of Fortaleza. A year earlier one of the Northeast's seven great droughts of the past century had begun.[31]

Although the wild rubber industry collapsed due to competition from plantation rubber in Asia and Africa after 1914, it never completely disappeared. Even today, *seringueiros* tap the heveas in remote parts of the basin. The industry also revived to some extent during the Second World War, when the United States and Brazilian governments signed an agreement to supply rubber for the Allied war effort. Once again, the people of Brazil's impoverished northeast were treated as expendable in the mini-boom. Up to 50,000 people were dragooned into service as "rubber soldiers" with the promise of 50 cents a day in wages and a ticket home at the end of the war. As many as half of them died of diseases such as yellow fever and beri-beri or were killed by wild animals. Alcidino dos Santos, a 19-year-old mason's laborer was one who survived. One morning in 1942 he was accosted by an army officer and told that it was his patriotic duty to go to tap rubber. He protested that he had a duty to support his widowed mother, but the officer refused to listen. Today, an old man, he still lives in a shack in Acre province and he never saw his mother again. "They treated us like donkeys," another rubber soldier told an American journalist in 2006. "We'd line up and the bosses of the rubber camps would pick the workers they wanted, favoring the strongest and fittest as if we were pack animals." Another told of frightful death rates. "They didn't have the proper medicines for diseases or snakebites there in the camps, so when someone died you buried him right there next to the hut and kept on working," Lupercio Freire Maia recalls. When peace came, the rubber bosses "feared an exodus and so many rubber soldiers were still there in the jungle years later, unawares," adds the historian Marcos Vinicius Neves.[32]

And yet there was worse suffering within the vast basin of the Amazon. The rubber boom generated such a demand for rubber that not even the human reservoirs of Ceará could meet the demand for labor. The idea of importing Chinese "coolies" was floated and dropped, although a certain number of free Japanese settlers came to the Amazon during the boom. Gringos were out, for according to the wisdom of the time, "full-blooded white men" could not possibly work in the heat of the tropics. In those circumstances, the rubber men's eyes turned to the Indians. If Jean-Jacques Rousseau considered that the self-interest of human beings was constrained by our capacity to feel pity for our fellows, there was precious little compassion for the Indians who were dragooned into service as slave laborers.

CHAPTER SIX

"There Is No Sin beyond the Equator"[1]: The Putumayo Devil Plant

Caoutchouc was first called "India rubber" because it came from the Indies, and the earliest European use of it was to rub out or erase. It is now called India rubber because it rubs out or erases the Indians.

—ROGER CASEMENT, 1910[2]

In October 2007, the anthropologist Richard Hill drew attention to the existence of a number of "lost" Peruvian rainforest tribes who shunned all contact with the outside world. Although the Peruvian government disputes the claim, Hill says that the evidence is incontestable: "We think there are 15 groups ... [and] many are the descendents of tribes contacted over 100 years ago, during the rubber boom, who fled the prospect of enslavement and decimation by new diseases."[3] For indigenous people throughout the tropical world, white sails on the ocean's horizon have often presaged death. For the Indians in the Amazon's green "ocean" in the late nineteenth and early twentieth centuries, death was heralded by the arrival of steam launches or gunboats bearing armed men hungry for rubber. Technology had moved on from the time of the conquistadors, and killing and slave-driving had become more efficient. Reclusive tribesmen living today in remote corners of the Peruvian *selvas* inherited the memory of a catastrophe proportional to the genocides of the Final Solution and the Armenian massacres.

The most infamous example of mass killing by the rubber men occurred along the Putumayo River on the remote and disputed borders of Peru and Colombia. A British House of Commons report published in 1912 estimated that some 32,000 mainly Huitoto tribesmen, women, and children had been murdered or worked to death within a five-year period, leaving a scant 8,000 survivors[4] to wander in the ruins of their world. In 1910, David Cazes, the English consul at Iquitos, told Roger Casement, the British consul general at Rio de Janeiro, that "The entire Indian population is enslaved in the *montaña* and whereon the devil plant, the rubber tree, grows and can be tapped. The wilder the Indian, the wickeder the slavery."[5] The ultimate cause of their suffering was the industrialized world's appetite for rubber. While local rubber barons were directly responsible for the atrocities, Roger Casement—scion of the Anglo-Irish ascendancy turned radical critic of Empire—had no doubts about the complicity of the industrialized world. An American geographer, writing in 1933, believed that the enslavement of the Indians in the Amazon basin only ended because "[t]he cessation of rubber gathering enables the Indian to return to his village home from the rubber camps, and he no longer has reason to retreat to the jungles to escape servitude."[6]

Centuries of Suffering in a Continent of Pain

The strict legal definition of genocide applies to cases where there is a deliberate attempt to exterminate a people, but the standard text on the subject regards the Putumayo killings as just that.[7] The river became a byword for torture and death, but as the American whistleblower Walt Hardenburg observed, it did not "stand alone."[8] While Hardenburg had exposed this particular horror to the world, Roger Casement claimed that slavery was practiced over "vast areas of South and Central America."[9] The Putumayo genocide came after centuries of oppression of the Amerindians. Similar atrocities occurred in other jungles and valleys of the basin, as well as in southern Mexico, Central America,[10] and in the Suarez rubber empire in Bolivia,[11] where the slaughter went on largely unremarked and unrecorded. The plight of the Huitoto people on the Putumayo became an international scandal due to the campaigning of three dissimilar men: a Peruvian Jewish Marxist, an American adventurer, and an eccentric Anglo-Irish diplomat. What they shared was a refusal to remain what the Israeli writer Amira Hass would later describe as "silent bystanders to human suffering."[12]

In 1542, shortly after the European arrival on the Spanish Main, Bishop Bartolemé de las Casas denounced the pillage, torture, rape, and murder of the Amerindians, hoping to convince his king to intervene.[13] Sadly, although the sixteenth-century Iberian kings forbade the enslavement of Indians provided they converted to Christianity,[14] such decrees carried little weight in the remote New World forests and the Indian population steadily declined. In 1542, friar Gaspar de Carjaval claimed that Indian villages along the Amazon's banks were situated just "a crossbow shot apart." Although the accuracy of his observations of "contact" population density has been disputed, it is clear from archaeological evidence that the population fell precipitously.[15]

From Huckster to Rubber Baron

The architect of the Putumayo genocide was the Peruvian businessman Julio César Arana, a former traveling hat salesman who had crossed over the Andes in 1899, at the age of thirty-six. Haberdashery provided a modest living, but rubber made him rich. Derided as "Fat César" by his competitors, Arana was an intelligent man determined to make his fortune at any cost. Arrogance and ruthlessness were among his salient qualities, and his gangster hubris was illustrated when he gratuitously "pardoned" Roger Casement on the eve of the latter's execution for his part in the 1916 Easter Rebellion in Ireland.[16] Although Arana was Peruvian, the company that he founded employed British supervisors, and more broadly, the enterprise greatly benefited the British rubber industry and the British ship-owners whose vessels transported what Casement later described as the "crimson rubber"[17] to English ports.

Unlike the boosters of Manáus who believed that the wild rubber boom would last indefinitely, Arana appears to have been acutely aware of the threat posed by the new Asian plantations. He knew he would have to extract the maximum profit from his newly acquired estates before the bubble burst and invest the proceeds elsewhere. Like the other rubber barons, however, his ambitions were stymied by an acute labor shortage. At first, Arana imported his tappers from drought-stricken Ceará in northeast Brazil, but the supply could not meet the demand. He turned to local Indians as an alternative labor force, his mind made up, according to some accounts, after some drunken Brazilian tappers physically assaulted him.[18]

In turning to the Indians, Arana was drawing on established practice in the basin. Back in 1879, the French traveler Jules Crevaux reported that on the upper Japurá River the Karihana tribe grew rich by selling members of other tribes to the white enslavers. "A suckling infant is reckoned to be worth an American knife; a girl of six years is valued at a machete or sometimes an axe; an adult man or woman fetches the price of a gun," he wrote.[19] There was also a *barraca* on the Madre de Dios River in Bolivia, which "concerned itself not with rubber but with breeding children for the slave market" and which "was said to have about six hundred women" as brood mares. In 1906, the American consul and journalist J. Orton Kerbey reported the existence of "slave pens" on the upper river "where the worst species of slave trade is practiced."[20]

Although Brazil had abolished slavery in 1888, Colombia in 1853, Bolivia in 1829, and Peru in 1854,[21] it nevertheless flourished, partly because in some cases the enslavers *were* the authorities, most notably Tomás Funes, the rubber tycoon who served as governor of Venezuela's Amazonas province in 1913. Young girls and older women were taken to traders "like cattle." Recalcitrant boys were beaten with a cat-o'-nine tails made of vines or with a "paddle-shaped club."[22] The letters of Lizzie Hessell, the Englishwoman who died on a rubber estate in the disputed territory of Acre, make it plain that slavery was considered normal and the laws abolishing it were ignored. In a letter from Bella Vista in 1896, Hessell wrote:

> There is a large slave trade carried out in these parts, a strong healthy girl costs £50. All your servants you have to buy, these are all kidnapped children, people bring them up and when they are about 14 years, sell them for enormous prices. When you buy them they are your own property and have to work them as hard as you like to make them, and if they don't work well, they are beaten dreadfully. Even the men have 50 or 100 strokes sometimes, with a stick which cuts like a knife and very often are half dead afterwards. If they try to run away they are punished more for that than anything else.[23]

The Indians, Hessell adds, were rounded up in hunts or *correrías*, during which the weaklings were tortured and killed and the stronger were enslaved.[24] The Royal Geographical Society's Colonel Percy Fawcett records the words of a bystander at the dock at Riberalta in 1907: "Here come the cattle!" "I looked where he pointed," Fawcett continued, "expecting to see beasts from the plains of Mojos coming in for slaughter . . . but instead it was a human cargo" that was soon "whipped ashore." They certainly were slaves, a customs officer agreed when Fawcett asked, looking surprised at being asked such a foolish question.[25]

Hessell reported to a friend in England that "Fred [her husband] is going to buy a little savage girl for me, they make splendid servants. . . . For a little girl of 10 or 12 he will have to pay about £10, boys cost more."[26] Lizzie Hessell did in fact have an eight-year-old boy slave, whom she treated "as a sort of child and servant at the same time," and who had wept for his mother when he first arrived.[27] The Englishman Paul Fountain anguished at the story of a former black slave whom he met on the Amazon. The man, whose back was a mass of scars from lashings, recalled how a succession of his wives had been sold away and would cry inconsolably when he spoke of his long-lost son.[28] Fawcett believed that the entire upper basin was "a land of perpetual whipping," beyond the law,[29] where an Indian was regarded as "nothing better than a wild animal."[30]

An American Engineer Seeks His Fortune

This was the harsh world that Walt Hardenburg, a fresh-faced twenty-one-year-old American engineer, entered just before Christmas 1907. Accompanied by his boyhood friend W. B. Perkins, Hardenburg had crossed the Andes to seek work on the Madeira-Mamoré railway. Previously, they had worked as laborers on the construction of the Panama Canal to "grubstake" themselves. For Hardenburg, the trip was the realization of a childhood dream, and initially he must have been delighted with the experience. The young Americans marveled at the snowclad peaks of the Andes and even the experience of being chased up a tree by a black caiman didn't diminish their boyish enthusiasm. Although naïve and romantic, Hardenburg had a strong dose of the Protestant work ethic and was capable of disciplined hard labor. Even after a day of work on the Panama Canal—a construction project that was a byword for disease and backbreaking toil—he would pore over his engineering books by candlelight. There is no evidence that the two young men were "on the make," as the American historian Michael Stanfield suggests.[31] They were adventurers, to be sure, but the evidence suggests that they hoped to make their fortunes by honest means.

By accident or design, Perkins and Hardenburg had entered the valley of the Putumayo, a river that rises in the Colombian cordillera and winds its way for a thousand miles before discharging into the Amazon two hundred miles downstream of Iquitos. A relatively minor stream, it is nevertheless two-thirds of a kilometer wide and twenty-five meters deep at its confluence with the Amazon, and is navigable for small steamers for much of its length. The valley was also richly stocked with wild Castilloa trees, and these had attracted Peruvian and Colombian entrepreneurs, who sold their produce on the London market as "Peruvian slab," "weak-fine," or "Putumayo tails." The year before Hardenburg's arrival, much of the territory had been ceded by treaty from Colombia to Peru, but the rivalry between Colombian and Peruvian rubber men continued and the Peruvian government actively supported Julio Arana as a guarantee of their continuing hold on the region. Arana was creating "facts on the ground" to establish Peruvian sovereignty over the region, and officials in faraway Lima weren't too concerned about how he did it.

Shadow on the Putumayo

Hardenburg entered the valley in high spirits, but he soon became aware that a shadow lay across the river. When he and Perkins left the mountain cataracts and entered the lowland forests, a Colombian man warned them of the danger of crossing Julio César Arana, who had effectively laid claim to the entire valley.[32] Frightened by what he saw, Perkins separated from his friend and continued south to the railroad construction job on the Madeira River in Bolivia. By this time, Arana was a formidable power in the land. He had built up a rubber and trading empire, with offices at Manáus and London for his Peruvian Amazon Rubber Company (PACO). He also monopolized transport on the river via his 168-ton steam launch, ironically named the *Liberal*, which was commanded by a man wanted for murder on the Pacific coast. Arana had been in the rubber trade for some years when he bought out the Colombian *estradas* at knockdown prices just before the Putumayo passed to Peruvian control.[33] The 12,000 square mile tract of jungle, for which he paid about £115,700, was to yield rubber worth £1,500,000 within a six or seven year period. (That is, around £10 million and £105 million in today's values.[34]) It is likely that he made the Colombians "an offer they could not refuse." Arana also knew the value of political power. By 1910, he had served as mayor of Iquitos and president of the local chamber of commerce and had twice been elected president of the Iquitos regional assembly.

The Indians who guided Hardenburg around the cataracts of the upper Putumayo refused to enter the lowlands and told him disturbing stories of the cruelty inflicted on Indians by Arana's men. One tale spoke of children slaughtered and cut up for dog food and of women burned alive in kerosene after gang rapes. One of Arana's overseers would blindfold young Indian girls and use them for target practice. In another contest, an Indian would be tied to a tree, and the first marksman to shoot off the victim's penis was declared the winner. To a law-abiding U.S. citizen, full of youthful romantic enthusiasm for the world, such tales must have sounded too bizarre to be true. And yet the white Colombian rubber entrepreneur David Serrano, with whom the Americans stayed, confirmed the stories and added that Arana's men had stolen his rubber and raped his Indian wife before dragging her off along with their son into captivity and prostitution. Serrano offered Hardenburg a half-share in his business, perhaps figuring that his rivals would be less likely to attack if a *gringo* were involved in the company. If this were the intention, Serrano was mistaken, for the law of the Winchester rifle ruled on the Putumayo. In early 1908, Arana's lieutenant, Miguel Loayza, a man with a "peculiar snake-like smile," "arrested" Hardenburg, beat him, and incarcerated him in a stockade at the river post of El Encento. From the stockade, Hardenburg saw a number of emaciated Huitoto women with bodies scarred from whippings supervised by a Barbadian overseer armed with a tapir-hide whip. Another hut in the compound was nicknamed the "Convent" and housed young Indian girls of between nine and sixteen years who were forced into sexual slavery. The corpses of a number of Indians lay on the outskirts of the encampment, the smell prompting one of the guards to admit that some days he couldn't eat his food.[35]

Hardenburg was released after spending some days in Loayza's "custody" and traveled to Iquitos, where he contacted the U.S. consul, a dentist named Guy T. King, with a view to publicly exposing the atrocities. His hopes that the consul would share his indignation were dashed.[36] King already knew of the carnage—indeed his predecessor had informed the U.S. embassy in Lima about it—but he refused to help. Hardenburg was furious, but King no doubt had good reason to fear for his livelihood and perhaps his life, for he knew that the tentacles of Arana's power were everywhere in Iquitos. Shortly before, in a warning to the editor for publishing articles attacking Arana, a newspaper vendor had been found dead in an alley with his eyes sewn shut with cobbler's thread and his ears blocked with hot beeswax. Undeterred by King's rebuff, Hardenburg

called on Arana himself, naïvely assuming that the Peruvian was unaware
of the atrocities and would stop them once he learned what his subordinates were up to. Arana, who could be charming when it suited him, welcomed the American and pretended to be shocked by his "revelations."
Hardenburg prepared to leave Iquitos with the hope that things would be
put right, but he soon learned that the situation might in fact be much
worse than he'd imagined.

Saldaña Rocca's Lonely Campaign

Shortly afterwards, a young man named Miguel Saldaña called on
Hardenburg at his hotel with fresh allegations against the rubber baron.
The boy's father was Benjamin Saldaña Rocca, a left-wing Jewish journalist who for some time had been waging a war of words against Arana in
the columns of his newssheets, *La Felpa* and *La Sanción* (which the murdered news vendor had been selling). There are files of the papers in
Oxford University's Bodleian Library, their mastheads emblazoned with
calls for the dictatorship of the proletariat,[37] but Saldaña's great passion
was justice for the Putumayo Indians. Although Michael Stanfield dis-
misses Saldāna as a "muckraker,"[38] it clearly took great courage to stand
up to Arana, who had already used his influence to have him exiled to the
Pacific coast—where he died in poverty in 1912.[39] The murder of the
news vendor was a grisly warning to his son. In any case, the Saldañas
could hardly expect protection from Peruvian law. Percy Fawcett argued,
"No Government inspector who valued his skin would venture into the
rubber country and send back an honest report." Fawcett went on to
relate that a judge sent to investigate the murder of an Austrian traveler
discovered that powerful people were involved and found it prudent to
accept a bribe and return home with the case unsolved. "Who can blame
him?" the explorer opined.[40] Saldaña's allies, such as they were, lived in
faraway Lima and on the Pacific coast.[41]

Miguel Saldaña brought Hardenburg a sheaf of affidavits signed by
former employees of Arana. These showed that there was an organized
criminal enterprise on the Putumayo with Arana at its head; PACO's
operations relied on the forced labor of the Huitotos and other tribes in
the valley. Arana knew that slave labor was not efficient; the Indians would
abscond or fail to work unless closely supervised and terrorized. Thus, in
1904, he recruited two hundred West Indians from Barbados, among

them the giant Armando King, who doubled as chief cook and flagellator at the El Cento base. Hiring these men on two-year contracts was a "master stroke" by Arana, for they were British subjects and this fact could assist him in any tricky legal situation.[42] The Barbadians were supervised by the "reptilian" Loayza and Arana's brother-in-law, Bartolemé Zumaeta, whom Hardenburg describes as a "syphilitic sadist." Arana hired his supervisory staff on a commission or part-commission basis to give them the incentive to extract as much rubber as possible from the forests.

Huitotos of all ages and of both sexes were forced to work as unpaid tappers and porters, humping heavy loads of rubber through the forests on rations of little more than a cup of farinha and a tin of sardines each day. Roger Casement stated that he would not be able to walk three paces with the loads Indians carried through the wild, muddy and hilly countryside.[43] Yet they walked up to forty-five miles per day with loads of 80 pounds and some adult men carried up to 170 pounds. The children were not spared and Casement grieved for "the little boys, some of them 5 or 6 [years old] . . . with soft, gentle eyes and long eyelashes" who often carried "30 lbs or more on their tiny backs" and for children of no more than eight who sported "broad weals and lashes."[44] Arana's men also stole the Indians' crops, and as a lucrative sideline their women and children were sold into bondage "wholesale and retail in Iquitos," wrote Hardenburg, at prices ranging from £20 to £40 each. Others were forced into unpaid prostitution, and some women were held hostage to ensure the compliance of their menfolk. If the tappers failed to deliver their quotas of rubber, they might be flogged "until the bones are laid bare" and with no medical treatment were left to die, their backs eaten up by maggots. This applied as much to the children as to the adults. They might also be mutilated or castrated at the whim of the overseers, and tortured with fire and water or crucified. Young children were seized by the ankles and their brains dashed out on tree trunks. When too old or infirm to work, the slaves might be killed and men, women, and children were shot or burned alive for the amusement of Arana's men.[45]

Hardenburg was not the first *gringo* to visit Arana's domain. At the turn of the century, a young physician named Herbert Spencer Dickey had accepted the post of doctor at El Encento. Initially, Dickey had been impressed by the settlement, finding his own quarters "very agreeable," but he soon came to see Arana's men as brutes who groveled to their superiors and terrorized those in their charge. As the doctor recalled many years later, "I grew more and more certain that the Putumayo

District was one vast torture chamber, where a handful of rubber officials, whose word was law, tortured and killed and maimed as they, in their degeneracy, saw fit."[46] Although he initially did not believe that the manager, Loayza, was responsible for the crimes—still less Arana—he soon realized that the whole operation was criminal and decided to leave. This was not easy: he was forbidden for the duration of his contract from taking his vacations downstream, and in any case Arana's men controlled transport in the valley. In the end, Dickey made his way downriver to Manáus on his own and then to the West Indies, where some years later he met Roger Casement by chance in a Barbados bar and agreed to accompany him back to the river.[47]

Some months into 1908, Hardenburg's boyhood dream had turned into a nightmare. He revisited the U.S. consul at Iquitos to seek his assistance but was again rebuffed; if justice was to be done, he would have to do it himself. He translated the affidavits and took the originals to a solicitor to arrange for the signers to make sworn statements. Not surprisingly, given that the lawyer was in Arana's pay, he refused to help. Hardenburg traveled to Manáus, where he persuaded the editor of the daily *O Commercio* to publish an account of the atrocities. The article, entitled "Beasts in Human Shape," proved to be a solitary victory, for although Manáus was a thousand miles east of Iquitos, Arana maintained an office there. A dubious character ingratiated himself with Hardenburg and tried to fit him up so that he might appear as a blackmailer of the rubber baron. Hardenburg resolved to spend the rest of his rapidly dwindling savings on a steamer ticket to London, where he planned to alert the British public to the Putumayo horror and to confront PACO's board of directors.[48]

Hardenburg had no connections in London, but he was a determined and resourceful young man. Eking out what remained of his Panama grubstake in cold bedsitting rooms, he approached newspaper offices, seeking to interest indifferent or incredulous editors in his story. Some feared legal action should they publish his allegations against the ostensibly British company responsible for the atrocities, but his luck turned when he met officials of the recently formed Anti-Slavery Society, who suggested that he contact journalists on the weekly populist newspaper *Truth*, which enjoyed a wide circulation and was not afraid to take on the rich and powerful. The paper published an article entitled "The Devil's Paradise: A British-owned Congo,"[49] and this stirred up a great deal of public interest and outrage. PACO countered with allegations that Hardenburg was a blackmailer and Saldaña Rocca a disgruntled businessman with a grudge against Arana. Unwisely, the PACO men also tried to bribe inquisitive journalists and this added fuel to the growing scandal.[50]

This attracted the attention of the Foreign Office, which was worried that the involvement of a British firm might damage the country's reputation. The Foreign Minister, Sir Edward Grey, decided to investigate the allegations, but was faced with the problem that the Putumayo was in Peruvian territory and thus outside of British jurisdiction. Grey realized, however, that the fact that many of Arana's men were British subjects gave him the pretext to launch an inquiry. And he knew exactly who to put in charge.

The Casement Inquiry and Report

Sir Roger Casement, who was serving as the British Consul-General at Rio de Janeiro in Brazil, had already investigated allegations of mass murder, slavery, and cruelty in the Congo, and had excoriated the King of the Belgians, Leopold II, for his role in the rubber and ivory trade there. According to one of his biographers, Casement had already informed his superiors at Whitehall of rumors of atrocities on the Putumayo eighteen months before Hardenburg's revelations and had specifically mentioned the involvement of Julio Arana.[51] The Casement mission to the Amazon would also include PACO secretary Henry Gielgud; Walter Fox, a pipe-smoking rubber expert from the Royal Botanic Gardens at Kew; Louis H. Barnes, an expert in tropical agriculture; and the economist Seymour Bell.

Roger Casement was a dynamic and complex figure and remains a controversial one. Born into the Protestant Anglo-Irish ascendancy in County Antrim, he is still viewed as a traitor by the British establishment for his part in the 1916 Easter Rising, for which he was executed. He is remembered differently in Ireland; huge crowds turned out to show their respect when his remains were returned to Dublin for reinterment in 1965 and, because of his work in the Congo and Peru, he is regarded by many around the world as a great humanitarian. Casement was openly gay in a rampantly homophobic era, and the Tory establishment and other enemies later used this fact to discredit him on the veracity of his findings on the Congo and the Putumayo. They did so, quoting from the so-called "Black Diaries," which Casement purportedly wrote during the 1911 Putumayo investigation. The diaries give details of sexual athleticism with

Roger Casement (1864–1916)
documented British atrocities inflicted
on the Indian rubber workers on
the Putamayo River.

some of Arana's thugs and damn Casement for sexual exploitation of the
Indians he was sent to protect. For many years, their authenticity was
unchallenged, and although they were kept under lock and key, mutter-
ings about their contents were effective in tarnishing his name.[52] Recently,
however, the Irish scholar Angus Mitchell has cast serious doubt on
Casement's authorship and argued that the diaries are police forgeries
that "have poisoned the reputation of Casement and muddied the waters
of South American history."[53] The diaries themselves are now open for
public inspection in the British National Archives at Kew. Mitchell's
claims are not merely intelligent speculation,[54] but are based on a meticu-
lous study of the diaries themselves. Mitchell's expertise, more broadly,
derives from his superbly edited versions of Casement's authentic diaries
and letters.[55]

Herbert Dickey has left us a fair portrait of the doomed Irishman, published many years after Casement's death. En route to Iquitos aboard a
Booth Line steamer, Casement ran into Dickey's cabin in tears at the sight
of the ill-treatment of some mules. He was, Dickey continued, "a remarkably unusual person" and while "not exactly mad . . . [he] was extremely
eccentric," especially in his dress. Despite the humid heat on the Amazon,
Casement habitually wore a heavy "dark brown suit of Irish homespun"
and "his straw hat looked as if it had been taken from an ash can years
before." For protection, he carried a *shillelagh* (wooden walking stick and
club) two inches thick—and given the brutal types he was to meet, perhaps it was not an unnecessary adornment. His sole concession to the
tropical climate was to wear white shoes with rubber sides. Nonetheless,

Dickey considered his friend to be "generous, honest, [and] high principled."[56] Casement could not abide cruelty and what he saw in Arana's domain led him to a state of white-hot indignation.

The Casement Commission left England in July 1910 and arrived at Iquitos at the end of August. What Casement found sickened him, although he was no stranger to human suffering. His report, presented to the British government and tabled in the House of Commons in July 1912, confirmed Hardenburg's claims. In a letter to Sir Edward Grey dated February 5, 1912, Casement wrote of the deliberate killing of Indians by starvation and of "the destruction of crops over whole districts or inflicted as a form of the death penalty on individuals who failed to bring in their quota of rubber." He went on to note that the "deliberate murder by bullet, fire, beheading, or flogging to death . . . [was] accompanied by a variety of atrocious tortures" over the course of Arana's twelve years of operations on the Putumayo. He estimated that during that time at least 30,000 Indians had been killed out of a population of 50,000. Almost 4,000 metric tons of rubber had been "extorted" from the valley and in the six years up to the end of 1910, that rubber had been sold for £966,000 on the London market. He calculated that every ton of rubber cost seven human lives.[57] Moreover, the four officials who had accompanied Casement to the Putumayo, including PACO's Gielgud, had been provided with incontrovertible proof of the atrocities and finally clamored for "worse punishment than hanging" for the perpetrators, although they had initially sought to excuse or downplay what they saw.[58]

Casement as Anti-Imperialist

While the torments inflicted on the Indians were medieval, Casement had no doubt that the Huitotos' enslavement had been rendered easier by modern technology, and that the reasons for it extended far beyond the Amazon basin. "Slavery is spreading," he wrote in a letter to his friend Edmund "Bulldog" Morel, who had exposed the horrors of the rubber and ivory trade on the Congo. "The steamboat and steam engine and modern armaments & the whole scheme of the modern government [are] all aiding it—with the stock gambling and share markets the pillars of the scheme," Casement continued.[59] His views flatly contradict those of Michael Stanfield, who tried to stereotype Casement as a Protestant with an "imperial ideology" operating in the anti-Catholic tradition of the "black legend."[60] In fact, Casement did not exonerate Britain of complicity in the genocide. He rejected the view that the British directors of PACO were "entirely ignorant of the appalling state of things on the Putumayo."[61] He was also critical of what he saw as U.S. imperialism hiding behind the Monroe Doctrine:[62] "If the United States cannot let light into the dark places of South America," he argued, "then she must stand aside or be swept aside . . . [for] The Monroe Doctrine is a stumbling block in the path of humanity. Instead of being the cornerstone of American Independence it is the block on which these criminals behead their victims."[63] The indifference of the U.S. Embassy at Lima to reports from Consul King's predecessor in Iquitos bears him out. According to Howard and Ralph Wolf, the U.S. Government appointed a commission of inquiry following the Paredes and Casement Reports. This commission cast doubt on the earlier allegations, but the Wolf Brothers were skeptical, pointing out that the commission's members "went no closer to the Putumayo than Iquitos" and that they acknowledged the "kindness" of Pablo Zumaeta, whom Hardenburg and Casement condemn as one of the worst of Arana's men.[64]

Although Casement was born into the Anglo-Irish ascendancy, by the turn of the century his experiences were impelling him in the direction of radical anti-imperialism and revolutionary Irish nationalism. Casement's conversion to Catholicism on the eve of his execution is also significant: it was a way of showing his solidarity with the common folk of Ireland and it demolishes the suggestion that he was an Orange bigot likely to give credence to unsubstantiated gossip and rumors in the "black legend" tradition.

Following the presentation of the Casement report to the House of Commons in London in mid-1912, the British government formed a parliamentary select committee to inquire into PACO's activities.[65] One of those who voluntarily chose to give evidence before it was Julio Arana. His charm could not save his reputation, and one day, after a bruising tussle with interrogators, he left the inquiry and never came back. The committee's report branded him a public liar and his days as a rubber baron were effectively over. In 1914, he closed his Manáus office, and some years afterwards the disputed Putumayo territory reverted to Colombia.[66] The Castilloa trees of the Putumayo had been exterminated along with the Indians, and large amounts of cheaper plantation rubber from Asia were coming onto the world markets. Arana died in 1952, almost ninety years of age, leaving substantial assets for his family.

What Was the Degree of British Culpability?

Arana was never punished for his crimes, despite the fact that the Peruvian government had been forced by bad publicity to conduct its own investigation into PACO's operations. The Peruvian report, tabled in the Superior Court at Iquitos on September 30, 1911, found the evidence of atrocities to be too overwhelming to deny.[67] Moreover, the report, which was written by Dr. Rómulo Paredes, recommended that a large number of PACO employees be put on trial for their crimes. However, few, if any of Arana's ruffians were punished. Local officials dragged their feet, and the worst offenders disappeared. Arana himself was never under threat of prosecution. He became a Peruvian senator in 1923 and controlled vast tracts of land in the country.[68]

For Arana, the deaths on the Putumayo were a part of a business equation, a cold-blooded, private, commercial genocide in which death was necessary for an acceptable rate of profit. Roger Casement believed that the system on the Putumayo was "not merely slavery but extermination," for "a slave was well-cared for and well-fed, so as to be strong for his master's work [whereas] these . . . serfs had no master who fed them or cared for them, and they were simply here to be driven by lash and gunfire to collect rubber."[69] Rómulo Paredes tried to blame it all on the English when he traveled to the United States in 1912. Why, he asked, did David Cazes, the British Consul at Iquitos, keep silent about the massacres? He could have asked the same question about Guy King, but perhaps thought it prudent not to do so when he was in the United States on his mission of blame-shifting. In fact, we should record that King's predecessor, Charles C. Eberhardt, *had* attempted to alert the U.S. Embassy at Lima to what was happening, but his account was met with official indifference. Paredes, too, might have sounded more convincing if he had been on record as standing up on the issue; as proprietor of *El Oriente*, the newspaper with the largest circulation in the Iquitos region, he was in a prime position to have done so.[70]

The question remains, to what extent were the British directors of PACO culpable? The findings of the British parliamentary select committee absolved the British PACO directors of direct guilt, but charged them with "culpable negligence" and declared they were in need of "severe censure."[71] Other Britons, some with direct knowledge of the conditions in Amazonia, were more forthright. In a letter to *The Times* in 1912, Percy Fawcett stated, "The City knows perfectly well that in the conditions [on the Putumayo] wild rubber can hardly be produced at a profit, unless conditions of slavery prevail. Governments know it; indeed some of them know at this very moment where horrors of slave-owning and slave-trading are rampant, but they lock these reports away from a sensitive public. . . . "[72] An English journalist who reported the committee's finding in *Outlook* magazine in 1913 felt the directors deserved more than censure and questioned a system that allowed unscrupulous men such as Arana to set up dummy companies as respectable fronts for their activities. Probably the fairest conclusion is that some of the PACO directors were gullible and naïve, while others were accomplices willing to turn a blind eye just so long as they avoided opprobrium and the dividends kept rolling in. The fact that the board was willing to slander Hardenburg and attempt to bribe nosy journalists is extremely suggestive of their guilt.[73] Many years later, the words of the Polish writer Ryszard Kapuscinski are ironically apposite: "Money changes all the iron rules into rubber bands."[74]

Roger Casement was in no doubt of British culpability. He wrote to Grey in February 1912 that "what was being done was being done under British auspices—that is to say, through an enterprise with head-quarters in London and employing British capital and British labor." Moreover, he added, "The whole of the rubber output of the region, it should be borne in mind, is placed upon the English market, and is conveyed from Iquitos in British bottoms [ships' holds]."[75] The American medico Herbert Dickey believed that the ultimate cause of the tragedy was the industrialized world's greed. "It is interesting," he wrote, "that two of the more terrible commercial crimes of the modern world should have been due to the growing demand for rubber."[76] It is to the second of these crimes that we shall now turn.

CHAPTER SEVEN

Heart of Darkness:
Rubber and Blood on the Congo

[Africa] had got filled in since my boyhood with rivers and lakes and names. It had ceased to be a blank space of delightful mystery—a white patch for a boy to dream gloriously over. It had become a place of darkness.

—Marlow in Joseph Conrad's *Heart of Darkness*[1]

It is now fashionable in conservative circles to stress the "positive value" of colonialism and imperialism and gloss over their dark side. In 2005, the French parliament passed legislation requiring history textbooks to comply with this "negationist" vision of the past.[2] Former Australian Prime Minister John Howard waged the "history wars" to revise the grim facts of the European encounter with the aboriginal population and to silence dissenting historians. Right-wing Japanese politicians have expunged reference in school textbooks to their country's crimes in China in the 1930s and 1940s. Likewise, the Belgian monarchist right has always refused to acknowledge the facts of what might be European colonialism's greatest crime—the murder and pillage on the Congo—and has cast its architect as the maligned benefactor of the "Dark Continent." The roots of colonialism is a complex historical issue, but a century ago the English economist J. A. Hobson argued convincingly that, while other factors were involved, imperialism's "taproot" was economic; the European countries acquired colonies, especially in the tropical world, as sources of cheap raw materials and labor, markets for manufactures, and places in which to invest surplus capital.[3] King Leopold II of Belgium and the administrators of his "Congo Free State" might have privately agreed. Although Leopold II wrote, "History teaches that countries with restricted territory have a moral and material interest in spreading out beyond their narrow frontiers," and claimed that his Congo adventure was the "cause of humanity and progress,"[4] he knew, as did Marlow in Conrad's *Heart of Darkness*, that "[t]he conquest of the earth, which mostly means the taking it away from those who have a different complexion than ourselves, is never a pretty thing. . . ."[5] Beneath the rhetoric of the *mission civilisatrice*, it was a case of where there's rubber, there's money—and blood.

Trappings of Nationhood

King Leopold II cut a larger-than-life figure. As the American rubber mogul Harvey Firestone Junior told his American listeners in a radio broadcast in 1932:

> In physical appearance Leopold was as dominant a force as he was in the exercise of royal power. Towering six feet, eight inches, he typified what we all picture a king should be like. He had an amazing gift for dramatizing himself, even to the point of so glorifying his enormous square-cut white beard that "the beard of Leopold" was as famous in his day as "the beard of the Prophet" was in days of old. In dress he was the Beau Brummel of royalty; in sumptuous living he was the Solomon of his day.[6]

Leopold II was only the second king of the Belgians. In 1831, the European powers had chosen his father from the Saxe-Coburg family—the royal "stud farm of Europe" as one historian described it[7]—as the new state's first king. Leopold Junior ascended the throne in 1865 when he was thirty-five years old and was to rule until his death in 1909 at the age of seventy-nine. If nations are "imagined communities," as Benedict Anderson insists, then the rulers of this artificial amalgam of Flemings and Walloons faced a huge task of inventing the symbols of nationhood. Overseas colonies were one such symbol, and like his German-born father before him, Leopold II was a committed imperialist who cast his eye abroad in search of colonies without which he believed Belgium could not take its place in the sun.

King Leopold II (1835–1909):
"Belgium doesn't exploit the
world, it is a taste we have
got to make her learn."

The problem was that the Belgian people were not particularly interested in imperial adventures. If the people and parliament would not act,
Leopold II reasoned, he must make them realize that no state could be
great without an empire. Acquisitive to the core, he saw no contradiction
in piling up his own personal wealth in the process. Like some hulking
Mammon, he pored over the accounts in the Spanish colonial archives,
inspired by the example of the profits that colonial powers could gouge
from their colonies. Unlike the Spanish monarchs, who had largely frittered away their colonial loot, Leopold was the bourgeois king of one of
the first industrial states; the profits of empire would be plowed back into
the economy of the mother country—and into his own pockets for the glo-
rification of the dynasty. As a member of the Belgian Senate before his
father's death, Leopold II had pointed to the financial benefits the
Netherlands had gained from its "cultivation system" of Java. Between
1851 and 1860, remittances from Java accounted for about 32 percent of
Dutch state revenues. As the historian Merle Ricklefs has written, "These
revenues kept the domestic Dutch economy afloat: debts were redeemed,
taxes reduced, fortifications, waterways and the Dutch state railway built,

all on the profits forced out of the villages of Java."[8] The lesson was not lost on the young king-in-waiting of Holland's neighboring state. "Belgium doesn't exploit the world," Leopold reasoned, "it's a taste we have got to make her learn."[9]

Leopold was a cunning, determined, and persuasive man. In the 1880s, after failing to acquire overseas colonies in New Guinea, the Philippines, and the Transvaal, he turned to central Africa. Shrewdly, he created a so-called scientific institute, the International African Association (IAA), as cover for his colonial ambitions. The IAA sent expeditions to the center of the continent, some of them more or less reputable, others little more than intelligence gathering operations for a future land grab.[10] By the 1870s, the European powers were poised to devour Africa and Leopold feared that Belgium might be elbowed aside from the colonial trough. Posing as a disinterested philanthropist, he proposed that his IAA be converted into a protective state over the Congo basin. He was able to enlist powerful British and American allies, including the British Chamber of Commerce, the various Protestant missionary societies, and celebrities such as the explorer Henry Morton Stanley. Even the Aborigines' Protection Society, which today advertises itself with some justification as the world's oldest human rights association,[11] was tricked.

As we shall see, however, not everyone was seduced by Leopold's rhetoric. He was to meet with determined opposition from the London-based Congo reform Association, led by the socialist and humanitarian Edmund Morel, and from Morel's great friend Roger Casement. In Belgium itself, Socialist Party leader Emile Vandervelde and his Liberal ally Georges Lorand campaigned strenuously to put an end to Leopoldian atrocities. It took many years, however, before their work bore fruit and even then only after a demographic catastrophe had overcome the Congo.

The Congo Free State

The upshot of Leopold's scheming was the fourteen-nation West Africa Conference, convened in Berlin between November 1884 and February 1885 with British support and the endorsement of Germany's "Iron Chancellor," Otto von Bismarck. The Conference sanctioned Leopold's scheme to set up a "benevolent" personal protectorate in the heart of

Africa. His only wish, they agreed, was to deliver the denizens of the Congo from superstition, disease, and the depredations of cannibals and Arab slave raiders. As an added bonus, Leopold promised that trade would be free to all comers. The Great Powers chose to accept his arguments, as they used a similar rhetoric to justify their own imperialist projects. Leopold had astutely played them off against each other. The IAA signed separate treaties with each of the fourteen powers represented. The new state was formally created on August 1, 1885, and Leopold informed the Berlin signatories that he would be the sovereign of the "Congo Free State." The peoples of the State were never consulted, nor was he answerable to the Belgian parliament, which subsequently assented that year to his absolute personal rule over the territory. In effect, he was a private imperialist in the tradition of the Dutch and English East India companies but with even less constraint or oversight.

The severity of colonial regimes differed; some weighed comparatively lightly on the shoulders of the natives and were tempered by democratic checks and balances in the parliament and civil society of the "mother country" and even in the colonies themselves. This was not the case with the Congo. King Leopold II was a constitutional monarch in Belgium, but in Africa he was an autocrat who declared, "my rights on the Congo are indivisible . . . [and] none possess any right of intervention."[12] The Belgian Foreign Minister, M. de Favereau, agreed, insisting that the Congo was "to us, a foreign state, in whose administration the Belgian government has no right to interfere."[13] Until its annexation by the Belgian government in 1908, the Congo Free State was, as the influential British politician Herbert Samuel put it, "held as personal property by one individual, and administered by him on much the same principles as a landowner might administer a private estate."[14] While Leopold II did attempt to unload the colony onto Belgium in the mid-1890s, the onset of the wild rubber boom convinced him to hold on to it at all cost.

Following the Berlin conference, Leopold sent an expeditionary force to chart his new domain and lay the foundations for a new state. It was a formidable task, given the swamps and jungles of the basin, the mountain peaks of the far east of the realm, and the sheer size of the territory annexed. The Free State sprawled over 900,000 square miles of central Africa; it was the size of all of the Western European countries combined. Its major physical feature was the Congo River, in Joseph Conrad's words, "a mighty big river . . . resembling an immense snake uncoiled, with its head in the sea, its body curving afar over a vast country, and its tail lost in the depths of the land."[15] Although only the world's ninth-largest river in terms of length, in terms of discharge and the size of its drainage basin, the Congo is second in size only to the Amazon. A Scottish missionary noted that if a map of the Congo is superimposed over one of Europe, the river would rise in the remote Russian steppes and debouche in Albania.[16] The river, however, presented shipping difficulties of a kind not encountered on the South American stream.

While the Congo and its tributaries formed natural routes of communication in the interior of the Free State, the passage of ocean-going steamers and river craft was barred by a series of boiling cataracts on the extreme lower reaches of the river. These extended some two hundred miles downstream from Stanley Pool to the seaport of Matadi at the head of navigation on the estuary. Below the pool, the river crosses a band of hard crystalline rock and mountains rear up 3,000 feet above the channel. Just downstream from Matadi—Kikongo for "rocks"—the cliffs close in, choking the river within a narrow chasm not more than half a mile across, through which the immense discharge of the river pours in a bottomless flood. In the first years of the Free State, all goods and machinery from Europe had to be offloaded from steamers onto Matadi's iron piers and humped, dragged, or rolled across the mountains by gangs of African porters. Roger Casement's friend and colleague Edmund Morel recounts the story of a river steamer carried by 1,500 forced laborers around the cataracts. Passage was made easier when the Belgians, in conformity with the stipulations of the Berlin treaty, built a narrow-gauge railroad that twisted for 220 miles from Matadi to reach Leopoldville on Stanley Pool.[17] The railroad's builder, Lieutenant—later General—Albert Thys, admitted that construction cost the lives of 132 Europeans and 1,800 Africans between 1889 and 1895, but some writers regard this as an underestimate.[18] Only the European victims were given the luxury of headstones.[19] From the railhead, a fleet of shallow-draught, flat-bottomed wood-burning stern wheelers plied the 1,000 miles of the main river until the next set of impassable rapids. One of these was commanded by the Polish-born sailor and writer Joseph Conrad, most of the others by Scandinavians. The principal downstream cargo of these steamers was wild rubber along with ivory.

The railway terminated at Leopoldville, the Free State's capital, where Baron Théophile Wahis ruled as Leopold's first Governor General. As the Belgian state did not possess a colonial administrative apparatus, Wahis had begun from scratch, developing a colonial police force and civil service. The European end of the Congo operation was run by a coterie of talented but unscrupulous old courtiers and civil servants[20] from offices in the Rue Brederode in Brussels; a place described by Joseph Conrad as a "narrow and deserted street in deep shadow, high houses, innumerable windows with Venetian blinds, a dead silence, grass sprouting between the stones, imposing archways right and left, immense double doors standing ponderously ajar."[21] Conrad's words hint at the ominous purpose of the enterprise behind the staid Belgian façades. The whole private colonial enterprise was underwritten by a loan of over thirty million francs from the Belgian parliament, which also assisted with recruitment for the Congo administration at public expense. The loans were eventually written off, but this was not the end of Leopold's scams: in 1894, fearing that Parliament might take over the Congo, he invented a five million franc loan and then recouped it from the Belgian government. As a Belgian professor remarked, "Leopold thus repaid himself for an advance made by himself to himself, and done so with somebody else's money. Perhaps the angels wept, but Midas looked down in envy."[22]

From the start, behind Leopold's "civilizing" rhetoric the Free State was to be what the French called a *colonie d'exploitation*, with a profitable sideline in swindling the Belgian treasury. Moreover, regardless of the promises of free trade made in Berlin, non-Belgian merchants were from the start made unwelcome by the new administrators. Many of those Belgians who did take up the offer of employment in the Congo appear to have been men of low moral caliber, or callow youths easily molded by older colleagues. Some of these were to resurface in French Indochina, where they distinguished themselves as brutal overseers on rubber plantations.[23] The ranks of the armed colonial police—the so-called *Force Publique*—were filled with Africans, many of whom were deliberately recruited from the most savage tribes of the upper Congo and garrisoned away from their homelands to minimize the chance of them sympathizing with the locals. These mercenaries engaged in all kinds of rape and plunder. According to one Scottish missionary, they were even permitted to eat their victims.[24] The Englishman Marcus Dorman thought them "fine looking fellows with a very pretty uniform; blue wide cut breeches to the knee, the legs and feet being bare, blue shirt with red facings and belt, and a red fez."[25] Pretty they might have been, but they acted as sentinels to keep those Africans impressed into collecting rubber and ivory from running away, participated in punitive missions against rebellious tribes, and rounded up laborers for Leopold and his licensees. Armed with Albini

rifles and "cap-guns," this 18,000-strong private force was the most powerful army in central Africa.

Vacant Lands and Other Decrees

The commercial imperatives of the Free State were made clear in a series
of decrees promulgated early in Leopold's reign. First, all so-called
"vacant lands" were declared state property; only land directly cultivated
by Africans or occupied by native dwellings was excluded, apart from
some areas in the lower basin. While some land might well have been
terra nullius, it is clear that traditional African society and customary law
recognized the existence of communal village property, and the forests
were regarded as a common treasury for those who lived nearby. An old
"Africa hand" insisted in 1908 that

> The existence of collective property cannot be doubted. . . . The boundaries
> of these collective lands are frequently natural; more often they appear to be
> purely arbitrary. But they are sanctioned by immemorial tradition and they
> are perfectly well known and recognised to within a foot's length by the
> natives themselves.[26]

The Janssens Commission, which was sent by Leopold to investigate
at the height of the international scandal over his misrule, acknowledged
that private property had never existed in the Congo.[27] Although the
Commission justified the decision to take over the vacant lands as essential for "progress," in fact it was theft. The Janssens Commission was
stacked with Free State functionaries and rubber men,[28] but it could not
avoid contrasting the situation in the Free State with policy in the neighboring French Congo, which reserved pastures, forests, and cultivated
lands adjacent to villages for native use.

The purpose of Leopold's land policy was evident in other decrees,
promulgated in 1891–92, which reserved the produce of the "vacant
lands" for the benefit of the state and its licensees. The Free State was to
become a huge extractive reserve for Leopold's benefit. A secret decree of
September 21, 1891, declared that "the paramount duty of the officials of
the 'Congo Free State' [was] the raising of revenue, to take urgent and
necessary measures to secure for the State the domainal fruits . . . notably
rubber and ivory." There could be no sale of these commodities to private

traders because everything belonged to the state; the sellers would be
poaching state property and the buyers in receipt of stolen goods.
Another decree banned elephant hunting except under state license. This
prohibition was not enacted for sentimental or ecological reasons; the
ivory from the animals' tusks was prized for the manufacture of ornaments, jewelry, piano and organ keys, billiard balls, handles, and the like,
and fetched high prices.[29] The most important product of the new colony,
however, was wild rubber, which according to the Belgian Liberal deputy
Georges Lorand, made up six-sevenths of the overall export revenues of
the Free State.[30] At the height of the wild rubber boom around the turn of
the nineteenth century, a fleet of fifty steamships plied the Atlantic to
bring the rubber to Antwerp's markets. Share prices climbed to dizzy
heights.

Europeans probably became aware of the existence of African rubber-
bearing plants in the 1760s, after the publication of scholarly articles by
Fresneau and Condamine drew attention to hevea in South America and
prompted investigations in Madagascar. In 1805, French botanist Pelisot
de Beauvois described a rubber-rich West African plant he classified as
the *Landolphia*, and by the late 1870s some 220 tons of rubber annually
were being exported to Europe.[31] When the Belgians began the commercial exploration of the Congo basin after 1885, they found over twenty
species of rubber-bearing vines and shrubs, including several types of
Landolphia and the Clitandta vine.[32] Like other Europeans, they believed
that the Africans had no knowledge of latex or its potential uses. Whether
this was true or not, the Africans were soon to learn that the Belgians had
an insatiable appetite for the sticky substance. The major beneficiary of
the wild rubber trade was King Leopold II himself.[33] However, large
tracts of country were leased out to eight private companies,[34] and administered as they saw fit. Some British capital was involved in these companies, but the majority of it was Belgian and Leopold II's cronies formed
the core of the shareholders and directors.[35]

The Labor Problem on the Congo

The commercial exploitation of the tropical colonies everywhere presented the Europeans with a labor supply problem. This was true of Africa,
Asia, Latin America, and Oceania. The "common sense" of the day held
that whites could not withstand the rigors of hard labor in hot climates; a

view shared by the authors of the Janssens Report.[36] Leopold's African subjects, however, were reluctant to labor for the whites. They had their own traditions of subsistence farming and fishing and engaged in small-scale craft industries such as pottery and brassware for trade. Wage labor was an alien concept that often appeared pointless and smacked of slavery. For this reason, most of the African laborers on the lower Congo railway construction were imported from Senegal and British Africa, where they had become, to some degree, accustomed to wage labor. The large-scale importation of such labor throughout the vast basin was not a commercial option. Commissioner Janssens noted that all production, commerce, and all daily-life operations in the Free State depended upon the work of the natives The problem, he observed, was that the Africans were not disposed to work beyond what was necessary for subsistence, and given the fertility of the soil and the ready availability of land, they did not have to expend too much energy in doing so. They were satisfied with humble dwellings and a minimal amount of possessions. They work so as to be able to procure weapons, a wife and some ornaments, Janssens said, but once these had been acquired, they would lose interest.[37] The English traveler Marcus Dorman asserted after a visit to the Congo in 1905 that "the native's . . . main idea always is, to do as little work as possible and he will often take the greatest trouble in his effort to accomplish this project." He was particularly annoyed by the inefficiency of longshoremen unloading and loading his steamer, the *Flandres*.[38] The great white hunters Grogan and Sharp opined that "you can't get a day's work out of a buck nigger, even though he be starving," adding that "some of the lower class have really no ostensible claims to being human."[39]

The logic of such deeply racist attitudes was that if the "lazy natives" would not work willingly they must be compelled to do so. In the Congo, this would be achieved via what the Belgians called the *impôt en travail* (the labor tax). In return for their work, they would get beads, cloth, and brass rods or wire. As a visiting British naturalist observed, often the laborer had no desire for such trinkets, already having enough of them, "but he must take what he is offered or go without payment altogether."[40] A British termagant wrote of how in the Congo, one went aboard a boat "'pickaback' on the back of a nigger," a people she considered to be "lazy good-for-nothings." When a porter had the temerity to fall asleep by the roadside, she had him given "twenty-five of the very best" and agreed that given the stoicism with which he bore the torment, the man "must have had the *chicotte* [rhinoceros or hippopotamus hide whip] from the day of his birth."[41]

For the nineteenth-century colonialists, Africans were created to be hewers of wood and drawers of water for their European masters. It never seems to have occurred to Leopold II's apologists that the labor system in the Free State was essentially one of forced labor for private profit. While admitting to abuses, the Janssens Report did not deny the supposed absolute right of the state to dispose of the labor of the African population as it saw fit.[42] Another early Free State decree instructed officials to round up African villagers and force them into so-called "camps of instruction," where they were subject to *corvée*, that is, unpaid or poorly remunerated labor on "public" works, providing fuel and meat to government posts, or the collection of forest products, above all rubber. Roger Casement claimed that government posts were maintained by the "unremunerated or scarcely remunerated industry" of the local African people: "Nearly everything necessary for the upkeep of these stations is levied in kind each week from the natives of the immediately surrounding districts," he wrote.[43] Leopold had argued in Berlin that it was necessary to bring the Congo territory under his control to stamp out the Arab enslavers, but while the Arab slave trade was unconscionable, the Belgian "camps of instruction" were nothing more than forced labor camps. Although *corvée* was theoretically restricted to forty hours or the equivalent of five eight-hour days per month,[44] in practice the hours were at the discretion of local administrators. According to the Belgian Socialist leader Emile Vandervelde, following his fact-finding mission to the territory in 1909, villagers were compelled to stay in the forests for between fifteen and twenty days a month in order to collect their quotas of rubber.[45] Even the Janssens Commission could not deny the fact of widespread abuse, noting that villagers were often forced to spend between one and two days every fortnight traveling from their homes to the rubber-bearing districts and that, particularly on the lands of the concessionary companies, the forty-hour provision was flagrantly flouted.[46] A refinement of the system was the introduction of quotas of rubber. This, according to the Belgian geographer A. J. Wauters, meant that the collectors had to work until such time as the amount of rubber set by the white men was reached.[47] To this was added a diabolical twist, guaranteed to ensure further abuse: white overseers were paid under an incentive payment system that mimicked the methods of the Amazonian rubber barons. Officials were paid a bonus depending on the size and value of the harvest of "domanial fruits": the bigger the collection, the bigger the bonus. It was a policy calculated to bring out the worst in men.

Mutilated child worker from
the Congo Free State.

The quotas and wholesale labor requisition sorely damaged the native economy. Villagers were forced to neglect their farms, and traditional industries fell into a state of disuse for lack of labor. Casement contrasted the "flourishing and prosperous" government posts with the sickly, underfed and ill-housed natives who were prevented from working for their own livelihoods by such impositions.[48] If the Belgians were concerned about this, it was only a matter of what some now call "collateral damage"; the fact that they did not have any moral right to expect the Africans to labor for them never seems to have crossed their minds.

The villagers resisted as best they could. There were scattered revolts, including one in the ABIR concession between January and August 1905, in which 142 guards were killed or wounded,[49] but it was an unequal contest, given the firepower of the Force Publique. Many villagers fled to the forests, and whole regions along the rivers were depopulated. According to Edmund Morel, the population of the upper basin decamped en masse to the relative safety of British territory.[50] Elsewhere, others slipped across the border into French territory. Some villagers persisted in "stealing" wild rubber and selling it to non-Belgian traders, although they were severely punished if caught. Others refused to work or worked as inefficiently as they could—Dorman's "lazy" stevedores aboard the Belgian riverboats are a case in point. In retaliation, the government authorized the taking of hostages as a deterrent, and even after the practice was officially frowned upon, it continued and was regarded as perfectly legal. As the Janssens Commission admitted, "the desire to free their chief or regain their women stimulated the zeal" of the laborers to bring in their quotas of rubber.[51] It also ensured that they would not abscond into the forests or over the nearest border.

In the remote forests, exasperated white men resorted to increasingly barbarous methods, bearing out André Gide's observation that "[t]he less intelligent the white man is, the more stupid he thinks the black."[52] Moreover, the functionaries of the Free State and the concessionary companies could justify robust methods by reference to "reason" and even science. By the nineteenth century, assumptions of the Africans' inferiority were hegemonic among Europeans. A. D. Cureau, a Belgian doctor, assured his readers in 1904 that "as far as sensitivity goes, the Black is rather inferior to the European."[53] This was a recipe for the infliction of draconian punishments. The solution to the African laborers' supposed congenital idleness was liberal use of the *chicotte*, a type of whip inherited from the Portuguese enslavers. Although the apologist Marcus Dorman claimed that it "did not appear to be more painful than an ordinary birching at an English public school,"[54] it was an instrument of torture. Diana Strickland recalled the fate of an African man who was beaten with the *chicotte* for ceasing to work through tiredness:

> One of the prisoners [was] bleeding from the eyes and obviously in terrible pain. He was unable to stand or stoop and kept sinking to his knees, clutching at his side, but the next moment the heavy strokes of the whip on his bare back forced him to his feet again for a few more seconds only once more to collapse. The revolting spectacle was repeated for some time until the man sunk unconscious on the ground and was carried away. The next day, happily for himself, he was dead.[55]

Aberrations or a Systemic Pattern of Abuse?

These dismal events beg the question: were they isolated aberrations or were they part of a pattern of systemic abuse? The Akron rubber baron Harvey Firestone, Jr. was no radical anti-imperialist, yet in his estimation Leopold II was responsible for a "reign of terror over the Congo" during which the "natives" were forced to collect rubber and ivory under the guns of "black cannibal soldiers" commanded by European officers. There were "frightful atrocities," Firestone said, including murders, whippings, and the severing of the hands of those deemed slow or recalcitrant.[56] Firestone's words are significant: "reign of terror" suggests ongoing violence and oppression. His opinion is backed up by others who had a closer association with the Free State. When Joseph Conrad describes a flowerbed in a Belgian fort decorated with human skulls, he is drawing on his own experiences as a riverboat skipper in the Congo Free State: a Captain Rom near Stanley Falls adorned his outpost in precisely such a way and was never punished for it. Whole villages were burned down in collective reprisal. Women were raped. Crops were destroyed and people were starved. Firestone's mention of severed hands is likewise based on firsthand testimony. We know that the Belgians cut off the hands of recalcitrant villagers, including children who failed to meet their quotas of rubber. The Reverend Clark, a Protestant missionary, testified to Janssens that in the mid-1890s, he had seen a canoe loaded with what appeared to be smoked human hands, which were fed to an "anthropophagic dog." Roger Casement describes his first-hand experience of the activities of La Lulanga, a Belgian trading society that employed "in a hearty free-trade way, numbers of armed ruffians . . . to compel the native population of the Lower Lulanga country to bring in rubber and perform every kind of degrading task for the occupants of the 'factory.'" Here, in September 1903, Casement met "a mutilated boy, whose right hand had been hacked off quite recently" by an armed sentry. The boy told him that the same thing had happened quite recently to another child. Casement added that the "truly extraordinary thing (were it not willingly universal) is that here was a whole village terrorised—a European 'centre of civilization,' only some 6 miles off, whose authorized agent had committed these atrocious acts; and yet this man remained the terror of the community—no one of his victims dared speak—although each fortnight they took their 'imposition' of rubber to the Director who had armed him and put him in their midst."[57] Professor Wauters agreed with Casement's summation.[58] Grogan and Sharp, who passed through the upper reaches of the basin at the turn of the nineteenth century, believed that the horror they witnessed resulted from the colonial power "permitting a vast tract of country to be run merely as a commercial speculation without [a] more legitimate objective than that of squeezing as much rubber and ivory out of the natives as possible . . . [and] of making the administrators of districts to all intents and purposes farmers of taxes."[59] The pair condemned "the whole [Congo Free] State as a vampire growth, intended to suck the country dry, and to provide a happy hunting ground for a pack of unprincipled outcasts and untutored scoundrels."[60] These are strong words from men who were themselves deeply imbued with racist attitudes toward Africans.

The Results of Misrule

Most writers believe that while the regime in the lower Congo was comparatively humane, the same could not be said for the upstream rubber regions. In 1909, Emile Vandervelde noted that in the lower basin, near river stations such as Coquilhatville and Irebu, the villagers' complaints "were neither very numerous nor very acute" and referred generally to onerous rates of taxation. He argued, however, that "it was quite another thing when we penetrated into the rubber forest and for fifteen days traversed on foot the district of Mongala, which has been made notorious by the atrocities of the Société Anversoise."[61] Roger Casement made the same distinction and his assessment is worth quoting at length:

> In 1887, I spent several months in the Upper Congo, and I then travelled over some of the ground I am now revisiting, after an absence of sixteen years. The country I am now in was then thickly peopled; frequent and populous towns surrounded by large areas of cultivated ground met one on many sides.
>
> To-day these towns have often entirely disappeared, or are, often, only wretched collections of ruinous and ill-kept hovels, wherein a panic-stricken remnant of fugitives (there is no other word to apply to the average Congo householder I have interviewed for the last six weeks) toil, under ever-present dread of the rifle, the lash, or the chain-gang, to satisfy the unremitting demands of the local tax collector, who appears in the guise of a local 'trader,' to whom they and their labours have been made over, just as often as in that of a Government official.
>
> Many of the inhabitants have been killed by the Government in the process of imposing this law of continuous forced labour—not upon unwillingly contracted workmen it be noted, but upon the entire population supposed to be free men, and in the enjoyment of every legal protection—how many it would be impossible to say, but the slaughter which prevailed under this head from 1893 up to 1900 must have been, from the evidence laid before me, absolutely appalling.[62]

Casement estimated that the population of the district had diminished by over 60 percent during the sixteen years since his last visit; towns with a population of one thousand had dwindled to less than three hundred. While Casement did admit some recent improvement, he argued that the Africans were still kept hard at work "developing the riches of the country" for the sole profit of their masters and disobedience was treated as revolt.[63] The traditional economy of the region had gone into steep decline and food production had plummeted. In short, the basin had been stricken by catastrophe. According to his friend Edmund Morel, Casement believed that the population of the Free State had fallen by almost three million people, and although Morel thought this likely to be an overestimate, he concluded that the period of Leopold II's rule had cost one hundred thousand lives per year.[64] We might never know the true death toll, but it is likely that Morel's figures are unduly conservative. Morel, who had first become aware that something terrible was happening in the Free State when he was employed as a shipping clerk by the Elder Dempster Line, whose steamers worked the Atlantic rubber route to Matadi, was aware that sensationalism could play into Leopold II's hands. The Belgian press and the King's well-resourced apologists elsewhere in Europe and North America kept up a steady stream of propaganda. While it is commonly the case that reformers cannot afford to slip up on their facts, their opponents can tell colossal lies. Recent authors believe that the death toll was far higher than the estimates of Morel and Casement. Neal Ascherson believes that the population of the Free State might have been halved between 1880 and 1920, or that as many as ten million died.[65] Strictly speaking, what happened might not have been genocide, which the term's inventor Raphael Lemkin defined as "the deliberate extermination of a national or racial group."[66] However, whether one accepts such a definition or not, the fact remains that a demographic catastrophe occurred in the Congo. The estimated population of the Congo in 1911 was 8,500,000 compared to between twenty and thirty million in the 1880s.[67] Apologists for the Free State are quick to point to the epidemic of sleeping sickness (trypanosomiasis) spread by the tsetse fly as a way of shifting the blame for mass death from the regime, but even at the time, critics pointed to the role of overwork, starvation, unsanitary conditions, and general privation in reducing resistance to the disease. One anonymous hired hack claimed that depopulation was caused by the "nomadic tendencies" of the natives.[68] Most damning for the Leopoldian state was the allegation that "depopulation began long before sleeping sickness assumed alarming proportions,"[69] a fact attested to even by some of Leopold's sympathizers.[70] As Ascherson has pointed out, there had been a "gigantic disruption of African society" during which time a starving and homeless population, dispossessed of its land and in a debilitated condition, was easy prey to disease.

Mission civilisatrice?

Leopold's apologists in Belgium and abroad worked tirelessly to propagate a sanitized vision of the Free State. Their themes were well-worn: colonialism had brought immense benefits, including the suppression of the Arab slave trade, the prohibition of liquor trafficking, a justice system, and the construction of public works, including telegraphs, railways, ports and river steamers, telephones, and "fine stations" in the retreating wilderness. The lobby also insisted that Morel's Congo Reform Association and other Anglo-Saxon critics were motivated by the desire to take the Congo away from Belgium. English "Congophobes," asserted the royalist pamphleteer Roland de Marès, were operating "on behalf of the Liverpool merchants" who were "jealous" of the Belgian rubber trade.[71] Many Belgians were— and still are—convinced that Leopold II was the innocent victim of an English Protestant conspiracy to undermine Catholic Belgium's "great work" in Africa, and to ensure the continuing ascendancy of the "Liverpool rubber barons" over their Antwerp rivals. "The English campaign [against the Congo regime] . . . has a political and economic objective hidden behind the humanitarian screen," fumed one anonymous Belgian pamphleteer. The English are jealous because "Belgium has too rapidly derived great benefit from its colony," he continued, and this "is a great crime in the eyes of the imperialists who desire an Anglo-Saxon Africa from Cape to Cairo."[72] "In founding the Congo state," declared an Irish admirer, "King Leopold had been animated by noble ideas and much of the work carried out in the Congo under his instructions was most noble" and "[n]o just man can deny it."[73] Another ploy was to treat all criticism as a left-wing conspiracy to blacken the king's name. Belgian monarchists heaped particular scorn on "certain socialists and Belgian radicals, republicans . . . [who] only try to exploit the Congolese question in order to satisfy their own ill-wills."[74] Underlying such calumnies lay an "alliance of [Protestant] bigotry and untruthfulness" toward Catholics, claimed an anonymous pamphlet printed in Edinburgh.[75]

The Belgian Liberal deputy Georges Lorand condemned such stereotypes and described Leopold's Congo Press Bureau, as "an agency for
corruption and the poisoning of the public mind."[76] Moreover, as an
American writer noted at the height of the international scandal, Catholic
opinion in the United States was firmly *against* Leopold. The *Catholic
World Magazine* roundly denounced the Free State, which

> Started as a philanthropic attempt, under the auspices of the chief Powers . . .
> [but] soon eventuated into a sordid oppression. It will have served no good
> purpose if it affords yet another demonstration of the impatience for good of
> autocratic methods of government.[77]

Leopold II refused to admit to any misconduct even after the Janssens
Commission acknowledged his wrongdoing in the Free State. In an interview with an American journalist in late 1906, the King stoutly defended
his rule as a *mission civilisatrice*. It was "absolutely false," he said, to
claim that he was "financially interested in the Congo." Moreover, he continued, he had "not one cent invested in the Congo and had received no
salary as the Congo chief executive in 22 years." The journalist was
stunned by such effrontery.[78] The United States Consul General at
Leopoldville, Mr. Slocom, reported that the Free State was "nothing but
a vast commercial enterprise for the exploitation of the products of the
country, particularly that of ivory and rubber."[79]

The King had a finger in every lucrative Congo pie. From a starting
capital of £40,000, ABIR made a profit of £600,000 in four years, half of
which went to Leopold II, and in 1901 at the height of the speculative
boom, £40,000 worth of shares could be sold for £2,160,000.[80] In the
five years between 1895 and 1900, the value of the Free State's exports—
primarily rubber—grew from 11.5 million francs to 47.5 million, leading
Leopold to abandon his wish to palm off the territory onto the Belgian
parliament.[81] The Free State had become a kind of capitalist utopia,
untrammeled by regulation or oversight, in which "large areas became
the almost independent domains of Big Business"[82] as British Naval
Intelligence later concluded. The largest domain was the so-called
Domaine Privée, which occupied an area ten times the size of Belgium
(or slightly larger than Arizona), and which was administered in the
name of "the Duke of Saxe-Coburg-Gotha," that is, Leopold II himself.
The Belgian scholar Félicien Cattier estimated that the King's private
domains had made him a clear profit of £2,900,000 in the ten years

between 1896 and 1906. (Using the retail price index as a guide, this is the equivalent of over £223 million in 2007. This is a conservative estimate.[83]) On top of this, the King owned over half the stock in three of the other major rubber companies.[84]

The Janssens Report

Leopold had long envied the public works schemes of the neighboring Netherlands, which had been financed from the profits of the cultivation system in Java. Emile Vandervelde considered, in a "rough calculation," that during the years of the Free State, Belgium got sixty million French francs worth of public buildings and other works paid for by the forced labor of Africans. The irony was that, although Leopold had furnished Brussels with the national symbols for an imagined community and fed his own ego and filled his pockets in the process, the monuments were largely valueless in financial terms.[85] Massive and tasteless, they brood on the horizons of Brussels' boulevards, messaging the adulation of power and wealth.

The Janssens Report, following the Casement Report and the long agitation of Edmund Morel's Congo Reform Association, was the beginning of the end for the Free State. The Socialists and Liberals kept up a sustained attack on Leopold II in the Belgian Parliament. Although the Janssens Report sanitized or overlooked key facts (including the suicide of Governor General Costermans upon the return of the Commission to Leopoldville), not even the unquestioning loyalty of the Belgian conservative press could smother the truth. In 1908, the Belgian parliament moved to take over direct control of the Congo, granting Leopold II a hefty indemnity for his loss. He had always said that he would bequeath the Free State to Belgium upon his death, and he was nearing the end of his life. He had also fallen out with many of his old cronies, who had not received the bounty they felt they were owed, and they too joined the agitation for a Belgian takeover. Most importantly, the supply of rubber and ivory was dwindling. The extraction system, like that on the Putumayo in Peru, was ultimately unsustainable in both ecological and economic terms. The elephants had been largely hunted out by late the 1890s and rubber production began to fall from 1907. Unlike the South American hevea tree, the *Landolphia* vine could not long stand the extractive incisions and neither the impressed tappers nor their overseers had any incentive to use sustainable methods. The quota and bonus systems ensured that the maximum amount of latex was extracted in the short term, but the vines were killed in the process. Congo rubber often arrived on the docks of Europe and America rotten, infested with maggots, and full of impurities. In 1907, the value of rubber exports from the Belgian and French Congo territories amounted to almost 44 million French francs. The following year, they had fallen to below 31 million French francs, and the decline continued after Leopold's death in 1909.[86] Shortly afterwards, the rise of plantation rubber killed the wild rubber industry. At the height of the boom, Congo rubber fetched between six and eight shillings a pound; by 1913 it had fallen to between one shilling and sixpence and two shillings a pound and the amount collected, which had formerly made up 75 percent of the Free State's exports, had dwindled to negligible levels.[87]

How Was It Possible?

Greed, as is well known, will make men do atrocious things. The astronomical profit rates from Congo rubber cited above are a case in point. Perhaps the common claim that one African died for every ten kilograms of rubber was hyperbole, but the villagers' lives were of little account in the arithmetic of profit and loss. The Africans were seen as less than human; the imperatives of natural law thus did not apply to them. The atrocities were also facilitated by the peculiar circumstances of Leopoldian imperialism in which a vast territory was administered as a private fief, beyond the rule of law, beyond any checks and balances on Leopold II's absolute executive power. It was also beyond the ocean and a world away from the humdrum of existence in Belgium. The likelihood of officials or traders being punished for their crimes was slight,[88] and when the Belgian state took over direct rule of the Free State, the old functionaries remained in place. To this, too, we should add the willful blindness of a substantial portion of the Belgian population, who chose to believe whatever the King's propaganda machine chose to tell them. In 1906, the Antwerp Royal Geographical Society organized a *grand fête* "to commemorate the results obtained by Belgians in the Congo." There were toasts to the "enlightened sovereign who had added a glorious page to our history," speeches greeted with "frantic applause" and the playing of the *Brabançonne*.[89] As the saying goes, "There are none so blind as those who will not see. The most deluded people are those who choose to ignore what they already know."

Avarice is international, too, as is evidenced by heavy British investment in the ABIR concession and by a little-known American venture into
Congo rubber. The latter involved a U.S.-based consortium consisting of
Continental Rubber, the speculator and financial wizard Bernard Baruch
(supremo of the U.S. rubber industry during the Second World War), the
banker Thomas Ryan, and Senator Nelson W. Aldrich. The consortium
only pulled out of a deal with Leopold II after a campaign by what they
called "yelping socialists" made the Congo an international scandal and
forced the U.S. Congress to condemn the Free State regime.[90]

Leopold II's grandson Charles continued the family association with
rubber, studying American business methods with Firestone in Akron
under the name of Richard Trent.[91] Given this close association with rubber, one wonders if he ever felt unease at his grandfather's misdeeds.
Probably not, as the blindness continues in Belgium to this day. Visitors to
Brussels can see Leopold II's likeness cast in a towering bronze equestrian
statue outside the royal palace grounds in the Place du Trône and contem-
plate the massive architecture which he bestowed on the burghers of the
city. Not all Belgians approved of the events on the Congo. In a speech to
the Belgian Senate in 1905, Emile Vandervelde dubbed Leopold II's
colossal folly in Brussels—the *arcade du Cinquaintenaire* erected to mark
the fiftieth anniversary of the dynasty—"the arch of the severed hands"[92]
and the soubriquet has stuck. Vandervelde and his Liberal ally, Georges
Lorand, along with the half-French, half-English idealist Edmund Morel
and the doomed Irishman Roger Casement, waged a long struggle to end
the Congo crimes. If there is anything edifying in this tale, it is their
courage and decency. Although derided as puppets of the Liverpool rubber merchants, Casement and Morel were radical anti-imperialists who
challenged the assumptions of European manifest destiny. "The battle of
the Congo is the battle of all Negro-Africa . . . ," wrote Morel, "Africa which
is, and must ever remain, the black man's country. . . . "[93] However, more
than a century later, visitors to the great African museum at Tervuren on
the outskirts of Brussels will find no reference to the atrocities in the Free
State, and books abound attesting to the good works of the King. Facts
might be stubborn things, but so are Belgian burghers intent on preserv-
ing their national myths.

CHAPTER EIGHT

Gutta-Percha, Telegraphs, Imperialism, and Ecology[1]

The political unity of India, more consolidated, and extending farther than it ever did under the Great Moguls, was the first condition of its regeneration. That unity, imposed by the British sword, will now be strengthened and perpetuated by the electric telegraph.

—KARL MARX, 1853[2]

In 1857, a New York manufacturer told prospective customers: "Perhaps no material was ever discovered which was so soon extensively shipped as an article of commerce—taken up so eagerly and manufactured at once so extensively, as has been the article of gutta-percha."[3] Today, it is difficult to think of another leading commodity that has been so comprehensively forgotten. Once almost as ubiquitous as its close cousin rubber, it was used for a myriad of domestic and industrial purposes; first and foremost for the submarine electric telegraph cables which girdled the world from the mid-nineteenth century. It was—as Marx understood in 1853—essential for the consolidation of the vast new European colonial empires. In the end, however, the demand for the gum was so great that the rainforest trees from which it was extracted in the tropical colonies were exterminated a grim harbinger of the today's greater rainforest destruction.

When I asked several classes of my undergraduate students if they had heard of gutta-percha, not one hand was raised in response. This was not

surprising, for apart from dentists, botanists, and specialist historians and
geographers few people know about it. In contrast, few citizens of the
industrialized countries during the Victorian era would not have heard of
it. As one contemporary account noted,

> Almost every species of toy is made from this gum; the furniture, the decora-
> tions, and even the covering of our houses are constructed from it; and we make
> of it soles for our boots and shoes, and linings for our water cisterns. It is used
> for pipes, alike for the conveyance of water and sound. Ear-trumpets, of various
> sizes and forms, are made of it; we also now frequently find gutta-percha tubes
> carried from the door of the medical man to his bedside; we also, as often, meet
> with the *Domestic Telegraph* [emphasis in the original]—a gutta-percha pipe
> passing from one room to another by which messages can be carried to all parts
> of the house; and when a pew in church is occupied by a deaf owner, a similar
> pipe ensures the afflicted worshipper to hear the word of God. . . .[4]

It was widely used for domestic, medical, and industrial applications
for which we use plastic and similar synthetics today, including: boats,
furniture, upholstery, and surgical appliances. Hatters and fuse makers
used large quantities. As it was acid and water resistant, it was much
sought after by chemical factories and photographic and other laboratories.[5] One British company used it to make roof tiles.[6] Its most singular
use, however, was to seal and insulate undersea electric telegraph cables.

Gutta-percha—the name comes from a Malay word for gum or
resin[7]—is a natural plastic, the sap or gum of certain trees from Southeast
Asia, in particular the *taban*. At normal atmospheric temperatures it is a
hard, dark substance. Chemically, it is a stereoisomer of rubber, sharing a
similar chemical composition—polyisoprene.[8] Unlike its elastic cousin, it
will not bounce when dropped and nor will it stretch and return to its
original shape and size. It is very dense and watertight, more so than rubber; a gum plastic rather than gum elastic. Its remarkable qualities were
easy to overlook. The Englishman John Tradescant brought the "pliable
mazer wood"[9] back to Europe in 1656, but it remained a curiosity for
many years.[10] The Malays were aware of its singular qualities—hard at
normal temperatures, it becomes pliable when heated in hot water—and
they fashioned it into a variety of artifacts, including canes and handles for
whips, knives, and hoes. In 1832, the Scottish colonial sawbones William
Montgomerie reported to the Medical Board at Calcutta that for some
surgical applications, gutta-percha might prove superior to India rub-

ber.[11] Fifteen years later, Edwin Truman used it for dental fillings and it is still used in orthodontics today.[12]

The Electric Telegraph Revolution

In the same year, another inventor made a breakthrough that would change human society forever. American inventor Samuel Morse developed the electric telegraph and triggered a communications revolution that was as astounding in its day as that of the Internet today. For the first time in human history, the nexus between physical transportation and the transmission of information was broken. By the eighteenth century, the fastest horses, running in relays in good weather and over flat terrain, could travel one hundred miles in one day to deliver a message; it took thirty-two days to sail across the Atlantic; and in 1788 the First Fleet took over eight calendar months to reach Australia from England. Even by the nineteenth century, the speediest clipper ship took one hundred days to travel from London to Hong Kong; fifty-five days from New York to Rio de Janeiro; and an average of 187 days to San Francisco from the U.S. East Coast.[13] The optical telegraph was faster over short distances but was restricted to daylight hours and fine weather. The electric telegraph could be used both during the day and the night and could relay information almost instantaneously over long distances regardless of the weather.

The development of the telegraph coincided with the expansion and consolidation of European political and economic domination of the globe. It is a truism that empires rise and fall, victims of "imperial overstretch" in which the economic costs outweigh the benefits.[14] Their size was also constricted by "the tyranny of distance"[15] and time. The first white settlers at Port Jackson on the remote Australian shore could have learned of the fall of the Bastille only nine months after the event. Requests for reinforcements to quell mutinies in the Asian and African colonies could travel to London, Amsterdam, or Paris only as quickly as the fastest sailing ship. The electric telegraph changed all that.

Essential for Submarine Insulation

Apart from the copper for the wires, electric telegraphy depended on reliable insulation from the elements and/or water, and the most suitable substance for this purpose was gutta-percha. Ironically, the substance that proved indispensable to "strengthen and perpetuate"[16] imperial rule in the colonies was found only in the European colonies in the Far East. William T. Brannt considered that "if gutta-percha and its properties had not been known, submarine telegraph lines would perhaps never have been successful."[17] India rubber deteriorated rapidly in saltwater and was not as watertight as its cousin.

Eight species of trees yielded gutta-type latex.[18] The best of it came from the taban, the *Isonandra gutta*, or *Palaquium gutta*, named by Sir Joseph Hooker, the director of the Royal Botanic Gardens at Kew in London. Lucile Brockway has drawn attention to the key role of the scientific experts of the British and Dutch Botanic Gardens in the development of colonial plantation agriculture and forest exploitation.[19] The taban was an impressive tree, growing to between sixty and eighty feet in height, with a diameter of between two and five feet, and with great buttress root systems rising to up to fifteen feet off the ground.[20] First used by the German engineer Werner von Siemens as an insulator for land cables,[21] the gum proved perfect for submarine cables, which gradually linked the national telegraph networks together. In 1859, Valentia in Ireland was joined to Newfoundland by telegraph cables laid from Isambard Kingdom Brunel's steamship, the *Great Eastern*.[22] Six years later, Karachi was linked to London. Malta was connected to Alexandria in 1868; France to Newfoundland in 1869; India, Hong Kong, China, and Japan by 1870; Australia to the outside world in 1871; and South America by 1874. By this time, there was over 650,000 miles of landline, and by 1880 there were 100,000 miles of undersea cable,[23] which grew to 115,000 miles at the end of the decade.[24] By 1907, there were 200,000 nautical miles of submarine cable, which had been laid at a cost of between £150 and £200 per mile[25] or a total of between £97.5 million and £130 million.[26]

Given the laissez-faire economic orthodoxy of the period, the telegraph network was initially developed by private capital.[27] Its strategic value was soon noticed by colonial governments, which led to its subsidization. As the historian Daniel Headrick notes, the near-panic engendered by the Indian Mutiny of 1857 led to a chorus of urgent calls for the expansion of the telegraph system.[28] In the year of the Mutiny, British India boasted 4,555 miles of telegraph wire and by 1859 the authorities endorsed plans to link the subcontinent with London.[29] The Red Sea and India Telegraph Company, which operated the trunk line to India, was heavily subsidized, with the British government guaranteeing dividends for fifty years.[30] The cable formed part of what the British called the "all red line," strategically designed to connect their empire to London without ever passing over foreign soil.[31]

A Paradox

The cables were a marvel of Victorian technology. The first transatlantic cable was made up of seven 3/8 inches copper wires twisted tightly together, with the individual wires given three coats of refined gutta-percha. The cables were then sheathed in tarred hemp and wound tightly with iron wire for protection from submarine hazards. The cables—which were manufactured in hundred-mile-long lengths at the Gutta-Percha Company's works at Silvertown in London's East End—were spliced together aboard the cable-laying vessels on the high seas.[32] Strict quality control ensured a product that would withstand the corrosive effects of saltwater and undersea hazards.

As with the early India rubber factories, this "high-tech" industry rested on a paradox: although the copper and the iron for the wires were obtained from highly organized mines run as disciplined industrial undertakings, the gutta-percha was provided by primitive, precapitalist extractive methods in the remote jungles of empire. Braving the snakes, leeches, biting insects, malaria, and sharp bamboo stakes on the forest floor, Malay, Dayak or Chinese woodsmen would select a suitable tree, fence it with wooden staging, and fell it with their axes and machetes. The leaves and branches would be trimmed and incisions made in the trunk of the fallen giant to drain the latex into bowls or holes in the ground. The coagulated latex would be roughly washed several times and delivered in sheets to the Singapore merchants, who usually mixed several grades together and were not averse to adulterating it with stones, sago flour, and sawdust.[33] The fallen trees—which still contained the bulk of their latex—would be left to rot on the jungle floor.

While the method of extraction might have been sustainable for the small amounts of gum used by the Malays and Javanese in pre-colonial days, the demands of the gutta-percha factories in the metropolitan countries caused unsustainable pressures on the forests. The trees, which yielded a mere eleven ounces of gum on average, were soon threatened with extinction. In 1900, William Brannt warned that "with the irrational manner in which the juice is collected, the trees still in existence will become more and more decimated, and . . . there is a danger of a decrease in the exportation and finally of the entire exhaustion of the sources."[34] Two decades earlier, the Scottish botanist James Collins reported that the once flourishing isonandra tree was almost extinct in Singapore as a result of gutta-percha exports to Europe.[35] In Collins's estimation, some three million gutta-percha trees were destroyed in one region of Sarawak alone between 1854 and 1875.[36] According to the French expert Eugène Sérullas, the tree had disappeared from Singapore by 1857, from Malacca and Selangor by no later than 1875, and from Perak by 1884. In 1883, British authorities in the Straits Settlements banned further exploitation but by then "it was too late, indeed, to preserve the existence of the trees."[37]

M. Sérullas warned that a crisis was at hand.[38] If the destruction of forests did not move the industry and governments to act, the drying up of gum supplies did. In 1891, two French cable companies were "compelled to abstain from competing for cables between France and the north coast of Africa, recently offered to tender by the French Government, owing to the scarcity of gutta-percha of a suitable quality," he noted.[39] In 1902, *The New York Times* reported that the taban tree was no longer found growing wild in the explored parts of the Dutch Indies.[40] By the early 1890s, the cable industry was consuming four million pounds of gum per year.[41] More than 23 million trees were destroyed to provide for exports in 1898 alone.[42] Lesley Potter estimated that by 1900, at least one million gutta-percha trees had been cut down in Dutch Borneo.[43] Sérullas estimated that five million isonandra trees were destroyed in the region.[44] In 1900, there were 200,000 nautical miles of submarine cable around the world. A rough calculation indicates that the gutta-percha in these cables totaled at least 27,000 tons. On the basis of an average yield of eleven ounces of latex per tree, some 88 million gutta-percha trees must have been sacrificed to make this possible.[45]

However, it would be wrong to blame the Malay woodsmen for the near-extinction of the trees, as European observers tended to do. Their methods of extraction were primitive and wasteful, but it was European and North American industry that sent demand soaring. There are sad parallels between this ecological destruction and the mass destruction of human beings by colonialism—from the Madras famine of 1876,[46] to the unspeakable horrors committed in the so-called Congo Free State under Leopold II and on the Putumayo River in Peru. For better or worse, it was colonialism that remodeled Southeast Asia, stripping away the forests and raising up new cities such as Singapore in the process.

Horrified by the destruction, James Collins argued that for every taban cut down, the colonial authorities ensure that three or four more were planted on "well-regulated plantations."[47] Efforts to develop substitutes for gutta-percha were unsuccessful until the creation of artificial plastics many decades later and it appeared that an impasse had been reached. In 1890 or 1891, however, Eugène Sérullas developed a method for extracting the gum from the leaves and twigs of the trees. These were chopped up mechanically and then treated with acid to produce a liquor that was concentrated into a gum by steaming. This process opened the way to the orderly and sustainable cultivation and harvesting of taban bushes and trees on plantations.[48] The idea was slow to catch on, however, and thirty years after Collins wrote his report, Hubert Terry claimed:

> Comparatively little has been done in the way of gutta-percha plantations, and the results so far achieved go to show that the cultivation is not only hedged around with difficulties but also that, compared with rubber, a much longer time must elapse before any return is obtained from invested capital.[49]

Many years later, by the time that synthetic plastic alternatives were available, the Southeast Asian rainforests faced much direr threats from the activities of logging companies and other industries. In the twenty years before 1990, one-third of the forests of Sarawak disappeared, and despite a greater consciousness of the role of the forests in ensuring the health of the planet, the plunder continues. The slaughter of the wild taban trees was on a smaller scale, yet James Collins's words, written in 1878, are an ominous portent of things to come:

> When in Singapore my heart has often ached when I have fallen across clearings for pepper, gambier, and the like, to see with what recklessness mighty monarchs of the forest are cut, or as a rule, burnt down in all directions, the unused rotting on the ground. Thus a fair spot costing nature centuries to fill with her handiwork looks like a charnel house.[50]

. . .

THE RUBBER COMPANIES were among the first of the twentieth century's large corporations. In Europe during the period, the industry included Dunlop in Great Britain, Pirelli in Italy, and Michelin in France. In the United States, there was the Big Four: U.S. Rubber, Goodyear, Firestone, and B.F. Goodrich. The latter three corporations were first established in the Midwestern city of Akron. Originally comparatively small operations, over time the Akron firms were transformed into enormous horizontally and vertically integrated corporations whose activities spanned the globe. Most of their smaller rivals perished as a result of ruthless competition, or survived by concentrating on niche markets. Small profit margins and intense competition also meant that the rubber corporations were among the most relentlessly anti-union of American employers. Even though Akron was a frontline in the struggle for unionization of the industrial workforce, Goodyear Tire & Rubber, the city's largest employer, did not sign a contract with the United Rubber Workers of America until 1941.

PART THREE

Monopoly Capitalism in Akron

CHAPTER NINE

"Rubber's Home Town"[1]

In those days Akron was still a boomtown; she had grown so fast she hadn't caught up with herself. Main Street, Market Street, it all had an unfinished look, more like a boardwalk in some amusement park. Night clubs and eating places and pool rooms and sport shops, where you could play the numbers, and at that time they had cabarets with girls, and shooting galleries, and all such trash. Seems they didn't even have time to put in a decent sewer system, you could smell that too, and roads ran out into nowhere and the whole town was a jumble with too many folks, crowded in, sweating, swearing, and pushing each other out of the way.

—VICKI BAUM[2]

Akron's old-timers used to say that you could smell Rubber Town long before you saw it. The Ohio city is hidden in the low sandstone folds of the westernmost Alleghenies, but if the wind was right, the "tang of molten rubber"[3] carried as far as Wooster, thirty miles to the southwest. Some early pilots even claimed to know when they were over Akron because of the dirty diaper smell of sulfuretted hydrogen.[4] The vast rubber factories belched a pall of smoke over the city, plunging it into twilight "gloomier than Pittsburgh"[5] and often carpeting it with black snow. In its time, this Midwestern city housed the world's greatest concentration of rubber factories and for some eighty years it was known as "Rubber's Home Town."[6]

The Akron Rubber Barons

Nineteenth-century boosters bragged of making Akron the greatest industrial city in the world, the "Tip Top City." One person who listened was an ex-Civil War surgeon named Dr. Benjamin Franklin Goodrich, who traveled west in 1870 seeking an alternative location for his New York rubber mill. Goodrich had planned—or gambled—well. Markets aside, there were other indications that he had made a wise choice. Rubber, it is often said, is a thirsty industry, and Ohio is never short of water. Land was also cheap and plentiful in Akron and coal—a heavy, dirty, and bulky commodity—was available from local mines. Labor could be locally recruited, and labor costs tended to be cheaper than they were back East. The raw rubber itself would be imported from Brazil. In May 1871, Dr. Goodrich opened his factory on flat land lying between South Main Street and the Ohio and Erie Canal. Initially precarious, the business eventually prospered.[7] Goodrich was convinced that the key to success in a competitive market rested with continuous improvement of the finished product. His motto was: "Anything that can be made can be made better."[8] Twenty years after its inception, BF Goodrich was the fourth-largest industry in the city, employing almost four hundred men in its mills.

The second of Akron's rubber barons was Francis "Frank" Seiberling, the descendent of a shoemaker who had set up a farm machinery factory in the city.[9] Control of the factory eventually passed to Frank,[10] but as the effects of the 1890s trade depression hit home and the center of gravity of America's agricultural industry shifted further west, he went bankrupt.[11] Stubborn and unsentimental, he borrowed capital in 1898 to set up the Goodyear Tire & Rubber Company in East Akron. His new factory started with thirteen employees, making bicycle tires and solid carriage tires by hand.[12] Two years later Seiberling had 150 men on the payroll. In the early days, the workers would hang fishing poles out of the factory windows into the Little Cuyahoga River to catch their dinners while they worked.[13] Such homely touches would not last long.

In 1900, a Yankee engineer named Paul Litchfield arrived in Akron to take up his new position as Goodyear's plant superintendent: a grandiose title for a job in what he later described as "a rather dilapidated group of buildings alongside a creek."[14] Litchfield was an ambitious outsider, but he was no bird of passage and as he wrote later the East Akron plant "was to be my business home for the next half century." Litchfield was the epitome of the "gum-dipped" executive. The son of a Boston portrait photog-

Goodyear President P. W. Litchfield (third from left) with zeppelin engineers
Karl von Arnstein (smoking cigar) and Hugo Eckener, Akron, OH.

rapher[15] and a devout Unitarian, Litchfield was descended from pioneers
who had arrived in America aboard the *Mayflower*.[16] He had stumbled
into a career in rubber in New England, working first as a laborer in the
region's antiquated rubber mills during his long vacations from MIT. The
experience prepared him well, for although he was initially "nauseated"
by the smell of the raw rubber, he grew inured to it. In fact, the stench on
his clothing was so bad that railway conductors refused to let him ride
inside the trains and he had to stand on the back platforms.[17] An energetic, forceful, visionary young man, he also had an eloquence seldom
found among the sober fraternity of engineers and managers, and he was
to become an indefatigable speaker and writer on behalf of Goodyear and
the industry as a whole. In time, he was to supplant Frank Seiberling as
the head of the firm and supervise its transformation into a business
empire that, he said, "spread all over the globe so that the sun never sets
on the Goodyear factory."[18] By 1916, Goodyear was the country's largest
tire manufacturer and by 1926 it was the largest rubber company in the
world,[19] fed by capital from New York banks following a bailout by the
brokerage firm Dillon Read when the company faced bankruptcy in the
postwar slump.[20]

Meanwhile, a third major player-to-be had settled in Akron. Harvey
Firestone, Sr., pious Episcopalian, staunch Republican, and devout entre-

preneur, had grown up on a farm near Columbiana, some miles to the west of Akron. Like Seiberling he was a little Napoleon of a man, a scant five-foot-five in his socks, and possessed fearsome energy and a will to succeed. After learning the rudiments of bookkeeping in a Columbus, Ohio coal office, Firestone struck out on his own as a glorified snake oil seller, hawking patent cures around rural Ohio. After a stint in the rubber marketing business in Chicago, Firestone moved to Akron in January 1900.[21] He opened a small rubber factory in the summer of 1900, moving the following year to a bigger site on South Main Street.[22]

A fourth magnate, William "Bill" O'Neil, set up his East Akron plant in 1915 when the tire industry was firmly established, standing out as an Irish Catholic in an industry dominated by WASPs. O'Neil was "a compulsively competitive man with supreme confidence in the American system of private enterprise." He called the company he founded General Tire & Rubber, probably because he equated the word "General" with the success of industrial giant General Electric.[23] Although his company never rivaled Akron's Big Three, it resisted the fierce competitive pressures that sent most of the city's other small fry to the wall.

The Dawn of the Automobile Age

At the turn of the nineteenth century, Akron was still a minor center in the American rubber industry, which was concentrated in New England and New York State. The industry had grown up there after a Yankee sea captain brought the first rubber goods to Boston in 1820. In the early 1830s, Edwin M. Chaffee and partners opened an India rubber factory in Massachusetts.[24] In 1892, Charles Renlett Flint formed the U.S. Rubber Company, a corporate behemoth by the standards of the time, with a capital stock of $50 million.[25] Flint absorbed many of his competitors and by 1892 he employed over 150,000 rubber workers.[26] The Akron upstarts were aggressive competitors, quick to take advantage of mass advertising, proximity to expanding Midwestern markets, and the relatively low pay rates applying in their city—and they were determined to keep the unions out of their plants. They were also dedicated innovators and they were not burdened by investment in the antiquated machinery common in the factories of the Northeast. Goodrich's successors were also quick to see the potential of the new automobile industry that was to transform American life.

Until the automobile age, people seldom strayed far from their homes. As Harvey Firestone, Jr. told his listeners in a 1931 radio broadcast, older people thought five to ten miles by horse and buggy a long journey, and fifty to one hundred miles by railroad was considered "extraordinary." By the 1930s, however, he said that Americans considered a trip of fifty miles by car to be "nothing" and took the pneumatic tire for granted.[27] By 1900 the United States was on the brink of revolutionary changes in transportation. Before the advent of mass-produced cars, the major products of the Akron plants, as in New England, included bicycle tires and solid wheels for carriages. As late as 1900, the Goodyear Company bought extensive advertising space in national magazines for its rubber horseshoe pads.[28] Even Harvey Firestone, who recognized the potential for pneumatic tires before his rivals, rode to work in a horse and buggy during those early years.[29] Skeptical bystanders would often call out "get a horse!" when cars stalled in the muddy Akron streets.[30]

Automobiles were produced in U.S. factories from the late-nineteenth century and the first U.S. car race was held in Chicago in 1895.[31] Cars were widely regarded as an expensive novelty, but Firestone's friend Henry Ford was to change this. Ford was a prickly, ruthless, rude, anti-Semitic and driven man who despised "book learning" with redneck intensity, but he epitomized the American industrial pragmatist. He famously sneered, "History is bunk," and once claimed that his innovations were possible "because I haven't enough knowledge in my head to interfere with my thinking."[32] Ford revolutionized industrial processes, making mass production by semiskilled and unskilled operatives a modern substitute for the painstaking process of small-scale manufacture by skilled mechanics. In 1908, the first of 15,000,000 Model T Fords rolled off the production line at Dearborn, Michigan. In 1905, there were 77,000 motor registrations in the U.S. Five years later, there were 350,000, and on the eve of the First World War, there were 1.25 million. By 1929, there were 26.5 million.[33]

Akron Cashes In

Akron's rubber barons quickly took advantage of the fact that the mass market in automobiles brought with it the need for the mass production of pneumatic tires.[34] In 1909, the *India-Rubber Journal* named Akron as "probably the largest rubber manufacturing centre in the world," with

thirteen rubber companies and a total investment of over £4 million ster-
ling, or more than $554 million in today's values using the retail price
index as a guide.[35] The main product was tires, but the city's factories also
churned out "rubber goods of all descriptions, including both soft and
hard rubber articles."[36] The Firestone plant alone was manufacturing
over 600,000 tires per annum by 1913.[37] By 1915, the United States was
consuming some 70 percent of the world's raw rubber,[38] and in 1918
Akron took 60 percent of the country's imports of the commodity[39]—or
over 40 percent of the global production of raw rubber.[40] Looking back
from the Depression years, the journalist H. Earl Wilson remembered that
there were eighty millionaires in Akron during the great boom.[41]

Statistics tell only part of the story. The rubber companies at Akron
did not just take hold of readymade machinery and use it on a larger
scale. The Big Three were at the cutting edge of rubber technology,
sinking vast sums of money into research and development. The twin
spurs were competition and profit. Profit margins were slim and could
only be maintained by quality control, efficient production, economies
of scale, ruthless marketing, and the strict regimentation of the workforce. Alfred Lief estimates that the introduction of machine-built tires
around 1910 cut direct labor production costs by one-half.[42] Five years
earlier, Harvey Firestone had built a huge new plant in South Akron and
began to produce handmade automobile tires. Seven years later, his factory was mass producing machine-built tires.[43] If intense competition
meant continuous technological change, it also led to an obsession with
time and the introduction of the Taylor and Bedaux systems of "scientific management" to extract the maximum possible surplus value from
the workforce.

The effects on competitors were devastating. The rubber barons
detested each other and jealously guarded their innovations. Suspicion
about industrial espionage verged on paranoia. Goodyear's Paul
Litchfield records that when he went to Clermont-Ferrand in 1912, the
Michelin management refused to see him and set a private detective to
dog his footsteps in the French city's streets.[44] Michelin employees were
required to sign an undertaking not to reveal the company's "secrets" to
rivals or their industrial spies.[45] By 1937, outside of the Big Three in
Akron, only Mohawk Rubber, General Tire, and the Seiberling Company
at Barberton survived and the once substantial Swinehart, Marathon,
Mason, and Star and Portage rubber companies had been driven to the
wall or absorbed by their rivals.[46]

The Akron entrepreneurs were guided by the realization that "nothing is so perishable as an established product."[47] They also recruited talented chemists and engineers to ensure that they stayed ahead in the technical race. Waldo Semon drove his Model T Ford to Akron with his family and belongings from Seattle in 1926 and headed up the polymer research at BF Goodrich that led to the creation of PVC.[48] Other gifted scientists in the company's stable included Arthur H. "Dirty" Marks, a nickname earned because of his blackened fingernails from laboratory work,[49] and Dr. George Oenslager, who first used carbon black to strengthen and color tire rubber in 1912[50] and who pioneered the use of aniline dyes to speed up the vulcanization process.[51] The rubber companies were also quick to acknowledge the value of any innovation made elsewhere. One example of this was the invention of the Banbury internal mixer in 1916 by Dr. Fernley H. Banbury, a Cornish-born heavy engineering specialist who was rushed to Goodyear to put the machine into operation.[52] It radically improved the mixing of masticated rubber and chemicals to produce a uniform product and rendered the old two-roll open mill obsolete. Banbury mixers are still a standard feature of rubber factories today.[53]

The Wingfoot Express and the Silver Fleet

The new motorcars were joined on the roads by motor trucks that relied on the pneumatic tires the Akron industrialists were eager to produce. The numbers grew steadily: in 1904 there were only 700 registered trucks in the whole of the United States and these all rolled on solid tires. By 1920 there were over a million and by 1947 over six and a half million.[54] From 1916, Goodyear manufactured pneumatic truck tires and while the advantages of these were clear for short-distance haulage, there was considerable skepticism about their value for long-distance freight. Goodyear set out to prove the critics wrong and to create the demand for its products. From 1917, the company operated its own freight line, the Wingfoot Akron-Boston Highway Express, "to convince skeptics of the value of pneumatics for long distance hauling." From 1920, the company even built its own six-wheeler trucks that could travel at thirty miles per hour with a six-ton load. The other rubber companies followed suit. BF Goodrich, for example, maintained its famous "Silver Fleet" of trucks, which toured the United States from 1929 to the mid-1930s testing the company's tires on every conceivable type of road and in every climate and terrain.[55] Such a commitment involved a real leap of faith. The problems were not just of human perception; they involved physical obstacles of mud, dust, snow and ice, and rickety bridges. Manufacturers and wholesalers relied on the railroads for long and medium distance haulage because the country's roads had been designed for the horse and buggy. Indeed there was no properly integrated national highway system at all, as the crews of the Wingfoot Express discovered when "[o]riginal and subsequent runs left a well-marked trail of broken bridges, aged structures that were to prove unequal to modern transportation demands."[56]

In 1917, the first trucks Goodyear sent over the Alleghenies to Boston were bogged down fifteen miles out of Akron. Heavy rain had turned the dirt road into a quagmire, and the crew had to winch the trucks out. Hugh Allen, the company's public relations manager, recorded that after five weeks, twenty-three wrecked tires and countless damaged or destroyed bridges and telephone poles, the crew drove into Boston.[57] Undaunted, Vice-President Litchfield made what was at the time a startling prophecy: "With pneumatic tires, the truck is destined to become a lifeline of our economy. From city streets and alleys, trucking will spread over every mile of existing highways in the nation and over highways yet to come." Moreover, they would carry everything from heavy machinery to eggs.[58] The public's attention had been earlier drawn to the issue of long distance automobile travel in 1919–1920, when a convoy of army trucks under the command of the young army officer Lt. Col. Dwight Eisenhower took sixty days to cross America from the Atlantic to the Pacific.[59] Thirty-six years later, U.S. President Eisenhower ordered the construction of an all-weather national highway system—the National Defense Highway System[60]—and Litchfield's economic prediction was realized.

"Akron: Standing Room Only"

Swept up in the rubber boom that preceded the First World War, Akron grew swiftly from a sleepy Midwestern town into a booming industrial city. The barons' factories were built on a colossal scale, strung like immense brick battleships along East Market and South Main, puffing clouds of smut and smoke into the air. Akron became one of the most polluted cities in America, rivaling even Pittsburgh's claim to endure "darkness at noon."[61] The city also pulsed with crowds. At the shift changes,

Aerial view of Goodyear plant, Akron, in its heyday.

workers swarmed onto the streets and the air was full of the clanging of
streetcar bells. No city on earth, perhaps, could match the speed with
which the "Tip Top City" was growing as a result of the rubber boom.
Akron entered the twentieth century with a population of 42,000, most of
them locally born in what had been "a quiet and well-regulated Western
Reserve city."[62] Between 1910 and 1917, the city experienced a 202 percent population increase.[63] In 1910, Akron housed almost 70,000 people
and by 1920, there were 208,000, a third of whom worked in the city's
rubber mills.[64] Many more were directly or indirectly dependent on the
mills for their livelihood: gummers' wives and children, shopkeepers,
landlords, contractors of every sort, whores and bartenders, peddlers and
service workers. The days in which local boys could fish and swim in the
town's creeks[65] would pass forever as the river banks fell under the shadow of an American version of Blake's "dark Satanic mills." Everywhere
was the thick crush of people in a boomtown of saloons, brothels, cafés,
music halls, and speakeasies. Bartenders lined up pots of beer and shots
of rye for gummers coming off shift. Revues with dancing girls had midnight sessions. The city lived twenty-four hours a day, catering for the different shifts. It was quite a change from the pre-rubber days in Akron
when, as one prominent citizen remarked dryly, "a young man could
spend a hilarious evening until nine o'clock at the public library and then
go to the Union Station to see the Columbus train come in."[66]

The city center was strung out along the intersection of Main and Market Streets. The streets were largely unpaved, with wooden sidewalks lapped by the mud and dust stirred up by horses' hooves and steel-shod wooden wheels and later the tires that were to bring the city its fame. It was a city of extremes of wealth and poverty, both of which could be found along Market Street, which ran from the factory district of East Akron "to the svelte suburb of Fairlawn" many miles west. In the east and center, there were "the slums along the canal . . . where hardworking women keep their men" and in the west "elegant apartments where befurred women are kept by men who do no work at all," the Akron writer Burr McCloskey wrote.[67] The worst districts were down by the marshy river bottoms. Here, the city's African American population lived in abject poverty, harassed by local chapters of the Ku Klux Klan, and the racism of genteel white folk who wished to keep their suburbs racially "pure."

Storybook Palaces

For many years the city's swankest suburb was Fir Hill, adjacent to what is now the campus of the University of Akron. By the early twentieth century, however, the stench of the rubber mills had driven many of the city's rich folk to the less tainted air of West Exchange and Market Streets. It was there that the O'Neils of General Tire & Rubber built their palatial mansion and Harvey Firestone his sprawling Harbel Manor.[68] Frank Seiberling's mansion, Stan Hywet Hall, was built on the Portage Path, along which the Iroquois once hauled their canoes between the Cuyahoga and the Ohio rivers. Built in the American Tudor revival style to the specifications of an acclaimed architect, the house and grounds are today open to the public and give some inkling of the tremendous wealth generated at the height of the rubber boom.[69] The O'Neil mansion is now an upmarket bed and breakfast, but the visitor will search West Market Street in vain for any sign of Harvey Firestone's mammoth residence. Begun in 1912, Harbel Manor expanded year by year until it comprised 118 rooms, some of them with Italian marble fireplaces and teak paneling. The property included a swimming pool, stables for seventy-five horses and an indoor riding course, and a farm with thirty sheep and 5,000 White Leghorn chickens. Pulled down in 1959 and sold off as forty-five separate lots by a realty firm, the only traces of what an Akron journalist

called a "storybook palace . . . from the great days of the rubber boom"[70]
are a scale model of the main house and the original brass nameplate of
the premises.[71] Firestone, who also maintained a mansion in Miami, once
pondered, "Why is it that a man as soon as he gets enough money, builds
a house much bigger than he needs?"[72]

Less privileged folk who came looking for work were fortunate if they
found board and lodgings in the overcrowded city. Often the mill men had
no real homes to return to after work. The influx of workers had created
a massive housing crisis, with basements, attics, garages, and chicken
coops sublet to families and single workers at extortionate rents.[73] There
was "standing room only in Akron," the journalist Edward Mott Wooley
famously observed in 1917. "It was ridiculously easy to find a job, but
almost impossible to find a place to sleep."[74] Another journalist recalled,
"Amazing signs dotted the town. They said: 'FOR RENT: BED FOR THIRD
SHIFT.'"[75] Some incoming workers were housed in a tent city on the site
of the company housing subdivision of Goodyear Heights.[76] Akron's
"unique sleeping arrangements" had melancholy consequences during
the influenza epidemic of 1918. "The overcrowded conditions in the
city's rooming houses," a local journalist considered, "were exactly what
was needed to make the flu a great death-dealing machine."[77]

"The Capital of West Virginia"

Akron's factories had an insatiable appetite for young, strong laborers. Even
before foreign immigration was curtailed by federal legislation in 1924, the
factories looked south for supplies. As the labor historian Dan Nelson has
written, "Akron lay on the northern edge of a vast area of marginal farms and
underemployed workers" that encompassed southeast Ohio, southwest
Pennsylvania, and West Virginia.[78] Recruiters scoured the region for workers. Three-quarters of the newcomers to Akron were American-born and
many came from the impoverished "hollows," coal towns, and hill farms of
the Appalachians.[79] Many were desperate to escape poverty. The future
rubber union leader John House recalled that he had watched his father
work "harder than any man should" trying to make a decent living to support his family on a marginal farm in Georgia. He vowed he would not
spend his life in the same drudgery and went north to Akron.[80]

The recruiters bought advertising space in backcountry newspapers,
holding out the promise of a better life to restless and impoverished farm

boys. These mountain men were often bussed direct to factory gates, with colored tags emblazoned with their new employers' names stuffed into their buttonholes[81] to brand them like so many pieces of merchandise. Because so many of them took Route 21 north from the hills, vaudeville comedians dubbed Akron "the capital of West Virginia."[82] By 1920, there were between 50,000 and 77,000 white Southerners living in the city.[83] They stood out because of their distinctive accents and clustered together in their own neighborhoods with their own traditions: playing "old-timey" music on fiddles, guitars, and banjos, worshipping in their own chapels for "shouting Methodists" and holy rollers, listening as revivalist preachers castigated Akron as Sodom on the Cuyahoga.[84]

By the end of the First World War, the Akron West Virginia Club boasted 25,000 members and twice that many turned out to their annual picnics.[85] Native-born Akronites often derided them as "Snakes" or "Snake Eaters," although there was no evidence that serpents ever formed part of their diet.[86] Like Irish immigrants elsewhere, they were the butt of cruel jokes. One farm boy turned on a drinking fountain in the BF Goodrich mill, but "a very large stream of water hit him full in the face with almost enough force to knock him down." The fountain was malfunctioning, but the young man was convinced it was a practical joke, opining "[t]hat's the way the darned smart alex [sic] in town plays tricks on us farm boys."[87] In 1921, local journalist Joe Sheridan quipped that a man had been "sentenced to West Virginia for life" after an Akron judge granted the felon a suspended sentence on condition that he leave the city and go home to Appalachia. Akron's outraged West Virginians successfully mobilized in local elections against the Democratic Party and swore, "There will be no more criminals who should be in the penitentiary that will be exiled to West Virginia."[88]

The hill folk were "Akron's largest ethnic group"[89] and the preferred labor force for the rubber mills. Although Ruth McKenney noted that Akron was a largely white city,[90] and Alfred Winslow Jones testifies to its high proportion of "native born" Americans,[91] there were enclaves of other nationalities: Italians in North Hill, Hungarians, Slovenes, and other Slavs in Barberton, and Germans in Wolf Ledges. The city must have been a strange and frightening place to the European immigrants, many of whom went directly from the trains into the factories, often without taking stock of their new surroundings or even eating a meal. Homesick and isolated behind barriers of language, they were nevertheless to contribute enormously to their new country. In the end many prospered, but the rubber industry's appetite for labor and profits all too often cast a shadow over the American Dream. As Daniel Nelson observed, European immigrants—and American blacks—often did the dirtiest, heaviest, least skilled, and poorest paying jobs in the mills, such as opening and washing the bales of crude rubber,[92] slaving in the mill rooms, or pushing brooms through the soapstone dust that was used in tiremaking.

Klan Town

Racism was deeply entrenched in Akron, an irony given that the city was the home of anti-slavery martyr John Brown for many years, the scene of Sojourner Truth's celebrated address "Ain't I a Woman?"[93] and a major stop on the "underground railroad" that smuggled runaway slaves to Canada. In 1913, white residents of North Hill formed a committee to exclude blacks from the suburb.[94] When Goodyear and Firestone built housing estates for their workers in the years following the First World War, black employees were excluded from buying houses even though white non-employees could do so.[95] Segregation extended to the company's in-house welfare schemes, with its separate "Goodyear Colored Club."[96] In the rubber mills, black people were excluded from the skilled and high-paying jobs. In 1937, a Communist pamphlet drew attention to what it called "Jim-Crow conditions" in the Goodyear plant: black workers were not allowed to eat in the main canteen and were forced by the management "to eat in that dirty little hole in the wall called the Mill-room cafeteria."[97] Called "boys" regardless of their age, black workers' lives were full of casual insult and governed by the color bar. James Turner started work at Firestone in 1934 and despite a good education his skin color saw him put to work on the yard gang. It was, he recalled, one of the most "distasteful" jobs in the plant. In winter, the men dug the pipeline for the plant's water supply, often up to their knees in water in subzero-degree weather. In summer, they cleaned the heater pits, in "sweltering" temperatures. He was later "promoted" to janitor and ended his career in the mill room before being seconded to work for the international union.[98]

Akron was perhaps the largest center for the Ku Klux Klan outside of the South—for the white Southerners had brought more than shouting religion and banjo music with them. For a brief period in the 1920s, according to historian Karl Grismer, the Klan "practically ruled the city."[99] Blacks formed a tiny minority of the city's population—less than

6,000 out of a population of 208,000 in 1920. The Klan boasted 52,000 members in the city at the time and its rallies and cross-burnings attracted large crowds. Depending on the circumstances, the Klan could appear both pro and anti-union and Republican or Democrat, but at its core, it was a demagogic anti-Black, anti-Semitic, anti-Catholic, and anti-Labor organization the rubber companies happily coexisted with. The Klan's influence declined after a series of financial scandals in 1926, but contrary to some optimistic claims, it never disappeared from the city. The Jewish CIO organizer Rose Pesotta records that many staunch union members in the 1930s, including the legendary picket captain "Skip" Oharra, had been Klansmen. When the wife of a striker casually mentioned the Klan, Pesotta disingenuously asked what it was. The woman replied that it was "'A social and educational society' . . . in the manner of one explaining a local custom to an outsider."[100]

It was a case of the "tradition of all the dead generations weigh[ing] like a nightmare on the brains of the living."[101] Conservative white Southerners were imbued with the ideology of individualistic "pure Americanism" and hailed from regions where wages were low and farm work was excruciatingly hard. Moreover, they brought with them the ideology of racism from a society in which the races are divided in every walk of life. Their attitudes—or at least those of the industrial union leaders whom they produced and deeply respected—only began to change as a result of the radicalizing effects of the class struggle that broke out in Akron in the 1930s, and was recorded by Pesotta. Nevertheless, the first black tire builder only learned the trade in 1955, and many things did not begin to improve for black people in Akron until after the Civil Rights Act was passed in 1964.[102]

"Light Infantry of Capital"

The rubber companies preferred to employ white Southerners rather than Ohio locals, blacks, or foreign immigrants.[103] It was in the interests of the rubber bosses to have a floating population to depress wage rates and cut across possible worker militancy, ensure maximum production and profits, and replace those who left or were worn out. The mountain men were hard workers and often individualistic in outlook, reflecting their origins as fiercely independent small-owners of farmlands. Even those who had previously labored on the railroads or down in the mines of their home states had close connections to the soil, and many Akron gummers maintained their small properties "back home." European immigrants were seen as more susceptible to socialist and syndicalist ideas, making them less favorable to Akron's employers, who were often forced to hire them because of labor shortages.[104] There is a striking parallel between the hiring policies of the Akron mills and those of the Michelin rubber company at Clermont-Ferrand in France. As Herbert Lottman has written, Michelin's workers were drawn from the remote farm villages of the Auvergne. These strong young men were willing to work for low wages and "were hardly likely to be confused with their brothers in the industrial North—descendents of the Communards, ancestors of the Communists, Socialists and Trotskyists, or anarchists of our time . . ."[105] Clermont-Ferrand is the commercial center of the Auvergne. Much of the farmland is marginal and the Occitan-speaking population would have had much in common with the Appalachian mountain men who flocked to Akron.

Akron's proximity to Appalachia also meant that "excess" labor could be returned when not needed. Work in the rubber mills was often seasonal, with greater demand for tires in the warmer months. Supply and demand for labor power was also affected by the booms and busts of the business cycle. The sociologist Alfred Winslow Jones claimed that the Southern migrant proletariat in Akron had a relatively undeveloped class consciousness,[106] with their fierce individualism and American "nativism" conflicting with collectivist ideologies. Yet the proposition is dubious, or at best overdrawn. As Marx has insisted, consciousness develops from social being, and collective struggle can trigger leaps in class consciousness. The harsh conditions of life and work in Akron would turn this Southern "light infantry of Capital" into a veritable proletarian army in the bitterly fought class war in America. They would embrace the new creed of industrial unionism with the same fervor with which they embraced the gospels in their churches. Furthermore, this syndicalist consciousness translated into considerable support for an independent working-class political party. Akron—and the local organization of the United Rubber Workers in particular—was a bastion of the Farmer-Labor Party.[107]

CHAPTER TEN

The 1913 IWW Strike at Akron

The rubber manufacturers do not cut off the hands and feet of your children, but they take the food from their mouths.

—"BIG BILL" HAYWOOD, IWW leader, Akron, 1913[1]

When the men and women of labor resent the tyranny of industrial czars a cry is sent up appealing to the public to . . . "put down the lawless mob."

—SHERMAN H. DALRYMPLE,
International President URWA, 1936[2]

By the early twentieth century, the United States had developed into a formidable industrial power, but this "great leap forward" came at a steep price for the working class. Ruthless competition and an aggressively individualistic ideology meant that the class struggle in America was fought with astounding ferocity. Governments, the police, the National Guard, and the courts invariably supported the employers, who did not hesitate to use thugs, spies, private detectives, and illegal means to win. As Sherman Dalrymple, the International President of the United Rubber Workers of America, later observed: "The rich have looked upon the agencies of government as their private instrument to protect and defend them in their raids on labor's rights."[3] Like their counterparts in iron and steel, textiles, mining, and heavy engineering, the rubber barons were determined to crush the unions before they could gain a foothold in the mills. The first major industrial battle in the Akron rubber factories broke out in 1913 when the nonunionized gummers spontaneously struck and called on the "Wobblies," the radical Industrial Workers of the World (IWW), for assistance. The strike collapsed in the face of employer intransigence and ferocious repression by police and vigilantes and it was another twenty years before the dream of an independent class-conscious union would be realized.

"A Great Business Is Really too Big to Be Human"

The first rubber factories in Akron were small enough for the owners to know the names of all their employees, but this would not last. "A great business," observed Harvey Firestone's friend Henry Ford, "is really too big to be human."[4] For all the literary labors of Paul Litchfield to prove the contrary, the interests of "masters and men" were not identical. His slogan of "business for the people, and by the people"[5] was oxymoronic. Although the struggle for improved pay and conditions was a central focus of union activity, generations of Akron workers saw their fight as one for what we would today call *human rights*.

On the eve of the First World War, Akron was already a boomtown. A banner at the city's Union Station famously welcomed newcomers to "the City of Opportunity" and the rubber companies' promises of good wages and steady work kept them coming. In truth, the wages were not so high,[6] but for farm boys and rural mill hands fresh from the impoverished South they were welcome, particularly when overtime is taken into account. The evidence also indicates that wages did increase in the longer term, despite a general fall just prior to 1914[7] and fluctuations in the following decades. Large profits also meant that the companies could grant seemingly gratuitous wage increases in order to undermine the unions, as happened during an ill-fated attempt to unionize the industry in 1902.[8] Yet there were many other grounds for worker dissatisfaction. These included poor working conditions, the speeding up of work tempos, and the insecurity of seasonal work. The first consequence was a high rate of labor turnover, but the workers' displeasure occasionally manifested itself in spontaneous walk-offs.

Women workers had good reason for dissatisfaction. Their working conditions were often poor and even hazardous, and their pay rates lagged far behind those of their male colleagues. One of the first recorded strikes in the Akron rubber mills involved women at BF Goodrich.

Despite the conventional wisdom that women only entered the industry in any numbers during the Second World War, there had been "generations of 'Rosies'" in the U.S. rubber mills before 1939.[9]

Not only were women paid less than men for comparable work, as with black workers, they were excluded from the higher-paying jobs. It was not until the URWA was firmly established in the early 1940s that there was any talk of equality.[10] Without a union to protect them, adult women rubber workers were paid a maximum of

Percentage of Women Workers in the U.S. Rubber Industry, 1879-1930	
YEAR	AMOUNT
1879	47.6
1880	32.4
1890	39.9
1900	33.0
1910	21.8
1920	26.8

Based on Kathleen L. Endres, *Rosie the Rubber Worker: Women Workers in Akron's Rubber Factories during World War II* (Kent, OH: Kent State University Press, 2000), 21.

ten cents an hour for a ten-hour day, the same rate as boy laborers. Their working conditions were often squalid and many worked in dungeon-like rooms with waterlogged floors throughout their shifts.[11]

The Open Shop

Despite such conditions, the Akron mills were notoriously difficult to unionize. In 1900, a brief sit-down strike erupted to protest cuts to piece-work rates at Goodyear, but management was intransigent and the strike petered out.[12] The American Federation of Labor (AFL) rubber workers' union chartered an Akron local in 1902, but it collapsed after the secretary's home office was burgled and the records were stolen.[13] Tire builders at Akron's Diamond Rubber Company went on strike in 1908, only to be replaced by scabs.[14] The Akron local thereafter "slid quietly into oblivion."[15] Employers could not expect to keep unions out of Akron indefinitely, however. Just before the First World War, the AFL had established a Central Labor Union (CLU) in the city. This body was craft-oriented in line with the Federation's rules, but it was strongly influenced by the city's growing Socialist Party (SP) branch, whose principal organizer was the Canadian-born firebrand Marguerite Prevey, a close friend of the legendary labor radical Eugene V. Debs.[16] The SP supported the idea of all-inclusive industrial unionism, and this was reflected in the CLU, which gave priority to the city's unorganized and unskilled workers, the bulk of whom were in the rubber factories.

Fordism and Scientific Management

After 1900, Paul Litchfield began to reorganize the Goodyear plant along Fordist mass production lines, and the company's rivals were forced to follow suit. Although technological progress did tend to make work lighter,[17] this was offset by intensified work tempos based on the ideas of "scientific management" pioneered by Frederick Winslow Taylor.[18] Taylor's aim was maximum production in the shortest time with the minimum number of employees. Wages were based on performance, and the system rested on the detailed "scientific" division of labor at the enterprise level.[19] Time and motion studies conducted with stopwatch and clipboard allocated a specified time for completion for each task (often down to fractions of a second), tools and equipment were simplified and standardized, and tasks were broken down into tiny units. Brainwork was to be solely in the hands of management and workers were expected to carry out detailed orders.[20] The Akron rubber moguls were quick to see the potential benefits of the system. Men with stopwatches and slide rules appeared throughout the plants, timing the workers' every movement. Workers complained that time allocations were based on the performance of the very youngest and strongest workers: a "rawhide" system that pitted worker against worker.[21] There were big redundancies, too, combined with faster work, deskilling, and pay cuts,[22] mocking Taylor's claim that scientific management would create "maximum prosperity for the employee," as well as bigger profits for the companies. Paul Litchfield later admitted as much when he told New England businessmen that with the new techniques young workers were able "to command earnings equal to or greater than their elders" and moreover:

> A situation has been reached where a man in the factory reaches the peak of his earning power at a much earlier period of life than formerly. His usefulness on this kind of work starts to diminish at a much earlier age, thus making it more difficult for those who have passed the prime of life.[23]

These remarks contradict his public utterances, which blamed high labor turnover on a lack of "grit and stamina" on the part of new recruits[24] and railed against "outside agitators" stirring up trouble. Litchfield was describing a new system that turned on its head the custom and practice of millennia, in which older workers were valued for their wisdom and finely honed skills, which they imparted to the younger generation, and which gave them some control over the work process.

By 1913 the stage was set for "a revolution in the gum mines."[25] Workers walked off the job at the Firestone plant and the strike spread rapidly to the other Akron companies. For six weeks between February 11 and mid-March, up to 75 percent of the city's gummers were on strike.[26] It was a brief "carnival of the oppressed," with parades and militant speeches, mass pickets, and red banners billowing on the cold winter streets. Although the immediate cause of the strike was a 35 percent cut to piece rates by the Firestone management, there was simmering resentment in all the plants over the unpleasant and unhealthy working conditions. These factors, along with the lack of grievance procedures and awareness of the growing gap between wages and profits, were later recognized as the root causes of the strike by an Ohio State Senate investigation.[27]

The employers were adamant that there would be no concessions. They would talk to their workers directly as individuals but would not recognize any union.[28] The entry of the Industrial Workers of the World (IWW) into the dispute led to redbaiting outrage by the employers. Goodyear's Paul Litchfield insisted that the dispute was "an attempt on the part of a left-wing group to seize power."[29] Ohio State Senator William J. Potting claimed that Akron was witnessing "a conflict between the stars and stripes and the red flag of anarchy."[30] David M. Goodrich argued that the strike "was really a battle of the IWW vs. the AFL" and that "the AFL would have been terribly disappointed if the IWW had won their strike."[31] However, while it *is* true that the AFL did try to undermine the IWW, and would have welcomed the strike's defeat, it was a straightforward class battle, not a demarcation dispute between rival federations. The respected Akron historian Karl Grismer concludes that the strike began as a spontaneous walk-off by exasperated Firestone employees and that the IWW "merely fanned the smoldering fire into roaring flames."[32]

The Wobblies and Violence

The IWW had arrived in Akron in 1912, but counted less than fifty paid up members in the city when the strike erupted.[33] Perhaps the Firestone

strikers would have turned to the AFL, but in the absence of interest by
the "mainstream" federation, they went to the Socialist Party's Reindeer
Hall to seek assistance. Marguerite Prevey urged solidarity, sobriety, non-
violence, and IWW membership as the way to win.[34] Despite their wild-
eyed reputation, the Wobblies stuck to a pacific strategy throughout the
dispute.[35] The IWW doctrine of revolutionary syndicalism held that the
workers would organize themselves into "one big union" in order to wrest
power from the capitalists. The new society, they argued, would take
shape within the shell of the old. This was a doctrine of workers' self-
emancipation, not terrorism. Ultra-democratic, they also insisted that the
strikers make their own decisions.

The Wobblies were at first unable to handle the flood of recruits as the
Akron strike spread to over 16,000 out of the city's 22,000 gummers.
They were preoccupied with another large strike at Paterson in New
Jersey, but discipline was gradually imposed, with picket rosters, soup
kitchens, and a propaganda committee to publicize the workers' side of
the dispute. The Wobblies had an ear for the deft and ringing phrase. In
one speech, Big Bill Haywood drew parallels with the atrocities of the
British and Peruvian rubber companies in the Putumayo and the depredations of the King of the Belgians in the Congo. In the early days of the
strike, the workers were euphoric. The IWW *Strike Bulletin* asked:

> Will Akron ever forget one moment of that wonderful afternoon. The sun
> shining in joy over the revolters [*sic*]. A breeze fanning the cheeks of the
> slaves listening to the gospel of emancipation. John Brown's monument tow-
> ering above as though whispering encouragement to the newer John Brown's
> [*sic*] speaking below.[36]

It is a hard lesson of life, however, that the justice of a cause is no guarantee of its success. Like so many of the IWW's battles, the Akron strike
was a "noble failure." The strike's organization was fatally flawed, in large
part because the workers had not been able to build up an effective shop-
floor network before the strike began. Far from being awash with funds
and bristling with squads of organizers and strong-arm men, the IWW
was thinly spread and impecunious. Nor was it a rigid bureaucracy acting
on the orders of an American Kremlin. The Wobblies, in fact, abhorred
hierarchy and bureaucracy. In the words of strike organizer James P.
Cannon, their ideal organizer was "footloose and fancy-free," a reflection
of the IWW's origins among itinerant workers.[37] Also significant—as they

later admitted, the IWW did not realize the significance of the events in Akron until it was too late.

The Goons and the Ginks and the Company Finks

Paid informers also contributed to the strike's defeat. Both the IWW Akron Local and the rubber strike committee were riddled with company spies. The extent of the infiltration was revealed when John W. Reid, secretary-treasurer of the IWW Local, signed an affidavit admitting that he and all of the other main officers had been paid informers.[38] The secretary of the CLU was also exposed as a spy, and private spooks had also penetrated the local Socialist Party branch.[39] Most damaging of all for the union was the behavior of H. E. Pollack, the twenty-three-year-old tire builder who chaired the strike committee. Throughout the strike, Pollack's sister, who worked as Frank Seiberling's stenographer, typed up the union's minutes and gave the carbons to her boss.[40] In contrast, the strikers were naïvely trusting.

Another problem was that for some time the strike committee failed to formulate a list of concrete demands to put to the companies. This stemmed in part from the IWW's doctrine of self-emancipation, which held that the workers must develop their own demands without interference from outsiders. But there *was* no established union in the rubber mills and the workers were too inexperienced to draft a coherent log of claims without expert assistance. When a list of demands was finally worked up, it included the following: reinstatement, a wage increase, the eight-hour day, the abolition of piece work and the speed-up, recognition of the IWW local, and collective bargaining. Another problem was that between one-quarter and one-half of the gummers[41] remained at work throughout the strike, and this undermined unity, solidarity, and eventually morale.

"The Mob of the Rich": Reverend Atwater's Vigilantes

Pro-company accounts claim that the IWW was defeated by a combination of management fortitude, the steadfastness of worker "loyalists," and the growing realization among the strikers that they were being used by subversive outsiders. The companies also admit to "being aided materi-

ally by the organization of a citizens' group,"[42] which they claim helped
control "mobs of men wearing red badges [who] were patrolling the
streets and terrorizing the populance [sic]."[43] Such accounts gloss over
the brutal and illegal role of the vigilantes, special deputies, and police
that were unleashed by the rubber companies to crack heads without fear
of prosecution.

The companies could violate the strikers' constitutional rights with
impunity because Akron's "respectable" middleclass rallied against the
strikers. The rubber companies were able to frighten these citizens by
painting the strike as a revolutionary conspiracy. They flocked to the
"Citizens' Welfare League" (CWL), which was inaugurated at a meeting
in Fir Hill by the Reverend George Atwater, an Episcopalian minister
with robustly reactionary views and an energetic propagandist bent. The
CWL grew into a one-thousand-strong private army that included the
entire staff of the YMCA, along with assorted bigwigs from the local
Chamber of Commerce and gangs of muscular young men with time on
their hands.[44] If the famous English clergyman Hewlett Johnson was "the
Red Dean," Akron's Rev. Atwater was the White Archbishop. Litchfield
hints at the CWL's strong-arm methods when he alleges that the IWW's
Big Bill Haywood meekly got back on his train upon arrival at Union
Station when the CWL told him to do so.[45] Litchfield belittles a courageous opponent: Haywood did *not* get back on the train, despite a show
of force by five hundred baton-wielding police and 780 CWL special
deputies. Such thuggery prompted Haywood to observe that:

> The Constitution has been trampled under foot, the Declaration of
> Independence scattered to the winds, the Bill of Rights forgotten, all because
> the rubber bosses wanted to drive their slaves back to work.[46]

The violence was relentless. Many years later, a striker called Paul
Sebestyen recalled a police attack on a peaceful demonstration in downtown Akron:

> We went to John Brown's memorial, marching up there. [William]
> Trautmann was in front of me and I was lucky. The cop came along without
> any provocation, hit him in the head. He fell down, bleeding. He didn't hit
> me . . . I suppose they knew he was one of the leaders of the strike. They knew
> who to hit. I was just a small guy.[47]

An alliance of the rubber companies, local authorities, and private individuals had effectively suspended the rule of law insofar as it applied to the strikers and their supporters. It was perfectly legal to withdraw one's labor, to organize a union, parade in the streets, and exercise one's freedom of speech and publication, but the CWL and the local authorities consistently violated these rights. The union appealed to the Ohio Governor to call out the National Guard to protect the workers from "the mob of the rich,"[48] but the state backed the companies and their vigilantes. Under the guise of martial law aimed at keeping the peace, the vigilantes and police ran amok in what Grismer considers "mob rule" by the CWL.[49]

By mid-March, the strike was dying. There was a steady drift back to work and whereas the employers and the state forces stuck together, there was little solidarity on the other side of the tracks. Although the socialists called for a general strike to counter the CWL violence, the CLU dithered, probably under the influence of AFL national organizers Carl Wyatt and John L. Lewis, who had arrived in town determined to isolate the IWW.[50] Akron writer Kevin Rosswurm considers that the AFL "did a grave disservice to the labor movement, to the IWW and to the workers themselves" as a result of their "half-hearted attempt" to enroll rubber workers in the midst of their strike.[51] These factors, combined with the activities of the company spies, the inexperience of the strike leaders, and the fact that the CWL and police ran many of those they labeled as "undesirables" out of town, caused the strike to collapse. Strikers crept back to work humiliated, militants were blacklisted, and to cap it off, Paul Litchfield rewarded company loyalists with two weeks' paid holiday.[52] On Fir Hill, the Reverend Atwater and his vigilantes gloated over what they believed was the "victory of the moral forces of the city over lawlessness."[53]

The collapse of the strike brought profound disappointment for the gummers and their supporters. Apart from isolated wildcat strikes during the First World War and in the early 1920s, the mills were free of industrial action and organized unions for the next twenty years. Seven years after the strike ended, the IWW admitted that "Akron remains, to this day, the supreme mistake of the IWW."[54] Veteran Wobbly Fred Dawson summed up the lessons thus:

> A spontaneous strike is a spontaneous tragedy unless there is a strong local organization on the spot or unless a strong force of outside experienced men are thrown into the town immediately.[55]

Many years later, the URWA reached the same conclusion, noting that "Big Bill Haywood . . . came to Akron in 1913 to inspire the striking rubber workers. But fiery speeches and militant parades were not enough. There was no strong union to back up the strikers. They were defeated."[56] The veteran socialist and union activist Jim McCartan also noted something many critics ignore: "The IWW was not equipped to finance the strike . . . [and] the rubber workers were starved and had to go back to work."[57]

CHAPTER ELEVEN

Sisters, Brothers, Unite!
The Rubber Workers' Union in Akron

The company will not sign any agreement with the United Rubber Workers
even if a vote of employees shows that a majority wish to be represented by
the union.

—PAUL LITCHFIELD, President of Goodyear Tire & Rubber[1]

The failure of the IWW strike in 1913 was a massive blow to union
organization in Akron. Immediately after the end of the IWW strike,
Goodyear set up the Flying Squadron in the plants to suppress union
activity. Goodyear was worried that mass production had brought such
specialization of skills that a disturbance on one part of the production
line could impact the whole factory. Members of the Squadron were
trained as "master rubber workers," an elite force capable of doing any of
the production jobs in the factories, who were instilled with discipline,
esprit de corps, and fierce loyalty to the company.[2] They were widely
feared and hated as industrial mercenaries in the plants and envied for
their privileges. This model was adopted in Goodyear plants elsewhere
in North America and overseas.

The companies did not rely solely on "master rubber workers" to
improve their profits. War was also good for business, and the companies were able to grant substantial wage increases. While it was no doubt
exaggerated, the story of Ralph Hogan's jewelry business gives an indi-

cation of the kind of money that rubber workers could earn. Hogan told "how the workers would come to his place, drag out enough bills to leave him breathless, and command, 'Let's see the best diamond you've got!'"[3] Wage increases and ample overtime were coupled with the introduction of the eight-hour day, which Paul Litchfield insisted was the "direct outgrowth of mass production."[4] In later years, hours were cut still further, with four six-hour shifts working round the clock. Stories still abound in Akron of schoolteachers who worked nights or afternoons in the mills and put in a full day in the classroom, catching up on sleep during school vacations. These improvements, together with paternalist welfare measures, did much to perpetuate the open shop in Akron. The rubber firms also faced the problem of securing a stable workforce and limiting high rates of labor turnover. In boom times, the "light infantry of capital" were better able to pick and choose their work, and the resultant labor shortages helped convince the companies of the need for "capitalist welfarism."

Soon after the 1913 strike, both Firestone and Goodyear built model-housing tracts close to their factories. They followed the model of public housing in Europe and gave it a distinctively American twist. The Akron companies oversaw construction and design of the houses and the precincts, but unlike the European rental schemes, selected occupants of the houses bought their dwellings on cheap hire purchase terms.[5] The rubber companies must also have been aware of the ideological and social bonus involved in employee-owned housing. As William B. Wilson, the American Secretary of Labor, stated in 1919:

> I have found that the man who owns his home is the least susceptible to so-called Bolshevist doctrine and is about the last man to join in the industrial disturbances fomented by the radical agitators. Owning a home gives a man an added sense of responsibility to the national and local government that makes for the best type of citizenship.[6]

The radicals—already weakened by the post-1918 "Red Scare" repression—could only seethe impotently. In 1925, an Akron Wobbly gummer observed that debt was a good way of "keeping the workers' noses on the stone," but he was wide of the mark when he forecast the early collapse of "what they had the nerve to call houses . . . many [of which] will still be mortgages when they have fallen down."[7] Eighty years later, the houses remain defiantly perpendicular.

"Welfare Capitalism"

The housing tracts formed part of a broader vision of "welfare capitalism."[8] This was not restricted to Akron's rubber industry; Goodyear took the model with them to other cities and countries,[9] which led foreign competitors to develop a similar approach. Michelin, for instance, which became Clermont-Ferrand's largest employer in 1905, ran its own free pharmacy and health service, plus a housing scheme.[10] In 1920, the Republican presidential nominee Warren Harding (himself an Ohio man) opened Goodyear Hall, a seven-story building adjacent to the main factory on West Market Street. It still exists today, housing offices and a rubber museum, but its glory days are past. It originally contained a gymnasium, a theater with murals of Vesuvius and a South American rubber loading dock, an orchestra pit, and sixty-five rooms dedicated to the Goodyear Industrial University.[11] This "university" was a kind of private technical college, although the city's radicals sneered at it as Goodyear's "private head-fixing operation," dedicated as much to company propaganda as to imparting skills.[12] The hall also contained an indoor rifle range, which came in handy for Flying Squadron drills during the industrial upheavals a decade later.

Goodyear's welfarist schemes were copied by the other big Akron companies. BF Goodrich gave its workers a clinic, insurance, free legal advice, and sporting facilities.[13] Firestone had an even more highly developed system, with a country club and golf course for employees, a savings bank, barber shop, and a four-story clubhouse replete with gymnasium, swimming pool, library, and bowling alleys, plus medical and dental services.[14] All the major firms experimented with profit-sharing schemes, although these were sometimes restricted to workers deemed more worthy than others.[15] Harvey Firestone declared that his aim was to make "every employee a stockholder,"[16] but Paul Litchfield insisted that the larger portion must go to "the wise, persistent and industrious [rather] than the lazy, ignorant or slothful."[17]

"Yellow Unionism" at Akron

These welfare projects sprang from a broader philosophical tradition that counterposed class collaboration to class struggle and which sought to head off independent working class organization with "corporatist" structures. Goodyear boasted that its own corporatist system, introduced in 1919, was "unique in employee relations in American industry."[18] Known as the Industrial Assembly (IA), it was modeled on the U.S. Constitution, with a "House of Representatives," a "Senate," and a "President."[19] The members of the Goodyear "community" made up the "electorate" and were known as "Industrians."[20] Litchfield, however, was appointed President by the company and there were no constitutional provisions or conventions to limit how many terms of office he could serve. The Industrians could not impeach him and his veto was final.

Firestone, BF Goodrich, and General Tire had their own less elaborate versions of the IA. These organizations were variants of what the American working class came to know as "yellow" or company unions. For a while, they were successful in blocking independent organization, but most eventually folded up or were absorbed by the AFL and CIO. General Tire's yellow union folded in 1934 when the company signed a surprise agreement with the URW, the first with a large rubber company in Akron.[21] Between 1932 and 1935, however, company union membership in the United States grew more rapidly than that of the independent unions: from 40 percent to 60 percent.[22]

Although some writers claim the companies' desire to create stable workforces was the primary motivation for these schemes, Paul Litchfield clearly saw them as a means of blocking the gummers from organizing independently. Some old-school Goodyear managers were suspicious of what they saw as Litchfield's "socialistic ideas,"[23] but he strongly rejected the criticism.[24] On the surface, his rhetoric seemed radical. He argued that the antidote to worker militancy was for the United States to "democratize" its industry.[25] However, he was stridently opposed to Section 7 (a) of President Roosevelt's National Industrial Recovery Act, which recognized workers' rights to independent organization and collective bargaining.

The weakness of the company unions was highlighted in 1920 when they proved incapable of resisting management's demands for the workers to bear the brunt of a massive downturn in trade. Goodyear almost went bankrupt; there were huge stockpiles of tires; and the city's rubber workforce fell from 75,000 in June to 20,000 at the year's end.[26] The yellow unions were powerless to resist the companies' demands, so the workers took matters in their own hands. There was even a flashback to 1913 when strikers paraded in the streets behind flags and banners. When trade improved, the companies simultaneously granted a 10 percent wage increase and victimized "ringleaders."[27] The comparative prosperity of the late 1920s plus the ubiquitous company spies and plant police—many of whom were Klansmen—made it difficult to build an independent union in the plants. Rising prosperity had bolstered faith in the limitless possibilities of the American Dream. Union membership in the United States had declined steadily from a peak of over five million during the First World War to below three and a half million in 1929, most of whom were concentrated in a few industries and regions.[28] Why, many workers reasoned, would anyone want to join a union when they had well-paying jobs and food on the table, and there was every chance of home and car ownership?

"City of Opportunity"to "Metropolis of Despair"

Most Americans—including the Akron gummers—were unprepared for the Great Depression that followed the Wall Street "crash" of 1929. If the 1920 slump had struck Akron "like a thunderbolt,"[29] the 1930s Depression was a catastrophe on a different scale. The city was over-whelmingly dependent on rubber, and the industry was always suscepti-ble to fluctuations of the business cycle. Soon there were rubber compa-ny bankruptcies and steep falls in profits. The number of tires produced in Akron fell from almost thirteen million in 1929 to under seven million in 1933.[30]

The consequences were grim for Akron's rubber workers. There were mass layoffs, short-time shifts, factory closures, wage cuts, and increased speed-ups, as the employers struggled to stay afloat. Women and foreign-ers were laid off first, regardless of length of service.[31] At the time of the Great Crash, there were some 58,316 rubber jobs in Akron. Ten years later, there were only 33,285,[32] although part of the decline was due to new labor-saving machinery. The city of opportunity had become a metropolis of despair. Most gummers, their ranks thinned by mass layoffs, were too numbed by despondency and the daily grind of survival to turn to industrial combination as a solution to their common problems. By 1933, however, there was a slight economic upturn and with it, hope for the future.

The early thirties also saw the continuous streamlining of production methods within the rubber mills. The new methods resulted in increased productivity and lighter work, but also in ever-faster work tempos, further deskilling, and a radical reduction of the workforce. The Bedaux company was brought in, and men with stopwatches and slide rules crawled over the factories making runic calculations.[33] Steven Kreis argues that Charles Bedaux could make the average Midwestern Scrooge believe that he was a "public benefactor" and an enlightened employer, but to the workers his name was synonymous with sweated labor.[34] A report published by the U.S. Bureau of Labor Statistics calculated that in the decade before 1931, "the poundage output per man in the rubber industry tripled." While some of this was due to technological change, much of it was accomplished by the speed up and workers were well aware of this.[35] With no independent union to negotiate on their behalf, wages and conditions slipped backwards. The same issues that had driven the workers to take action in 1913 reemerged.

Given the interplay of economic and social forces sweeping America, it was no wonder that from the early 1930s more skilled rubber production and maintenance workers trickled into the AFL craft unions.[36] Membership was risky given the swarms of company spies; time had not softened the bosses' hostility to unions.[37] Between 1933 and 1942, the number of strikes in U.S. industry for union recognition never fell below 30 percent of the total of stoppages and rose to almost 60 percent in 1937.[38] This trend was true of Akron, where the rubber companies had pioneered yellow unions and the union-busting methods known elsewhere in America as "the Mohawk Valley Formula."[39]

Wilmer Tate: Keeping Unionism Alive in Akron

Throughout those grim years, a small group of Akron unionists stubbornly kept alive the dream of an independent rubber workers' union. Their work finally paid off. While they were skilled craftsmen and members of craft unions themselves—Wilmer Tate was a machinist and James McCartan a typographer for example[40]—they were socialists who advocated industrial unionism—the organization of all the workers in an industry in one union, regardless of skill or trade. By 1933, there was an upturn in the market for finished rubber goods and by July, BF Goodrich and Goodyear had rehired some 7,000 laid-off workers. This gave the gummers fresh hope and confidence, and it strengthened their resolve not to accept the conditions they had endured after the Crash.[41] Many were skeptical, too, of the old assumptions of the American Dream. The chance to organize the gummers stemmed from a combination of circumstances:

the worst of the Depression was over; there was rising discontent in the mills, and confidence in the yellow unions' ability to shield workers was badly damaged; a core of union leaders was crystallizing inside the mills with support from the Akron CLU; and there was a sense of hope. Another crucial factor was the passage of a number of pro-labor federal laws in the last days of the Hoover administration and the first days of its successor. In 1933, President Franklin Delano Roosevelt signed into law the National Industrial Recovery Act (NIRA).

The NIRA introduced the thirty-six-hour week for industrial workers, set a federal minimum wage of forty cents an hour, abolished child labor, and legally guaranteed unions the right to organize and to bargain collectively with employers. The latter provisions, contained in Section 7(a), were anathema to management. Although the U.S. Supreme Court declared the NIRA unconstitutional in 1935, the same year saw the passage of the Wagner Act,[42] which empowered a National Labor Relations Board to order secret ballot elections to allow workers to decide whether or not they wished to be represented by an independent union. Employers were forbidden to interfere with their employees' rights to organize and had to bargain collectively if the unions won a ballot.[43] In theory, the legislation granted organized labor important rights long denied by politicians, employers, and the courts.

Union organizers campaigned under the slogan "PRESIDENT ROOSEVELT WANTS YOU TO ORGANIZE."[44] The New Deal gave organized labor and the American working class an enormous psychological boost, and union membership soared as a result. Section 7(a) was the greatest legal and political opportunity American labor had ever received. However, R. W. Fleming cautions that while "Section 7(a) proved helpful in many ways . . . [it was] illusory in others . . . for industry professed to find nothing in the law inconsistent with the formation of company unions, and defied the [Labor Relations] Board whenever it attempted to proceed against them."[45]

This is precisely what happened in Akron. Barberton's Seiberling Rubber told its employees that "a written working agreement [with the union] would serve no good purpose and is wholly unnecessary and the company declines to sign . . . an agreement."[46] Goodyear's Paul Litchfield claimed, "We believe in unions, we believe in the right of men, encourage the right of men, to unite to promote the general welfare and to provide for their common defense against injustice. . . . "[47] However, the "union" he had in mind was the Industrial Assembly (IA), which "effectively rep-

166 THE DEVIL'S MILK

resents our employees . . . [and which] provides a method of collective bargaining which is eminently satisfactory to, and voluntary on the part of our employees." Litchfield concluded that because the IA had "brought maximum benefits to our employees and peace and harmony . . ." no "outside" union would be recognized.[48] He denounced the "epidemic" of strikes he saw stemming from NIRA. "The dying embers of class consciousness were fanned into new flames [by agitators]," he declared, and if the right to strike was "inherent in a free nation," so was "the right to work" without hindrance from unions.[49]

A Homegrown Leadership

In the summer of 1933, the CLU organized a meeting open to all the city's rubber workers. When the doors opened on the evening of June 30, over 5,000 rubber workers packed the Armory Hall and listened as Wilmer Tate and other militants passionately denounced the employers and exhorted the gummers to stick together for their rights. Tate, a tall, redheaded man with a booming voice, lived and breathed the cause of Labor. He had begun life on an Iowa farm, but moved to the city as a teenager and learned the machinist's trade, at which he became unusually skilled. (He once complained of having to leave jobs because the bosses wanted to promote him to foreman and his heart was always in the union!) After Tate spoke that evening, gummers signed up for union cards on the spot. One of them was John D. House, a farm boy from Georgia who had joined the Goodyear Flying Squadron back in 1925, and who was to become a URWA international organizer and educational director. House had first stepped off the train at Union Station in September 1923, drawn to Akron by the promise of good wages and steady work. He had expected an industrial Mecca but found instead its tawdry simulacrum, with what he recalled as "deplorable" working conditions in the factories that left men "broken at 40." "Without a union," he recalled many years later, "there wasn't a damned thing we could do but take it." [50]

Together with fellow Southerners ex-marine Lieutenant Sherman H. Dalrymple and George Bass from BF Goodrich, Labor Party activists N.N. Eagles and L. L. Callahan from Goodyear, and Walter Kriebel and the former Indiana schoolmaster L. S. Buckmaster from Firestone, House was to form a core part of URWA organization in the city's mills. Dan Nelson notes that these men shared the "ability to inspire confidence among their fellow workers" and were driven by "a fierce anti-authoritarianism"[51] that bonded them to the ordinary gummers. They were honest and immune to enticements and threats. The sociologist Alfred Winslow Jones points to an "almost evangelist approach to unionism,"[52] which set these men apart from the careerists so common in the AFL. They provided the kind of sincere and capable "indigenous" leadership that had been so disastrously lacking in the 1913 IWW strike. House and his friends were able to build functioning locals of the URW for the first time in Akron's history. It was an astonishing development in an open shop town.

When Wilmer Tate organized the summer rally at the Akron Armory, the CLU was on its last legs, with as few as 400[53] and no more than 2,000[54] union members in the city, hardly any of whom were gummers. By November 1933, its ranks had grown to 30,000 and more were flocking in every day. Much of the growth was in the rubber plants, with as many as 90 percent of the workers in the smaller factories joining up. Over 7,000 of BF Goodrich's 10,000 workers had joined,[55] and even with comparatively low representation at Goodyear, estimates were that 60 percent of Akron's rubber workers had been brought into the new "federal" unions by rank-and-file organizers as 1933 drew to a close.[56] Akron had become a solid union town to an extent difficult to imagine today. Looking back from today's individualistic, neoliberal age, mid-1930s Akron's collectivist ethos seems foreign—a vibrant alternative to mass capitalist culture that resembles German working-class life in the heyday of the Social Democratic Party before the First World War. There were union picnics, dances, quiz nights, boxing matches, boating excursions, dinners, and barbecues. As John Borsos stresses in his study of organized labor in Barberton, the Summit County unions were working-class community organizations,[57] a far cry from the later business union template imposed by the AFL-CIO. Coupled with this was an instinctive commitment to the industrial as opposed to craft union model of organization that predated the rise of the CIO.

But it is one thing to recruit union members and quite another to know what to do with them. By late 1933, Capital and Labor in Akron circled each other warily like boxers at the beginning of a fight. In the red corner, the unions now had the muscle to take on their opponents, but they realized that a premature strike might prove fatal to their cause. In the opposite corner, the rubber bosses were also feeling their way. In July 1933, Goodyear, always the most intransigent and confrontationist employer, sacked four URW activists, only to back down after federal government intervention on the workers' behalf. Goodyear grudgingly gave way, but the company had no intention of retreating on the broader questions of union recognition and collective bargaining rights.

Craft vs. Industrial Unionism

Shortly after the meeting at the Armory, Wilmer Tate traveled to Washington, D.C., to seek assistance from William Green, the ex-Ohio State Senator who had succeeded Sam Gompers as AFL President in 1924.[58] Although an ex-coal miner from an industrial union himself, Green was an AFL man of the old school—cautious, conservative and devoted to craft unionism, top-control, and class collaboration. He was later criticized within the movement for his inept handling of union affairs in Akron, but at this stage he was sufficiently impressed by Tate's account of developments to dispatch an AFL international organizer,[59] Coleman Claherty, to the city. A ruddy-faced Cleveland Irishman and former metal worker, Claherty arrived in Akron one month after the Armory meeting, opened an office in the swank Savings & Loans Building on South Main Street, and hired Tate as assistant organizer of the URWA in the city.[60] Claherty had worked alongside William Z. Foster, the militant union leader and later Communist, in the great national steel strikes of 1919 and had organized chicken packers in San Francisco. He told a reporter for the *Akron Beacon Journal* that he had "many times fled" the "loaded shotguns of mine owners' Cossacks," but believed that with the advent of the Roosevelt government and Section 7(a) of the NRA, "it's fair sailing now."[61] Green reinforced Claherty's approach at a 6,000-strong rally of rubber workers shortly afterwards. He argued that unionists must put their faith in Roosevelt and the NRA, strive for respectability, and aim for a constructive partnership with the employers. This, in essence, was the philosophy of Samuel Gompers, the "grand old man" of the AFL, whom Paul Litchfield had praised as the "best friend" of the American worker in the obituary he wrote for Gompers in *The Wingfoot Clan*.[62]

Any suggestion of union organization along industrial lines was anathema to the spirit and rules of the Federation. Rather than organize all the workers in a particular industry into a common industrial union—an approach long advocated by radicals and which made sense to most gummers—Claherty and Green believed in craft organization in which workers in a plant or industry would be divided up into different unions according to trade. Electricians, for example, would belong to the electrical union, machinists to the machinists, carpenters to the carpenters' union, and so on. The unskilled and semi-skilled laborers were regarded as "fair-weather unionists," and were suspected of being unstable and even untrustworthy elements. Such an approach might have made sense in the small-scale industries of the early to mid-nineteenth century, but militants saw it as an impediment to effective organization in the Fordist mass production industries of the twentieth. They believed the craft approach would lead to demarcation disputes, erode unity and solidarity, foster parallel bureaucracies, and generally waste resources.

The mass of the newly organized rubber workers grew impatient with Claherty's approach. By 1934, the AFL had made a significant breakthrough in terms of membership, with perhaps 40,000 recruits in the Akron mills, but it was becoming obvious to the local militants that the AFL leaders had no precise plans for action, given that the rubber companies had never rolled over and accepted the implications of the NRA. Nor were the employers interested in the AFL's "partnership" approach. They might have accepted, for the moment, that many of their employees had chosen to join AFL affiliates, but they remained committed to the open shop and the yellow unions, so collective bargaining with independent unions was out of the question. Claherty could still deliver a rousing speech at a union rally, but it had no effect on hardboiled Harvey Firestone or Paul Litchfield. Members of the URW began to slowly drift away.

URW Breakthrough at General Tire

Other rank-and-filers preferred to work within the union for change. In early 1934, there was a brief sit-down strike at the Mansfield Tire & Rubber plant, southwest of Akron,[63] and in mid-March of that year, URW members at the O'Neil family's General Tire & Rubber factory in Akron felt strong enough to threaten action.[64] As pressure built up, Claherty began to resemble King Canute,[65] unable to impose his will on the increasingly stormy industrial sea. In January 1934, two local officers of the URW in Akron were removed for their advocacy of industrial unionism.[66] By June, the militants at General Tire & Rubber in East Akron had run out of patience with what they perceived as the AFL's cowardice. Fifteen-hundred strikers walked off the job on June 19, exasperated by the Bedaux system and Claherty's dithering. They did not ask for permission from Claherty or Green, who moved to contain the wildcat, warning that members who attempted to extend the strike would be expelled from the union. The General Tire strikers picketed and settled in for a protracted battle. After some weeks Bill O'Neil met with strikers' representatives over coffee and sandwiches and agreed to end all support for the plant's yellow union (the General Tire Employees' Joint Council), to reinstate the strikers, and to meet with their representatives to consider the principle of seniority in layoffs.[67] Shortly afterwards, following a sit-down strike, the company signed a formal agreement with the union.[68] General was a relatively small firm and had every reason to fear predatory raids on its markets by its larger rivals if the disturbances continued, but the agreement was a landmark for the union.[69]

The big rubber companies were alarmed by the union's victory. Publicly, they presented a "reasonable" face, but in July 1934, Firestone was again building barbed wire fences and erecting floodlights in preparation for a lockout.[70] Firestone and BF Goodrich hired Colonel Joseph Johnson, a strike-busting veteran of the Ohio National Guard, to train supervisors and company loyalists, and at Goodyear the Flying Squadron were drilling in the Goodyear Hall indoor rifle range.[71] Later in the year, there was an unsuccessful attempt to set up a bogus "independent" union to outflank the URW,[72] but few workers were fooled and the outfit died. Another company ploy was to tie the union up with court battles and injunctions. Shocked by the union breakthrough at General Tire, the Big Three refused to allow NLRB elections in their plants, arguing that the company unions already served as collective bargaining agents. Even when the federal government ordered that the elections go ahead, the companies sought court injunctions to block them.[73] More often than not, the courts gave them what they wanted. Incensed, the union took a strike vote at Barberton's Seiberling Rubber, and it was ratified by a margin of four to one. The company was forced to negotiate but even though an agreement was reached and posted on plant notice boards, the company would not actually sign it.[74] The following January, a URW strike ballot at Firestone was lost, as it failed by thirteen votes to achieve the three-fourths majority necessary for ratification under the AFL's restrictive rules.[75] Green appears to have been relieved by the result, but fretted that "[t]he situation in Akron is becoming tense and anything is liable to break loose most any time." He added, "We will try to keep the situation in hand and if any action is taken, it will be taken in an orderly manner." Three months later, the companies were still stalling for time, but the pressure from below had become so intense that at a huge mass meeting held in Akron on March 27, Claherty agreed to hold a fresh strike vote in all the big plants.[76] The companies fortified the factories with barbed wire and sandbags and armed plant police with submachine guns and tear gas. Searchlights were set up around the factory perimeters and stockpiles of food were brought in together with thousands of camp beds for strike-breakers. The warehouses, too, were full to the rafters with stockpiled tires.[77] In an echo of the 1913 IWW strike in which the Rev. George Atwater's vigilantes had played a pivotal role, "concerned citizens" set up the Akron Civic Justice Council, which was backed by the local Lions and Rotary clubs. The local authorities came out on the companies' side, with Summit County Sheriff Flower swearing in one thousand special deputies and declaring that he would break any picket lines.[78]

Double Cross in Washington

Frances Perkins, Roosevelt's Secretary of Labor, summoned representatives from both sides to a conference in Washington. The employers refused to meet with the union delegates in the same room. In a touch of opéra bouffe, Perkins had to walk back and forth between separate rooms, like a marriage counselor attempting to broker a deal between warring spouses. This behavior worsened when the companies agreed to meet with workers' delegates, only to qualify this later to mean representatives of the yellow unions. It was a cheap trick, but it worked: Green and Claherty agreed to call off the strike ballot pending final resolution of court proceedings initiated by the companies. Labor Relations Board elections to decide who would have the right to collective bargaining rights were postponed. Claherty presented it as a victory to the incredulous membership back in Akron, but at this stage the URW had no formal independent international union charter and, as such, the membership and local officials had little say in the decisions of the union. Union membership again dropped off; the promise of a strong union in the plants had failed so many times before that many gummers had little confidence it would succeed this time. A further blow fell in May, when the U.S. Supreme Court ruled that Section 7 (a) of the National Recovery Act was unconstitutional: "six old men . . . have seized the nation by the throat," fumed Wilmer Tate during an Akron radio broadcast.[79] Although the Roosevelt administration passed the Wagner Act to reassert the rights stripped away by the judges, their ruling could not have come at a worse time for the URWA's organizing drive. Inside the plants, the company spies and police redoubled their efforts, buoyed by the union setback, but there was a sign of things to come when Sherman Dalrymple's BF Goodrich union local called for an international union charter to take control of disputes away from Green and Claherty.

Akron's Rebellion against Green

Green had other ideas about the type of union needed and whom it would represent, but he was pressured by the Akron militants to call the first national convention of the URWA in Washington in August 1935. From the start of the proceedings, he was determined to keep control of the union with assistance from Claherty. He unveiled the URWA's new charter at the convention, which stipulated that craftsmen would be farmed out to the appropriate craft union regardless of their wishes. He also informed the convention that it had no choice but to accept his nominee for URW president. Worse still, Green stated that it was not up to the delegates to accept, reject, or modify the new URW charter; that right was his alone. When the delegates objected, Green told them that the AFL would not provide money for the URWA unless they accepted Claherty as president. For a man used to dealing with a submissive membership, that must have seemed like the final word, but the delegates made the first move in what would become an open breach with Green and the AFL by electing Sherman Dalrymple as president and Thomas Burns as vice-president. There had been only one Green supporter on the international executive.

Green, in his belief that the experience of trying to run the union without money would bring the rebels to heel, underestimated the resolve of these men to build a strong, active, and democratic industrial union in Akron. The first edition of the union's *United Rubber Worker* approvingly quoted the legendary socialist leader Eugene V. Debs: "When I rise it will be with the rank and file, not from them."[80] In October 1935, the URWA delegation listened with intense interest to the key debate at the AFL convention in Atlantic City: which way forward for American labor—the old, conservative path of business and craft unionism, or fighting industrial unionism? They watched as John L. Lewis, president of the miners' union and an advocate of the industrial path, frustrated by the craft unionists' stalling tactics, punched Willy Hutcheson of the

Carpenters' Union in the jaw. The issue which precipitated the blow was Hutcheson's obstructive use of procedure to have motions from Summit County unions supporting the labor party idea ruled out of order.

Intransigence of the Rubber Companies

Shortly after the AFL convention, Goodyear declared that its factories would go back to working an eight-hour day, rather than working in six-hour shifts. As a result, over a thousand workers were laid off. The other companies followed suit, anxious to maintain their competitive edge. The union said that it would fight the changes, but after the membership hemorrhage that followed the foot-dragging of Green and Claherty earlier in the year, the employers believed it was too weakened to resist. They were mistaken. The URWA now had a solid core of militants in the factories and had fallen under the national and local control of men who wanted to build a sustainable industrial organization. With William Green sulking in Washington and Coleman Claherty sidelined, Akron was about to enter into the greatest period of industrial turmoil in its history. The winter of 1935–36 was bitterly cold but this did not deter the militants from launching an audacious campaign that caught the bosses by surprise. In early January of 1936, when blizzards swept down from Canada and ice choked the Cuyahoga, the miners' leader John L. Lewis appeared in Akron to drum up support for the newly formed Committee for Industrial Organization (CIO), which although still part of the AFL,[81] was dedicated to the idea of building strong industrial unions.[82]

Sit-Down Strikes

The sit-down—or sit-in, factory occupation, or stay-in—strike became synonymous in the American labor movement with the cities of Detroit, Toledo, and Akron. Former Akron Communist Ruth McKenney credits inspiration for the first Akron sit-down strike to Alex Eigenmacht, a left-wing Akron printer, who recalled it being used during his youth in Hungary and mentioned it to friends from the rubber factories when they were discussing tactics for the imminent industrial battles.[83] In fact, there had already been a sit-down strike at Goodyear in Akron in 1900, but Eigenmacht's memories did act as a catalyst in 1936. The sit-in idea was attractive because a key reason for the failure of the 1913 IWW rubber strike had been the large numbers of strikebreakers who kept the plants running at reduced capacity, thus contributing to the demoralization of the strikers. The sit-down strike, when properly organized, is a powerful tool for workers in an industrial dispute and one that employers find very difficult to counter. Occupation of a key part of a plant could block production in an integrated factory, even if substantial numbers of workers did not join in. The tactic was such a threat to the employers' power that in 1939 the U.S. Supreme Court declared it illegal in the Fansteel case.[84] Until then, the sit-down strike tactic effectively turned the tables on the employers by paralyzing factory machinery at the point of production, although as the Fansteel example showed, sit-down strikes could be broken by ruthless methods. In 1936, sit-down strikes symbolized union power, but they ebbed toward the end of the decade because of the opposition of increasingly conservative officials such as Sherman Dalrymple[85] as well as the fear of legal action.

On January 29, 1936, the first sit-down strike at Akron broke out in the truck tire-building section of the main Firestone plant after a union committeeman was suspended from work for fighting with a non-unionist. At two o'clock in the morning, according to a prearranged plan, there was a sudden silence as the union stopped the conveyor belts. By three o'clock in the morning, the Firestone No. 1 plant had stopped and the workers had sat down. The tactic caught the plant superintendent by surprise, and two days later the company backed down and reinstated the union man. It was an impressive demonstration of the workers' power. No sooner had the Firestone dispute ended than another sit-down erupted at Goodyear in East Akron, in protest of an arbitrary 10 percent pay cut on workers in the curing pit. One week later, workers sat down at BF Goodrich on South Main, again over a pay cut, and the company caved in. At the same time, workers in the Goodyear No. 2 plant put their feet up and played cards in protest at the layoffs of seventy-eight men. When attempts to intimidate them back to work failed, they were sacked but then reinstated without loss of entitlements. Word of such victories traveled quickly, and between March and December of 1936, there were reportedly no fewer than fifty-two sit-down strikes in the Akron rubber mills.

The Mohawk Valley Formula

In response, the companies stepped up their infiltration and surveillance, both inside and outside the plants. Union activists reported receiving threatening telephone calls and claimed they were attacked and beaten by company thugs.[86] These methods formed part of what became known as the "Mohawk Valley Formula" in the U.S. labor movement, after a "scientifically" organized union-busting campaign by the Remington Rand Company in 1934 at Ilion in the Mohawk Valley of New York State.[87] The formula involved the following steps: form a "citizens' committee"; label union organizers "outside agitators"; stir up violence and fear of violence; apply for court injunctions prohibiting picketing; have a state-of-emergency situation declared and call on the National Guard; organize a "back-to-work" movement and have the back-to-workers march back into the plant with police protection. Although the formula was named after the strikebreaking activities of the Remington Rand Company, it also sums up the tactics developed during the 1913 IWW strike in Akron and honed by the city's rubber companies in the 1930s. The Goodyear Tire & Rubber Company was among the most obstinate of the anti-union corporations in America and resisted signing a union contract until 1941.[88] Under Cliff Slusser, the company vice-president, it employed an army of finks, bullies, spies, and gun thugs.[89] These included members of the fascist Black Legion and the Ku Klux Klan at the Gadsden plant in Alabama. In one notorious instance, Slusser threatened that URW organizers in Gadsden would "leave town on a stretcher."[90] Indeed, a number of the union's organizers and rank-and-file supporters, including Sherman Dalrymple and John House, were savagely bashed at Gadsden.[91] In 1936, rubber workers in Goodyear's Akron plants staged spontaneous sit-down strikes to protest the Gadsden thuggery.[92] It did not stop. In one instance in the summer of 1936, two hired gun thugs attacked J. L. Miller, a union member, at 2:30 a.m. in his own home. In the words of B.T. Garner, the union's southern representative, in a letter to Sherman Dalrymple:

> Our old friend Marvin (Speedy) Brock held the gun on Miller for Leon Long, another well known thug, to do the beating . . . but Miller floored Long with the first blow, when Brock fired at him with the gun he missed him. It seems that Miller proceeded . . . [and] knocked Long into the bath tub . . . turned scalding hot water on him and . . . [backed] Brock into a room gun and all and making it so damned hot for him until Brock jumped out of a second story window.[93]

Garner concluded that "This fellow Miller, Dal, is just a quiet, unassuming country boy. I believe they got him to where he just had to fight and he did a hell of a good job of it."[94] More usually, however, the thugs and scabs attacked in overwhelming force. The following year, scabs wielding blackjacks jumped the URW recording secretary as he left the showers inside the Gadsden factory. Another unionist defended himself with a mill knife when set upon by the same goons.[95]

The allegations of violence and intimidation were not all one way; the Goodyear archives contain material concerning allegations of violence by union militants against so-called "Red Apples"[96] and supervisory staff. For instance, a supervisor on the night shift claimed, "a group of union members, numbering from fifty to seventy-five men all carrying tomahawks [sic] and other weapons of destruction came to the fifth floor to see whether we had resumed operations." "Any employee who did not see fit to join the union," he continued, "and the supervisors as well, were terribly abused by foul language which was used by this riotous mob of union men." It seems that the worst cases of violence by unionists were reserved for members of the plant police, special deputies, and the Flying Squadron for whom the gummers had a particular hatred. These instances, however, seem trivial when compared to the bashings regularly meted out to union members by hired goons and gun thugs. In fact, rubber workers had a whole vocabulary to describe "specialists" in repression, snooping and violence. These included:

Fink—low class strikebreaker, recruited from barrooms and gangster sections; Noble—Triggerman; Missionary—goes round workers' houses to dissuade strikers' wives, posing as a salesman; Hooker—detective who recruits spies to make reports on workers—keeps them hooked by threatening to tell the union; Gorilla—hard guy, who uses guns, clubs, gas or knife on strikers; Hookedman—spy inside plant—$50–$60 a month; Roper—follows or shadows union men.[97]

The Great Goodyear Strike of 1936

In the end, the URW relied on more traditional strike strategies to achieve its aims. Shortly after the sit-downs in the Goodyear plants, frustrated by the refusal of the company to negotiate or recognize the union, the URW called an all-out stoppage. On the night of February 17, despite a blizzard, the union shut down the Goodyear plants in East Akron.[98] Remarkably, given the driving snow, bitter cold, and the intimidation of police and deputies, the union was able to maintain picket lines strung out over a distance of eleven miles for the duration of the strike.[99]

It was the biggest work stoppage since 1913, and despite the Mohawk Formula the strikers stood solid until they won a partial victory. Spies were everywhere in the factories, the going rate was now $100 to $200 per month for their services, but the companies received some bad publicity when AFL President Green testified about their activities at the La Follette Senate committee hearings in Washington, D.C.[100] La Follette also produced evidence that Goodyear had paid scabs to attack unionists at the Gadsden plant in Alabama.[101] Contrary to company claims and an hysterical campaign waged by Akron's mayor, C. Nelson Sparks, to whip up a climate of fear and violence, the strike was largely peaceful. In a radio progam, Sparks denounced the "red" subversion and spoke of forming a 1913-style "law and order league" to run agitators out of town. Sparks's claims that over 30,000 men had joined his committee rang hollow.[102] This time few were listening, and the union laughed at "the sparks of fascism" that failed to ignite.[103] In contrast to 1913, when the city's middle class had rallied behind the rubber companies, this time they were either neutral or pro-union. Although the *Akron Beacon Journal* was pro-Republican, its proprietor John S. Knight editorialized on February 18 that there was "No Room for Vigilantes" in Akron.[104]

The movement for industrial unionism was gathering momentum across America. Less than one week after the strike erupted, miners' union leader John L. Lewis stormed into town with an entourage of seasoned organizers from the CIO. This was a far different Lewis to the one who had come to Akron two decades earlier to undermine the IWW strike. This time the message was one of solidarity and industrial unionism. In the process, old-style AFL men such as Coleman Claherty lost any credibility they still had in the city.

The marginal importance of the Communist Party in Akron did not deter the companies and their apologists from red-baiting attacks on the union in the press and on the radio. A key ingredient of the Mohawk Valley Formula was to blame industrial unrest on "outside agitators." "Reds under the beds" was a stock in trade for employer propaganda. Typical of this was a piece entitled "Revolution in Michigan": recycled for an edition of the *Wingfoot Clan* during the Akron strike, it savagely attacked CIO organizers.[105] The socialist Powers Hapgood, for example,

was described as a "veteran rabble rouser." John Brophy, the executive
director of the CIO, was accused of being "a paid agent of the Soviet government," and Rose Pesotta was described as a "lady comrade who currently represents the downtrodden garment workers of Manhattan."[106]
This kind of red-baiting fell flat in 1936.

Nor were the other strikebreaking methods effective. There were public meetings of foremen and "loyal workers." Substantial numbers of Red
Apples stayed inside the plant, but not enough to ensure more than a tiny
fraction of usual production. It is difficult to believe Litchfield's claim
made some years later that the strike was a time of "great happiness" for
him because of the loyalty of what he claimed were some 1,500 scabs.[107]
Nor was the anti-picketing injunction obtained from a Summit County
judge effective. The union asked, "Who will enforce the injunction?"
Akron's Sheriff Flower was reluctant to do so when faced with a union
that had the support of many Akronites. On the morning of March 7,
Flower's deputies made a half-hearted attempt to break the picket lines,
but unionists mobilized across the city. When the CLU threatened to call
a general strike, Flower backed off.[108]

A Political Education

For many of the mountain men and women on the picket lines, the strike
provided a rapid political education. Rose Pesotta records that many
strikers were, or had been, members of the Ku Klux Klan. Picket captain
Skip Oharra, for example, whose courage and energy inspired the strikers, had been a member as recently as six months before the strike
began.[109] Pesotta tells how the wife of a striker told her that the KKK was
"'a social and educational society' . . . in the manner of one explaining a
local custom to an outsider." When some picketers asked Pesotta about
her ethnic background, assuming that she was Italian, she stunned them
by her admission that she was "a full-blooded Hebrew." This sparked a
spirited discussion about Jews, with the Southerners reeling off the
names of prominent capitalists to support their anti-Semitism. Powers
Hapgood responded by pointing to the many Gentile tycoons, including
Henry Ford, Paul Litchfield, Harvey Firestone, John D. Rockefeller, and
J.P. Morgan.[110]

There was even time for some lighthearted tomfoolery, as when two
old-time mountain men appeared with their guitars outside Paul

Goodyear pickets arriving outside the plant
during the 1936 strike.

Litchfield's office. They began to sing about him to the tune of "Old
MacDonald Had a Farm": "Old Man Litchfield had a shop, ee-i-ee-i-o!
And in that shop he had some scabs [machines/Red Apples, etc.]" for
hours until he fled to the Mayflower Hotel downtown.[111] The strike was
not always cheerful, however. Toward the end of the strike, the authorities
tried to clear the streets of the strikers' shanties, one of which was named
Fort Roosevelt. In the end, confronted with mass pickets and the possibility of a general strike, the authorities agreed to a compromise: the huts
would go, but the picketers would remain unmolested and could use their
automobiles as shelter from the elements.[112]

Although the company declared that they would not negotiate until
the pickets were lifted, the strikers were not fooled by this obvious ploy.
Litchfield showed his hand when he said that he would not sign an
agreement even if a clear majority of workers voted for the URW.[113]
However, by the twentieth day of the strike, he realized negotiation was
inevitable. On March 8, representatives of the company and the union
met secretly for what appears to have been the first time. Goodyear
remained intransigent on key demands, but in order to head off any neg-
ative spin that the company might put on the outcome of the talks, the
union put the company terms to a membership ballot. Although the

media tried to whip up a "return to work" movement and Goodyear claimed they conducted a poll showing the overwhelming majority of its employees wanted to go back on the union's terms, the strike continued until an agreement was reached.

The agreement was only accepted after a spirited debate in which the militants challenged their more conservative but still respected president, Sherman Dalrymple.[114] The union did not get all that it wanted: the union itself was not recognized and the Industrial Assembly continued.[115] However, given the company's earlier avowals that they would never negotiate with the URW, it was a partial victory and paved the way for a comprehensive agreement and union recognition in 1941 and the closed shop after the Second World War.[116]

"Firestone Whipped"

In the meantime, the epicenter of struggle shifted to the Firestone factories in South Akron, where an eight-week battle erupted in March 1937 following the company's insistence on negotiating only with the company union.[117] According to historian Alfred Lief, the company closed the factory to punish the union for staging a number of short stoppages. The union responded with mass pickets around the factories in a dispute that was to last fifty-six days before the company capitulated. Although General Tire & Rubber and a number of smaller companies had already signed agreements with the URW, Firestone was the first of the big employers to do so.[118] The agreement, signed on April 28, 1937, was to run for one year. There was to be a standard thirty-six-hour week of six six-hour days. Overtime was to be paid at the rate of time and a half, and paid holidays, insurance, and other welfare measures previously granted by the company would continue. There would be negotiations with the union in the event of layoffs and union preference and seniority in rehiring.[119] Firestone agreed to bargain collectively with the URWA and pledged not to interfere "with the right of its employees to become members of the union." The company also agreed to disband the yellow union and recognize the URWA as the sole representative of the workers. In return, the union agreed not to "cause or tolerate any sitdown or stay-in strikes or other stoppage of work in any of the plants of the Company during the term of the Agreement."[120] Jubilant at the breakthrough, Firestone workers danced in the streets and the *United Rubber Worker* trumpeted

"Union Whips Firestone" in a banner headline.[121] By the following year, when the yellow union at BF Goodrich was closed down on the orders of the National Labor Relations Board, Akron had become famous in America as a union town.

. . .

THE EXTRACTION OF LATEX from wild trees was a costly, time-consuming, and inefficient business. As the demand for raw rubber grew exponentially to feed the rubber factories in the advanced capitalist world, it became clear that the wild industry could not keep pace, nor assure the quality of the product. Wild rubber had also received bad publicity as a result of the atrocities on the Congo and Putumayo. Although the first hevea plantations predated those scandals, the movement toward making rubber an agribusiness crop was further stimulated by them. Initially, European planters were reluctant to switch from established commodities such as sugar, cotton, coffee, and tea for a new product whose success was far from being assured. Nevertheless, even before the First World War, plantation hevea had caught up with and then outstripped wild rubber production. The new plantations were run along industrial, mass production lines with regimented workforces. Often, in order to assure supplies and to cut costs, the rubber manufacturing companies established their own plantations: this was true of Michelin in French Indochina, Dunlops in Malaya, Goodyear in Sumatra, and Firestone in Liberia. The industry was to significantly alter the social relations, ecology, and ethnic makeup of the colonies, transplanting millions of laborers across the seas. In the most extreme case—that of Firestone in Liberia—a nominally independent state was reduced to a commercial satrapy to a startling extent. Although many other commodities were cultivated in the tropical colonies for the benefit of capitalism, perhaps none were as crucial to the system as rubber and its close cousin, gutta-percha.

PART FOUR

Plantation Hevea:
Agribusiness and Imperialism

CHAPTER TWELVE

The Triumph of Plantation Hevea

> The short life of the [rubber] industry has been marked by alternating booms and depressions of remarkable intensity. The boom of 1910, the scramble to increase acreage and output, the depression of the following years culminating in the despair of 1921; the recovery by means of compulsory restriction and the second boom of 1925, are the sensational points in a series which simply reflects the general course of capitalist production.
>
> —*British Imperialism in Malaya*, Labour Research Department, Communist Party of Great Britain, 1926[1]

The huge industrial complexes of Akron and elsewhere were initially built on the back of the wild rubber industry in the Amazon and Africa, but the system was ultimately unsustainable. The solution was the orderly cultivation of rubber on tropical plantations. The tale of how Henry Wickham purloined Brazil's rubber patrimony is one of the romantic legends of the British Empire. By his own account, in 1876 Wickham collected over 70,000 hevea seeds from the forests along the Tapajós River. Then, he smuggled the seeds to Joseph Hooker, the eminent botanist who served as director of the Royal Botanic Gardens at Kew. Wickham was handsomely rewarded for his trouble at the rate of £10 per 1,000 seeds, or £700 for the lot.[2] This seed stock formed the basis of the rubber plantations in Asia and destroyed the Amazonian wild rubber trade in the process.[3] Had Wickham been American, his exploits might well have been dubbed "the great Amazon rubber heist." Even the Germans of the Hitler era were inspired: the film *Kautschuk* (Rubber) (1938) was a box-office hit in the Reich. Loosely based on Wickham's jungle exploits, the drama showed him fighting for his life in the coils of a giant boa constrictor and outwitting his Latin competitors.

Whether Wickham's mission was a "jolly-good show" of British imperial legend or the "brazen and lucrative robbery" alleged by his critics,[4] it seems likely that the Brazilian customs men were indifferent to what must have seemed to them a quixotic venture. Small-scale hevea plantations did exist in Amazonia at this time, but it is only with hindsight that we know that transplanting seeds overseas would supplant the Brazilian industry. As late as 1907, some foreign experts considered that wild rubber would always dominate world markets.[5] This attitude was dangerously complacent for the wild rubber producers; Wickham had been contracted to collect seeds by the Royal Botanic Gardens, the prestigious scientific center set up by King George III and directed and funded by the British state since 1841. As anthropologist Lucile Brockway has shown, the Kew Gardens had placed their formidable scientific expertise at the service of the Empire's commercial interests;[6] Kew was a place of applied rather than pure science where the personnel who provided the research and development for colonial agribusiness were trained. Malaya, opined British Prime Minister Joseph Chamberlain, was "an undeveloped estate,"[7] and the same might have been said of the rest of the Empire. Kew was central to this project, and without its expertise it is difficult to imagine the rise of the plantation industries, which allowed transplanted crops such as coffee, tea, sisal, cinchona, and rubber to flourish for the benefit of the Mother Country.

An Idea that Came into Its Time

The British Government—and in particular the India Office—had become interested in the idea of rubber cultivation some time before Wickham's mission, and they had naturally sought the support of the management of the Kew Gardens. In 1872, anxious to procure reliable supplies, the India Office commissioned Mr. James Cross, a botanist from Edinburgh, to draw up a report on the feasibility of transplanting South American rubber trees to India.[8] Rubber farming was a radical concept, but the idea was not entirely new. The periodical *Bea* had raised the idea as early as 1791, and seven years later an Englishman named Howison had suggested the introduction of the hevea tree to India and Malaya.[9]

The rubber manufacturer and inventor Thomas Hancock had also flagged the plantation idea in an 1855 edition of the *Gardener's Chronicle*.[10] There were already some small-scale rubber plantations in Brazil from 1865 and possibly a little later in Peru, with their product sold on the London market as fine pará sheet.[11] The Government of India also established a number of *Ficus elastica* plantations at Charduar in Assam in 1873,[12] and by 1893 the latex was the most lucrative minor forest product from the province, with a value of 1,307,819 rupees per annum.[13] Reports and correspondence from the Kew Gardens archives show that the decision to transplant hevea and castilloa seeds from the Amazon and Central America to Asia was taken at the very highest levels of the Indian Government and the India Office in London.[14]

Even before Wickham's expedition, Kew Gardens' personnel had brought rubber seeds back from the Amazon. The ex-naval officer Clements Markham, for instance, sent 2,000 hevea seeds to Kew in 1873, and although only a dozen germinated, some of these were successfully transplanted in the Royal Botanic Gardens in Calcutta. Robert Cross brought 134 castilloa seedlings from Panama to Kew in 1875 and forwarded them to India the following year. Cross also imported a considerable quantity of hevea seeds from Brazil, of which 2,000 survived and were sent to botanical gardens in Ceylon, Buitenzorg, and Singapore. A Mr. Ferris also delivered around 2,000 seedlings to Kew around the same time. Some of these seedlings arrived at the Peradiniya Gardens in Ceylon in 1876, a date that the organizers of the 1908 Colombo rubber exhibition believed marked the start of the industry on the island[15] and which predates the arrival of Wickham's seeds. Others were sent to the botanical gardens in Singapore. Perhaps the significance of Wickham's mission was its larger scale, but it is clear that his talent for self-dramatization obscured the contributions of others. In the process, his story became a sustaining myth of empire. The whole project was authorized, paid for, and even initiated by the India Office in London, with the former naval officer Clements Markham acting on behalf of the Secretary of State for India in his dealings with the Gardens.[16]

No Assurance of Success

Even after Wickham's mission, the development of a large-scale rubber plantation industry in Asia was by no means assured. The hevea seedlings

failed to adapt to Indian conditions,[17] and an early attempt to cultivate
rubber in the botanic gardens at Saigon in Cochin China was also unsuccessful.[18] More importantly, Southeast Asian planters ignored the new
crop for nearly twenty-five years after Wickham's mission, preferring to
stick to established commodities such as tobacco, coffee, tea, indigo, and
sugarcane. Rubber had its supporters, but they were considered oddballs.
The director of the Singapore Botanic Gardens, Henry Ridley, for example, was an enthusiast but planters dubbed him "Rubber Ridley" and less
politely as "Mad" Ridley for what they saw as an unrealistic obsession.[19]
Civil servants perhaps agreed; the veteran Malayan colonial administrator
Frank Swettenham later recalled that rubber was regarded as a "hopeless
gamble."[20] Even Wickham himself, who had done so much to bring the
possibility of hevea plantations to public attention, turned to copra farming and *bêche-de-mer* collection in New Guinea.[21] Lack of scientific
knowledge and technical know-how reinforced the fear that rubber planting was a risky proposition. This was shown in 1877 when a Mr. Sowerby
of the Royal Botanic Society in London advised a planter called
Underdown at Penang to crush the fresh leaves and branches of hevea
trees in rollers to extract the "juice," admitting that this fanciful method
"has yet to be tried."[22] The fact that it takes rubber trees six years to
achieve profitable maturity also did not appeal to skeptical planters
maneuvering in fickle markets.

"We Owe a Lot to the Rats"

Plantation rubber came into its own as a result of the collapse in commodity prices during the 1890s depression. Between 1889 and 1900, the number of tobacco estates in the Deli region of Sumatra fell from one-hunred-
five to seventy-four and the membership of the Planters' Association from
forty-three to twenty-two.[23] Across the Straits of Malacca, British coffee
and sugar planters were also facing bankruptcy and turned to rubber as a
last resort. The established firm of Harrisons and Crosfield in Ceylon had
even earlier changed to rubber when their tea plantations were stricken
with blight.[24] Malayan sugarcane too "would have to struggle hard if it is
not to become a dead industry," wrote the planter Dick Ramsden to his
father in 1895, worrying about competition from the European beet industry.[25] A Chinese businessman called Tan Choy Han was probably Malaya's
first successful rubber planter, interplanting hevea with tapioca, although a

planter named Low had experimented with Ceará rubber in Perak as early as 1878.[26] Cautiously, the European planters followed Tan's suit, combining hevea with tea, sugar, and coffee.[27] The results were so promising that in 1899 the Selangor Rubber Company decided to concentrate exclusively on hevea. The case of Penang Sugar Estates, which was another of a large group of companies controlled by the Ramsden family, was fairly typical. The company began to plant rubber from 1900, but it was reluctant at first to end sugar production because of its considerable capital investment in sugar plant and machinery. The Ramsden executive E. L. Hamilton fretted about labor shortages and fickle markets, lamented white ants and root disease attacking the hevea seedlings, and worried about "the risk of an artificial substitute for rubber being found."[28] In the end, the appetites of sweet-toothed rodents played a significant role in propelling the Ramsden companies into full-scale rubber production. "We owe a lot to the rats," Hamilton wrote to Sir John Ramsden, for without them "we might not have started [rubber planting] until a much later date."[29] By 1905, all the Ramsden companies had embarked on large-scale hevea planting, and in 1910 Penang Sugar Estates officially changed its name to Penang Rubber Estates.[30] Thereafter, the company progressively abandoned sugar on the rest of its plantations.[31]

The period from 1900 to the end of the First World War was the "Golden Age" of the rubber planters. By 1915, rubber had overtaken tin as Malaya's most important export, worth 40 percent of the colony's total export value up until 1941 and accounting for four-fifths by volume of all agricultural produce. As early as 1906, at the suggestion of an upcountry planter named James Ryan, the rubber growers of Ceylon staged a rubber exhibition in Sinhalese-style pavilions in the Royal Botanic Gardens at Peradiniya. The exhibition was a great success, with countries from around the world displaying their wares. Malaya won first prize for its block rubber. The major plantation rubber regions were always Malaya and Sumatra, but smaller plantations were established elsewhere in the tropical world. The British New Guinea Development Company and some smaller operations began commercial production of hevea rubber in 1906, with trees brought from Malaya,[32] although indigenous rubber vines had been commercially exploited even earlier on the island.[33] A number of plantations were started in the Belgian Congo and German East Africa before the First World War. The first large hevea plantations were started in French Indochina in 1905[34] and began production by 1914.[35]

The year 1913 marked a watershed in rubber history, with the output on the Asian plantations exceeding that of Amazonia by 25 percent.[36] From then on, the fortunes of the wild industry waned, and although Amazonian production actually *increased* in the short term, by the end of the 1920s it had fallen into a slump from which it never recovered, save for a brief revival during the rubber-hungry years of the Second World War. The Brazilian government began to encourage the development of plantations by the end of the first decade of the twentieth century, but it was too late to counter the foreign threat,[37] and their efforts were thwarted by the appearance of hevea leaf blight, which affected plantation trees in Latin America but not those growing in the wild. Until mass-produced synthetic rubber appeared during the Second World War, the overseas plantation product was supreme. Wild rubber producers could not compete with an industry based on cheap regimented labor and systematic cultivation under the supervision of scientific experts. During the halcyon days during and up to the First World War production boomed. Many of the original plantations in Malaya and Ceylon were small-scale affairs run by owner-operators, but from at least 1910 there was a shift toward joint stock companies and large-scale production. Many small planters cashed out at a handsome profit, and some stayed on as managers on the estates they had founded. The process accelerated after the First World War, with the difference that small planters were now buffeted by fickle markets and had to sell on much less advantageous terms.[38]

The Price Roller Coaster and Stevenson

Paradoxically, the plantation industry's success undermined its profitability. The efficiency of the rubber estates ensured ever-greater volumes of quality rubber. Consumers were able to stockpile for their needs and producers faced a buyers' market. Prices fell and they never again climbed to the dizzy heights that wild rubber had fetched during the great boom years. From a price of six to eight shillings per pound in 1910, rubber was selling at between one and sixpence to two shillings per pound in 1913.[39] This was offset by bigger output and large sales generated by the war and lower wage rates and associated costs. In 1914 the average wage for an adult male Asian rubber "coolie" was around one shilling a day without rations, compared to six shillings and eight pence per day in Brazil.[40] The end of the war was followed by a world trade slump that sent the demand for rubber tumbling at a time when ever-greater supplies of it were available. Prices plummeted, ruining the smaller producers and forcing their larger rivals to make stringent economies. At the war's end, prices were so low that Australian planters in Papua begged for government subsidies.[41] Three years later, when prices fell below the cost of production, one of Papua's largest rubber estates was saved from bankruptcy by generous government loans.[42] The pattern of an industry beset by roller coaster price fluctuations was set, with short-lived booms alternating with longer slumps, steadily declining prices, and government bailouts. Planters in Papua and New Guinea, for example, claimed only one year of prosperity between the early 1920s and 1942, and production virtually ceased in 1922 when the price of rubber fell to seven pence a pound.[43] In Malaya, the Ramsden estates tapped trees on alternate days and postponed all but the most necessary work until trade improved.[44]

Although the planters in Malaya and elsewhere were fierce advocates of the free market, many admitted that some kind of regulation was needed if they were to halt the downward price spiral. The Rubber Growers' Association (RGA), an influential London lobby group for the colonial planters, campaigned for quotas on production in order to stabilize prices. The rubber manufacturing firms were less keen on the idea, fearing that their profits would be undermined as a result, but the RGA prevailed. In 1922 the British government introduced the Stevenson plan, named after the chairman of the committee that drafted it, Sir James Stevenson, who was described by a Goodyear executive as "a hard-headed businessman who had made a fortune as the distiller of Johnnie Walker whiskey." Significantly, although British planters were represented on the committee, British rubber manufacturers were not.[45] The Plan proposed that rubber producers would be allocated strict quotas to prevent the "over-supply" from further eroding prices.

Generally, the British planters in Malaya cooperated with the Stevenson Plan, although Malay smallholders were fiercely hostile and disturbances almost turned into full-scale riots in some areas of the colony.[46] In 1929, the British authorities in Malaya admitted to "coercing" Muslim *bumiputras* into abstaining from tapping on Sundays,[47] a move that gained support from European clerics anxious to maintain the sanctity of the Christian Sabbath.[48] A Colonial Office memo calculated that the ban would result in a 12 to 14 percent decrease in output.[49] By 1934, the Governor of the Straits Settlements, Sir Cecil Clementi, secretly proposed that 70,000 acres of illegally planted land in Johore State should be destroyed "by force if necessary," followed by "punitive action" against Chinese squatters. His critics in the British government and press warned that draconian measures would cause "riots and bloodshed, probably bordering on civil war" and Clementi backed off.[50]

From the beginning, the Stevenson Plan was undermined by its complexity. A British plantation director quipped, "there are only three persons who ever understood the intricate complexities of Restriction: Lord Stevenson, who is dead; a Professor of Economics, who has gone mad; and Mr. Ormsby-Gore, who was always misrepresented."[51] Although three of the "Big Four" U.S. manufacturers were at least lukewarm to the idea of price stabilization, the rebarbitive Harvey S. Firestone denounced the plan as a price-fixing British cartel. The Dutch authorities and planters in the Indies were also recalcitrant, partly out of self-interest and partly from a stubborn attachment to free market principles, despite a request by the Dutch Rubber Growers' Association to join the plan.[52] French planters in Indochina refused to cooperate and big Chinese planters in Malaya were suspicious. Rubber theft and smuggling—often carried out by the Chinese and Malays—were perennial problems for the colonial authorities throughout the six years of the Stevenson Plan. However, huge profits were made by smuggling rubber through Sumatra and Thailand. Singapore continued to act as a port for black market rubber despite the vigilance of colonial authorities.[53]

"The Little Brown Man Breaks the Monopoly"

In the end, it was obvious that the Stevenson Plan did not serve British interests. For the Dutch planters, however, it had been a bonanza. Between 1923 and 1927, the total area under rubber in the Netherlands East Indies (NEI) multiplied sevenfold.[54] The NEI had increased their share of the world rubber market to almost 50 percent,[55] and the vice president of the U.S. firm Lee Tire & Rubber claimed that the actual production of rubber in the Dutch Indies increased by 300 percent between 1922 and 1927.[56] The most striking expansion in the Indies was in native smallholdings, whose production soared from 6,000 tons in 1921 to 95,000 in 1927. By 1940, native rubber smallholdings in the NEI occupied an area equal in size to that of the large European plantations. Goodyear executive Hugh Allen believed that "it was the little brown man who in the end broke the British monopoly." The smallholder could do so because:

He had no town sites to keep up, no payrolls to maintain, no managing directors. His overheads were zero, his tastes were simple, he had no tailor bills,
no Scotch-and-soda chits, no sons to be educated in Europe, no daughters to
be presented at court. Give him his holiday festivals and enough to eat and he
was content. He was not a businessman, had no ambition to build an industrial empire. His challenge was that of numbers, of the vast areas of trees that
he held.[57]

There is a certain ironic justice in native smallholders challenging the
colonialists at their own game. Following a campaign led by the pro–free
trade Beaverbrook press, the Hambling Committee recommended scrap-
ping the plan and the British government closed it down in November
1928.[58] Prices tumbled immediately from 37.5 cents to 28.5 cents per
pound,[59] a harbinger of the Great Depression soon to come.

The Barons Grow their Own

The big rubber manufacturing companies also threatened to compete
directly with the growers. Leading the charge was Akron's Harvey S.
Firestone, who appears to have seen himself as a "field marshal of U.S.
industry." Firestone was not content to merely criticize what he saw as bla-
tant price fixing by the British. Stockpiling and recycling scrap rubber
were one way to counter Stevenson, and his firm also established its own
purchasing arm in the Far East, buying rubber directly from planters and
smallholders and processing it in a Singapore plant.[60] Rubber manufacturing firms were among the world's first multinational corporations, with
factories and outlets wherever they could find or create markets. It was
logical that they would become vertically integrated concerns, in which
they grew their own rubber, shipped it across the oceans, processed it in
their huge factories, and sold it through their own outlets. Nevertheless,
Firestone's U.S. rivals—Goodyear, Goodrich, and U.S. Rubber—initially
welcomed Stevenson as "a chance to escape the Depression-born nightmare of rubber inventories fluctuating wildly from month to month."[61]

Firestone was also concerned for patriotic reasons about British and
Dutch control of the world's rubber supplies. In his eyes, the perils for
American business had been highlighted in November 1914 when the
British government imposed an embargo on rubber to stop it falling into
German hands. While the British did allow the United States to continue

importing rubber during the war, they strictly regulated the trade in line with their own strategic interests. For Firestone, the Stevenson Plan was the last straw, but even earlier, in 1915, he had concluded that the United States had to grow its own rubber and began to search for plantation sites in the Philippines, Malaya, and Sumatra.[62] In 1923, he persuaded the U.S. Congress to subsidize the quest with an initial appropriation of half a million dollars.[63] Initially, Firestone favored the Philippines, since 1898 a U.S. colony, as the site for his proposed plantations, but he was frustrated by the colony's land laws, which forbade foreigners from owning more than 2,500 acres of agricultural land. Manuel Quezon led Filipino nationalists in blocking a Firestone-inspired push in the Manila parliament to lift the ceiling,[64] warning that "[e]very dollar of American capital is one more nail in the coffin of independence."[65] The political class of the Republic of Liberia would have done well to heed Quezon's words.

Firestone's Liberian Satrapy

Following his rebuff at the hands of the Filipino nationalists in 1923, Harvey Firestone, Sr., switched his attentions to the impoverished African Republic of Liberia. Originally settled by freed slaves from the United States in 1822, Liberia was chronically underdeveloped and had drifted close to bankruptcy several times. Its status as a sovereign state was in serious doubt; although U.S. Secretary of State Elihu Root admitted in 1910 that Liberia was a de facto American colony,[66] the U.S. government had neglected the country's economic and social development. Dominated by a small coastal oligarchy of "Americo-Africans" (known colloquially as "Congos"), the hinterland was a commercially undeveloped wilderness inhabited by resentful indigenes who occasionally rose in rebellion against the government in Monrovia.[67] In late 1923, Firestone sent his assistant, the Scotsman Donald Ross, to investigate the possibilities of hevea culture in Liberia. When Ross advised that the terrain and climate were favorable, Firestone arranged with the U.S. State Department to prepare the way for plantations.[68] In 1925, he signed a ninety-nine year lease on the use of up to one million acres of land with the Liberian government and swore "to make England realize that America is now . . . in the rubber business in earnest."[69] All told, the million-acre Firestone lease amounted to one-twenty-fifth of the surface area of the West African republic,[70] although only a fraction of this was actually developed for rubber production. Firestone, in the argot of his kind, "thought big." Proposing to invest $100 million in the country and eventually employ hundreds of thousands of workers, Firestone experimented with hevea on a small plantation at Mt. Barclay, which he had purchased from a bankrupt British company. This plantation, which came back on line in 1925, was a pilot project for a much more ambitious undertaking on the Du River, forty-five miles from Monrovia. Under Ross's supervision, African laborers cut down a huge swathe of jungle with axes, machetes, and crosscut saws and cleared the river of trunks and roots to act as a transport artery.[71] The giant plantation, which was greatly expanded during the Second World War, is still in production today under the ownership of the Japanese company Firestone-Bridgestone.[72]

The other large rubber firms also entered the plantation business. Goodyear bought out a number of existing Dutch-owned estates as early as 1916, opened new ones in Sumatra after 1927, and experimented with smaller estates on Mindanao in the Philippines and in Costa Rica, Panama, Guatemala, and Brazil.[73] The Michelin Company of France entered into the plantation industry in Cochin-China and Cambodia in the 1920s, and British-owned Dunlop moved into Malaya and Sumatra. By 1933, the journalist M. J. Kennaway reckoned that Dunlop's Malayan estates, extending over 100,000 acres, were "the biggest enterprise in the plantation industry in the British Empire today."[74]

Firestone's West African initiative was probably the most spectacular single undertaking in rubber plantation history, and it is still hailed by some as a milestone in the economic and social development of Liberia.[75] During the Second World War, it was the largest producer of natural raw rubber for the Allied war effort. The terms of the lease agreement bound Firestone to build a modern seaport at Monrovia,[76] plus roads and other essential infrastructure in a country which had hitherto lacked the amenities of modern life. Until Firestone built this port, all goods brought in or out by sea had to travel offshore in surfboats to freighters in the Atlantic.

From the outset, however, critics assailed both Firestone and the U.S. government for what they saw as an imperialist venture that threatened Liberia's sovereignty.[77] In 1925, Liberia was in poor shape to resist Firestone's demands. Its financial affairs were in the hands of international receivers following a default on loan repayments, its frontiers were in dispute, and its sovereignty was menaced by neighboring colonial powers. The Americo-African oligarchy at Monrovia was split over whether to embrace or reject Firestone. Under the terms of the agreement with the

Liberian government, Firestone leased its land for a mere six cents a year per acre, or $60,000 per annum. The rate was fixed for the ninety-nine years of the concession and any gold, diamonds, or other minerals discovered on the land were Firestone's property. Exports of rubber were to be taxed at a flat rate of 1 percent of earnings at New York market prices. Firestone's supporters claimed that the company had brought steady employment, a modern infrastructure, educational and health facilities, and socioeconomic development to the country. However, its critics pointed out that while the company made immense profits, very little of these actually remained inside the country and those that did primarily benefited the Monrovia oligarchy. In 1944, Liberia's exports were worth $10,306,308; 90 percent of these, or $9,418,282, came from rubber.[78] Of this, Liberia received only an amount equal to 1 percent via export taxes. It was small wonder that a number of U.S. academics, journalists, and union activists roundly criticized the Firestone venture. The United Rubber Workers' Union decried the wages and conditions of the plantation laborers, and Raymond Buell of the Foreign Policy Association in Washington, D.C., charged Firestone and the Liberian government with using forced labor.[79] There were also land problems. The overwhelming bulk of the population were Kru and other tribal Africans, many of whom now risked eviction as a result of their land and its minerals being given away by the government of Liberia.[80]

The vast size of the concession and its minimal cost to Firestone were not the only complaints of the anti-imperialist lobby. After a preliminary agreement had been reached with the Liberian government, Firestone unilaterally added "Clause K" to a list of minor amendments made by the U.S. State Department. The clause made the plantation lease and the building of associated infrastructure contingent on the Liberian government's acceptance of a $5,000,000 loan to be raised from the National City Bank of New York by the Finance Corporation of America, a Firestone subsidiary. Initially, the Liberian government balked, but following intense pressure by the U.S. Secretary of State, Frank Kellogg, Liberian President Charles King had little choice but to sign an agreement that saddled his country with a debt that was only wiped out thirty years later. Moreover, acceptance of the loan meant that Liberia agreed to supervision of its financial affairs by the United States—and must pay the salaries of the officials appointed to do so. As the American writer J. H. Mower points out, "service charges and advisors' salaries amounted to a fixed charge of nearly $220,000 a year, constituting 20 percent of govern-

Workers at Firestone's Harbel plantation, Liberia, 1930s.

ment revenues in 1928, and about 50 percent in 1931."[81] According to Raymond Buell, "Firestone insisted upon the loan. . . in order to establish financial control over the Liberian government, exclude foreign competition and to prevent the government from getting a loan from any other foreign source."[82]

When the Great Depression struck, the loan became a crippling burden for the Liberian people: the interest had been set at 7 percent or $350,000 per annum, in addition to the charges detailed above. When in 1933 it appeared that Liberia might default on its payments, Harvey Firestone clamored for the dispatch of a U.S. warship to Monrovia. The Roosevelt administration rejected gunboat diplomacy, but repayments to Firestone were nevertheless put ahead of the needs of the Liberian people. The salaries of government employees were cut by 50 percent, and the state education system was closed and taken over by missionaries. Whatever Firestone might have done in terms of infrastructural "development," the agreement was of the kind that the Liberians could not refuse. In 1936, the United Rubber Workers charged that "Firestone was going to loan Liberia money to improve the country for Firestone, and in addition was going to pay Firestone interest on the loan." The financial advisors' role, moreover, was to ensure that the loan money was used "wisely," that is, for Firestone's benefit. The URWA also pointed out that

Firestone was granted a complete monopoly over the sale of rubber products in the country.[83]

The upshot was that Liberia's sovereignty was compromised. Nominally independent, the treatment of the Republic epitomized what was later known as "neocolonialism," although Firestone's power also harkened back to the private imperialism of Leopold's Congo Free State. The United Rubber Workers accused Firestone of being the "virtual dictator" of Liberia,[84] and many Americans agreed. A writer in the *Philadelphia Record* alleged that Harvey Firestone "is much closer to being the off-stage ruler of Liberia than Mussolini can claim of Ethiopia."[85] When Liberia finally repaid the loan and interest in 1956, the Liberian government erected a commemorative plaque in Monrovia, which read:

> This Monument erected by the people of Liberia is dedicated to the great relief brought to the Country by the Tubman Administration in the retirement of the 1927 Loan with its humiliating and strangulating effects on the economy of the Nation.[86]

Henry Ford and the Leaf Blight

In contrast to Firestone's lucrative Liberian venture, an attempt by the automobile tycoon Henry Ford to build a plantation industry in Brazil proved an expensive disaster. Ford wanted to make his business empire, based on his Rouge automobile plant near Detroit, a model of vertical integration. The Rouge plant boasted its own tire-making department and from the mid-1920s, for reasons similar to those of his good friend Harvey Firestone, Ford decided to produce his own raw rubber. In 1927, he bought one million acres of land in the Tapajós valley in Brazil, extended an existing estate, and set up the Belterra and Fordlandia rubber plantations. In 1928, the steamer *Lake Ormuc* left Dearborn, Michigan, towing the heavily laden barge *Lake LaFarge*. Some months later, the craft dropped anchor in the Tapajós and unloaded a cargo of bulldozers, a steam shovel, locomotives, prefabricated buildings, an ice plant, and other equipment. He built an American-style town in the jungle, Boa Vista, and constructed roads, railways, schools, hospitals, sawmills, a power station, machine shops, a hotel, churches, a floating dock, and other costly infrastructure.[87]

Ford had lost faith in his friend Thomas Edison's belief that native North American latex-bearing shrubs might be commercially viable and sufficient for America's needs. Unfortunately for Ford, the trees he acquired in Brazil were struck by *Dothidella nisi* (leaf blight). Combined with the depredations of caterpillars, lace bugs, and other tropical insect and plant pests, the mold proved a formidable enemy, thwarting the best efforts of Ford's expert botanist James Weir to find a solution. Labor troubles also contributed to his plantations' problems. Ford upset the Brazilian laborers with his strong-arm tactics and riled them up with a ban on drinking and smoking in the plantations, including their own homes. The project also ran afoul of Brazilian Integralist politicians and army officers, but Ford persevered, convinced that American technical know-how and diplomacy would triumph.[88] By 1934, however, with the Depression eroding profit margins and no sign of a technical fix, he began losing interest. Ford's failures were repeated in the Goodyear plantations in Central America.[89] Goodyear and U.S. government scientists eventually developed an antidote to the mold, but by that time cheap synthetic rubber was widely available and the pressure to open new plantations had disappeared. In 1945, with synthetic rubber plants churning out most of America's wartime rubber, Ford admitted defeat and sold his lot to the Brazilian government for $250,000.[90] All told, Ford had sunk up to $30 million into his Brazilian adventure.

Depression and Recovery

The effects of the Great Depression after 1929 further sapped the economic viability of the New and Old World plantations. Firestone virtually mothballed his Liberian plantations as prices slumped below the cost of production to seventeen cents a pound.[91] Goodyear recalled key managerial personnel from its Asian plantations and set them to menial jobs in Akron during the economic downturn. Throughout the plantation industry, many others were laid off, and there was hardship and distress. Following the end of the Stevenson plan in 1928, before the Wall Street Crash, rubber prices had tumbled.

By the late 1930s, however, the worst of the Depression was over, and rubber prices and production rose steadily. In 1934, *India Rubber World* calculated the world's production of rubber amounted to the equivalent of a solid column as big as the Empire State Building, 1,250 feet high and

173 square feet.[92] The International Rubber Regulation Agreement of
1934–1943—a more successful incarnation of the Stevenson Plan involv-
ing the French, Dutch, and the British—also contributed to healthier
profits and shielded the industry to some extent.[93] In 1939, an official
French colonial document hailed what it saw as "the miracle of
Indochinese rubber," which had been heavily subsidized during the
Depression years, but was once again profitable.[94] On the eve of the
Second World War, the French plantations employed close to 100,000
laborers, who drew more than one quarter of the wages paid in all of
French Indochina.[95] The Malayan industry was also booming, with 2.1
million acres planted in rubber on some 2,500 estates employing 325,000
laborers and accounting for almost 40 percent of the world's supply of
raw rubber.[96] The industry was now larger than before the onset of the
Depression[97] and although Malay smallholders were increasingly turning
to rubber as a sideline, 75 percent of the total acreage was still in
European hands, unlike in Sumatra.

Enormous Industrial Undertakings

The larger rubber estates were disciplined industrial undertakings, with
enormous workforces and considerable investment in infrastructure.
Many of the early planters were owner-managers, and while this white
smallholder class never completely disappeared, after 1910 their estates
were increasingly absorbed into concerns owned by joint-stock companies. There was an influx of ex-servicemen onto Malayan smallholdings
after the Great War, but many went bankrupt during the Depression and
their estates were taken over by companies such as Guthrie and
Dunlop.[98] The scale of operations on the estates was described by the
Ramsden company secretary E. L. Hamilton following a visit to Malaya
in 1906; after meeting with the general manager, John Turner, in the
main offices at Penang, Hamilton took the ferry to Prye and then traveled
by car over "20 miles of good road" in seventy minutes to the company's
estates at Caledonia and elsewhere. He noted shipping wharves, hospitals, "coolie lines,"[99] and spacious European bungalows. The company
had also built its own brickworks, engine repair shops, and a water
pumping plant. A private road network had been cut from the jungle, and

a system of embankments and sluices kept high tides from flooding the plantations. The rubber itself was treated in the company's own on-site factories, where it was washed, dried, and pressed hydraulically into blocks and sheets of required size with machinery powered by steam from a nearby boiler house.[100] Almost thirty years later, the huge Dunlop estate at Johor was treating 7,000 lbs. of rubber each day in its on-site factory using state-of-the-art technology.[101] Many plantations boasted their own electricity generating plants and light rail systems, with the locomotives maintained in well-equipped workshops staffed by European craftsmen and their Asian laborers. Even the smaller estates in Malaya were self-contained, with their own cattle sheds, blacksmiths, carpenters' shops, and basic hospitals.[102] Harvey Firestone built his own hydroelectric power station close to the Du Plantation in Liberia and shipped block latex downstream aboard "queer-looking power-lighters [which] resembled submarines." These craft moored alongside ships riding offshore until the company built the country's first deep-water port at Monrovia. The Du Plantation was in direct radio telegraphic contact with the firm's Akron headquarters.[103]

War Clouds

For planters in Southeast Asia, the outbreak of war in 1939 had contradictory effects. Prices boomed as a result of the upsurge in demand, but people were jittery about the possibility of a Japanese invasion. Firestone vastly expanded its operations in Liberia out of reach of the Japanese (although he never provided the 350,000 jobs promised at the time of the lease agreement with the Liberian government). Domestic consumption had also soared with the easing of the Depression. Sales of cars skyrocketed in the United States, with the Office of Production Management estimating that "Sunday drivers on the day of the sneak attack on Pearl Harbor . . . [were wearing] out 5,000 tons of rubber."[104]

Fears of Japanese aggression were well-founded. The subsequent advance of the Japanese armies into Malaya and Sumatra cut off almost 80 percent of the world's rubber supplies.[105] While this was partially offset by a vast expansion of the Liberian plantations, with the revival of the Amazon wild rubber industry, stringent rationing, recycling of scrap and the "slaughter tapping" of rubber trees to increase yield, the Allies were still faced with chronic shortages. The shortfall was made up for by the expansion of the synthetic rubber industry. As a writer noted in the *Sydney Morning Herald* in 1945, "some [U.S.] Government-owned factories . . . [were] producing synthetic rubber cheaper than the natural rubber cost before the war."[106] This was not the only change. The Japanese occupation, albeit short-lived, was to shatter the old colonial system and with it, the world of the rubber planters and their European assistants.

CHAPTER THIRTEEN

The Planters' World

> He hadn't much to talk about but rubber and games, tennis, you know, and
> golf and shooting; and I don't suppose he read a book from year's end to
> year's end. He was the typical public school boy. He was about thirty-five
> when I first knew him but he had the mind of a boy of eighteen. You know
> how many fellows when they come out East seem to stop growing.
>
> —SOMERSET MAUGHAM, pen portrait of a planter called Bronson[1]

Their pink and white skins peeled or burned crayfish-red under the tropical sun. Their pale European eyes surveyed an ocean of brown and black
faces, the owners of which must have regarded these planters as beings as
exotic as the hevea trees they brought with them to Africa and Asia. They
sipped at *stengahs* (whisky and sodas) and bitter beer, clad in sweat-
stained khakis or tropical whites and *sola topees* [safari helmets], sum-
moning a "boy" with teapot or gin bottle to the veranda at the end of
another hot day. They carried stout sticks to ward off cobras coiled in the
rows of rubber trees. They sent their children to boarding schools in
Singapore, or Australia, or "back home" in Europe. They were, *Tuan
Besars* and *Tuan Kechils*—"great gentlemen" and "junior masters" in
Malay respectively; *pukka sahibs*—masters or lords in Hindi or *mem-
sahibs* if they were female; *bwanas*—sirs in Swahili; or more generally
great white fathers; lording it over the "boys," "coolies," *amahs*, "Marys,"
and *dhobi wallahs* who served them.[2] Noel Coward lampooned them.
Writers such as W. Somerset Maugham, Lázló Székely, Anthony Burgess,

and Madelon Lulofs left accounts of their lives varying from the subtle, sympathetic, or nuanced to the bluntly disparaging. Some of them have left eloquent memoirs. There is much that we today would despise about them: they were racists and fervent advocates of imperialism. Brutality— to a greater or lesser degree—was built into the colonial system, and at best they treated the coolies with an insufferable paternalism, serene in the belief that they were the bearers of a higher civilization for the benefit of the natives. Most of them would have applauded the sentiments of Sir Malcolm Watson, the conqueror of malaria in Malaya, who declared that "if we have done well out of Malaya, we deserve it."[3] The best of them had some admirable qualities, not the least their doggedness in adversity and their resourcefulness. Many of them were fair linguists, picking up Tamil, Malay, Javanese, or the Chinese dialects; indeed employment on some estates was dependent on learning the coolies' tongues. Some took up with young Malay or Tamil women—dubbed "sleeping dictionaries" in colonial argot—but the more orthodox approach was to pore over *Well's Coolie Tamil*.[4] On the other hand, the Brazilian tappers at Fordlandia joked that after one year the American staff had learned enough Portuguese to say *"uma cerveja"* (one beer) and after two years, *"duas cervejas"* (two beers).[5] They were often profoundly lonely, and many took to the bottle for solace. They were an essential part of Empire, for as the writer Daniel Green has observed, it is not "just a conceit to claim that the British Empire was, to a certain extent at least, a vegetable empire."[6] The same was true, to varying degrees, of the French, Dutch, Belgian, German, and American empires. Those formal empires have gone and with them, by and large, the rubber planters.

A Strong Pair of Lungs to Bellow

Most of the Europeans employed on the estates were young assistant planters. The smooth running of the plantations depended on a steady supply of these men, for the color bar prevented coolies from rising beyond the level of clerk, *tandil*, or *mandur*.[7] Many of those who made their way to the Far East were restless young men dissatisfied with the prospect of dull European office jobs. The starting salary for a plantation assistant in the Dutch Indies was two hundred guilders a month, plus 5 percent of the net profits of the plantation, in addition free lodging, servants, a bungalow, medical attention, and postal expenses. Every eight years, you were entitled to eight months' leave back home on full salary. The only qualifications needed were white skin and a strong pair of lungs to bellow at the coolies! Lázló Székely didn't mull it over for long; his Uncle János had worked as a clerk for the Hungarian State Railways for thirty years and still wasn't earning that much. If he stayed home, Lázló could look forward only to boredom "under the eye of a quarrelsome, pretentious boss." Székely boarded the S.S. *Prince Ludwig* at Genoa, bound for the Netherlands Indies via Suez. He was twenty years old and without a profession, one of thousands of young men for whom the lure of the Orient and the promise of fortune proved irresistible.[8] Similarly, the ex-public schoolboy Leopold Ainsworth, overcome with revulsion for his job in a tea and rubber broker's in London, was granted a transfer to Malaya, though his boss cursed him as a fool for leaving a comfortable berth.[9]

The Social Origins of the Assistants

In the early days of plantation rubber, the planters scoured Southeast Asia for suitable employees, but this area yielded only a small pool of labor and was soon drained. The Dutch writer Jan Breman believes that the plantations attracted "a surprising number of misfits and black sheep who were either forced by misfortune to migrate . . . or were sent into exile there by their families."[10] The archives of the Ramsden companies in Malaya[11] are replete with tales of assistants discharged as alcoholic, mentally ill, or as shiftless idlers, but it would be a mistake to generalize from these cases. Many assistants were the younger sons of genteel families of limited means "whose chief qualification for Colonial life is that there is no room for . . . [them] at home."[12] This observation echoes James Mill's aphorism that the British Empire was a "vast system of outdoor relief for the British upper classes."[13] The Scots, disproportionately, made up "as many as a third" of the planters in Malaya,[14] and there was "a pronounced Edinburgh flavour" on the estates.[15] During the "Malayan Emergency" after the Second World War, the rubber companies were less fussy about educational standards. Harrisons and Crosfield hired Robin Bryant after a brief interview in the company's London headquarters. "I was an immediate success," he recalled, "[because] I could play rugby and cricket. For the crusty, mean, miserable company directors this was of infinitely higher priority than knowing the physiology of a rubber tree."[16]

Playing Fields of Eton

If the playing fields of Eton provided much of the officer caste of Empire, they also furnished much of the British plantation supervisory staff. Many of the assistants in Malaya had attended one of the "great" English public schools—Eton, Winchester, Harrow, Rugby, Shrewsbury, Charterhouse, or Westminster—or were educated at select state grammar schools such as Manchester and Bedford. Others had attended "lesser" public or grammar schools.[17] Many of the Scots had been educated at Fettes School in Edinburgh or other exclusive private schools. Molded from early childhood into unquestioning acceptance of imperialism, these young men were unlikely to sympathize with the hardship of the coolies or their nationalist aspirations and could generally be relied upon to eschew anything that was "not cricket" for the companies' interests. The backgrounds of the European personnel found on American-owned plantations reflected the relatively egalitarian nature of U.S. society. Whereas the British plantations maintained the fixed class divisions of "home," it was easier for working-class Americans to rise through the ranks. However, the American companies' comparative liberalism did not extend to race: Afro-Americans endured Jim Crow conditions in the Akron mills, and the color bar was a *sine qua non* of social organization on the Firestone estates in Liberia and on the Goodyear plantations on Sumatra.

Things were different on the French plantations in Indochina. The Communist organizer Tran Tu Binh remembered the entire European staff on the Michelin plantation where he worked as former Foreign Legion men. The manager, M. Triai, a Corsican, had been a captain in the Legion, and his deputy, a cruel man who "looked liked a gibbon," was an old first lieutenant from the same force.[18] A disproportionate number of assistants and managers on the French plantations were Belgians, some of them unsavory types such as Jacques Verhelst and Antoine d'Ursel.[19] The French assistants were likely to be from a petty bourgeois or working-class background, a reflection of the demographic differences between the French and British empires.[20]

Living and Working Conditions

Living and working conditions for the planters and assistants varied depending on the size of the estate, the nationality of the owners, and the

stage of development of the plantation. For the European employees of
the biggest enterprises, whole new towns were conjured up. Firestone's
white employees enjoyed electric light, ice machines, cold storage rooms,
and purified running water.[21] Amid the heat and enormity of the African
bush on the Du estates, Firestone's doctors and nurses ran well-equipped
hospitals and, in what was a first for Liberia, the town's waste was treated
in a modern sewage plant.[22] Harvey Firestone also built a housing estate
for his white employees three miles from the center of Singapore and
named it Firestone Park, after the company's model precinct at Akron.
The houses were built of solid teak to resist white ants and boasted the
"first modern bath rooms ever to be installed in Singapore."[23]

Firestone was a "can do" American businessman, but his rivals also
did not spare expense when it came to the well being of their European
supervisory staff. On Goodyear's Wingfoot and other plantations in
Sumatra, the Americans lived in neat brick and stucco houses with tile
roofs, large windows with insect screens, wired-in porches, and "wide
expanses of lawn," which were manicured by servants. Most white
employees had refrigerators in their houses and ate imported ice cream.
They had the run of golf courses, movie theaters with films from "home,"
football and baseball fields, and tennis courts. Goodyear's Americans
could also go cycling or horseback riding, and there were regular dances
and parties at the well-appointed club rooms. Wild animals were usually
kept at bay—or were hunted for sport—and streams and swampy areas
were sprayed to prevent malarial mosquitoes from breeding.[24] This was
the cutting edge of American capitalist society in a Third World setting,
and there was little, if anything, for the Americans to do around their comfortable bungalows. A family of two, noted Goodyear assistant D.W.
Peabody, "usually have about five servants in the home." Nor were the
American assistants' tasks too onerous. All the physical work was done by
the coolies. In Sumatra, the Americans would begin at 7:00 a.m., when
the air was still cool, and return to their homes for "Tiffin" at midday, after
which they would enjoy a two-hour siesta. After this, they would put in
another two and a half hours before finishing for the day at 4:30 p.m.[25]

The large British companies were equally solicitous of their white
employees' needs. Following a visit to Dunlop's Johor estates, a journalist stated, "I doubt if any other company operating in Malaya can claim
to have studied the well-being of its employees so much."[26] Michelin's
managerial staff on its Indochinese estates enjoyed similar luxuries. Tran
Tu Binh recalled the manager of one Michelin estate was "like the prince

of the plantation." He owned several cars and employed dozens of servants, secretaries, "boys,"[27] cooks, servant girls, and gardeners. His European assistants lived in "spacious rooms, high and dry" from the mud and floods in separate houses with glass windows, shutters, ventilation, and polished veneer furniture.[28] Perhaps the most fanciful house ever built on a rubber estate was that of an eccentric Malayan planter called Douglas Money. Resembling a Chinese pagoda, it rose six storeys high above his plantation and the surrounding jungle, and was fashioned from reinforced concrete. Like many of his fellow planters, Money had become addicted to alcohol, but after he had overcome his problem he preferred to cool off in his indoor swimming pool, the only one in Malaya at the time. He liked to play cards on the roof with his cronies, but this sundeck also acted as a kind of panopticon from which he could keep an eye on the laborers toiling below.[29]

Primitive Conditions on Smaller Estates

The smaller estates could not provide such luxury for their European staff. Margaret Shennan, who grew up in British Malaya, recalls that living conditions were often primitive, with no running water, electric light, or refrigerators; beer and soda would be kept reasonably cool by immersion in wells, but it was a far cry from the ice-cold beverages enjoyed by Firestone's employees. In the monsoon, the rains would make a terrific racket on corrugated iron roofs, but this was perhaps preferable to the thatch used on many estates, which was home to snakes, insects, rats, owls, and other strange creatures.[30] The Scottish assistant Ian Matheson lived on a Sumatran rubber estate in the 1920s and recalls that his wooden bungalow leaked during downpours. There was no running water or electricity and bathing was done in a cement tank filled up daily by servants with kerosene cans. The lavatory was "a thunder box, which needs no description," he added.[31] Leopold Ainsworth describes his first home as a novice assistant or "creeper" in Malaya as a gloomy room in an estate manager's house in Kedah province. He writes that his spirits sank as he saw, by the "miserable dreary light" of an oil lamp, a smelly mattress damp with mildew, with a "Dutch wife"—a long pillow or bolster placed between the legs to circulate air. During the night a violent monsoon sent "a solid, streaming, crashing wall of water" cascading onto his bed through holes in the roof.[32] He had wandered aimlessly around Penang on arrival after nobody had met him at the wharf, 8,000 miles from England, where he had landed with ten pounds and a five-year contract in his pocket, feeling as lonely as on his first day at school. Ainsworth traveled all day in the terrible heat from Penang to a new plantation cut from the jungle under Kedah Peak, first aboard a flimsy boat up a crocodile-infested creek and then in a bullock cart piloted over rough roads by a drunken Tamil. The estate manager, a sullen and taciturn Scotsman, demanded to know what had taken Ainsworth so long, grunted his disapproval, thrashed the cart driver who was the cause of the delay, and retired to bed. Things scarcely improved for Ainsworth as the evening wore on. The Chinese cook served him a "disgusting" meal consisting of tinned soup with ants floating in it, fried fish roe on toast, tinned beef, hard tack akin to dog biscuits, and bananas fried in rancid canned butter. The coffee was strained through one of the manager's old socks.[33] Such fare was not uncommon; much of what the planters ate came out of cans, particularly the ubiquitous turtle soup, and foodstuffs were sold at outrageous markups by Singapore victualers.[34] With his bowels outraged, Ainsworth fell into a fitful sleep, only to be awoken in the morning by the manager hammering on the door and bawling "get up you lazy b— — [sic]." Ainsworth threatened fisticuffs and a grudging truce followed, although the manager's habits never ceased to amaze him. The Scot spent his evenings sawing "scotch tunes" from an ancient violin, and enlivened his mealtimes by shooting at rats and tarantulas with a .22 caliber air rifle from the table.[35]

The Assistants' Work

Ainsworth came to admire and respect the resourcefulness of this Celtic nonpareil who had had little choice but to be a jack-of-all-trades, "a master of everything from road-making to midwifery."[36] He also expected the same from his subordinates. Soon after Ainsworth's arrival on the estate, the manager charged him with responsibility for the installation of the heavy machinery for a new rubber mill, a task the newcomer was able to complete despite his utter lack of experience with all things mechanical.[37] The assistants' duties could be monotonous, but they might be called upon at any time to solve difficult problems. Most days, they would supervise the roll call of laborers in the pre-dawn cool, making sure that none had absconded from their contracts and rousting latecomers from their beds if necessary. Later, as the sun crept blazing into the sky, they would check and recheck the coolies' work. Other assistants would sweat inside the rubber mills where the raw latex was dried and compressed into block or sheet rubber, the tropical heat and humidity intensified by proximity to steam engines and boilers. Probably the worst job of all was supervising the clearing of jungle on new plantations, for although the heavy physical work was carried out by the laborers, the assistants had to ensure that the work was done properly, all the while watching out for snakes and sharp slivers of bamboo that could pierce a man's boot.

It could also be a lonely life, particularly on the smaller estates in the interior. In 1939, an opinionated New Guinea planter named Eckhoff informed an Australian politician that while there were great opportunities in the colony, they would only suit "the right type" and that "we want the men who do not regard leaving the empty hollow life of our Cities as a 'sacrifice,' but a pleasure."[38] His words were self-serving, but contained a great deal of truth. Many planters spent their entire working lives on the plantations, far from what they generally thought of as "home." In 1909, John Turner had served thirty-six years in the tropics, first on sugar estates in British Guiana and then almost twenty years at Penang when he petitioned Ramsdens to retire to Scotland.[39] Turner had combined his managerial responsibilities with membership of the Straits Legislative Council[40] and sat on numerous boards along the length of the Malayan peninsula. He was an indefatigable worker who demanded the same dedication from his employees, and took a Presbyterian view of alcoholic drink, which was something of an occupational hazard for planters. Such Puritanism was widespread. Smoking was banned on Harrisons and Crosfield premises until the 1960s,[41] and Henry Ford prohibited smoking and drinking on his Fordlandia and Belterra estates in Brazil, although the *seringueiros* treated the edict with contempt.

Insects, Snakes, and Wild Beasts

With thunder boxes and leaking roofs, the smaller plantations in particular were no place for the faint-hearted. Nor would they appeal to those frightened of tropical bugs and creepy crawlies. Given their proximity to jungles, swamps, rivers, and tidal lagoons, and the great heat and humidity, there was no shortage of animal and insect pests on the plantations. Enormous swarms of mosquitoes—many of them malarial—emerged after sunset from swamps and waterways. The prevention for malaria, quinine, was taken orally twice a week, and often left many planters feeling woozy or retching uncontrollably.[42] There were multitudes of ants, some of them capable of inflicting nasty bites; stinging scorpions and spiders; and centipedes, locusts, and beetles that fell into food and drink.[43] Goodyear man Walter Klippert recalls leeches known as *"patjats"* on Sumatra, which were one-inch long before they had sucked blood. Snakes—including the frightful black cobra—slithered through the bush and sometimes lurked inside houses to terrify the unwary. The planters would carry clubs with them on their tours of inspection to ward off the reptiles. Klippert lists numerous alarming creatures on the Goodyear plantations in Panama, including a variety of poisonous snakes such as pit vipers, the *fer-de-lance* (spearhead), and the bushmaster, together with repulsive insects such as chiggers, bocaza flies, the anigua, a small louse that burrowed under the toenails to lay its eggs, and screw worms, which laid their eggs under the skin.[44] Safe home in "England's green and pleasant land," Margaret Shennan still shuddered to recall the "loathsome reptile life" in the Malayan rivers.[45] In 1913, C. J. Mason, the manager of Ramsden's Sungei Serarap Estate in Johore, report-ed large numbers of deaths due to *sampans* (flat-bottomed wooden boats) capsizing and casting coolies into crocodile-infested waters. Mason lived in dread of ending his days as "a meal for a crocodile."[46] In the same year, another Ramsden plantation manager reported the death of a Tamil coolie woman who was taken by a crocodile while doing her laundry at the land-ing pontoon of the Nova Scotia Estate.[47] Goodyear files from Sumatra include photographs of "natives" and American *tuans* posing with the body of a large crocodile that had earlier "dined on a coolie."[48] Leopold Ainsworth was startled one day to find a black panther in his room and was relieved when it left peacefully.[49] A Malayan planter's wife remembered that tigers would come "moaning around the house about once a week general-ly"[50] and in 1905, John Turner reported that a tiger killed two men near a company estate in Sungei.[51]

Rabid animals, too, were not uncommon. The Ramsden files contain numerous examples of employees sent from Malaya to the Pasteur Institute at Saigon after being bitten. In 1913, for example, Dr. Jesser Coope, an Indian physician employed by Ramsden, was bitten by a mad dog while visiting the Kurau Estate and sent to Indochina for treatment.[52] Rabid dogs, allegedly, had much in common with Englishmen in Asia. According to Noel Coward's amusing ditty, only "mad dogs and Englishmen go out in the midday sun."

Noel Coward, who visited Malaya in 1932, was dismissive of British colonial society, quipping famously that Malaya was "a first rate country for second rate people." In contrast, at a meeting of the Royal Geographical Society at London in 1942, Dr. Malcolm Watson, the director of the Ross Institute of Tropical Hygiene, praised "the wonderful work done by the rubber planters," adding that "I have seen it stated that these people in Malaya lived a luxurious and riotous life. Believe me, it was the best of our race who built up Malaya in the old days when everyone was frequently down with malaria. The Europeans used to be knocked senseless by it." Watson's efforts in Malaya had gradually brought the disease under control; Mr. G. E. Cator told the same meeting that "during the fifteen years before I left Malaya I should have been as surprised to get a bout of malaria as I should have been to be bitten on the leg by a sheep."[53] The planters also had to contend with numerous waterborne diseases such as cholera, typhoid, and dysentery. These diseases were distressingly common, particularly on new plantations. Although the estate laborers were usually hardest hit by these diseases, the microbes responsible did not spare their European masters. The same applied to venereal diseases, according to Shennan.[54]

"Tropicalia"

When the first rawness of the spaces carved from the jungles had faded, the plantations could display a kind of beauty, at least to the eyes of some. "Set out in perfectly straight rows . . . [the] young green leaves of the rubber trees were indeed beautiful to behold," Tran Tu Binh grudgingly admitted.[55] However, Madelon Lulofs, once married to a rubber planter in Sumatra, paints a picture of monotony in her semi-autobiographical novel *Rubber*: "The hard white road ran through the rubber trees. On either side the heveas with their dark green leaves formed endless rows. Porcelain cups were suspended from the stems and into them slowly dripped the coagulating latex."[56] A French economist wrote of the "melancholy gloom" of the plantations in Indochina following a visit during the Second World War.[57] The Scottish planter Bruce Lockhart believed "[t]here is nothing beautiful about a rubber estate—only a monotony of regularity which corrodes one's outlook on life."[58] Small wonder, then, that the strain proved too much for some assistants and they went mad. According to Australian popular wisdom, Europeans could easily be driven mad by the heat in tropical latitudes. In Australian slang this was known as "going troppo."[59] An Australian newspaper dubbed the condition "Tropicalia" and claimed that most whites in New Guinea suffered from a touch of the condition and were extremely "touchy" as a result.[60] The Ramsden files contain numerous examples of assistants who went mad or became aggressive, particularly under the influence of liquor. In 1913, the manager of the Gedong plantation, for example, informed John Turner that he had suspended a man called Langham who was "addicted to drink" and in the habit of picking fights with his fellow assistants. The final straw came when Langham knocked the manager into a drainage ditch.[61] In the same year, another young man named Gall developed delusions of persecution and had to be escorted back home to England aboard the S. S. *Syria* under the watchful eye of Sergeant Ross of the Straits Settlements Police.[62] Another unfortunate man named Farquharson declined a free passage home after being discharged by the company for insobriety and poor work. Some months later, he was seen "begging food and shelter at the Bungalows of Assistants and Government Rest Houses" and later, on board the S. S. *Palawan* bound for Bombay, he was charged with "cheating."[63] An assistant named McAuley was placed in the Singapore Lunatic Asylum prior to being shipped home, and a man called Wrottersley from the same estate was detained for displaying "homicidal tendencies," which was a problem as no ship's master could be found to take him "home."[64]

Boom and Bust and the Assistants

In the late-nineteenth century, trainee planters in Ceylon and Malaya were known as "creepers" and their families had to pay £100 for the privilege of their "apprenticeship."[65] They often had to pay their own fares and to give evidence of good character, family, and education. As the industry expanded, however, the estates became less choosy and had to pay the creepers' fares, expenses, and salaries.[66] They could still be picky in times of downturn, but had to be considerably less so in boom years. In 1910, at the height of the pre-war rubber boom, Ramsden's John Turner noted sourly that good times brought with them a high turnover of personnel, with assistants breaking their contracts to accept higher-paying jobs on rival plantations. The company was forced to pay higher salaries and offer assistants blocks of shares at preferential rates as enticements for them to

stay.[67] On the other hand, as in the 1921 downturn and during the Great
Depression of the 1930s, the company took advantage of slump to sack
assistants it deemed unsatisfactory and slash the pay and conditions of the
others.[68] During the recession of the early 1920s, Guthrie's, the largest
rubber company in Malaya, sacked many of its younger assistants and
retained the more experienced middle-aged men on half pay. Conversely,
some other owners sacked their older assistants and hired new, younger
men on lower rates of pay.[69]

The ISP: A Quasi-Trade Union

It is not surprising that the assistants in Malaya found it necessary to
organize a quasi–trade union separate from the Rubber Growers'
Association (RGA), which represented the employers' interests. The
Incorporated Society of Planters (ISP) was founded in October 1919,
with a subvention from the RGA. The original aim was that the ISP would
be a professional association. Of Scots yeoman stock or English ex-public schoolboys, they were the kind of people who volunteered to break the
1926 British General Strike out of class solidarity and a sense of patriot-
ism. We are "not a trade union and cannot become one," declared the ISP.
Nevertheless, the assistants *were* employees whose interests were distinct
from those of the growers. The ISP performed many of the functions of a
white-collar union.[70] In neighboring Dutch Sumatra, plantation assistants
set up a more militant and avowedly syndicalist organization to protect
their wages, jobs, and conditions.[71]

Conditions remained harsh during the 1930s. A character in a
Somerset Maugham story set in Malaya during the Depression says, "I've
known of planters sleeping in the street because they hadn't the price of a
night's lodging. I've known them stop strangers outside the 'Europe' and
ask for a dollar to get a meal. . . ."[72] The colonial government set up
European Unemployment Committees in Kuala Lumpur and other towns
to provide relief for "DBSs" (Distressed British Subjects) laid off from the
rubber and tin industries and paid a stipend for young men who had been
laid off to join the volunteer rifles.[73] Others had their passage paid
"home," only to find themselves working in jobs they must have considered below their station. They could be found "doing the most odd
assortment of jobs," recalled one planter, "taxi-driving, Stop-Me-and
Buy-One ice cream selling, driving delivery vans—anything in fact." If

things were hard for the assistants, they were often intolerable for smallholders and a number took their own lives, including a Malayan rubber
planter called Captain Lester.[74]

A White Man Rampant, with a Boy Couchant, Bearing a Bottle of Beer Proper

It could be lonely for the young assistants, especially when the tropical
sun dipped below the horizon and the long hours had to be wiled away.
Some chose to do so with drink; a Sydney brewer appealed to expatri-
ates in the New Guinea colonies to enjoy "Resch's Pilsner in the famous
long bottle—the drink which eases the white man's burden."[75] Alcohol
often had unfortunate consequences. When young Douglas Money started as a rubber planter in Malaya, he soon became "a victim of thirst,"
writes Daniel Green, and downed prodigious quantities of iced beer and
stengahs. An exception to the rule among planters, Money gave up the
booze relatively early in life and drank jugs of cold water instead,
although for some strange reason he decided this too was sinful and took
cold baths instead![76] H. E. Solbe, who arrived in Malaya from Ceylon,
was another reformed drunkard who had once fitted the "prototype of
the whiskey-swilling planter." Acquaintances said that he would "go to
bed with a case of whiskey, and would not get up until he had finished
it." He became a teetotaler after the Salvation Army discovered him
rolling drunk in a Colombo gutter.[77] In 1912, John Turner demoted the
manager of Ramsden's Rubana estate, hinting that the man's bouts of ill
health and his poor bookkeeping were due to alcoholic excess.[78]
According to Madelon Lulofs and Lázló Székely, the Dutch planters in
Sumatra were stupendous soaks. Shortly after arriving on Sumatra,
Székely attended a dinner with other planters in a local hotel. The
planters "put away incredible quantities of beer at an incredible pace,"
with whiskey on the side. Soon, they were so inebriated that they were
throwing food around the room and tipping jugs of beer over each
other's heads.[79] Lulofs, too, recounts a bacchanalian evening in a hotel
where the planters gathered to eat, drink, and be merry. The fun began
when a novice planter was whitewashed from head to foot. Plates of hors
d'oeuvres were hurled across the room, the floor covered in food, and the
tablecloths sodden with beer. When more drink had been taken, an assistant was coated in mustard and butter and an ox was commandeered

from a passing cart driver and ridden round the dining room. Eventually the rider fell off and lay unconscious among the smashed tableware, with the hotel manager vainly appealing for decorum.[80] Predictably, Lulofs' book triggered a storm of outrage.

In Papua and New Guinea, too, alcoholism was a real danger for the planters.[81] In 1924, a journalist reported, "If the Mandated Territory ever wants a coat of arms it might have it, a white man rampant, with a boy couchant, bearing a bottle of beer proper."[82] Across the planters' world, the eternal cry echoed, "Boy! Beer!" with the "boys" impassively observing their masters' excesses. According to a former assistant named Robin Bryant, the Harvey Wallbanger cocktail was invented by a planter's cook in order to knock out the garrulous wives of planters whom he detested.[83] Margaret Shennan believes that "the wear and tear of jungle work together with whisky in excess killed many a man" in Malaya, and cites cases of young white women who had to be guarded from the nocturnal attentions of drunken assistants.[84]

The Planters and Women

Part of the problem, perhaps, was that European women, who might have acted as a civilizing force, were very rare on the plantations. Many rubber companies forbade their assistants from marrying. Harrisons and Crosfield, for example, did not allow assistants to marry until the fourth year of their contracts and anyone wishing to marry had to give the company secretary one month's notice. Failure to comply resulted in instant dismissal. The company also enforced a total ban on employees marrying Asian women.[85] The RGA considered the prohibition was reasonable, asking a critic if he would "go so far as to advocate an inexperienced youth of 21 being engaged and sent out to an Eastern plantation with the blessings of a wife and say, a brace of twins—all at the Company's expense!"[86] Similar rules applied on the Dutch plantations in Sumatra, although the rules were gradually relaxed to allow the more senior assistants to bring back brides from periods of leave in the Netherlands.[87] One result was that the brothels of Kuala Lumpur, Singapore, Batavia, and other towns did a steady trade. The Batu Road in Kuala Lumpur was renowned for its Malay "kip shops," where a planter on a spree could buy a cold beer or a Malay, Siamese, or Japanese girl. Other bordellos specialized in imported European women, including Hungarians, Poles, and Russians.[88]

Another result, according to the RGA, was a "vast number of irregular alliances . . . between the mercantile assistants and native ladies, in a few instances ending in marriage."[89] Indeed, many white men enjoyed sexual relations with Asian women—even setting them up as "housekeepers"—but generally such liaisons were psychologically and emotionally stunted by racism and it was extremely uncommon for European men to marry their "colored" paramours. One exception was Robert Munro, of the Permatang Estate in Selangor, who had two children by his Tamil mistress and married her shortly before his death in 1919.[90] Interracial marriage was *illegal* in Papua and New Guinea until well after the Second World War. Some assistants admitted only to ogling the pretty Tamil or Javanese women.[91] Depending on the degree of license applying to their particular plantation, others openly embarked on liaisons with the coolie women; Asian concubines were known in Malaya as "keeps."[92] One former Ramsden's assistant came to blows with his estate manager when the latter "refused to sanction the redemption of an Indentured woman belonging to the labour force of this Estate, which he required for the purpose of prostitution."[93] Public opinion could be ruthlessly judgmental: an assistant named Hammond in Somerset Maugham's story "The Letter" is judged capable of the rape of a white woman, a neighbor, because he was living openly with a Chinese woman.[94] According to Margaret Shennan, after the First World War it became increasingly unacceptable for whites to keep Asian mistresses and children. At the same time, the number of white women was increasing: by 1931, they accounted for 28 percent of Malaya's European population and the proportion had grown further by the outbreak of war.[95]

The planters could be sexually predatory. According to Tran Tu Binh, the French staff at the hospital on the Michelin plantation where he worked would demand sexual favors from their patients in return for treatment. He reports one manager was a homosexual rapist who forced himself on the Vietnamese coolies.[96] Margaret Shennan mentions similar incidents in Malaya.[97] Perhaps saddest of all were the cases in which European planters lived with Asian women and fathered children by them, only to abandon them when they brought a white wife from "home." This is the theme of Somerset Maugham's short story "The Force of Circumstance," in which a newly arrived English bride, Doris, notices "two little boys who were much whiter than the others" in the nearby Malay kampong.[98] When she confronts her husband with her discovery, he admits that it is true, but justifies it by saying that five out of six white men do it.[99] He feels nothing for the children, he assures her, but will send them to school in Singapore out of a sense of duty. As for his Malay concubine, it is not possible that she, as an Asian woman, could feel anything for him, he opines. Doris leaves him, full of jealousy and bitter reproach: "I think of you holding those little black babies in your arms. Oh, it's loathsome."[100] Madelon Lulofs writes of a Sumatra planter she calls Van Der Meulen who plans to retire to Holland and leave his Japanese "housekeeper," Okubo San, who would "of course" return to Japan. Deep down, however, the man agonizes because he knows that emotionally he will never be able to do without her, even though he could never take her "home" with him.[101]

Sexual Politics and Plantation Society

The politics of colonialism was perhaps nowhere thrown into more sharp relief than in the matter of interracial sexual relations. White planters did have casual sexual encounters with coolie women, and such liaisons were regarded with varying degrees of tolerance by "polite" white society. Yet, while the white man might sleep with Caliban's wives or daughters, woe betide the coolie who entertained the idea of sexual relations with a white woman! Octave Mannoni argued in his book *Prospero and Caliban*[102] that white women were greater racists than white men in colonial society; and many were morbidly obsessed with the idea of rape by a "colored" man. For their part, white men were happy to enforce strict "protection" of "their" women because the idea of Caliban sleeping with them threatened the whole edifice of white supremacy on which the plantation system rested. Mannoni's book focused on Madagascar, but the racial sexual taboo existed across the colonial world. As the historian Edward P. Wolfers writes of Australian Papua:

> The world of Papua's expatriate settlers before the war was a dusty, lower middle class, Australian version of the British Raj. . . . Its security derived less from a sense of pride in its technological superiority and splendour than from a mean and pedantic insistence on the importance of innate racial differences. Nonetheless, its sexual fantasies about its subjects rivalled those of the French in Malagasy. . . .[103]

This ideology impelled the Australian colonies—and plantations above all—into a system of "separate development." An enormous body of laws and ordinances dictated what the "native" might and might not do. These included: a strict curfew; a prohibition on singing, dancing, playing cards, and gambling; a ban on the consumption of alcohol and kava[104] and staying overnight in towns; the institution of whites-only parks, beaches, swimming pools, and cinemas; and the penal provisions of the Native Labor Ordinance. All in all, it was a strict racial separation that foreshadowed apartheid in South Africa. Some of the most draconian aspects of the system were clearly motivated by sexual hysteria. Native men were forbidden under the White Women's Protection Ordinance of 1926 from marrying European women in New Guinea, and the weight of white public opinion ensured that there was no such union in neighboring Papua until the late 1950s. Moreover, the sentences that a Papuan male could receive for sexual assault far outweighed the penalties for Europeans found guilty of such crimes, and it was a crime for native man to have consenting intercourse with a white woman unless she was his wife. Predictably, there was no legal stricture against a white man having sexual relations with a Papuan woman.[105]

Prowling around Bedrooms

Members of the white community began agitating for the sexual color bar and differential sentencing for Papuan sex offenders some years before it was made law. In 1914, for example, Arthur W. Reynolds, editor of the *Papuan Times,* fulminated against those he perceived to be "mollycoddling the natives." There was more than a hint of the lynch mob in his warning that such behavior "may lead to the violation of our women, whom it will soon be impossible to protect, and the stern retaliation which must follow will astonish the namby-pamby advocates of this weak and silly policy."[106] Seven years later, replying to hostile questions about the flogging of Papuans by planters, Australian Prime Minister William "Billy" Hughes stoked the fires of racist sexual paranoia when he declared that a more "serious menace . . . is the frequency with which natives are caught prowling in and around the bedrooms of European women." The outburst was prompted after one culprit had been caught, deemed to be "insolent," flogged, and jailed.[107]

By the 1920s, the Australian colonies were seething with hysteria. On January 13, 1926, a Papuan "boy" was found guilty on one count of an unspecified sexual offense against a European woman and was sentenced to two years with hard labor and fifteen strokes of the cane. The Melbourne *Argus* noted that "[p]ublic feeling is very high against these offenders, who are often civilised boys employed at European residences, and in constant association with white women and children."[108] The offender was sentenced under the new White Women's Protection Ordinance, which prescribed disproportionate punishment for Papuan offenders, who could be sentenced to death for rape or attempted rape, life imprisonment for indecent assault, with or without whipping, and up to fifty strokes of the birch, strap, or cat-o'-nine-tails for less serious offenses. Those under sixteen years could receive up to twenty-five strokes.[109]

Bearing out Mannoni's observations about their racism, white women featured prominently in the agitation for the new ordinance. Mrs. F. L. Clarke, the wife of a planter, argued that the new law was necessary because "white women . . . were living in constant dread of molestation by natives." Prison was no deterrent, she opined, as the natives regarded it as "a home away from home." She concluded with the following statement that railed against individual offenders and collectively indicted Papuans:

> Public flogging is the only way to deal with natives. A flogging is the only form of punishment which will inspire them with dread and respect for authority. We who live among them know and understand them too well.[110]

As a result of the hysteria, the colonial authorities were able to impose an apartheid-style system of laws and regulations on the Papuans. Not only were they coerced by the head tax into leaving their villages to work in the mines and plantations, but when they got there, every aspect of their lives was controlled. Mrs. Clarke indignantly rebuffed a Melbourne cleric's suggestion that there ought to be equality before the law, demanding to be apprised of his degree of knowledge about conditions on the island. The Hobart *Mercury* approached local clergyman John Hunt for comment. The Rev. Hunt, who had spent twenty years in New Guinea, said that he was very surprised by the new ordinance because such assaults were actually few and far between.[111]

The Days Were All Alike

The planters' world was dominated by males, and there was often little for their women to do in days in of empty idleness and ennui. Some busied themselves with charitable work or developed a keen interest in gardening or pets, which Shennan says abounded in planters' homes.[112] In Lulofs' *Rubber*, an assistant's wife laments, "All days were alike . . . always the children, the household, the servants. And the summit of the pyramid was the man. Their own man. . . . Did those women feel no other needs? Literature, music, the theatre. . . . Did they want nothing outside this eternal sameness?"[113] Lulofs later ran off from her rubber planter husband with Lázló Székely to seek fulfillment in a literary life in the Netherlands.

The social attitudes of the plantation were deeply conservative. Any suggestion that women might be gainfully employed in the industry would have been ridiculed, but there were rare instances of women owning and running rubber plantations. One remarkable example is Madame Rivière de la Souchère, described in one account as the "princess of hevea," whose plantation lay close to the fifty-third-kilometer milestone between Saigon and Cape Saint-Jacques. It has been documented that the stylish white buildings of her establishment struck a "gay note" in the monotony of the *terres grises* (grey soil). A noted beauty who dressed in men's tropical whites, Mme. de la Souchère began operations in 1910, carving her estate from bamboo forests. Fluent in Vietnamese, she was said to have enjoyed the respect and loyalty of her 800 laborers. In 1912, she lost 50,000 young hevea trees to fire, but ten years later, she had prospered.[114] In the 1920s she was vice-president of the Rubber Planters' Association of Indochina.[115] A prospectus issued in June 1929 claimed her estates were worth some thirteen million francs,[116] but it seems that she was bankrupted by the Great Depression and forced to return to France.

The Twilight of the Tuans

Although the Depression-struck industry had returned to health by the end of the 1930s, the threat of approaching war cast long shadows over the plantations. It is likely, however, that many planters were only dimly aware of the war's imminence. Secure in a racist cocoon, the Europeans believed that Singapore was an impregnable fortress and that the Japanese army would be seen off by the British soldiery. By 1940, however, the Japanese were amassing on the northern frontiers of French Indochina, and after France's capitulation to the Nazis on the European continent, the Vichy authorities at Hanoi were forced to grant the Japanese unrestricted passage through the colony, together with military bases and a supply of raw materials, including rubber, at low prices. In alliance with Thailand, they were soon poised ready for a lightning advance down the Malay Peninsula, and the end came for Singapore and the Dutch East Indies with terrible swiftness. Symbolically, as the historian D. J. M. Tate records, "one of the first buildings to be destroyed in the [Southeast Asian] war was Guthrie's head office in Raffles Place during the Japanese air raid on Singapore in the early morning of 8 December 1941. . . . "[117] The Goodrich employee A. C. Brett claims that nobody on the American plantations in the Dutch Indies foresaw the speed of the Japanese advance. This included the manager of an estate on Sumatra, who "made his getaway in classic style through the back door" as Japanese soldiers erupted through the front gates of the plantation. He survived to tell Brett that, "At 2:00 o'clock I was drinking a scotch-and-soda on the veranda with Jim; at 6:00 o'clock we were both running like hell . . . "[118] Many fled without a thought for the servants and coolies they left behind, although they later suffered agonies of guilt for it.[119] The Japanese placed many of those who remained in internment camps. With the exception of French Indochina, the plantations fell into desuetude. In Tate's words: "The estates lay silent in ghostly neglect, their managers' bungalows empty and derelict, their labour lines depleted of many of their occupants, their rubber trees rarely tapped and their trunks gradually becoming enveloped in secondary jungle."[120] Many of the Tamil coolies were conscripted for work on Japanese war projects, including the infamous Burma railway. Very few survived the ordeal. The Chinese estate laborers fled, terrified of the brutalities the Japanese reserved for them, either to set up as small farmers in the jungles, or to join the Communist guerrillas of the Malayan People's Anti-Japanese Army.[121]

Although the British, the Dutch, and the French came back to their plantations in late 1945 and production gradually restarted, things would never be the same again. The Dutch were faced with a revolutionary nationalist movement led by Sukarno and Hatta. Independence also came to Indochina in 1954 after the defeat of the French at Dien Bien Phu. In June 1948, a rubber planter called A. E. Walker was murdered at the London Asiatic Estate in Perak, followed by two other planters on nearby estates. The twelve-year-long Communist Emergency had begun. A report from Ramsden's Penang estates in 1950 noted that Communist "bandits" were always active in the region. They had burned down plantation buildings and the European bungalows were wired-in as a precaution against grenade attacks. "European staff still carry arms at all times," noted the reporter, "and move around with personal guards."[122] Today, some of the European rubber companies have survived, but the nationalist policies of the independent states have meant that the estates are largely in Asian hands. Harrisons and Crosfield, for example, was restricted to 30 percent of the equity in their former Malayan estates.[123] Today, the world's largest producer of natural rubber is Thailand, which was never directly colonized by the Europeans. A world the planters had thought secure vanished barely half a century after it began.

CHAPTER FOURTEEN

The Coolie Diaspora

> If a surplus labouring population is a necessary product of accumulation or
> of the development of wealth on a capitalist basis, this surplus-population
> becomes, conversely, the lever of capitalistic accumulation, nay, a condition of
> the existence of the capitalist mode of production. It forms a *disposable
> reserve army* [emphasis added], that belongs to capital quite as absolutely as
> if the latter had bred it at its own cost.
>
> —KARL MARX[1]

In 1848, Marx and Engels forecast that the requirements of the expanding market would "chase the bourgeoisie over the entire surface of the
globe."[2] To effect this transformation, imperialism needed the workforces
to run the mines, mills, and plantations thrown up across the tropical
world. This involved the resettlement—permanent or temporary—of millions of human beings. Rubber was central to the new international economic order; thus many of the transplanted laborers toiled on the plantations of rubber multinationals such as Michelin, Firestone, Dunlops,
Guthrie's, Ramsdens, and Goodyear. The scale of migration was so great
that the ethnic composition of whole nations was permanently altered, as
in Malaya where the native Malay population now lives side by side with
huge Indian and Chinese minorities, and Sri Lanka, where the Sinhalese
live alongside a restive Tamil minority.

As the American writer Virginia Thompson observed in 1947, "prior
to the development of plantation agriculture, there was no labor problem

in Southeast Asia as a whole."[3] Across the region, peasants lived as they had done for millennia on smallholdings under traditional land tenure systems. The Spanish had created some *latifundia* (landed estates) in the Philippines after their arrival in the sixteenth century, and the Dutch coerced smallholders into cash crop production under the *Cultuurstelsel* or "Cultivation System" in mid-nineteenth-century Java,[4] but large-scale plantation agriculture dates from the late-nineteenth century. Rubber only appeared after the 1890s depression had taken its toll on earlier commodities. With the development of agribusiness came a myriad of labor problems, including finding ongoing supplies of workers for large undertakings, enforcing work discipline, and preventing high rates of labor turnover. Eventually, the creation of a large agrarian proletariat was to spark sharp class struggles, as was the case in late 1930s Malaya and a decade earlier in French Indochina.

The Vast Scale of Labor Migration

The larger rubber estates were enormous industrial undertakings that soaked up all available local labor and thirsted for more. Only a minority of "coolies"[5] were native to the regions or countries in which they worked. Most laborers in Sumatra and Malaya were imported on contract from densely populated regions of China, India, and Java. Likewise, the majority of workers on the French plantations in Cochin-China and Cambodia were shipped south from the "rice deficit" regions of Tonkin and northern Annam after the French decided against importing Chinese labor.[6] In 1911, the native Malays made up little more than 7 percent of the total workforce on the rubber plantations in Malaya,[7] with the figure rising to just below 13 percent by 1940.[8] The Australian-owned estates in New Guinea were worked by impressed laborers from the expanding "labor frontier" of the recently pacified interior.[9] The size of the population movement necessary to feed the plantations' appetites for labor was enormous. By 1912, some 550,000 Tamils had been imported from India for agricultural work in Ceylon, where they worked alongside 150,000 Sinhalese laborers. By 1927, there were over 700,000 migrant workers in Ceylon, although not all of them worked on the rubber estates.[10] In 1911, the rubber coolies in Malaya numbered just over 179,000, of whom 100,000 were from India, almost 18,000 from Java, and roughly 46,000 from China.[11] The descendents of Javanese coolies are still to be found

"Coolies from Annam disembarking at Saigon"

across the tropical world in the former colonies of Malaya, Indochina, New Caledonia, Surinam, Sarawak, New Guinea, Christmas Island, the Cocos-Keeling islands, Réunion, and East Africa.[12] On the eve of the Japanese invasion in 1941, there were over 350,000 coolies working on plantations in Malaya, mostly in rubber. The vast bulk came from overseas: including over 220,000 from India and 86,000 from China.[13] By 1929, there were some 41,000 Tonkinese on the rubber estates of Cochin-China and Cambodia, and the planters were clamoring for an additional six to eight thousand every year and demanding the relaxation of "over-zealous" recruitment regulations.[14] The number had grown to 100,000 in Cochin-China alone by the Second World War.[15]

"Pig Business"

By the turn of the nineteenth century, Malaya had become "a great emporium of labor."[16] Not only were hundreds of thousands of workers imported for the mines and plantations of the peninsula itself when Malaya became the world's largest producer of rubber, it also acted as a labor entrepôt supplying workers to surrounding countries, the Dutch East Indies in particular. Initially, the majority of Malayan coolies were recruited in South China, using existing Chinese recruitment channels. The Chinese government, however, had become increasingly hostile to the labor trade. Reports had trickled back of poor treatment on the plantations, and nationalists were embarrassed by the exposure of what the English writer Persia Campbell described as a "veiled slave trade" run by "crimps and compradors."[17]

In a trade known as "pig business," recruits were transported by sea to Malayan coastal towns and kept in lodging houses until they could be hired out to the highest bidder. In 1890, a British commission of inquiry instituted a system of regular inspections. In 1904, the trade was further tightened following an Anglo-Chinese Convention on indentured labor. While government intervention might be said to have stemmed from humanitarian motives, the cost of Chinese labor was significantly reduced after the elimination of the pig business middlemen. William Duncan, writing to Ramsden's London office from the Caledonia Estate in 1910, had complained of the problems of recruiting Chinese because of "the middlemen who wax fat out of the Chinese coolie traffic."[18] Ramsden had tried to cut out the middlemen as early as 1890 by directly hiring Chinese laborers, but the crimps were tenacious.[19] Decades later, they were still selling Chinese laborers to planters at £10 a head. Known as "Kongsi men," the laborers were paid ten cents a day and had to pay off the £10 for their passage and lodgings within the three-year period of their contracts. Armed Sikh guards stood over them to prevent desertion or mutiny. Leopold Ainsworth described the Kongsis as "a labour force [which] was to all intents and purposes comprised of slaves conveniently camouflaged under the 'officially approved' sounding title of 'indentured labour.'"[20]

The Tamil Immigration Fund

As European agribusiness expanded, the Chinese labor trade was overshadowed by recruitment in India. The planters regarded the Indians—"the mild Hindoo"—as more docile and tractable than their Chinese counterparts. The British authorities also wanted to ensure that no one ethnic group predominated in Malaya. The skeptic might argue that this fitted with an unofficial policy of divide and rule. Most Indian laborers came from the Madras region, the Tamil districts, and the Coromandel Coast: southerners were preferred as they were stereotyped as being milder in temperament than their northern cousins. From the 1880s onwards, immigration was handled by a quasi-official body known as the Indian Immigration Committee, which supervised the activities of labor recruiters and attempted to regularize hiring practices and streamline the trade. The system had been rife with abuse and was lambasted by the Sub-Collector of Tanjore, Mr. Hathaway, as "a regularly organised system of kidnapping." In 1907, the British authorities in Malaya created the Tamil Immigration Fund. Known after 1914 as the Indian Immigration Fund, the scheme required employers of Indian workers to pay into a central fund on the basis of their labor requirements, and they were allocated workers on the basis of the amount paid in. Employers who chose not to participate could lose their licenses to employ imported labor.[21]

The Labor Question on the Estates

At the outset, the rubber estates were faced with the problem of how to secure an abundant, flexible, and reliable labor force. The new plantations were often situated in thinly populated remote areas such as the red soil (*terres rouges*) areas of Cambodia and Cochinchina, the jungles of Sumatra and Malaya, and the wild interior of Australian New Guinea. The indigenous populations of these regions were often hostile to the idea of wage labor, preferring to work their smallholdings or collective gardens rather than toil for foreigners. This was the case with the Malays and Bataks on Sumatra, for example,[22] and generally with the Malays on the peninsula and in Borneo. In Cambodia and Australian New Guinea, the Khmers and Papuans preferred to remain in their villages and as a rule shunned wage labor.[23] Wage labor was alien to many of the peoples of Southeast Asia, Oceania, and Africa, who lived in traditional cultures practicing subsistence agriculture—ways of life instilled with "the authority of 'the eternal yesterday'" as Max Weber once put it.[24] Life as a permanent wage laborer meant being regimented by the clock and not by the seasonal and diurnal rhythms—dawn and dusk, summer and winter or wet and dry seasons, planting and harvests, festivals and the milestones of life and death—that the peasant was used to. Industrial work— in factories, mines or plantations—meant submitting to rigid discipline. To the villagers it seemed pointless.[25] In Europe, Asia, Africa, and Oceania, whites regarded the indigenes' attachment to traditional life as evidence of congenital stupidity. This was exemplified by the racist stereotyping of the Danish author J. Lyng, who believed that, "Mentally, the Papuans and Melanesians range with European children of about twelve years of age. Their gift to assimilate ideas has the same limitation.

For instance, the white man's device for reckoning time is beyond their comprehension. . . ."[26]

Plantation work meant toiling for low rates of pay or even for worthless trinkets. As Parmer has noted, the Malay *bumiputra* might offer himself for wage labor, but only if the price were high enough,[27] and would scorn the wages paid to foreign workers on the estates. In Australian Papua and New Guinea, where the indigenes were *forced* into wage labor, the effects of deracination were devastating for indigenous cultures.

One solution to the labor problem might have been mass immigration of whites, as was the case from Europe to the temperate regions of North America, Australasia, and Argentina, but the ideology of the "high imperialist" era held that Europeans could not perform hard manual work in tropical climates. In 1910, for example, a writer in the Sydney *Daily Telegraph* claimed that "all concur" that white men could not possibly carry out laboring work on the new rubber plantations in the Papuan colony.[28] The French economist Paul Leroy-Beaulieu even divided colonies into the categories of *colonies du peuplement* and *colonies d'exploitation*.[29] Given these ideological constraints, the only possible solution lay in the transportation of "colored" labor to "labor deficit" regions.

The Labor Systems

Although the rubber planters rarely sank to the depravity witnessed during the scramble for rubber in the Congo Free State and the Amazon basin, they still relied on coercive labor systems and penal sanctions.[30] Four systems can be identified: free or day labor; contract or indentured labor; the *kangani* system[31]; and the tax bondage model used in Australian Papua and New Guinea. Free or day labor was the planters' least preferred option because workers employed on a daily wage could leave whenever it suited them to do so. The tapping and processing of latex requires a stable workforce, and rubber company files are filled with examples of the disruptive effects of workers lured away to higher-paying employment, or simply going home. For the Papuan horticulturalist or the Khmer or Malay peasant, wage labor was unnatural, unpleasant, and unnecessary. At most, the Malay or Khmer peasant might hire himself by the day or for the duration of a particular task, in particular clearing forest to make way for a plantation, but he had little interest in settling into the drudgery of plantation work. Free Chinese laborers brought from Penang to Dutch plantations on Sumatra were notorious among planters for leaving their employers for higher-paying work. Many smallholders in Malaya, Sumatra, and Java preferred to grow rubber on their own account, and by the 1930s this accounted for a huge slice of total production. A substantial number of Indian and Chinese coolies paid their own passage to the Southeast Asian colonies to obtain work on a day labor basis, but this was not enough to meet the plantations' needs.

Indentured Labor

The solution for the planters was to import bonded laborers. These were generally obtained in regions fraught with problems of landlessness, overpopulation, poverty, and famine. These included China, India, Tonkin and northern Annam in French Indochina, and Java. Modern Indian immigration to Malaya began in 1833, although the British authorities used Indian convict labor on public works at Penang even earlier.[32] There were some drawbacks, however, which led to the abolition of the system in Malaya in 1910 and the Dutch East Indies in 1931, but it survived until much later in French Indochina and, in a peculiar variant, in Australian New Guinea until the end of the Second World War. The system of Indian indentured labor began in Malaya in 1840 and lasted until 1910, when it was replaced by the *kangani* system.[33] The importation of Chinese, Tamils, Siamese, Javanese, and Klings from the Coromandel Coast of India into Sumatra was established by the late 1860s.[34] By the turn of the nineteenth century some 7,000 Javanese indentured laborers were imported annually by the Sumatran estates.[35] The contract system was forbidden on Java itself, where it was not necessary because its large population ensured a steady supply of labor.[36]

Wages and conditions were generally set by government decree. In Tonkin, for example, contract laborers signed on for three-year terms, renewable upon expiration of the period of service. They worked a ten-hour day with one unpaid day off per week, or two consecutive days in a fortnight. Wages were set at forty cents per day for males and thirty cents for females. They were also entitled to free medical attention, lodging, and food; the latter primarily in the form of rice.[37] According to M. Delamare of the Inspection du Travail in Indochina, laborers' wages and conditions were inferior to those existing in other colonies in the region.[38]

Trickery and coercion might obtain recruits for a while, but as word of the real conditions on the plantations filtered back to the villages of Java or China, the supply dried up. Hunger and poverty were always the best recruiting agents, as Yeap Joo Kim noted in her novel *Moon Above Malaya*.[39] After dismissing the idea of importing Chinese coolies for the rubber estates in southern Indochina, the French authorities predicated their labor policies on the emigration of poor, landless, and often undernourished peasants from overpopulated Tonkinese villages.[40] In 1929, the population density of Tonkin, almost 200 people to the square kilometer (430 within the Red River delta), was in sharp contrast to the average density for French Indochina as a whole, which stood at twenty-five persons to the square kilometer. "The planter," the French Colonial Institute noted, "is therefore placed in an embarrassing dilemma, in which he must set himself up in almost deserted mountainous regions, or stay in the populated zones, which lack suitable land."[41] Shortly afterwards, by decree of the Governor General, the colonial administration set up a central Inspectorate of Labor to regulate and control the overall organization of labor in the colony.[42] The General Manpower Office in Hanoi supervised the recruitment process.[43] As a rule of thumb, good harvests in India, Tonkin, or China meant fewer recruits, bad times meant long lines of misery at the recruitment depots. In a letter to Ramsden's London head office in 1907, general manager John Turner noted that "very few indentured coolies are arriving just now due to its being a time of plenty in southern India."[44] In 1909 his colleague William Duncan remarked that it "will demand constant hustling on the part of the individual Managers to secure their share of labor"[45] because the fields of India were so bountiful.

The Kangani System

By 1910, it had become apparent in Malaya that an indentured labor system could not assure a regular supply of suitable workers for the estates. The system was abolished in Malaya in 1910 and the Dutch East Indies followed suit in 1931 (with some exceptions in the Outer Islands). Although preferable to free labor from the planters' point of view, the system was far from perfect for their interests, regardless of the existence of draconian labor legislation. With recruitment effectively out of their hands, the planters had to take whatever workers were available, regardless of age, health, or prior occupation. "Many were weavers, dhobis, 'coolies' and other workers with no experience in agriculture," complained one employer, and others were chronically sick or aged "hospital birds" who became a burden on the estates before they had done a day's work. Desertion was also common: 610 laborers out of a total workforce of 1,026 absconded from the Gula Plantation in Perak province in 1895, for instance.[46]

They turned, therefore, to the kangani system. In operation to a small degree in Malaya from 1890 and in Ceylon from even earlier, it involved sending a trusted Tamil or Kling foreman back to his home village in India to recruit laborers directly for his employer. Each "kangani" was expected to recruit twenty or so coolies and had to possess a recruiter's license issued by the Deputy Controller of Labour in Malaya and countersigned by an agent of the British Indian administration. The scheme generally assured the planters of a workforce accustomed to field labor, and the kanganies could be held responsible for weaklings, the aged, or the infirm.

At its best, the kangani system helped create a sense of community among the estate laborers, who were more likely to stay on the plantation if they were among people from their own home villages. In this new system, however, there was ample scope for corruption on the part of the overseers. This was especially the case in Ceylon, where planters paid wages in the form of a lump sum, which was distributed to the laborers by their overseer.[47] The foremen could very easily pocket a portion of the wages.

All in all, the planters considered it a great success. A Ramsden manager, for example, noted that system ran at "little or no cost to [the] estate beyond the passage money which is paid from the Immigration Fund and recovered in the form of assessment." He concluded that "[t]his is the perfect system of recruiting and that which we aim at."[48] The system might have been ideal for the employers, but it brought no general improvement of living standards for the estate laborers—and nor was it intended to. In the 1930s, one British planter admitted that "when one compares . . . [the laborers'] wages with those of even the lowest paid of our own country-men, one wonders how they can possibly exist as human beings."[49] The system remained in force until the eve of the Second World War when, under pressure from rising nationalist agitation in India, the British authorities banned assisted passages to Southeast Asia.

The Tax Bondage System in New Guinea

The system in Australian New Guinea[50] differed in important respects from those in Southeast Asia. The small Australian rubber industry faced the same labor supply problem as its counterparts in Asia, but with added complications. Many planters and some politicians—and indeed the British government while it still had jurisdiction in Papua—were eager to import workers from China and other parts of Asia, as the Germans had done prior to the First World War in the northeast part of the island. The Australian government and public opinion, however, was opposed to Asian immigration into Australia or its "overseas territories"—the circumlocution for Australian colonies in the South Pacific. The White Australia Policy was a central plank of the national consensus after Australia became a federation in 1901 and as the "first grandchild of the Empire," Papua would be subject to the same restrictions on "colored" labor that had applied in the former German territory. Given the belief that Europeans could not perform heavy manual work in the tropics, the policy meant that the planters turned to the Papuans for their labor requirements. The problem was that Papuan people, like the Khmers and Malays, were wedded to traditional lifestyles and therefore reluctant, indifferent, and even hostile to the idea of wage labor. While Papua was admirably suited for hevea cultivation and fantastic profits were possible in the boom that preceded the First World War, "workers [in Papua] cannot be had for love or money," noted one writer in the Sydney *Daily Telegraph*.[51] Recruiters scoured the countryside with scant success. One "recruiting captain" managed to enlist only twenty-seven laborers on the Papuan coast in a three-month period in 1910, for example.[52]

Most Papuans lived in villages outside of the European cash economy and were able to meet their needs from horticulture, fishing, and hunter-gathering. "The natives are not particularly fond of work," lamented one observer. "The reason is they have very little need of it in order to exist, because they have their villages, a system of trading which has been in force for years, and they prefer to allow their wives to cultivate their gardens and keep the pot boiling."[53] Even when enticed onto the plantations, Papuans were likely to leave once they had saved enough money for whatever they wanted to buy, or once the novelty had worn off, he added. For most whites, such behavior was evidence of "laziness" and "stupidity," although unbiased observers pointed out that the Papuans were very industrious within their own traditional economies. In 1911, Senator

New "recruits" going ashore at a New Guinea plantation.

Allan McDougall reported on "beautifully cultivated gardens . . . full of yams, taro, coconuts, sugar cane, bread fruit, sweet potatoes, and other things" that were cooperatively run and capable of feeding an entire village.[54] A Sydney journalist agreed: "The man in the street will say Papuans are the laziest people on earth," but they actually work very hard on their own account in their villages, he noted.[55] No doubt the villagers were also afraid of overwork and high mortality rates on the plantations. The recent gold rush and rubber boom had been responsible for the deaths of five hundred natives. One Sydney journalist cited the example of a plantation that had recruited twenty-two "boys" from one village, of whom only seven survived.[56] The debate in Australian newspapers coincided with the high point of the prewar rubber boom, which saw prices rise to giddy heights.

The Nigger Caught Up in the Backwash of Civilisation

Australian planters and their advocates believed they were losing windfall profits because of the "lazy natives." "The reason the boys don't want to work is their conservatism," said the Right Reverend Dr. Sharp, the Anglican Bishop of New Guinea. "Their parents have never worked, and they do not see why they should."[57] The solution, which dovetailed with the rhetoric of the *mission civilisatrice*, was that the natives should be *forced to work.* The left-wing *Barrier Daily Truth* warned that "a number of capitalistic hirelings have sought a remedy for Papuan labor problems in a system of enforced labor." "The chief of these," the article continued, was Miss Beatrice Grimshaw, "who has travelled extensively in Papua."[58] Grimshaw's views received strong support from the Australian establishment. Earlier, a number of letters published in the Sydney *Daily Telegraph* urged the introduction of a head tax to force the Papuans into the cash economy and wage labor.[59] The most prominent advocate of compulsion was Sir Hubert Murray, an Irish-Australian lawyer serving as the Lieutenant Governor of Papua who had commanded a detachment of the NSW Rifles in the Boer War.[60] Murray told the Melbourne newspaper *Age* that unless the natives were compelled to work, then the colony would not be developed and they would become "useless betel-chewing louts."[61] Murray pointed to South Africa, where

> They accomplished the task by direct taxation, imposing a money hut tax on all the natives under their control. The natives were of course destitute of money, but they had money's worth in the labor of their hands. Finding themselves obliged to pay the tax, they worked to produce it, either as servants of the whites or as producers and tillers of their own soil.[62]

Murray also introduced a stringent Native Labor Ordinance to regulate the terms and conditions of laborers' work under a system of contracts.[63] The Papuans called the head tax "throw-away money."[64] Underlying Murray's reasoning was the belief that the whites had a *right* to employ the Papuans for whatever purposes they saw fit. Bishop Sharp argued that "a term of service does them good" and a white expatriate appealed to historical inevitability: "The fact is that the nigger has been caught up in the backwash of civilisation, and he must put up with the consequences."[65] As Marx's ghost might have said, the Papuan labor force belonged to Capital "quite as absolutely as if the latter had bred it at its own cost."[66]

Critical voices such as the *Barrier Daily Truth* and the New Zealand Methodist Church[67] were lost in the clamor. Between 1909 and 1941 there were over 200,000 contracts in Papua and between 1920 and 1940 almost 280,000 in the neighboring mandated territory.[68] Considering the size of the island and its population, the labor trade was huge. As the anthropologist Chris Gregory notes, the plantations "survived by exploiting cheap unsophisticated labour from the labour frontier," with a constant supply of new labor recruited from "new" areas opened up by government officials.[69] Once an area was "pacified," recruiters would move in and take out long lines of "signed on boys," often roping them together to prevent them from escaping.[70]

"Really Rather like Slavery"

With surprising candor, Governor Murray admitted to a meeting of the Anti-Slavery Society in London in 1929 that the system was "really rather like slavery," yet he justified it as the only way with which the colony could be developed. Puzzlingly, attendants of the meeting gave Murray a hearty vote of thanks and opined that Papua was a model of how colonies should be run.[71] However, Florence Harding, a former student of the Australian anthropologist Professor Adolphus Elkin, concluded that Australians had complacently accepted "an emergent caste system; for as the situation stands today the native is merely 'a hewer of wood and a drawer of water.'"[72] A system based on the methodical discrimination against the natives had been created, and it should be viewed as apartheid. Its defining features were the Native Labor Ordinance, the head tax, and the bonded labor system. When the indentured labor system was abolished in 1945, the majority of the laborers simply went home to their villages.[73]

CHAPTER FIFTEEN

The Coolies' World

A crow on a far-off bough,
Outlined against the falling snow,
Is such a picture as will find
An echo in my heart.
—Chinese coolie lament[1]

What a mistake to enter the rubber lands,
Like life imprisonment without a jail.
—Vietnamese coolie song[2]

Only one rubber coolie, Tran Tu Binh, has left us an account of his life on the plantations.[3] His account is invaluable, but the seminary-educated Tran, who enlisted as a coolie in order to carry out Communist agitation among the Michelin estate laborers, is not representative of his fellows. For the historian, the reconstruction of the coolies' world is based largely on second- and third-hand accounts from official documents, newspapers, works of fiction, and the memoirs of European colonialists. Coolie folklore still awaits detailed ethnographic study for what it can reveal about the rubber estates. In 1920, for example, J. Neville Whymant published an annotated collection of coolie songs he had transcribed while serving with a Chinese labor battalion in Europe during the First World War.[4] Novels, poems, and songs were an important ingredient in the social rebellion of peasants in China[5] and they were also part of coolie life in

Malaya. In 1925, Orientalist Lily Strickland-Anderson noted unsympa-
thetically: "The Chinese coolie (and there are thousands of them in
Malaya) chants his barbaric and untuneful folk-songs as he works in mine
or field. . . . His songs are the almost unconscious accompaniment of his
labours and his moods."[6] Forty years later, the ethnologist Ved Prakash
Vatuk recorded close to one hundred protest songs sung in creolized
Hindi by sugar cane workers in British Guiana, telling of their forefathers'
recruitment, the ocean voyage, and labor on the estates.[7] I have drawn on
these in this chapter, for they must surely also give voice for the Indian
rubber workers of Southeast Asia.

To the Foreign Shore

Hunger is always the sharpest spur to impel a person to leave his native
land. As the Singaporean novelist Yeap Joo Kim writes:

> Malaya was the obvious choice. Even in our remote village we had heard all
> about the prosperity of that haven where milk and honey took the form of
> rubber and tin. The lure to Malaya was intensified by the call of the British
> rulers for more labourers, and by our unabatable hunger and misery at
> home.[8]

In bad times, the peasants flocked to the recruiting stations, drawn by
the recruiters' promises and their own rumbling bellies. Chinese peasants
sang:

> How difficult to live!
> The daily labour has no price;
> The body has no rest from toil,
> But starves in poverty.
> The birds have each their sustenance,
> Who toil not in the fields;
> The barn-rat has food enough to spare,
> The plough-ox has no grass for food.[9]

"The French colonialists had a shortage of workers," wrote Tran Tu
Binh, "so the [recruiting] advertisements were overflowing with words of
sugar and honey."[10] Ruki, the Javanese hero of Madelon Lulofs' novel

Tran Tu Binh (1907–1967):
Vietnamese labor organizer and
revolutionary, led a brief uprising
at Michelin's Phu-Riêng plantation. Later became a general and
ambassador for the Democratic
Republic of Vietnam.

Coolie, is accosted by a richly dressed stranger from Batavia who extols
the benefits of life on a faraway plantation; "All those who have gone have
come back wealthy a few years later," he tells the trusting youth. Shortly
afterwards, after a journey on foot and by train to the city, Ruki makes his
mark on a document proffered by a clerk in a language he doesn't understand while a mighty *tuan* stands by. A seasoned old coolie shakes his
head at the sight of yet another youngster caught up in the plantation
machine.[11] Lulofs' account is not "authentic," but it is a sympathetic
reconstruction by the former wife of a rubber planter of what must have
happened countless times in the villages of Java. A Hindi song from
British Guiana sums up the bitterness and regret felt by Indian emigrants,
and it would surely have been echoed half a world away on the rubber
estates of Malaya:

> Oh recruiter, your heart is deceitful,
> Your speech is full of lies!
> Tender may be your voice,
>   articulate and seemingly logical,
> But it is all used to defame and destroy
> The good names of the people.[12]

The Kongsi Laborers

In China, the new recruits were kept in "pig stations" until a large enough cargo could be assembled for shipment south. Should they be deemed unfit after a medical examination, they might be cast destitute into the streets, far from their villages.[13] The Kongsi laborers would be met on the docks of Singapore, Penang, Surabaja, or Belawan by a Chinese labor contractor, who would cram them into a lodging house until they were sold to the planters. Before the introduction of the kangani system in 1910, their Indian counterparts would sign on in Madras, the Coramandel Coast, or the Tamil regions of South India and be held in a camp at Avadi, which had a capacity of 6,000 people, or another at Melpakem which could accommodate 2,000.[14] The Tonkinese recruits were taken to a bamboo-and-thatch camp at the Haiphong docks, or to Ha-ly, where they broiled in steel-roofed sheds, surrounded by a swamp of sewage, Tran recalls.[15] If they were lucky they would not wait long before the *Claude Chappe*, the *Merlin*, the *Commandant Dorier*, or another French freighter took them to Saigon, or in the case of the Indians, for a British steamer to ferry them across the Bay of Bengal to Singapore or Penang.

They would be fed on board and in the holding pens, but the food was often of poor quality and there was not enough of it. Tran Tu Binh writes that instead of the promised beef, fish, and fragrant rice, their rations were rotten and "stank like roach dung."[16] Like the *cablocos* (landless peasants) of Ceará en route to Amazonia, the coolies traveled as livestock, sleeping on mats on the open decks in the sun or rain, or confined to the ships' holds. In Papua and New Guinea, "blackbirding" contractors led new recruits from the "labor frontier" through the jungles, with individuals roped together, ostensibly to prevent them from being picked off by hostile tribesmen but perhaps to prevent them from escaping. People also became ill when forced to eat putrid food and share filthy latrines, but some were already sick and malnourished when they embarked. According to painstaking analysis by John McDonald and Ralph Shlomowitz, the mortality rate for Indian migrant labor aboard ship from Calcutta in the years 1872/3–1917 was 7.1 percent.[17]

Police Swarmed like Flies

The story of neglect, threats, and actual violence continued once the French steamers docked at Saigon. Tran tells us that French and Vietnamese guards stormed aboard and "used canes on the heads of the recruits, counting us like animals" after which the recruits were "driven ashore . . . like a herd of cattle." Once down the gangplank they ran the gauntlet of police who "swarmed like flies," flailing their clubs and screaming insults to herd them into the Saigon "arrival department," a holding depot run by the Labor Inspectorate for Southern Vietnam, which Tran describes as "exactly like a concentration camp."[18]

As the historian Anthony Reid notes in his preface to Tran's memoir, many of today's readers will be skeptical of such a relentlessly gloomy story. He concludes, however, that "overall, Tran's account . . . may be assessed as exaggerated in tone, yet essentially reliable in substance." This judgment is supported by the reports of French labor inspectors at the time, although they stressed that conditions varied among the rubber estates in Southern Indochina, and it should be noted that conditions did improve as a result of their efforts and agitation by the workers themselves. The Đoàn Report of June 1928, for instance, found that the workers on Michelin's Dau-Triêng estate were treated well, but that the coolies rightly regarded the company's Phu-Riêng plantation, where Tran worked, "as a hell."[19] The Governor of Cochin-China admitted that the new arrivals at Saigon had once been kept in "a kind of prison" at Xom-Chieu, but were now kept in more salubrious quarters in the Khanh-Hôi quarter.[20] The reports of labor inspector E. Delamare revealed grave abuses, and the apologias of later writers such as Webby Silupya Kalikiti cannot reasonably be sustained.[21]

The same picture, broadly speaking, was found in other parts of the rubber plantation world. In 1904, the Rhemrev Report to the Dutch parliament roundly condemned the recruitment system and working and living conditions on the plantations in the Dutch East Indies. In 1924, the Ainsworth Report took a similar stance toward the indentured labor system in the Australian colonies on New Guinea. The publication of Madelon Lulofs' novel *Coolie* in 1931 outraged planters and their supporters in Holland, but the substance was correct. Colonial officials in British India, too, were often very critical of the conditions of Indian laborers in Malaya. As for Indochina, when nationalists assassinated René Bazin, the French official who supervised labor recruitment in Tonkin in 1929, few coolies mourned his passing.

After arrival at holding depots in Saigon, Penang, Singapore or Belawan, the recruits would be allocated to the rubber estates. The Vietnamese recruits were trucked to nearby plantations in Cochin-China, or loaded aboard river steamers for the long journey up the Mekong to Cambodia. They arrived in a strange new world governed by gongs and whistles, and of fines for the slightest infraction of work discipline, in which the whites were the masters. In Australian Papua, indigenous workers might be fined for insolence, yet there were no legal limits on the verbal abuse a planter might rain on their heads—and few barring physical violence. The laborers had entered what the Australian writer Peter Fitzpatrick, echoing Erving Goffman, described as a "total institution—a small state—with the employer as the ruler."[22]

"A World Cut in Two"

"The colonial world," as Frantz Fanon reminds us, was "a world cut in two"[23] along a sharp cleavage of color and class. The frontiers between the whites and the "colored" workers were marked out with barracks and police stations. The cheapness of the rubber relied on the super-exploitation of the estate workers. Sometimes the authorities admitted it, as in 1935, when the Australian *Pacific Islands Yearbook* confessed, "success in tropical agriculture can be achieved only when labour . . . was paid on a scale far below the standard of whitemen's wages."[24] The planters and their supporters derided those who sought to reform the system. One Port Moresby journalist insisted that Australia has "to decide whether she is going to maintain, at great expense, a huge brown benevolent asylum, with a few old women to run it, for the benefit of the natives, or whether she is going to own a prosperous Territory. . . ."[25]

Ultimately, as Fanon reminds us, the colonial system rested on "pure force"[26] and the celebrated Australian anthropologist C. D. Rowley believed that violence and the threat of it was the "basic labour incentive" in New Guinea. To the European planters, the coolies were seldom recognized as fellow creatures with individuality, intelligence, feelings, and what today we would call human rights. As Colin Palmer has argued in his book *Worlds of Unfree Labour*, "servitude was always justified by ideology." This ideology dehumanized the victims of colonialism and was justified in a densely woven discourse that stretched back centuries. The sixteenth-century Aristotlean scholar and polemicist Juan Ginés de

Sepúlveda, for example, claimed that there was as much difference between Europeans and the "barbarians" of the New World as between men and apes.[27] The planters of Virginia drew on the experiences of planters in Ireland, where the Irish were regarded as "a species of wild people" and under the "exception of Irishry" law, the penalty for killing an Irish man or woman was a fine of seventy shillings, payable to the lord of the victim.[28] Peter Kleintitschen, a German missionary, dismissed the people of the Gazelle Peninsula as "deceitful, suspicious, callous, cowardly, avaricious, untruthful, thieving, hypocritical, ungrateful, and lazy [and] in fact . . . utterly beyond redemption." This was, he insisted, the opinion of all white traders and planters.[29] By the time the rubber plantations were set up, the ideology had become "common sense" for planters, colonial officials, and most of the public in the metropolitan countries. The editor of *The Papuan Times* approvingly quoted Lord Methuen, who had told the Pretorian Diocesan Association that "it was right that the black should be ruled with a rod of iron, but justly and fairly. He should always be made to realise that the white was the master."[30]

Boys, Marys, and Monkeys

At best the rubber coolie was regarded as childlike; the oldest Cantonese, Annamite, or Tamil was a "boy" to an assistant fresh off the boat from Tilbury or Rotterdam. Harvey Firestone, Jr., told American radio audiences that the white supervisor on the Liberian estates "soon gains the love and respect of the trusting and childlike people working under him," for they were "confident that his wisdom is infallible and his judgment unerring."[31] A Dutch planter on the Orang Kebenaran estate in Borneo told the *Sydney Daily Telegraph* that the local Malays and Dyaks took to rubber work well, but "they were like big children, and sometimes became a bit stubborn."[32] Just before the First World War, an English writer claimed that Malays were "simple, jungle-bred children—half savage and half child . . ." and that "they look upon the white man as a quite superior being."[33] Papuan laborers were called "boys" until they turned forty, when they mutated into "grandfathers."[34] The Papuan women servants were all "Marys," and child laborers were "monkeys."[35] A Port Moresby journalist told his readers, "Natives are like children and should be punished in the same way. No one would permit a child to be treated with inhumanity. On the other hand it is often necessary to chastise him."[36] The flip side to such paternalism was fear and mistrust. At worst the plantation laborer was seen as a dangerous Caliban, an unfathomable Other lurking across an ontological divide.

Collectively, in Asia at least, the laborers were "coolies," a word of South Dravidian origin that came to have racist overtones.[37] If individual planters or assistants knew their coolies' names—and we can assume they often did, as some degree of proficiency in native languages was required on many estates—they rarely recorded them for posterity. The files of the Ramsden companies fill a score of spools of microfilm, but the reader will search in vain for a laborer's name, whereas those of even the most insignificant whites were recorded. Firestone's American overseers in Liberia affected not remembering their African laborers' names, and bellowed out "funny" nicknames such as "Beercase," "Ginger," "Teacup," and "Julius Caesar" at roll calls instead.[38] Generally, only when individual laborers committed some crime or became known as "agitators" were their names written down for posterity.

Obsession with Color

Frantz Fanon's observation that colonial society was "a world divided into compartments" is supported by a number of European writers. The former assistant Lázló Székely wrote in his autobiographical novel *Tropic Fever* that "the first thing I learned in Sumatra was that there are two kinds of people in the world: white and coloured. The white man is the master, master and ruler in the strictest sense of the word."[39] A veteran planter, horrified that Székeley had lifted his own luggage on the Belawan docks, upbraided him: "What are you thinking of? You as a European can't lug your baggage! Nothing like that here. Please don't forget the prestige of the whites." Soon afterwards, kitted out in crisp tropical whites, young Székely was confirmed in his place as a member "of the race that ruled the world." In New Guinea, unwritten rules dictated that a planter never spoke directly to his laborers, but always gave orders via his "boss boy," for there could be no social contact between planter and laborer.[40] From 1921 in the Australian colony, contract laborers required written permission from their employers to wear singlets, shirts, or sweaters and were expected to wear loincloths instead of shorts.[41]

The color bar was absolute and at its heart was a racial division of labor. Even a Hindu millionaire would bow before the humblest white, though he be "runaway sailor or a card-sharper or a swindler," considered Székely.[42] The Invercargill-born New Guinea magistrate Captain Charles Monckton insisted that "one of the chief industries of the coloured people always must be that of serving the whites," a stance he justified because "white men and especially white women, cannot possibly live in the tropics without a plentiful supply of coloured servants."[43] The servant cooked the white master's food, washed his clothes, emptied his thunder box, trimmed his lawns, fetched his beer, and wiped his children's bottoms. The Malay, Kikuyu, Vietnamese, or Tamil girl (or boy) might join the white man in his bed or on the earth between the rubber trees but there was little chance of marriage across the color lines. Such miscegenation resulted, often enough, in "half-caste" children, but there were very few Eurasians in positions of authority in most of the colonies. This was shown when John Turner, the general manager of the Ramsden estates in Malaya, agonized about hiring a potential assistant from British Guiana because "Mr. Craigen has a slight tinge of dark blood from his mother's side." Turner knew the young man's father to be a well-respected member of the Demerara legislature, and the mother to be "a highly educated woman," but the slight pigmentation of his skin was a barrier to employment in a colony obsessed by color.[44] On the Australian rubber plantations in Papua, half-castes were employed as overseers or mechanics and "paid usually at higher rates" than "full-blood" Papuans,[45] but they were still segregated from Europeans because of their "dark" blood. In the Dutch East Indies, Eurasians "had little chance of being accepted into . . . [European] ranks" and rarely rose above clerk, according to Jan Breman.[46]

The Coolie Lines

The new recruits must have had mixed feelings when they first sighted the plantations. The ordeal of the ocean voyage was over, but they were in a strange country where the locals spoke foreign languages. There were wild animals in the surrounding swamps, mountains, and jungles and clouds of insects. In addition to the malarial mosquitoes, Tran Tu Binh shuddered at the memory of biting "ox-flies, round as castor beans and purplish red," that "left gaping wounds which quickly grew deeper and wider." There were also army ants, which moved in great columns, with "bodies as big as the joint of a man's finger" and which left their pincers embedded deep in the flesh.[47] There were often foremen of their own nationality, but the real bosses in the place were the whites. The hevea trees stretched out in straight lines, their dark green foliage glistening wet in the monsoon season or drab and dusty in the dry season. There were smoking chimneys and throbbing machinery where the latex was processed, lighters moored at wharves, and light railways where panting engines ran on steel rails, prompting Chinese coolies to sing:

> These strange things which barbarians have,
> Have devil-bellies which make them go.
> But we are happier people,
> Who do not ally ourselves with the devil.[48]

Whether the laborers were happier or not is a moot point. They were inevitably housed in barracks; long low structures made from a variety of materials and in varying states of repair. In the British colonies they were called "the coolie lines," less often the "labor lines." Although partitioned into compartments, the internal walls rarely stretched all the way to the ceiling, or roof, and privacy was impossible. Within a small space a family or a group of single men or women would sleep, wash, cook, and while away the hours after work. Tran recalls that Michelin's Phu-Riêng barracks were each divided into ten sections. Five people shared each section, making a total of fifty persons per barrack. There were no windows and, under the corrugated iron roofs, "We felt that we were living in ovens the whole year round," Tran wrote.[49] Other barrack blocks in Indochina housed up to one hundred people and were built either of corrugated iron or woven bamboo, with the internal screens made of wattle and daub.[50]

"Sucked Oranges"

On the worst estates, the housing conditions were appalling by any standard. The barracks at Phu-Riêng, for example, flooded during the monsoon,[51] and on the Mimot plantation in Cambodia the rains poured through a four-inch gap in the roof where the ridge-capping should have been.[52] Mimot and Phu-Riêng were singled out by the French labor inspectors as the very worst of the plantations in terms of the physical conditions of life and work, but the high rates of sickness and death on estates elsewhere in Southeast Asia testify that poor living conditions were widespread. Apart from malaria, the most prevalent illnesses were

bowel complaints caused by poor sanitation and polluted water supplies.
Tran records that the barracks at Phu-Riêng were surrounded by pools of
stagnant water, and latrines were often little more than open drains. This
was true even of the comparatively well-run Thmar Pitt estate in
Cambodia, where the lavatory consisted of an open concrete drain covered with a thatched roof. According to Inspector Delamare, "The
[waste] matter remains in the gutter, exposed to the air and flies, and from
time to time is expelled with a jet of water."[53] Poor hygiene led to alarming rates of sickness and death. On the Indochinese estates there were epi-
demics of cholera, dysentery, and other waterborne diseases. Malaria was
endemic, together with tropical ulcers and trachoma. Psychiatric ailments
such as depression were common, and other frequent afflictions included
nephritis, scabies, the mange, and respiratory complaints such as bron-
chitis. Other diseases, including beriberi and pernicious anemia, were
due to deficient diet.[54] When criticized by Inspector Bui Bang Doan
about the high rates of sickness and death on the Budop plantation in
Cochin-China, Monsieur Gatille, the manager, retorted that the plantation
was only just starting and that "it is necessary to make sacrifices." The
inspector wondered if Monsieur Homberg, the president of the owners,
the Société des Cultures Tropicales, in France, would agree.[55]

Some coolies fared worse. Writing in 1919, a Dutch writer described
the living conditions of laborers in the new rubber district of Asahan in
Sumatra ten years earlier, basing his summation on a district officer's
report:

At the point of destination there was no accommodation whatsoever. Mud
and dirt were their mattress. Many were starving because they had sold their
rice rations to some sly Malay. There were no permanent houses or *pondoks*.
In the makeshift hospital no Vaseline, iodine or castor oil was available.
Mortality was high, reaching as much as 30 per cent because of the appalling-
ly poor washing facilities.[56]

As Inspector Delamare noted, such a regimented life was psychologically damaging for people who were used to private family life and individual liberty in their native villages. He urged that the plantation companies should try to replicate village life as far as possible; that it would not
be expensive to house the workers in maisonettes, with streets, court-
yards, gardens, and wells. In such a setting, they could retire in the
evenings to the company of their families and friends, with photographs,

knick-knacks, furniture, and other affirmations of their humanity. His recommendations were ignored.[57]

Physical conditions on the French plantations did improve, partly as a result of the efforts of the labor inspectors, but also because of the agitation of the plantation laborers themselves.[58] According to Governor General Pierre Pasquier, the An-Viêng estate, for example, suffered a death rate of 27 percent in 1927, but this fell to 17 percent in 1928 and to 2.47 percent in 1929. Pasquier claimed that the overall death rate on the rubber plantations in Cambodia and Cochin-China fell from 4.5 percent in 1928 to 2.8 percent in 1929. The rubber companies, he noted, had heeded the advice of the Pasteur Institute at Hanoi, which recommended better drainage to reduce the habitat of mosquitoes, coupled with free rice rations and better quality food in general, free distribution of quinine, and regular government inspections.[59] No doubt, fear of the spread of infection to the European staff was another factor in improved hygiene. During one epidemic at the Kantroy plantation in Cambodia, "the entire European staff fled to Saigon and the native nurses likewise left their posts."[60] In a desperate effort to ward off cholera during an epidemic in Malaya's Kedah province, Leopold Ainsworth claimed that he ingested potassium permanganate washed down with a bottle of brandy a day![61] The dismal side effects of taking quinine also made it necessary for the estates to introduce prophylactic methods such as draining swamps and spraying the breeding grounds of the *Anopheles* mosquito with DDT.

The coolies' health conditions were little better in Malaya, particularly in the early years of the rubber estates. The employers blamed the workers' poor health on their condition on arrival, but as George Netto points out, "the principal diseases from which the workers suffered were ulcerated legs, chronic diarrhoea, dysentery and debility,"[62] contracted after their arrival in Malaya. In 1890, Dr. S. Patrao, the Acting Civil Surgeon at Negapatam in India drew attention to what he called the "deplorable" death rates of Tamil laborers in Malaya, attributing them to "the unhealthiness of most of the estates and the climatic influence, the low rate of wages and the long term of their contracts, or overwork." In his opinion, Tamil laborers returned home after the expiration of their contracts "like sucked oranges."[63]

The Ramsden Company's files reveal some dismal statistics. While the death rate at the Byram Estate between April and November 1905 was slightly in excess of 5 percent, at Victoria it was 13.69 percent, at Gedong 19.65 percent, and 33.83 percent at Caledonia.[64] The company's records also disclose that it had to be badgered by government medical officers and inspectors to improve conditions. In 1905, one manager fretted about sickness among "weaklings from India" whom he believed "only serve to build up our Hospital bill," and claimed that the rate of bowel complaints would improve if the company obtained "better class labourers."[65] In 1910, the general manager was issuing the same complaints about the poor health of new arrivals, whom he blamed for the high rates of death and illness from dysentery, cholera, and diarrhea. The Indian immigration service was not impressed with such evasions and forced the company to provide a new supply of fresh water to the coolie lines as a condition for bringing in more labor.[66] In 1908, Dr. MacDowell, a government medical officer, had also condemned the "insanitary state" [sic] of the coolie lines on the company's Caledonia Estate and ordered their replacement with solidly built barracks raised five feet off the ground.[67]

Out of a total of 100,000 Tamil laborers working in the Malayan rubber plantations in 1910, almost 5,000 died from malaria, dysentery, and diarrhea: almost fifty deaths per thousand workers.[68] Nevertheless, the overall death rate of Indian laborers in Malaya did decline steadily after 1912.[69] In 1930 the Principal Medical Officer for the Federated Malay States reported that the death rates on the estates were an average of 22 percent below those for the Malayan population as a whole. This, however, was uneven; at 41.5 per thousand, the death rates for rubber plantations in Pahang West province were far in excess of the Malayan average of 26.4 per thousand.[70] Put another way, estates with a death rate in excess of 45.6 per thousand had a laboring population of 13,767. The remaining estates, with a population of almost 151,000, had a death rate of 12.9 per thousand. The very worst places were the malarial Old Seremban Estate in Negri Sambalan, with a death rate of 99.2 per thousand; and the equally pestilential Hendra Estate in Perak, which had 85 deaths per thousand.[71]

The Stinkers

Although the rubber companies would never admit it publicly, hard work combined with poor nutrition and physical debility took its toll. In 1906, in an internal memorandum to John Turner, the manager of Ramsden's Gedong Estate, Mr. D. Ritchie, admitted the role of overwork in the coolies' ill health. With over seventy coolies hospitalized on any given day on the estate, Ritchie forecast that, "Now that the pressure of work in factory and punt loading is over, there is every indication that the numbers in hospital will materially decrease."[72] Healthwise, the worst work was forest clearing. Tran Tu Binh was employed on this work at Phu-Riêng close to the border with Cambodia, clearing an area of jungle and upland scrub twenty kilometers long and ten wide with hand tools.[73] There was constant danger of death or injury from falling trees or from poisonous snakes and insects underfoot. Another constant threat was injury from sharp slivers of bamboo, which could pierce right through a naked foot. Often the wounds would turn septic, which caused the Dutch overseers on Sumatran plantations to dub those afflicted as "stinkers." The use of the epithet was later extended to the coolies as a whole.[74]

A Culture of Violence

As Tran Tu Binh soon discovered, casual violence was a fact of life for the coolie. The hero of Madelon Lulofs' novel, Ruki, is stunned to receive a punch in the face for misplacing his spade while clearing a choked waterway. Confused, the lad smiles, only to further enrage his Dutch manager, who curses him for "impertinence," calls him a monkey, and shoves his face in muddy water.[75] An Indian protest song laments that if the new recruits objected to being given food inappropriate for Hindus or Muslims, the clerks in the holding depots on the coast would use force:

> They beat us with a cane, lifting us over their
> heads,
> They threw us on the floor;
> In abusive language they called us *sālā* and other
> names.[76]

On the Saigon wharves, the police flailed at the heads of the new recruits, cursing them as "animals," "savages," and "motherfuckers."[77] Lest the reader consider this an exaggeration, the published memoirs of European planters attest that casual violence was endemic on the estates. Leopold Ainsworth recalls his first morning on a rubber estate when a European assistant stormed into the coolie lines, seized a sleeping "malingerer" by the ankles "and with a quick jerk pulled him straight off the platform, so that he fell quite two feet on the ground with a resounding and impressive bump." Ainsworth soon found himself doing the same, and admits that he "actually enjoyed it as a new and rather amusing form of sport." When a gang of Maliartum coolies refused to work because the manager had postponed their payday, the manager appeared "quivering with rage," and while the creepers covered the "mutineers" with Schneider rifles, he "proceeded to beat the stuffing out of them" one by one. Ainsworth also saw a gang of Chinese Kongsi laborers guarded by Sikh overseers armed with guns and heavy whips which they used on the laborers.[78] In 1912, Helge Holm, the manager of the Robinson River Estate in New Guinea, got off scot-free after kicking a laborer to death.[79]

An article published in the Melbourne *Herald* in 1923 claimed that the law forbidding the thrashing of plantation laborers in New Guinea "is flagrantly disobeyed." The Australians had inherited the culture of violence from German planters for whom the use of "a heavy but pliant piece of hosepipe securely nailed to a stout handle" on the "pachydermous hides" of the natives was the rule. One planter told the *Herald*, "I do my own punishing, and the *kanaka*, who steps over the rope of good behaviour gets a good solid whack with a stick or a punch on the jaw. They understand that . . ."[80] Such attitudes were not confined to the often ill-educated soldier-settlers who took estates in New Guinea after the First World War. Dr. R.W. Cilento, the director of the institute for tropical medicine in Townsville, told Melbourne Rotarians that the Papuans were "the least intelligent race on earth," and although sullen and hostile, once under control they "admired force."[81] The historian D. C. Lewis noted that:

> The white men came from societies in which the corporal punishment of children and young males was still socially and legally sanctioned, and the plantations invariably invited comparisons with boarding schools and the conditions of life on board ship or in the army. And Papuans of any age, physically smaller generally than the Europeans and culturally backward or immature in the eyes of most white people, could indeed be regarded just as they were routinely described, as 'boys.'[82]

Although the Canning Report of 1923–24[83] absolved the New Guinea estates of the use of violence, it was immediately challenged by a planter called Acherley, who denounced it as "a tissue of lies"[84] and the Australian government was forced to commission a new investigation headed by Colonel Ainsworth, the former Chief Native Commissioner in Kenya. Ainsworth's report was a "slashing indictment" of the culture of violence in the colony, declared the Melbourne *Herald*.[85] Nevertheless, in the decades that followed, few planters were prosecuted and those who were received derisory sentences. In 1939, for instance, a European found guilty of the "unlawful killing" of a Papuan was sentenced to twelve months' hard labor. In the same year, fifteen planters were found guilty of assaulting laborers and received very light sentences.[86] In 1932, thirty-nine Europeans were convicted of assaulting "natives," but in the same year 268 Papuans were convicted of breaching the Native Labor Ordinance and received stiffer punishments. At the same time, the planters clamored for the right to "thrash . . . lazy and cheeky boys."[87] The treatment of Papuan plaintiffs was in stark contrast with the leniency with which magistrates dealt with whites. In one case noted by Ainsworth, a magistrate dismissed a case brought by an indentured laborer who had been forced to do unpaid overtime. The magistrate sentenced the plaintiff to three months jail for conspiracy![88] Similar patterns were found in other parts of the British Empire. When an assistant named W. R. C. Gray beat two Javanese women so severely on a Malayan estate in 1910 that the matter came to the attention of the police, he was heavily fined and quietly transferred to another plantation. Ramsden's general manager, William Duncan, argued that it was not necessary to sack him because "he gets on so well with his coolies."[89] On the other hand, in the same year Ramsden's did sack an assistant named Bruce Petrie following repeated sadistic excesses.[90]

Violence on the Estates in Indochina

On the Michelin estates in Indochina almost twenty years later, Tran Tu Binh claims that laborers were often beaten on the buttocks with sticks. Others were caned on the soles of the feet until the skin was shredded and were afterwards locked in a dark room with their legs shackled and deprived of food. Tran alleges that soldiers trampled on escapees and broke their bones. One of the worst thugs was a Corsican overseer whom Tran calls "Triai," a former Foreign Legion captain, who carried a thick rattan cane he used to beat a number of people to death. Most brutal of all was an overseer Tran calls Monte,[91] whose beatings were so severe that he regularly wore out his canes. When the coolies turned on him and killed him, the overseers took their revenge indiscriminately, Tran alleges, even burying some victims alive and torturing and kicking others to death.[92]

Tran's accounts are backed up by the reports of Delamare and other French labor inspectors. Perhaps even worse than Tran's Phu-Riêng plantation was the Mimot estate in Cambodia. Emile Desenlis, the French *Résident* at Kompong Cham, considered that the Mimot coolies were treated like "human livestock, terrorized by the overseers" and as a result "they don't dare complain for fear of bullying and cruelty."[93] When Delamare inspected Mimot in 1927 after several hundred laborers had deserted en masse, he found unhealed scars from whippings on the their bodies. The culprit, a Belgian overseer named Jacques Verhelst, was convicted of assault and expelled from Indochina. Verhelst had once whipped a group of women, one of whom was pregnant, with telephone wire for drinking water without his permission.[94]

For all the humanity of officials such as Delamare, the French authorities themselves were sometimes guilty of grave violence against the estate workers. One of the worst instances occurred in December 1932 during a strike called to protest wage and ration cuts on the Michelin plantation at Dau-Tiêng. A detachment of 120 militiamen under the command of Lieutenant Noblot turned out to block the strikers from marching on the nearby town of Thudaumot to present their grievances to the authorities. Noblot gave the order to open fire with live rounds. When the cordite smoke cleared, four strikers lay dead and another three were wounded. Word leaked out to France, and when the case became a scandal, the local authorities rushed to absolve themselves of blame. Noblot, according to a *Sûrêté* report, had lost his head when confronted with a large crowd of demonstrators, despite the fact that they were unarmed and showed no evidence of aggression. In the final analysis, the policeman held Michelin responsible for illegally cutting pay and rations. The report does not say, however, why it was thought necessary to send such numbers of heavily armed men to the plantation in the first place.[95]

The Rhemrev Report

In 1904, a report on the Sumatran plantations landed on the desk of the conservative Dutch colonial minister, A. W. F. Idenburg. The contents of the report, which was written by J. L. T. Rhemrev, the public prosecutor in Batavia, was so explosive that Idenburg refused to table it in parliament and buried it in the state archives, where it languished until 1987. All that the Dutch government would say was that there was no evidence of systematic abuse of plantation laborers and that any cases of violence were deplorable aberrations. Yet, as Jan Breman argues, "Rhemrev made it quite clear . . . that the use of physical coercion and of other forms of force against the workers was linked indissolubly to the plantation economy." What the report revealed also mocked the so-called "Ethical Policy," which asserted that one of the primary goals of the Dutch colonial state was the advancement and well-being of the natives. The Rhemrev Report did not fall from a clear sky. Two years earlier, a lawyer called Van den Brand had published an attack on the plantation system under the title *De Millioenen uit Deli*, in which he had asserted that violence was integral to the system. The Socialist and Liberal oppositions had seized upon the revelations in Van den Brand's pamphlet to launch a ferocious attack on the government, but neither Van den Brand nor Rhemrev were left-wing radicals.[96]

As in New Guinea and Malaya, private violence by the Dutch planters was forbidden by law,[97] but Breman argues that after the Rhemrev Report it continued as before, if more discreetly. The savagery of the indentured labor system had also been exposed by the writer H. Van Kol, who described what he had seen as:

> In general, these physically weak people seem to be overcome by a sort of apathy; many lose all desire to live; they can be seen, frequently, still quite young, indifferently waiting for death. Investigation of their past would probably bring to light a long sequence of misery and deprivation; these people are all too often the victims of grinding toil and insufficient food. Their blank faces, their staring eyes—I can see them in front of me whenever I think back to my visits to some of the Deli hospitals.[98]

Melancholy Effects on Indigenous Cultures

One of the most melancholy aspects of the indentured labor system in Australian Papua and New Guinea was the destruction of the indigenous cultures. John Decker noted that "the advent of European-controlled government, religion and employment has been followed by the pathetic melting away of the native population." Whole villages and districts were "bled white," with scarcely a man of employable age left in them. It was not surprising, given the brutal cultural encounter, that anthropologists noted a profound "loss of interest in life" among the Papuan population.[99] Life had been rendered meaningless, with the dazed native trapped in Weber's "polar night of icy darkness" in an "iron cage" of rules and regulations, performing tasks he found pointless, his villages emptied of able bodied men and boys. Many planters shrugged off the population decline as evidence of the "innate degeneracy" of the natives, but the anthropologist Pitt-Rivers insisted there was no history of decline before colonialism.[100]

Did the white planters sitting on their verandas in the cool of evening quaffing their stengahs ever reflect on their common humanity with their laborers, one wonders? Perhaps some did, but to do so openly would risk running afoul of a system predicated on race prejudice. Chinese laborers were regarded with particular disdain by their white bosses. While these *sinkehs* were often illiterate, their songs and laments reveal a world steeped in ancient philosophical and literary wisdom that contrasts sharply with the shallow mental universe of the planters as revealed by writers such as Somerset Maugham. Revolt, too, can be an affirmation of humanity:

> Why waste your years in hot dispute?
> Do not give way to anger;
> Be slow to spend your time in envy;
> Soon your hair will be snowy white.[101]

There might be a sly dig at the pretensions and transience of worldly power in the words:

> How changing are the ways of this world!
> The flower blooms only to wither;
> When your power and position are gone
> Even those who served you will hurry to insult you.[102]

There could be joy, too, in milestone events affirming the coolie's humanity:

> It is not the Feast of Lanterns,
> It is not my birthday feast.
> Nor has any moon arisen;
> Yet I have a gift today—
> A little baby boy![103]

CHAPTER SIXTEEN

Coolie Revolts

If estates cannot pay a living wage, the estate should be shut down. It is usually the estate that is best off that is the worst payer or worst employer and should be black listed by the government.

—E. A. DICKSON, *Old Malaya Hand*, 1934[1]

The Selangor strikes have shown very clearly the growing strength of Indian political organisations in this country. . . . The second series was purely a strike against authority, in protest against the arrest of a sedition-monger, who had posed as the champion of oppressed labour against the employers.

—SIR SHENTON THOMAS, High Commissioner, Federated Malay States, May 17, 1941[2]

The plantation system was based on the super-exploitation of labor. Pay was so low that the English assistant Leopold Ainsworth wondered how the Tamil workers and their families could "possibly exist as ordinary human beings" on the wages paid on his boss's Malayan plantation.[3] In 1926, the cost of a Papuan indentured laborer was 20 percent of that of a white worker, 25 percent of that of an employed estate manager, and 10 percent of that of a white unskilled laborer.[4] Racist humiliation, insult, and cruelty were part of the everyday lives of the coolies: "I've been greeted only with cudgels/And a pot-bellied, red-faced French colon/Who swears all day long: 'shit, pig, scum!'" laments a Vietnamese *vè* poem about work in the colonial era.[5] The plantation workforces were largely made up of new proletarians from a peasant background. Peasants often tend toward individualistic solutions to socially based problems. Moreover, these peasants-turned-workers often came from outside the regions where the rubber estates were situated. In the case of Sumatra and Malaya in particular, the new plantation proletariat was ethnically heterogeneous, riven by barriers of language, culture, and belief. In addition, many of the workers were transient and would return to their homes upon the expiration of their contracts, although as the present-day ethnic composition of Singapore and Malaya shows, many of them stayed on in their adopted countries.

Class consciousness and the internationalist values of the labor movement have to be learned, and the classic forms of workers' resistance often have to be reinvented afresh. While stoical fatalism might be an understandable response to factors beyond an individual's control in a traditional setting, in the plantation context it was a barrier to collective action. The uprooted peasant might also regard cruelty and injustice as a normal part of life to be endured, or even as somehow justified. When Sir Maori Kiki, a future Prime Minister of independent Papua New Guinea, was a boy in both senses of the word, a white planter poured a cup of scalding hot tea over his chest because Kiki had accidentally slopped some in the saucer. Kiki was scarred for life but, "At the time," writes Hank Nelson, "He accepted the punishment. That was the way things were. It was only later when he was filled with hate."[6]

Primitive Protests

The first coolie protests often took the form of spontaneous and sometimes murderous assaults on overseers. In 1911, for example, in the Bila district of Sumatra, estate laborers murdered an English manager and two of his Swiss counterparts with hoes and knives. Given what we know from the Rhemrev Report, the official explanation that there was no provocation seems dubious.[7] Sometimes the overseers got off lightly, as when an arrogant assistant called John Mair was attacked on a Ramsden estate in Malaya and had a finger chopped off.[8] Vengeful assaults were not uncommon on the plantations in French Indochina, as in 1929 when irate coolies attacked a surveyor named Pellen with machetes and tapping knives on the Kantroy plantation in Cambodia, forcing him to seek shelter in a cesspit.[9] Tran Tu Binh records the murder of the French overseer

Monteil, who he calls "Monte," on the Phu-Riêng plantation.[10] The murders sparked off a wider mutiny, which was only quelled when the estate director and his staff fired on the coolies, killing several and causing others to flee into the jungle.[11] Labor inspector Texier concluded that the attack was not premeditated, but had erupted after Monteil, frustrated that he did not receive an expected promotion, caned a coolie for "arrogance" and for neglecting his work.[12] Another French official assured the Colonial Minister that there was no political character to the affair,[13] but from what Tran says about Monteil, the coolies would have seen his killing as retribution for his excesses. Occasionally, physical attacks yielded results for the aggrieved coolies, as on the Sabrang Estate in Malaya in 1913. An assistant named Paton thrashed a Tamil coolie with a stick for "impertinence" and was afterwards set upon by "the whole of the coolies in the lines." The police arrived to quell the disturbance and arrested three laborers, but when the manager learned that the coolies intended to complain to the immigration department, Paton was discharged.[14] More generally, the planters and police cracked down on "mutineers"; for example, the alleged ringleader in the murder of Monteil was executed. While the French characteristically downplayed any element of political protest in such episodes, the Dutch made public examples of the perpetrators of violence against the planters. This was the case on a Dutch estate in 1881, when two Javanese coolies named Tasmin and Kzomo di Rono were publicly hanged for their part in the murder of a Dutch planter. As Jan Breman argues in his book *Taming the Coolie Beast*, their execution was a "stage performance" enacted "to dramatize colonial power."[15] The dangling corpses of Tasmin and Kzomo di Rono on the plantation where they had committed the murder was a grim warning to all other coolies of the consequences of revolt. In contrast, no matter how onerous the life of a European "wage slave," work discipline was not enforced by "thanatocratic" methods.[16] Marx argued that the element of direct force distinguishes slavery from wage labor, but as Ravindra K. Jain observes, the lines between the two were blurred on the plantation,[17] where violence and the threat of it were always present. It follows, then, that when the estate laborers were aroused, industrial struggles would be bitter, and a direct political element was often present.

Individual and Mass Desertions

The strike is the classical form of workers' resistance, but a more rudimentary form of defiance, desertion, sometimes en masse, was common in
the rubber plantations. Although desertion was illegal and punishable by
imprisonment and fines, the planters continually complained about
"absconders." Sometimes these workers deserted to other plantations or
mines on the promise of higher wages. According to Akers, up to a quarter of all indentured Chinese laborers working on Malayan plantations
before the First World War deserted, many of them attracted by the higher wages in the tin mining industry.[18] In November 1910, the manager of
the Selaba Estate grumbled that eight Chinese coolies had absconded and
not been retaken, adding, "I am afraid the chances of capturing them are
very small."[19] Another Malayan manager complained in 1916 that
although recruiters in India had recently sent seventy-five new coolies,
seventy had either left legally at the termination of their contracts or had
absconded and the estate was suffering an acute labor shortage as a
result.[20] The desertion rates in French Indochina, particularly in the early
years, were strikingly high. In 1927 alone, according to the Vietnamese
inspector Bui Bang Doan, 3,001 laborers deserted from plantations in
Cochin-China. Many more fled over the border from estates in
Cambodia.[21] At Tran Tu Binh's place of work, the Michelin plantation at
Phu-Riêng, no less than 161 fled out of a total workforce of 990 between
June 1927 and March 1928.[22] The French authorities posted cordons of
armed guards to apprehend deserters, and those who were caught were
often brutally assaulted before being returned to their place of employment, and were sometimes murdered.[23]

    While spontaneous assault, sabotage, and desertion were serious nui-
sances for the estate owners, the results for the coolies were mixed. While
some might have escaped, others perished in the jungles and swamps or
were apprehended and punished. Those found guilty of physical attacks
during breakouts could expect little mercy from the authorities.
Meanwhile, the system of super-exploitation continued without serious
challenge, with fresh supplies of labor brought in to replace those who ran
off. Much more serious from the planters' point of view was that the concentration of large numbers of laborers enduring similar conditions led to
collective resistance. The planters often responded by calling on state
power to quash the strikers. Trade unions were illegal: in the case of
Papua New Guinea until 1962, where the planters were even opposed to

racially exclusive white unions because of the "possible demonstrative effect" on the Papuans.[24] The same situation was true of Malaya, where organizations such as the Communist-led Nanyang Federation of Labor were illegal until 1941.[25] It was also illegal for indentured laborers to strike or refuse to obey orders across the plantation world. Nevertheless, strikes and other forms of collective action erupted no matter how hard the authorities cracked down. Jan Breman notes instances of strike action on Sumatran plantations from as early as 1878, predating the rubber era and bequeathing a legacy of struggle.[26] For a number of years from the late 1920s, the estates in French Indochina were convulsed with industrial disorders and a similar pattern unfolded toward the end of the 1930s in Malaya and Singapore.

The Strike Wave in French Indochina

One of the crucial ingredients for the emergence of effective trade union-ism in the repressive environment of the rubber estates was the creation of a class-conscious and politically aware workers' leadership capable of winning the workers' trust, drawing conclusions from experience, and mapping out strategies which could lead the workers to at least partial vic-tory. The strike wave that erupted across the plantations of southern Indochina in the late 1920s marked the beginning of the Indochinese Communist Party's involvement in mass workers' struggles. The Communists were able to win mass support by skillfully combining their anti-imperialist program with the direct, economic demands of the work-ers.[27] In some respects, this mass mobilization was easier for Tran Tu Binh and his comrades than for their counterparts in Malaya. Vietnam boasted a long history of proto-nationalist opposition to foreign occupa-tion going back to the time of Chinese overlordship and developing into modern nationalism during the period of French colonialism after 1858. The Tonkinese peasants, too, had a strong tradition of mutual assistance that marked them off from the more individualistic farmers in other coun-tries. In addition, the plantation proletariat in French Indochina was eth-nically and culturally homogeneous to a much greater extent than was the case in Malaya or Sumatra. While the French employed some Khmers and hill tribesmen, primarily in forest clearing operations, the vast bulk of the coolies were Vietnamese. These factors made it easier for the Communists to develop and foster the ideas of cooperation, class struggle, and solidarity without which trade unionism—and militant political action—is not possible.

Although Tran Tu Binh does not say so explicitly, it seems clear that he enlisted as a coolie and went south under the direction of the Communist Party. By 1928, reports of shocking conditions on the plantations had trickled back to Tonkin and anti-recruiting leaflets were circulating. One of these was intercepted at the Phy Ly post office by the *Sûreté*:[28]

> Fellow countrymen and women!
> Our country is ruined, we are wretched, we pay heavy taxes and duties, we are beaten and thrown in prison for the slightest offence. Now they are recruiting coolies, whom they first stupefy with drugs, then forcibly transport far away to their deaths![29]

By his own account, Tran was already an ardent Communist when he went south. The well-educated product of a Catholic seminary, he was also naturally rebellious and gifted with leadership qualities and high intelligence. He led a successful hunger strike aboard the *Commandant Dorier* during the passage to Saigon in protest against the poor food served by the ship's galley and even managed to gain the support of the French sailors.[30] He arrived at Michelin's Phu-Riêng plantation already respected as a man who would stand up against injustice. Finding the estate seething with discontent, Tran set to work to channel the inchoate anger into organized revolt.

The reports of the labor inspectors confirm that in its early years the Phu-Riêng estate was a "hell on earth," with poor sanitary conditions, sadistic overseers, insufficient and inferior food, relentless work, and unsanitary barracks. Individual protests, no matter how peaceful, were brutally repressed, such as when Tran's outspoken older friend Phan was bashed and then shackled in a dark shed for remonstrating with the bosses after the estate manager kicked a young man to death. Violent resistance to this reign of terror was met with greater violence, and peaceful protest was equally ineffective.[31] When an assistant battered a Vietnamese foreman to death, the workers filed a legal complaint. The court found him guilty of "negligent manslaughter" and awarded his victim's widow five piastres in damages—roughly eight days' pay for a male coolie[32]—a modern French version of the "exception of Irishry" laws. Disgusted, the workers responded with sabotage, slowing down production and slashing the roots of hevea saplings just before planting and killing up to a third of the trees.[33] Dying in droves from sickness, overwork, and despair, tormented by the insults and blows of the overseers, and forbidden by law from leaving until the expiration of their contracts, the laborers were increasingly receptive to Tran's advocation of militant collective action.

The Tết Strike at Phu-Riêng

When the strike wave broke at Phu-Riêng and other plantations during the Tết festivities in late January 1930, Tran and his comrades prepared the workers for the battle. As Tran knew from experience and Marxist theory, the strength of the working class lies in its numbers and in disciplined organization. Expecting that the planters would try to starve them back to work, they had built up hidden caches of food. Expecting violent repression, they had stockpiled knives and other homemade weapons. During extensive discussions at secret meetings in the coolie lines, they had formulated a list of demands to be served to the rubber companies. Tran lists these as:

- The prohibition of beatings and other ill-treatment
- Exemption from taxation
- Paid maternity leave
- An eight-hour day, including traveling time
- Accident pay
- Freedom for the imprisoned Communist leader, Tran Van Cung
- Workers to be returned to their homes at the bosses' expense upon termination of their contracts[34]

The labor inspector J. G. Herisson noted that the workers also demanded the dismissal of two of the most brutal assistants employed at Phu-Riêng.[35] In spite of the findings of earlier labor inspectors regarding the unfair and unfit conditions of the laborers, Herisson considered the strike was unjustified.[36] This is incredible, given that the workers' economic demands were not especially radical; indeed much of what they wanted was theoretically guaranteed in their contracts. The contracts stipulated an eight-hour working day, six days a week, but in practice they were made to perform unpaid overtime and free time on Sundays was spent performing compulsory unpaid work around the coolie compound.

The demand to free the imprisoned Communist leader, however, was a calculated political move. As the strike unfolded, up to 5,000 strikers were parading behind red banners and sending delegations to put their grievances to the state authorities.[37] Michelin considered closing the plantation and sending the coolies home but decided to call in the police and militia instead. The disturbances continued for some months and ended with massive repression by the state forces. On April 10, 1930, Governor Jean-Félix Krautheimer wired his superior at Hanoi to report that over a dozen workers had been imprisoned for their part in the strike. Three of these, including Tran, were sentenced to five years, four to three years, and the others received lesser sentences.[38] The Governor reported that the workers had been sentenced at a court in Bien Hoa for "impeding freedom of work and for actions compromising public security."[39]

Bloody Confrontation at Dau-Tiêng

In Hanoi, Governor General Pierre Pasquier professed to be puzzled by the strike, which he assured the Colonial Minister at Paris was solely the result of Communist manipulation. He could not understand the outbreak, he claimed, because the Michelin workers were treated particularly well at Phu-Riêng.[40] Either he was lying or he had not been reading the reports of his own inspectors, Delamare and Doan, who were highly critical of Michelin. The strike spread to other plantations, despite the arrest and banishment of the ringleaders from Phu-Riêng. In late April 1930, the manager on the Thuan Loi plantation reported to Michelin headquarters in Clermont-Ferrand that 1,300 coolies had put their tools down. He added that reinforcements of militia were being sent in to keep order.[41] Two years later, the disturbances were to culminate in a massacre of unarmed workers on Michelin's Dau-Tiêng rubber estate. The latter strike erupted when Michelin cut wages from forty to thirty cents a day and reduced the rice ration from 800 to 700 grams for males to 600 grams for females. Michelin justified the cuts as austerity measures brought on by the trade slump. Confronted with the strike, the estate manager, Monsieur Planchon, panicked and called out a detachment of militia. On the orders of their commander, Lieutenant Noblot, the militiamen opened fire, killing three coolies and wounding four others. This time the authorities had gone too far, and a cover-up was not possible. Word of the shootings leaked out and caused a wave of outrage in France, with parliamentary deputies and newspaper editors censuring the government. The *Sûreté* condemned Michelin for its illegal pay and ration cuts, and concluded that the strikers had shown no signs of aggression before they were shot down.[42]

By now, however, the Great Depression had begun in earnest and the workers' resolve to fight was waning. Contrary to popular wisdom, industrial militancy is more likely to occur during periods of economic upturn, when there is hope for the future. Conversely, during hard times, the workers are more concerned with survival than strikes and revolution. Moreover, by this time, the very worst conditions on the plantations had been ameliorated both as a result of the estates becoming more established and the practice of regular inspections. The colonial authorities and the rubber companies realized that it was not in their best interests to provoke the coolies into rebellion. The worst of the overseers had been dismissed and some were expelled from the colony.

Many of the leading militants were also in jail on the island of Poulo Condore (Con-Son) in the South China Sea. One can imagine *vè* poems being recited on the deck of the French ship Tran was aboard:

> As I look at the prison island
> Still a small dot in the distance
> I feel a surge of hatred unbound
> As deep as the blue sea around.[43]

Tran spent five years on an island that for many political activists was a university of revolution. There, imprisoned high-ranking cadres of the Communist Party gave political lectures and their students discussed and debated the burning political and social questions of the hour: independence from France in particular. Seasoned in struggle and jail, Tran was to rise rapidly through the ranks of the Party after his release, becoming deputy secretary of the Viet Minh's Central Military Committee, commander of the army's military academy, and chief inspector of the Vietnam People's Armed Forces.[44]

The Strike Waves in Malaya

There were also serious strike waves on the plantations in Malaya. As the historian Charles Gamba has pointed out, prior to the Second World War, "there were no trade unions in Malaya in the Western sense of the term."

This was partly due to repression. Trade unions were not legalized in Malaya and Singapore until 1941,[45] and before then both the Kuomintang[46] and the Malayan Communist Party (MCP) were banned by the British authorities.[47] Despite the ban, both continued throughout the 1930s, and this suggests deeper causes for the rudimentary state of the unions, stemming from what Gamba describes as "the special organisation of Malay, Chinese and Indian society." The Malays remained largely outside the wage economy at this stage and were thus indifferent to labor organization and to nationalist politics.[48] For most of the prewar period, the Chinese were organized in trade guilds—corporate institutions that included both employees and employers—and until the end of the 1930s the Indian workforce was comparatively docile and was looked down on by the Indian middle class, the Europeans, and most Chinese and Malays.[49] Such prejudices and ethnic insularities stunted the development of both class solidarity and multi-ethnic nationalism. Gamba argues that both the Kuomintang and the Chinese-dominated Malayan Communist Party "seemed inclined to think of Singapore as an extension of China."[50] Other Communists and radicals were aware of the block this placed on labor organization. One of these was the legendary Indonesian Communist Tan Malaka. René Onraet, the director of the Criminal Intelligence Department in the Straits Settlements, noted that "Tan Malaka had put on record his opinion that Malaya was, on account of the language difficulty, a difficult country [in which] to organize proletarian movements and Alimin[51] told me in 1927 that it was impossible to lead the masses in Malaya on account of the different nationalities it contained."[52] There was also a certain amount of deliberate divide-and-rule involved on the part of the British authorities. Sir Frederick Weld, who served as Governor of the Straits Settlements in the 1880s, believed "it is advisable that, in a country like this, the preponderance of any one Eastern nationality should not be excessive," particularly "because the Indians are a peccable and easily governed race." The historian J. Norman Parmer argued that "[f]rom Weld's administration onward, the Indians were cast in the role of a counterpoise to the Chinese,"[53] who were regarded as much less tractable.[54]

Nevertheless, examples of militancy, desertion, sabotage, and other forms of protest abounded from the beginning of the industry, particularly among the Chinese. On the eve of the First World War, C. E. Akers noted that the Chinese coolies had a reputation for being "difficult": the 1911 Revolution in China had "unsettled" them, and evidence of "a tur-

bulent spirit on several estates" had led to the intervention of the police
and the military. Akers added that the Javanese, too, could be unruly[55]: a
point on which John Turner, the longtime general manager of the
Ramsden estates, agreed. Writing to the London head office in January
1908, he reported that many Javanese coolies had been employed in
recent times but that "they are inclined to be troublesome." As a result,
the estates had cancelled orders for more of them, and those involved in
unrest had been "severely dealt with."[56]

Militancy among the Chinese Laborers

By 1927 at least, the colonial authorities were seriously worried about the
subversive potential of the Chinese population in Malaya. One official
worried that "[m]any of our Chinese immigrants are highly undesirable
politically,"[57] and a colleague informed the Colonial Secretary that the
"police are constantly discovering secret societies and centres of communist revolutionary and anti-British organisations" in the colony. With an
excess of unskilled labor in Malaya, the official added, it might be possible to halt the flow of Chinese immigrants.[58] Nevertheless, the planters
themselves believed that they could "see off" so-called "Celestial" trou-
blemakers.[59] This belief was apparently confirmed when Chinese bud-
ders[60] struck on the Dunlop estates in 1929, demanding a raise in pay
from $1.50 to $2.00 a day. The management refused to negotiate, despite
the loss of $7,000 worth of budwood, and "the Chinese, recognising the
firm hand, returned to work at the old rate and have never given any further trouble since," a government journalist reported.[61]

    As in French Indochina, labor militancy tended to die down during
the worst years of the Great Depression. There had been widespread layoffs. Many coolies had returned to India or China. There were also wage
cuts, but with a worldwide glut of rubber, the workers were in no position
to mount serious resistance. C. D. Ahearne of the Federated Malay States
Labor Department reported, "there were no strikes or serious disturbances of note" in 1932, with "the relations between employers and
employed being harmonious."[62] On April 13, 1937, Police Commissioner
C. H. Sansom wrote:

> For the past 3 or 4 years throughout the period of depression in this country
> the Communist Party has been moribund, partly due to police action, partly

due to lack of funds but chiefly, perhaps, owing to the innate reasonableness
of the Chinese character moulded by generations of adversity.[63]

A wave of strikes swept across the plantations and on April 27, the
Financial News reported that the number of rubber workers on strike in
Malaya had jumped in the space of twenty-four hours from 10,000 to
24,000, with forty-four estates affected by the unrest.[64] Alarmed by the
tide of discontent, Governor Shenton Thomas banned a huge range of
"subversive" books, pamphlets, and newspapers. The Colonial Secretary
at London offered his support for the prevention of what he called "the
circulation of deliberate revolutionary propaganda amongst ignorant and
excitable people" but regretted that in his haste, the Governor had
banned a number of classics of English literature and the publications of
the Phoenix Book Company, which was "innocent" of any leftist affilia-
tion.[65] By May, the colonial authorities were writing of the "alarming situation" in Malaya. Thomas claimed that "the critic at home does not
realise that what may be harmless to an English undergraduate may be
most unwholesome food for a Chinese, Tamil or Malay youth . . ."[66]

An Explosion of Strikes

The planters and the colonial government in Malaya were soon faced with
an explosion of strikes based in the Chinese population and orchestrated
in large part by the Malayan Communist Party (MCP) through its General
Labor Union (GLU). The strike wave began in March 1937 among
Chinese workers on rubber estates in Selangor and Negri Sambilan
provinces and spread beyond the plantations to the collieries at Batu
Arang.[67] However, while the MCP was an avowedly revolutionary organization, dedicated to overthrowing British rule on the peninsula, the
Colonial Office privately admitted that "the strikers had, for the most
part, genuine grievances in regard to their rates of pay, no effort having
been made to raise them, as the price of rubber increased." The strikers
were demanding $1.00 a day, an increase of around thirty-five to forty
cents. After a half-hearted attempt at conciliation, the High
Commissioner ordered the police to raid the plantations and arrest the
"leading agitators." With the abandonment of evenhandedness by the
authorities, the disturbances grew more violent. In one case in mid-1937,
the police opened fire on strikers who had converged on a local adminis-

trative center. In another, four plainclothes detectives who were spying on a crowd were set upon and fired their revolvers, wounding two of their assailants. As the strikes dragged on, such clashes became more frequent, with hundreds of arrests. When the workers organized flying pickets to close down plantations, the authorities responded by flooding the plantations with police, backed by the bayonets of the Punjab Regiment and the Malay Rifles.[68] On March 2, 1937, the manager of the Malayan Rubber factory, Mr. Grice, telephoned the police to report that he had been "taken prisoner" by a group of striking women. It was only with difficulty that the police were able to "extricate" him from the women's clutches. The male strikers stoned the officers in retaliation, and in the mélêe a police revolver went missing. The police retreated with two arrested strikers whereupon the workers formed themselves into a 1,200-strong procession and marched on the police barracks to demand their comrades' release. C. H. Sansom, the Commissioner of Police, admitted that the demonstration was "orderly," but considered "their attitude was one of insolent defiance." The strikers "literally took possession of Klang town for 3 hours and stipulated a reply [to their demands] within 24 hours." They dispersed only after the police trucked in massive reinforcements.

Strikes also engulfed the plantations in the Kajang district some thirteen miles from Kuala Lumpur, with militants cycling round the estates to spread the action. Matters came to a head when strikers overpowered an undercover policeman and stole his notebook. The police responded by raiding the plantation and arresting seventeen strikers, after which the workers decided to march on Kuala Lumpur to present their grievances directly to the colonial government. When the procession neared the Bolton Estate they found the road blocked by a phalanx of more than150 police under the command of an Inspector Dickinson. Dickinson gave the order to baton charge the strikers, whereupon "the mob broke and was driven all the nine miles back to Kajang" where "110 arrests were made." Coolies on a nearby estate responded by roughing up some Chinese plainclothesmen—an action that Commissioner Sansom claimed was unprovoked—and more arrests were made. Later, the police were incensed by events on the Wardieburn Estate in Ulu Klang, where female tappers flew a red flag and stopped work to observe International Women's Day; "one of the days decreed for celebration by the Communist Party of Russia," fumed Commissioner Sansom. At the same time, he claimed that the strikers had lodged "exorbitant wage demands" and other "supplementary and unreasonable demands." These included the provision of childcare for children under the age of five, schools for the coolies' children, and "no dismissals or fines without cause and new labourers to be introduced by the present labour force." In response, the coolie lines on the nearby Hawthornden Estate were raided and the strike leaders dragged off. When the workers held a protest meeting on the lines, the police and soldiers of the Punjabi Rifles attacked with force. Sansom's report read, "For three weeks this unruly gathering had been a law unto itself, definitely anti-European and defiant." This strike wave was later crushed by the state authorities.[69]

Other officials were critical of the authorities' handling of the distur-bances. Mr. S.W. Jones, the British Resident at Selangor, was unimpressed by what he saw as the "unscrupulous" behavior of planters, who had refused to negotiate in good faith despite the modest demands of the work-ers. "The police have forgotten for the moment certain vital circumstances," he observed. Generally, there had been an "insufficient element of unlawful-ness . . . to justify strong measures. Meetings only call for dispersal when they threaten a breach of the peace; picketing is not defined as an offense under any law of this country; and in the early days intimidation in actuali-ty hard to discover and proof was only 'information received.'"[70] Jones rep-resented the part of the colonial establishment that favored a more concilia-tory approach, believing that trade unions should be legalized in order that moderate leadership might displace the militants.[71] Trade unions were not legalized in Malaya until the eve of the Japanese invasion of 1942, but if the authorities believed that they had cowed the Chinese workers into submis-sion, they were soon forced to rethink this.

May Day Riot and Firestone Occupation

Another wave of unrest rolled across the plantations in 1940, with fifty-seven strikes in the Selangor province alone. The unrest spread to the rubber factories in Singapore and culminated in the occupation of the Firestone plant, an action which itself followed directly from spectacular riots that erupted on May 1, 1940. The Malayan Communist Party called for a "monster demonstration" and general strike "in sheer defiance" of the authorities' wishes, noted a police inspector. The police shot two demonstrators dead and wounded another two. Predictably, a white jury found the shootings to have been justified.[72] The Firestone plant, which employed almost 300 men and women and which was said to have con-

Civil unrest in Singapore, Syed Alwi Bridge, May 1940.

tained "a strong communist cell," went on strike the following day after the manager refused to discuss "an entirely unreasonable" log of claims served on him by the GLU. The evidence is contradictory, however, it seems that the manager locked out the workers, whereupon they occupied the plant. A sit-down strike lasted for two months, during which time the police observed that the coolies held "continuous anti-British meetings" on the premises and organized a workers' militia to repel attempts to evict them. In the meantime, the strike spread to other rubber factories and there were continuous disturbances, with the police shepherding blacklegs into work through angry picket lines. In at least one instance, the workers fought a pitched battle with police, defending themselves with "wooden staves, stones, iron bars and hammers." On July 1, 1940, the police stormed the Firestone factory and ended the occupation, arresting forty-six workers in the process and initiating deportation procedures against a number of "subversives." Firestone's management immediately rehired the workforce, minus those it deemed to be ringleaders, and granted a general increase in pay. These were tried and true tactics honed back home in Akron. "The result was a complete defeat for the General Labour Union at that factory," observed a colonial official with some satisfaction. Just to make sure, the company built a high fence around the property and instituted a strict surveillance over its employees,[73] again a staple of Akron-style union busting.

The strike wave and occupation had severely rattled the British authorities. A Colonial Office mandarin calculated that there had been

130 strikes in Singapore alone since the outbreak of the Second World War, but conceded that this reflected "genuine discontent with the failure of wages to follow the cost of living in spite of increased profits . . ."[74] A journalist at the *Manchester Guardian* agreed and claimed that the strikes could have been averted if the management had been willing to negotiate in good faith. The solution, the journalist believed, was to legalize trade unions and create mechanisms for the conciliation of disputes.[75] In fact, a bill was introduced into the colonial legislature later in the year with precisely that intention.[76] At the same time, the authorities claimed to see a Japanese connection behind the strikes, and clamped down hard on known Japanese "agitators," some 1,000 of whom were rounded up and placed in detention prior to deportation to Hong Kong and Amoy. The Chinese Government made urgent representations to ensure that the deportees were not delivered into the hands of the Japanese and their "puppets."[77]

Myth of the "Mild Hindoo" Shattered

The wave of strikes by Indian estate laborers in 1941 shattered the stereotype of "the mild Hindoo." While Tamils had launched sporadic industrial action over the years, including a wage dispute at Ramsden's Sabrang estate in 1912,[78] and numbers of "undesirables" had been deported to India,[79] in general they had been comparatively subdued. If the Klang strikes in Selangor province in 1941 came as a shock to the planters, they also caught Malaya's Communists napping. The local MCP branch was rebuked by the Party's central committee for failing to foresee or involve itself in the upsurge and thus missing an opportunity to extend the Party's influence beyond the Chinese community.[80] The Tamils moved separately into industrial struggle after the massive Chinese strike wave of 1940 had died down. We should note, too, that whereas the planters were represented by powerful industry lobby groups (the Rubber Growers' Association and the United Planters' Association of Malaya), the Indian laborers lacked any semblance of trade union organization until the strikes actually started. Although the Central Indian Association of Malaya (CIAM) included the furtherance of the interests of the laborers among its aims, it had a mainly middle-class, North Indian leadership.[81]

The epicenter of the strikes was in the Klang district of Selangor Province, with its chief town at Port Swettenham on the Straits of Klang

to the west of Kuala Lumpur. The stoppages began at the Demansara
Estate,[82] on March 17, 1941 when four laborers were arrested for allegedly intimidating the others into ceasing work.[83] As a Colonial Office report
noted, there were actually three consecutive strike waves. The first broke
out early in the year and was inspired by the desire for parity in wage rates
with Chinese plantation workers and by widespread resentment that
despite a vast increase in profits since the Depression, wage cuts had not
been restored.[84] The synchronicity of the strikes with similar demands
was made possible by the formation of a new illegal workers' organization,
the Klang District Indian Union, by two "agitators" called Y. S. Menon
and R. H. Nathan (whom the British described as members of the Indian
National Congress with "strong socialist sympathies").[85] Further support
came from the Indian Communist R. K. Thangaiah and the CIAM's Mr.
Raghaven. The strikes were successful in that the Indian laborers were
granted a general wage increase to sixty cents a day for men and fifty cents
for women, although this still fell short of the rates paid to their Chinese
counterparts.[86]

The second wave broke on April 16 and was not directly wage-relat-
ed. The Colonial Office considered the motives political and that, "[t]he
underlying cause of the strikes was probably the fact that the earlier strikes
had given the labourers an idea of their power and their victory had gone
to their head." The workers demanded the right to wear "Gandhi hats"
and fly Congress flags in their compounds, and wanted the abolition of
the custom of coolies having to dismount from their bicycles if they met a
planter's car on the roads.[87] Such "insolence" outraged the High
Commissioner, Sir Shenton Thomas, who told CIAM leaders, "the strike
was a disgrace to the Indian community" and a "politically inspired . . .
challenge to authority." Nevertheless, Thomas downplayed the significance of the affair by claiming that "the men will soon get tired of the new
fashion" of Gandhi caps. Sounding like the Wodehouse character Bertie
Wooster, he claimed, "It is the custom of India to dismount from a bicycle when meeting a superior . . . just as we take off our hat to a lady."[88]
Arguably, the laborers were demanding to be treated with respect, and
this collided with the racist stereotyping common among planters and
British officials. Puzzled that "their" Tamils had become unruly, the
British police blamed the whole situation on "agitators." They reasoned,
"if they could get rid of them, the rest of the labour force would be perfectly contented."[89]

The Third Strike Wave

High Commissioner Sir Shenton Thomas ordered the arrest of Nathan and Thangaiah, whom he blamed for leading the Tamils astray. In the monochrome world of racial stereotypes common to men of Thomas's rank and class, it was inconceivable that "the mild Hindoo" could act without outside influence. There is evidence that he had already decided to arrest the agitators before the start of the second wave of strikes but was waiting for the most opportune moment to act and thus behead the strike movement. The laborers, however, were incensed by the arrests, which added to their growing list of unresolved grievances. After his deportation to India, Nathan listed the strikers' demands as follows:

- Pay parity between Indian and Chinese [laborers]
- Removal of "brutal" Ceylonese and Malayili staff and replacement with Tamils
- Proper education for children
- An end to the molestation of laborers' womenfolk by Europeans and "black" Europeans
- Proper medical facilities
- Closing of toddy shops
- Freedom of speech and assembly
- Free access to estates for family and friends
- Laborers to remain mounted on bicycles in front of European and Asian staff
- Abolition of 10–12-hour days
- No victimizations
- Permission to form associations to represent their interests[90]

These were scarcely trivial matters. A new spirit of solidarity and a deep yearning to be treated with dignity had swept through the Tamil coolie lines. The laborers' demands were a mix of classical trade unionism with nationalist aspirations and the desire for what we today would call human rights. The arrests reignited the movement and drew in wider groups who had held aloof from the first and second waves. At its height, the strikes involved over 20,000 laborers from close to one hundred estates. Young militants fanned out on bicycles to spread the message of revolt over the 1,500 square miles affected. Police inspector Bagot concluded they were "the best organised and most widely spread strikes

among Indian labourers that Malaya has yet encountered."[91] The historian H. E. Wilson later argued that had there been even better organization,
the disturbances could have been pan-Malayan in scope.[92]

High Commissioner Shenton Thomas was full of the patrician direct-
ness common among upper-class Englishman in the colonies. Sir Robert
Menzies, the grand old man of Australian conservatism, considered him
"compact, brisk and I should think efficient," unlike the usual "tropical
service Englishmen."[93] For a man like Thomas, the place of the Tamil
laborer was at his master's gate. His attitude toward Asian people was
shown in 1942 when the Japanese invaded Malaya. He is reputed to have
said to the army commanders, "Well, I suppose you'll shove the little men
off." The Tamils' "insolence" infuriated him, particularly as the strikes
were affecting vital war production. Even then, he might have temporized,
as some colonial officials advised and as the Government of India
demanded. He could have released Nathan, recognized the laborers'
union, and appointed a conciliation commission. Instead, he sent in the
military. The commander of Australian troops stationed nearby declined
to be involved in civil disturbances, so Thomas relied on Indian soldiers
under the employ of British officers.[94] The coolies armed themselves with
sticks, batons, stones, and "anything they could find," complained
Thomas. They cut down telephone wires in some instances. On May 15,
1942, a frightened assistant barricaded himself in his house on a Klang
rubber estate. The military arrived and opened fire, killing three demonstrators outright and injuring another two, one of whom later died of his
wounds.[95] When the echoes of the shots died away, five strikers lay dead
and a further sixty were wounded.[96] The strikers gradually flooded back
to work.[97]

The government and planters prevailed, but Thomas had overstepped
the mark. It had been a moral defeat for British power. Indian nationalist
opinion was outraged by the shootings, British politicians were demanding explanations, and the Government of India was considering what sanctions it could bring to bear on the administration in Malaya. At the urging
of the Colonial Office, the FMS Government appointed a Commission of
Inquiry into the disturbances. Thomas was furious; he claimed such a
course could only lead to a recrudescence of militancy.[98] The initiative
was, however, out of his hands and the Commission, presided over by a
Malayan Supreme Court judge and a European judge from India, was critical of his handling of the crisis. The planters and officials, however, soon
had more pressing concerns. The Japanese invasion came shortly after-

wards and as a Colonial Office mandarin noted, "This document is now only of historical importance but the issues raised by speakers in the debates will be heard again if we re-occupy Malaya [and] still more if Indian troops play a large part in the re-occupation."[99]

Syndicalism and Nationalism

In both Malaya and Indochina, the struggles of the rubber workers were to combine economic with revolutionary nationalist political demands. The Vietnam plantations remained strongholds of the underground Communist movement over thirty years later during the Second Indo-China War.[100] The same picture was broadly true of the relationship between the Chinese rubber workers and the MCP, which endured until the period of the "Malayan Emergency" when the Party launched guerrilla war against the British. As for the Indian laborers, they too wanted independence from Britain. A police spy noted that a secret meeting of the Sepang (Selangor) Indian Association at the Sungei Pelek plantation in 1941 resolved to:

> Unite & work for independence, Give their lives for independence. . . . ALL INDIAN labourers should be instructed not to help the BRITISH in present war. They should not retreat when they are confronted with troubles. They should work in the same way as IRELAND did when she gained her independence.[101]

It is interesting to speculate what might have happened in Malaya had the Japanese not invaded. Class solidarity might have overcome entrenched ethnic divisions, and the plantation laborers might have united in a multi-ethnic political-industrial movement to challenge the planters and British rule. After the invasion, the plantations ceased production and many Chinese coolies fled to the jungle as guerrillas or squatter-farmers. Tragically, Indian estate laborers made up a large proportion of those whom the Japanese deported to work and die on the infamous Burma Railway. After the war, Malayan politics crystallized into the three-way communalist pattern that continues to this day.

The brief Japanese occupation of Southeast Asia had far-reaching consequences. The planters returned in the baggage train of Mountbatten's armies—or were released from Japanese prisons and concentration camps.

The coolies returned to the lines, and the masters to their bungalows. The rubber estates were brought back into production. The encroaching jungle was cut back, and the rusting machinery was oiled and restarted. Freighters again plied the seas with their cargoes of block, biscuit, and sheet rubber. Eventually, the Malayan workers were to form an enduring union: the National Union of Plantation Workers. But the world had changed. A huge synthetic rubber industry had emerged in the Allied countries to compete with the natural product. The returning colonialists were confronted by determined independence fighters, many of them former rubber workers, and within the space of a decade and a half, most of the countries of the colonial world had achieved independence.

RUBBER HAS A DISTURBING HISTORY. As an essential and profitable industrial commodity, corporations and private firms have been willing to use brutal methods to obtain assured supplies of raw rubber at low prices. And still we have not yet plumbed the depths of the brutality and avarice to which men were willing to stoop to get it. We must now turn our attentions to Europe during the Second World War, when a fanatical and lawless regime was murdering countless human beings in order to guarantee an assured supply of rubber. At IG Farben's Auschwitz synthetic rubber and oil plant, the Nazis soaked the Silesian soil in blood. In the Auschwitz rubber plant and the nearby experimental Kok-Saghyz farm, human corpses were regarded as waste products.

The Nazis' Allied opponents, too, were reminded of the crucial place of rubber in a modern economy when the lightning advance of the Japanese armies into Southeast Asia cut off their supply of natural rubber from Sumatra and Malaya. The solution for both sides in the conflict was to launch colossal projects to build synthetic rubber plants. The Allies, however—in the west at least—used free labor, whereas their opponents preferred slaves. Adolf Hitler was well aware of the need of an assured rubber supply and made it central to the Four-Year Plan that his government launched in 1936 to put Germany on a war footing. The west muddled through, wedded to the free market, with the more farsighted among the politicians and captains of industry battling complacency and dogma, and an obstructive secretiveness on the part of one major corporation that verged on treason. Had the farsighted not prevailed, the outcome of the war might have been very different.

PART FIVE

Synthetic Rubber, War, and Autarky

CHAPTER SEVENTEEN

The Long Road to Monowitz

The mass production of synthetic rubber must also be organized and achieved with the same urgency. From now on there will be no talk of processes not being fully determined and other such excuses. It is not a matter of discussing whether we are to wait any longer; otherwise time will be lost and the hour of peril will take us by surprise.

—ADOLF HITLER, 1936[1]

The Chemist

The middle-aged man who stares into the camera lens is well-fed and groomed, his darkening blond hair and mustache neatly trimmed and combed. He probably smells of soap and aftershave. He looks intelligent— if a trifle pedantic—and used to being in charge, so the situation he finds himself in is clearly uncomfortable for him. But he looks pleasant enough and so in fact his U.S. military warders found him to be. He speaks with a soft South German accent, and is educated and polite. These attributes might explain the slightly bewildered, perhaps embarrassed air with which he holds the card with his name neatly lettered on it against the breast of his tweed coat. He doesn't match any of the conventional visual criminal stereotypes: he could be a professor or a well-to-do businessman and a good Christian gentleman. And, in fact, he was all three.

Herr Doktor Otto Ambros—he insisted on the use of his title at his trial—was one of twenty-three top IG Farben executives who found themselves in the dock at Nuremberg in 1947 charged with using slave labor and plundering the occupied nations of Europe. He was one of thirteen convicted. Like many of his co-accused, he was a brilliant man and had he lived in a different time and place, we might perhaps honor his memory. His theoretical work, which helped make possible the development of magnetic recording tape in 1932,[2] would alone have assured him a place in the annals of science.

In 1926, he had joined IG Farben as a twenty-five-year-old chemist and established a reputation as a talented researcher and administrator. Recognizing the young man's promise, the Nobel laureate Richard Willstätter took him under his wing. Whether from cowardice, prejudice, or expediency, Ambros did not protest when Willstätter was driven out of IG Farben and into foreign exile during the anti-Semitic purges after Hitler came to power in 1933.[3] Perhaps Ambros rationalized the incident in some way; a British intelligence officer described him as "an adroit wriggler."[4] With hindsight we can see that the incident was a significant milestone in Ambros's and IG Farben's moral decline. Interestingly, Ambros was an old school friend of Reichsführer Heinrich Himmler,[5] the head of the SS, with whose fortunes those of Ambros and IG Farben were entwined.

Ambros also came to the attention of another company bigwig, who sent him on an extended trip to the Far East. "It was," Ambros later recorded, "the climax of my life when Dr. [Fritz] ter Meer sent me to the forests of Ceylon and the Malay States, to study how nature produces rubber." Afterwards, Ambros rapidly climbed the company ladder and was entrusted by ter Meer with the development of Buna (synthetic rubber).[6] By 1935, he was the driving force behind IG Farben's Buna program and chairman of the company's Committee for Rubber and Plastics.[7] In 1941, by his own admission, he first visited the Auschwitz concentration camp. There he discussed the plans for a massive new synthetic rubber plant with the commandant, Rudolf Höss, who was later to share hunting trips and convivial Christmases within sight and smell of the crematoria with Ambros's colleague Walter Dürrfeld. Although he probably never personally abused a prisoner, as director of the Auschwitz Buna plant Dr. Ambros bears full responsibility for the crimes committed during the construction of that factory.

Whether he ever secretly felt remorse is doubtful, given his public utterances; the best a character witness could offer was that like a "good Christian" Ambros had been "distressed" when the Monowitz church was demolished to make space to house IG Farben's forced laborers.

When confronted at his trial, he said repeatedly, "I was just a chemist" and insisted that "I still do not understand why I am here."[8] Two years later, despite ample opportunity for reflection and repentance in his cell in Landsberg Prison, "Dr. Ambros stated that he could not regard himself in any way guilty" because "what he had done [he] had done in the line of duty and what he had been accused of had been done over his head and without his knowledge."[9]

The Nuremberg war crimes court had not agreed. Ambros was convicted of enslavement and plunder and sentenced to eight years' imprisonment. The American prosecutor later complained that the IG Farben sentences "were light enough to please a chicken thief, or a driver who had irresponsibly run down a pedestrian."[10] Nor did those convicted serve their full term. Ambros was released in 1951 and achieved prominence as an industrial consultant in both his native country and the United States. When he died at Mannheim in 1990 at the age of eighty-nine, he had enjoyed a long and privileged life, save for his short period of imprisonment. He had never known the privation, hunger, unbearable cold and damp or the miseries of chronic, untreated illness inflicted on people working in the factory that he designed. He had never been forced to work at giddy heights in all weathers without a safety harness. He had never been beaten, starved, humiliated, and worked beyond the limits of physical and psychological endurance like the slaves at Auschwitz, dying in droves in the process. He had stood the old maxims that "virtue is its own reward" and "the wages of sin is death" on their heads. In contrast, a number of survivors of the "extermination through work" program at Monowitz committed suicide, among them the writers Primo Levi—himself a chemist—and Jean Améry (Hans Mayer), who left chilling records of their time in the factory and associated concentration camp.

•

Napoleon once observed that an army marches on its stomach. Over a century later, Adolf Hitler knew that the mechanized army he planned to subjugate Europe with would have to roll on pneumatic rubber tires. By the early twentieth century, rubber had become indispensable for a myriad of military uses and was one of a handful of raw materials essential for the industrial power that underpinned military might. In 1911, during the Amazon rubber boom, J. Orton Kerbey, the American consul at Pará, wrote:

THE DEVIL'S MILK

> The product is necessary for our civilization, and a war, blockading the
> Amazon and creating a rubber famine, would cripple the electric age, which
> depends upon rubber for insulation of telegraph and telephone wires,
> motors, lights and railroad air brakes; to say nothing of the increasing
> demand for bicycle and automobile and other tires, belting and packing for
> machinery, roofing, flooring, clothing and its use in the arts etc.[11]

The consul's prophecy of rubber famines created by military blockade
was soon vindicated.

Rubber Famine in Germany, 1914–1918

Soon after the outbreak of the First World War, Germany lost its colonies
in Africa and the Pacific. This meant an abrupt halt in the shipments of
rubber from German plantations in New Guinea and East Africa.
Production had been modest, but Germany needed every kilogram of rubber it could lay hands on, given that its enemies controlled the bulk of the
world's wild and plantation rubber production. Britain also ruled the
waves, despite prodigious efforts by the German High Command to catch
up with the Royal Navy. This superiority enabled the Allies to protect their
own merchant shipping and impose a crippling naval blockade on the
Central Powers, whose warships and freighters were bottled up in port for
most of the war. Theoretically, Germany might expect to be able to count
on supplies of plantation rubber from the neutral Dutch East Indies, but
Allied naval commanders regarded such cargoes as contraband.

By 1918, German industry was dangerously short of vital raw materials
despite strict rationing and prohibition of the use of rubber for nonessential, non-war-related purposes. The rubber shortage was so desperate that
Germany sent submarines to Baltimore and Connecticut to break the
British blockade and fetch modest cargoes of rubber, much to the outrage
of the British government.[12] While these stunts might have boosted
German morale, they only highlighted the nation's industrial weakness.

With no domestic sources of natural rubber, the government turned to
the chemical industry, which had begun experimenting with synthetic
substitutes before the outbreak of war. The Bayer chemists Fritz
Hofmann and Carl Coutelle had already succeeded in synthesizing a rub-
ber-type substance from coal tar in 1909. A year later, the company began
small-scale commercial production, although the product was largely of

novelty value and could not compete in terms of price and quality with natural rubber. Still, the results were encouraging enough to warrant further research and development. Bayer presented Kaiser Wilhelm with a set of tires made from synthetic rubber, mounted on a Daimler car. It was not the best time to seek markets, however, for just before the outbreak of the war the price of rubber fell drastically as the Far Eastern plantations began production. That might have been the end of the story, but wartime shortages provided the impetus for further research and made synthetic rubber an attractive commercial proposition.

After experimenting with byproducts of grains and potatoes, the industry settled on limestone and coal as the basic raw materials. The result was poor stuff compared with natural rubber. It could be used for car tires, but they became sticky in hot weather and brittle during cold. Still, Bayer's scientists persisted as the effects of the Allied blockade intensified. By dint of trial and error, the quality improved. Toward the end of the war, the company produced three basic types of rubber: H (hard rubber), which was adequate for casings of U-boat batteries, magnetos, and wireless sets; W (soft rubber), which was a poor substitute for natural rubber in car tires; and B-rubber, which was suitable for electrical insulation. Technical difficulties meant that wartime production never rose beyond 150 tons per month, and it took up to six months for the rubber compound to coagulate into useable form. Still, by the end of the war, Bayer was building new synthetic rubber plants with a capacity of almost 8,000 tons per annum. Commercial production halted after the Armistice when the synthetic product was once again forced to compete with natural rubber.[13]

An Austrian Corporal Draws Conclusions

Under the terms of the Treaty of Versailles, Germany was assigned sole blame for the war and was stripped of its colonies and large tracts of its own territory. The Treaty also demanded massive reparations from Germany, and forbade the country to maintain a standing army of more than 100,000 men or a navy of any size. The Armistice and Treaty of Versailles were bitterly resented by Germans and especially by the returning veterans. Among the streams of discharged German soldiers was Adolf Hitler, a young Austrian who had served as a corporal in a Bavarian regiment on the Western Front. Back in his adopted city of Munich,

Hitler gravitated toward the lunatic fringes of politics, the proto-fascist militias and mystical nationalist political movements, from which he formed the Nazi Party.

Even as he was building up the Nazi Party to overthrow the Weimar Republic, Hitler was thinking ahead to the coming war. The lessons from the First World War were clear. If Germany lacked vital natural raw materials and was dependent on others to supply them, the coming war would repeat the failure of the first. He was an early convert to the new ideas of *Blitzkrieg* (lightning war) and mechanized warfare. The war machine would rely on efficient and well-supplied German industry. Hitler was an admirer of Fordist technology[14] and vowed to build a solid economic foundation for his imperial dreams. In the words of Jeffrey Herf, he was a "reactionary modernist."[15]

The war machine would rely on two key commodities Germany was not naturally endowed with: oil and rubber. Steel was also vital, but it was more easily obtainable. The Allies had stripped Germany of her colonies, and German-owned plantations in the territories of her rivals would be subject to sequestration in the event of war. In order to wage the coming war, Germany had to make itself self-sufficient in those vital raw materials, regardless of the normal laws of capitalist economics.

The IG Farben Octopus

Before he came to power in 1933, Hitler had already decided on a policy of autarky or economic self-sufficiency, at least for vital raw materials that were not naturally present in Germany. He turned to Germany's foremost industrial combine, the Frankfurt-based IG Farben—*Interessen Gesellschaft Farbenindustrie* or the "Dyestuffs Trust"—to put his plans for war into action. One of the key components of the giant company was the Bayer firm, which had been responsible for Imperial Germany's wartime synthetic rubber program. By the late 1920s, IG Farben was the largest corporation in Europe and smaller on a worldscale only than General Motors, U.S. Steel, and Standard Oil of New Jersey.[16] In 1939, "the nominal capital of this huge concern was Reichsmarks (RM) 720 million"[17] and it was the largest chemical company in the world, controlling over half of Germany's prewar chemical production, with monopolies and near-monopolies over a number of key products. It was also prewar Germany's "largest single source of foreign exchange. Its exports greatly exceeded its imports, and its income from dividends, royalty payments, and sale of patents outside Germany was considerable." Like many other Transnational Corporations (TNCs), IG Farben was coy about the real extent of its empire and took pains to camouflage the extent of its overseas operations.[18]

IG Farben was a powerhouse of managerial and scientific expertise: the foundation of its strength was its formidable "research and technical know-how," which it "protected by aggressive patent tactics."[19] The company's board was made up of ruthless men, many of them brilliant chemists, including Dr. Carl Bosch and his hard-nosed successor, Professor Dr. Carl Krauch. At lower levels, the company employed what the writer Joseph Borkin described as a "scintillating range of scientific talent."[20]

After his accession to power in 1933, Adolf Hitler forged a close partnership with the corporation; this was central to his plans for war. In a survey of IG Farben's role in 1945, the U.S. intelligence officer Hyman Ritchin concluded that without the company, Hitler would never have been able to wage war for as long as he did. Hitler's legions swarmed over Europe, ferried in vehicles fueled to a large extent by IG Farben's synthetic petrol and rolling on tires made from the company's Buna.

Bayer had been engulfed by the IG Farben octopus in 1925, and although it had abandoned commercial production after the Armistice, research continued on technical issues. One of these was the inordinate length of time involved in production: soft rubber had to be stored in barrels for up to six months before it could be used. During the interwar years, IG Farben's chemists were able to cut this down to a matter of a few days. Some of their product's other problems appeared insoluble—poor resistance to low temperatures, difficulties of adhesion, and the tendency to build up heat under working conditions, for instance—but it did have some decided advantages over natural rubber. It was superior to the natural product in its resistance to abrasion, petrol, oil, and other corrosive liquids, making it eminently suitable for applications such as lining aircraft fuel tanks.[21]

There were some other breakthroughs during the 1920s. Researchers had been wedded to the idea of reproducing a synthetic product based on the chemical composition of the "real thing" rather than seeking to reproduce the qualities of rubber from different ingredients. As with many scientific breakthroughs, the discovery of an acceptable rubber substitute was largely accidental. In 1923, Julius Nieuwland, a Belgian-American

Jesuit and professor of chemistry, synthesized a superior rubber-like substance as a spin-off of his research into poison gases. The new substance
could be polymerized into synthetic rubber much faster than the older
products, and its suitability for vulcanization overcame problems of stick-
iness and brittleness. The DuPont corporation began commercial production of the new synthetic material they called "Du Prene" at their New
Jersey plant in 1931. It was comparable and in some respects superior to
natural rubber for the manufacture of automobile tires. It was, for
instance, densely waterproof and resistant to sunlight and chemicals.[22]

During this period, partially spurred by artificial shortages of natural
rubber created by the Stevenson Plan, there was new interest in USSR
and Germany in synthetics, known as "Sovprene" and "Buna" respectively, but essentially the same as the U.S. product.[23] By the end of the 1920s,
the technical problems had been largely solved through a process using
coal and limestone to produce calcium carbide, which was converted into
acetylene gas and then polymerized into synthetic rubber by treatment
with hydrochloric acid. The only barrier to large-scale production was its
cost. However, advocates of the new product were convinced that the
price would drop if large plants were built to allow for economies of scale.

The Nazification of IG Farben

Although IG Farben was dominated by patriotic German gentlemen, not
all of them were enthusiastic Nazis from the beginning. Carl Bosch, the
chairman of the board, for example, was known for his coolness toward
the National Socialists, although this may have stemmed from patrician
contempt for the unsavory Nazi street brawlers. From Hitler's point of
view, the company was suspect because it was "riddled" with Jewish managers and researchers. During the last days of Weimar, Nazi propagandists
had attacked the company as a bastion of "Jewish international finance
capital" and lampooned it as "Isidore G. Farber" and "IG Moloch." Some
of the company's leading figures were indeed Jews, including the Nobel
Prize–winning chemists Fritz Haber and Richard Willstätter.

Aware of the growing electoral support for the Nazis, Bosch's fellow
directors trimmed their sails to the Nazi winds. What clinched it for them
was their fear of a possible seizure of power by the growing German
Communist Party. Bourgeois gentlemen such as Carl Bosch put their
scruples aside to work with Hitler, who they viewed as a bulwark against

the greater evil of Communism. A number of employees who were already Nazi Party members were promoted to senior executive positions, including the "racial geographer" Heinrich Gattineau, who was put in charge of the company's press office in 1931. His promotion illustrates the growing convergence between big business and the Nazis.[24] During the dying days of Weimar, IG Farben joined Krupp, Thyssen, Siemen, and other leading industrialists in donating generously to the Nazi coffers. According to the IG Farben executive Georg von Schnitzler, the company's subventions to the Nazis and other parties of the extreme right amounted to around 400,000 Reichsmarks in each of the elections leading up to 1933. They gave a further donation of 400,000 Reichsmarks to the Nazis alone in February 1933. IG Farben's donations to the Nazi Party exceeded three and a half million Reichsmarks in 1933, seven and a half million in 1939, and peaked at almost thirteen and a half million marks in 1942.[25] They were to reap rich rewards as a result: between the outbreak of war in 1939 and 1943, IG Farben's sales soared to over RM 3.1 billion, with net profits of some 300 million "despite steeply rising taxes."[26]

Carl Bosch Meets Hitler

In 1932, the patrician Carl Bosch had a fateful meeting with Adolf Hitler. For Germany's tycoons, striking a deal with the Nazis was painful but necessary. For his part, Hitler knew that IG Farben would be indispensable in his plans to make Germany supreme in Europe. Like many sociopaths, Hitler could be charming when it suited him. Bosch was impressed by Hitler's knowledge of the technology involved in producing IG Farben's synthetic rubber and his grasp of the political-economic realities involved in Germany's defeat in the First World War. Hitler sketched his plans to make Germany self-sufficient, and Bosch, as a patriotic German and as a businessman bent on making profits, complied with him.

However, when Bosch remarked that the removal of prominent Jewish scientists from their work at IG Farben might set back German science by a century, Hitler screamed: "Then we'll work a hundred years without physics and chemistry!" before storming from the room.[27] The message was clear: politics trumped science and economics, regardless of the cost. The Party's anti-Semitism was not negotiable.[28]

When the Brownshirts came to power the following year, many of the company's top executives joined the Nazi Party. Party recruits included

292 THE DEVIL'S MILK

Heinrich Bütefisch, a leading chemist and researcher into synthetic gasoline, who accepted an *Obersturmbannfuehrer*'s (colonel's) commission in the SS and would later become one of the top IG Farben executives in the Monowitz plant at Auschwitz in Poland. The company's Jewish employees were laid off and many left the country. Fritz Haber, for example, died in exile in Basel in 1934 and Otto Ambros's mentor Richard Willstätter left for the United States. The company also took the opportunity to suppress and purge its workforce of left-wing militants and the factory walls were "plastered over" with the Nazi slogan *Arbeit Macht Frei* (Work Brings Freedom).[29]

By 1935, Hitler and IG Farben were on the road to war. According to the testimony of Rudolf Höss, the commandant of Auschwitz, IG Farben representatives visited the Dachau concentration camp outside Munich as early as 1935 to investigate the use of prisoners as forced laborers.[30] Later, a number of IG Farben executives would claim at their Nuremberg trials that they only reluctantly and belatedly cooperated with the Nazis, but their claims are at variance with the facts.

Blueprint for Autarky and War: The Four-Year Plan

IG Farben's Buna was a vital raw material for the war machine Hitler was building in defiance of the Treaty of Versailles. In mid-1936, Hitler drew up the blueprints for a Four-Year Plan that aimed to make Germany ready for war by the end of the decade. Public works schemes would be expanded, in particular the construction of Autobahns, under the centralized coordination of the Todt Organization; agricultural production would be boosted; armaments production would be massively stepped up; and, "with iron determination," Germany would become 100 percent self-sufficient in vital raw materials, especially metals and synthetics.[31] The Plan stitched together the major areas of Nazi policy. "The Final Solution," Hitler wrote, "lies in the extension of our living space, and/or the sources of the raw materials and food supplies of our nation."[32] His goal with Germany's autarky was predicated on expansion to the east.[33] He wrote:

> There is no doubt by now we could have been completely independent of
> foreign countries in the fields of fuel, crude rubber and partly also iron ore
> supplies. Just as we produce 700,000 or 800,000 tons of gasoline at the pres-

ent time, we could be producing 3 million tons. Just as we produce several
thousand tons of synthetic rubber, we could already be producing 70,000 or
80,000 tons per year . . .[34]

The Four-Year Plan was officially launched on October 18, 1936, at
Hitler's mountain retreat at Berchtesgaden in the Bavarian Alps.[35] It was
placed under the supreme control of Minister President Hermann
Goering, although Economics Minister Hjalmar Schacht was initially
given an important role. Both the military and the economy were to be "fit
for war" within four years, although the goal was actually achieved earlier.
The Plan was to have expired in 1940, but in practice Goering's "Office
of the Four-Year Plan" continued until its mission of permanent economic warfare was taken over by Albert Speer in 1942.

Farben Anxious to Oblige

Critically for IG Farben, Hitler's plan specifically drew attention to the
need for the mass production of synthetic rubber and oil regardless of
production costs.[36] IG Farben was anxious to oblige, and threw its enormous industrial capacity and technical and managerial know-how into the
race. Even before the plan, in early 1936, the company had set up an
experimental unit to produce synthetic rubber in the Rhenish town of
Ludwigshafen and followed this up with the establishment of a larger pilot
plant at Schkopau in Saxony at the end of the year. By early 1937, Farben
was turning out Buna at the rate of approximately 5,000 tons per
annum.[37] It was of such good quality that the rubber was awarded a Gold
Medal at the Paris Exposition of 1937, where it was exhibited in a pavil-
ion designed by Albert Speer.[38] Thereafter, the production of Buna
climbed steeply. The British War Office estimated that IG Farben's plants
were producing around 55,000 tons per annum when the Schkopau plant
came into full production at the end of 1939 and 70,000 tons when the
Hüls plant in the Ruhr was opened in late 1941. By late 1943, when a new
plant was completed at Ludwigshafen, the company was turning out rubber at a rate of over 100,000 tons per annum, despite temporary setbacks
caused by Allied bombing.[39] Rising from perhaps 1,000 tons in 1936,
German synthetic rubber production rose to almost 20,000 tons in 1939,
about 40,000 in 1940, and around 75,000 tons in 1942. By 1944 it had
soared to around 100,000 tons.[40]

In 1935, IG Farben explored the possibilities of using concentration camp inmates as forced laborers. By 1940, the company entered into agreements with the SS for the use of slave labor, and negotiations were under way for a massive new synthetic rubber and gasoline plant at Monowitz, near Auschwitz in occupied Polish Silesia. The project was to be one of the darkest chapters in the history of rubber. For reasons of greed, expediency, and conviction, IG Farben's executives moved into the inner circles of the hell created and run by Himmler's SS. Had Hitler won the war, the "vision of the future" would have been identical to that of Orwell's image of "a boot stamping on a human face forever."[41] The boot's synthetic rubber sole would have been courtesy of IG Farben.

Natural Rubber Famine after 1939

In 1940, the Western democracies controlled about 93 percent of the world's production of natural rubber.[42] Around 77 percent was from plantations in British Malaya and the Netherlands East Indies,[43] with smaller amounts from French Indochina[44] and elsewhere. Germany's enemies also consumed the bulk of the world's supply of natural rubber. The United States imported more than half and Britain over 13 percent. Before 1939, Germany consumed less than 8 percent of the world's natural rubber production.[45] After 1939, Germany's imports of natural rubber dried up except for several tens of thousands of tons which were railed across Siberia to the Reich from the Soviet port of Vladivostok courtesy of the Stalin-Hitler Pact.[46]

Although the Allies lost control of the Far Eastern plantations after the Japanese invasion of 1942, this did not result in a diversion of production to the Axis industry. The Japanese lacked the manpower, management, and technical skills to exploit the plantations, and strategic military imperatives caused them to divert much of the plantations' Asian workforce to immediate practical needs such as construction of the Burma railway. Nor could Japanese ships pass the Allied blockade, and the Far Eastern plantations lay largely untouched until after the Japanese surrendered in 1945.

British Foreign Office analysts concluded that "Germany should be suffering from a severe shortage of rubber soon after the first year of the war," with a probable deficiency of between 50,000 and 60,000 tons. They estimated Germany's prewar net consumption of crude rubber from all sources at 130,000 tons per annum and that Germany had entered the war with a total stockpile of 50,000 tons. They calculated a maximum recoverable amount of 20,000 tons "from cars laid up owing to petrol rationing."[47] Germany, therefore, might face a similar situation to that during the First World War, when the government was reduced to such desperate measures as sending submarines to the U.S. to buy small amounts of rubber. However, Hitler's decision to expand Buna production had paid off: by 1944, the Buna plants were turning out over 140,000 tons per annum,[48] and the war machine carried on despite dwindling stocks of natural rubber. In late 1941, German tires contained an average of 37 percent natural rubber, but this declined to around 8 percent in February 1943.[49] In 1940, the planners' eyes had turned east for a suitable site for a massive factory close to raw materials and labor, and as far as possible from the threat of Royal Air Force (RAF) bombs. The long road to Monowitz was nearing its end.

CHAPTER EIGHTEEN

Monowitz: "A Bulwark of Germandom"

[Locating the Buna plant at Auschwitz will] fulfill a high moral duty and contribute to building a firm cornerstone for a healthy and powerful Germandom in the East.[1]

—OTTO AMBROS

Before the outbreak of war, IG Farben considered a number of possible sites for the new Buna plant. Rattwitz, near Breslau in Lower Silesia, initially appeared to be the best choice,[2] and the firm began preparatory work there for a new plant in 1940.[3] Auschwitz, on the other hand, lay in Upper Silesia within occupied Poland, and although it was close to ample supplies of raw materials and on a main railroad line, its disadvantages at first seemed to outweigh its advantages.

The Town of Auschwitz

Auschwitz lies at the confluence of the Sola and Vistula rivers, approximately halfway between the Polish university city of Kraków and the industrial city of Kattowitz.[4] The region around Auschwitz was part of Austrian Silesia until 1918 and its population in 1939 was ethnically mixed. Out of a total of 13,000 inhabitants, 7,000 were Polish, 4,000 were Jewish, and 2,000 were Germans.[5] From IG Farben's point of view, Auschwitz's greatest disadvantage was its lack of an adequate pool of local

The IG Farben synthetic rubber plant (the Buna) under construction
at Monowitz during World War II.

skilled workers. However, Auschwitz had distinct advantages from the
standpoint of economic geography and Nazi geopolitical theory. Upper
Silesia had been incorporated into the German Reich after the invasion of
Poland, the Upper Silesian coalfields had double the reserves of those in
the Ruhr, and the type of coal from the mines at nearby Fürstengrube and
Janinagrube was ideal for the carbide process needed for making Buna.
Large deposits of limestone were also locally available, and the Vistula
River and its tributaries guaranteed the supply of the large volumes of
water needed for synthetic rubber production. Finally, there was ample
flat land above the level of the Vistula's spring floods for the site of a large
factory just outside the town.[6]

According to German accounts, Auschwitz was a scruffy little town
before the Nazis marched in. The IG Farben engineer Max Faust said that
in the beginning it was "a miserable dirty hole,"[7] and a Belgian interpreter
later told the British that many of the company's engineers preferred to
drive the seventy kilometers or more round trip from Kattowitz or
Gleiwitz each day.[8] Chief engineer Walther Dürrfeld, a fanatical Nazi who
held a commission in the SS, sneered that in the beginning, "The 'town'
of Auschwitz was not a town in the usual German way of seeing things."[9]
There were not enough houses and they were not fit for Germans, he
complained. The fact that Auschwitz soon became a vast chamber of horrors did not endear it either, and IG Farben had to pay its German civil-

ian employees generous bonuses to compensate for relocating there.[10] In the end, IG Farben agreed on the site because it feared that the state might step in to build and run the proposed Auschwitz plant and thus potentially cost them billions of marks in profits.[11]

"Historical Destiny"

The driving force behind locating the factory at Auschwitz was Heinrich Himmler, SS *Reichsführer* and Chief of the German Police. After the invasion of Poland in 1939, Hitler appointed him "Reichskommissar for the Reinforcement of Germandom in the East," charged with the assimilation and what would be known to later generations as the "ethnic cleansing" of the former Polish territories. The claim that Germany needed *Lebensraum* (living space) in the east was a central tenet of Nazi geopolitical ideology, and after Hitler himself, no other Nazi leader was as fanatical about it as Himmler. "Fanatics have their dreams," Keats once observed, "wherewith they weave a paradise for a sect."[12] Himmler's dream was of hardy "Nordic" pioneers colonizing vast swathes of land stretching to the steppes of Central Asia. The grandiose work was to start in Upper Silesia where some seventeen new German towns were to be built to house hundreds of thousands of settlers.[13] Central to the plan was a huge new factory complex around Auschwitz,[14] which Himmler hoped would drag the center of gravity of German industry eastwards and eclipse the Ruhr. *Ostexpansion*, he claimed, was Germany's "historical destiny."[15] The decision to relocate in Silesia also reflected conflicts within the Nazi hierarchy. The involvement of the SS in the assimilation of Upper Silesia would enable Himmler to expand the economic arm of the SS, the *Wirtschaftverwaltungshauptamt* (hereinafter the WVHA, or in English, the SS Business Administration Main Office) at the expense of the Four-Year Plan's boss, Hermann Goering.

Otto Ambros's "high moral purpose" and "cornerstone for Germandom" was to be steeped in the blood of slave laborers. The WVHA was a gigantic "system of slavery and murder" directed by Oswald Pohl, a former Navy paymaster who was personally appointed by Himmler. Pohl was to develop the doctrine of "extermination through work," which was to be epitomized in the industrial slave complex at Auschwitz.

Slave labor was the Nazis' solution for the labor shortage in Upper Silesia. In 1935 IG Farben had investigated the use of concentration camp inmates at Dachau as slave laborers and, after the outbreak of war, IG Farben and many other German businesses rushed to take advantage of the sudden appearance of large numbers of prisoners of war and other captives as laborers in their factories. While this was done partly because of the Nazis' genocidal ideology, it also dovetailed with practical necessity. Millions of male German workers, including many with valuable industrial skills, were conscripted into the armed forces, and Nazi anti-feminist ideology meant the regime was reluctant to replace them with women. The SS was only too keen to hire out prisoners as slave laborers for big capital. By 1944, there were about 700,000 slave laborers in the Nazi empire, and IG Farben's workforce expanded by over 45 percent during the first four years of the war.[16]

The "High Moral Duty" at Monowitz

Ambros and his staff began serious investigations into the Auschwitz site in late 1940[17] following assurances by Himmler that the nearby town would be emptied to make room for German families. The SS would expel all Jews and Poles from the town of Auschwitz and replace them with German colonists. These would be the advance guard of what the WVHA planners foresaw as a model German city of 40,000 inhabitants.[18] The IG Farben executives also noted the presence of the nearby concentration camp as a source of unpaid labor for the project.[19] Heinrich Bütefisch announced that he had floated a new company to exploit the coal deposits at Fürstengrube, some eight miles from the town center.[20] Himmler appointed his chief of staff, SS *Gruppenführer* Karl Wolff, to liaise directly with IG Farben on all matters relating to the Auschwitz plant,[21] and Rudolf Höss, the Auschwitz camp commandant visited, existing Buna plants to familiarize himself with requirements. Himmler himself visited Auschwitz in March 1941 and outlined his grandiose plans for the region. He brought an entourage including the local Nazi Gauleiter Herr Bracht and all the high police and SS officers of Silesia, along with high executives of IG Farben. According to Rudolf Höss:

> The intention of the *Reichsführer* was that Auschwitz was to become one immense prison-cum-munitions centre. What he said during his visit in March of 1941 made this perfectly plain. The camp for 100,000 prisoners, the ear-marking of 10,000 prisoners for the synthetic rubber factory, all of

this emphasised the point. But the numbers envisaged were this time something entirely new in the history of concentration camps.[22]

Auschwitz was to become the center of the armaments industry of the
entire Reich and the concentration camp was intended to hold 30,000
prisoners even after Germany had won the war.[23]

The Buna Site

At IG Farben's request, the SS drove local Polish farmers from their land
without compensation to prepare the way for the new Buna site. The site
lay on flat land about five miles from the Auschwitz concentration camp
and about three miles from the town center, near the Dwory railroad station on a spur of the main Kattowitz-Kraków line, and extended as far as
the village of Monowitz.[24] Work on the new site began in March 1941.[25]
Overseen by Karl Bischoff, an old Nazi who had fought with the *Freikorps*
after the First World War,[26] concentration camp inmates dug foundations
and leveled the ground for roads. The work continued throughout the
spring, summer, and autumn and "despite the extraordinarily bad winter
of 1941–42," chief engineer Walther Dürrfeld noted with satisfaction,
foundation work, concreting, sewer lines, and roadwork had been completed. By the spring of 1942, work was "well advanced," on the power
station, the carbide plant, the acetylene gas plant, and the works railway
station.[27] It was, Dürrfeld enthused, "a bulwark of Germandom thrown
up against the East."[28]

IG Farben made an initial investment of over 330 million
Reichsmarks.[29] The company also received government tax writeoffs of
over 60 million Reichsmarks paid in advance.[30] The plant that took shape
was much larger than IG Farben's existing Buna factories in Germany proper. According to Borkin, when the Auschwitz plant was fully operational, it
would have furnished three-quarters of its output for military uses[31] and
consumed more electricity than the city of Berlin.[32] By 1944, the plant
employed tens of thousands of slave and civilian workers and was fringed
with concentration and POW camps and civilian workers' barracks. British
wartime analysts believed that the workforce at any one time was in the
region of 17,000,[33] but subsequent estimates run as high as 29,000.[34]

However, the construction schedule had fallen behind in mid-1942
and this, coupled with the effects of Allied bombings and the inefficien-

cy of slave labor, meant that the plant never played the role the Nazis
hoped in the German war effort. As more than one former inmate later
recalled with satisfaction, the Auschwitz plant never produced as much
as one pound of rubber[35] despite the monumental efforts of the Nazi
engineers. Preventing the factory from starting production was essential
from the Allied point of view. In 1942, an RAF intelligence officer noted
that the Auschwitz area was becoming "the most important war arsenal
in all the Axis territory," and that the Buna plant "ought to be flattened
even at great risk."[36] Although the Allies bombed the plant on a number
of occasions, work continued intermittently until the Red Army had
advanced into southern Poland in 1945. As Primo Levi wrote, only at the
very end, when "the ravaged Buna [lay] under the first snows, silent and
stiff like an enormous corpse" with the Russians fifty miles away and
"three of the four acetylene gasometers . . . blown up"[37] did the Nazis'
"iron determination" flag.

CHAPTER NINETEEN

The Only Way Out Is Up the Chimney

As I am no longer a man, my body will be burnt as excrement, as planned.
Everything is programmed in the Auschwitz principality; everything ends up
in the crematorium chimney.

—WILLI BERLER, Monowitz slave laborer[1]

Nor could our treatment be considered exactly slavery. For throughout history it was in the slaveowners' interest to keep their slaves alive. The Nazis had no such motivation, since in reviving the custom of slavery they did it with the difference that they *wanted* their slaves to die. After all, they were never threatened with a shortage of forced manpower.

—SIM KESSELL, Jaworzno colliery slave[2]

Farben's site engineer Max Faust ordered that "the Jews in Buna must be assigned only the most menial tasks and compassion . . . [will not be] tolerated."[3] The English prisoner Leon Greenman watched an off-duty SS man cuddling a pet and mused how "men could care for rabbits while their human brothers were dying from their wounds, hunger and lack of kindness."[4] The colliery slave Sim Kessell noticed two young SS guards

who were sincerely amused by our appearance—not particularly hostile or even insulting. They just gazed at us as if we were clowns in a circus. They knew perfectly well what awaited us, but it had no meaning . . . they obvious-

ly considered us broken-down robots, still-breathing carcasses who must
now be disposed of.[5]

For the SS and IG Farben, the corpses at the Buna plant were mere
"waste material"[6] in an essential war project that doubled as a disposal
center for political and "biological" enemies. Although the SS and IG
Farben destroyed many of their records, it is clear that several hundred
thousand slaves labored on the Buna production between 1942 and
January 1945.[7] Joseph Borkin estimates that 25,000 slave laborers were
worked to death at the Buna plant.[8] An estimate of the mortality at
Monowitz is much higher; according to one statement at Nuremberg,
370,000 were killed.[9] As the SS camp physician at Monowitz, Dr.
Friedrich Entress, later admitted, "The turnover of inmates in Monowitz
was enormous. The inmates were weak and malnourished. It should be
emphasized that the performance demanded of the inmates was not in
accord with their living conditions and nutrition."[10] It is also certain that
the IG Farben management were aware of the role of Buna production in
this Nazi principality of death. The American prosecutor at Nuremberg
put the welter of statistics into human perspective when he said that the
construction of the main factory chimney at Monowitz cost 300 lives: a
life for every foot of its height.[11]

The Monowitz survivors included a number of men who bore eloquent witness to the suffering of their fellows. Foremost among them was
Primo Levi, the master of modern Italian prose. In the spring of 1944 he
was arrested in his native Turin after taking part in an abortive partisan
operation, and found himself aboard the cattle car of a train chugging
north across the Alps toward Monowitz. Others who recorded their experiences at Monowitz included Willi Berler and the French boxer Sim
Kessell. Berler arrived on a transport of 1,600 prisoners from Mechelen
in Belgium: a journey that was brightened by a daring train hold up by
three Belgian Communists who, armed only with a revolver and a lantern
covered in red paper, freed over 200 prisoners.[12] The Austrian
Communist prisoner Hermann Langbein also recorded many details
about Monowitz in his monumental book *People in Auschwitz*.[13]

By 1942, occupied Europe was a vast asylum run by lunatics who
graded human beings according to racial stereotypes. The very center of
this madhouse was the Auschwitz industrial and extermination complex,
described by the Nazi doctor Heinz Thilo as *anus mundi*—the anus of the
world—a term which accurately reflects the Nazi obsession of cleansing

the world of what they regarded as human biological waste.[14] Over 1,200 of Willi Berler's consignment of 1,300 Dutch and Belgian prisoners were gassed, leaving the remaining ninety-six to trudge to Monowitz. Upon arrival at the Monowitz camp, they were stripped of their clothing and valuables, their heads were shaven, they were showered, disinfected, and issued with the camp clothing: coarse shirts and trousers in blue and white vertical stripes, insufficient to keep out the biting Silesian wind and changed only once every six to eight weeks. Next, they were tattooed with identifying numbers on the outside of the left forearm. The same needle was used for all prisoners without any concessions for hygiene. Willi Berler received the number 117,476, Primo Levi 174,517, and Leon Greenman 98,288.[15] These figures give some indication of the vast numbers of prisoners involved.

Once inducted, the new prisoners were the branded property of IG Farben and the Third Reich, destined to disappear through the *anus mundi* after every scrap of value had been squeezed from them. There was no escape. As Paul Kozwara, the Silesian criminal whom the SS appointed as *Lagerältester* (camp elder) told newcomers: "There is only one way out of here, through the chimney."[16]

The Monowitz Camp

When Primo Levi arrived in the winter of 1944, there were about 11,000 inmates at the Monowitz camp, crammed into fifty wooden barracks in a square of 600 yards. Each hut contained 148 bunks arranged in three tiers, with two men occupying each bunk. When Levi arrived, another ten huts were under construction to house additional incoming workers.[17] Other camps in the vicinity housed British POWs, young Silesians earmarked for assimilation into the German nation, and civilian workers from across Europe. Rearing up behind the camp were the carbide tower, the gasometers, smokestacks, and pylons of the Buna, which occupied an immense rectangle of flat land stretching to the outskirts of the town of Auschwitz. The foothills of the Carpathian Mountains rose up to the south of the camp, visible from the *Appelplatz* or muster yard in the middle of the camp.

The Monowitz camp—also known as Auschwitz III[18]—was created in 1942, the year after work began on the Buna plant. It was originally under the command of a Bavarian SS officer named Vincent Schöttl, who was replaced by the more bloodthirsty and fanatical Heinrich Schwarz in late 1943.[19] Previously, the laborers had been marched back and forth in all weather, from the worksite to Auschwitz I, the original concentration camp. In December 2005, I walked the fourteen kilometers' return between the two camps through snow and sleet. It was not an easy journey, despite my warm clothing, well-shod feet, full stomach, and good health. As I trudged along the black waters of the Sola in the bitter cold and damp, I caught a glimpse of what it must have been like for the malnourished, overworked, and often sick slaves, clad in their thin pajamas and ill-fitting wooden clogs, driven on with shouts and blows, and the example of instant death for anyone who lagged behind. The move to the IG Farben camp at Monowitz, however, was not made because of any humanitarian scruples but simply to reduce the travel time which ate into the working day.[20]

The barracks were never a place of sanctuary after the arduous workday was over. Prussian barracks discipline was carried to the limit, and the prisoners were made to realize they were creatures utterly bereft of rights, individuality, and even the smallest personal autonomy. On his first day at Monowitz, tormented by thirst, Primo Levi stretched out his hand to an icicle hanging outside the barracks window, only to be stopped by a guard. When he asked why, the guard replied, "*Hier ist kein warum*" (Here there is no why).[21] Levi had gotten off lightly for his unwitting misdemeanor. Casual brutality was an integral part of camp life, and prisoners might be beaten to death for incurring an SS man's displeasure. A prisoner could be forced into a so-called "standing cell," a confined space in which he could not stand upright, kneel or lie down.[22] A whipping block and a gallows stood on the *Appelplatz* as warnings of the consequences of insubordination. Primo Levi was forced to watch over a dozen hangings, carried out to the strains of the camp band as punishment for such things as attempted escape, sabotage, and theft from the camp's kitchens.[23]

Deceit of IG Farben

Against all the evidence, IG Farben boss Fritz ter Meer declared that the camp was well run. Under oath at Nuremberg, ter Meer even claimed not to have noticed the SS guard towers around the perimeter of the camp when he visited in 1943.[24] Ter Meer knew that he was on dangerous ground, because while the SS were responsible for the labor supply (for which they charged the firm four Reichsmarks a head) and for discipline and security in the Monowitz camp, it was a private institution in which IG Farben oversaw the health of their forced laborers. It is true that the Monowitz prisoners were generally better fed and housed than their compatriots in the Auschwitz I and II camps, but this was only a matter of degree. Cold showers did exist at Monowitz, and the prisoners received a small ration of low-grade soap, but this was only because the inmates worked alongside German civilian workers, not because of any concern with the health of those marked for extermination. The prisoner Ronald Berger later wrote that the "Buna was an improvement on Birkenau. The barracks were neat and clean, and the bunk beds were covered with straw. Unlike Birkenau, only two inmates were assigned to each bunk. On first impression I felt that survival was possible here."[25] Berger did notice, however, that while some inmates looked well fed, others were emaciated. He soon learned that survival depended on one's ability to "organize" additional supplies of food. Jan Sehn, the Polish prosecutor at Auschwitz, said food intake at Auschwitz averaged between 1,300 and 1,700 calories per day. While forced laborers were supposed to receive 2,150 calories per day, thefts reduced this considerably. Even so, Sehn calculated a worker on light duties actually needed 3,600 calories per day and a forced laborer on heavy work 4,800 calories. According to Monowitz's prisoner-physician Robert Waitz, by October 1943 a slave's daily food intake consisted of 350 grams of bread, supplemented by twenty-five grams of margarine five days a week; seventy-five grams of semi-vegetable sausage issued five times a week; twenty grams of jam once a week; and two teaspoons of skimmed-milk cheese given out from time to time. This, Waitz estimated, was the equivalent of between 1,000 and 1,100 calories per day.[26] Even when IG Farben introduced a daily allowance of one liter of watery "Buna soup," prisoners suffered an average weight loss of between 6½ and nine pounds per week and soon resembled walking skeletons.[27]

On average, the life expectancy of a Jewish slave at Monowitz was between three and four months, although skilled workers tended to fare better than unskilled laborers. In IG Farben's coal mines at Janinagrube and Fürstengrube, the survival rate was between four and six weeks.[28] Those who could not "organize" additional food and did not master techniques of appearing to work hard while doing the bare minimum were doomed to slow death or risked being selected for the gas chambers. The water supply at the camp was unfit for human consumption and was responsible for outbreaks of debilitating diarrhea. Given the poor diet, the slightest wound could turn into a suppurating sore, and if bad enough this would be a passport to Birkenau. "Death," recorded Primo Levi, "begins with the shoes."[29] New inmates were supplied with used boots or clogs without regard to size or condition, and an SS doctor later admitted that wearing the clogs was tantamount to a death sentence. The prisoners' feet would swell with edema, forcing them to risk a visit to the camp hospital where the seriously ill were always candidates for the mass selections the SS periodically organized to weed out those deemed incapable of work. One of these caused the gas chambers to work overtime after 7 percent of the whole Monowitz camp and between 30 and 50 percent of the sick were judged unfit.[30] The historian Peter Hayes claims that selections made during the late winter of 1943 were carried out at IG Farben's instigation and that the engineer Walther Dürrfeld was present when the SS sent some 1,750 prisoners to the gas chambers.[31]

Working on the Buna

Prisoners who wre assigned to work on outside "commandos" could not expect to survive long. Willi Berler was set to work in a gang carrying huge pieces of timber. His torment was exacerbated when he was made to lump leaky cement bags on his wounded shoulders, but perhaps the worst job he had to do was on the "*Scheisskommando*" (shit detail) standing to his waist in a cesspit and filling buckets on a rope to empty it.[32] Primo Levi was initially paired up with a youth unloading steel pipes at a railway siding. Like many inmates, the boy, whom he called "*Nul Achtzehn*" (Zero Eighteen) from the last three digits of the number tattooed on his arm, had given up all hope. He made no effort to avoid accidents or work with the minimum of effort. Indifferent to what happened to him, Nul Achtzehn was doomed; he was one of the walking dead.[33] Michael Berger dug ditches and unloaded sacks of cement in a block-making plant. He was punched and kicked by the kapos to make him work harder, constantly craving food on the starvation rations.[34] Everything had to be done at the infamous "SS trot" and the work continued regardless of the weather, except when the Germans feared the prisoners might escape under cover of fog. The French Resistance fighter Sim Kessell was selected for work in the Jaworzno coal mines, some six miles from Auschwitz. A former boxer with a powerful physique, he survived his work in the mines for three months. His first month's work, he recalls, was "painful," the second "excruciating," and "by the third a kind of mad desperation had set in."[35]

The British POWs at Monowitz

As the Auschwitz Museum archivist Piotr Setkiewicz has observed, it is "baffling" why IG Farben's management agreed to use British prisoners of war for construction work on the Buna. British POWs had been used elsewhere in Upper Silesia, including at the Janinagrube colliery, but Walther Dürrfeld insisted that "they be sent away as quickly as possible" because they had no interest in producing coal for the German war effort. Nevertheless, British POWs from North Africa began to arrive in September 1943 and by the end of the year some 1,200 were held in a special compound one mile away from the concentration camp at Monowitz and employed in a variety of tasks on the Buna.[36] Better housed and treated than the concentration camp inmates,[37] the POWs insisted on being treated according to the conventions of war, and enjoyed a remarkable sense of solidarity.[38] As was the case in the Janinagrube mine, the British prisoners were hostile to the construction of a facility that was vital to the German war effort. According to former British prisoner of war Arthur Dodd's account,[39] if the POWs thought they could get away with go-slows or sabotage, they would do it and their productivity was no greater than that of the half-starved forced laborers. Indeed the POWs' "insolent" attitudes enraged the IG Farben engineers, such as Max Faust, who complained about them receiving Red Cross parcels and sharing them with German civilian workers as well as the slaves.[40] A large number of POWs died during an American bombing raid on August 20, 1944. After January 1945, the remaining British POWs at Monowitz were removed to Czechoslovakia before the arrival of the Red Army.[41]

Experimental Rubber Plants at Rajsko

A few miles from Auschwitz at the village of Rajsko the Nazis ran a large experimental plant-breeding station. The facility consisted of a cluster of glasshouses, warehouses, and laboratories, surrounded by twelve thousand hectares of cultivated fields and seedbeds. The director of this enterprise, which was run under the auspices of the SS *Landwirtschaft*

The SS experimental plant station at Rajsko near Auschwitz
during World War II.

(Agricultural Department), was Dr. Joachim Cäsar, an agronomist with
the rank of Lieutenant Colonel in the SS.[42] Cäsar had earlier made his
mark by planting a "cosmic garden" at Birkenau to screen the killing facilities from the arriving victims.[43] The main focus of the Rajsko project was
the rubber-bearing plant known as *Kok-Saghyz*, or Russian dandelion,
which had been discovered growing wild in the Tien-Shan Mountains of
Kazakhstan by Russian botanists in 1931.[44] The plant could yield significant amounts of good-quality rubber, and the Nazis believed that it could
make a significant contribution to wartime production. The Nazis had
harnessed many of Germany's leading scientists behind the quest for
alternative rubber sources, particularly via the Kaiser Wilhelm Institute.[45]
The Institute's Richard Boehme moved to Auschwitz in 1944 to continue his work.[46]

The practical possibilities of this project at Rajsko reinforced one of
the primary obsessions of Nazi ideology—agricultural self-sufficiency.
The Nazi Party's Agriculture Minister Walther Darré's aim was to make
Germany self-sufficient in "organic" agricultural produce. Darré's vision
was an integral part of the Nazis' aim of autarky and expansion for living
space in the east for a self-sustaining "racial community."[47] Thus,
although Auschwitz was to be the center of a new Ruhr in the east, it was
also a center of agricultural experimentation. Commandant Rudolf Höss
revealed that although Himmler inspected the Buna plant "minutely," the
Rajsko facility "was of far greater interest to him,"[48] which is not surprising, given the SS *Reichsführer*'s cranky biologic obsessions.

The Rajsko facility depended on the labor of several thousand female slaves.[49] Although working and living conditions were said to be better than elsewhere, and Cäsar personally was said by some inmates to be relatively humane,[50] it was all a matter of degree. The punishment for infraction of the rules was transfer to Birkenau's gas chambers. That the conditions were only better comparatively speaking than elsewhere in Auschwitz is attested to by details from the Rajsko medical register, which is full of entries indicating that many of the young women suffered ailments normally found in the middle-aged and elderly. Helene Baümgarten and Janine Trypka, for example, were both thirty-four-years old when they contracted typhus and were sent to the gas chambers. Sofia Augustyn and Rosalie Zuber were only twenty-two and twenty-one respectively when they suffered the same fate. Aurelia Kziqikowska suffered a blood disorder, was kept in the hospital for five days, then sent to Birkenau. Wanda Gora was twenty-eight years old when she developed angina and was gassed. Klara Herz, aged twenty-one, was also diagnosed with angina and sent to Birkenau. Maria Szaglai, thirty-one years old, gave birth to a child in the Rajsko infirmary on November 4, 1943. Four days later, mother and child were sent to Birkenau.[51] There is no indication of who the father was or how Maria managed to conceal the pregnancy.[52]

Attitude of Civilian Workers at the Buna

IG Farben employed many thousands of civilian workers at Monowitz, and it is inconceivable that they could not have observed the sufferings of the slaves nor been ignorant of the purpose of the Birkenau camp. In May 1944, "ethnic Germans" made up between 20 and 30 percent of the total workforce of 27,000 to 29,000 at the Buna; foreign "free" workers accounted for 40 to 50 percent; and the remaining 30 percent were inmates of the slave and POW camps.[53] According to Walther Dürrfeld, there were some 20,555 civilian employees on the worksite in the fall of 1942.[54]

Ernst Levin recalled that the civilian workers "saw the living corpses [of the slave laborers] marching daily into their territory . . . some of them nothing more than skin and bones."[55] Several survivors have left accounts of their dealings with these civilian workers, and former slaves and British POWs testified under oath at Nuremberg about the treatment of slave laborers by IG Farben management and other personnel. When Primo Levi was transferred to professional work in the IG Farben laboratories at

Monowitz in early 1945, he was shunned by his German coworkers and invariably referred to as a "*Stinkjude*" (stinking Jew).[56] The prisoners were "untouchables" to the majority of civilians, non-Germans included.[57] Sim Kessell was soon disabused of the notion that the German civilian *Meisters* (bosses) in the Jaworzno mines would treat him better than the kapos and SS men. Nor were the rank-and-file colliers much better: "These civilian German miners we'd looked forward to working with were not inclined to throw us any scraps from their meals, and seemed to find every incentive for exploiting us," Kessel recalls.[58] According to the evidence of a British POW, in one typical instance, an IG Farben supervisor set forced laborers to work carrying hundredweight bags of cement: "It took four men to lift one bag and to put it on the back of one man. When the inmates couldn't go along quickly enough to satisfy the Farben Meister, the Meister beat them with sticks and iron bars and punched them with his fists and kicked them. I have often seen them beaten to death with iron bars."[59] According to Rudolf Vrba, who deliberately entered the Auschwitz complex in order to report to the Allies on what was happening there, "there were only two kinds of workers at the Buna site: the quick and the dead." His report of the scene at Monowitz in June 1942 bears repeating:

> Men ran and fell, were kicked and shot. Wild-eyed kapos drove their blood-stained path through rucks of prisoners, while SS men shot from the hip, like television cowboys, who had strayed somehow into a grotesque, endless horror film; and adding a ghastly note of incongruity to the bedlam were groups of quiet men in impeccable civilian clothes, picking their way through corpses they did not want to see, measuring timbers with bright folding yellow rules, making neat little notes in black leather books, oblivious to the blood-bath. They never spoke to the workers. . . . They never spoke to the kapos, the gangsters. Only occasionally they murmured a few words to a senior SS NCO, words that sparked off another explosion . . .[60]

According to the testimony of Rudolf Höss, IG Farben civilian personnel mistreated the inmates, both because it was policy and of their own accord.[61] While there are reported instances of words or acts of kindness by German civilian workers, they were isolated occurrences. Jean Améry, for instance, recalls a chemicals foreman named Matthäus "who said to me with an anguished sigh on June 6, 1944 [D-Day]: 'Finally, they have landed! But will the two of us hold out until they have won once and for all?' One German shared his last cigarette with Améry and another gave him bread.[62] In contrast, Hermann Langbein, an Austrian Communist who spent many years in the camps, records the indifference and even hostility of many German civilians to the inmates. The prisoners would intently study the reactions of civilians to their misery, because they believed it relayed what the German people as a whole thought.[63]

Racial Pecking Order

The evidence suggests that by 1944 most of Auschwitz's civilian workers had become coarsened to human suffering. As the war ground on, they were themselves put on short rations of ersatz food, and this undermined whatever sympathy they may have had for the inmates. It is also a sad fact that many people will cling to whatever privileges mark them off from those around them. This was pronounced at Auschwitz. At Monowitz, recalled Améry:

> There was a strict ethnic hierarchy imposed by the Nazis on all of us. A German from the Reich was regarded more highly than a German from an eastern country. A Flemish Belgian was worth more than a Walloon. A Ukrainian from occupied Poland ranked higher than his Polish compatriot. A forced labourer from Eastern Europe was more poorly regarded than an Italian. Far down on the bottom rungs of the ladder were the concentration camp inmates, and among them, in turn, the Jews had the lowest rank . . .[64]

Piotr Setkiewicz concurs: there was a racial pecking order even on the buses delivering civilian workers to the Buna from Auschwitz, with all nationalities forced to stand for Germans of whatever age, rank, or trade.[65]

Auschwitz was considered a hardship posting for German civilians and IG Farben made substantial social contributions for its civilian workers and their families. Families with children received a subsidy of 20 Reichsmarks for the first child and a further 10 marks for subsequent children. There was an allowance for wives, which increased with the number of children they had.[66] In the beginning, Auschwitz was hardly fit for Germans to live in, sneered Dürrfeld, but gradually the amenities of life were extended, with gymnasiums, games, swimming, hiking tours, winter sports, soccer, handball, boxing, and athletics.[67] By 1943, the engineer could boast of the cultural facilities available for the civilian workers, with approximately RM 3,000 per month spent on such things as the "Strength through Joy" works library and the Works Choir. The Prague Philharmonic Orchestra visited and performed a selection from Johann Strauss. The Dresden State Theater appeared, along with the State Theater Orchestra of Kattowitz and the State Theater of Zagreb, the latter for the benefit of the Croatian civilians working on the Buna. A variety revue attracted 1,800 people to a packed hall.[68]

The IG Farben supervisory staff and management were well rewarded for resettling to what Max Faust regarded as "a miserable dirty hole." Walther Dürrfeld's salary was RM 20,500 when he first arrived, but by May 1944, with allowances, his salary stood at RM 33,000. The executives were also allocated private hunting grounds in Upper Silesia after Dürrfeld complained to the provincial governor that hunting hares around the Monowitz plant was not very interesting.[69] In 2007, the United States Holocaust Memorial Museum published what in some respects is the most shocking collection of photographs from the Holocaust.[70] Chilling in their banality, these record the SS men and women of the Auschwitz garrison at play: a group singing along to an accordion, friends eating blackberries and drinking wine, fellows joking and relaxing on a sundeck, a contingent marching grim-faced during the funeral of colleagues killed by Allied "terror flyers" who had bombed the Buna. In the midst of the misery at Auschwitz—the gas chambers and the slave laborers—civilian workers and their families appeared to live "normal" lives.

The claims by IG Farben management and German civilian personnel that they did not know what was happening around them are self-serving. An SS man testified at a later trial that "when the ovens were burning, the leaping flame was five meters high and could be seen from the railroad station. That station was full of civilians." Another witness said, "the pitch-black smoke clouds [from the crematoriums] could be seen and heard for kilometers. The stench was simply unbearable. The flames . . . could also be seen from afar." A German railway official said that the flames could be seen from a distance of fifteen to twenty kilometers "and that people knew that human beings were being burned there." They could also see columns of people marched into Birkenau by the SS. Farben office manager Georg Heydrich was told by a "shaken and tearful SS man" of the crematoriums, where people were sometimes cast alive into the flames.[71] Christian Schneider, a member of IG Farben's Board of Directors, exposed the deceit of his fellow executives when he testified: "The smokestacks of the KZ Auschwitz were visible from the IG Auschwitz. I heard that IG people who visited Auschwitz—for example Walther Dürrfeld and other engineers—smelled the odour of burning bodies. Those gentlemen told me it was a terrible stench."[72] British POW Charles Coward testified: "Everyone to whom I spoke gave the same story—the people in the city, the SS men, the concentration-camp inmates, foreign workers. All the camp knew it. All the civilian population knew it; they complained about the stench of the burning bodies. Even among the Farben employees to whom I spoke, a lot of them would admit it. It would be utterly impossible not to know."[73] In 1944, a naïve Austrian clerical employee asked the Monowitz prisoner Ernst Levin, "What's going on over there in Auschwitz? This smell and these chimneys: what are they doing there?" "After all," Levin recalled, "when the wind was right, you smelled the corpses burning. I said to him, 'Well, those are crematoriums.'"[74] And yet if we are to believe the IG Farben managers and engineers, they knew nothing. Gustav Murr, the firm's site overseer at Monowitz, typified the response of his colleagues at the 1948 IG Farben trial at Nuremberg when he claimed that he didn't know what the crematoria chimneys were for, and that he had no idea of what happened to slave laborers after they were "sacked" for weakness.[75]

The concept of "collective German guilt" for the Holocaust remains controversial, with one writer describing the German people as "Hitler's willing executioners."[76] There is not much evidence, however, to indicate that many of the Germans and other "free" workers showed much sympathy for the slaves who worked alongside them. By 1941, when the construction of the Buna began, the German people had been inundated for eight years with Nazi propaganda extolling the supposed superiority of the Aryan race and the corresponding inferiority of Jews and Eastern Europeans. Auschwitz was to be turned into a model German town at the center of a new Ruhr in annexed Polish territory. Many of the Germans who settled in the town were attracted by the promise of material benefits and it seems likely that others were motivated by ideological conviction: the wish to "do their bit" for the "high moral purpose" of *Ostexpansion*. Others may well have been drafted to work on the Buna by the Nazi authorities. Regardless of the reasons for their going to live and work in the *anus mundi*, precious few of them showed much compassion for those who left this world via the chimneys of Birkenau or through overwork and malnutrition at Monowitz.

The Beginning of the End

Although IG Farben and the Nazi leadership had chosen Monowitz as the site of the Buna partly because it lay out of range of British bombers, the Allied armies advanced relentlessly upon the Buna after Stalingrad and D-Day. A huge air attack on August 25, 1944, destroyed the plant's acetylene production facilities.[77] The bombing continued and ensured that the production of buna "was gradually postponed until the Germans no longer talked about it."[78] Although the most fanatical of the SS and the German civilian workers clung doggedly to the belief that they would win the war, the end was drawing near for the Monowitz factory and the Nazi regime. As early as September 1944, Fritz ter Meer planned the destruction of the most incriminating of the company's files in the likely event that the firm's Frankfurt headquarters was overrun by advancing U.S. soldiers.[79] By January 1945, the continuous rumble of artillery could be heard across the Silesian plains as the Red Army front lines drew closer to Auschwitz. On January 16 and 19, Soviet planes bombed the plant and destroyed its water and gas supplies. Shortly afterwards, after burning as many of the camp records as they could, the Nazis withdrew, taking some 58,000 surviving prisoners with them on a death march deep into Germany. Only a handful of the very sick and those who managed to hide were left behind, some 650 in total.[80] By midday on Saturday January 27, the first Russian, soldiers had arrived at the Monowitz camp. Primo Levi describes their arrival:

> They were four young soldiers on horseback, who advanced along the road that marked the limits of the camp, cautiously holding their sten-guns. When they reached the barbed wire, they stopped to look, exchanging a few timid words, and throwing strangely embarrassed glances at the sprawling bodies, at the battered huts, and at us few still alive.
>
> To us they seemed wonderfully concrete and real, perched on their enormous horses, between the grey of the snow and the grey of the sky, immobile beneath the gusts of damp wind which threatened a thaw.[81]

The young soldiers were members of a reconnaissance group of the 100th Infantry Division of the 106th Red Army Corps.[82] They had fought their way thousands of kilometers across their homeland and into Upper Silesia, but they did what they could for the emaciated creatures left behind in the principality of death, dressing their wounds, administering medicines and sharing their rations. Meanwhile, back in Germany, Otto Ambros and IG Farben's other leading men prepared for the arrival of the Allied armies, convinced that they bore no responsibility for what had been done at the Buna and prepared to lie their way out of trouble.

CHAPTER TWENTY

The Allied Struggle for Rubber in the Second World War

For more than 100 years we accepted rubber as a matter of course. We used some 35,000 products made from it, and we committed what came close to being a fatal error—we took rubber for granted. We had given little, if any, thought to rubber from the strategic angle. I suspect we didn't realize how important it was in that respect.

—CONGRESSMAN WRIGHT PATMAN
in the U.S. House of Representatives, September 28, 1943[1]

In 1942, American journalist Robert Reiss noted that the Nazis had rolled into Paris and Athens and across the Russian steppes on "inflated elastomers"—not tires made of natural rubber.[2] They were forced out of Russia, he later added, by mechanized units of the Red Army rolling "on the same ersatz equipment."[3] Hitler was acutely aware of the crucial importance of rubber for his war machine and had suspended normal market principles to develop substitutes for the natural product. Under Joseph Stalin, the Soviets were also willing to ignore commercial considerations in the country's synthetic rubber industry,[4] both for pragmatic reasons and because of Stalin's commitment to the autarky of "socialism in one country." Both the centrally planned Soviet economy and the state-directed autarky of Nazi Germany were able to mobilize and coordinate rubber production to wage total war. This was not so easy for the Western democracies; only an eleventh-hour, state-directed crash program to expand synthetic production averted a crippling rubber famine for the Allies.

In 1941, 99 percent of the American rubber industry's raw material was natural. By October 1945, this figure had slipped to only 11 percent.[5] The bulk of America's synthetic rubber was produced in state-owned factories that were then leased to the private rubber corporations. Yet this was not the "creeping socialism" imagined by some critics. It was not the nationalization of industry but a state-private partnership in which the government provided the capital and the corporations reaped fantastic profits. It also laid the basis for an expanded postwar rubber and plastics industry as part of what some writers described as the corporate welfare state, or the massive subsidization of the corporate sector by the taxpayer, a form of state-directed capitalism.[6]

At the outbreak of the Second World War in 1939, Great Britain controlled just under half of the world's natural rubber supplies. The bulk of this supply was from the Malayan plantations, which accounted for some 39 percent of world production. Dutch Sumatra accounted for another 38 percent; so taken together with the neighboring colonies they produced over three-quarters of the world's rubber.[7] By far the bulk of this was consumed in North America: the United States took 52.3 percent; the United Kingdom 13.1 percent; Germany 7.9 percent; France 5.3 percent; Japan 5.3 percent; the USSR 2.6 percent; and Italy 2.0 percent.[8] The United States imported 95 percent of its rubber from the "danger area" menaced by the Japanese armies, which had reached French Indochina and were poised to invade the rest of the region.[9] The U.S. Department of Agriculture *Yearbook* for 1927 noted America's reliance on foreign rubber from a vulnerable region, warning that "[o]ur dependence on foreign rubber would place us in a critical condition if supplies were restricted or interrupted, as might be the case, in the event of war."[10] This was an echo of Consul Kerbey's words two decades earlier when he warned against the danger of a wartime rubber famine.[11]

Battle against Insouciance

In 1939, the British merchant marine carried much of the rubber to the industrial centers of the northern hemisphere. They were protected by the Royal Navy, and Singapore stood as an apparently impregnable fortress athwart the Straits of Malacca. The U.S. Pacific fleet, based at

Pearl Harbor, was another bulwark against possible Axis expansion. Even President Franklin Delano Roosevelt did not realize the crucial importance of rubber for the coming war. He believed that the Allies would quickly crush the Japanese and that existing stockpiles of rubber would be sufficient for a short war.[12] Many British leaders shared his views, as did numerous opinion makers, as exemplified by an article that appeared in the June 29, 1940, edition of *The Magazine of Wall Street*. "Revolution in Rubber?" it asked. It replied: "Probably, but no near term famine in the natural product is indicated [and] prospects for new products . . . would seem to lie considerably in the future."[13] On the eve of the Japanese invasion of Malaya, an internal British Colonial Office report advised against building synthetic rubber plants, arguing that Henry Ford's Fordlandia plantations in Brazil could provide the Allies with sufficient rubber to replace any that might be lost in Southeast Asia. A handwritten annotation suggests that the author based his assessment on an article in *Reader's Digest*.[14]

The Geneva Bourse, however, was pessimistic, reporting a steep fall in rubber share prices in July 1941 triggered by Japan's imminent southward thrust.[15] Around the same time, public opinion makers in the Allied camp slowly awoke to the seriousness of the situation; the influential American journalist I. F. Stone spoke for many when he demanded to know whether America was "to wait until Japan seizes the Dutch East Indies before trying to increase synthetic rubber production?"[16]

In early June 1940, BF Goodrich President John Lyon Collyer staged an effective public relations stunt at the Waldorf-Astoria Hotel in New York. "Ninety-seven percent of our crude rubber . . . is coming from the Far East," Collyer informed his guests. "Ordinarily it travels the short route by way of the Suez Canal and the Atlantic." On a screen behind him, a model steamship was traveling across a painted ocean, bound for the United States. Just as he said "the sea lanes were precarious," there was a sharp "pop" and the little ship blew up behind him. "On the clock of history," he concluded, "it was already getting late." Shortly afterwards, Collyer testified before the Senate Committee on Military Affairs, where he called on the government to commence building two new synthetic rubber plants to increase production to the one million ton mark.[17] Collyer estimated that in October 1940 the United States had only a four months' supply of raw rubber, plus another three months' worth aboard ships en route from the plantations, and another four months' worth in finished goods.[18]

Although Collyer recognized that federal government intervention was needed for the immense task of planning, building, and coordinating synthetic rubber production, this smacked of socialist heresy to many Americans. Robert A. Solo, in a lengthy report for the U.S. Congress, noted: "We had neither the habit, the values, nor the competence for collective choice and action. . . . The prerogatives of individualism [were] surrounded with an aura of sanctity."[19] This dogmatism went to the very top: President Roosevelt was reluctant to fund the construction of the factories and believed that the rubber companies should do it themselves.[20] It was the catastrophe at Pearl Harbor, combined with the Japanese victories in Southeast Asia, that brought home the truth. Solo insisted the rubber problem could only "be resolved at the level of public action,"[21] not by leaving so important a matter to the vagaries of the free market.

The IG Farben– Standard Oil Cartel

There were other serious obstacles to be overcome. While John Collyer and the rubber company executives were willing to cooperate with the government to harness U.S. industry to win the war, other industrialists placed their own patents and profits first. The powerful farm lobby campaigned to ensure that it too got its "share of the action" regardless of patriotic or strategic considerations.[22] While that lobby's strength was considerable, it doesn't fully explain why America's synthetic rubber capacity was so small.

The U.S. rubber companies had developed commercial-grade synthetic rubber by the end of the 1930s. In 1938, BF Goodrich marketed a synthetic product that was particularly useful for gasoline and oil hoses. In 1940 they put their Ameripol synthetic tires on the market, claiming that the decision was not just a commercial matter but one of national security. Goodrich also provided the market with Koroseal, a fire-resistant product suitable for electrical insulation, especially aboard warships. The other big rubber companies developed similar products.[23]

However, Goodrich ran afoul of Standard Oil of New Jersey,[24] which, since its beginnings in 1870 under J. P. Morgan and the Rockefellers, had epitomized robber baron capitalism.[25] In 1929, when Standard Oil was one of the world's three largest multinational corporations, it had formed a cartel with Germany's IG Farben to carve up the world's synthetic rubber and chemical markets. The two megacorporations had negotiated a division-of-fields agreement that gave the German firm supremacy in chemical markets around the world outside of the United States and granted Standard Oil worldwide supremacy in the world's oilfields outside of Germany. Standard also secured patent rights for the Buna synthetic rubber process outside of Germany. However, the corporation was only interested in producing Buna S rubber from oil wastes and refused to grant other U.S. firms patent rights to manufacture the superior Buna N type rubber from other raw materials.[26] A web of cross investment linked the two giant firms: IG Farben was the second largest shareholder in Standard after the Rockefellers, and this propinquity had been increased by the formation of the jointly owned JASCO (the Joint American Study Company) in 1930 under a rotating chair system.[27]

Whether this collusion with the Nazi-run corporation was intentional or merely naïve is a matter for debate, but as Robert Solo pointed out, Standard Oil was not dealing with a "free agent" in its relations with IG Farben. After 1933, the German corporation acted as "an instrument and agency for the policies of the Nazi government,"[28] and even before the Nazi seizure of power it had thrown its support behind Hitler. It is clear that Standard Oil deliberately put its own commercial advantage before the interests of the nation in the looming war against the Axis powers and ignored the deadly partnership between Farben and the Nazis in their drive to war.[29]

Standard Oil held the U.S. patents for the IG Farben processes to produce superior grades of synthetic rubber from coal and grain alcohol, but was reluctant to license production to other manufacturers. Indeed, they were willing to go to great lengths to prevent this from happening. For example, during the rubber emergency period of 1941, Standard Oil served notice of patent infringements on Goodyear and the BF Goodrich subsidiary Hycar,[30] claiming they had stolen its—or Farben's—technology.[31] A Goodrich report countered that while "[m]any have the erroneous belief that . . . [synthetic rubber] 'know-how' came from Germany . . . Hitler saw to it that no such information left [the country]."[32] Shortly after this incident, Thurman Arnold of the U.S. Justice Department blasted Standard Oil at a session of the Truman Congressional Committee, blaming the nation's shortage of synthetic rubber on the corporation's cartel with Farben.[33] In fact, American rubber companies had been trying without success for the best part of a decade to obtain licenses and technical know-how from the German corporation. Goodrich's president, James D. Tew was fobbed off when he visited the Farben headquarters in 1936 and

1937. The firm's leading scientist, Dr. Waldo L. Semon, was shadowed by the Gestapo when he visited Germany.[34] Firestone's Swiss branch manager, however, gained entry to Farben's Leverkusen plant in 1938[35] and warned that Germany was gearing up for a war the United States was unprepared for.[36] At the same time, Farben's U.S. subsidiary, Chemnyco, carried out industrial espionage to discover whatever it could about the U.S. synthetic rubber and chemical industries.[37] Even when the other U.S. rubber firms won the rights to produce Buna rubber without consulting Farben, Standard imposed "onerous royalty terms [and] limitations on [its] use and sale."[38]

In 1944, an article in *The New Republic* magazine ran a fiercely critical piece on Standard Oil's role in blocking production of the superior butyl rubber (which was practically leakproof for tire inner tubes and other applications) until 1943. "Most accounts," the author wrote, "have assumed that Standard was either under some strange form of commercial hypnosis, or that Farben took advantage of Standard's ingenuous ignorance of cartel methods." However, the writer continued, "from all the visible facts . . . it is more logical to assume that Standard was just not interested in making rubber, but only in retaining the monopoly rights." The writer added that many of IG Farben's U.S. patents were held by Standard Oil's patent attorney W. E. Currie "for safekeeping" and that the corporation had "refused to pledge that it . . . [would] not join up with Farben [after the war], although it has been specifically requested to do so by minority stockholders."[39] If, as Joel Bakan has argued, the behavior of corporations often resembles that of pathological individuals, then Standard is surely a case in point.[40]

The Hopkins Audit

In June 1940, the looming crisis finally prompted President Roosevelt to empower his advisor Harry Hopkins to audit the nation's rubber reserves. Hopkins concluded that the U.S. had rubber stockpiles only for five to six months—much of it from reclaim—"crap" in the indelicate language of the trade—and recommended the formation of a government 'rubber reserve' company to coordinate its accumulation and use.[41] In July 1941, the lawmakers passed the Rubber Supply Act, which would have committed the country to the production of rubber from grain alcohol and sidelined coal and oil as raw materials. Later in the month,

Roosevelt vetoed the act[42]: he had finally realized that rubber from coal and oil was a better proposition. The agribusiness lobby continued stubbornly to press for the expansion of guayule farms as a major part of the rubber program.[43] According to a wildly optimistic article in the New York *Daily News*, for example, "Guayule, desert shrub, can yield 25% of rubber needed in [the] U.S."[44] The dispute was settled when FDR's "Rubber Tsar," William Jeffers, ruled that the land could be better used for food production and could not produce the volumes of rubber needed for the war effort.[45]

Baruch and "Bull" Jeffers

The figure in the United States's expansion of the synthetic rubber industry was a technocrat and former banker named Bernard Baruch.[46] In August 1942, President Roosevelt put him at the head of a three-person Rubber Survey Committee charged with assessing the state of the nation's rubber industry and recommending measures to ensure that enough rubber could be provided for victory. In September 1942, the Baruch Committee came to the alarming conclusion that:

> Of all critical and strategic materials, rubber is the one which presents the greatest threat to the safety of our Nation and the success of the Allied cause . . . if we fail to secure quickly a large new rubber supply, our war effort and our domestic economy will collapse.[47]

President Roosevelt also created the Office of Rubber Director with wide powers over technical research and development as well as the purchase, sale, requisition, stockpiling, and manufacturing of rubber. While this was scarcely socialism, as some free marketers claimed it to be, it did amount to centralized state direction of the industry. Its success bears out Robert Solo's observation that some things can only be achieved through public action (although the profits remained strictly private). Roosevelt's first Rubber Director was the flamboyant William M. "Bull" Jeffers, the president of Union Pacific Railroad. Although Jeffers "knew nothing about rubber and said so," he studied the Baruch Report closely and warmed to his new job. He was said to have

Marched out of his home city [Omaha, Nebraska] behind a brass band and high-stepping drum majorette, and arrived in Washington accompanied by his secretary and a personal publicity expert whose salary was reported to be more than that paid to the President of the United States.[48]

By 1943, a huge new industry had been created by the Roosevelt government to reach Baruch's target of 1 million tons of synthetic rubber. Production soared from 40,000 tons in 1942 to 900,000 by the end of 1943, which meant that within two years the United States had "duplicated the capacity of the entire world's natural rubber plantations."[49] The synthetic program cost more than $750 million, according to BF Goodrich.[50] Fifty-one new factories were built between 1942 and 1945, when production of Buna S reached 1,230,000 tons.

The synthetic program was coupled with strict rationing. Tire rationing was not lifted until December 1945 in the United States. The Allies also banned or restricted the manufacture of a vast number of nonessential rubber products. A list of rubber products restricted by the British authorities included: "Artificial flowers, baby drawers or pants, badminton shuttlecocks, golf bags, sports balls, toy balloons, billiard table cushions, dog biscuits, door buffers, pencil erasers, pacifiers, sink plugs, [and] tap [faucet] washers."[51] Jeffers imposed a 35 mph speed limit on all road traffic to conserve tire rubber. By 1944, not much rubber was available for essential domestic items, prompting an American schoolgirl named Diane Berntzen to demand of the Rubber Administrator:

> When are you going to give us that elastic you promised. My panties fell down . . . at school and all the kids lauffed [sic]. I betcha Mrs. Roosevelt's panties don't fall down cause she is our President's wife and I betcha you give her all the lastic she wants . . .[52]

The Allies also scoured the world for whatever other rubber they could find. Firestone's Liberian plantations were greatly expanded, with almost 5,000 additional acres of hevea trees reaching maturity each year.[53] On May 12, 1942, the Vargas government[54] of Brazil signed a Rubber Agreement with the United States, that provided that the United States would get all of the country's wild rubber in excess of Brazil's domestic needs. The United States purchased the rubber at the fixed rate of 39 cents per pound with a bonus for rubber in excess of 10,000 tons exported.[55] Brazil would deploy 100,000 men—about the same number employed in the Akron war factories—to harvest 50,000 tons of wild rubber every year.[56] The United States underwrote the program with a $100 million subvention, but it was only modestly successful: Brazilian wild rubber production increased by 1944 to slightly more than half of the total in the peak production year of 1912.[57] The Brazilian venture was not without an element of buffoonery. According to one account, William Graham, the executive in charge of U.S. operations, "spends part of his time collecting monkeys and rare birds" and much of the energy of his 200 direct employees—including machinists, carpenters, and welders— was spent on his private projects: "foreign jobs" in workers' argot. The reporter alleged that a carpenter spent a whole Sunday making cages for Graham's menagerie, for which he earned a week off on full pay from his boss. Another worker was employed stenciling winged alligators on Graham's yacht. Graham lived in an opulent mansion and chartered the Manáus opera house to watch American movies. It was little wonder, grumbled the reporter, that the United States received only "a fraction of the rubber expected."[58] This was despite the mobilization of some 50,000 Brazilian "rubber soldiers" who were transplanted, often against their will, from Ceará to the Amazon basin to tap the heveas.[59]

Further agreements were reached with other Latin American countries including Panama, Colombia, and Mexico,[60] as well as with Portugal for wild rubber from West Africa.[61] Landolphia vines were once again exploited in French Equatorial Africa[62] And poor-quality wild rubber was once again collected after a forty-year break in Papua and New Guinea.[63] In 1943, the Shada Corporation,[64] which appears to have been a subsidiary of the United Fruit Corporation, floated a scheme to plant several million rubber-bearing cryptostagic vines on 100,000 acres near Gonaives in Haiti. Critics assailed the Shada project for its dependence on cheap labor, and for taking land away from food production[65]; and the scheme died because of the hostility of the Haitian government and people[66] who had already suffered decades of U.S. occupation and meddling.

So great was the hunger for rubber that in 1943 the Australian government ordered planters to begin "slaughter tapping"[67] on hevea estates in New Guinea to increase output,[68] as did Firestone in Liberia.[69] Somewhat farcically, in 1942 some former Far Eastern "old hands" cooked up a scheme to smuggle raw rubber from occupied Singapore from under the noses of the Japanese.[70]

The Allied rubber program was a colossal operation, without which the war could not have been won. Even then, stockpiles often fell to dangerously low levels and Harvey Firestone Jr.'s boast to the Economic Club in Detroit in 1944 that "the rubber crisis has been licked"[71] was a trifle complacent. Production only caught up with demand in the second quarter of 1944 and six months later, during the Battle of the Bulge, the U.S. stockpile had dwindled to between 80,000 and 90,000 tons, much of it "crap." Following the D-Day landings in the summer of 1944, a journalist observed that "[a]ll estimates of the army went out the window after the breakthrough in France . . . [for] we had outrun our supplies . . . at one period they were ruining 5,000 tires a day, and that was only one of a half dozen similar lines. It was then that the crisis of rubber became acute. It is still acute and will keep on that way until we finish off the Japs. . . . Rubber was the original great problem of the war and will continue to be one until the end."[72] Frank Chalk concludes his study of the U.S. wartime rubber industry with the observation that "only the stockpiling of rubber in the United States before the fall of the Dutch East Indies and the mushrooming of synthetic rubber production in 1945 saved the country from military paralysis in the last year of the war."[73]

The synthetic rubber produced by this immense effort was used for tens of thousands of military and industrial purposes. It was superior for some applications to the natural product. The Rubber Manufacturers' Association considered that Buna S had "remarkable resistance to oxygen, [and] tear and abrasion" and was almost immune to most chemicals including concentrated nitric and sulfuric acids, along with oils and greases. The downside was that it had less bounce than natural rubber and that the first synthetic tires performed only 50 percent as well as natural tires due to a heat buildup in the carcass, which caused them to spread under load.[74] As we have seen, Buna N, or butyl rubber, was of a much superior quality but the manufacture had been restricted because of the patent wrangles of Standard Oil. American scientists displayed great ingenuity in making up the shortfall: Goodrich scientists succeeded in producing a good quality rubber from mushrooms,[75] and others produced lactoprene rubber from the lactic acid in milk combined with molasses, starch, and other carbohydrates.[76]

One use synthetic rubber was particularly well suited for was the internal self-sealing linings of aircraft fuel tanks. Before this was developed, aircraft would swiftly become "flying coffins" if bullets hit their tanks. Another was slip and flame resistant coating on battleship decks.[77] BF Goodrich also developed a rubber that, unlike other elastomers, acted as an electrical conductor rather than insulator. This was useful in drain-

ing off static electricity from machinery, gasoline pump nozzles, power
tools, and aircraft tires.[78] Goodyear's medical director, H. R. Conn, developed a pneumatic tourniquet which did not break blood vessels and was
effective in the prevention of gangrene.[79] Other rubber products mass
produced for the war effort included run-flat and divided rim tires, which
were fitted to almost a million trucks and artillery pieces; over one billion
belt links for machine guns; gas masks; hundreds of thousands of plastic
rifle butts; countless steel helmet liners; battery cases for walkie-talkies;
foamex mattresses for military hospitals; rubberized life vests and belts;
rubber rafts; tank tracks; filler for aircraft wings; lighting buoys; inflatable
boats and pontoons (including for the D-Day landings in 1944); barrage
balloons; oxygen cylinders for high-altitude flights; rubber filament mosquito netting; rubber pup tents; special tires to enable aircraft to land in
snow or mud or on aircraft carrier decks; and even pneumatic dummies
of artillery pieces and other weapons designed to deceive the enemy.[80]
The enormous demand can be visualized by the statistics of military aircraft and truck and bus tires. The British firm Dunlop produced enormous amounts of rubber products for the war effort, including the bulk of
the 32.7 million vehicle and 47,000,000 bicycle tires made by British
industry, along with 600,000 aircraft tires and six million pairs of rubber
boots.[81] This output was dwarfed by U.S. production. In 1939, the
American military purchased 33,000 aircraft and 7,680,000 truck and
bus tires; in 1941, the figures were 170,000 and 11,148,000 respectively;
and by 1944 these had jumped again to 1,417,000 and 14,627,000. The
U.S. military also wore out 45,000,000 pairs of rubber boots and shoes,
along with 127,000,000 rubber soles and 181,000,000 rubber heels in
1943 and 1944 alone.[82] This war production relied almost totally on synthetic rubber. We should not forget the human cost of war. One example
is the Akron researchers' pioneering use of unvulcanized rubber to camouflage soldiers' faces disfigured by war wounds. These included false
ears and noses that could be removed at night for the comfort of those
fated to wear them.

The wartime profit bonanza for the American rubber companies,
which operated in factories paid for by the U.S. government, was
immense. This is illustrated by the story of the run-flat tire. When the
British firm Dunlop allowed U.S. rubber firms to use its invention, the
Americans modified it and then tried to sell the manufacturing rights back
to Dunlop![83] Such behavior was in stark contradiction to the attitude of
the American working class. As William Green, the president of the

American Federation of Labor, declared: "We need no longer pledge that free labor will outproduce slave labor. The workers of America are already doing it. They have broken every production schedule. They are setting new records every day. They are producing the weapons of war in literally unheard of quantities."[84] It is to the contribution of the American workers that we shall now turn.

CHAPTER TWENTY-ONE

War Is Good for Business

> Government promises to . . . curb the high cost of living, company war-time profits and management's salary hikes have not been kept. The no-strike pledge of our union has therefore boomeranged on us.
>
> —URWA Local 5, Akron, Ohio, September 1944[1]

> [Goodyear] has gone back to their old 1936 and 37 way of driveing [sic] the members out of the Union, the same old thug gang has quit working and just gang up in the plant and cuss and abuse the members until they are driveing [sic] them from the plant faster than we can get them in the Union, the ones that have guts enough to defy the thugs, the Company will get them out by either fireing [sic] them or makeing [sic] life so miserable . . . that they will either walk out or work a notice and quit.
>
> —Union steward at Goodyear's Gadsden plant in Alabama, June 1941[2]

In his poem "Questions from a Worker Who Reads," Bertolt Brecht famously reminds us that although the history books credit the great monuments and cities of antiquity to kings, the kings did not "haul up the lumps of rock" for their construction.[3] Similarly, in books dealing with America's mammoth synthetic rubber project during the Second World War, you will find the names of the politicians, generals, and captains of industry. Industrial "kings" like Paul Litchfield did not actually build the great towers and factories that sprouted across America. These tasks were carried out by ordinary men and women, whose efforts in the U.S.' wartime industrial project helped vanquish the Axis powers. As the URW's Sherman Dalrymple reminded listeners in a prewar radio broadcast: "Labor is the foundation of all civilization."[4] From their taxes and war bonds, the American people provided the government with the finance it needed to build the new synthetic rubber plants. As Eric Hobsbawm has written, "collectively, if not as individuals, such men and women are major historical actors. What they do and think makes a difference. It can and has changed culture and the shape of history, and never more than in the twentieth century."[5]

Mushroom Farm of a Community of Giants

There are some records of what it was like for American rubber workers during wartime. New York *Daily News* journalist Russ Simontowne has written a vivid account of his visit to the Port Seches construction site on the Texas coast in the summer of 1943. The Port Seches plant, built with U.S. government finance, was one of three giant Buna S synthetic rubber plants on the Texas oilfields.[6] It played a major role in the race for production against the Nazis, who were building the Monowitz complex in Silesia at the same time.

Over 8,000 men toiled at Port Seches. It was one of the largest industrial projects in American history. A larger version of a pilot plant at Baton Rouge in Louisiana, it looked like "the mushroom farm of a community of giants," wrote Simontowne. There were sixty silver towers, forty-five of which were about 170 feet tall, each weighing over 225 tons. Each tower took a mere two weeks to build.[7]

Living conditions for the Port Seches workers were poor: "Even the so-called purified drinking water tastes and smells as though it were about to hatch into a chicken," Simontowne recalled. As for the housing, it was "pretty bad," he observed, although carpenters were assembling hundreds of wooden cottages on the flats. Mostly, however, the workers and their families were crammed into government-owned trailers in bleak parks adjacent to the towers. There were many hardships, including the heat and humidity, the primitive housing and the soaring cost of living, which spiraled above what their wages could buy, but the workers would have been aware that the project was essential for the Allied war effort.

Akron: Standing Room Only, Again

In Akron too, it was once again "standing room only." "Rubber's home town" was bursting at the seams with workers crammed into single rooms, sheds, rooming houses, garages, chicken coops, and trailer parks on the city's outskirts. For some, it was again a matter of occupying beds in shifts. New synthetic plants rose against the skyline, along with new factories to turn the synthetic rubber into the myriad of products necessary for the war effort. Women workers glued the joints of huge barrage balloons and inflatable pontoons. One advertisement placed by the city's War Job Enrollment Center declared that AKRON WAR PLANTS NEED WORKERS NOW! It added that:

> Women who have never done a day's work in their lives are finding new thrills in war work. Physically handicapped men and women are learning new usefulness as they help turn out the weapons of Victory . . . [8]

By late 1942, the city's plants were hiring 2,000 extra workers every week,[9] labor scouts were scouring Appalachia for workers, and men were brought in from Mexico, Jamaica, and Barbados to fill in the gaps. Members of America's persecuted Japanese-American minority were brought in to replace agricultural workers who had been drafted into the war industries. By early in the following year, the Akron workforce had swollen to 117,000, over 64,000 in the rubber plants, according to a survey carried out by the city's chamber of commerce.[10] The 1942 edition of the *Encyclopedia Britannica* said that Akron was once again a city enjoying "phenomenal growth,"[11] a startling turnaround from 1939, when the national census had revealed "a sorry picture indeed, [with] declining production figures, slumping employment totals and diminishing industrial income."[12]

In 1943, Ohio State Senator Joseph I. Ross introduced a bill to allow a general increase in working hours for women, girls, and boys. The bill also proposed to suspend penalties for violations of labor laws and to remove the right of state inspectors to monitor working conditions. Governor John W. Bricker approved a modified version of the bill a few months later despite vehement union protests.[13] Given the URW's no-strike pledge for the duration of the war, there was little workers could do in practical terms against the new legislation.

The influx of new workers generated a social crisis in the city: once again, Akron's industries had grown so fast that there was nowhere for the new workers to live. In the summer of 1943, the Goodyear Aircraft Corporation made an appeal for housing in the city's daily paper, the *Akron Beacon Journal*:

> Wanted! Any vacancy for war workers; furnished or unfurnished; houses or apartments; light housekeeping rooms or sleeping rooms. No commission charged.[14]

The previous year, an article in the *Beacon Journal* complained of trailer parks with "tiny and dingy" accommodation that violated the city's trailer ordinance. There were over 85,000 houses in Greater Akron, but only eighty-five of them were for rent at Christmastime in 1943.[15]

The price of food also rose steadily during the war years. According to figures published in the *CIO Economic Outlook* in 1942, retail food prices rose by 21 percent between March 1940 and December 1941, and there was an overall rise of 12 percent in the cost of living in the same period.[16] On occasion, food shortages, or rumors of them, led to panic buying. This even caused restaurants to run out of food to serve.[17]

War Is Good for the Rubber Business

Despite the public squalor and chaos generated by the war boom, the rubber barons managed to rake in unprecedented profits. By 1940, Firestone Tire & Rubber reported a net profit of $8.6 million, and its sales amounted to $187.2 million.[18] When the synthetic rubber program got going, the rubber companies' profits soared further. According to URW Local Union 5 at BF Goodrich in Akron, in March 1942 the employer had "amassed a net profit of 40.6 per cent over and above" the previous year. This, however, told only part of the story as a further $6 million of clear profit went into the company's contingency fund and was not distributed to stockholders. The union estimated that the company had made an after-tax profit of 138.6 percent over the previous year.[19] The *United Rubber Worker* claimed that the rubber industry as a whole had increased its profits sevenfold from $43,279,000 in 1936–39 to $307,368,000 in 1943.[20] The profit bonanza continued for the remainder of the war and into the prosperity of the 1950s.

Following the attack on Pearl Harbor in December 1941, the union's international officers imposed a no-strike pledge for the duration of the war[21] and the ban was ratified by all of the union's subsequent wartime national conventions. Sherman Dalrymple and the other officers of the union were determined that organized labor should play its part in the battle against the Axis. It was, however, often difficult to enforce the ban on the rank and file and on the more militant of the union's locals. This was particularly true of Akron, where the local unions took positions consistently to the left of the international leadership. While the workers were being called upon to sacrifice for victory over the Axis, their employers were making windfall profits and taking advantage of the no-strike pledge to avoid serious negotiations with the union, and even to undermine it. The six-hour day came under attack as early as 1940. The Akron URW official L.L. Callahan retorted that "[t]he talk that lengthening the working day is necessary for national defense is bunk. We have millions of workmen in this country without jobs. Put them back to work first. Then, if there is a shortage of labor, we will do whatever is necessary for the welfare of the country."[22] As the war dragged on and production surged, however, all available labor was absorbed and a huge shortage of workers arose. Conservative opinion kept up the pressure, with *Time* magazine holding Dalrymple personally responsible for "forcing the six-hour day and slowdown in the rubber industry."[23] In October 1942, the six-hour day was abolished for the duration in the Akron war plants,[24] but the anti-labor forces were not satisfied. Republican Congressman John Cattlett introduced a bill into the state legislature to further control unions, wherein workers could be sued, a cooling-off period was to be required before strike action, and unions were to be forbidden from making financial contributions to political parties and individual candidates.[25] The latter measure was clearly aimed at the Democrats, but the Republicans were also spooked by the idea of a Labor Party, which had been strong in Summit County.

Discriminatory Hiring Practices

Nor was the union impressed with the xenophobia of the rubber corporations, which had fired many hundreds of "aliens." The *Akron Beacon Journal* reported on January 4, 1942, for example, that a sixty-year-old Polish man named Peter Duda had been fired from the mill room in his factory despite the fact that Poland was under Nazi occupation and Duda had three sons serving in the U.S. military.[26] These kinds of firings were applied "on a wholesale scale" at BF Goodrich, General Tire & Rubber, and American Hard Rubber, with isolated cases at Goodyear.[27] Goodrich alone had laid off 282 aliens in the week after Pearl Harbor, many of them British, Irish, French, Belgian, and Dutch nationals.[28] The *Akron Beacon Journal* reported that the FBI had more than doubled its surveillance in Akron in 1940, fearing the possibility of sabotage and espionage. The article quoted the Bureau's Cleveland boss describing Akron as a "fertile field" for such activities because of its "polyglot population" and "large output of war supplies."[29] President Roosevelt made a direct appeal to employers not to lay off aliens, the union stood firmly against what it saw as "the hysteria of the times," and the foreigners were reinstated.[30]

The Akron unions struggled against other discriminatory hiring practices of the city's rubber companies. Despite an ostensible labor shortage, there were thousands of unemployed and precariously employed people in the city. Many were denied work because of "age, sex, color, size, education, lack of experience, or just plain bureaucratic red tape," declared Local 5's newsletter, *The Air Bag*.[31] Black people suffered from racism at every level in the city's Goodyear factories, from its hiring practices to its everyday dealings on the shop floor. They were the last to be hired and the first to be fired, and were employed only in the most menial jobs. A color bar excluded them from "white" cafeterias and other facilities.

Although there had been large numbers of female workers in the rubber factories since before the turn of the century, the industry's appetite for wartime labor considerably boosted their numbers. However, there were widespread claims that the city's women faced discrimination in the factories' hiring practices. In early 1942, according to the War Manpower Commission, as few as one in ten women applying for a job actually got it, with many told that they lacked experience, were "a little too old," that they "didn't look like a good factory worker," or that they were too thin or too fat, and so forth.[32] Others were prevented from work by a dearth of childcare facilities in the city.[33] Increasing numbers of women and girls were to find their "traditional" occupations barred to them. In one instance, probation officer Fanny Grable investigated a complaint "that pulchritudinous young war workers were swapping their riveting guns for G-strings" in a burlesque show on Main Street.[34] Undoubtedly, the war brought fresh opportunities for many other women. In one case a "gum chewing, slang-using Cuyahoga Falls girl" escaped ill-paid part-time drudgery for a well-paid war plant job when she appealed to the War Manpower Commission panel. "The guy we work for knows we're froze[35] on our jobs," she complained, "and told us we would work that way and like it." The employer was checked for "labor hoarding"—a common-enough complaint at the time—and the young woman was allowed to take a better job. Nevertheless, a panel member reflected the misogyny of the times when he quipped that the young woman was "a decided blonde—she decided last week."[36]

In her absorbing account of women workers in the Akron factories, Kathleen Endres argues that although the message behind the wartime hiring was that women were working in industry for patriotic reasons and would quit once the war was over, many needed the work to support themselves. Pauline Rohrbaugh, who worked in the Goodyear fuel cells department, spoke for many when said that while she wanted to help defeat the Axis, she also needed the income. Once hired, the women faced a system of organized industrial patriarchy, with the more skilled and highly paid jobs regarded as men's work. In 1942, women at Goodyear staged an "illegal" sit-down strike and although they won their claims against the company's piecework system, they were cast as "unpatriotic," and disowned by their own union's international officers. Although union locals had come out against discrimination and supported equal pay,[37] the first union contract signed with Goodyear at Akron in 1941 set minimum hourly rates at 85 cents for men and 65 cents for women.[38] And at the end of the war, women were laid off in droves.[39]

Growing Gulf between Wages and Profits

The rubber industry had been the site of ferocious class battles since 1913 and although the war dampened these conflicts, they did not entire-ly disappear. In late September 1941, Goodyear signed its first contract with the union at Akron, raised pay rates, and agreed to restrict the activ-ities of the Flying Squadron.[40] This contract was a breakthrough against one of America's most intransigent anti-union corporations.

Aware of the growing gulf between wages and profits, and of the rising cost of living, in the following year, the URW's local unions demanded substantial pay increases. In early 1942, Local 5 in Akron lodged a claim for a 10 percent increase for BF Goodrich workers, claiming that cost-of-living rises meant that the company's workers were working for 15 to 20 percent less in real terms than in May 1941 when the last agreement was signed. Despite reporting record profits, the management retorted that

increases "cannot be justified at this time."[41] The union retaliated by
pointing out that company president John Collyer received $130,000 in
1941, around sixty-five times the annual wage of a rubber worker. Despite
the discrepancy, the corporations, conservative politicians, and newspa-
permen routinely presented the unions as unpatriotic and hinted at sinister motives on the part of its officials. In 1939, the "Chicago red hunter"
Elizabeth Dillard "revealed" at a meeting in the Akron Armory that
Sherman Dalrymple had been a student at a "Trotskyite school,"[42] and in
1944 the Congressional Dies Committee claimed he was a Communist.[43]
The early war years also saw an attempt to revive the 1919 "Red Scare,"
with the Dies Committee claiming to have unearthed 11,000
Communists in Northeast Ohio, many of them in union positions in
Cleveland and Akron.[44] In fact, Dalrymple, who was among the most conservative of the URW leaders, was a lifelong Democrat. More radical local
unionists such as Wilmer Tate who had supported the Farmer-Labor
Party also supported the war effort, while demanding labor's right to
defend itself against the corporations in wartime. The Akron militants
were also anxious to dispel anti-labor propaganda in the armed forces.
Local 5's newsletter, *The Air Bag*, was delivered to former URWA members serving in the military, and the union took delight in publishing their
letters, many of which urged the local to keep up the pressure for wage
justice and not to let the employers take advantage of the war to undermine the union. One soldier, Ralph Squires, even wrote that "many men
feel there's a strong need for a union in the army."[45]

Fobbed Off

In June 1942, the major Akron rubber companies agreed to small wage
increases for some workers, but some firms still refused to recognize the
union's other main demand: the closed shop.[46] By that year, it had
become clear that without the strike weapon, the URWA was relatively
powerless, despite boasting 100,000 members and 162 active branches
nationwide.[47] Meanwhile, the companies' earnings continued to skyrock-
et: corporate profits in 1942 were 400 percent higher than in 1939 and
the union claimed that salaries of corporate executives had risen by 218
percent over 1941 levels.[48] According to Local 5, the rank-and-file workers were so angry that they organized a "spontaneous" petition to the War
Labor Board (WLB) demanding wage justice. The local, which was the

largest and most radical of the URWA's affiliates, warned that "[i]f at the end of the war we do not have our union strong to maintain our jobs, our standards and our civil rights; then every sacrifice we and our brothers in uniform have made will have been in vain."[49]

Seven months after the union's petitions had been delivered to the WLB, the local had not received an answer and a general meeting passed a resolution calling for recission of the no-strike pledge. Although BF Goodrich settled a number of long-standing grievances,[50] the WLB did not yet consent to arbitrate on wages, despite figures produced by the union that indicated that the purchasing power of $100 in 1939 had fallen to $78 in 1940, $69 in 1941, $60 in 1942 and $43 in 1943.[51] When the Board handed down its decision in April, it recommended a flat eight cents an hour pay increase, which was later reduced to three cents. This fell far short of what the union had called for.[52] Provoked by an editorial in the *Akron Beacon Journal* which denounced "inflationary" wage claims, Sherman Dalrymple took out full-page advertisements stating what he saw as the facts of dwindling wages and soaring profits.[53] He stopped short, however, of endorsing industrial action. This was not enough for the militants in his union. The stage was now set for wildcat strikes—including sit-downs—at Akron and for a battle between the conservative international union officials and their radical local union counterparts.

Mohawk Valley Formula at Gadsden, Alabama

Meanwhile, a bitter industrial battle was being fought in Gadsden, Alabama. In 1930, in Etowah County on the edge of a vast upland area that was home to poor Southern dirt farmers, the Goodyear Tire & Rubber Company had opened a major plant as part of a plan to decentralize operations away from Akron. Although Goodyear president Paul Litchfield claimed that the reasons for decentralization were purely economic,[54] the URWA knew that he wanted to undermine their Akron power base. True to form, Goodyear set up a yellow union, recruited a Flying Squadron, and launched a reign of terror against the URW in the Gadsden plant and in union activists' homes. The company enjoyed the full cooperation of the local police. In 1936, the URW's international president, Sherman Dalrymple, was severely beaten by up to thirty company goons in the union's Gadsden offices while the local sheriff watched and mildly remonstrated.[55]

Sit-down strikers at Goodyear, Akron, OH, 1942.

The United Rubber Worker warned: "We must organize 100 percent. Otherwise the rubber barons will take work from Akron gum miners and force it upon unorganized workers whom they exploit ruthlessly."[56] Almost five years later, the union noted that Goodyear had "consistently and uniformly resisted every attempt at peaceful organization, relying on violence against union organizers and members to prevent organization. It is the only major company in the rubber industry that has refused to negotiate and sign a contract with the United Rubber Workers of America."[57] The continuing pattern of violence against union activists at the Gadsden plant increased during the crisis years leading to the Second World War. In February 1941, former Akron rubber worker and CIO organizer John House was hospitalized after five men attacked him with lengths of insulated electric cable in his office at Gadsden.[58]

Even after the company signed its first contract at Akron in 1941, it held out in Alabama. In May 1943, the Gadsden workers voted 1144 to 327 in a NLB ballot to join the URWA[59] following a U.S. Appeals Court ruling that ordered Goodyear to desist in discriminating against union members, stop the physical assaults, and halt all other forms of interference, restraint, and coercion. The court had also ordered Goodyear to restrain the Flying Squadron from interfering with the workers' rights to organize and bargain collectively, to reinstate victimized unionists, and to disband the "yellow" company union in the plant.[60] While federal government legislation contributed to the victory, it could never have been achieved without the solidarity of the Gadsden workers themselves.

Wildcats in Akron

Back in Akron, there was a spate of unofficial strikes as workers walked off the job in protest at the three cents an hour raise finally awarded by the War Labor Board. *The Air Bag* reported the complete closure of the BF Goodrich plants in May and another wildcat of 52,000 workers at Goodrich, Goodyear, and Firestone in late June 1943. The strikers only returned to work after President Roosevelt threatened to draft them into the armed forces.[61] The September 1943 Convention of the URWA was a stormy affair, and although it again ratified the no-strike pledge, a significant minority of delegates, many of them from Akron, voted to end it.[62] Matters came to a head in early 1944 when Dalrymple expelled seventy-two band room workers from Local 9 at Akron without a hearing for striking at General Tire & Rubber.[63] Although sixty-two of the strikers were reinstated, the atmosphere in the plant was so acrimonious that a referendum organized by the officers of Goodrich Local 5 voted by a margin of 1,419 to 626 to expel Sherman Dalrymple from his own local union. Dalrymple's actions were also condemned by the CIO's Akron Industrial Union Council as "hasty, ill-advised, illegal and unconstitutional."[64] Dalrymple managed to face down his critics and his expulsion was over-turned by the international union officers.[65] While he admitted there was a long list of justified grievances, he was adamant that the no-strike clause had to be maintained throughout the war.[66] Dalrymple resigned his post in September 1945[67] to work as a CIO railroad organizer in California, and later on a recruiting drive in the South until his death in 1962.[68] He was an honest man, as even his radical critics in the labor movement will admit, and had suffered bashings and privations in the struggle to build the union.

Victory over the Axis

The war dragged on for three and a half weary years after Pearl Harbor. American industry, long crippled by the Great Depression, expanded with astonishing speed to equip the war machine. The rubber industry absorbed all available labor and clamored for more. Incredible amounts of overtime were worked as the industry went into overdrive. Akron was labelled "the arsenal of democracy," with its factories churning out the weapons of victory over the Axis. Enormous synthetic rubber plants squatted on the hills and plains of America. The war brought some social gains: women and Afro-Americans found themselves working in occupations previously closed to them, and although the peace brought retrenchments, the experience was salutary and would inspire later feminists and black activists to fight for equality. The union remained strong: the URWA fought a long-running battle to ensure that the workers' hard-won gains were not eroded by the rubber corporations whose patriotic rhetoric masked colossal greed. They held the line, although not without massive internal conflicts. Wages were eroded, but on-the-job union organization was maintained and even strengthened. White-collar workers were brought into the union and even Goodyear, which was possibly the most virulently anti-union corporation in America, signed an agreement with the URWA. This was not the "business unionism" so dear to the "labor lieutenants of capital" and so despised by worker radicals. It was social unionism: campaigning, democratic and militant, its watchword the recruitment of all workers regardless of color, gender, creed, or skill in industrial unions. Its spirit was encapsulated in the person of Wilmer Tate, the socialist and union activist, known as "the father of the CIO" in Akron, who had dedicated his life to the cause of the working class. Tate died in 1944, still working as a CIO organizer, before the victory over the Axis that his members had worked for. Years before, Tate and other Akron militants had championed the cause of Republican Spain against fascism. At least one Akron rubber worker, Steve Miletich, had been killed in action in Spain, dying as a member of the Abraham Lincoln Brigade in the siege of Belchite in 1936. Countless others had perished on the battlefields of Europe and the Pacific in the following world war. Tate would have savored the Axis defeat, while looking askance at American capitalism, personified by Harvey Firestone, the Akron rubber baron who had sold tires on cheap credit terms to Franco.

•

The war ended suddenly. On VJ Day, September 2, 1945, the *Akron Beacon Journal* broke the news of the Japanese surrender in a banner headline.[69] Among its readers were the thousands of rubber workers coming off shift. Four months earlier, the newspapers had announced Nazi Germany's unconditional surrender. The war could not have been won without the astonishing Soviet victory at Stalingrad, or the hard-fought British and American campaigns in the Pacific, North Africa, and Europe. However, the victory was also due to the harnessing of America's immense industrial power to churn out the tanks, guns, warships, aircraft, and all the other deadly paraphernalia of war. Rubber was a crucial ingredient of the war machine, and the fact that the nation had been able to build synthetic rubber plants with a greater capacity than all of the prewar hevea plantations put together was to the credit of the masses of workers who toiled on the construction sites and in the factories.

Rubber in the Postwar World

If people want to develop as natural beings, they must develop further as social beings, and achieve an explicit socialization of the natural conditions of production . . . if we want to live with nature, we must master our social organization.

—PAUL BURKETT[1]

Rubber is inextricably bound up with the rise of capitalism, imperialism, and modernity. Despite its ubiquity and indispensability in modern life, it is only five hundred years since the Spanish, the Basques, and the Portuguese brought rubber to Europe. While this might seem a long time, we can put the "Rubber Age" in better perspective by recalling that the Copper Age began around 5,500 years ago, the Bronze Age 4,000 years ago, and the Iron Age 3,200 years ago.[2] Rubber was used by the Amerindian peoples for a variety of sacred and secular purposes, but in Europe it largely remained a curiosity for the best part of 300 years. It wasn't until after the Industrial Revolution that rubber became an essential part of society.

The decades since 1945 are a brief period in historical time, but given the restless nature of capitalism, with its irresistible drive to change, tear down, rebuild, relocate, and innovate, the rubber industry has not stood still. In terms of its utility value, rubber is indispensable: without it, society as we know it might perish, perhaps literally so given the importance of latex condoms in the battle against HIV/AIDS. Yet at the same time rubber has delivered such benefits to humanity, it has also brought huge social and ecological problems, and it is still true that where there is rubber there is often human suffering.

•

In 1945, the regime that had signed forty-year forward contracts for raw materials for the Monowitz slave factory was utterly smashed. In the Allied countries, many people hoped this humanitarian victory would bring sweeping social and economic reforms to their own countries after the war. In Britain, voters swept Winston Churchill from office in 1945 and elected a Labour government. The United States lacked a mass labor party, but the labor party idea had always been relatively strong in Akron and Summit County and a number of the city's rubber workers kept the idea alive until the weight of the Democrat ascendancy and McCarthyism put an end to it in the 1950s.[3]

Economic reconstruction came soon enough, but the hopes for sweeping social change gradually faded. In the United States, the government-owned synthetic rubber plants were sold off cheaply to corporations as befitted the "the land of the free," where stock markets are equated with democracy. Risk had been socialized, but the profits and means of production were privatized. The world was headed into the postwar boom that historian Eric Hobsbawm has called "the Golden Age."[4]

After Victory in Europe (VE) Day, the Allies pondered Germany's fate. The Henry Morgenthau school of thought wanted to deindustrialize Germany, to 'pastoralize' it into an agricultural society incapable of waging modern war: it was to become a "potato field," as Goebbels had warned.[5] The British Foreign and Colonial offices debated the fate of the German rubber factories, for despite the ferocity of the Allied bombings, the bulk of these had survived. Some Colonial Office mandarins wanted to emulate the Russians, who busily shipped whole factories back home from the Eastern Zone—including parts of the Leuna Works near Merseburg, which had produced synthetic gasoline and rubber along with fertilizers.[6] Given the Russians' forcible reparations program, it is not surprising that the Leuna Works and the former IG Farben Buna plant at Schkopau were centers of the workers' uprising of 1953 against the East German regime.[7] Across the Iron Curtain, the British mandarins were keen to stop economic competition from Continental Tires[8] and other German manufacturers. One report reveals that the Colonial Office

was anxious that the Allies should not "foster a permanent [German rub-
ber] industry, the suppression of which would be in the interests of the
Colonial Empire."[9]

How the majority of German tire plants were still functioning in 1945
is an interesting question. Asked by British military intelligence about the
possible effects of "systematic aerial attacks on the rubber industry,"
Albert Speer replied that if the industry had been systematically bombed
"it would have been no longer possible to produce the required number
of new tanks, vehicles or aircraft . . . [and the] lack of supplies of tyres,
etc., would have brought many units at the front to a standstill." In short,
the Nazi war machine would have been crippled. Failure to bomb the
plants meant that the Luftwaffe and the Wehrmacht did not run short of
tires until the war's end.[10]

The behavior of the rubber corporations and government mandarins
reveals agendas that differ little from those of the blimps and profiteers of
the First World War. In the United States and other highly industrialized
countries, the war only strengthened the economic hegemony of the large
rubber corporations, already flush with profits from war contracts and
state subsidies. As the economist Walter Adams noted in 1968, "In synthetic rubber, the wartime operations of the government plants gave a
handful of large firms enormous patent and know-how advantages for the
post-war period, and the subsequent disposal program resulted in the sale
of twenty-five plants to three firms controlling 47 percent of the industry's
capacity."[11] The rubber corporations' direct sales of rubber and rubber
products to the military normally accounted for only a small proportion
of their profits. The one exception, General Tire & Rubber, made 37 percent of its earnings from government contracts in 1970 because of direct
sales to the military by its subsidiary Aerojet.[12] However, indirect sales of
a myriad of other rubber products to U.S. government contractors such
as Lockheed and McDonnell Douglas firmly cemented the rubber firms
into the military-industrial complex where they remain a cornerstone of
late capitalism's new world order.

To the Utmost Ends of the Earth?

After the Allied victory, IG Farben was broken up into a number of smaller companies (including BASF, Bayer, and Hoechst) and twenty-four of
its chief executives were put on trial in August 1947 at Nuremberg. The

Monowitz synthetic rubber plant was taken over by the Poles when they regained Upper Silesia after the German retreat in 1945. They completed the Buna, and it remains a functioning chemical plant to this day. There is a monument to the slave laborers at the main gates and over the concrete perimeter walls many of the structures built by the Nazis are still clearly visible. The guard towers and barbed wire fences that surrounded the adjoining concentration camp have gone, but the fields are dotted with crumbling concrete air raid shelters. The SS guard post, a concrete blockhouse weathered by the elements and daubed with graffiti, still squats in the Monovice village like some monstrous beetle.

Most of the slaves who toiled on the Buna perished from gassing and other forms of torture, overwork, malnutrition, and lack of medical care. In contrast, most of the SS men who had guarded them reentered civilian life.[13] We should not forget, however, that while the SS provided Monowitz with its slaves and enforced discipline over them, the Buna was a private institution, funded and run by IG Farben for the benefit of its shareholders.[14]

Although Roosevelt, Churchill and Stalin had earlier declared that the Allies would "pursue . . . the Nazi criminals to the uttermost ends of the earth,"[15] the sentences that were handed down at the IG Farben trial in Nuremberg were more appropriate for white collar miscreants.[16] Of the twenty-four accused, thirteen were found guilty on one or more counts of the indictment and sentenced to prison terms ranging from one and a half to eight years, including time already served; ten defendants were acquitted of all charges; and another was discharged for medical reasons. The Monowitz rubber supremo Otto Ambros was sentenced to seven years at Nuremberg but was released in 1950 and soon rose to prominence in his profession.[17] The Axis was smashed but the new dawn of peace, liberty, and social equality that had inspired the anti-fascist struggle was waning.

New World Order

When the economist John Maynard Keynes and other Allied representatives met at Bretton Woods in 1944, many hoped they were laying the foundations of a more just and stable world order. Since Bretton Woods there has been no repeat of the catastrophic economic slump of the 1930s,[18] but the price of commodities has not been stabilized. Rubber prices have always been mercurial and have always fluctuated wildly. In

1974, there were reports of Malaysian rubber tappers starving because of a slump in rubber prices.[19] Malaysian plantation wages have been in long-term decline, and the rubber estate housing stock has been deteriorating for some years.[20] Skilled rubber workers—many of them women whose families have lived on the Malayan estates for generations—have been forced to take on unskilled, unhealthy, and poorly paid work as rubber is squeezed out by the more profitable oil palm.[21] The oil palm, which grows rapidly to maturity, yields high quality vegetable oil that is used to manufacture a variety of products. Highly lucrative, it is also ecologically destructive and the chemicals used on the plantations are often injurious to workers' health.

The Firestone operations in Liberia have been criticized since the company first began operations there in the mid-1920s. The firm, which was taken over by the Japanese giant Bridgestone in 1988, is still regular-ly assailed in the international media for its labor and ecological practices. A report published by the United Nations in 2006 stated that:

> Many [rubber] workers lack effective trade union representation. Living and working conditions on the plantations violate fundamental human rights standards. The situation is particularly poor in relation to child [ren]; child labour is indirectly encouraged by work practices and lack of access to edu-cation. Health care facilities are scarce and poorly equipped. Living condi-tions, hazardous working conditions and the impact of industry on the local environment exacerbate health concerns.[22]

While the report concerns Liberian rubber plantations as a whole, the essence of it applies to the Firestone operations on the huge Harbel estate.[23] The Harbel estate is reputedly the world's largest rubber planta-tion, employing around 10,000 people at the wage of $3.00 per day. Harbel's entire production is exported to the U.S. In 2006, journalist Ariane Chemin published an article in the British *Guardian Weekly* describing the Harbel workers' living conditions:

> Most of them occupy mud huts with corrugated iron roofs. Families, often more than 10 people, cram into one, maybe two rooms. There is neither run-ning water nor electricity, just a pump connected to the river. At one end of the camp are the latrines and a shower.

Chemin's article claims that effluent from the estate's processing plant flows into the nearby river, thereby seriously polluting it. According to a seventy-five-year-old retired plumber from the plant, the chemicals made him blind.[24] Conditions on the plantation led the US-based NGOs Samfu and the International Labor Rights Fund to file a federal class-action suit against Firestone in 2005 for what they called "a gulag of misery."[25] Firestone denied the charges, pointing out that it was the only major company not to walk away from the country during its fourteen years of civil war.[26]

For many years, Firestone enjoyed a cozy relationship with the leaders of the Firestone Agricultural Workers' Union of Liberia (FAWUL). For all intents and purposes a company union, FAWUL allowed child labor, and workers were given no say in the negotiation or ratification of collective bargaining agreements. Disgruntled plantation workers formed an aggrieved workers' committee, organizing wildcat strikes in February 2006 and April 2007, demanding wage increases and union elections. In July 2007, the group won every union position with overwhelming majorities, but Firestone refused to recognize the new leadership and continued to forward union dues to the ousted officials. Further strikes ensued and the police were called on a number of occasions to quash the unrest. During this period, Firestone-Bridgestone made huge profits but continued to pay its Liberian workers a pittance. Worldwide, the company made a profit of $1.1 billion in 2007, with plantation workers' wages ranging from $2.65 to $3.38 a day. The workers were paid on a piece-work basis and could make the higher amount if they tapped 750 trees a day and lugged the buckets of latex some miles to the weighing station.

In 1990, a Firestone executive told *The New York Times*, "The best way to think of it [the Liberian rubber estate] is as an old Southern plantation." The victory of the aggrieved workers' committee in the 2007 FAWUL elections made Firestone think again. Liberia's Supreme Court intervened after a series of strikes for recognition of the new leadership convulsed the industry. Firestone was forced to recognize the elected officials and negotiate a new collective bargaining agreement. While the victory had been made possible by the solidarity of the plantation workers, the union acknowledged the assistance of labor rights organizations and the United States Steelworkers' Union, which had absorbed American rubber workers some years before.[27]

New Dickensianism

As we have seen, rubber factory workers often endured dangerous and unhealthy working conditions. While conditions have generally improved since the days of Banbury's "blue men" sickened by aniline dyes in early twentieth-century U.S. factories, the same cannot be said of factories in the Third World and the Newly Industrializing Countries (NICs), where conditions remain Dickensian. One long-term study by Chinese medical researchers found significant increases in mortality in a Chinese rubber factory employing almost 1,600 workers. The most common causes of excess deaths were cerebrovascular disorders and cancers of the lung, pancreas, and liver.[28] Given the rate of growth of the Chinese economy and the proliferation of unregulated industry since this research was completed in December 1997, it is likely that the situation has worsened. The Chinese rubber industry has expanded at such breakneck speed that plantations in Yunnan have eaten up all available land. The industry has looked south to Laos, where large areas of jungle are now being cleared for rubber.[29] Chinese workers in the export zones of Guangzhou endure low pay and long hours, forced overtime, dangerous machinery, and toxic chemicals in the workplace; they often sleep in crowded and unsanitary dormitories adjacent to their places of work. Free trade unions are illegal, making it difficult for workers to defend themselves against unscrupulous employers. Ironically, under a self-styled Marxist government, workers suffer conditions similar to those once endured by European workers whose plight roused Marx and Engels to white-hot fury. Even if trade unions in some other developing countries are technically legal, as in Mexico, for example, this has not prevented the state and employers from colluding in ferocious attacks on workers exercising their legal rights. This, for instance, was the case at the Tornel Rubber Company, Mexico's largest tire plant, when workers struck against poor occupational health and safety practices and declining wages and sought to join a more militant union in 1989.[30]

The Death of the Akron Rubber Industry

Class struggle, social upheaval, and technological change: all of these things have long been associated with the rubber industry. Akron, Ohio, was once "Rubber's Home Town," and housed the largest concentration of rubber manufacturing plants in the world. In its heyday the city consumed up to two-thirds of the world's raw rubber and employed over 60,000 workers. If Akron's "gummers" did not invent the sit-down strike, they certainly used it to devastating advantage—in a series of strikes in the 1930s they turned the city from a bastion of the open shop into a citadel of organized labor. Postwar union agreements assured Akron's rubber workers high wages, permanent jobs, and generous pensions and health-care benefits, but this ended in the late 1970s, when the city joined the "rust-belt" manufacturing centers of northeast America. Today, Akron is eerily quiet. As with many other industrial American cities, business has moved to shopping malls in the suburbs, a development made possible by the automobile. Ironically, the proliferation of privately owned automobile was made possible by the mass production of rubber tires. But the decline of the city also reflects the death of its rubber industry: this is a cause of grief and nostalgia for Akronites old enough to have grown up with the "black snow" and sulfur smells of the mills. In Steve Love and David Giffels's book on their city's rubber industry, they wrote: "By 1983, there were virtually no tire-building jobs in Akron."[31] What this meant for Akronites was poignantly expressed by Love and Giffels:

> There are places in this town where the wind blows clean through with nothing to stop it. Places where men and women once worked, where they drank, prospered, argued, and manufactured lives for themselves. Massive sections of this town are gone, yet we can still feel their presence, the way an amputee swears to God he can still feel his missing limb.[32]

By the turn of the twenty-first century only Goodyear—the second oldest and the largest of Akron's Big Three—maintained a manufacturing presence in the city, with 3,000 employees and its advertising blimp constantly circling overhead. Even so, in December 2007, only a last-minute government deal prevented the company from pulling out of the city.[33] Earlier, in 1986, the company had only just survived a "greenmail" attack by the British corporate raider Sir James Goldsmith. The bid failed but reputedly cost Goodyear $2.66 billion. Goldsmith walked away with $90 million. In 2001, the nation's last remaining rubber glove company at nearby Massillon closed its doors and shifted production to Malaysia and India, throwing 200 people out of work.[34] The closure highlighted a long-term decline in which the Akron region's rubber industry was first "decentralized" to other parts of the United States, and then exported off shore. Fifty or even forty years ago, few would have believed that "Rubber's Home Town" would one day see its last remaining rubber firm threaten to close, but Akron bears out Marx's famous observation that under capitalism "all that is solid melts into air."[35] The rubber workers' national union membership declined from a peak of 200,000 in 1960 to 94,000 in 1995, prompting a merger with the U.S. Steelworkers' Union.[36] In late 2008, the collapse of the U.S. automobile industry was only averted by massive government loans and subsidies. The crisis flowed on to the rubber industry. Over seventy years ago, when Harvey Firestone died, his company erected a bronze statue of him in a South Akron park overlooking the huge factories he had created. Today the Akron factories are dead and only vandals and birds pay attention to the statue which is as much a testament to impermanence and vanity as the broken stone image of the poet Shelley's King Ozymandias.

The Logic of Capitalist Accumulation

The Akron rubber firms grew from modest beginnings into giant corporations—and then outgrew their birthplace. By 1929, the three largest Akron tire companies were firmly established multinational corporations and among the fifty largest U.S. firms, with international webs of marketing outlets, plantations, factories, and links with New York banks. The process had begun in 1910, when Goodyear established a Canadian manufacturing subsidiary. In 1916, the company bought land on Sumatra for its first rubber plantations. This was followed in 1927 by factories in Australia and Britain; in Argentina in 1930; Java in 1934; and Brazil and Sweden in 1938. For its part, BF Goodrich expanded its manufacturing operations to France in 1910, Canada in 1923, and the United Kingdom in 1924.[37] The post–Second World War period also saw a rapid acceleration of the U.S. rubber corporations' overseas investments. By 1970 Uniroyal—the successor to US Rubber—reaped three-quarters of its earnings abroad; Goodyear 30 percent; and Firestone 25 percent.[38]

Although Marx's analysis of capitalism dealt with an earlier laissez-faire period, with a multiplicity of small producers (or "capitals" as he calls them), he forecast that such an economy could not last—and for the rubber industry it didn't. The competitive logic of the system led to the development from the last quarter of the nineteenth century to what we now know as monopoly capitalism. As Marx put it, "The battle of competition is fought by cheapening commodities. The cheapness of commodities depends, *ceteris paribus*, on the productiveness of labor, and this again on the scale of production. Therefore, the larger capitals beat the smaller."[39] The logic of capitalist accumulation drove the corporations to expand their operations around the world in search of markets, raw materials, and cheap labor. The "decentralization" of the Akron industry was a step in the process we now call globalization.

The rubber barons might have eventually shifted out of Akron even if it had remained an open-shop town where they could cut wages at will and lay off "the light infantry of capital" during downturns. Conveniently, the rise of the URWA allowed conservative commentators to blame the workers for decentralization. As the *India Rubber Journal* editorialized in 1936, "The [Akron] workers have allowed themselves to be swayed by the mass oratory of those who have nothing to lose and everything to gain by perpetrating the disturbances," and the result "will be unemployment in a ruined city."[40] The workers' rejoinder to such speciousness is summed up in a union song of Depression-era America:

> I get the fairest pay on earth,
> I belong to the Company union.
> I'm paid exactly what I'm worth.
> I belong to the Company union.
> I think the Company is fair
> They lay me off, but I don't care
> I belong to the Company union. . . .[41]

The rubber corporations will always decentralize to low-wage areas and blame factory closures and unemployment on the workers they leave behind in ruined cities. Thus, it was in mid-2008 when Goodyear announced the closure of its plant at Somerton in Australia, while at the same time it expanded its operations in low-wage, non-unionized China.[42] Tires are no longer produced in Australia. The logic of the system means that perhaps one day, rubber workers in Guangzhou will note that:

> Money moves without a whisper,
> Money has no home or nation,
> It has no friends and it won't stay long.[43]

There is no room for morality or social responsibility in the corporate boardrooms. Lives are destroyed and meager savings are swallowed up when decisions to relocate factories are made or when corporate raiders target other firms for quick pickings. As Noam Chomsky has observed, individuals who behave like the modern corporation are called sociopaths, yet TNCs that behave badly are rewarded for their antisocial behavior.[44]

•

If the social and economic blessings of rubber have been accompanied by disturbing downsides, its relationship with ecology has also been problematic. Rubber has been inseparable from the major development of the second phase of the Industrial Revolution: the internal combustion engine. It is difficult to imagine trucks and automobiles running on steel or iron wheels (illegal since the 1930s in the United States)[45] and it seems impossible for aircraft to land without rubber wheels. Aircraft, ships, automobiles, trucks, and all manner of stationary engines, electrical and telegraphic systems, civil constructions, and other industrial machines and domestic appliances rely on rubber. In 1937 a trade journal noted that there were 121 rubber parts excluding tires in a Buick and 142 in an Oldsmobile.[46] Earlier, an article in *India Rubber World* claimed 400 in the average automobile.[47] Rubber is used for seismic bearings in buildings in earthquake zones, and the 6,600-metric-ton sills at the base of the Thames flood barrier in London rest on rubber bearings.[48] Rubber is incorporated in satellites, and a variety of lowly adhesives have a rubber base. But the most common and visible use of rubber is the pneumatic tire. When pneumatic tires were introduced, few if any people foresaw the possible ill effects of so "obvious" a boon to humanity. In 1948, R. H. Seaman, a member of the Goodyear plant police in Akron, retired after twenty-five years' service. When asked if there was anything he regretted, he replied that he had never used a streetcar in all of his years of service; he had always driven in his own car. He planned "to ride a city bus soon just to see what the experience is like" and considered that it was "too bad that the streetcars no longer run."[49] Many years earlier, when Goodyear's Paul Litchfield enthused about the coming revolution that would see trucks carry everything from eggs to heavy machinery, and Harvey Firestone waxed lyrical about the benefits of passenger vehicles, they had little inkling of the threat that climate change would pose for the planet.

Thomas Edison's prediction that the electric battery-powered automobile—already developed in the early twentieth century—would "put the gasoline-powered auto out to pasture in company with the horse," may yet prove true, but in the long years since the inventor's words, electric cars have been a rarity.[50] If Francis Fukuyama's claim that the future of humanity is America writ large, then we might ponder John Steinbeck's observation that:

> The new American finds his challenge and his love in traffic-choked streets, skies nested in smog, choking with the acids of industry, the screech of rubber and houses leashed in against one another, while the townlets wither a time and die.[51]

In February 2008, Australian scientist Ross Garnaut released an interim report warning that the country would have to make huge adjustments to its way of life if it was to meet its targets for cuts in greenhouse gas emissions.[52] Since then, the country's emissions have increased inexorably,[53] for all the "greenwash" emanating from Australia's government. Other scientists warn that we will have to learn to go without automobiles altogether and to live more decentralized and less peripatetic lifestyles. We should also not forget the effects of flying around the planet—an activity again impossible without rubber. The assumption has been since the automobile revolution that faster and farther is always best—but is it?

Biological Time Bomb

The tropical rubber plantations and smallholdings on which the world still relies for between a third and a half of its rubber might be "natural" in that they grow trees in the soil, but huge areas of forest must be cleared to plant what is an exotic species outside of its native Amazonia. Blasted by fire, defoliants, and bombs during the American war, the forests of Laos are now threatened by the demands of the Chinese rubber industry. Nevertheless, plantation rubber is preferable to the synthetic product, which depends on dirty raw materials such as coal and petroleum refinery wastes. The alternative of using grain alcohol as the raw material for synthetics diverts scarce agricultural land and resources away from food production.[54] Although some rubber is recycled, often scrap rubber is seen as garbage, and some of it is burned in great pyres, with abysmal

effects on air quality. We would do well to systematically recycle whatever we can and to introduce conservation measures to reduce our consumption of rubber. This is not likely to happen anytime soon. Rubber is
ubiquitous, taken for granted, questions about its origins and production
scarcely asked.

There is also another lurking biological time bomb, whose ticking gets
ever more imminent as a result of globalization and mass international air
travel. The *Hevea brasiliensis* tree is native to the South American rainforests, but attempts to cultivate it in orderly plantations in Brazil failed
due to leaf blight. Henry Ford's Fordlandia rubber plantation, which
occupied a belt of land equal in size to Rhode Island, now molders in the
Brazilian wilderness, a victim of the blight. One rubber expert describes
the blight as "the AIDS of the rubber industry" and another believes that
if it jumped the oceans from Amazonia, it would kill off the Asian plantations within five years. If this happened, the world would become almost
completely dependent on the synthetic rubber industry, which has never,
despite all of its successes, been able to manufacture a product as good as
natural rubber. In the past, when international freight and passengers
traveled mainly by ships, it was a very remote possibility that blight's thin
spore walls could survive the lengthy ocean voyages. Now, with international air traffic the norm,[55] many other human, animal, and plant diseases
have already spread far beyond their places of origin. Ironically, during
the Second World War the United States poured vast sums of money into
research in the Amazon aimed at isolating blight-resistant hevea trees.
With victory in 1945, and the triumph of the massive synthetic rubber
project, this promising research project was scrapped.[56] Even if it is possible to genetically modify the hevea to be blight-resistant, the cost of
replacing the world's stock of rubber trees would be enormous and it
would be many years before the resilient trees became productive. The
decision to end the Amazon research program was based on the assumption that humanity is somehow immune to the laws of nature. Yet, as
Frederick Engels cautioned well over a century ago:

> Let us not, however, flatter ourselves overmuch on account of our human vic-
> tories over nature. For each such victory nature takes its revenge upon us.
> Each victory, it is true, in the first place brings about the results we expected,
> but in the second and third places it has quite different, unforeseen effects
> which only too often cancel the first.[57]

The challenge, as Engels recognized over a century ago, is for humanity to realize that it is part of nature, to learn the laws of nature and to live within them. Such an insight, however, flies in the face of the logic of capitalism, whose raison d'être is the accumulation of capital regardless of the social and ecological consequences.

Chico Mendes, the Jungle, and the Hevea

From the mid-1970s, Francisco Alves Mendes Filho—better known to the world as Chico Mendes led a courageous struggle to save the rainforests from the depredations of ranchers, miners, and loggers. Central to his vision of the preservation of the Amazon jungles was the creation of publicly owned "extractive reserves" in which clear-felling, ranching, and other destructive practices would be forbidden. Economic activity would be restricted to sustainable activities such as rubber tapping and the collection of Brazil nuts. Mendes realized that, far from "standing outside of nature like a conqueror," as Engels had insisted, we are part of nature and must learn to live with its laws if we—and the planet we inhabit—are to survive. For the ranchers, loggers, and other the vested interests, however, Mendes and his rubber tappers' union were subversive eco-Luddites blocking progress; which in their eyes was indistinguishable from the short-term maximization of profits.

A series of forty-five successful *empates* in which rubber tappers staged mass occupations to prevent forests from being clear-felled and burnt provoked the Brazilian landowners to take violent measures. In late December 1988, the forty-four-year-old Mendes was shot down by thugs hired by ranchers as he stood in the doorway of his house in Xapuri.[58] If the vested interests thought that had put an end to the matter, they were soon proved wrong. In 1990, the Brazilian government inaugurated the first two extractive reserves, the largest of which, named after the murdered activist, comprises almost one million hectares of jungle. By early 2004, there were thirty-five reserves with a total area of over five million hectares.[59] It is fitting that Mendes, who began life as a humble *seringueiro*, tapping heveas along his *estrada* in remote Acre, is today an enduring international symbol of resistance to environmental and social rapine.

The Devil's Milk

Karl Marx held that "At the first glance, a commodity seems a common-place sort of thing . . . [but] it is a very queer thing indeed, full of meta-physical subtleties and theological whimsies."[60] This is certainly true of rubber. We tend to take the superficially humble, black substance for granted, but it contains within it the whole buried world of social and eco-logical relations. My investigation into these relations began two decades ago while repairing the Banbury mixer in a Melbourne tire plant.

Clearly, rubber is an essential commodity for modern society in terms of its utility. Yet, as my investigation has shown, the oozing latex has also been the devil's milk. The story of rubber is a potent illustration of our alienation both from nature and from our own humanity. As the American Marxist writer Paul Burkett reminds us, even if we are no longer so direct-ly dependent upon nature as in the past, if we want to live in harmony with nature we must *master our own social organization*.[61] If we can do that, we might begin to use commodities such as rubber to meet human needs in an ecologically sustainable and socially responsible manner.

The human encounter with rubber has brought out the best and the worst in people. We take the inventions of men such as Robert Thomson, John Dunlop, Thomas Hancock, Charles Macintosh, and Charles Goodyear for granted, and yet they are indispensable for life as we know it. Among the human rights campaigners who refused to remain silent in the face of the injustices of the rubber industry are Edmund Morel, Walt Hardenburg, Roger Casement, Emile Vandervelde, and Benjamin Saldaña Rocca. Among the labor movement activists who struggled to make a difference for the poor, the outcasts, and the forgotten were the Vietnamese Communist Tran Tu Binh, the Americans Sherman Dalrymple, John House, Wilmer Tate, and the Brazilian *seringueiro* Chico Mendes. It is perhaps fitting to conclude with mention of a retired American rubber worker named Lilly Ledbetter, who was seventy years old at the time of writing. Ledbetter worked for almost twenty years as a supervisor at the Goodyear Tire & Rubber plant in Gadsden, Alabama. During that time she did the same work as men, but was always paid sub-stantially less. After her appeals to the company for equal pay failed, Lilly took her case to the U.S. Supreme Court. In 2007, the court voted five to four to reject her plea for wage justice. All avenues for redress were blocked by an alliance of business interests, judges, politicians—and the Bush administration.

Goodyear Tire & Rubber has been a ruthless opponent of labor since the days when company vice-president Cliff Slusser threatened that any union organizer who went to Gadsden during the 1936 organizing drive would "get his head knocked off."[62] The Supreme Court, too, has a long history of siding with capital against labor. Lilly's struggle finally bore fruit in the form of the first bill signed into law by the incoming president, Barack Obama, in January 2009. The Lilly Ledbetter Fair Pay Restoration Act overturned the 2007 Supreme Court ruling and cleared the way for other women workers to seek redress.[63] Lilly herself will not benefit, but the act named after her is a monument to her long fight and shows that people can change the world, though it takes courage, patience, and determination to do so.

Bibliography

ARCHIVAL SOURCES

Akron Beacon Journal newspaper archives, Akron
Archives d'outre-mer, Aix-en-Provence
Archives des Ministère des Affaires Etrangères, Brussels
Archives of the Royal Botanic Gardens, Kew, London
Archives of the State Museum at Auschwitz
Bowling Green State University Center for Archival Collections, Bowling Green
British National Archives, Kew, London
Chandler Papers, Asian Studies Library, Monash University, Melbourne
Ginaven Collection, Akron-Summit County Public Library, Akron
National Archives of Australia, Canberra and Melbourne
National Archives of Cambodia, Phnom Penh
Ohio State Historical Center, Columbus
Pennington of Muncaster files, State Library of Victoria, Melbourne
University of Akron Archives, Akron

BOOKS AND JOURNAL ARTICLES

Adams, Ian, *Stan Hywet Hall & Gardens* (Akron: University of Akron Press, 2001).
Adams, Walter, "The Military-Industrial Complex and the New Industrial State,"
    The American Economic Review, Vol.58, No. 2, Papers and Proceedings of the
    Eightieth Meeting of the American Economic Association, May 1968.
Ainsworth, Leopold, *The Confessions of a Planter in Malaya: A Chronicle of Life
    and Adventure in the Jungle* (London: H.F. and G. Witherby, 1933).
Akers, C.E., *The Rubber Industry in Brazil and the Orient* (London: Methuen,
    1914).
Allen, Hugh, *Rubber's Home Town: The Real-Life Story of Akron* (New York:
    Stratford House, 1949).
Allen, Michael Thad, *Hitler's Slave Lords: The Business of Forced Labour in
    Occupied Europe* (Stroud, Gloucestershire: Tempus, 2004).

Amarchi, Azeem, Good, Kenneth, and Mortimer, Rex, *Development and Dependency: The Political Economy of Papua New Guinea* (Melbourne: Oxford University Press, 1979).

Améry, Jean (Hans Mayer), *At the Mind's Limits: Contemplations by a Survivor of Auschwitz and Its Realities*, trans. Sidney Rosenfeld & Stella P. Rosenfeld (Bloomington: Indiana University Press, 1980).

Anissimov, Myriam, *Primo Levi: Tragedy of an Optimist*, trans. Steve Cox (London: Aurum Press, 1998).

Annuaire des Syndicats des Planteurs de Caoutchouc de l'Indochine (Saigon: Syndicats des Planteurs de Caoutchouc de l'Indochine, 1926).

Anon., "War Department to Send Motor Convoy from Washington to Los Angeles," *Highway Engineer and Contractor: A Journal of State and City Engineering and Construction Problems* (Chicago: June 1920).

Anstey, Roger, *King Leopold's Legacy: The Congo under Belgian Rule* (London: Oxford University Press, 1966).

Arden, Stanley, "Report on Hevea Brasiliensis in the Malay Peninsula" (Kuala Lumpur: Perak Government Printing Office, 1902).

Ascherson, Neal, *The King Incorporated: Leopold the Second and the Congo* (London: Granta, 1999).

Bakan, Joel, *The Corporation: The Pathological Pursuit of Power* (New York: Free Press, 2004).

Baldwin, Neil, *Edison: Inventing the Century* (New York: Hyperion, 1995).

Barham, Bradford L., and Coomes, Oliver T., *Prosperity's Promise: The Amazon Rubber Boom and Distorted Economic Development*, Dellplain Latin American Studies No. 4 (Boulder: Westview Press, 1996).

Barham, Bradford L., and Oliver T. Coomes, "Reinterpreting the Amazon Rubber Boom: Investment, the State, and Dutch Disease," *Latin American Research Review*, Vol. 29, No.2 (1994).

Barnhardt, Robert J. (ed.), *The Barnhart Dictionary of Etymology* (New York: H. & W. Wilson, 1988).

Barns, T. Alexander, *An African Eldorado: The Belgian Congo* (London: Methuen, 1926).

Bauer, P.T., *The Rubber Industry: A Study in Competition and Monopoly* (London: Longmans, Green, 1948).

Baum, Vicki, *The Weeping Wood* (London: Michael Joseph, 1945).

Baxter, P.J., and J.B. Werner, *Mortality in the British Rubber Industries, 1967–76* (London: Health and Safety Executive, 1980).

Beasley, Norman, *Men Working: A Story of the Goodyear Tire & Rubber Co.* (London: Harper Bros., 1931).

Berger, Ronald J., *Constructing a Collective Memory of the Holocaust: A Life History of Two Brothers' Survival* (Niwot, CO: University Press of Colorado, 1995).

Berkowitz, Henry, "In the Sweat Shop," from the Yiddish of Morris Rosenfeldt, *The Jewish Quarterly Review*, Vol. 15, No. 3 (April 1903).

Berlage, Jean, *Répertoire de la Presse du Congo Belge (1884–1954) et du Ruanda-Urundi (1920–1954)* (Brussels: Commission Belge de Bibliographie, 1955).

Berler, Willi, *Journey through Darkness: Monowitz, Auschwitz, Gross-Rosen, Buchenwald* (Portland, OR: Vallentine Mitchell, 2004).

Biskup, Peter, "Foreign Coloured Labour in German New Guinea," *The Journal of Pacific Studies*, Vol. 5 (Suva, Fiji: 1970).

Blackford, Mansel G., and Austin K. Kerr, *B.F. Goodrich: Tradition and Transformation, 1870–1995* (Columbus: Ohio State University Press, 1996).

Blanchard, Peter, *Slavery and Abolition in Early Republican Peru* (Wilmington, DE: Scholarly Resources, 1992).

Blainey, Geoffrey, *Jumping Over the Wheel* (St. Leonards, NSW: Allen & Unwin, 1993).

Bloor, Janet, and John D. Sinclair, *Rubber! Fun, Fashion, Fetish* (London: Thames and Hudson, 2004).

Blower, Arthur H., *Akron at the Turn of the Century; 1890–1913: Recollections of Arthur H. Blower* (Akron: The Summit County Historical Society, 1955).

Boillet-Robert, J., *Léopold II et le Congo: nos fils au continent noir* (Paris: Bureau de Vente des Publications Coloniales Officielles, 1912).

Borkin, Joseph, *The Crime and Punishment of IG Farben* (New York: The Free Press, 1978).

Borsos, John, "'We Make You This Appeal in the Name of Every Union Man and Woman in Barberton': Solidarity Unionism in Barberton, Ohio, 1933–41," in Staughton Lynd (ed.), *"We Are All Leaders": The Alternative Unionism of the Early 1930s* (Urbana and Chicago: University of Illinois Press, 1996).

Boulter, R., *Economic Conditions in British Malaya to 28th February 1931* (London: Department of Overseas Trade, 1931).

Bramwell, Anna, *Blood and Soil: Richard Walther Darré and Hitler's "Green Party"* (Abbotsbrook, Bourne End, Bucks: The Kensal Press, 1985).

Brannt, William T., *India Rubber, Gutta-percha and Balata* (London: Sampson Low, Marston, 1900).

Braverman, Harry, *Labor and Monopoly Capitalism: The Degradation of Work in the Twentieth Century* (New York: Monthly Review Press, 1974).

Brecht, Bertolt (ed. John Willett and Ralph Manheim with Erich Fried), *Bertolt Brecht Poems 1913–1956* (New York: Eyre Methuen, 1976).

Breman, Jan, *Taming the Coolie Beast: Plantation Society and the Colonial Order in Southeast Asia* (Delhi: Oxford University Press, 1989).

Brocheux, Pierre, "Le prolétariat des plantations des hévéas au Vietnam méridional: aspects sociaux et politiques," *Le Mouvement Social*, No. 90 (Ivry, France: Association le mouvement social, Jan–March 1975), 55–86.

Brockway, Lucile H., "Science and Colonial Expansion: The Role of the British Royal Botanic Gardens," *American Ethnologist* (Davis, CA: American Ethnological Association, August, 1979): 449–465.

Brooks, Peter, *Zeppelin: Rigid Airships, 1893–1940* (Drexel Hill, PA: Putnam Aeronautics, 1991).

Brow, Jessica, Nora Mitchell, and Michael Bresford (eds.), *The Protected Landscape Approach: Linking Nature, Culture and Community* (Gland, Switzerland: International Union for the Conservation of Nature, 2005).

Bryant, Robin, *Fading Pictures* (Lewes, East Sussex: The Book Guild, 2004).

Burkett, Paul, *Marx and Nature: A Red Green Perspective* (New York: St. Martin's Press, 1999).

Burns, E. Bradford, "Manáus, 1910: Portrait of a Boom Town," *Journal of Inter-American Studies*, Vol. 7, No. 3 (July 1965).

Burrow, T., 1986, Review of R.L. Turner (ed. J.C. Wright), "A Comparative Dictionary of the Indo-Aryan Languages: Addenda and Corrigenda," in *The Bulletin of the School of Oriental and African Studies*, Vol. 49, No. 3 (London: SOAS, University of London, 1986): 593.

Butcher, John G., *The British in Malaya 1880–1941: The Social History of a European Community in Colonial South-East Asia* (Kuala Lumpur: Oxford University Press, 1979).

Campbell, Persia Crawford, *Chinese Coolie Emigration to Countries within the British Empire* (London: Frank Cass, 1932).

Camus, J. J., *L'Oeuvre Humaine et Social dans les Plantations de Caoutchouc d'Indochine* (Paris: Société d'Editions Techniques Coloniales, 1949).

Chalk, Frank, and Kurt Jonassohn, *The History and Sociology of Genocide: Analysis and Case Studies* (New Haven, CT: Yale University Press, 1990).

Chalk, Frank Robert, "The United States and the International Struggle for Rubber, 1914–1941," unpublished Ph.D. History thesis (Madison: University of Wisconsin, 1970).

Chalk, Frank, "The Anatomy of an Investment: Firestone's 1927 Loan to Liberia" in *Canadian Journal of African Studies*, Vol. 1, No. 1 (March 1967).

Charny, Israel W., *Encyclopaedia of Genocide* (Santa Barbara: ABC-CLIO, 2003).

Childe, Vere Gordon, *The Bronze Age* (Cheshire, CT: Biblo and Tannen, 1963).

Clendinnen, Inga, *Aztecs: An Interpretation* (Cambridge: Cambridge University Press, 1991).

Coates, Austin, *The Commerce in Rubber: The First 250 Years* (Singapore: Oxford University Press, 1987).

Collier, Richard, *The River that God Forgot: The Story of the Amazon Rubber Boom* (London: Collins, 1968).

Collins, James, "Report on the Gutta-percha of Commerce" (London: Geo. Allen, 1878).

Committee of Anti-Fascist Resistance Fighters in the German Democratic Republic, *IG Farben, Auschwitz, Mass Murder* (Berlin: 1974).

Conlin, Joseph R., *At the Point of Production: The Local History of the IWW* (Westport, CT: Greenwood Press, 1981).

Conrad, Joseph, *Heart of Darkness and Selections from the Congo Diary* (New York: The Modern Library, 1999).

Corden, W.M., and J.P. Neary, "Booming Sector and Deindustrialization in a Small Open Economy," in *The Economic Journal*, No. 92 (London: Royal Economic Society, 1982): 825–848.

Cornwell, John, *Hitler's Scientists: Science, War and the Devil's Pact* (London: Penguin Books, 2004).

Crawford, D., *Thinking Black: 12 Years without a Break in the Long Grass of Central Africa* (London: Morgan and Scott, 1913).

Crocker Green, Edward, *Rethinking AIDS Prevention: Learning from Success in Developing Countries* (Westport, CT: Greenwood Publishing, 2003).

Cureau, A.D., "Essai sur la psychologie des races nègres de l'Afrique Tropicale. Première Partie: sensibilité et affectivité," *Revue Générale des Sciences Pures et Appliquées* (Paris: Librairie Armand Colin, 15 July 1904).

Daniels, John, "The Congo Question and the 'Belgian Solution,'" in *The North*

American Review, Vol. CLXXXVIII (New York: December 1908): 891–902.
Davin, Eric Leif, "The Very Last Hurrah? The Defeat of the Labor Party Idea, 1934–36," in Staughton Lynd (ed.), *"We Are All Leaders": The Alternative Unionism of the Early 1930s* (Urbana and Chicago: University of Illinois Press, 1996).
Davis, Mike, *Late Victorian Holocausts: El Niño Famines and the Making of the Third World* (London: Verso, 2001).
Davis, Wade, *One River: Explorations and Discoveries in the Amazon Rain Forests* (New York: Simon and Schuster, 1996).
De Kalb, Courtney, "Nicaragua: Studies on the Mosquito Shore in 1892," *Journal of the American Geographical Society of New York*, Vol. 25, (New York: 1893).
De las Casas, Bartolomé, A *Short Account of the Destruction of the Indies*, ed. and trans. Nigel Griffin (Harmondsworth: Penguin, 1992).
Dean, Warren, *Brazil and the Struggle for Rubber: A Study in Environmental History* (Cambridge: Cambridge University Press, 1987).
Decker, John Alvin, *Labour Problems in the Pacific Mandates* (London: Oxford University Press, 1940).
DeMali Francis, David W., and Diane, *Images of America: Akron* (Charleston: Arcadia Publishing, 2004).
Denoon, Donald, and Snowden, Catherine (eds.), *A Time to Plant and a Time to Uproot: A History of Agriculture in Papua New Guinea* (Port Moresby: Institute of PNG Studies, 1981).
Department of Statistics, Straits Settlements and Federated Malay States, *Malaya's Rubber Statistics, 1930: Acreage, Crops, Imports and Exports*, Revised Edition (Singapore: Government Printing Office, 1930).
Dibner, Bern, *The Atlantic Cable* (New York: Blaisdell, 1964).
Dickey, Herbert Spencer (in collaboration with Hawthorne Daniel), *The Misadventures of a Tropical Medico* (London: John Lane and the Bodley Head, 1929).
Doyle, Arthur Conan, *The Crime of the Congo* (London: Hutchinson, c. 1910).
Drew, David, *The Lost Chronicles of the Maya Kings* (London: Weidenfeld and Nicolson, 1999).
Drewe, Robert, *The Shark Net* (Camberwell, VIC: Penguin Books, 2004).
Dubois, Josiah E., Jr., and Edward Johnson, *Generals in Grey Suits: The Directors of the International "I.G. Farben" Cartel, their Conspiracy and Trial at Nuremberg* (London: The Bodley Head, 1953).
Dürrfeld, Walter, *Leistungskampf der Deutschen Betriebe 1942–1943* (Auschwitz: IG Farbenindustrie Aktiengesellschaft Werk Auschwitz OS, 1943).
Dwork, Deborah, and Robert Jan van Pelt, *Auschwitz: 1270 to the Present* (New York and London: W.W. Norton, 1996).
Dwyer, R.E.P., "Rubber Production in New Guinea and Papua," in *The New Guinea Agricultural Gazette*, Vol. 17, No. 4 (Rabaul: Department of Agriculture, Territory of New Guinea, November 1941): 249–279.
Dyer, Joyce, *Gum-Dipped: A Daughter Remembers Rubber Town* (Akron: University of Akron Press, 2003).
Edelman, Marc, "A Central American Genocide: Rubber, Slavery, Nationalism, and the Destruction of the Guatusos-Malekus," *Comparative Studies in Society and*

History, Vol. 40, No. 2 (Ann Arbor: Society for the Comparative Study of Society and History, April 1998).

Ellis, Edward S., *The Rubber Hunters or Adventures in Brazil* (London: Cassell, 1903).

Emmer, P.C., and Shlomowitz, Ralph, *Mortality of Javanese Labour in Surinam (1890–1936) and Malaya (1912–1933)*, Working Papers in Economic History No. 64 (Adelaide: Flinders University, 1995).

Emmer, P.C., "The Meek Hindu; the Recruitment of Indian indentured labourers for Service Overseas, 1870–1916," in P.C. Emmer (ed.), *Colonialism and Migration: Indentured Labour Before and After Slavery* (Dordrecht: Martinus Nijhoff, 1986).

Endres, Kathleen L., *Rosie the Rubber Worker: Women Workers in Akron's Rubber Factories during World War II* (Kent, OH: Kent State University Press, 2000).

Engels, Frederick, *The Part Played by Labour in the Transition from Ape to Man* in *Dialectics of Nature*, trans. Clemens Dutt (Moscow: Progress Publishers, 1934).

Evans, Susan Toby, *Ancient Mexico & Central America: Archaeology and Culture History* (London: Thames and Hudson, 2004).

Ewans, Martin, *European Atrocity, African Catastrophe* (London: Routledge Curzon, 2002).

Fanon, Frantz, *The Wretched of the Earth* (New York: Grove Press, 1963).

Faul, Denis, and Murray, Raymond, *Rubber and Plastic Bullets Kill and Maim* (Belfast: International Tribunal into Deaths and Serious Injuries Caused by Rubber and Plastic Bullets in N. Ireland, 1981).

Fawcett, Percy Harrison, *Exploration Fawcett* (London: Phoenix Press, 2001).

Feldenkirchen, Wilfried, *Werner von Siemens: Erfinder und Internationaler* (Berlin: Siemens Aktiengesellschaft, 1992).

Fédération pour la défense des interest belges à l'étranger, *La Verité sur le Congo* (Brussels: 1906).

Fifer, J. Valerie, "The Empire Builders: A History of the Bolivian Rubber Boom and the Rise of the House of Suarez," in *Journal of Latin American Studies*, Vol. 2, No. 2 (London: Institute for the Study of the Americas, November 1970).

Finley Lewis, Clarice, *A History of Firestone Park* (Akron: Firestone Park Citizens' Council, 1986).

Firth, S.G., "The New Guinea Company, 1855–1899: A Case of Unprofitable Imperialism," *Historical Studies* 15 (59) (Melbourne: Department of History, University of Melbourne, 1972): 361–377.

Fitzpatrick, Peter, "Really Rather like Slavery," in E.L. Wheelwright and Ken Buckley (eds.), *Essays in the Political Economy of Australian Capitalism*, Vol. 3, (Sydney: Australia and New Zealand Book Company, 1978), 102–118.

Fleming, R.W. "The Significance of the Wagner Act," in Milton Derber and Edwin Young (eds.), *Labor and the New Deal* (New York: Da Capo Press, 1972).

Fortey, Richard, *Life: An Unauthorised Biography: A Natural History of the First Four Thousand Million Years of Life on Earth* (London: Flamingo, 1998).

Foster, Lynn V., *Handbook for Life in the Ancient Maya World* (New York: Facts on File, 2002).

Fountain, Paul, *The River Amazon: From Its Sources to the Sea* (London: Constable, 1914).

French, M.J., "The Emergence of a U.S. Multinational Enterprise: The Goodyear

Tire and Rubber Company, 1910–1939," *Economic History Review*, New Series, Vol. 40, No. 1 (London: Economic History Society, February 1987).

Frischauer, Willi, *Goering* (London: Odhams Press, 1951).

Furneaux, Robin, *The Amazon: The Story of a Great River* (London: Hamish Hamilton, 1969).

Galeano, Eduardo, *Open Veins of Latin America: Five Centuries of the Pillage of a Continent*, trans. Cedric Belfrage (New York & London: Monthly Review Press, 1976).

Galey, John, "Industrialist in the Wilderness: Henry Ford's Amazon Venture," *Journal of Interamerican Studies and World Affairs*, Vol. 21, No. 2 (Miami: University of Miami, May 1979): 261–289.

Galloway, Jonathan, "The Military-Industrial Linkages of U.S.-Based Multinational Corporations," in *International Studies Quarterly*, Vol. 16, No. 4 (International Studies Association, December 1972): 491–510.

Gamba, Charles, *The Origins of Trade Unionism in Malaya: A Study in Colonial Labour Unrest* (Singapore: Eastern Universities Press, 1962).

Gann, L.H., and Duigan, Peter, *The Rulers of Belgian Africa (1884–1914)* (Princeton, NJ: Princeton University Press, 1979).

Gareau, Frederick H., "Morgenthau's Plan for Industrial Disarmament in Germany," *The Western Political Quarterly*, Vol. 14, No. 2 (Salt Lake City: Western Political Science Association, June 1961): 517–535.

Geer, William C. *The Reign of Rubber* (London: George Allen and Unwin, 1922).

Gide, André, *Travels in the Congo*, trans. Dorothy Bussey (Harmondsworth: Penguin, 1986).

Giffels, David, "'Readin' Writin' and Route 21: The Road from West Virginia to Ohio," in Evans, Mari-Lynn et al. (eds.), *The Appalachians: America's First and Last Frontier* (New York: Random House, 2004).

Ginaven, Marlene, *Not For Us Alone* (Akron: Stan Hywet Hall Foundation, 1985).

Giuliani, Massimo, *A Centaur in Auschwitz: Reflections on Primo Levi's Thinking* (Lanham, MD: Lexington Books, 2003).

Goldhagen, Daniel Jonah, *Hitler's Willing Executioners: Ordinary Germans and the Holocaust* (New York: Vintage Books, 1997).

Goodyear Tire & Rubber Company, *A Study of the Labour Movement* (Akron: 1920).

Goulding, Michael, Nigel J.H. Smith, and Dennis J. Maher, *Floods of Fortune: Ecology and Economy along the Amazon* (New York: Columbia University Press, 1996).

Graves, Adrian, "Colonialism and Indentured Labour Migration in the Western Pacific, 1840–1915," in P.C. Emmer (ed.), *Colonialism and Migration; Indentured Labour Before and After Slavery* (Dordrecht: Martinus Nijhoff, 1986).

Green, Daniel, *A Plantation Family* (Ipswich: The Boydell Press, 1979).

Green, Edward Crocker, *Rethinking AIDS Prevention: Learning from Successes in Developing Countries* (Westport, CT: Greenwood Publishing, 2003).

Greenman, Leon, *An Englishman in Auschwitz* (London: Vallentine Mitchell, 2001).

Gregory, C.A., *Gifts and Commodities* (London: Academic Press, 1982).

Grismer, Karl H., *Akron and Summit County* (Akron: Summit County Historical Society, c. 1951).

Grogan, Ewart S., and Arthur H. Sharp, *From the Cape to Cairo: The First Traverse of Africa from South to North* (London: Hurst and Blackett, 1900).

Grubb, Kenneth G., *From Pacific to Atlantic: South American Studies* (London: Methuen, 1933).

Guérin, Daniel, *Fascism and Big Business* (New York: Pathfinder Press, 1938).

Guttery, T.E., *Zeppelin: An Illustrated Life of Count Ferdinand Von Zeppelin, 1838–1917* (Aylesbury, Bucks: Shire Publications, 1973).

Hancock, Thomas, *Personal Narrative of the Origin and Progress of the Caoutchouc or India-Rubber Manufacture in England* (London: Longman, Brown, Green, Longmans and Roberts, 1857).

Hanson, Earl, "Social Regression in the Orinoco and Amazon Basins: Notes on a Journey in 1931 and 1932," in *Geographical Review*, Vol. 23, No. 4 (New York: American Geographical Society, October 1933).

Hardenburg, W.E. [ed. C. Reginald Enock], *The Putumayo: The Devil's Paradise: Travels in the Peruvian Amazon Region and An Account of the Atrocities Committed upon the Indian Therein* (London: T. Fisher Unwin, 1912).

Harp, Stephen J., *Marketing Michelin: Advertising and Cultural Identity in Twentieth-Century France* (Baltimore: The Johns Hopkins University Press, 2001).

Harris, Christina Phelps, "The Persian Gulf Submarine Telegraph of 1864," *The Geographical Journal*, Vol. 135, No. 2 (London: Royal Geographical Society, June 1969): 169–190.

Harris, Nigel, "World Crisis and the System," *International Socialism*, 1st Series, No. 100 (London: Socialist Workers Party, July 1977).

Hart, Henry M., "The Fansteel Case: Employee Misconduct and the Remedial Powers of the National Labor Relations Board," *Harvard Law Review*, Vol. 52, No. 8 (Cambridge, MA: Harvard Law Review Association, June 1939): 1275–1329.

Haury, Emil W., "A Pre-Spanish Rubber Ball from Arizona," *American Antiquity*, Vol. 2, No. 2 (Washington, D.C.: Society for American Archaeology, September, 1937): 556–557.

Haye, Amy de la, "'Travellers' Boots, Body-Moulding, Rubber Fetish Clothes: Making Histories of Sub-Cultures," in Gayor Kavanagh (ed.), *Making Histories in Museums* (London: Leicester University Press, 1996), 143–151.

Hayes, Peter, *Industry and Ideology* [Second Ed.] (Cambridge: Cambridge University Press, 2001).

Headrick, Daniel, R., *The Tentacles of Progress: Technology Transfer in the Age of Imperialism, 1850–1940* (London: Oxford University Press, 1988).

Heim, Susanna, *Autarchie und Ostexpansion. Pflanzenzucht und Agrarforschung in Nazionalsozialismus* (Göttingen: Wallstein Verlag, 2002).

Hemming, John, *Amazon Frontier: The Defeat of the Brazilian Indians* (London: Macmillan, 1987).

Henderson, John S., *The World of the Ancient Maya* (Ithaca: Cornell University Press, 1981).

Henderson, Peter V.N., "Modernization and Change in Mexico: La Zacualpa Rubber Plantation, 1890–1920," *The Hispanic American Historical Review*,

Vol. 73, No. 2 (Durham, NC: Conference on Latin American History, May, 1993): 235–260.

Herbert, Vernon, and Bisio, Attilio, *Synthetic Rubber: A Project that Had to Succeed* (Westport, CT: Greenwood Press, 1985).

Herf, Jeffrey, *Reactionary Modernism: Technology, Culture, and Politics in Weimar and the Third Reich* (Cambridge: Cambridge University Press, 1986).

Herrara y Tordesillas, Antonio de, *The General History of the Vast Continent and Islands of America, commonly call'd the West Indies*, Vol. 1, trans. Capt John Stevens (London: Jer. Batley, 1725).

Hessell, Lizzie, compiled by Tony Morrison, Ann Brown, and Anne Rose, *Lizzie: A Victorian Lady's Amazon Adventure* (London: BBC, 1985).

Hett, Walter S., "The Games of the Greek Boy," *Greece and Rome*, Vol. 1, No. 1 (Cambridge: The Classical Association, October, 1931): 24–29.

Hobhouse, Henry, *Seeds of Wealth: Four Plants that Made Men Rich* (London: Macmillan, 2003).

Hobsbawm, Eric, *Age of Extremes: The Short Twentieth Century, 1914–1991* (London: Abacus, 1995).

Hobsbawm, Eric, *Uncommon People: Resistance, Rebellion and Jazz* (London: Abacus, 1999).

Hobson, J.A., *Imperialism: A Study* [Revised Ed.] (London: Constable, 1905).

Hochschild, Adam, *King Leopold's Ghost* (New York: Mariner Books, 1998).

Hoess, Rudolf, *Commandant of Auschwitz: The Autobiography of Rudolf Hoess*, trans. Constantine Fitzgibbon (London: Phoenix Press, 1995).

Homze, Edward L., *Foreign Labor in Nazi Germany* (Princeton, NJ: Princeton University Press, 1967).

Horter, John C., "Cultivated Rubber," *Bulletin of the American Geographical Society*, Vol. 37, No. 12 (New York: American Geographical Society, 1905): 720–724.

House, James S., *Occupational Stress and the Mental and Physical Health of Factory Workers*, Survey Research Center, Institute for Social Research (Ann Arbor: University of Michigan, 1980).

Howard, Frank A., *Buna Rubber: The Birth of an Industry* (New York: D. van Nostrand, 1947).

Howard, Gene L., *The History of the Rubber Workers in Gadsden, Alabama, 1933–1983* (East Gadsden, AL: URWA Local 12, 1983).

Ingham, John N., *Biographical Dictionary of American Business Leaders* (Santa Barbara: Greenwood Press, 1983).

International Institute of Synthetic Rubber Producers, *Synthetic Rubber: The Story of an Industry* (New York: International Institute of Synthetic Rubber Producers, 1973).

International Rubber and Allied Trades Exhibition, *A Short History of the Rubber Industry in Ceylon* (Colombo: Olympia, 1908).

Jain, Ravindra K., "South Indian Labour in Malaya, 1840–1920: Asylum, Stability and Involution," in Kay Saunders (ed.), *Indentured Labour in the British Empire, 1834–1920* (London: Croom Helm, 1984), 158–182.

Johnson, Eric A., and Karl-Heinz Reuband, *What We Knew: Terror, Mass Murder and Everyday Life in Nazi Germany* (London: John Murray, 2005).

Johnson, George (ed.), *The All Red Line: The Annals and Aims of the Pacific Cable Project* (Ottawa: James Hope, 1903).

Johnston, Harry, *George Grenfell and the Congo*, Vol. 1 (London: Hutchinson, 1908).

Jones, Alfred Winslow, *Life, Liberty and Property: A Story of Conflict and a Measurement of Conflicting Rights* (Philadelphia: J.B. Lippincott, 1941).

Jones, Geoffrey, "The Multinational Expansion of Dunlop, 1890–1939," in Geoffrey Jones (ed.), *British Multinationals: Origins, Management and Performance* (London: Gower, 1986), 24–42.

Jones, Geoffrey, "The Growth and Performance of British Multinational Firms before 1939: the Case of Dunlop," in Mira Wilkins (ed.), *The Growth of Multinationals* (Aldershot, Hants: Edward Elgar, 1991).

Kadir, Abdul Aziz bin S.A. et al. (eds.), *Portrait of the Global Rubber Industry: Driving the Wheel of the World Economy* (Kuala Lumpur: International Rubber Research and Development Board, c. 2006).

Kalikiti, Webby Silupya, "Plantation Labour: Rubber Planters and the Colonial State in French Indochina, 1890–1939" (unpublished Ph.D. thesis) (London: SOAS, University of London, 2000).

Kaur, Amarjit, "A History of Forestry in Sarawak," *Modern Asian Studies*, Vol. 32, No. 1 (Cambridge: Cambridge University Press, February 1998).

Kennaway, M.J., *Some Agricultural Enterprises in Malaya, 1933–1934* (Kuala Lumpur: Dept. of Agriculture, Straits Settlements and Federated Malay States), 1934.

Kennedy, Paul, *The Rise and Fall of the Great Powers: Economic Change and Military Conflict from 1500 to 2000* (London: Unwin Hyman, 1988).

Kennedy, P.M., "Imperial Cable Communications and Strategy, 1870–1914," *The English Historical Review*, Vol. 86, No. 341 (Oxford: Oxford University Press, October 1971): 728–752.

Kerbey, J. Orton, *The Land of To-morrow: A Newspaper Exploration Up the Amazon and Over the Andes to the California of South America* (New York: W.F. Brainard, 1906).

Kerbey, J. Orton, *An American Consul in Amazonia* (New York: William Edwin Rudge, 1911).

Kessel, Sim, *Hanged at Auschwitz*, trans. Melville and Delight Wallace (London: Coronet, 1973).

Killeffer, David H., *Banbury the Master Mixer: A Biography of Fernley H. Banbury* (New York: Palmerton, 1962).

Klemperer, Victor, *I Shall Bear Witness* (London: Orion, 1999).

Klippert, Walter E., *Reflections of a Rubber Planter: The Autobiography of An Inquisitive Person* (New York: Vintage Press, 1972).

Knepper, George W., *Akron: City at the Summit* (Akron: Continental Heritage Press, 1981).

Korman, Richard, *The Goodyear Story: An Inventor's Obsession and the Struggle for a Rubber Monopoly* (San Francisco: Encounter Books, 2002).

Kreis, Steven, "The Diffusion of Scientific Management: The Bedaux Company in America and Britain, 1926–1945," in Daniel Nelson (ed.), *A Mental Revolution: Scientific Management since Taylor* (Columbus: Ohio State University Press, 1992).

Kurlansky, Mark, *The Basque History of the World* (London: Vintage, 2000).

La Botz, Dan, *Mask of Democracy: Labor Suppression in Mexico Today* (Boston: South End Press, 1992).

Labour Research Department, *British Imperialism in Malaya*, Colonial Series No. 2 (London: Labour Research Department, CPGB, 1926).

Langbein, Hermann, *People in Auschwitz*, trans. Harry Zohn (Chapel Hill: University of North Carolina Press, 2004).

Lange, Algot (ed. in part by J. Odell Hauser), *In the Amazon Jungle: Adventures in Remote Parts of the Upper Amazon River, including a Sojourn among Cannibal Indians* (New York: G. P. Putnam's Sons, 1912).

Las Casas, Bartoleme de, *A Short Account of the Destruction of the Indies*, ed. & trans. Nigel Griffin (Harmondsworth: Penguin, 1992).

Le Bras, Jean, *Introduction to Rubber*, trans. J.H. Goundry (London: MacLaren and Sons, 1965).

Lemkin, Raphael, *Axis Rule in Occupied Europe: Laws of Occupation, Analysis of Government, Proposals for Redress* (Washington, D.C.: Carnegie Endowment for International Peace, Division of International Law, 1944).

Lenin, V.I., *Imperialism, The Highest Stage of Capitalism* (New York: International Publishers, 1939).

Leonhart, Wolfgang, *Child of the Revolution*, trans. C.M. Woodhouse (London: Ink Links, 1979).

Leroy-Beaulieu, Paul, *De la colonisation chez des peuples modernes* (Quatrième Édition) (Paris: Guillaumin, 1891).

Letter of the King to M. Beernaert, August, 5 1889, in "The King's Testament," *American Journal of International Law*, Vol. 3, No. 1, Supplement: Official Documents, 1909, 27.

Levi, Primo, *The Periodic Table*, trans. Raymond Rosenthal (London: Abacus, 1986).

Levi, Primo, *If This Is a Man*, trans. Stuart Woolf (London: Orion Press, 1960).

Levi, Primo, *The Truce* (London: New English Library, 1962).

Levitt, Sarah, "Manchester Mackintoshes: a history of the rubberized garment trade in Manchester," *Textile History* 17 (1986).

Lewis, D.C., *The Plantation Dream: Developing British New Guinea and Papua, 1884–1942* (Canberra: The Journal of Pacific History, 1996).

Li Kei and Yu Shunzang, "Mortality in a Chinese Rubber Factory: A Prospective Cohort Study," *Journal of Occupational Health*, Vol. 44, No. 2 (2002): 76–82.

Liebrechts, Ch., *Congo: Suite à mes Souvenirs d'Afrique: Vingt années à l'Administration centrale de l'État Indépendant du Congo (1885–1908)* (Brussels: Office de Publicité, 1920).

Lief, Alfred, *The Firestone Story: A History of the Firestone Tire & Rubber Company* (New York: McGraw-Hill, 1951).

Linebaugh, Peter, *The London Hanged: Crime and Civil Society in the Eighteenth Century* (London: Verso, 2003).

Linn, Ruth, *Escaping Auschwitz: The Culture of Forgetting* (Ithaca, NY: Cornell University Press, 2004).

Litchfield, Paul W., *Industrial Voyage: My Life as an Industrial Lieutenant* (New York: Doubleday, 1955).

Litchfield, Paul, *The Republic of Business* (Akron: Goodyear Tire & Rubber, 1920).

Loadman, John, *Tears of the Tree: The Story of Rubber—a Modern Marvel* (Oxford: Oxford University Press, 2005).

López de Gómara, Francisco, *Cortés: The Life of the Conqueror by his Secretary*, trans. & ed. Lesley Bird Simpson (Berkeley: University of California Press, 1965).

Lottman, Herbert R., *The Michelin Men: Driving an Empire* (London and New York: I.B. Taurus, 2003).

Love, Steve, and Giffels, David, *Wheels of Fortune: The Story of Rubber in Akron*, (Akron: University of Akron Press, 1999).

Lulofs, Madelon, *Coolie*, trans. G.J. Renier and Irene Clephane (Singapore: Oxford University Press, 1982).

Lulofs, Madelon, *Rubber*, trans. G.J. Renier and Irene Clephane (Singapore: Oxford University Press, 1987).

Lynd, Staughton, "A Chapter from History: The United Labor Party, 1946–1952," *Liberation* (December 1973).

Lyng, J., *Our New Possession (Late German New Guinea)* (Melbourne: Melbourne Publishing, 1919).

MacDonnell, John de Courcy, *The Life of His Majesty Albert, King of the Belgians* (London: John Long, 1915).

Macedo Soares, José Carlos de, *Rubber: An Economic and Statistical Study* (London: Constable, 1930).

Maloney, William, *The Forged Casement Diaries* (Dublin and Cork: The Talbot Press, 1936).

Mannoni, Octave, *Prospero and Caliban: The Psychology of Colonization*, trans. Pamela Powesland (London: Methuen, 1956).

Maretti, Claudio C. et al., "From Pre-assumptions to a 'Just World Conserving Nature': The Role of Category IV in Protecting Landscapes," in Jessica Brown, Nora Mitchell, and Michael Beresford (eds.), *The Protected Landscape Approach: Linking Nature, Culture and Community* (Gland, Switzerland: International Union for the Conservation of Nature, 2005).

Marès, Roland de, *The Congo* (Brussels: J. Lebègue, c. 1904).

Marin, Flores, *La explotación del Caucho en el Perú* (Lima: Consejo Nacional de Cienca y Tecnología, 1987).

Markham, Clements, "The Cultivation of Caoutchouc-yielding Trees in British India," *Journal of the Society of Arts* (London: April 7, 1876): 475–481.

Martin, G., "Competitive Rubber Plants," *Journal of the Royal Society of Arts*, (London: February 18, 1944): 146–155.

Marx, Karl, *A Critique of Political Economy*, Vol. 1, trans. Ben Fowkes (New York: Penguin Books, 1990).

Marx, Karl, *Capital*, Vol. 1, trans. Eden and Cedar Paul (London: J.M. Dent, Everyman's Library, 1972).

Marx, Karl (ed. Shlomo Averini), *Karl Marx on Colonialism and Modernization: His Despatches and Other Writings on China, India, Mexico, the Middle East and North Africa* (Garden City, New York: Doubleday, 1969).

Marx, Karl, and Frederick Engels, *The Communist Manifesto* in *Selected Works* (Moscow: Progress Publishers, 1970).

Marx, Karl, *The Eighteenth Brumaire of Louis Bonaparte*, in Karl Marx and

Frederick Engels, *Selected Works*, Vol. 1 (Moscow: Progress Publishers, 1969).

Maugham, W. Somerset, *Altogether* (London: William Heinemann, 1934).

Mayhew, Henry, *London Labour and the London Poor* (Harmondsworth: Penguin Books, 1985).

McAlister, Hugh (pseudonym of Margaret Alison Johansen), *Steve Holworth of the Oldham Works: The Story of a Boy Who Chose a Career in the Rubber Industry* (Akron: Saalfield Publishing, 1930).

McClain, Shirla Robinson, *The Contributions of Blacks in Akron: 1825–1975* (Akron: Akron Gallery of Black History Curriculum Committee, 1996).

McCloskey, Burr, *He Will Stay Till You Come, The Rise and Fall of Skinny Walker* (Durham, NC: Moore Publishing, 1978).

McDonald, John and Ralph Sholomowitz, *Mortality of Indian Labour on Ocean Voyages, 1843–1917*, Working Papers on Economic History No. 28 (Adelaide: Flinders University, 1989).

McKay, Donald Vernon, "Colonialism in the French Geographical Movement, 1871–1881," *Geographical Review*, Vol. XXXIII (New York: American Geographical Society, 1943): 214–232.

McKenney, Ruth, *Industrial Valley* (New York: Greenwood Press, 1939).

McMillan, James, *The Dunlop Story: The Life, Death and Rebirth of a Multinational* (London: Weidenfeld and Nicolson, 1989).

Melby, John, "Rubber River: An Account of the Rise and Collapse of the Amazon Boom," *The Hispanic American Historical Review*, Vol. 22, No. 3 (Durham, NC: Conference on Latin American History, August 1942).

Mendes, Chico, and Tony Gross, *Fight for the Forest* (London: Latin American Bureau, 1989).

Meyer, Bruce M., *The Once and Future Union: The Rise and Fall of the United Rubber Workers, 1935–1995* (Akron: University of Akron Press, 2002).

Mitchell, Angus (ed.), *The Amazon Journal of Roger Casement* (London: Anaconda, 1997).

Mitchell, Angus (ed.), *Sir Roger Casement's Heart of Darkness: The 1911 Documents* (Dublin: Irish Manuscripts Commission, 2003).

Morel, E.D ., *Great Britain and the Congo: The Pillage of the Congo Basin* (London: Smith, Elder, 1909).

Morel, E. D. *Red Rubber: The Story of the Rubber Slave Trade Flourishing on the Congo in the Year of Grace 1906* [Second Ed.] (London: T. Fisher Unwin, 1907).

Morel, E. D. *King Leopold's Rule in Africa* (London: William Heinemann, 1904).

Morgenthau, Henry, *Germany Is Our Problem: A Plan for Germany* (New York: Harper Bros, 1945).

Mosco, Maisie, *Almonds and Raisins* (London: New English Library, 1979).

Mountmorres, Viscount, *The Congo Independent State: A Report on a Voyage of Enquiry* (London: Williams and Norgate, 1906).

Mower, J.H., "The Republic of Liberia," *The Journal of Negro History*, Vol. 32, No. 3 (July 1947).

Mundey, Jack, *Green Bans and Beyond* (Sydney: Angus and Robertson, 1981).

Musée du Congo, 1903, *Annexe aux Annales du Musée du Congo. Ethnographie et anthropologie*. Série IV: Fascicule I. E. *Le pays et ses habitants; documents historiques*. Tome I. *L'État Indépendant du Congo—Documents sur le pays et ses habitants* (Brussels: Musée du Congo, 1903).

Naval Intelligence Division, *The Belgian Congo* (London: Geographical Handbook Series, 1944).

Nelson, Daniel, *American Rubber Workers & Organized Labor, 1900–1941* (Princeton, NJ: Princeton University Press, 1988).

Nelson, Hank, *Taim Bilong Masta: The Australian Involvement with Papua New Guinea* (Sydney: Australian Broadcasting Commission, 1982).

Netto, George, *Indians in Malaya: Historical Facts and Figures* (Singapore: George Netto, 1961).

Newbury, Colin, "The Imperial Workplace: Competitive and Coerced Labour Systems in New Zealand, Northern Nigeria, and Australian New Guinea," in Shula Marks and Peter Richardson (eds.), *International Labour Migration: Historical Perspectives* (London: Institute of Commonwealth Studies, 1984).

Nguyen Ngoc Phach, *Life in Vietnam: Through a Looking Glass Darkly* (Melbourne: Nguyen Ngoc Phach, 2005).

Nichols, Kenneth, *Yesterday's Akron: The First 150 Years* (Miami: E.A. Seeman, 1976).

Noakes, Jeremy, and Pridham, Geoffrey (trans. & eds.), *Documents on Nazism, 1919–1945* (London: Jonathan Cape, 1974).

O'Neill, Dennis J., *A Whale of a Territory: The Story of Bill O'Neil* (New York: McGraw Hill, 1966).

Olin, Oscar Eugene, *Akron and Its Environs: Historical: Biographical: Genealogical* (Chicago and New York: Lewis Publishing, 1917).

Orwell, George, "Charles Dickens," *Inside the Whale and Other Essays* (London: Victor Gollancz, 1940).

Orwell, George, *1984* (New York: New American Library, 1983).

Ostermann, Christian F., and Byrne, Malcolm, *Uprising in East Germany* (Budapest: Central European University Press, 2003).

Palmer, Bryan D., *James P. Cannon and the Origins of the American Revolutionary Left, 1890–1928* (Urbana and Chicago: University of Illinois Press, 2007).

Palmer, Colin A., *The Worlds of Unfree Labour: From Indentured Servitude to Slavery* (Aldershot: Ashgate Variorum, 1998).

Parmer, J. Norman, *Colonial Labor Policy and Administration: A History of Labor in the Rubber Plantation Industry in Malaya, c. 1910–1941* (Locust Valley, NY: J.J. Augustin for the Association of Asian Studies, 1960).

Paternoster, G. Sidney, *The Lords of the Devil's Paradise* (London: Stanley Paul, 1913).

Perlman, Selig, *A Theory of the Labor Movement* (New York: Augustus M. Kelly, 1928).

Perry, Elizabeth J., "When Peasants Speak: Sources for the Study of Chinese Rebellion" in *Modern China*, Vol. 6, No. 1 (January 1980): 72–85.

Pesotta, Rose (ed. John Nicholas Beffa), *Bread upon the Waters* (Ithaca, NY: ILR Press, 1987).

Polanyi, Karl, *The Great Transformation: The Political and Economic Origins of Our Time* (Boston, MA: Beacon Press, 1957).

Polasky, Janet, *The Democratic Socialism of Emile Vandervelde: Between Reform and Revolution* (Oxford: Berg, 1995).

Porritt, B.D., *The Early History of the Rubber Industry* (London: Rubber Growers' Association, 1927).

Potter, Lesley, "Community and Environment in Colonial Borneo: Economic Value, Forest Conversions and Concern for Conservation, 1870–1940" in Reed L. Wadley (ed.), *Histories of the Borneo Environment: Economic, Political and Social Dimensions of Change and Community* (Leiden: Verhandelingen van Het Koninklijk Instituut voor Taal, Landen Volkenkunde, 2005).

Priestley, Joseph, *A Familiar Introduction to the Theory and Practice of Perspective* [Second Ed.] (London: J. Johnson, 1789).

"Prospectus of the United States Vulcanized Gutta-percha Belting and Packing Co." (New York: United States Vulcanized Gutta-percha Belting and Packing Co., 1857).

Pugh, Peter, et al. (ed. Guy Nickalls), *Great Enterprise: A History of Harrisons and Crosfield* (London: Harrisons and Crosfield, 1990).

Quine, C.R. (ed.), *The Akron Riot of 1900* (Akron: C.R. Quine, 1951).

Rahn, Joan Elma, *More Plants that Changed History* (New York: Atheneum, 1985).

Ramachandran, Selvakumaran, and Bala Shanmugan, "Plight of Plantation Workers in Malaysia: Defeated by Definitions," *Asian Survey*, Vol. 35, No. 4 (April 1995): 394–407.

Regli, Adolph C., *Rubber's Goodyear: The Story of a Man's Perseverance* (New York: Julian Messner, 1941).

Reid, B.L., *The Lives of Roger Casement* (New Haven, CT: Yale University Press, 1976).

Revkin, Andrew, *The Burning Season: The Murder of Chico Mendes and the Fight for the Amazon Rain Forest* (London: Collins, 1990).

Ricklefs, M.C., *A History of Modern Indonesia c. 1300 to the Present* (Houndmills, Basingstoke: Macmillan Education, 1981).

Rivera, Jose Eustasio, *The Vortex*, trans. E.K. James (London: Putnam, 1935).

Robequain, Charles, *The Economic Development of French Indo-China*, trans. Isabel A. Ward (London: Oxford University Press, 1944).

Roby, Marguerite, *My Adventures in the Congo* (London: Edward Arnold, 1911).

Rodden, Robert G., *The Fighting Machinists: A Century of Struggle* (Washington, D.C.: Kelly Press, 1984).

Ross, Eric B., "The Evolution of the Amazon Peasantry," *Journal of Latin American Studies*, Vol. 10, No. 2 (London: Institute for the Study of the Americas, November 1978): 193–218.

Roth, Joseph, *The Radetzky March*, trans. Eva Tucker and Geoffrey Dunlop (Harmondsworth: Penguin, 1974).

Rowe, J.W.T., *Studies in the Artificial Control of Raw Material Supplies*, Special Memorandum No. 34, No. 2, *Rubber* (London: London and Cambridge Economic Service, London School of Economics, 1931).

Rushton, Colin, *Spectator in Hell: A British Soldier's Story of Imprisonment at Auschwitz* (Chichester, West Sussex: Summersdale, 2001).

Russell, W.H., *The Atlantic Telegraph* (London: Day and Son, c. 1865).

Said, Edward, *Orientalism* (Harmondsworth: Penguin Books, 1978).

Santos, Roberto, *História Econômica da Amazônia* (São Paulo: Quieroz, 1980).

Sawai, Charles, "Plantation Labour Recruitment in New Guinea in the Period 1922 to 1942," in *Yagl-Ambu: PNG Journal of the Social Sciences and Humanities*, 4 (4) (Port Moresby: University of Papua New Guinea, 1977): 294–314.

Sawyer, Roger, *Casement: The Flawed Hero* (London: Routledge and Kegan Paul, 1984).

Schidrowitz, P., and Dawson, T.R. (eds.), *History of the Rubber Industry* (Cambridge: W. Heffer and Sons, 1952).

Schidrowitz, Philip, *Rubber* (London: Methuen, 1911).

Scott, Charles Payson Gurley, "The Malayan Words in English," *Journal of the American Oriental Society*, Vol. 18, (New Haven : American Oriental Society, 1887).

Serier, Jean-Baptiste, *Histoire du Caoutchouc* (Paris: Editions Desjonquères, 1993).

Serier, *Les Barons du Caoutchouc* (Paris: Editions Kathala, 2000).

Sharer, Robert J., *Daily Life in Maya Civilization* (Westport, CT: Greenwood Press, 1996).

Shennan, Margaret, *Out in the Midday Sun: the British in Malaya, 1880–1960* (London: John Murray, 2000).

Shlomowitz, Ralph, and Lance Brennan, *Mortality and Indian Labour in Malaya, 1877–1933*. Working Papers in Economc History, No. 38 (Adelaide: Flinders University, 1990).

Shlomowitz, Ralph, *The Internal Labour Trade in Papua (1884–1941) and New Guinea (1920–1941): An Economic Analysis*, Working Papers in Economic History No. 15 (Adelaide: Flinders University, 1987).

Shuy, Roger W., "Tireworker Terms," *American Speech* (Durham, NC: The American Dialect Society, Duke University Press, 1964).

Slack, Charles, *Noble Obsession: Charles Goodyear, Thomas Hancock, and the Race To Unlock the Greatest Industrial Secret of the Nineteenth Century* (New York: Hyperion, 2002).

Slade, Ruth, *King Leopold's Congo: Aspects of the Development of Race Relations in the Congo Independent State* (London: Oxford University Press, 1962).

Slocomb, Margaret, *Colons and Coolies: The Development of Cambodia's Rubber Plantations* (Bangkok: White Lotus Press, 2007).

Solo, Robert A., *Synthetic Rubber: A Case Study in Technological Development under Government Direction: Study of the Subcommittee on Patents, Trademarks, and Copyrights of the Committee of the Judiciary* (Washington, D.C.: United States Senate, U.S. Government Printing Office, 1959).

Soustelle, Jacques, *Daily Life of the Aztecs on the Eve of the Spanish Conquest*, trans. Patrick O'Brian (London: Phoenix, 2002).

Spire, Camille, and Spire, André, *Le Caoutchouc en Indochine: etude botanique, industrielle et commerciale* (Paris: Augustin Challamel, 1906).

Standage, Tom, *The Victorian Internet: The Remarkable Story of the Telegraph and the Nineteenth Century's Online Pioneers* (London: Phoenix, 1999).

Stanfield, Michael Edward, *Red Rubber, Bleeding Trees: Violence, Slavery, and Empire in Northwest Amazonia, 1850–1933* (Albuquerque: University of New Mexico Press, 1998).

Steele, Valerie, *Fetish: Fashion, Sex and Power* (New York: Oxford University Press, 1996).

Steinbeck, John, *Travels With Charley: In Search of America* (London: Pan Books, 1965).

Stern, Theodore, *The Rubber-Ball Games of the Americas* (New York: J.J. Augustin, 1948).

Sternstein, Jerome L., "King Leopold II, Senator Nelson W. Aldrich, and the Strange Beginnings of American Economic Penetration of the Congo," *African Affairs*, Vol. 68, No. 271 (April 1969): 189–204.

Stonelake, Alfred R., *Congo, Past and Present* (London: World Dominion Press, 1937).

Strickland, Diana, *Through the Belgian Congo* (London: Hurst and Blackett, 1926).

Strickland-Anderson, Lily, "Music in Malaya," *The Musical Quarterly*, Vol. 11, No. 4 (October 1925).

Sweezy, Paul, "Monopoly Capitalism," in John Eatwell, Murray Milgate, and Peter Newman (eds.), *The New Palgrave Dictionary of Economics* (Basingstoke: Palgrave Macmillan, 1987).

Székely, Ladislao (Lázló), *Tropic Fever: The Adventures of a Planter in Sumatra*, trans. Marion Saunders (New York: Harper Bros, 1937).

Tambs, Lewis A., "Rubber, Rebels, and the Rio Branco: The Contest for the Acre," in *The Hispanic-American Historical Review*, Vol. 46, No. 3 (Durham, NC: Conference on Latin American History, August 1966).

Tarbell, Ida M. (ed. David M. Chalmers), *The History of the Standard Oil Company* (New York: Harper & Row, 1966).

Tate, D.J.M., *The RGA History of the Plantation Industry in the Malay Peninsula* (Kuala Lumpur: Oxford University Press, 1996).

Tawney, R. H. *Religion and the Rise of Capitalism: A Historical Study* (Harmondsworth: Penguin, 1938).

Taylor, A.J.P., *The Origins of the Second World War* [Second Ed.] (Greenwich, CT: Fawcett, 1965).

Teed Apha, *By Jungle Track and Paddy Field to Rubber Plantation and Palm Grove* (Liverpool: Henry Young and Sons, 1913).

Terry, Hubert L., *India-Rubber and Its Manufacture, with Chapters on Gutta-Percha and Balata* (London: Archibald Constable, 1907).

"The King's Testament" in *American Journal of International Law*, Vol. 3, No. 1, Supplement: Official Documents (Danvers, MA: American Society of International Law, 1909).

Thompson, E.P., "Time, Work-Discipline, and Industrial Capitalism," *Past and Present*, No. 38 (December 1967): 56–97.

Thompson, *The Making of the English Working Class* (Harmondsworth: Penguin, 1968).

Thompson, Virginia, *Labor Problems in Southeast Asia* (New Haven, CT: Yale University Press, 1947).

Thornton, Jonathan, "A Brief History of the Early Practice and Materials of Gap-Filling in the West," *Journal of the American Institute for Conservation*, Vol. 37, No. 1 (Spring 1998).

Thurber, John Newton, *Rubber Workers' History (1935–1955)* (Akron: Public Relations Office, URCLPWA, AFL-CIO, 1956).

Tomlinson, H.M., *The Sea and the Jungle* (London: The Citadel Press, 1927).

Trades Union Congress, *The Case Against Latex: Rubber Banned?* (London: Trades Union Congress, 2001).

Tran Tu Binh (as told to Ha An), *The Red Earth: A Vietnamese Memoir of Life on a Colonial Rubber Plantation*, ed. David G. Marr and trans. John Spragens, Jr.

(Athens, OH: Center for International Studies, 1985).

Tully, John, *Cambodia under the Tricolour: King Sisowath and the Mission Civilisatrice in Cambodia, 1904–1927* (Clayton, VIC: Monash Asia Institute, 1996).

Tully, John, *France on the Mekong: A History of the Protectorate in Cambodia 1863–1953* (Lanham, Maryland: University Press of America, 2002).

Tully, John, "A Victorian Ecological Disaster: Imperialism, the Telegraph and Gutta-Percha," *The Journal of World History*, Vol. 20, No. 4 (Honolulu: University of Hawaii, 2009): 559–579.

Unsigned, *Annexe aux Annales du Musée du Congo. Ethnographie et anthropologie, série IV fascicule I, Le Pays et ses habitants; documents historiqies:* Vol. I, *L'état Indépendant du Congo. Documents sur le pays et ses habitants* (Brussels: Musée du Congo, 1903).

Unsigned, "Employee Misconduct under the Wagner Act: developments since the Fansteel Case," *Columbia Law Review*, Vol. 39, No. 8 (December 1939): 1369–1382.

Ure, John, *Trespassers on the Amazon* (London: Constable, 1986).

URWA, *25 Years of the URW: A Quarter Century of Panorama of Democratic Unionism* (Akron: United Rubber, Cork, Linoleum and Plastic Workers of America, AFL-CIO, 1960).

Van Tuerenhout, Dirk R., *The Aztecs: New Perspectives* (Santa Barbara: ASC Clio, 2005).

Vandervelde, Emile, *Politique Coloniale, Caoutchouc et Mains Coupées* (Ghent: Volksdrukkerij, 1903).

Vatuk, Ved Prakash, "Protest Songs of East Indians in British Guiana," *Journal of American Folkore*, Vol. 77, No. 305 (July 1964): 220–235.

Venter, Jewell, "Possibilities of Rubber Production in Central America," *Economic Geography*, Vol. 4, No. 4 (October 1928): 381–384.

Wallace, Alfred Russel, *A Narrative of Travels on the Amazon and Rio Negro with an account of the native tribes and observations on the climate, geology and natural history of the Amazon valley* (Glasgow: Grand Colosseum Warehouse, n.d.).

Watson, Malcolm, "The Geographical Aspects of Malaria," *The Geographical Journal*, Vol. 99, No. 4 (London: Royal Geographical Society, April 1942).

Wauters, A.J., *Histoire du Congo Belge* (Brussels: Pierre van Fleteren, 1911).

Weber, Max, *The Protestant Ethic and the Spirit of Capitalism* (London: Unwin Paperbacks, 1985).

Weinstein, Barbara, *The Amazon Rubber Boom 1950–1920* (Stanford: Stanford University Press, 1983).

Whaley, W. Gordon, and John S. Bowen, *Russian Dandelion (Kok-Saghyz): An Emergency Source of Natural Rubber* (Washington, D.C.: United States Department of Agriculture, 1947).

Wheen, Francis, *Karl Marx* (London: Fourth Estate, 1999).

Whymant, A. Neville J., "Chinese Coolie Songs," in *Bulletin of the School of Oriental Studies*, Vol. 1, No. 4 (London: SOAS, University of London, 1920).

Wickham, Henry, *On the Plantation, Cultivation and Curing of Para Indian Rubber* (London: Kegan Paul, 1908).

Wiesel, Elie, *Night*, trans. Stella Rodway (Harmondsworth: Penguin Books, 1982).

Wilcock, Richard C., "Industrial Management's Policies towards Unionism," in

Milton Derber and Edwin Young (eds.), *Labor and the New Deal* (New York: Da Capo Press, 1972).

Wilkins, Mira (ed.), *The Growth of Multinationals* (Aldershot, Hants: Edward Elgar, 1991).

Willis, J.C., M. Kelway Bamber, and E.B. Denham (eds.), *Rubber in the East: Being the Official Account of the Ceylon Rubber Exhibition Held in the Royal Botanic Gardens, Peradiniya, in September, 1906* (Ceylon: H.C. Cottle Government Printer, 1906).

Wilson, H.E., *The Klang Strikes of 1941: Labour and Capital in Colonial Malaya*, Research Notes and Discussion Paper No. 25 (Singapore: Institute of Southeast Asian Studies, 1981).

Wilson, Jack, "In a Billion Dollar Industry," *New International*, Vol. 2, No. 2 (New York: March 1935).

Wolf, Howard, and Ralph Wolf, *Rubber: A Story of Glory and Greed* (New York: Convici- Friede, 1936).

Wolf, Ralph, "La Capitale du Caoutchouc," *Revue Générale du Caoutchouc*, Vol. 35, No. 6 (June 1958).

Wolfers, Edward P., "Trusteeship without Trust: A Short History of Interracial Relations and the Law in Papua and New Guinea," in F.S. Stevens (ed.), *Racism: The Australian Experience, A Study of Race Prejudice in Australia*, Vol. 3, *Colonialism* (Sydney: Australia and New Zealand Book Company, 1972).

Wollaston, A.F.R., *From Ruwenzori to the Congo: A Naturalist's Journey across Africa* (London: John Murray, 1908).

Wolmar, Christian, *The Subterranean Railway: How the London Underground Was Built and How it Changed the City Forever* (London: Atlantic Books, 2005).

Woodroffe, Joseph F. [ed. Harold Hamel Smith], *The Rubber Industry of the Amazon and How Its Supremacy Can Be Maintained* (London: John Bale, Sons and Danielsson, 1915).

Woodruff, William, *The Rise of the British Rubber Industry during the Nineteenth Century* (Liverpool: Liverpool University Press, 1958).

Wright, Herbert, *Rubber Cultivation in the British Empire: A Lecture Delivered to the Society of Arts* (London: MacLaren and Sons, 1907).

Yeap Joo Kim, *Moon above Malaya* (Singapore: Graham Brash, 1991).

Zimet, Susan, and Victor Goodman, *The Great Condom Cover-Up: A Condom Compendium* (New York: Civan, 1988).

Zinoman, Peter, *Colonial Bastille: A History of Imprisonment in Vietnam, 1862–1940* (Berkeley: University of California Press, 2001).

OTHER PERIODICALS

Advertiser, Adelaide
Age, Melbourne
Air Bag, Akron
Akron Beacon Journal, Akron
Akron Strike Bulletin, (IWW), Akron
Akron Times-Press, Akron, Ohio
American Review of Reviews

Annuaire des Syndicats des Planteurs de Caoutchouc de l'Indochine, Saigon
Anti-Slavery Reporter and Aborigines' Friend, London
Argus, Melbourne
Atlantic Monthly, Boston
Australasia, Sydney
Barrier Daily Truth, Broken Hill
Bulletin Financier Suisse, Lausanne
Business Week, New York
Ceylon Observer, Colombo
Chronique Coloniale, Paris
Collier's Weekly, New York
Congressional Record, Washington, D.C.
Contemporary Review
Daily Mirror, London
Daily News, New York
Daily Telegraph, Sydney
Engineering Magazine, London
Financial News, London
Fortnightly Review, London
Fortune Magazine, New York
Gardener's Chronicle, London
Goodyear: A Family Magazine, Akron
Goodyear News, Akron
Goodyear Worker, Akron
Guardian Weekly, London
Guardian, London
Harper's Magazine, New York
Hecht, Levis & Kahn's "Caoutchouc Report" for 1885
Herald, Melbourne
Highway Engineer and Contractor: A Journal of State and City Engineering and Construction Problems, Chicago
India Rubber World, Akron
India-Rubber and Gutta-Percha Trades Journal, London
Indochine Financière et Economique, Paris
Industrial Pioneer: An Illustrated Labor Magazine, Chicago
Industry Record, Washington, D.C.
Liberty Magazine, New York
L'Impartial, Saigon
La Verité sur le Congo, Brussels
Liberty Magazine, New York
London Review of Books, London
Magazine of Wall Street, New York
McClure's Magazine, New York
Mercury, Hobart
Midi-Coloniale, Paris
New Republic, New York
The New York Times, New York

North American Review, New York
Outlook, London
Papuan Times, Port Moresby
Petit Journal, Saigon
Philadelphia Inquirer
Philadelphia Record
Reader's Digest
Rubber Growers' Association Bulletin, London
Scientific American, New York
Sun, Melbourne
Sun, Sydney
Sydney Morning Herald
Time Magazine
Tire Review
United Rubber Worker, Akron
Walkabout, Melbourne
Westways
Wingfoot Clan, Akron
Worker, Sydney

UNPUBLISHED MATERIALS

Beasley, Norman, undated, "Beasley Manuscript" (undated, unpublished typescript
    history of BF Goodrich. Copy in University of Akron Archives [UAA]).
Borsos, John E., "Talking union: The labor movement in Barberton, Ohio,
    1891–1991" (Bloomington, IN: Indiana University, unpublished Ph.D. thesis,
    1992).
Brett. A.C., "All in the year's work: a story of wartime Washington." Unpublished
    typescript in University of Akron Archives. No date.
Chalk, Frank Robert, "The United States and the International Struggle for
    Rubber, 1914–1941" (Madison: University of Wisconsin, unpublished Ph.D.
    History thesis, 1970).
Clausen, Carl, Ann Van Tine, and Patricia Curran, Interview with James Tuner,
    Retired Fair Practices Director Rubber Workers International (Akron: Ohio
    Labor History Project, 1975). Bowling Green State University Center for
    Archival Collections, MMS 922.
Dürrfeld, Walter, "Leistungkampf der Deutschen Betriebe 1942–1943" (Auschwitz:
    IG Farbenindustrie Aktiengesellschaft Werk, Auschwitz OS, 1943).
Frazier, Kevan Delaney, "Model Industrial Subdivisions: Goodyear Heights and
    Firestone Park and the Town Planning Movement in Akron, Ohio" (Kent:
    unpublished M.A. thesis, Kent State University, 1994).
Goodrich, B.F., "Rubber," unpublished typescript, c. 1946, UAA.
Goodrich, B.F., "Biographical History of the Rubber Industry," undated typescript,
    UAA.
House, John D., Microfilm, "Birth of a Union," unpublished book manuscript
    (Columbus: Ohio Historical Society, 1981).

Huy Kanthoul, "Mémoires," undated, unpublished French language typescript,
     copy in Chandler Papers, Monash University Asian Studies Library.
Kalikiti, Webby Silupya, "Plantation Labour: Rubber Planters and the Colonial State in
     French Indochina, 1890–1939" (London: SOAS, University of London, 2000).
Litchfield, P.W., "Crossing the Red Sea: The reveries of an Industrial Lieutenant: A
     Study in Industrial Economics," unpublished typescript, c. 1920, UAA.
Rosswurm, Kevin Michael, "A Strike in the Rubber City: Rubber Workers, Akron,
     and the IWW, 1913," 13. (Kent: Unpublished M.A. thesis, Kent State
     University, 1975).
Sam Pollock Papers. Bowling Green State University center for Archival
     Collections, MS 468 Box 9, Folder 16. Undated and unpublished fragment
     written by James McCartan on the 1913 rubber strike in Akron.
Setkiewicz, Piotr, "British POWs at IG Farben," unpublished typescript c. 2005,
     provided to the author at the Archives of the State Museum of Auschwitz.
Shilts History, 1912–1916, undated, unpublished bound typescript, UAA.
Shrake II, Richard W., "Working-Class Politics in Akron, Ohio, 1936: The United
     Rubber Workers and the Failure of the Farmer-Labor Party" (Akron: unpub-
     lished M.A. thesis, University of Akron, 1974).
Wolf, Howard, "The Akron Beacon-Journal: The First 100 Years" (Akron: unpub-
     lished typescript, 1939). Courtesy of the Akron Beacon Journal archives.
Wortman, Roy, Oral History Interview with Mr. Paul Sebestyen [Sebastian] on
     Akron's Rubber Strike and General Ideological Background (Columbus, OH:
     Dept. of History, Ohio State University, July 8, 1969). Bowling Green State
     University, Center for Archival Collections, p OG 2563.

ELECTRONIC SOURCES (INCLUDING RADIO)

1936 Reichsgesetzblatt, part I, p. 887, available online at
     http://www.adolfhitler.ws/lib/proc/fouryear.html.
ATSDR Agency for Toxic Substances and Diseases Registry. ToxFAQs for Aniline.
     Available online at http://www.atsdr.cdc.gov/tfacts171.html.
Avert: AVERTing HIV and AIDS (2007). Available online at
     http://www.avert.org/condoms.htm.
BBC, History of the Condom (2006). Available online at
     http://www.bbc.co.uk/dna/h2g2/A375446.
Black, Edwin, "At Death's Door: Archivist Finds IBM Site near Auschwitz,"
     Forward (October 11, 2002). Available online at
     http://www.nizkor.org/ftp.cgi/camps/auschwitz/Hollerith-machines-located.
Bolton, Diane K., "Stoke Newington: Economic history," in A History of the County
     of Middlesex: Volume 8: Islington and Stoke Newington Parishes Vol. 8 (1985),
     184–94. Available online http://www.british-history.ac.uk/report.asp?com-
     pid=10548.
Bulletin de la fondation pour le mémoire de la déportation, Mémoire Vivante
     trimestriel, No. 41 (March 2004). Available online at
     http://www.fmd.asso.fr/updir/37/memoire_vivante41.pdf.
Charles Booth Online Archive. Charles Booth, 1840–1916—a biography. London

School of Economics. Available online at http://booth.lse.ac.uk/static.c/2.html.
De Miranda, Alvaro, "Creative East London in Historical Perspective," occasional
    paper (University of East London, 2007). Available online at
    http://www.uel.ac.uk/risingeast/archive07/academic/miranda.pdf.
Dempsey, Mary A., "Fordlandia," *Michigan History* (1994). Available online at
    http://www.michiganhistorymagazine.com/extra/fordlandia.html.
Dorman, Marcus R.P. [eds. Brendan Lane and Martin Pettitt], *A Journal of a Tour
    in the Congo Free State*. Available online at
    http://www.gutenberg.org/files15240/15240-h/15240-h.htm.
Dwight D. Eisenhower Library, "Interstate Highway System." Available online at
    http://www.eisenhower.archives.gov/dl/InterstateHighways/InterstateHighways
    documents.html.
Ebrahim-zadeh, Christine, "Dutch Disease: Too Much Wealth Managed Unwisely,"
    in *Finance and Development: A Quarterly Magazine of the IMF*, Vol. 40, No. 1
    (March 2003). Available online at
    www.imf.org/external/pubs/ft/fandd/2003/03/ebra.htm.
Firestone Natural Rubber Company website, available online at http://www.firesto-
    nenaturalrubber.com/.
Firestone, Harvey S., Jr., "Leopold II: 'Reign of Terror over the Congo,'" The
    Romance and Drama of the Rubber Industry: radio talks delivered by Harvey
    S. Firestone Jr., in "The Voice of Firestone" programs over the nationwide net-
    work of National Broadcasting Company, September 1931 to September 1932,
    (Akron, OH: Firestone Tire & Rubber, 1932). UAA Transcript.
"Garnaut Climate Change Interim Report to the Commonwealth, State and
    Territory Governments of Australia." Available online at http://www.garnautre-
    view.org.au/CA25734E0016A131/pages/reports-and-papers.
Heim, Susanne, "Science Without Scruples," Max Planck Research Project on the
    History of the Kaiser Wilhelm Institute Under National Socialism (2005).
    Available online at http://www.mpg.de/english/illustrationsDocumentation/mul-
    timedia/mpResearch/2005/heft03/3_05MPR_60_65_pdf.pdf.
Herodotus, *The History of Herodotus*, Book One, I, 94, trans. George Rawlinson,
    1994. Available online at http://classics.mit.edu/Herodotus/history.html.
Hoad, T.F. (ed.), *The Concise Oxford Dictionary of English Etymology*, Oxford
    Reference Online, OUP, Victoria University of Technology. Available online at
    http://0-www.oxfordreference.com.library.vu.edu.au:80/views/ENTRY/html?
    subviewMain&entry=t27.e3385.
Issac, John R, "History of the Atlantic Cable & Submarine Telegraphy," 2007.
    Available online at http://www.atlantic-cable.com/Books/1857Isaac/index.htm.
Jones, Ronald, *Caesar's Cosmic Garden*, Institutionen för Konstoch
    Musikvetenskap, Lunds Universitet, Stockholm, January 29 to February 20,
    2000. Available online at http://www.arthist.lu.se/discontinuities/inscriptions/rj-
    caesar-eng.htm.
Keats, John, "The Fall of Hyperion – A Dream." Available online at
    http://www.john-keats.com/gedichte/the_fall_of_hyperion.htm.
Knowles, Richard D., "Transport shaping space: differential collapse in time-space"
    in *Journal of Transport Geography*, Vol. 14, No. 6 (November, 2006), 407–425.
    Available online at http://ntlsearch.bts.gov/tris/record/tris/01041310.html.

Labor Rights and Press. Available online at
    http://www.laborrights.org/press/index.html.
"Liberté pour l'Histoire!" in *RFI Actualité* (December 13, 2005). Available online at
    http://www.rfi/fr/actfr/articles/072/article_40466.asp.
Li Kei and Yu Shunzang, "Mortality in a Chinese Rubber Factory: A Prospective
    Cohort Study" in *Journal of Occupational Health*, Vol. 44, No. 2 (2002):
    76–82. Available online at http://joh.med.uoeh-u.ac.jp/e/E/44_2_03.html.
Lifton, Robert J, "The Nazi Doctors: Medical Killing and the Psychology of
    Genocide." Available online at http://www.mazal.org/Lifton/LiftonT147.htm.
Madeira-Mamoré Railway Society website. Available online at
    www.ferrolatino.ch/FLBMexChileMadMamEng.htm.
Measuringworth.com. Available online at http://www.measuringworth.com/calcula-
    tors/uscompare/result.php.
Menzies' 1941 Diary. Entry for January 29, 1941. Available online at
    http://www.oph.au/menziesonpeople.htm.
Sojourner Truth, "Ain't I A Woman?" Speech to the Women's Convention, Akron,
    Ohio, December 1851. Available online at
    http://www.fordham.edu/halsall/mod/sojtruth-woman.html.
Morrison, Allen, "The Tramways of Manaus, Amazonas State, Brazil," (n.d.).
    Available online at www.tramz.com.br.mn.html.
MSN Encarta. Available online at http://encarta.msn.com/encyclope-
    dia_761556347_5/Rubber.html.
National Defense Highway System. Available online at
    http//www.globalsecurity.org/military/facility/ndhs.htm.
Orwell, George, "Charles Dickens" (1940). Available online at
    http:www.orwell.ru/library/reviews/dickens/e_chd.
Shuy, Roger W., "Language Call. Benny Come Home" (2007). Available online at
    http://itre.cis.upenn.edu/~myl/languagelog/archives/004012.html.
Siemens, "Milestones." Available online at
    http://www.siemens.com/index.jsp?sdc_p=ft4mlsu20o1236410i1264228pCO
    RPcz4&sdc_bcpath=1233808.s_0,&sdc_sid=934834636&.
Slivinski, Steven, "The Corporate Welfare State: How the Federal Government
    Subsidizes US Business" in *Policy Analysis*, No. 592 (Washington, DC: The
    Cato Institute, May 14, 2007). Available online at http://www.cato.org/pub_dis-
    play.php?pub_id=8230.
Staudenmaier, Peter, "Fascist Ecology: the 'Green Wing' of the Nazi Party and its
    Historical Antecedents." Available online at
    http://www.scribd.com/doc/8750846/Eco-Fascism-Fascist-Ideology-the-Green-
    Wing-of-the-Nazi-Party-and-Its-Historical-Antecedents-by-Peter-Staudenmaier
Stenou, Katérina (ed.), "Struggles Against Slavery: International Year to
    Commemorate the Struggle Against Slavery and Its Abolition" (Paris:
    UNESCO, 2004). Available online at
    http://unesdoc.unesco.org/images/0013/001337/133738.pdf.
Straumann, Lukas, "Nazis: Pflanzenzüchtung für de End-Sieg" (2004). Available
    online at http://www.onlinereports.ch/2004/.
Taylor, Frederick Winslow, *Principles of Scientific Management* (1911). Available
    online at http://melbecon.unimelb.edu/het/taylor/sciman.htm.

Tilzey, Paul, "Roger Casement: Secrets of the Black Diaries" (2002). Available online at http://www.bbc.co.uk/history/british/britain_wwone/casement_05.shtml.

Trotsky, Leon, *Fascism—What It Is and How to Fight It*, Ch. 6. Available online at http://history.eserver.org/fighting-fascism/.

United Nations, "Human Rights in Liberia's Rubber Plantations: Tapping into the Future" (May 2006). Available online at http://www.stopfirestone.org/liberiarubber.pdf.

Weber, Max, "Politics as a Vocation." Lecture delivered at Munich University in 1918. Available online at http://www.ne.jp/asahi/moriyuki/abukuma/weber/lecture/politics_vocation.html.

World Rainforest Movement, "Malaysia: Women Plantation Workers' Conditions in Oil Palm Plantations" (2006). Available online at http://www.wrm.org.uy/bulletin/105/Malaysia.html.

Notes

AUTHOR'S PREFACE: WHY A BOOK ON RUBBER

1. On the engineer's story, see David H. Killeffer, *Banbury the Master Mixer: A Biography of Fernley H. Banbury* (New York: Palmerton, 1962).
2. Karl Marx, *Capital*, Vol. 1, trans. Eden & Cedar Paul (London: J.M. Dent, Everyman's Library, 1972), 43–44.
3. John Tully, *France on the Mekong: A History of the Protectorate in Cambodia 1863–1953* (Lanham, MD: University Press of America, 2002).
4. Vicki Baum, *The Weeping Wood* (London: Michael Joseph, 1945), vii.
5. Jack Mundey, *Green Bans and Beyond* (Sydney: Angus and Robertson, 1981), 148. Mundey was a leader of the celebrated green bans movement, which allied members of Mundey's union—the NSW branch of the Builders Labourers' Federation—with environmental activists. Although the union was crushed by a coalition of employers, developers, gangsters, governments, and venial union officials, its ideas live on. Mundey's union gave the world the word "green" as a synonym for ecological consciousness.

INTRODUCTION: THE MUSCLES AND SINEWS
OF INDUSTRIAL SOCIETY

1. University of Akron Archives (hereafter UAA). Goodyear Files. Goodyear Labor (Personnel) Box 1. Paul Litchfield talk to the American Chemical Society, Boston, Massachusetts, September 13, 1939.
2. Linotex was invented by Bernard "Wilkie" Wilkinson, who had begun working life in the rubber industry as a plantation assistant in Malaya. It was patented in 1923. See Peter Pugh et al, *Great Enterprise: A History of Harrisons and Crosfield*, ed. Guy Nickalls (London: Harrisons and Crosfield, 1990), 102.
3. Fordyce Jones, "Early History to 1826" in P. Schidrowitz and T.R. Dawson (eds.), *History of the Rubber Industry* (Cambridge: W. Heffer and Sons, 1952), 1.
4. Richard Fortey, *Life: An Unauthorised Biography: A Natural History of the First Four Thousand Million Years of Life on Earth* (London: Flamingo, 1998), 96.
5. International Institute of Synthetic Rubber Producers, *Synthetic Rubber: The Story of an Industry* (New York: IISRP, 1973), 8.

6.   William T. Shenkell, "Rubber—Little Giant of an Industry," *Akron Times-Press* (Akron: October 4, 1934).

7.   Unsigned, "Footwear From Old Tires," *India Rubber World*, Vol. 78, No. 3 (Akron: June 1, 1928): 78.

8.   Vernon Herbert and Attilio Bisio, *Synthetic Rubber: A Project that Had to Succeed* (Westport, CT: Greenwood Press, 1985), ix.

9.   T.R. Dawson, "Chronology of Rubber History," in Schidrowitz and Dawson.

10.   Karl Marx, *Capital*, Vol. 1, trans. Eden & Cedar Paul (London: J.M. Dent, Everyman's Library, 1972), 43–44.

11.   Ibid., 45.

12.   According to the writer W.H. Johnson (cited in Philip Schidrowitz, *Rubber* (London: Methuen, 1911), 2) the French word *caoutchouc* is derived from the Amerindian word *cauchu*, itself derived from the words *cau* (wood) and *ochu* (to run or weep). The German variation is *Kautschuk*.

13.   See for example. C.E. Akers, *The Rubber Industry in Brazil and the Orient* (London: Methuen, 1914), 2.

14.   Joseph Priestley's preface to his *Familiar Introduction to the Theory and Practice of Perspective* (1770 edition). (Cited in William C. Geer, *The Reign of Rubber* (London: George Allen and Unwin, 1922), 6.) The 1780 edition of the book, published in London by J. Johnson, omits the reference to rubber and "a few crumbs of soft bread" is recommended instead as an eraser, which suggests that *caoutchouc* was expensive and hard to come by.

15.   B.D. Porritt, *The Early History of the Rubber Industry* (London: Rubber Growers' Association, 1927), 5.

16.   This is how we still describe sheets of thin and pliable rubber today.

17.   Robert J. Barnhart (ed.), *The Barnhart Dictionary of Etymology* (New York: H. and W. Wilson, 1988), 579.

18.   *MSN Encarta* online at http://encarta.msn.com/encyclopedia_761556347_5/ Rubber.html. See also Abdul Aziz bin S.A. Kadir et al (eds.), *Portrait of the Global Rubber Industry: driving the wheel of the world economy* (Kuala Lumpur: International Rubber Research and Development Board, 2006).

19.   Warren Dean, *Brazil and the Struggle for Rubber: a study in environmental history* (Cambridge: Cambridge University Press, 1987), 8–9.

20.   John Loadman, *Tears of the Tree: The Story of Rubber—A Modern Marvel* (London: Oxford University Press, 2005), 276.

21.   G. Martin, "Competitive Rubber Plants," *Journal of the Royal Society of Arts* (London: Royal Society of Arts, February 18, 1944), 146.

22.   Ibid.

23.   Ibid. Only about 0.2 percent of the common European dandelion is rubber and 0.4 percent of salsify root.

24.   Neil Baldwin, *Edison: inventing the century* (New York: Hyperion, 1995), 380–381.

25.   "Scouts Soviet Oil Rubber," *India Rubber World*, Vol. 84, No. 3, (Akron: June 1, 1931).

26.   James McMillan, *The Dunlop Story: The Life, Death and Rebirth of a Multinational* (London: Weidenfeld and Nicolson, 1989), 36.

27.   However, eschewing steel, some of the most advanced rail systems, following the lead of the Paris *Métro*, now employ solid rubber wheels (an innovation which first appeared, albeit with mixed success, on the French SNCF's Micheline railcars during the 1930s).

28.   See Geoffrey Jones, "The Growth and Performance of British Multinational Firms before 1939: The Case of Dunlop," in Mira Wilkins (ed.), *The Growth of Multinationals* (Aldershot, Hants: Edward Elgar, 1991). See in particular Wilkins's introduction to the book.

29.   This is a point that Francis Wheen emphasizes in his biography of Marx. (Francis Wheen, *Karl Marx* (London: Fourth Estate, 1999).)

30.   Karl Marx and Frederick Engels, *Manifesto of the Communist Party* in *Selected Works* (Moscow: Progress Publishers, 1970), 39.

31.   UAA. Goodyear Files. Advertising Box 1.

32.   Michelin's innovative advertising is the subject of a superb book by University of Akron historian Steve Harp. (See Stephen J. Harp, *Marketing Michelin: Advertising and Cultural Identity in Twentieth-Century France* (Baltimore: The Johns Hopkins University Press, 2001).

33.   Herbert R. Lottman, *The Michelin Men: Driving an Empire* (London: I.B. Taurus, 2003), 95.

34.   *1884–1909: The Quarter Century Number of the India-Rubber Journal: A Souvenir* (London: Maclaren and Sons, 1909.

35.   Robert Drewe, *The Shark Net* (Camberwell, VIC: Penguin, 2000), 29.

36.   Walter E. Klippert, *Reflections of a Rubber Planter: The Autobiography of an Inquisitive Man* (New York: Vintage Press, 1972).

37.   Drewe, 29.

38.   Joyce Dyer, *Gum-Dipped: A Daughter Remembers Rubber Town* (Akron: University of Akron Press, 2003), 91.

39.   Ibid., 171.

40.   UAA. JB1-24. BF Goodrich Files. Copy of the *Congressional Record: Proceedings and Debates of the 78th Congress*, First session, September 28, 1943. Speech by Mr. Patman.

41.   UAA. JA1-72. BF Goodrich Files. RMA publication, "We Had to Have Rubber," 1945.

42.   UAA. JA1-23. BF Goodrich Files. "Mushroom rubber."

43.   Austin Coates, *The Commerce in Rubber: The First 250 Years* (Singapore: Oxford University Press, 1987), 3.

44.   Jean-Baptiste Serier, *Histoire du Caoutchouc* (Paris: Editions Desjonquères, 1993), 7

Part One—From the Sacred Essence of life to the Muscles and Sinews of Industrial Society

ONE: RUBBER IN MESOAMERICAN CIVILIZATION

1.   Antonio de Herrara y Tordesillas, *The General History of the Vast Continent and Islands of America, commonly call'd the West Indies*, Vol. 1, trans. Capt. John Stevens (London: Jer. Batley, 1725), 349.

2.   Herodotus, *The History of Herodotus*, Book One, 1, trans. George Rawlinson (1994): 94. Available online at http://classics.mit.edu/Herodotus/history.html. I am indebted to Herodotus specialist Dr. Julia Kindt of Sydney University's Department of Classics and Ancient History for confirming my observations.

3.   See for example Walter S. Hett, "The Games of the Greek Boy," *Greece and Rome*, Vol. 1, No. 1 (October 1931): 24–29.

4.   The claim was made by Fordyce Jones' "Early History to 1826," in P. Schidrowitz

and T.R. Dawson (eds.), *History of the Rubber Industry* (Cambridge: W. Heffer and Sons, 1952). This claim is somewhat repeated by John Loadman, *Tears of the Tree: The Story of Rubber – A Modern Marvel* (London: Oxford University Press, 2005), 1. Most likely, as in later European societies, the "very bouncy balls" were made of animal bladders.

5. An encyclopedia alleged that the chariot was shod with solid two-inch thick tires. Expert advice was that the chariot's wheels had been cushioned with leather. Editorial, "Rubbered Egyptian Chariot Hoax," *India Rubber World*, Vol. 85, No. 6, (Akron: February 1, 1931).

6. Mesoamerica refers to the region of Central America inhabited by the most technologically advanced Indian societies, such as the Aztecs, Maya and Olmecs, in the period before the Spanish conquest.

7. There are a number of other rubber-bearing plants in North America and elsewhere, including guayule, but extraction of the rubber is more difficult and the yields are not as great as those from tropical rubber trees.

8. Rubber trees grow in a thick belt from Chiapas province in southern Mexico through to Panama and into Colombia in South America. See, for instance, Jewell Venter, "Possibilities of Rubber Production in Central America," *Economic Geography*, Vol. 4, No. 4 (October 1928): 381–384.

9. Susan Toby Evans, *Ancient Mexico & Central America: archaeology and culture history* (London: Thames and Hudson, 2004), 113.

10. Howard and Ralph Wolf, *Rubber: A Story of Glory and Greed* (New York: Convici-Friede, 1936), 211.

11. See B.D. Porritt, *The Early History of the Rubber Industry* (London: Rubber Growers' Association, 1927), 2; Jean Le Bras, *Introduction to Rubber*, trans. J.H. Goundry (London: MacLaren and Sons, 1965), 7; John Hemming, *Amazon Frontier: the defeat of the Brazilian Indians* (London: Macmillan, London, 1987), 271. Porritt and Le Bras cite Antonio de Herrara as the source of this information. I was unable to locate this in the copy of Herrara's work in the British Library's collection. It is possible that they might be referencing another edition.

12. Austin Coates, *The Commerce in Rubber: the first 250 years* (Singapore: Oxford University Press, 1987), 3.

13. T. R. Dawson, "Chronology of Rubber History" in Schidrowitz and Dawson, ix–xxiv.

14. Peter Martyr's *De Orbe Novo* (1511). (Cited in Coates.)

15. F.J. de Torquemada, *Monorbia Indias*, Vol. 2 (1615): 603. (Cited in G.L. Hammond, "Rubber in Medicine and Surgery" in Schidrowitz and Dawson, 260.)

16. Ibid.

17. Herrara. The book was originally published in Spain in 1601.

18. See, for instance, Dirk R. Van Tuerenhout, *The Aztecs: New Perspectives* (Santa Barbara, California: ASC Clio, Santa Barbara, 2005); Jacques Soustelle, *Daily Life of the Aztecs on the Eve of the Spanish Conquest*, trans. Patrick O'Brian (London: Phoenix, 2002); Inga Clendinnen, *Aztecs: An Interpretation* (Cambridge: Cambridge University Press, 1991); John S. Henderson, *The World of the Ancient Maya* (Ithaca: Cornell University Press, 1981); Susan Toby Evans, *Ancient Mexico and Central America: Archaeology and Culture History* (London: Thames and Hudson, 2004); Robert J. Sharer, *Daily Life in Maya Civilization* (Westport, CT: Greenwood Press, 1996); and Lynn V. Foster, *Handbook for Life*

in the Ancient Maya World (New York: Facts on File, 2002). An earlier work was Theodore Stern, *The Rubber-Ball Games of the Americas* (New York: J. J. Augustin, 1948).

19.   Van Tuerenhout, 196. Van Tuerenhout records that men in Sinaloa today play a similar game with a heavy, solid rubber ball, wearing leather loincloths for protection.

20.   Joseph F. Woodroffe, *The Rubber Industry of the Amazon and how its supremacy can be maintained*, ed. Harold Hamel Smith (London: John Bale, Sons and Danielsson), 26.

21.   A ball court was discovered in Arizona in 1935 and a pre-Spanish rubber ball even earlier, in 1909. See Emil W. Haury, "A Pre-Spanish Rubber Ball from Arizona," *American Antiquity*, Vol. 2, No. 2 (September 1937): 556–557. It is possible that the rubber for the balls was extracted from the Guayule shrub, which is native to what is now the U.S. Southwest, but this is speculation on my part.

22.   Herrara, 340.

23.   Dawson, ix.

24.   Jean-Baptiste Serier, *Histoire du Caoutchouc* (Paris: Editions Desjonquères, 1993), 253

25.   Herrara, 342.

26.   Inga Clendinnen, *Aztecs: An Interpretation* (Cambridge: Cambridge University Press, 1991), 143.

27.   Herrara, 341.

28.   Francisco López de Gómara, *Cortés: The Life of the Conqueror by his Secretary*, trans. & ed. Lesley Bird Simpson (Berkeley: California University Press, 1965), 146. The book was originally published in Zaragoza in 1552.

29.   Herrara, 341. Spelling in the original.

30.   Clendinnen, 144.

31.   Herrara, 340.

32.   David Drew makes the claim in his book *The Lost Chronicles of the Maya Kings* (London: Weidenfeld and Nicolson, 1999), 235. Evans claims that an Aztec ball team toured Europe 500 years ago, but does not give a source for the information (113).

33.   Gómara, 390.

34.   Clendinnen, 144

35.   Evans, 113–114.

36.   Ibid.

37.   Serier (1993), 18.

TWO: RUBBER IN THE INDUSTRIAL REVOLUTION

1.   Inventor of the Week Archive, Lemelson-MIT Program. Available online at http://web.mit.edu/invent/iow/goodyear.html. This version omits the first sentence, but it is included in "Charles Goodyear and the Strange Story of Rubber," *Reader's Digest* (January 1958).

2.   Austin Coates, *The Commerce in Rubber: The First 250 Years* (Singapore: Oxford University Press, 1987), 15.

3.   B.D. Porritt, *The Early History of the Rubber Industry* (London: Rubber Growers' Association, 1927), 2.

4.   C.E. Akers, *The Rubber Industry in Brazil and the Orient* (London: Methuen, 1914), 2.

5.   John Hemming, *Amazon Frontier: The Defeat of the Brazilian Indians* (London: Macmillan, 1987), 271.

6.   Howard and Ralph Wolf, *Rubber: A Story of Glory and Greed* (New York: Convici-Friede, 1936), 28.

7.   Hemming, 272.

8.   Porritt, 5.

9.   Mark Kurlansky, *The Basque History of the World* (London: Vintage, 2000), 104.

10.   Bertolt Brecht, "The Tailor of Ulm," in John Willett and Ralph Manheim (eds.) with the cooperation of Erich Fried, *Bertolt Brecht Poems 1913–1956* (New York: Eyre Methuen, 1976), 243.

11.   The process was invented by the physician L.A.P. Hérissant and the chemist Pierre Joseph Macquer. It was patented by Samuel Peel in 1790 or 1791. See Le Bras, 12.

12.   Coates, 16–17. A popular account of these incidents is to be found in Henry Hobhouse, *Seeds of Wealth: Four Plants that Made Men Rich* (London: Macmillan, 2003), 127.

13.   There are a number of books on the subject of Zeppelins. A recent publication is Peter Brooks, *Zeppelin: Rigid Airships, 1893–1940* (Drexel Hill, PA: Putnam Aeronautics, 1991).

14.   Coates, 16–17.

15.   James McMillan, *The Dunlop Story: The Life, Death and Re-birth of a Multinational* (London: Weidenfeld and Nicolson, 1989), 67. See also M.J. Kennaway, *Some Agricultural Enterprises in Malaya, 1933–1934* (Kuala Lumpur: Department of Agriculture, Straits Settlements and Federated Malay States, 1934), 53.

16.   Anon., "A chronological history of the trade," *1884–1909, The Quarter Century Number of the India-Rubber Journal: A Souvenir* (London: Maclaren and Sons, 1909).

17.   International Institute. See also William C. Geer, *The Reign of Rubber* (London: George Allen and Unwin, 1922), 7.

18.   Cited in Hemming, 272.

19.   Coates, 16–17.

20.   McMillan, 34.

21.   It would appear that Stoke Newington's rubber industry died in the ashes of the factory. Economic historian Diane Bolton does not mention it in her history of the borough. Diane K. Bolton, "Stoke Newington: Economic History," in *A History of the County of Middlesex: Islington and Stoke Newington parishes*, Vol. 8. (1985): 184–194. Available online at http://www.british-history.ac.uk/report.asp?compid=10548.

22.   Sarah Levitt, "Manchester Mackintoshes: A History of the Rubberized Garment trade in Manchester," *Textile History* 17, (1986): 51. It would seem that Macintosh added the "k" to his firm's name for easier recognition in marketing.

23.   Cited in McMillan, 34–35.

24.   Coates, 25.

25.   Levitt, 58. Salford, which became part of the sprawl of Greater Manchester, was administered separately.

26.   Ibid., 67.

27.   University of Akron Archives (UAA). BF Goodrich Files. JA1-37. Biographical History of the Rubber Industry (n.d.).

28.   Schidrowitz, 4.

29.   Charles Goodyear's story has been told by a number of authors. Two widely avail-

able recent texts are: Richard Korman, *The Goodyear Story: An Inventor's Obsession and the Struggle for a Rubber Monopoly* (San Francisco: Encounter Books, 2002), and Charles Slack, *Noble Obsession: Charles Goodyear, Thomas Hancock, and the Race to Unlock the Greatest Industrial Secret of the Nineteenth Century* (New York: Hyperion, 2002).

30.   Howard and Ralph Wolf, 34.
31.   International Institute, 12.
32.   Henry Mayhew, *London Labour and the London Poor* (Harmondsworth: Penguin Books, 1985), 167.
33.   Levitt, 52.
34.   Abdul Aziz bin S.A. Kadir et al (eds.), *Portrait of the Global Rubber Industry: driving the wheel of the world economy* (Kuala Lumpur: International Rubber Research and Development Board, c. 2002).
35.   Schidrowitz, 5–7.
36.   John Loadman, *Tears of the Tree: The Story of Rubber – A Modern Marvel* (London: Oxford University Press, 2005), 236–236.
37.   Thomas Hancock, *Personal Narrative of the Origin and Progress of the Caoutchouc or India-Rubber Manufactures in England* (London: Longman, Brown, Green, Longmans and Roberts, 1857).
38.   Ibid., 169–181.
39.   UAA. BF Goodrich Files. Box NA1-1, "Chronology of BF Goodrich."
40.   Christian Wolmar, *The Subterranean Railway: How the London Underground Was Built and How It Changed the City Forever* (London: Atlantic Books, 2005), 42–43.
41.   Ibid., 137.
42.   T.R. Dawson in Dawson and Schidrowitz, xx.
43.   Howard and Ralph Wolf, 34.
44.   UAA Goodyear Files. Goodyear History, Box 4, "Chronological Data Rubber History Book 2."
45.   Korman, 7.
46.   Ambrose Foster, "Fifty Years in the Trade, 1884–1909," *The Quarter Century Number of the India-Rubber Journal: A Souvenir* (London: Maclaren and Sons, 1909). Foster's father was Lavater's financial backer.
47.   *India Rubber Journal*, Vol. IV, No. 12 (London: July 9, 1888). (Hereinafter *IRJ*.)
48.   Ibid., Vol. VII, No. 2 (September 8, 1890).
49.   Ibid., Vol. V, No. 3 (October 8, 1888).
50.   Ibid., Vol. V, No. 4 (November 8, 1888) and Vol. VI, No. 3 (October , 1889).
51.   George Orwell, "Charles Dickens," *Inside the Whale and Other Essays* (London: Victor Gollancz, London, 1940). This essay does not appear in the 1962 Penguin edition, but is available online at http:www.orwell.ru/library/reviews/dickens/e_chd.
52.   Susan Zimet and Victor Goodman, *The Great Cover Up: A Condom Compendium* (New York: Civan, 1988).
53.   Ibid., 3.
54.   Ibid., 14.
55.   Robert Drewe, *The Shark Net* (Camberwell, VIC: Penguin), 308–309.
56.   Geoffrey Blainey, *Jumping Over the Wheel* (St. Leonards, NSW: Allen & Unwin, 1993), 238.
57.   Zimet and Goodman, 15.
58.   *Avert: AVERTing HIV and AIDS* (2007). Available online at http://www.avert.org/condoms.htm.

59.   BBC, History of the Condom (2006). Available online at http://www.bbc.co.
      uk/dna/h2g2/A375446.
60.   Zimet and Goodman, 23.
61.   Figures calculated from Edward Crocker Green, *Rethinking AIDS Prevention:
      Learning from Successes in Developing Countries* (Westport, CT: Greenwood
      Publishing, 2003), 102.
62.   Ibid., 148.
63.   Janet Bloor and John D. Sinclair, *Rubber! Fun, Fashion, Fetish* (London: Thames
      and Hudson, 2004), 9.
64.   Nick Barlay, "Mr. and Mrs. Blowup and Chums," *The Guardian* (London:
      August 2, 2000).
65.   "Style for Bathing Accessories," *IRW*, Vol. 82, No. 1 (Akron: May 1, 1930).
66.   Damon Guppy, "Blow-up Sex Doll Suspect Arrested in Cairns," *Cairns Post*
      (Cairns, QLD: January 21, 2009).
67.   "Scalp Massage Device," *IRJ*, Vol. 79, No. 2 (London: November 1, 1928).
68.   *Akron Times-Press*, undated clipping from the archives of the *Akron Beacon
      Journal*.
69.   Pres Bergin, "Dy-Dee Dolls Conquer Even 'Prude' Group," *Akron Times-Press*
      (December 2, 1937).
70.   Ken Nichols, "Santa's Helper Keeps an Eye on Toyland," *Akron Beacon Journal*
      (December 20, 1980).
71.   McMillan, 36.
72.   Denis Faul and Raymond Murray, *Rubber and Plastic Bullets Kill and Maim*
      (Belfast: International Tribunal into Deaths and Serious Injuries Caused by
      Rubber and Plastic Bullets in N. Ireland, 1981), 3–5.
73.   Helen Waterhouse, "Noses, Ears of Rubber Give Surgery New Speed," *Akron
      Beacon Journal* (June 11, 1940).
74.   Howard and Ralph Wolf, 378–379.
75.   Ibid., 406; Schidrowitz, 6; McMillan, 3. The first two sources claim that
      Thomson was English. McMillan, who has seen the original patent, says that he
      was a Scot, born in Kincardineshire in 1822.
76.   Schidrowitz, 6.
77.   Hancock's book contains a number of illustrations of inflatable boats and pon-
      toons. T.R. Dawson records that a Mr. J. Clark took out a patent for inflatable
      beds, pillows, and cushions in 1813.
78.   I am indebted to James McMillan's book *The Dunlop Story* for the details in the
      following paragraphs.
79.   Huy Kanthoul, "Mémoires," unpublished French-language manuscript (n.d.),
      18, located in the Chandler Papers, Monash University. Cited in John Tully,
      France on the Mekong: A History of the Protectorate in Cambodia, 1863–1953
      (Lanham, MD: University Press of America, 2002), 58.
80.   McMillan, 8.
81.   Hemming, 273.

THREE: THE DARK SIDE OF THE RUBBER REVOLUTION

1.   Cited in D.H. Killeffer, *Banbury the Master Mixer: A Biography of Fernley H.
      Banbury* (New York: Palmerton, 1962), 93.
2.   "Highlights in Dalrymple's Radio Talk on Akron Strike," *Akron Beacon Journal*
      (February 28, 1936).
3.   F. I. Tuckwell, "Personnel in the Rubber Industry," in P. Schidrowitz and T.R.

Dawson (eds.), *History of the Rubber Industry* (Cambridge: W. Heffer and Sons, 1952), 356–357.

4.   *The India Rubber and Gutta Percha and Electrical Trades Journal: A Record of the Caoutchouc, Gutta Percha, Asbestos and Allied Industries*, Vol. IV, No. 9 (London: April 9, 1888). (The name of this publication is henceforth abbreviated as *IRJ*.)

5.   Tuckwell, 356.

6.   "The Introduction and Cultivation of the Hevea in India," *IRJ*, (London: January 20, 1902).

7.   Sarah Levitt, "Manchester Mackintoshes: A History of the Rubberized Garment Trade," *Textile History*, 17 (1) (1986).

8.   *IRJ*, Vol. VII, No. 12 (London: January 8, 1891).

9.   Ibid., Vol. I, 1884–85, 300. (Cited in Levitt, 54.)

10.   Letter to the *IRJ*, 1887. Cited in Levitt, 55.

11.   "'Sweating' in the waterproof trade," *IRJ*, Vol. V, No.11 (London: June 8, 1889).

12.   Henry Berkowitz, "In the Sweat Shop," trans. from the Yiddish of Morris Rosenfeldt, *The Jewish Quarterly Review*, Vol. 15, No. 3 (London: April 1903).

13.   Maisie Mosco, *Almonds and Raisins* (London: New English Library, 1979).

14.   Levitt, 64.

15.   Ibid., 65.

16.   Mosco, 47.

17.   Ibid., 50.

18.   Ibid.

19.   Ibid., 182.

20.   *IRJ*, Vol. VII, No. 2 (London: September 8, 1890).

21.   Levitt, 64–65.

22.   Howard and Ralph Wolf, *Rubber: A Story of Glory and Greed* (New York: Convici Friede, 1936), 499.

23.   *New York Times*, June 15, 1919

24.   John D. House, "Birth of a Union," unpublished book manuscript (1978). Microfilmed in 1981 by the Ohio Historical Society, Columbus, Ohio.

25.   David Giffels, "Readin', Writin' and Route 21: The Road from West Virginia to Ohio," in Mari-Lynn Evans et al. (eds.), *The Appalachians: America's First and Last Frontier* (New York: Random House, 2004), 147.

26.   "The Pit: As It Was and Is in the Rubber Shops," *Akron Beacon Journal* (October 10, 1926).

27.   Ibid.

28.   Kevin Michael Rosswurm, "A Strike in the Rubber City: Rubber Workers, Akron, and the IWW, 1913," unpublished MA thesis (Kent, OH: Kent State University, 1975), 70–71.

29.   Kathleen L. Endres, *Rosie the Rubber Worker: Women Workers in Akron's Rubber Factories during the First World War* (Kent, OH: Kent State University Press, 2000), 99.

30.   University of Akron Archives (UAA). URW Box 9–15. International Industrial Hygiene, Misc. K–P Before 1980. Box 2 of 2. See also P.J. Baxter and J.B. Werner, *Mortality in the British Rubber Industries, 1967–76* (London: Health and Safety Executive, 1980).

31.   Or disulfide (CS2). This chemical easily evaporates at room temperature and is absorbed into the body via the respiratory system.

32.   Cited in Levitt, 55.

33.   "The Use of Bi-sulphide of Carbon," *IRJ* (London: September 30, 1898).
34.   UAA. URW Box 9–15. International Industrial Hygiene, Misc. K–P, before 1980. Box 2 of 2.
35.   UAA. URW Local 5 (BF Goodrich), Box A1, *The Airbag* (Akron: October 4, 1942).
36.   Roger W. Shuy, "Language Call: Benny Come Home." Posted January 6, 2007. Available online at http://itre.cis.upenn.edu/~myl/languagelog/archives/004012. html. Shuy reports that he was recently approached by lawyers representing workers who were suing their employers over diseases contracted by benzene use. Shuy had noted the routine use of "benny" in an article published in a scholarly journal in 1964. See note 42.
37.   This is only one of a plethora of the deleterious effects of aniline dyes on the human body. See ATSDR Agency for Toxic Substances and Diseases Registry, "ToxFAQs for Aniline." Available online at http://www.atsdr.cdc.gov/tfacts171.html.
38.   UAA. BF Goodrich. NA1-1. "Chronology of BF Goodrich (1870–1948)."
39.   Howard and Ralph Wolf.
40.   UAA. BF Goodrich. NA1-1. "Chronology of BF Goodrich (1870–1948)."
41.   Joyce Dyer, *Gum-Dipped: A Daughter Remembers Rubber Town* (Akron: University of Akron Press, 2003), 95.
42.   Roger W. Shuy, "Tireworker Terms," *American Speech* (Durham: The American Dialect Society, Duke University Press, 1964), 268–269.
43.   Endres, 75.
44.   Ibid., 89.
45.   UAA. URW International Files Box 9–19. I.H. Heat Stress. Box 2 of 2.
46.   The equivalent of the AFL-CIO in the U.S.
47.   Trades Union Congress, *The Case Against Latex: Rubber Banned?* (London: TUC, Organisation and Services, 2001), 3–4.
48.   "The Strike in the Elastic Web Trade," *IRJ*, Vol. IV, No. 9 (London: April 9, 1888).
49.   "Strike at Myer Rubber Company," *IRJ*, Vol. V, No. 1 (August 8, 1888).
50.   The following issues of the *IRJ* contain extensive coverage of the Silvertown dispute: Vol. VI, No. 3 (October 8, 1889); Vol. VI, No.4 (November 8, 1889); Vol. VI, No. 5 (December 9, 1889); Vol.VI, No. 6 (January 8, 1890).
51.   Ibid., Vol. VII, No. 1 (August 8, 1890).

Part Two—Wild Rubber: A Primitive "Mode of Extraction"

1.   See Karl Polanyi, *The Great Transformation: The Political and Economic Origins of Our Time* (Boston, MA: Beacon Press, 1957), ch. 3.

FOUR: THE AMAZON RUBBER BOOM
1.   H. M. Tomlinson, *The Sea and the Jungle* (London: The Citadel Press, 1927, first published 1912).
2.   For details of the physical geography of the Amazon basin see, for instance, Robin Furneaux, *The Amazon: The Story of a Great River* (London: Hamish Hamilton, 1969) and Michael Goulding, Nigel J.H. Smith, and Dennis J. Maher, *Floods of Fortune: Ecology and Economy along the Amazon* (New York: Columbia University Press, 1996).
3.   One author believes that the basin might have supported as many as 6.8 million

people before the arrival of the Portuguese: Eric B. Ross, "The Evolution of the Amazon Peasantry," *Journal of Latin American Studies*, Vol. 10, No. 2 (November, 1978): 193–218. See also Goulding et al., 25.

4.   Hevea was the more important source; the Castilloa accounted for only 23 percent of rubber exports from the Amazon in 1913. See C.E. Akers, *The Rubber Industry in Brazil and the Orient* (London: Methuen, 1913), 4.

5.   Manaos is the old spelling of Manáus. See A.M. and F. Ferguson (eds.), *India Rubber and Gutta Percha: being a compilation of all the available information respecting the trees yielding these articles of commerce and their cultivation; with notes on the preparation and manufacture of rubber and gutta percha*, second ed. (Colombo: *Ceylon Observer*, 1887), 132.

6.   John Hemming, *Amazon Frontier: The Defeat of the Brazilian Indians* (London: Macmillan, 1987), 276.

7.   Algot Lange, *In the Amazon Jungle: Adventures in Remote Parts of the Upper Amazon River, Including a Sojourn among Cannibal Indians*, ed. in part by J. Odell Hauser (New York: G.P. Putnam, 1912), 149.

8.   Jean-Baptiste Serier, *Les Barons du Caoutchouc* (Paris: Editions Kathala, 2000), 55.

9.   Hemming, 276.

10.   Lizzie Hessell, compiled by Tony Morrison, Ann Brown, and Anne Rose, *Lizzie: A Victorian Lady's Amazon Adventure* (London: BBC, 1985), 58.

11.   Ibid., 101.

12.   José Eustasio Rivera, *The Vortex*, trans. E.K. James (London: Putnam, 1935).

13.   Bradford L. Barham and Oliver T. Coomes, "Reinterpreting the Amazon Rubber Boom: Investment, the State, and Dutch Disease," *Latin American Research Review*, Vol. 29, No. 2 (1980): 80.

14.   J. Orton Kerbey, *The Land of To-morrow: A Newspaper Exploration Up the Amazon and Over the Andes to the California of South America* (New York: W.F. Brainard, 1906), 26.

15.   Lewis A. Tambs, "Rubber, Rebels, and the Rio Branco: The Contest for the Acre," *The Hispanic-American Historical Review*, Vol. 46, No. 3 (August 1966): 258.

16.   Howard and Ralph Wolf, *Rubber: A Story of Glory and Greed* (New York: Convici Friede, 1936), 69.

17.   Kerbey, *The Land of To-morrow*, 73.

18.   E. Bradford Burns, "Manáus, 1910: Portrait of a Boom Town," *Journal of Inter-American Studies*, Vol. 7, No. 3 (July 1965): 400–421.

19.   Howard and Ralph Wolf, 68.

20.   Calculated using the MeasuringWorth website. See http:www.measuringworth.com/calculators.html.

21.   Hemming, 274.

22.   Barham and Coomes, 73.

23.   Collier, 26.

24.   British Foreign Office report.

25.   John Melby, "Rubber River: An Account of the Rise and Collapse of the Amazon Boom," *The Hispanic American Historical Review*, Vol. 22, No. 3 (August 1942): 453.

26.   Charles Booth Online Archive, "Charles Booth, 1840–1916—a biography." Available online at http://booth.lse.ac.uk/static.c/2.html.

27.   Burns, 413.

28. Tambs, 254.
29. Barbara Weinstein, *The Amazon Rubber Boom 1950–1920* (Stanford: Stanford University Press, 1983). According to Weinstein, the total rubber production in the Amazon in 1827 was a little more than 310 metric tons. It had risen to over 670 in 1846, but soared to over 1,446 in 1850, 1,906 in 1856 and 2,673 in 1860. See also Melby, 452–453.
30. Melby, 456–457.
31. Barham and Coomes, 81.
32. Alfred Lief, *The Firestone Story: A History of the Firestone Tire & Rubber Company* (New York: McGraw-Hill, 1951), 50. Akers, 5, gives the total production in 1912–13 as 43,362 tons, all but 12,000 tons of it from the upper reaches of the basin. He also indicates that the total production had been around 10,000 tons at the start of the great boom.
33. J. Orton Kerbey, *An American Consul in Amazonia* (New York: William Edwin Rudge, 1911), 95.
34. *India Rubber Journal* (March 11, 1907).
35. National Archives of Australia. A1/15, Item 6478. BNG: proclamation re: "Protection of Wild Rubber Trees."
36. Kerbey, *The Land of To-morrow*, 213.
37. P. H. Fawcett, *Exploration Fawcett*, ed. Brian Fawcett (London: Phoenix Press, 2001), 77.
38. John C. Horter, "Cultivated Rubber," *Bulletin of the American Geographical Society*, Vol. 37, No. 12 (1905): 720–724.
39. Marc Edelman "A Central American Genocide: Rubber, Slavery, Nationalism, and the Destruction of the Guatusos-Malekus," *Comparative Studies in Society and History*, Vol. 40, No. 2 (April 1998): 359.
40. Courtney de Kalb, "Nicaragua: Studies on the Mosquito Shore in 1892," *Journal of the American Geographical Society of New York*, Vol. 25 (1893): 259.
41. Cited in Hemming, 273.
42. Howard and Ralph Wolf, 65.
43. Unsigned, "Wild Scramble for Rubber Shares in the City," *The Daily Mirror* (London: April 19, 1910), 9.
44. "'Cosmopolitan,' Through Mincing Lane, 1884–1909," *The Quarter Century Number of the India-Rubber Journal: A Souvenir* (London: Maclaren and Sons, 1909), 52.
45. Collier, 27.
46. "Rubber in the Congo Territory," *India Rubber Journal*, Vol. V, No. 2 (London: September 8, 1888).
47. Hecht, Levis & Kahn's "Caoutchouc Report" for 1885. Copy in the Royal Botanic Gardens Archives, Kew London. Director's Correspondence Mexico and Central America Vol. 204, ff 57–536, Central America and British Guiana Letter 1865/1900.
48. UAA. Summit County Historical Society Box 35. Business. Rubber companies. Harvey S. Firestone Jr., "'The Rubber Boom of 1910,' The Romance and Drama of the Rubber Industry: Radio talks delivered by Harvey S. Firestone, Jr., in 'The Voice of Firestone' programs over the nationwide network of National Broadcasting Company, September 1931 to September 1932" (Akron: Firestone Tire & Rubber, 1932).
49. Howard and Ralph Wolf, 72.
50. Hemming, 278.

51. Furneaux, 161–164.
52. Hemming, 278.
53. Furneaux, 165.
54. Akers, 13.
55. J. Valerie Fifer, "The Empire Builders: A History of the Bolivian Rubber Boom and the Rise of the House of Suarez," *Journal of Latin American Studies*, Vol. 2, No. 2 (November 1970).
56. Edwin McDowell, "By Train to the Middle of the Amazon Jungle," *The New York Times* (New York: November 26, 2007). See also the Madeira-Mamoré Railway Society website at www.ferrolatino.ch/FLBMexChileMadMamEng.htm.
57. Kerbey, *An American Consul*, 299.
58. Barham and Coomes, 73.
59. Unsigned, "Rubber Planters Seek Assistance," *The Argus* (Melbourne: August 5, 1918).
60. D. C. Lewis, *The Plantation Dream: Developing British New Guinea and Papua, 1884–1942* (Canberra: *The Journal of Pacific History*, 1996), 213.
61. Woodroffe, 48–49.
62. Akers, 291.
63. Ibid., 126–127.
64. For an account emphasizing the ecological aspects of Amazonian rubber's decline, see Warren Dean, *Brazil and the Struggle for Rubber: A Study in Environmental History* (Cambridge: Cambridge University Press, 1987). Edelman, 359, notes another biological pest: the grubs of harlequin beetles, which killed tapped Castilloa trees in Central America.
65. Brazilian plantation rubber was sold as Pará sheet in London in 1907. This was reported in *India Rubber World*, Vol. 37, No. 6, (Akron: March 1908), 185. See also Warren Dean, cited in Bradford L. Barham and Oliver T. Coomes, *Prosperity's Promise: the Amazon Rubber Boom and Distorted Economic Development* in *Dellplain Latin American Studies*, No. 34 (Boulder, CO: Westview Press, 1996), 80.
66. Royal Botanic Gardens Archives, Kew, London. Director's Correspondence, Mexico and Central America, Vol. 204, ff 57–536, Central America and British Guiana, Letters 1865/1900. For instance: J. Moreur, Belize planter to D. Morris, Assistant Director, Kew, March 29, 1889; John Miller, general manager Jaltipan Estate, Chiapas, to "the Governor of the Gardens, Kew," June 1, 1898; and Edward Sturridge, Chalmette Plantation, Bluefields, Nicaragua, to Mr Morris, June 30, 1896. See also Horter, de Kalb, and Peter V.N. Henderson, "Modernization and Change in Mexico: La Zacualpa Rubber Plantation, 1890–1920," *The Hispanic American Historical Review*, Vol. 73, No. 2 (May 1993): 235–260.
67. Akers, 33.
68. Fawcett, 69.
69. Ibid.
70. Earl Hanson, "Social Regression in the Orinoco and Amazon Basins: Notes on a Journey in 1931 and 1932," *Geographical Review*, Vol. 23, No. 4 (New York: American Geographical Society, October 1933): 597.
71. Many of these theorists are Latin American. See in particular Eduardo Galeano, *Open Veins of Latin America: Five Centuries of the Pillage of a Continent*, trans. Cedric Belfrage (New York and London: Monthly Review Press, 1973). Specifically on rubber, see for example Flores Marin, *La explotación del Caucho en el Perú* (Lima: Consejo Nacional de Cienca y Tecnología, 1987).

72.   Weinstein, 2.

73.   Ibid., 12.

74.   Michael Edward Stanfield, *Red Rubber, Bleeding Trees: Violence, Slavery, and Empire in Northwest Amazonia, 1850–1933* (Albuquerque: University of New Mexico Press, 1998), 41.

75.   Weinstein, 9.

76.   Collier, 20.

77.   Ibid., 24.

78.   Burns, 403.

79.   Collier, 24.

80.   Royal Botanic Gardens, Kew, Economic Botany Library. Box File No 2. British Foreign Office, "Brazil: Diplomatic and Consular Reports, State of Amazonas" (June 1900): 22.

81.   Howard and Ralph Wolf, 65; Goulding et al, 34; "Brazil: Diplomatic and Consular Reports" as above.

82.   "Brazil: Diplomatic and Consular Reports" as above.

83.   Roberto Santos, *História Econômica da Amazônia* (São Paulo: Queiroz, 1980), 178. Cited in Barham and Coomes, "Reinterpreting the Amazon Rubber Boom," 88–89.

84.   See W.M. Corden and J.P. Neary, "Booming Sector and Deindustrialization in a Small Open Economy," *The Economic Journal*, No. 92 (1982): 825–848. In 1960, natural gas was discovered off the Netherlands coast. The resulting boom sucked investment capital from other less profitable sectors of the economy and also inflated the guilder, thus rendering Dutch exports more expensive. See also Christine Ebrahim-zadeh, "Dutch Disease: Too Much Wealth Managed Unwisely," *Finance and Development: A Quarterly Magazine of the IMF*, Vol. 40, No. 1 (March 2003). Available online at www.imf.org.

85.   Hanson, 584.

86.   Ibid., 588.

87.   Ibid., 584.

FIVE: THE LIVES OF THE *SERINGUEIROS*

1.   Cited in Eduardo Galeano, *Open Veins of Latin America: Five Centuries of the Pillage of a Continent*, trans. Cedric Belfrage (New York and London: Monthly Review Press, 1973), 99.

2.   A contrast Barbara Weinstein sums up as between "a highly advanced 'metropolitan' industry" and an "essentially precapitalist 'colonial' economy." Barbara Weinstein, *The Amazon Rubber Boom, 1850–1920* (Stanford: Stanford University Press, 1983), 9.

3.   Joseph F. Woodroffe, *The Rubber Industry of the Amazon and How Its Supremacy Can Be Maintained*, ed. Harold Hamel Smith (London: John Bale, Sons and Danielsson, 1915), 29.

4.   Kenneth G. Grubb, *From Pacific to Atlantic: South American Studies* (London: Methuen, 1933), 104.

5.   *Gardener's Chronicle* (London: December 9, 1876).

6.   Lizzie Hessell, *Lizzie: A Victorian Lady's Amazon Adventure*, eds. Tony Morrison, Ann Brown, and Anne Rose (London: BBC, 1985), 135.

7.   Paul Fountain, *The River Amazon: From Its Sources to the Sea* (London: Constable, 1914), 144–145.

8.   Algot Lange, *In the Amazon Jungle: Adventures in Remote Parts of the Upper Amazon River, Including a Sojourn among Cannibal Indians*, ed. in part by J. Odell Hauser (New York: G.P. Putnam, 1912), 234.

9.   P. H. Fawcett, *Exploration Fawcett*, ed. Brian Fawcett (London: Phoenix Press, 2001), 82.

10.   C. E. Akers, *The Rubber Industry in Brazil and the Orient* (London: Methuen, 1914), 12.

11.   Hessell, 137.

12.   Cited by J.H. Harris, "Native Races and Rubber Prices," *The Contemporary Review*, No. 104 (London: November 1913): 653.

13.   Fawcett, 64.

14.   A person of mixed race, generally European and Indian.

15.   A. M. and J. Ferguson (eds.), *India Rubber and Gutta Percha: Being a compilation of all the available information representing the trees yielding these articles of commerce and their cultivation; with notes on the preparation and manufacture of rubber and gutta percha* (Colombo: Ceylon Observer, 1887), 132.

16.   Woodroffe, 111.

17.   Akers, 56.

18.   Hessell, 100.

19.   Weinstein, 16.

20.   Akers, 68.

21.   Royal Botanic Gardens Archives, Kew London. (Hereinafter KEW.) Misc. Reports India. India Office. Caoutchouc II c.1874–1903. Imperial Institute Series, Handbooks of Commercial products Indian Section, No. 25, "India-Rubber from Fiscus elastica" (Calcutta: Government of India, 1873).

22.   See Howard and Ralph Wolf, *Rubber: A Story of Glory and Greed* (New York: Convici Friede, 1936), 1–19; Robin Furneaux, *The Amazon: The Story of a Great River* (London: Hamish Hamilton, 1969), 149; and Akers, 64 and 91, for details of the tapping and curing processes. Harmless in small concentrations and an ingredient of many soft drinks, large amounts of carbonic acid are toxic and damaging to the respiratory system in particular.

23.   John Hemming, *Amazon Frontier: The Defeat of the Brazilian Indians* (London: Macmillan, 1987), 274.

24.   Ibid., 295.

25.   Hessell.

26.   Hemming, 292.

27.   Richard Collier, *The River that God Forgot: The Story of the Amazon Rubber Boom* (London: Collins, 1968), 46.

28.   Akers, 54.

29.   Howard and Ralph Wolf, 75.

30.   J. Orton Kerbey, *The Land of To-morrow: A Newspaper Exploration Up the Amazon and Over the Andes to the California of South America* (New York: F. Brainard, 1906), 60.

31.   Galeano, 100.

32.   Larry Rohter, "Brazil Forgets Its 'Rubber Soldiers,'" *The Age* (Melbourne: November 25, 2006).

SIX: THE PUTUMAYO DEVIL PLANT

1. Cited in Richard Collier, *The River that God Forgot: The Story of the Amazon Rubber Boom* (London: Collins, 1968), dedication page.

2. Roger Casement, "Notes on the Peruvian Frontier on board the Huayna—Friday 26th August 1910," National Library of Ireland, MS 13.087 (24). Cited in Angus Mitchell (ed.), *The Amazon Journal of Roger Casement* (London: Anaconda, 1997), 85.

3. Cited in John Vidal, "Tribes that Hide from Mankind," *The Guardian Weekly* (London: October 26–November 1, 2007), 26.

4. Roger Casement's report to the British Parliament is entitled *Correspondence respecting the treatment of British Colonial Subjects and Native Indians employed in the collection of rubber in the Putumayo District*, PP 1912–1913 (Cd 6266), LXVIII.

5. *The Amazon Journal*, "Statements made by David Cazes to me [Roger Casement] from 31 August to 14 September during my stay at Iquitos," NLI MS 13.087 (26/ii).

6. Earl Hanson, "Social Regression on the Orinoco and Amazon Basins: Notes on a Journey in 1931 and 1932," *Geographical Review*, Vol. 23, No. 4 (New York: American Geographical Society, October 1933): 584.

7. Frank Chalk and Kurt Jonassohn, *The History and Sociology of Genocide: Analysis and Case Studies* (New Haven: Yale University Press, 1990).

8. W. E. Hardenburg, *The Putumayo: The Devil's Paradise: Travels in the Peruvian Amazon Region and an Account of the Atrocities Committed upon the Indian Therein*, ed. C. Reginald Enock (London: T. Fisher Unwin, 1912), 39.

9. Ibid., 425–427. Letter to Henry Nevinson, 1911.

10. See, for instance, Marc Edelman, "A Central American Genocide: Rubber, Slavery, Nationalism, and the Destruction of the Guatusos-Malekus," in *Comparative Studies in Society and History*, Vol. 40, No. 2 (April 1998): 356–390.

11. Angus Mitchell (ed.), *Sir Roger Casement's Heart of Darkness: The 1911 Documents* (Dublin: Irish Manuscripts Commission, 2003), 436n. Mitchell states that Suarez exterminated the Caripuña people on the Madeira River in Bolivia.

12. Robert Fisk, "Life under Israeli Occupation—by an Israeli," *The Independent* (London: August 26, 2001). Amira Hass is an Israeli writer and human rights activist who lives and works on the West Bank. The daughter of Holocaust survivors, she recalled her mother's description of civilians who stood by indifferently as a column of emaciated women were marched into the Bergen Belsen camp.

13. Bartolomé de las Casas, *A Short Account of the Destruction of the Indies*, ed. and trans. Nigel Griffin (Harmondsworth: Penguin, 1992). The book was originally published in Spanish in 1542.

14. Robin Furneaux, *The Amazon: The Story of a Great River* (London: Hamish Hamilton, 1969), 56.

15. Michael Goulding, Nigel J.H. Smith and Dennis J. Maher, *Floods of Fortune: Ecology and Economy along the Amazon* (New York: Columbia University Press, 1996), 20–25. The decline was of the magnitude of 90 percent in some regions.

16. British National Archives (hereinafter BNA) PRO FO 371/2798. Telegram to Roger Casement in the Tower of London, June 1916.

17. Casement, Letter to Nevinson.

18. Collier, 45.

19. Cited in John Hemming, *Amazon Frontier: The Defeat of the Brazilian Indians*

(London: Macmillan, London, 1987), 301. The same point could be made about African involvement in the slave trade.

20. J. Orton Kerbey, *The Land of To-morrow: A Newspaper Exploration of the Amazon and Over the Andes to the California of South America* (New York: W.F. Brainard, 1906), 91.

21. See Peter Blanchard, *Slavery and Abolition in Early Republican Peru* (Wilmington, DE: Scholarly Resources, 1992). More generally, see Katérina Stenou (ed.), 'Struggles Against Slavery: International Year to Commemorate the Struggle Against Slavery and Its Abolition," UNESCO (Paris 2004). Available online at http://unesdoc.unesco.org/images/0013/001337/133738.pdf.

22. Kerbey, 91.

23. Lizzie Hessell, *Lizzie: A Victorian Lady's Amazon Adventure*, eds. Tony Morrison, Ann Brown, and Anne Rose (London: BBC, 1985), 82.

24. Ibid., 58.

25. Percy Harrison Fawcett, *Exploration Fawcett*, ed. Brian Fawcett (London: Phoenix Press, 2001), 95.

26. Ibid., 110.

27. Ibid., 132.

28. Paul Fountain, *The River Amazon: From Its Sources to the Sea* (London: Constable, 1914), 213–215.

29. Fawcett, 97.

30. Ibid., 44.

31. Michael Edward Stanfield, *Red Rubber, Bleeding Trees: Violence, Slavery, and Empire in Northwest Amazonia, 1850–1933* (Albuquerque: University of New Mexico Press, 1998), 128.

32. Collier, 60.

33. Ibid., 61.

34. The MeasuringWorth calculator is available online at http://www.measuring-worth.com.

35. Howard and Ralph Wolf, *Rubber: A Story of Glory and Greed* (New York: Convici Friede, 1936), 5.

36. The account of Hardenburg's campaign against the rubber company in the following paragraphs is derived from Hardenburg's book, cited above, and Richard Collier's book, which itself draws heavily on Hardenburg's accounts.

37. See for instance, *La Felpa, Quincenario Politico, Satirico y con Caricaturas, Iquitos*, Ano. 1, No. 5, (Iquitos, Peru: November 1, 1907). Held at the Bodleian Library, University of Oxford, N.2343 b.10 (1).

38. Stanfield invariably describes the journalist as a "muckraker" (e.g., xv, 125) and his publications as "muckraking," despite by his own admission never having seen them.

39. Mitchell, *Heart of Darkness*, 265.

40. Fawcett, 44.

41. Saldaña's allies included Eugenio Robuchon, who wrote an account of the atrocities and attacked the collusion of the Peruvian government with Arana, and the Lima paper *El Comercio* that had earlier carried articles attacking slavery in the interior. (Sawyer, 78–80).

42. Collier, 64.

43. "Putumayo Diary," Mitchell, *The Amazon Journal*, 263–264.

44. Ibid.

45. Hardenburg, 180–181.

46.   Herbert Spencer Dickey, *The Misadventures of a Tropical Medico* (London: Bodley Head, 1929), 160.

47.   Ibid.

48.   Collier, 164–165.

49.   The allusion is to the activities of Belgian rubber men in King Leopold's so-called "Congo Free State," discussed in chapter 7.

50.   Collier, 180–181.

51.   Roger Sawyer, *Casement: The Flawed Hero* (London: Routledge and Kegan Paul, 1984), 69.

52.   There is a file of press clippings about the "Black Diaries" in the British National Archives: HO 144/23489.

53.   Mitchell, *The Amazon Journal of Roger Casement*, 8.

54.   An example of a book that challenged the diaries' authenticity in this way was William Maloney, *The Forged Casement Diaries* (Dublin and Cork: The Talbot Press, 1936).

55.   In 2002, the diaries were subjected to forensic examination by Dr. Audrey Giles as part of an investigation funded by the Irish RTE and the BBC. Dr. Giles concluded that the diaries were genuine. (See Paul Tilzey, "Roger Casement: Secrets of the Black Diaries" (2002). Available online at http://www.bbc.co.uk/history/british/britain_wwone/casement_05.shtml.) This forensic examination, however, has been challenged as insufficiently rigorous and the controversy is not yet over.

56.   Dickey, 156–163.

57.   BNA FO 881/10080. Consul General Sir R. Casement to Sir Edward Grey.

58.   Mitchell, *Heart of Darkness*, 23, and "The Putumayo Diary," 176.

59.   Ibid., 215.

60.   Stanfield, 27, 211–212.

61.   BNA FO 371/1201. Notes for Mr. Mullett written by Roger Casement.

62.   Mitchell, *Heart of Darkness*, 255.

63.   "Putumayo Diary," 313.

64.   Howard and Ralph Wolf, 101. Hardenburg was a U.S. citizen, but after his part in exposing the Putumayo scandal, he married an Englishwoman and emigrated to Canada. It is possible that his dismay about the U.S. government's attitude toward the events in Putamayo influenced his decision to not return to the land of his birth.

65.   BNA CAB 41/33, August 7, 1912.

66.   Collier, 295–300.

67.   BNA FO 881/9970. Précis of the Paredes Report by Roger Casement for Edward Grey.

68.   Howard and Ralph Wolf, 99–101.

69.   "The Putumayo Journal," 142–143.

70.   Anon., "Peruvian Rubber and International Politics," *The American Review of Reviews*, Vol. 46 (New York: September 1912): 325–328.

71.   The House of Commons Select Committee report of 1913 is House of Commons Paper 148 XIV.

72.   Colonel Percy Fawcett, letter to *The Times* (1912. Cited in J.H. Harris, "Native Races and Rubber Prices," *The Contemporary Review*, No. 104 (November 1913): 653.

73.   Unsigned, "Rubber and Humanity," *The Outlook*, Vol. 104 (June 28, 1913): 404–405.

74.   Ryszard Kapuscinski, *Shah of Shahs* (New York: First Vintage, 1992).

75.   BNA FO 881/9977.
76.   Dickey, 155. The book was published thirty years after Dickey's stint in the jungle.

SEVEN: HEART OF DARKNESS: RUBBER AND BLOOD ON THE CONGO
1.   Joseph Conrad, *Heart of Darkness and Other Stories* (Ware, Hertfordshire: Wordsworth Editions, 1999), 35–36.
2.   For the angry responses of a number of eminent French historians to this bizarre decree, see "Liberté pour l'Histoire!" in *RFI Actualité* (December 13, 2005). Available online at http://www.rfi/fr/actfr/articles/072/article_40466.asp.
3.   J. A. Hobson, *Imperialism: A Study* (Ann Arbor: University of Michigan, 1965).
4.   Letter of the King to M. Beernaert, August 5, 1889, in "The King's Testament," *American Journal of International Law*, Vol. 3, No. 1, Supplement: Official Documents (1909): 27.
5.   Conrad, 34.
6.   UAA. Summit County Historical Society. Box 35. Business. Rubber Companies. Harvey S. Firestone, Jr., "'Leopold II: 'Reign of Terror over the Congo,' The Romance and Drama of the Rubber Industry: Radio talks delivered by Harvey S. Firestone, Jr. in 'The Voice of Firestone' programs over the nationwide network of National Broadcasting Company, September 1931 to September 1932" (Akron: Firestone Tire & Rubber, 1932), 47.
7.   Martin Ewans, *European Atrocity, African Catastrophe* (London: Routledge Curzon, 2002), 12.
8.   M. C. Ricklefs, *A Modern History of Indonesia, c. 1300 to the Present* (Houndmills, Basingstoke: Macmillan, 1981), 117.
9.   Cited in Neal Ascherson, *The King Incorporated: Leopold the Second of the Congo* (London: Granta, 1999), 55.
10.   E.D. Morel, *Red Rubber: The Story of the Rubber Slave Trade Flourishing on the Congo in the Year of Grace 1906*, second ed. (London: T. Fisher Unwin, London, 1907), 11–13. For a discussion of the importance of the "geographical movement" in impelling European countries toward colonialism, see Donald Vernon McKay, "Colonialism in the French Geographical Movement, 1871–1881," *Geographical Review*, Vol. XXXIII (1943): 214–232.
11.   Today it's known as Anti-Slavery International.
12.   Cited in H.L. Samuel, "The Congo Free State and the Commission of Inquiry," *Contemporary Review*, Vol. LXXXVIII (London: July–December 1905): 872.
13.   Cited in E.D. Morel, "The Congo Question," *The Outlook* (New York: February 18, 1905): 40–443.
14.   Samuel, 872.
15.   Conrad, 36.
16.   D. Crawford, *Thinking Black: 12 Years Without a Break in the Long Grass of Central Africa* (London: Morgan and Scott, 1913), 164.
17.   Demetrius C. Boulger, "The Railways of the Upper Congo," *The Engineering Magazine*, Vol. XXXIII, No. 4 (July 1907): 571–582.
18.   Ewans, 114.
19.   Diana Strickland, *Through the Belgian Congo* (London: Hurst and Blackett, c. 1926), 21.
20.   Ewans, 19.
21.   Conrad, 37.

22. Cited in Ascherson, 193.

23. See Part Four.

24. D. Crawford, *Thinking Black. 12 Years Without a Break in the Long Grass of Central Africa* (London: Morgan and Scott, 1913), 331–332

25. Marcus R.P. Dorman *A Journal of a Tour in the Congo Free State,* eds. Brendan Lane and Martin Pettitt, 17. Available online at http://www.gutenberg.org/files15240/15240-h/15240-h.htm. Originally published in 1905 by J. Lebègue, Brussels and Kegan Paul, Trench, and Trübner, London.

26. Vice Consul Beck, *Africa,* No. 1 (1908). (Cited in E.D. Morel, "The Belgian Parliament and the Congo" in *The Contemporary Review,* Vol. XCIV (London: September 1908): 351.)

27. Archives des Ministère des Affaires Etrangères, Brussels. Papiers Janssens, III, Rapport de la Commission d'enquête, Bulletin Officiel de l'Etat Indépendent du Congo, Nos. 9 & 10. Rapport au Roi-Souverain. October 30, 1905. (Hereinafter Janssens Report.)

28. As was revealed in a speech by Emile Vandervelde in the Belgian parliament. Apart from Janssens and three others, Vandervelde claimed, the others were in fact "the principal accused" and shared responsibility for "organizing the system of exploitation of the natives." Archives des Ministère des Affaires Etrangères, Brussels. Chambre des Réprésentants—Annales Parliamentaires, Séance du mardi, 20 février 1906.

29. The decrees are discussed in Morel, *Red Rubber,* and in British parliamentary papers. The basic facts of the land and labor questions were verified by the Janssens Report.

30. Georges Lorand, "Belgian Opinion on the Congo Question," *Contemporary Review,* Vol. XCIII (London: February 1908): 187.

31. Howard and Ralph Wolf, *Rubber: A Story of Glory and Greed* (New York: Convici-Friede, 1936), 103.

32. Musée du Congo, *Annexe aux Annales du Musée du Congo. Ethnographie et anthropologie. Série IV: Fascicule I. E. Le pays et ses habitants; documents historiques. Tome I. L'État Indépendant du Congo—Documents sur le pays et ses habitants* (Bruxelles: Musée du Congo, 1903), 80–83.

33. Morel, *Red Rubber,* 150.

34. These were: the Anglo-Belgian Rubber Company (ABIR), the Société Anversoise, the Compagnie du Kasai, the Commercial Congolais, the Grand Lacs concern, the Comité Spécial du Katanga, and the Busira and Lomani companies.

35. Ibid., 142. Also see Ewans, 159–160. The biggest shareholders were: A. Van den Nest, Count J. d'Outremont, Baron Brown de Tiège, Alexis Mols, Count Horace van den Burgh, J. van Strappen, and Leopold II himself. The chairman of ABIR was a shady Englishman, Colonel North, another royal crony.

36. Janssens Report.

37. Ibid.

38. Dorman.

39. Ewart S. Grogan and Arthur H. Sharp, *From the Cape to Cairo: The First Traverse of Africa from South to North* (London: Hurst and Blackett, 1900), 198.

40. A.F.R. Wollaston, *From Ruwenzori to the Congo: A Naturalist's Journey Across Africa* (London: John Murray, 1908), 209.

41. Marguerite Roby, *My Adventures in the Congo* (London: Edward Arnold, 1911), 121 and 209.

42. Janssens Report.

43. British National Archives (BNA). FO 629/11. Congo Confidential. Consul Casement to the Marquess of Lansdowne, September 5, 1903.

44. Janssens Report.

45. Emile Vandervelde, "Belgium and the Reforms on the Congo," in *The Contemporary Review*, Vol. XCVI (London: December 1909): 653.

46. Janssens Report.

47. A. J. Wauters, *Histoire du Congo Belge* (Brussels: Pierre van Fleteren, 1911).

48. Casement to Lansdowne.

49. Janssens Report.

50. Morel, *Red Rubber*.

51. Janssens Report.

52. André Gide, *Travels in the Congo*, trans. Dorothy Bussey (Harmondsworth: Penguin, 1986), 12.

53. A. D. Cureau, "Essai sur la psychologie des races negrès de l'Afrique Tropicale. Première Partie: sensibilité et affectivité." *Revue Générale des Sciences Pures et Appliquées* (Paris: Librairie Armand Colin, July 15, 1904).

54. Ibid., 33.

55. Strickland, 187.

56. Firestone, 47–48.

57. BNA FO 629/11. Consul Casement to the Marquess of Lansdowne, Stanley Pool, September 15–16, 1903.

58. Wauters.

59. Grogan and Sharp, 154.

60. Ibid., 227.

61. Vandervelde, 652.

62. Casement to Lansdowne, September 5, 1903.

63. Ibid.

64. Monkswell, "'The Government and the Congo Free State: A Plea for British Consular Jurisdiction," *The Fortnightly Review*, No. CCCCLXXXIII, New Series, (London: March 1, 1903): 479.

65. Ascherson, 9. See also Adam Hochschild, *King Leopold's Ghost* (New York: Mariner Books, 1998).

66. Raphael Lemkin, *Axis Rule in Occupied Europe: Laws of Occupation, Analysis of Government, Proposals for Redress* (Washington, D.C.: Carnegie Endowment for International Peace, Division of International Law, 1944). For a general discussion, see Frank Chalk and Kurt Jonassohn, *The History and Sociology of Genocide: Analyses and Case Studies* (New Haven: Yale University Press, 1990). For a broader definition of genocide, see Israel W. Charny, *Encyclopaedia of Genocide* (Santa Barbara: ABC-CLIO, 2003).

67. Howard and Ralph Wolf, 103.

68. Anon., "Dr. Guinness Self Refuted. Inconsistency of the Congo Balolo Missionaries" (Edinburgh: Oliver and Boyd, 1905). With a few exceptions, Leopold's no doubt well-paid supporters preferred to remain anonymous.

69. Monkswell, 480.

70. For example, see Wollaston, 225.

71. Roland de Marès, *The Congo* (Brussels: J. Lebègue, c. 1904), 50. Morel riposted that the jealousy was more likely to be the other way around. Between 1900 and 1903, Liverpool imported 74,318 tons of rubber compared with 22,667 for Antwerp. Morel, "The Congo Question."

72. Fédération pour la défense des interest Belges à l'étranger, *La Verité sur le Congo*

(Brussels: February 15, 1906).

73.   John de Courcy MacDonnell, *The Life of His Majesty Albert, King of the Belgians* (London: John Long, 1915), 65.

74.   Fédération pour la défense.

75.   Anonymous, "Dr Guinness Self Refuted. Inconsistency of the Congo Balolo Missionaries" (Edinburgh: Printed by Oliver and Boyd, no publisher listed, 1905)

76.   Lorand, 184.

77.   Cited in John Daniels, "The Congo Question and the 'Belgian' Solution," *The North American Review*, Vol. CLXXXVIII (December 1908): 902.

78.   Anonymous, "King Leopold's Self-Defense," *The Outlook* (New York: December 22, 1906): 945–6.

79.   Cited in Daniels, 902.

80.   Samuel, 874.

81.   Janet Polasky, *The Democratic Socialism of Emile Vandervelde: Between Reform and Revolution* (Oxford and Washington, D.C.: Berg, 1995), 58.

82.   Naval Intelligence Division, *The Belgian Congo* (London: Geographical Handbook Series, 1944), 4–5.

83.   Calculated using the MeasuringWorth website at http://measuringworth.com. Accessed on January 15, 2009.

84.   Cited in Ascherson, 241.

85.   Ewans, 172.

86.   Vandervelde, 653–654.

87.   J. H. Harris, "Native Races and Rubber Prices," *The Contemporary Review* 104 (November 1913): 650.

88.   Between 1901 and 1902, seventeen Europeans were put on trial in the Free State for various offenses, apparently including ones against other Europeans. (BNA FO 629/11 Roger Casement: Congo Atrocities, 1903.)

89.   Anonymous, "The Antwerp Congolese Fête," reprinted by the Fédération pour la défense des intérêts Belges à l'Etranger, *La Verité sur le Congo* (Brussels: February 15, 1906). The Brabançonne is the Belgian national anthem.

90.   See Jerome L. Sternstein, "King Leopold II, Senator Nelson W. Aldrich, and the Strange Beginnings of American Economic Penetration of the Congo," *African Affairs*, Vol. 68, No. 271 (April 1969): 189–204.

91.   Robert Gunning, "Belgian Tragedy Touches Akron; Recall Prince's Visit," *Akron Beacon Journal.* Clipping in *Akron Beacon Journal* archives (no date).

92.   Ewans, 172.

93.   E. D. Morel, "The Belgian Parliament and the Congo," *The Contemporary Review*, Vol. XCIV (September 1908): 355. Far from being a puppet of British capitalist and imperialist interests, Morel was later jailed for his opposition to the First World War, and later became a left-wing Labour MP at Westminster.

EIGHT: GUTTA-PERCHA, TELEGRAPHS, IMPERIALISM, AND ECOLOGY

1.   This chapter is based on my article "A Victorian Ecological Disaster: Imperialism, the Telegraph and Gutta-percha," *The Journal of World History*, Vol. 20, No. 4 (Honolulu: University of Hawaii, 2009): 559–579.

2.   Karl Marx, "The Future Results of British Rule in India," in Shlomo Averini (ed.), *Karl Marx on Colonialism and Modernization: His Despatches and Other Writings on China, India, Mexico, the Middle East and North Africa* (Garden City, NY: Doubleday, 1969), 133.

3.   *Prospectus of the United States Vulcanized Gutta Percha Belting and Packing Co.*
       (New York: United States Vulcanized Gutta Percha Belting and Packing
       Co,1857), 4.

4.   Cited in Alvaro de Miranda, "Creative East London in Historical Perspective"
       (2007), occasional paper, University of East London. Available online at
       http://www.uel.ac.uk/risingeast/archive07/academic/miranda.pdf.

5.   William T. Brannt, *India Rubber, Gutta Percha and Balata* (London: Sampson
       Low, Marston and Company, 1900), 227; Hubert L. Terry, *India-Rubber and Its
       Manufacture, with Chapters on Gutta-Percha and Balata* (London: Archibald
       Constable, 1907), 277.

6.   "Gutta-percha Leaves as Roof Tiles," *IRJ*, V, No. 2 (London: September 8,
       1888): 39.

7.   Charles Payson Gurley Scott, "The Malayan Words in English," *Journal of the
       American Oriental Society*, Vol. 18 (1887): 54.

8.   Jonathan Thornton, "A Brief History of the Early Practice and Materials of Gap-
       Filling in the West," *Journal of the American Institute for Conservation*, 37, No.
       1 (Spring 1998).

9.   James Collins, *Report on the Gutta Percha of Commerce* (London: Geo. Allen,
       1878). No page numbers. Rare. There is a copy in the Royal Botanic Gardens
       Archives at Kew, London: MR Malaya Rubber, Misc. 1852–1908, f205.

10.   Terry, 271.

11.   Brannt, 225. James Collins gives the date of Montgomerie's findings as 1822.

12.   Brannt, 227; Terry, 277.

13.   Richard D. Knowles, "Transport Shaping Space: Differential Collapse in Time-
       space," *Journal of Transport Geography*, Vol. 14, No. 6, 407–425. Available online
       at http://ntlsearch.bts.gov/tris/record/tris/01041310.html.

14.   Paul Kennedy, *The Rise and Fall of the Great Powers: Economic Change and
       Military Conflict from 1500 to 2000* (London: Unwin Hyman, 1988). The term
       "tyranny of distance" was perhaps coined by the Australian historian Geoffrey
       Blainey. [Geoffrey Blainey, *The Tyranny of Distance: How Distance Shaped
       Australia's History* (Melbourne: Macmillan, 1968).]

15.   See note 14.

16.   Tully, "A Victorian Ecological Disaster: Imperialism, the Telegraph and Gutta-
       percha," *The Journal of World History*, 559–579.

17.   Brannt, 270.

18.   The different types of gum exported from Sarawak included gutta-percha, gutta-
       jangkar and gutta-jetulong. (See Amarjit Kaur, "A History of Forestry in
       Sarawak," *Modern Asian Studies*, Vol. 32, No. 1 (February 1998): 124.)

19.   Lucile H. Brockway, "Science and Colonial Expansion: The Role of the British
       Royal Botanic Gardens," *American Ethnologist* (August, 1979): 449–465.

20.   Brannt, 228–230.

21.   Wilfried Feldenkirchen, *Werner von Siemens: Erfinder und Internationaler*
       (Berlin: Siemens Aktiengesellschaft, 1992).

22.   W. H. Russell, *The Atlantic Telegraph* (London: Day and Sons, c. 1865). See also
       Bern Dibner, *The Atlantic Cable* (Norwalk: Burndy Library, 1999) and Tom
       Standage, *The Victorian Internet: The Remarkable Story of the Telegraph and the
       Nineteenth Century's Online Pioneers* (London: Phoenix, 1999), 96–97.

23.   Standage, 96–97.

24.   "Ocean Cable Service," *IRJ*, V, No. 6 (London: January 8, 1889): 126.

25.   Terry, 278.

26.   Or between £7 billion and £9.5 billion in today's values using the retail price
       index as a guide. Calculated using tables from MeasuringWorth.com. Available at
       http://www.measuringworth.com/ukcompare/.
27.   Of the eight cables laid across the Atlantic between Europe and America by 1889,
       four were owned by the Anglo-American Cable Company and two by Western
       Union. See "Ocean Cable Service."
28.   Daniel R. Headrick, *The Tentacles of Progress: Technology Transfer in the Age of
       Imperialism, 1850–1940* (Oxford: Oxford University Press, 1988), 99.
29.   Christina Phelps Harris, "The Persian Gulf Submarine Telegraph of 1864," *The
       Geographical Journal*, Vol. 135, No. 2 (June 1969): 169–170.
30.   Headrick, 100.
31.   George Johnson (ed.), *The All Red Line: The Annals and Aims of the Pacific Cable
       Project* (Ottawa: James Hope, 1903). See also P.H. Kennedy, "Imperial Cable
       Communications and Strategy, 1870–1914," *The English Historical Review*, Vol.
       86, No. 341 (October 1971): 728–752.
32.   See Russell, Dibner, and Standage.
33.   Ibid., 236.
34.   Brannt, 233.
35.   Collins.
36.   Ibid.
37.   "M. Sérullas on Gutta-Percha," *IRJ*, Vol. VII, No. 6, (London: January 8, 1891),
       112–113.
38.   Ibid. Also see: "A Paper Read before the Société d'"Encouragement by M.
       Sérullas," *IRJ*, Vol. VIII, No. 11 (London: June 8, 1892), 329–330.
39.   "M. Sérullas on Gutta-Percha," 162–163.
40.   Unsigned, "Trade in Gutta Percha," *The New York Times* (New York: May 24,
       1902).
41.   *IRJ*, Vol. VIII, No. 3 (London: October 8, 1891).
42.   Based on figures from Terry, 280.
43.   Lesley Potter, "Community and Environment in Colonial Borneo: Economic
       Value, Forest Conversions and Concern for Conservation, 1870–1940" in Reed
       L. Wadley (ed.), *Histories of the Borneo Environment: Economic, Political and
       Social Dimensions of Change and Community*, (Leiden: Verhandelingen van Het
       Koninklijk Instituut voor Taal, Landen Volkenkunde, 2005), 116.
44.   "M. Sérullas on Gutta-Percha," 162–163.
45.   Author's calculations based on figures from Terry, 280.
46.   See Mike Davis, *Late Victorian Holocausts: El Niño Famines and the Making of
       the Third World* (London: Verso, 2001).
47.   Collins.
48.   "New Process for Recovering Loss of Gutta-Percha," *IRJ*, Vol. VIII, No. 3
       (October 8, 1892): 90. Reprinted from the *Kew Bulletin*. See also "A Gutta-
       Percha Revolution," *IRJ*, Vol. VIII, No. 11 (London: June 8, 1892): 337–338.
49.   Terry, 273–274.
50.   Collins.

Part Three—Monopoly Capitalism in Akron

NINE: "RUBBER'S HOME TOWN"

1. I have borrowed the title of this chapter from Hugh Allen, *Rubber's Home Town: The Real-Life Story of Akron* (New York: Stratford House, 1949). For many years Hugh Allen was Goodyear's public relations supremo and he authored a number of books on the industry.. Before that he worked as managing editor of the *Akron Beacon Journal*.
2. Vicki Baum, *The Weeping Wood* (Garden City, New York: Doubleday, Doran, 1943).
3. Steve Love and David Giffels, *Wheels of Fortune: The Story of Rubber in Akron* (Akron: University of Akron Press, 1999), xiii.
4. P. W. Litchfield, *Industrial Voyage. My Life as an Industrial Lieutenant* (New York: Doubleday, 1954), 69.
5. Karl H. Grismer, *Akron and Summit County* (Akron: Summit County Historical Society, c. 1951), 377.
6. Allen.
7. Mansel G. Blackford and Austin K. Kerr, *B.F. Goodrich: Tradition and Transformation, 1870–1995* (Columbus: Ohio State University Press, 1996). See also Howard and Ralph Wolf, *Rubber: A Story of Glory and Greed* (New York: Convici-Friede, 1936), 403.
8. UAA. BF Goodrich Files. Box NA 1, File Na 1-27. Beasley Manuscript. Unpublished typescript history of BF Goodrich by Norman Beasley, 4.
9. Alfred Winslow Jones, *Life, Liberty and Property: A Story of Conflict and Measurement of Conflicting Rights* (Philadelphia: J.B. Lippincott, 1941), 25.
10. Grismer, 194.
11. UAA. Goodyear Files. Goodyear History 16 A009. "Mr F.A. Seiberling's speech to the SSS," undated.
12. Seiberling's speech to the SSS
13. Norman Beasley, *Men Working: A Story of the Goodyear Tire & Rubber Co.* (New York: Harper Bros., 1931), 53.
14. Litchfield, 9.
15. "Industry: No Time to Relax," in *Newsweek* (October 11, 1954).
16. Litchfield, 28.
17. Ibid., 58.
18. UAA. Goodyear Files. Goodyear Labor (Personnel) Box 1. Notes for a talk by PW Litchfield, September 1934.
19. UAA. Goodyear History Box 2. Shilts History, 1912–1916. i, unpublished bound typescript.
20. Jack Wilson, "In a Billion Dollar Industry," *New International*, Vol. 2, No. 2 (March 1935): 69; and John L. Ingham, *Biographical Dictionary of American Business Leaders* (Santa Barbara: Greenwood Press, 1983), 808.
21. Alfred Lief, *The Firestone Story: A History of the Firestone Tire & Rubber Company* (New York: McGraw-Hill, 1951), 3.
22. Ibid., 9–15.
23. Dennis J. O'Neill, *A Whale of a Territory: The Story of Bill O'Neil* (New York: McGraw-Hill, 1966), 1–52.
24. UAA. BF Goodrich Files. JA1-37. "Biographical History of the Rubber Industry," unpublished typescript.
25. *India Rubber and Gutta-Percha and Electrical Trades Journal* (November 8, 1892).

26.   Howard and Ralph Wolf, 409–411.
27.   UAA. Summit County Historical Society Box 35. Business. Rubber Companies. Harvey S. Firestone, Jr., "The Romance and Drama of the Rubber Industry: radio talks delivered by Harvey S. Firestone Jr. in 'The Voice of Firestone' programs over the nationwide network of National Broadcasting Company, September 1931 to September 1932" (Akron: Firestone Tire & Rubber, 1932).
28.   UAA Goodyear Files. Advertising Box 1. Clipping from *Collier's Weekly* (December 15, 1900).
29.   Lief, 27.
30.   Arthur Blower, *Akron at the Turn of the Century, 1890–1913: Recollections of Arthur H. Blower* (Akron: Summit County Historical Society, 1955), 37.
31.   Lief, 33.
32.   Cited in the Beasley manuscript, 97.
33.   Lief, 23, 56, 75, 170.
34.   Tires were not the only use for rubber in automobiles. A 1937 trade article noted that there were 121 rubber parts excluding tires in Buicks and 142 in the Oldsmobile. "Rubber," *Tire Review* (September 1937). UAA. BF Goodrich Files, JA1-5.
35.   Calculated using the Measuringworth website at http://www.measuringworth.com/ukcompare/.
36.   *Quarter Century Number*, xix.
37.   Lief, 70.
38.   Howard and Ralph Wolf, 401.
39.   Lief, 94.
40.   Employment in the U.S. rubber industry grew steadily. In 1849, there were just 2,602 rubber workers (exclusive of clerical and staff employees). In 1889, there were 20,152. By 1909, there were 49,264 and by 1929 the figure had risen to 158,549. Many of these employees lived and worked in Akron by that time. F.I. Tuckwell, "Personnel in the Rubber Industry," in P. Schidrowitz and T.R. Dawson (eds.), *History of the Rubber Industry* (Cambridge: W. Heffer, 1952), 358.
41.   H. Earl Wilson, "Crash! And beggars walked city streets in silk shirts," *Akron Beacon Journal* (January 8, 1934).
42.   Lief, 66
43.   Ibid.
44.   Litchfield, 133.
45.   Herbert R. Lottman, *The Michelin Men. Driving an Empire* (London and New York: I.B. Taurus, 2003), 59.
46.   Jones, 41.
47.   Beasley Manuscript, 19.
48.   Ibid., 159.
49.   Ibid., 118.
50.   UAA. BF Goodrich Files. JA1-37.
51.   UAA. BF Goodrich Files. NA1-1. "Chronology of BF Goodrich (1870–1948)."
52.   UAA. Goodyear Files. Goodyear History, Box 7.
53.   David H. Killeffer, *Banbury the Master Mixer: A Biography of Fernley H. Banbury* (New York: Palmerton, 1962).
54.   UAA. Goodyear Files. Goodyear History Box 4. "Address by E.J. Thomas, Goodyear President, to the American Trucking Company," October 29, 1947.
55.   "Business, Rubber Companies." UAA. Summit County Historical Society Box 35.

56.   UAA. Goodyear Files. Goodyear History Box 4. "Typed notes."

57.   Ibid. See also Hugh Allen, "Tires Popped: Curious Caravan Proves Truck
       Pneumatics' Abilities for Transport in 1917," *Goodyear News* (Akron: Goodyear
       Tire & Rubber, 1917).

58.   Ibid. and *The Wingfoot Clan* (Akron: Goodyear Tire & Rubber, 1960).

59.   Ibid. See also Anonymous, "War Department to Send Motor Convoy from
       Washington to Los Angeles," *Highway Engineer and Contractor: A Journal of
       State and City Engineering and Construction Problems* (June 1920).

60.   National Defense Highway System. Available online at http//www.globalsecuri-
       ty.org/military/facility/ndhs.htm. Also the Dwight D. Eisenhower Library's
       "Interstate Highway System," available online at http://www.eisenhower.
       archives.gov/dl/InterstateHighways/InterstateHighwaysdocuments.html.
       Eisenhower was also impressed by what he saw of the German Autobahn system
       in the First World War.

61.   Grismer, 377.

62.   C. R. Quine (ed.), *The Akron Riot of 1900* (Akron: C.R. Quine, 1951), 10.

63.   Jones, 57.

64.   Grismer, 378.

65.   Blower, 3.

66.   Unpublished paper of George Parkin Atwater (1928), cited in Kevin Michael
       Rosswurm, "A Strike in the Rubber City: Rubber Workers, Akron, and the IWW,
       1913," unpublished MA thesis (Kent: Kent State University, 1975), 13. Copy in
       UAA.

67.   Burr McCloskey, cited in William Bierman, "An Author's Akron: The Way It
       Was," *Akron Beacon Journal* (October 21, 1979).

68.   Kevan Delaney Frazier, "Model Industrial Subdivisions: Goodyear Heights and
       Firestone Park and the Town Planning Movement in Akron, Ohio," unpublished
       MA thesis (Kent: Kent State University, 1994), 58.

69.   For an illustrated history of the premises, see: Ian Adams, *Stan Hywet Hall &
       Gardens* (Akron: University of Akron Press, 2001).

70.   Joseph E. Kuebler, "Firestone's Harbel Manor Sold to Realty Developer," *Akron
       Beacon Journal* (January 25, 1959).

71.   The mansion's name was a contraction of the given names of Harvey Firestone
       and his wife, Idabelle. The nameplate and model are in the University of Akron
       Archives.

72.   Kenneth Nichols, "Expandable Palace Grew with Akron," *Akron Beacon Journal*
       (January 25, 1959).

73.   Grismer, 379.

74.   Edward Mott Wooley, "Akron: Standing Room Only!" in *McClure's* (July 1917).

75.   H. Earl Wilson, "Crash!"

76.   Kenneth Nichols, *Yesterday's Akron: The First 150 Years* (Miami: E.A. Seeman,
       1976), 56.

77.   H. Earl Wilson, "'Good Old Days' Embraced Rugged War Time Doings–Flu
       Horror," *Akron Beacon Journal* (February 8, 1934).

78.   Daniel Nelson, *American Rubber Workers & Organized Labor* (Princeton, NJ:
       Princeton University Press, 1988), 53.

79.   Grismer, 378.

80.   Charlene Nevada, "The URW at 50: An Old Timer Recalls Those Early,
       Desperate Years," *Akron Beacon Journal* (September 1, 1985).

81.   Ibid.

82.   Grismer, 379.
83.   Jones, 61.
84.   Giffels.
85.   Jones, 61.
86.   Grismer, 378.
87.   UAA. BF Goodrich Files. Box NA1-11.
88.   Cited in Howard Wolf, "The First 100 Years," *The Akron Beacon Journal*, 634–635.
89.   Knepper, cited in Giffels, 145.
90.   Ruth McKenney, *Industrial Valley* (New York: Greenwood Press, 1939), 2.
91.   Jones, 20. In 1931, around 12.38 percent of Akron's population (31,568 out of 255,000 people) was foreign born. This was down from 37,889 in 1920. The main groups of "foreign-born white persons" were: 4,345 Italians, 3,860 Hungarians, 3,238 Yugoslavs, 2,712 Germans, 2,537 English, 1,759 Poles, and 15,556 Czechoslovaks. "31,568 Akronites Are Foreign-Born," *Akron Beacon Journal* (June 25, 1931).
92.   Nelson, 54.
93.   Modern History Sourcebook: Sojourner Truth: "Ain't I A Woman?" Speech to the Women's Convention, Akron, Ohio, December 1851. Available online at http://www.fordham.edu/halsall/mod/sojtruth-woman.html.
94.   Shirla Robinson McClain, *The Contributions of Blacks in Akron: 1825–1975* (Akron: Akron Gallery of Black History Curriculum Committee, 1996).
95.   Frazier, 50.
96.   Klippert. 34
97.   UAA. Goodyear Files. Labor Relations, Box 1. *The Goodyear Worker* (February 1937).
98.   Bowling Green State University Center for Archival Collections. MMS 922. Ohio Labor History Project 14.4.1 Mr. James Turner, Retired Fair Practices Director Rubber Workers International. Interview conducted December 4, 1975, by Carl Clausen, Ann Van Tine and Patricia Curran in Akron.
99.   Grismer, 403. The most complete account of the KKK in Akron is an unpublished thesis: John Lee Maples, "The Akron, Ohio, Ku Klux Klan, 1921–1928," MA History thesis (Akron: University of Akron, 1974).
100. Pesotta, 198–199 and 211–212.
101. Karl Marx, *The Eighteenth Brumaire of Louis Bonaparte*, in Karl Marx and Frederick Engels, *Selected Works*, vol. one (Moscow: Progress Publishers, 1969), 398.
102. Love and Giffels, 114–117.
103. Nelson, 90.
104. Blackford and Kerr claim that almost half of the BF Goodrich workers in 1917 were noncitizens (71).
105. Lottman, 41 and 58.
106. Jones, 305.
107. See, for instance, Eric Leif Davin, "The Very Last Hurrah? The Defeat of the Labor Party Idea, 1934–36," in Staughton Lynd (ed.), *"We Are All Leaders": the Alternative Unionism of the Early 1930s* (Urbana and Chicago: University of Illinois Press, 1996), 117–171; and Richard W. Shrake II, "Working-Class Politics in Akron, Ohio, 1936: The United Rubber Workers and the Failure of the Farmer-Labor Party," unpublished MA thesis (Akron: University of Akron, 1974).

TEN: THE 1913 IWW STRIKE AT AKRON

1. Cited in Howard and Ralph Wolf, *Rubber: A Story of Glory and Greed* (New York: Convici-Friede, 1936), 503.
2. "Highlights in Dalrymple's Radio Talk on Akron Strike," *Akron Beacon Journal* (February 28, 1936).
3. Ibid.
4. Cited in URWA, *25 Years of the URW: A Quarter Century of Panorama of Democratic Unionism* (Akron: United Rubber, Cork, Linoleum and Plastic Workers of America, AFL-CIO, 1960).
5. Paul Litchfield, *The Republic of Business* (Akron: Goodyear Tire & Rubber, 1920).
6. University of Akron Archives (UAA). BF Goodrich Files. Labor Relations Box D2, BF Goodrich D2-13, Wage Scale 1902; *25 Years of the URW*; Daniel Nelson, *American Rubber Workers & Organized Labor, 1900–1941* (Princeton, NJ: Princeton University Press, 1988), 10; Kevin Michael Rosswurm, "A Strike in the Rubber City: Rubber Workers, Akron, and the IWW, 1913," unpublished MA thesis (Kent: Kent State University, 1975), 9, 12; Karl Grismer, *Akron and Summit County* (Akron: Summit County Historical Society, c. 1951), 365.
7. Rosswurm, 15.
8. Ibid., 23.
9. Kathleen L. Endres, *Rosie the Rubber Worker: Women Workers in Akron's Rubber Factories during World War II* (Kent: Kent State University Press, 2000), 18. Endres' allusion is to "Rosie the Riveter," an image created during the Second World War by the U.S. War Advertising Council to lure women into industrial jobs. (Ibid., 1.)
10. The URW leaders were often very progressive on women's rights. During the Second World War the union's international president, Sherman Dalrymple, favored extension of the standard work week rather than "see housewives work eight hours in a factory and then another eight hours at home." He believed housework should be shared equally.
11. Endres, 21 and 28.
12. According to Rosswurm, this was possibly the second recorded sit-down strike in U.S. labor history (9). Details are scant apart from a mention in P.W. Litchfield, *Industrial Voyage: My Life as an Industrial Lieutenant* (New York: Doubleday, 1954), 77.
13. John Newton Thurber, *Rubber Workers' History (1935–1955)* (Akron: Public Relations Department, URCLPWA, AFL-CIO, 1956), 3–4; Nelson, 12 and 21; and Alfred Winslow Jones, *Life, Liberty and Property: A Story of Conflict and Measurement of Conflicting Rights* (Philadelphia: J.B. Lippincott, 1941), 74.
14. Rosswurm, 25.
15. Howard and Ralph Wolf, 497–499.
16. Nelson, 8.
17. Rosswurm notes that eventually mechanization meant that women could physically do most jobs, including even tire building, which had been done by only the strongest young men (31). It had also been the most skilled of the production jobs, but was gradually deskilled.
18. Frederick Winslow Taylor, *Principles of Scientific Management* (1911). Available online at http://melbecon.unimelb.edu.au/het/taylor/sciman.htm.
19. The classical division of labor was between different crafts, for instance carpenter and blacksmith, potter and weaver. As Adam Smith, Marx, and others showed, in

NOTES TO PAGES 152–155

the capitalist factory system, the older crafts were broken down into a myriad of semi-skilled and unskilled jobs—a new division of labor at the enterprise level. This deskilling led to alienation and loss of control by the worker. See, for instance, Harry Braverman, *Labor and Monopoly Capitalism: The Degradation of Work in the Twentieth Century* (New York: Monthly Review Press, 1974).

20. Taylor, chapter 1: "Fundamentals of Scientific Management."

21. For a nightmarish fictionalized description of Taylorism and its Bedaux version in the Akron tire factories see Burr McCloskey, *He Will Stay Till You Come, The Rise and Fall of Skinny Walker* (Durham, NC: Moore Publishing, 1978). McCloskey, then a young Communist, worked as a tire builder in Akron in the 1930s. The book has been heavily criticized for presenting a distorted picture of Akron, the rubber workers, and their union. Skinny Walker, the book's antihero, bears little resemblance to the URW officials others remember. Perhaps this is not surprising, given McCloskey's gravitation to the right in politics.

22. Rosswurm, 32–34.

23. UAA. Goodyear History Box 9. P.W. Litchfield, "Current Trends in Industry," address given November 20 in Boston, Mass. To New England Council, local business association organized by New England state governors in 1929."

24. Cited in Nelson, 20.

25. Grismer, 366.

26. Ibid., i.

27. Rosswurm, 89–90. The chairman of the committee, Ohio State Senator William Green, had close links with the rival AFL and later became its president. The committee also shied away from any criticism of what amounted to a reign of terror against the strikers. The committee's findings only came out after the end of the dispute and were thus a dead letter.

28. Evidence of Frank Seiberling, E.C. Shaw (BF Goodrich) and Harvey Firestone to the Ohio State Senate investigative committee, Akron, 1913. Cited in Rosswurm, 72.

29. Litchfield, 131.

30. Cited in the *Akron Beacon Journal* (February 25, 1913).

31. UAA. BF Goodrich Files. Box NA1-48. "Reminiscences of David M. Goodrich."

32. Grismer, 365.

33. Howard and Ralph Wolf, 499.

34. Ibid., 501.

35. This was often the case in IWW disputes. Despite the revolutionary rhetoric, the IWW behaved in many respects like an orthodox union. See Joseph R. Conlin, *At the Point of Production: The Local History of the IWW* (Westport, CT: Greenwood Press, 1981).

36. UAA. BF Goodrich Labor Relations Box D2-18. "*Akron Strike Bulletin*, 3/18/13." The legendary abolitionist John Brown lived and worked in Akron as a wool classer.

37. Cannon later joined the Communist Party via the Socialist Party and was for many years the national secretary of the Trotskyist Socialist Workers Party. Cannon's role in the Akron strike is discussed in Bryan D. Palmer, *James P. Cannon and the Origins of the American Revolutionary Left, 1890–1928* (Urbana and Chicago: University of Illinois Press, 2007), ch. 3 and 60–67.

38. Rosswurm, 92.

39. Ibid., 92–93.

40. Nelson, 35.

41. Ibid. Rosswurm gives the lower figure, company sources the higher. Grismer says a maximum of 15,000 went on strike (367).
42. Shilts. 101.
43. Litchfield, 131.
44. Rosswurm, 82.
45. Litchfield. 131.
46. UAA. BF Goodrich Labor Relations Box D2-18. *"Akron Strike Bulletin,* 3/18/13."
47. Bowling Green State University Center for Archival Collections. pOG 2563. Oral History Interview with Mr Paul Sebestyen [Sebastian] on Akron's Rubber Strike and on General Ideological Background, July 8, 1969, by Roy Wortman, Department of History, Ohio State University, Columbus. Trautmann was the founding General Secretary of the IWW. Sebestyen was a socialist and Hungarian immigrant.
48. Rosswurm, 83.
49. Grismer, 368.
50. Lewis's role is curious, given his later role in the formation of the CIO in the 1930s. His own union, the United Mine Workers, was already an industrial union. (Howard and Ralph Wolf, 502; Nelson, 31.)
51. Rosswurm, 42.
52. Shilts, 102.
53. Rosswurm, 88.
54. Cited in Shilts, 110–111.
55. Cited in Palmer, 66.
56. *25 years of the URW.*
57. Jim McCartan, unpublished and undated fragment in the Sam Pollock Papers, MS 468. Box 9, Personal Papers, Folder 16. Bowling Green State University Center for Archival Collections. Bowling Green, Ohio.

ELEVEN: SISTERS, BROTHERS, UNITE! THE UNITED RUBBER WORKERS AT AKRON

1. URWA, *25 Years of the URW: A Quarter Century of Panorama of Democratic Unionism* (Akron: United Rubber, Cork, Linoleum and Plastic Workers of America, AFL-CIO, 1960); see also Ruth McKenney, *Industrial Valley* (New York: Greenwood Press, 1939), 343.
2. Ibid., 121.
3. H. Earl Wilson, "Crash! And Beggars Walked City Streets in Silk Shirts," *Akron Beacon Journal* (January 8, 1934)
4. P. W. Litchfield, *Industrial Voyage: My Life as an Industrial Lieutenant* (New York: Doubleday, 1954), 107. See also Alfred Lief on the voluntary introduction of the eight-hour day without loss of pay at Firestone. Previously, shifts had been of ten or twelve hours. Alfred Lief, *The Firestone Story: A History of the Firestone Tire & Rubber Company* (New York: McGraw-Hill, 1951), 80.
5. See Kevan Delaney Frazier, "Model Industrial Subdivisions: Goodyear Heights and Firestone Park and the Town Planning Movement in Akron, Ohio," unpublished MA thesis (Kent: Kent State University, 1994). See also Clarice Finley Lewis, *A History of Firestone Park* (Akron: Firestone Park Citizens' Council, 1986).
6. Cited in Frazier, 28.
7. Anonymous, "Rubber Slavery in Akron," *The Industrial Pioneer; An Illustrated Labor Magazine* (Chicago: Industrial Workers of the World, August 1925).

8.   Mansel G. Blackford and K. Austin Kerr, *B.F. Goodrich: Tradition and Transformation, 1870-1995* (Columbus: Ohio State University Press, 1996), 57. The term appears to have been coined in the 1920s: see Selig Perlman, *A Theory of the Labor Movement*, (New York: Augustus M Kelly, 1928), 207-209. The idea itself seems to have originated in Europe. For instance, the Siemens electrical engineering company pioneered a wide-ranging system of employee benefits in the nineteenth century and built the Siemensstadt housing estate in Berlin in 1921. Siemens's welfarism was in part impelled by a fear of the powerful socialist movement in Germany. See, for example, Siemens, "Milestones." Available online at http://www.siemens.com.

9.   Goodyear took the welfarist approach to new plants in Gadsden, Alabama, Wolverhampton in England and in Scotland. For information on the former, see, for example, Gene L. Howard, *The History of the Rubber Workers in Gadsden, Alabama, 1933-1983* (East Gadsden, AL: URWA Local 12, East Gadsden, 1983), 3. For the latter, see the Ginaven Collection, 1930-1978, held in the Akron-Summit County Public Library. This collection of documents and photographs was bequeathed by Howard "Piggy" Ginaven, a Goodyear executive who worked in the Flying Squadron at Akron before helping set up the Wolverhampton plant. He retired in 1975 after forty-one years of service.

10.   See, for example, Herbert R. Lottman, *The Michelin Men: Driving an Empire* (London and New York: I.B. Taurus, 2003), 82-83.

11.   UAA. Goodyear History, Box 4. *Goodyear: A Family Magazine*, Vol. IX, No. 5 (Akron: Goodyear Tire & Rubber, May 1920).

12.   "Rubber Slavery in Akron,".

13.   Blackford and Kerr, 71. Alfred Winslow Jones considers that Goodrich had a more lukewarm approach than Goodyear and Firestone. Alfred Winslow Jones, *Life, Liberty and Property: A Story of Conflict and Measurement of Conflicting Rights* (Philadelphia: J.B. Lippincott, 1941), 51.

14.   Lief, 73, 78, 221.

15.   Lottman, 61.

16.   Lief, 83.

17.   University of Akron Archives (UAA) Goodyear Files. Unpublished typescript by P.W. Litchfield, "Crossing the Red Sea: The Reveries of an Industrial Lieutenant. A Study in Industrial Economics" (c. 1920).

18.   Arthur Pound, "An Industrial Republic: The Goodyear Program for Employee Representation and Education," *The Atlantic Monthly* (March 1935).

19.   UAA. Goodyear History Box 19. The system is also discussed in Daniel Nelson, *American Rubber Workers & Organized Labor, 1900-1941* (Princeton, NJ: Princeton University Press, 1988), 57-59.

20.   Ibid.

21.   UAA. International President Local Unions, Box 1-3.

22.   Richard C. Wilcock "Industrial Management's Policies towards Unionism," in Milton Derber and Edwin Young (eds.), *Labor and the New Deal* (New York: Da Capo Press, 1972), 288.

23.   UAA. Goodyear Labor, Box 12. Comments by Hugh Allen on the launch of Litchfield book *Industrial Voyage*, 1954.

24.   Litchfield, *Industrial Voyage*, 133.

25.   Litchfield, "Crossing the Red Sea."

26.   Howard Wolf, "*The Akron Beacon Journal*: The First 100 Years" (Akron: unpublished manuscript, 1939), 623. (Courtesy of the *Akron Beacon Journal* archives.)

27.   "Rubber Slavery in Akron" and Nelson, 96.
28.   Milton Derber, "Growth and Expansion," in Derber and Young, 3.
29.   H. Earl Wilson.
30.   Lief, 222.
31.   Karl H. Grismer, *Akron and Summit County* (Akron: Summit County Historical Society, c. 1951), 450.
32.   Ibid., 489.
33.   Nelson, 84–86.
34.   Steven Kreis, "The Diffusion of Scientific Management: The Bedaux Company in America and Britain, 1926-1945," in Daniel Nelson (ed.), *A Mental Revolution: Scientific Management Since Taylor* (Columbus: Ohio State University Press, 1992). Charles Eugène Bedaux lacked formal qualifications and originally made his living in the United States as a sand hog in New York City tunnels. Charming but unsavory, he was also a thug, gangster, and a Nazi collaborator during the Second World War.
35.   Cited in McKenney, 117–118.
36.   Lief, 223.
37.   Wilcock, 293.
38.   R. W. Fleming, "The Significance of the Wagner Act," in Derber and Young, Table 1, 131.
39.   The "formula" was based on the tactics of the Remington Rand Company at Ilion, New York.
40.   Tate was eventually expelled from the AFL machinists' union for his support of the industrial approach and McCartan voluntarily transferred members of the typographers' union inside the rubber mills to the URWA. Tate "died in harness" as a CIO steelworkers' union organizer in 1944. McCartan retired from the *Akron Beacon Journal* print room some years later and died in 1967 a staunch union man. Unlike the URWA leaders, who were mainly Southerners, Tate began life on an Iowa farm and McCartan came from a family of Irish immigrants who worked on the Ohio coalfields at New Industry, or "Slabtown" as it was more prosaically known.
41.   McKenney, 99.
42.   Named after the pro-Labor Democrat Senator Robert F. Wagner, who sponsored the Bill.
43.   Derber, 129.
44.   Ibid., 10.
45.   Fleming, 126.
46.   "Notice to employees of the Seiberling Rubber Company."
47.   UAA. Goodyear Labor, (Personnel) Box 1. "Men of Goodyear" speech, February 23, 1939.
48.   UAA. URW International President Local Unions, Box 4. Notice from Goodyear management, November 14, 1934, in response to proposal lodged by the URW to open negotiations.
49.   Ibid. Address delivered by PW Litchfield in the Forum of Liberty, November 1, 1934, Broadcast No. 3.
50.   John D. House, 1978, "Birth of a Union," unpublished book manuscript, microfilmed in 1981 by the Ohio Historical Society, Columbus, Ohio. See also Charlene Nevada, "The URW Hits 50: An Old Campaigner Recalls Those Early, Desperate Years," *Akron Beacon Journal* (September 1, 1985).
51.   Nelson, *Rubber Workers*, 119.

52.   Winslow Jones, 86.
53.   McKenney, 63.
54.   Howard and Ralph Wolf, 510.
55.   Ibid. Blackford and Kerr, say 7,500 (124).
56.   Howard and Ralph Wolf, McKenney, 122.
57.   John E. Borsos, "Talking Union: The Labor Movement in Barberton, Ohio, 1891–1991," unpublished Ph.D. thesis (Bloomington: Indiana University, 1992). An abbreviated version of the thesis is more widely available: John Borsos, "'We Make You This Appeal in the Name of Every Union Man and Woman in Barberton': Solidarity Unionism in Barberton, Ohio, 1933–41," in Staughton Lynd (ed.), "We Are All Leaders": The Alternative Unionism of the Early 1930s (Urbana and Chicago: University of Illinois Press, 1996), 238–293.
58.   McKenney, 104.
59.   The federation was international in the sense that it had a Canadian affiliate.
60.   Ibid., 108.
61.   Harry Harrison, "Union Labor's New Air of Business-like Dignity is Called its Just Recognition," Akron Beacon Journal (October 6, 1933).
62.   Paul Litchfield, obituary for Samuel Gompers in The Wingfoot Clan (Akron: December 17, 1924).
63.   Nelson, 133.
64.   McKenney, 140.
65.   King Canute or Knut was an 11th-century English king famous for demonstrating to his courtiers the limits of royal power by showing that he could not halt the incoming tide. More usually, the tale implies that Canute was arrogant.
66.   James S. Jackson, "Ouster of two rubber union officials to bring showdown, testing power of federation of labor," Akron Beacon Journal (January 20, 1934). The two officers were Frederick L. Phillips and Clark C. Culver, financial secretaries of the BF Goodrich and Goodyear locals respectively.
67.   Howard and Ralph Wolf, 512; McKenney, 156; Nelson, 142.
68.   UAA, URW International President Local Unions, Box 1-3.
69.   The Big Three must also have been apprehensive about the spread of union militancy to their overseas plants. In January 1935, for example, the workers at Goodyear's Granville factory in Sydney, Australia, struck for fourteen days. A photograph of a strike meeting can be seen online at http://acms.sl.nsw. gov.au/search/simpleSearch.aspx?authority=place&ID=38238. State Library of NSW, Manuscripts, Oral History and Pictures. Accessed March 19, 2010. Three years later, there was a strike of engineering workers in the Dunlop factory at Drummoyne, Sydney. See Geoffrey Blainey, Jumping Over the Wheel (St. Leonards, NSW: Allen & Unwin, 1993), 168. Blainey gives few details except that the strike was because Dunlops did not pay overtime for Saturday work.
70.   UAA, URW International President Local Unions. Box 4. Letter to Coleman Claherty from O.H. Boseley, Recording Secretary, Firestone Local No 18321 (AFL), Akron, July 13, 1934.
71.   Nelson, 154.
72.   URW International President Local Unions. Letter from C.E. Huggins, "Chairman Organization Committee Independent Rubber Workers Vertical Union 1238 South Main Street Akron Ohio." Dated November 9, 1934.
73.   McKenney, 182. UAA, URW International President Local Unions Box 4, Seiberling Rubber, November 27, 1934 and Goodyear, November 14, 1934.
74.   URW International President Local Unions Box 4, Seiberling Rubber.

75.   UAA, URW International President Local Unions Box 1-5. Letter from William
       Green to HT Wilson, January 14, 1935.
76.   McKenney, 192.
77.   Howard and Ralph Wolf, 514.
78.   McKenney, 194 and 200.
79.   "Court Assailed in Tate Speech," in *Akron Beacon Journal* (May 23, 1936).
80.   McAlister Coleman, "Spirit of Debs Guides Tire Strike," *United Rubber Worker*,
       Vol. 1, No. 1 (Akron: URWA, 1936). The editor was the well-known Akron
       Trotskyist B.J. Widick, a former journalist for the *Beacon Journal*.
81.   The Committee changed its name to the Congress of Industrial Organizations
       when it formally split from the AFL in 1938 with the URW as one of its flagship
       affiliates.
82.   McKenney, 248; Lief, 225.
83.   McKenney, 251. Eigenmacht seems to have been a member of the Communist
       Party of the United States, or at least close to it, and so we should be cautious of
       McKenney's claims, given her inflation of the importance of the Party in the
       Akron struggles. While the Party did have influence in the Firestone plant in par-
       ticular, and its members were on friendly terms with Wilmer Tate and other
       socialist unionists, it was not as influential as McKenney claims. There was also
       some distrust of the Party because of its earlier espousal of ultra-left sectarian
       "Third Period" policies of building separate "Red" unions which had prevented
       it from working with the union mainstream. On the other hand, we should also be
       skeptical of the tendency of the more conservative URW leaders to disparage the
       Party's work in the period.
84.   "When 63 gassed, weeping, retching sit-downers fled from two North Chicago
       plants in 1937, they presented U. S. Labor and jurisprudence with the celebrat-
       ed case of *NLRB v. Fansteel Metallurgical Corp.*," reported *Time* magazine. Two
       years later, the U.S. Supreme Court reversed the NLRB's order to the company
       to reinstate the strikers, ruling that they had no right to occupy company proper-
       ty and this effectively made the tactic illegal. See "Sit-Down Out," *Time* (Monday,
       March 6, 1939) for a report on the ruling. For legal discussions see Henry M.
       Hart, "The Fansteel Case: Employee Misconduct and the remedial powers of the
       National Labor Relations Board," *Harvard Law Review*, Vol. 52, No. 8 (June
       1939): 1275–1329, and "Employee Misconduct under the Wagner Act:
       Developments since the Fansteel Case," *Columbia Law Review*, Vol. 39, No. 8
       (December 1939): 1369–1382.
85.   John Newton Thurber, *Rubber Workers' History (1935–1955)* (Akron: Public
       Relations Department, URCLPWA, AFL-CIO, 1956), 3.
86.   Ibid. Letter from E.B. Harper of URW Local 18323 to Dalrymple, April 14,
       1936.
87.   Wilcock, 293. See also Robert G. Rodden, *The Fighting Machinists: A Century of
       Struggle* (Washington, DC: Kelly Press, 1984).
88.   "Goodyear's Gadsden Workers Vote URWA," *United Rubber Worker*, Vol. 8, No.
       5 (Akron: URWA, May 1941).
89.   Howard.
90.   "Hypocrites Cackle," *United Rubber Worker*, Vol. 1, No. 3 (Akron: URWA, June
       1936).
91.   Ibid. Also Nevada, and Ed Heinke, "Ask US Quiz after Beating on Trip South,"
       Akron Beacon Journal (June 9, 1936).
92.   James S. Jackson, "New Sitdown Ends Tonight," *Akron Beacon Journal* (June 10, 1936).

93.   UAA. Box 1-3. URW International President Local Unions. B.T. Garner, URW southern representative to Dalrymple, June 16 1937.
94.   Ibid.
95.   Ibid. Letter from C.S. Holmes to S.H. Dalrymple. Not dated but describes events of January 5 1938.
96.   A gummers' term for anti-union workers with echoes of "an apple for the teacher."
97.   "Fink Lingo," *United Rubber Worker*, Vol. 1, No. 6 (Akron: URWA, September 1936)
98.   "Heroes Fight Wintery Blast," *United Rubber Worker*, Vol. 1, No. 1 (Akron: URWA, April 1936).
99.   *25 Years of the URW.*
100. "Wintery Blast."
101. Gene L. Howard, *The History of the Rubber Workers in Gadsden, Alabama, 1933-1983*, (East Gadsden: URWA Local 12, 1983), 9
102. Rose Pesotta, *Bread Upon the Waters*, ed. John Nicholas Beffa (Ithaca, NY: ILR Press, 1987), 220.
103. Ibid.
104. John S. Knight, "No Room For Vigilantes," *Akron Beacon Journal* (February 18, 1936).
105. Pesotta, 214.
106. UAA. Goodyear Files. Goodyear Labor Relations Box 1. Article reprinted from "Revolution in Michigan."
107. UAA. Goodyear Files. Goodyear Labor, Box 1, Paul Litchfield, "Men of Goodyear" speech, February 23, 1939.
108. McKenney, 343 & 348.
109. Pesotta, 198–199.
110. Ibid., 211–212.
111. Ibid., 214.
112. Nelson, 196.
113. *25 Years of the URW;* McKenney, 343.
114. Nelson, 198–199.
115. *United Rubber Worker*, Vol. 1, No. 1.
116. *25 Years of the URW.*
117. "Firestone Shuns URWA," *United Rubber Worker*, Vol. 1, No 3 (Akron: URWA, March 1938).
118. Lief, 226–229.
119. Ibid.
120. UAA. URW International President Local Unions, Box 1-2, File 7, 1934–1955. Copy of agreement signed April 28, 1937 between Firestone Tire & Rubber and URW Local No. 7 in Akron.
121. "Union Whips Firestone," *United Rubber Worker*, Vol. 2, No. 5 (Akron: URWA, May 1937).

Part Four—Plantation Hevea: Agribusiness and Imperialism

TWELVE: THE TRIUMPH OF PLANTATION HEVEA

1.   *British Imperialism in Malaya*, Colonial Series No. 2 (London: CPGB Labour Research Dept., 1926), 4. Copy in British National Archives, CO 273/539/12. 1927 Straits Malay States. Item No. 28150.

2.   Royal Botanic Gardens Archives (Kew, London) (hereinafter KEW). MR Malaya Rubber, Misc. 1852–1908, f205. Stanley Arden, "Report on Hevea Brasiliensis in the Malay Peninsula" (Perak: Government Printing Office, 1902).

3.   For the collector's own story, see Henry Wickham, *On the Plantation, Cultivation and Curing of Para Indian Rubber* (London: Kegan Paul, 1908).

4.   John Hemming, *Amazon Frontier: The Defeat of the Brazilian Indians* (London: Macmillan, 1987), 283.

5.   Herbert Wright, *Rubber Cultivation in the British Empire: A Lecture Delivered To the Society of Arts* (London: MacLaren and Sons, 1907), 46.

6.   Lucile H. Brockway, "Science and Colonial Expansion: The Role of the British Royal Botanic Gardens," *American Ethnologist* (August 1979): 449–465.

7.   J. Norman Parmer, *Colonial Labor Policy and Administration: A History of Labor in the Rubber Plantation Industry in Malaya, c. 1910–1941* (Locust Valley, NY: J.J. Augustin for the Association for Asian Studies, 1960), 5.

8.   "The Future Supply of India-Rubber," *The India-Rubber and Gutta-Percha and Electrical Trades Journal* (June 9, 1890).

9.   B.D. Porritt, *The Early History of the Rubber Industry* (London: Rubber Growers Association, 1927), 14.

10.   Abdul Aziz bin S.A. Kadir et al (eds.), *Portrait of the Global Rubber Industry: Driving the Wheel of the World Economy* (Kuala Lumpur: International Rubber Research and Development Board, c. 2006), 46.

11.   Bradford L. Barham and Oliver T. Coomes, *Prosperity's Promise: The Amazon Rubber Boom and Distorted Economic Development*, Dellplain Latin American Studies, No. 34 (Boulder, CO: Westview Press, 1996), 80.

12.   KEW. Miscellaneous Reports. India. India Office. Caoutchouc II, c. 1874–1903. This file contains a number of documents pertaining to the Assam plantations, including Gustav Mann, Deputy Conservator of Forests "Report on the Caoutchouc Plantations in Assam and the Yield of Caoutchouc from the '*Ficus Elastica*'" (Assam: June 10, 1875).

13.   KEW. Miscellaneous Reports. India. India Office. Caoutchouc II, c. 1874–1903. Imperial Institute Series. Handbooks of Commercial Products. Indian Section. No. 25 India-Rubber from *Ficus elastica* (Calcutta: Government of India, 1893).

14.   See, for instance, KEW India Office Caoutchouc I. Letter from India Office to Sir Joseph Hooker, Kew Gardens, May 7, 1873, signed Duff.

15.   International Rubber and Allied Trades Exhibition, *A Short History of the Rubber Industry in Ceylon* (Colombo: Olympia, September 14, 1908).

16.   This is clear from numerous letters and other documents in the Kew Gardens Archives. See, for instance, KEW India Office Caoutchouc I, which contains relevant correspondence between the Secretary of State for India, Clements Markham, Joseph Hooker, Robert Cross, Henry Wickham, and others.

17.   KEW. India Office Caoutchouc I. Memo from Dr G. King, Superintendent Royal Botanical Gardens, Howrah to the Acting Assistant Secretary to the Government of Bengal, February 22, 1876.

18.   Jean Le Bras, *Introduction to Rubber*, trans. J.H. Goundry (London: MacLaren and Sons, 1965), 24.

19.   Ridley's efforts are detailed in D.J.M. Tate, *The RGA History of the Plantation Industry in the Malay Peninsula* (Kuala Lumpur: Oxford University Press, 1996), 193–197. The soubriquet of "Mad" Ridley is mentioned in Daniel Green, *A Plantation Family* (Ipswich: The Boydell Press, 1979), 133. For a general discus-

sion of rubber's early days in Malaya, see C.E. Akers, *The Rubber Industry in Brazil and the Orient* (London: Methuen, 1914), 166.

20. Quoted in Tate, 194.

21. D. C. Lewis, *The Plantation Dream: Developing British New Guinea and Papua, 1884–1942* (Canberra: *The Journal of Pacific History*, 1996), 26–27.

22. Pennington of Muncaster (Cumbria Record Office, The Castle, Carlisle, Cumbria) (Australian Joint Copying Project, National Library of Australia and the State Library of NSW). Microfilm No. JAC 239 D/PEN/Malaya. Letter from Mr. Sowerby, Royal Botanic Society of London to Mr. Underdown at Penang on the cultivation of India Rubber Trees, May 3, 1877. These files are those of a group of British sugar and rubber companies in Malaya. [Hereinafter, this source will be referred to as as MUNC plus file numbers and document title.]

23. Jan Breman, *Taming the Coolie Beast: Plantation Society and the Colonial Order in Southeast Asia* (Delhi: Oxford University Press, 1989), 70.

24. Peter Pugh et al., *Great Enterprise: A History of Harrisons and Crosfield*, ed. Guy Nickalls (London: Harrisons and Crosfield, 1990), 27.

25. MUNC JAC 242. Letter from Dick Ramsden to his father, March 2, 1895.

26. Tate, 193 & 195. Also KEW MR Malaya Rubber, Misc. 1852–1908 f 205. Notes by Mr. Ridley, Botanic Gardens, Singapore, October 20, 1897.

27. Akers, 166.

28. MUNC M1345 JAC 243 D/Pen/Malaya Report to the directors, Penang Sugar Estates, March 14, 1907.

29. MUNC JAC 272. Rubana Rubber: E.L. Hamilton's correspondence 1910–1911. Letter from E.L. Hamilton to Sir John Ramsden, April 13, 1910.

30. MUNC M1349 JAC 261 D/PEN/Malaya/2/15. Letters, July–December 1910.

31. MUNC M1351 JAC 263 2/24. Telegram from the directors to Penang. March 25, 1913.

32. National Archives of Australia (NAA) A518/1, Item 105013, ANGPCB – Rubber – Rubber Production – General. Memorandum for the PCB in Australia, NG from the Dept. of External Territories, "Rubber Industry in Papua and New Guinea" by J. R. Halligan.

33. Lewis, 28.

34. J. J. Camus, *L'Ouevre Humaine et Sociale dans les Plantations de Caoutchouc d'Indochine* (Paris: Société d'Editions Techniques Coloniales, 1949).

35. François de Tessan, "Impressions de Cochinchine: chez les planteurs d'arbre à caoutchouc," *L'Impartial* (Saigon: November 7, 1921). Also see Le Bras, 24.

36. Akers, 291.

37. "Rubber in Brazil," *The Scientific American*, Vol. 103 (October 8, 1910), 272. See also J. Orton Kerbey, *An American Consul in Amazonia* (New York: William Edwin Rudge, 1911), 278.

38. Parmer, 10.

39. J. H. Harris, "Native Races and Rubber Prices," *The Contemporary Review*, Vol. 104 (London: November 1913): 650.

40. Akers, 122.

41. "Rubber planters seek assistance," *The Argus* (Melbourne: August 5, 1918).

42. NAA A1 (A1/15) 43764 Loans to Kemp, Welch and New Guinea Rubber Estates Ltd., Home and Territories Department memo 25/16087.

43. Lewis, 213 and 216.

44. MUNC JAC275 D/PEN/Malaya. Sabrang Rubber Estates Quarterly Annual Reports, 1921–1922. J. Cruickshank to Chairman and Directors, February 13, 1922.

45.   UAA. Goodyear History Box 2. Typescript: Revised House of Goodyear. Third Period, Goodyear in the 1920s. Section 2, Depression on the Plantations. By Hugh Allen.

46.   Tate, 355.

47.   British National Archives (BNA) CO 717/68/20. Item 62499. Malay States 1929 Rubber tapping prohibition of tapping on Sundays. Note to Sir E. Birch from M. Gent, November 20, 1929.

48.   Ibid. Maurice Maude to A.M. Samuel, House of Commons, December 14, 1929.

49.   Ibid. Sir E. Birch to Lord Passfield, November 19, 1929.

50.   BNA CO 717/104/7. Item No 33352. Unfederated Malay States 1934. "Native Rubber Planting."

51.   H. B. Egmont Hake, a director of Harrisons, Baker and Co., cited in Tate (355). W.G. Ormsby-Gore was the British Colonial Secretary at the time.

52.   J. W. F. Rowe, *Studies in the Artificial Control of Raw Material Supplies*, Special Memorandum No. 34, No. 2, *Rubber* (London: London and Cambridge Economic Service, London School of Economics, 1931), 6. Copy in BNA CO717/76/9. Item 72487. Malay States, 1930.

53.   Tate, 347–357.

54.   Ibid., 363.

55.   Ibid.

56.   A.A. Garthwaite, "The Rubber Situation," *India Rubber World*, Vol. 78. No. 1 (Akron: April 1, 1928): 70.

57.   Allen, "Depression on the Plantations" (no page numbering).

58.   Tate, 364.

59.   G. E. Perry, "Abolition of Rubber Restriction," *India Rubber World*, Vol. 78, No. 2 (Akron: May 1, 1928): 53.

60.   UAA. Summit County Historical Society. Box 35. Business. Rubber Companies. Typescript of Harvey S. Firestone, Jr., "'The Romance and Drama of the Rubber Industry: radio talks delivered by Harvey S. Firestone, Jr., in 'The Voice of Firestone' programs over the nationwide network of National Broadcasting Company, September 1931 to September 1932" (Akron: Firestone Tire & Rubber, 1932), 82.

61.   Frank Chalk, "The Anatomy of an Investment: Firestone's 1927 Loan to Liberia," *Canadian Journal of African Studies*, Vol. 1, No. 1 (March 1967): 15.

62.   Alfred Lief, *The Firestone Story: A History of the Firestone Tire & Rubber Company* (New York: McGraw-Hill, 1951), 89–92.

63.   Chalk, 16.

64.   Ibid.

65.   Harvey Firestone, Jr., 77–78.

66.   Cited in J.H. Mower, "The Republic of Liberia," *The Journal of Negro History*, Vol. 32, No. 3 (July 1947): 275.

67.   For details of Liberia's history and its relations with the United States, see Mower, 265–306.

68.   Chalk, 17.

69.   Cited in "The Rubber Business," *Age* (Melbourne: October 16, 1925).

70.   "Liberia's Planting Progress," *India Rubber World*, Vol. 78, No. 6 (Akron: September 1, 1928).

71.   Firestone, 104. See also Lief, 144–159.

72.   The headquarters of their subsidiary, the Firestone Natural Rubber Company, remain in Akron, Ohio. The company's current Liberian operations are discussed in the Epilogue to this work.

73.   UAA. Goodyear Files. Goodyear Property Box 1 (Plantations). See also Walter E.
      Klippert, *Reflections of a Rubber Planter: The Autobiography of An Inquisitive
      Person* (New York: Vintage Press, New York, 1972). Klippert was a longtime man-
      ager of Goodyear's estates in Sumatra and Central America.
74.   M. J. Kennaway, *Some Agricultural Enterprises in Malaya, 1933–1934* (Kuala
      Lumpur: Department of Agriculture, Straits Settlements and Federated Malay
      States, 1934), 44 and 63.
75.   See the Firestone Natural Rubber Company's website at http://www.firestonenat-
      uralrubber.com/.
76.   With a $300,000 subvention from the Liberian government, it should be added,
77.   Firestone is still under attack today for its labor policies and the ecological effects
      of its Liberian plantations. For a compendium of recent news articles on
      Firestone's Liberian operations, see Labor Rights and Press Online at
      http://www.laborrights.org/press/index.html.
78.   Mower, 280.
79.   James Wright, "Liberia Loses its Freedom under Regime of Firestones," *United
      Rubber Worker*, Vol. 1, No. 5 (Akron: URWA, August 1936).
80.   Mower.
81.   Ibid., 288.
82.   Ibid., 284–285.
83.   Wright.
84.   Ibid.
85.   Arthur D. Howden Smith, "The Men Who Run America," *Philadelphia Record*
      (Philadelphia: November 22, 1935).
86.   Cited in Chalk, 32.
87.   "The Ford Rubber Plantation," *India Rubber World*, Vol. 82, No. 5 (Akron:
      August 1, 1930): 62.
88.   See Greg Grandin, *Fordlandia: The Rise and Fall of Henry Ford's Forgotten
      Jungle City* (New York: Metropolitan, 2009).
89.   Klippert, 76.
90.   For another detailed account of Ford's Amazon venture, see John Galey,
      "Industrialist in the Wilderness: Henry Ford's Amazon Venture," *Journal of
      Interamerican Studies and World Affairs*, Vol. 21, No. 2 (May 1979): 261–289.
      For easily accessible but shorter accounts, see Robin Furneaux, *The Amazon:
      The Story of a Great River* (London: Hamish Hamilton, 1969), 244–246;
      Warren Dean, *Brazil and the Struggle for Rubber: A Study in Environmental
      History* (Cambridge: Cambridge University Press, 1987),76–84; Michael
      Goulding, Nigel J.H. Smith, and Dennis J. Maher, *Floods of Fortune: Ecology
      and Economy along the Amazon* (New York: Columbia University Press, 1996),
      35; John Ure, *Trespassers on the Amazon* (London: Constable, 1986), 143–146.
      An interesting account of a visit by Mary A. Dempsey, entitled "Fordlandia,"
      which originally appeared in the July–August 1994 edition of *Michigan
      History*, is available online at http://www.michiganhistorymagazine.
      com/extra/fordlandia/fordlandia.html. This account is accompanied by histor-
      ical photographs from the Ford Museum at Dearborn and contemporary pho-
      tographs taken by Dempsey.
91.   Lief, 170.
92.   *India Rubber World*, Vol. 91, No. 5 (Akron: February 1, 1935).
93.   See, for instance, Parmer, 10–12. Goodyear's Hugh Allen also describes the
      agreement in some detail and denounces it as a price-fixing cartel.

94.   Archives d'outre-mer (AOM), Aix-en-Provence. Agence FOM Carton 190
       Dossier 106. Indochine: caouchouc: culture, production, main d'oeuvre.
95.   Camus.
96.   Parmer, 9.
97.   BNA, CO 273/573/22. Item No 82081. 1931 Straits Malay States, "Malaya
       Rubber Statistics," 1930.
98.   Margaret Shennan, *Out in the Midday Sun: the British in Malaya, 1880-1960*
       (London: John Murray, 2000), 83.
99.   In Asia, the laborers' quarters were invariably referred to as "coolie lines."
100.   MUNC. M1354 JAC 269 6/1. Notes by E.L. Hamilton, Thursday November 22,
       1906.
101.   Kennaway, 49.
102.   Ainsworth, 46.
103.   "Voice of Firestone," 119 and 121.
104.   Lief, 253 and 271.
105.   BNA. FO 837/112. Commodities Priority Committee. Sub-committee on
       Rubber, etc., and Tyres (1940).
106.   "Future of Rubber: U.S. Synthetic Cheaper," *Sydney Morning Herald* (Sydney:
       January 19, 1945).

THIRTEEN: THE PLANTERS' WORLD

1.   W. Somerset Maugham, "Footprints in the Jungle," *Altogether* (London: William
       Heinemann, 1934).
2.   Boy = male servant; *amah* = Chinese nursemaid or female servant; Mary =
       female servant in New Guinea but Japanese concubine of white man in Malaya;
       dhobi wallah = Hindi for servant who does washing. There were a variety of
       other *wallahs*, including drinks *wallahs*, boot *wallahs*, and box *wallahs* (itiner-
       ant pedlars).
3.   Sir Malcolm Watson, "The Geographical Aspects of Malaria," *The Geographical
       Journal*, Vol. 99, No. 4, Discussion (April 1942).
4.   Margaret Shennan, *Out in the Midday Sun: the British in Malaya, 1880-1960*
       (London: John Murray, 2000), 172.
5.   James C. Scott, "Duas Cervejas," *The London Review of Books*, Vol. 31, No. 19
       (London: October 8, 2009): 31. This is a review of Greg Grandin, *Fordlandia:
       The Rise and Fall of Henry Ford's Forgotten Jungle City* (New York: Metropolitan,
       2009).
6.   Daniel Green, *A Plantation Family* (Ipswich: The Boydell Press, 1979), 5.
7.   The former was a Chinese term for foreman, the latter the Javanese equivalent.
8.   Ladislao (Lázló) Székely, *Tropic Fever: The Adventures of a Planter in Sumatra*,
       trans. Marion Saunders (New York and London: Harper Bros., 1937), 8-10.
9.   Leopold Ainsworth, *The Confessions of a Planter in Malaya: A Chronicle of Life
       and Adventure in the Jungle* (London: H.F. and G. Witherby, 1933), 15.
10.   Jan Breman, *Taming the Coolie Beast: Plantation Society and the Colonial Order
       in Southeast Asia* (Delhi: Oxford University Press, 1989), 77.
11.   Pennington of Muncaster (Cumbria Record Office, The Castle, Carlisle,
       Cumbria). (Australian Joint Copying Project, National Library of Australia and
       the State Library of NSW.) Microfilm No JAC 239 D/PEN/Malaya. Letter from
       Mr. Sowerby, Royal Botanic Society of London to Mr. Underdown at Penang on
       the cultivation of India Rubber Trees, May 3, 1877. These files belong to a group

of British sugar and rubber companies in Malaya. Hereinafter, references from this source are given as MUNC plus file numbers and document title.

12.   John G. Butcher, *The British in Malaya 1880-1941: The Social History of a European Community in Colonial South-East Asia* (Kuala Lumpur: Oxford University Press, 1979), 44.

13.   Cited in J.A, Hobson, *Imperialism: A Study* (London: Constable, 1905), 46.

14.   Butcher, 34.

15.   D.J.M. Tate, *The RGA History of the Plantation Industry in the Malay Peninsula* (Kuala Lumpur: Oxford University Press, 1996), 193.

16.   Bryant, 3-4.

17.   Butcher, 34. The "public" schools of upper class England are actually elite private establishments. Grammar schools were in those days elite state institutions.

18.   Tran Tu Binh (as told to Ha An, trans. John Spragens Jr., and ed. with an introduction by David G. Marr), *The Red Earth: A Vietnamese Memoir of Life on a Colonial Rubber Plantation* (Athens: Ohio Center for International Studies, 1985), 24 and 34.

19.   John Tully, *France on the Mekong: A History of the Protectorate in Cambodia, 1863-1953* (Lanham, MD: University Press of America, 2002), 312 and 317.

20.   John Tully, *Cambodia Under the Tricolour: King Sisowath and the Mission Civilisatrice in Cambodia, 1904-1927* (Clayton, VIC: Monash Asia Institute, 1996).

21.   University of Akron Archives (UAA). Summit County Historical Society. Box 35. Business. Rubber Companies. Harvey S. Firestone, Jr., "The Romance and Drama of the Rubber Industry: radio talks delivered by Harvey S. Firestone, Jr., in 'The Voice of Firestone' programs over the nationwide network of National Broadcasting Company, September 1931 to September 1932" (Akron: Firestone Tire & Rubber, 1932). Typescript.

22.   Ibid.

23.   Ibid., 83.

24.   UAA. Goodyear Files. Goodyear Property Box 1 (Plantations).

25.   D.W. Peabody, "Three Years on a Rubber Plantation."

26.   M.J. Kennaway, *Some Agricultural Enterprises in Malaya, 1933-1934* (Kuala Lumpur: Department of Agriculture, Straits Settlements and Federated Malay States, 1934), 44.

27.   The English term "boy" was used in all the colonies of Southeast Asia and Oceania, regardless of the mother tongue of the colonialists and regardless of the age of the servant.

28.   Tran Ta Binh, 24.

29.   Green, 123-125. Surprisingly, given that the tower was a do-it-yourself affair with techniques gleaned from the *Encyclopaedia Britannica*, the structure lasted until well after the Second World War, when the foundations cracked and it was blown up.

30.   Shennan, 174.

31.   Cited in Peter Pugh et al, *Great Enterprise: A History of Harrisons and Crosfield*, ed. Guy Nickalls (London: Harrisons and Crosfield, 1990) 97.

32.   Ainsworth, 41-42.

33.   Ainsworth, 41.

34.   Shennan, 25.

35.   Ainsworth, 50.

36.   Ibid., 62.

37. Ibid., 62.

38. National Archives of Australia (NAA). B30/1 (180). New Guinea – rubber, ginger, cocoa, etc. Letter from H.G. Eckhoff, Bewapi Plantation, Markham Valley, New Guinea to Albert E. Green, MHR, Canberra, December 12, 1939.

39. MUNC. JAC 246 D/PEN/MALAYA. Letter from Turner to Mr. Hamilton, January 19, 1909.

40. *1884–1909, The Quarter Century Number of the India-Rubber Journal: A Souvenir* (London: Maclaren and Sons, 1909).

41. Pugh, 88.

42. Shennan, 174.

43. Ibid., 25.

44. Walter E. Klippert, *Reflections of a Rubber Planter: The Autobiography of an Inquisitive Person* (New York: Vintage Press, 1972), 70 & 77.

45. Shennan, 25.

46. MUNC JAC 261 D/PEN/MALAYA 2/15. C.J. Mason at Sungei Separap Estate, Batu Pahet, Johore to W. Duncan, May 5, 1913.

47. MUNC JAC 271 D/PEN/MALAYA. SRC Letters from Penang July–December 1913. W.B. Murray, Nova Scotia to General Manager, Caledonia, October 13, 1913.

48. UAA. Goodyear Files. Goodyear Scrapbooks. Box D2-4, 1925–1933. Rubber 27 Goodyear Rubber Plantations.

49. Ainsworth, 78.

50. Shennan, 25.

51. MUNC M1356 JAC 271 D/PEN/MALAYA. JAC 245 Sungei Bogak Quarterly Report, written by W. Duncan, June 29, 1910.

52. MUNC JAC 271 D/PEN/MALAYA SRC. Letters from Penang, July–December 1913. D. Ritchie to W. Duncan, October 29, 1913.

53. Watson.

54. Shennan, 172.

55. Tran Tu Binh, 30.

56. Madelon Lulofs, *Rubber*, trans. G.J. Renier and Irene Clephane (Singapore: Oxford University Press, 1987), 116.

57. Charles Robequain, *The Economic Development of French Indo-China*, trans. Isabel A. Ward (London: Oxford University Press, 1944), 212–215.

58. Shennan, 174.

59. The term is believed to be a corrupt diminutive of the Italian *troppo caldo* (too hot), which Anglo-Celtic Australians may have heard on the lips of Italian cane cutters in North Queensland.

60. "All Whites Have Grievances in New Guinea," *The Herald* (Melbourne: June 13, 1929).

61. MUNC. JAC D/PEN/MALAYA 6/3. SS Co. Letters from Penang (July to December 1909). C. Renwick, Acting Manager at Gedong to John Turner, September 29, 1909.

62. MUNC JAC 270 D/PEN/MALAYA 7/5 SRC Letters from Penang 1910. W. Duncan to Taylor, September 9, 1910 and October 14, 1910.

63. MUNC. JAC 266 D/PEN/MALAYA 5/1. Evans to Taylor, June 13, 1913.

64. Ibid., Duncan to Taylor, January 16, 1914.

65. The practice was also common for blue-collar apprenticeships and clerkships at the time. £100 in 1900 values translates into almost £8,000 in today's values using the retail price index as a guide.

66. Butcher, 97.

67.   MUNC. M1355. JAC 270 D/PEN/MALAYA/6/3. Duncan to Taylor, April 8,
      1910. Ramsdens lured an American from Massachusetts named J.M. Kydd for a
      four-year contract on the promise of £200 for the first two years, £250 for the
      third, and £300 for the fourth, plus free passage. (MUNC JAC
      D/PEN/MALAYA/2/15. Letter to Kydd from Jas. Fraser for John Turner, 1909.)
68.   MUNC. JAC 270 D/PEN/MALAYA/7/3. J. Cruickshank to F.E. Maguire (Sec.),
      August 2, 1921.
69.   Tate, 324–331. An assistant named Brandon also took Dunlop to court for swin-
      dling him out of the half-pay leave due at the end of his contract.
70.   BNA CO 273/602/22 1934. Straits. Rubber Estates: Salaries and General
      Conditions of Planters.
71.   Tate, 330.
72.   Somerset Maugham, "Footprints in the Jungle."
73.   BNA CO 273/575/15 1931 Straits. Reports by HM Trade Commissioner.
      Singapore (Boulter Report).
74.   Shennan, 183.
75.   *Pacific Islands Monthly*, cited in Hank Nelson, *Taim Bilong Masta: The
      Australian Involvement with Papua New Guinea* (Sydney: Australian
      Broadcasting Commission, 1982), 137.
76.   Green, 120.
77.   Tate, 193.
78.   MUNC JAC 272 D/PEN/MALAYA 8/6. Rubana Rubber, letters from Penang.
      Duncan to Mr. J. Wilson, June 14, 1912.
79.   Székely, 55–57.
80.   Lulofs, 49–51.
81.   Nelson, 68.
82.   A special representative, "Boys and Bosses. Work at Five Shillings a Month.
      Labour in New Guinea," *The Sun* (Melbourne: October 7, 1924).
83.   Bryant, 29.
84.   Shennan, 66.
85.   Pugh et al., 88.
86.   Editorial, *Rubber Growers' Association Bulletin*, Vol. 2, No. 2 (March 1920): 89.
      (Copy in MUNC files.)
87.   Breman, 79.
88.   Shennan, 68–69, 172.
89.   *Rubber Growers' Association Bulletin.*
90.   Shennan, 68.
91.   Bryant, 13.
92.   Shennan, 68.
93.   MUNC. Renwick to Turner September 29, 1909.
94.   W. Somerset Maugham, "The Letter," *The Complete Short Stories of W. Somerset
      Maugham*, Vol. III (London: William Heinemann, 1951), 1431–1432.
95.   Ibid, 188–189.
96.   Tran Tu Binh, 27 and 61.
97.   Shennan, 67.
98.   W. Somerset Maugham, "The Force of Circumstance," *The Complete Short
      Stories of W. Somerset Maugham*, Vol. I (London: William Heinemann, 1951),
      484.
99.   Ibid., 496.
100. Ibid., 501.

NOTES TO PAGES 218-222

101.   Lulofs, 165.
102.   Octave Mannoni, *Prospero and Caliban: The Psychology of Colonization*, trans. Pamela Powesland (London: Methuen, 1956).
103.   Edward P. Wolfers, "Trusteeship Without Trust: A Short History of Interracial relations and the Law in Papua and New Guinea," in F.S. Stevens (ed.), *Racism: The Australian Experience, A Study of Race Prejudice in Australia*, Vol. 3, *Colonialism* (Sydney: Australia and New Zealand Book Company, 1972), 75.
104.   Kava is a relatively mild narcotic derived from the *Piper methysticum* plant, a relative of black pepper.
105.   NAA, A452 (A452/1) Item 3471497 Law Revision–Discriminatory Legislation –Papua and New Guinea, December 28, 1961. Includes report of December 20, 1961 by the Assistant Secretary of the Department of Territories, and a speech given by Sir Dallas Brooks at the opening of the Legislative Council of Papua New Guinea on April 10, 1961.
106.   Arthur W. Reynolds, "The Colour Question: Mollycoddling the Natives," *The Papuan Times* (Port Moresby: July 15, 1914).
107.   "New Guinea Affairs: Allegations of Floggings," *Argus* (Melbourne: November 22, 1921). At the time, Hughes was basking in the limelight of his intervention at Versailles, where he had blocked the insertion of a clause banning racial discrimination in the charter of the League of Nations.
108.   "Offences by Papuans," *Argus* (Melbourne: January 13, 1926).
109.   "Women in New Guinea," *Argus* (Melbourne: January 11, 1926) and "A Papuan Ordinance: Protection of European Women and Children," *The Age* (Melbourne: February 3, 1926). In contrast, the Queensland criminal code stipulated a maximum sentence of imprisonment for life, with or without whipping, for rape, fourteen years for attempted rape, and two years hard labor, with or without whipping, for indecent assault.
110.   *Herald* (Melbourne: February 6, 1926).
111.   *The Mercury* (Hobart: February 13, 1926). The Australian government only moved under strong international pressure to dismantle this oppressive legal apparatus in December 1961, by which time there were forty ordinances or sets of regulations in Papua and forty-two in neighboring New Guinea, along with over one hundred other laws in both colonies that contained discriminatory provisions. The Papuan regulations had included clauses which made it illegal for "(a) a European woman to permit a native man (not her husband) to have intercourse with her; and (b) a Native man to have, or to attempt to have intercourse with a European woman (not his wife) with her consent." In NAA, A452 (A452/1). Item 3471497.
112.   Shennan, 207.
113.   Lulofs, 162.
114.   François de Tessan, "L'ouevre d'une Française en Indochine," *Le Petit Journal* (Saigon: May 1, 1923).
115.   *Annuaire des Syndicats des Planteurs de Caoutchouc de l'Indochine* (Saigon: 1926). Archives d'outre-mer, Aix-en-Provence (AOM), BIB AOM A119.
116.   AOM Agence FOM Carton 190 Dossier 106 Indochine: caoutchouc: culture, production, main d'ouevre, 1921–1953. Photographs of Mme. de la Souchère's estates and their proprietor can be found in the *Annuaire des Syndicats des Planteurs de Caoutchouc de l'Indochine* cited above.
117.   Tate, 495.
118.   UAA BF Goodrich Files. Box NA-1. NA-37. A. C. Brett, "All in a day's work; a story of wartime Washington," unpublished manuscript.

119. Shennan, 236–237.
120. Tate, 496.
121. Ibid.
122. MUNC JAC 264 D/PEN/MALAYA 3/2. Penang Rubber Estates. Annual Reports (whole estate) 1914–1916, 1921–1922, 1948–1952. Report of 1950.
123. Pugh, 174.

FOURTEEN: THE COOLIE DIASPORA

1.   Karl Marx, *Capital,* Volume One, Part Seven: "The Accumulation of Capital," Chapter XXIII. Section 3. "Progressive Production of a Relative Surplus Population or Industrial Reserve Army," trans. Eden and Cedar Paul (London: Everyman, 1972), 698.

2.   Karl Marx and Frederick Engels, *The Communist Manifesto* in *Selected Works* (Moscow: Progress Publishers, 1970), 38.

3.   Virginia Thompson, *Labor Problems in Southeast Asia* (New Haven: Yale University Press, 1947).

4.   The Cultivation System was enormously lucrative. The peasants were compelled to sell cash crops to the Dutch authorities at low fixed prices. The Dutch then resold the produce at market prices. See for instance M.C. Ricklefs, *A History of Modern Indonesia c. 1300 to the Present* (Houndmills, Basingstoke: Macmillan Education, 1981), ch. 11, "Java, 1830–1900." While many historians rightly give credit to Dutch reformers for abolishing the system under the so-called Ethical Policy, they are mute on its replacement with indentured labor on plantations in the Outer Islands.

5.   I have used this word throughout, for although it had racist overtones, it is convenient as a term meaning Asian laborer and is used by many writers. It is also the title of a novel by the Indian writer Mulk Raj Anand, who was a passionate anti-colonialist and social justice campaigner. (Mulk Raj Anand, *Coolie* (Harmondsworth: Penguin Classics, 1994).)

6.   Archives d'outre-mer (AOM), Aix-en-Provence, France, Fonds Ministériels 7 Affeco/25. Copie d'une note adressée par le consul général de France à Batavia M. le gouveneur général de l'Indochine, en date du 10 mai 1928.

7.   C.E. Akers, *The Rubber Industry in Brazil and the Orient* (London: Methuen, 1914), 195.

8.   Author's calculation based on figures from Ravindra K. Jain, "South Indian Labour in Malaya, 1890–1920: Asylum, Stability and Involution," in Kay Saunders (ed.), *Indentured Labour in the British Empire 1834–1920* (London and Canberra: Croom Helm, 1984), 45.

9.   Colin Newbury, "The Imperial Workplace: Competition and Coerced Labour Systems in New Zealand, Northern Nigeria and Australian New Guinea," in Shula Marks and Peter Richardson (eds.), *International Labour Migration: Historical Perspectives* (London: Institute of Commonwealth Studies, 1984), 225.

10.   AOM Fonds Ministériels 7 Affeco/25 Main d'ouevre en Indochine. Memoire addressé par le Comité de l'Indochine (du Commerce et l'industrie et de l'agriculture) au Ministre des Colonies, 5 Juin 1929.

11.   Akers, 161 and 195.

12.   Jan Breman, *Taming the Coolie Beast: Plantation Society and the Colonial Order in Southeast Asia* (Delhi: Oxford University Press, 1989), 64.

13.   Jain, 45.

14.   Comité de l'Indochine, 5 Juin 1929.

15. AOM Fonds Ministériels 86 Agence FOM, Carton 189, Dossier 105, Caoutchouc: planteurs 1922–1948. Also J.J. Camus, *L'Ouevre Humaine et Sociale dans les Plantations du Caoutchouc d'Indochine* (Paris: Société d'Editions Techniques Coloniales, 1949).

16. J. Norman Parmer, *Colonial Labor Policy and Administration: A History of Labor in the Rubber Plantation Industry in Malaya, c. 1910–1941* (Locust Valley, NY: J.J. Augustin for the Association for Asian Studies, 1960), 16.

17. Persia Crawford Campbell, *Chinese Coolie Emigration to Countries within the British Empire*, preface by W. Pember Reeves (London: Frank Cass, 1923), xii.

18. Pennington of Muncaster (Cumbria Record Office, The Castle, Carlisle, Cumbria) (Australian Joint Copying Project, National Library of Australia and the State Library of NSW.) (Hereinafter MUNC.) JAC 245 D/PEN/MALAYA 1907–1913 2/11A Penang Sugar Estates Quarterly Reports B–R. Caledonia Quarterly Report, October 19, 1910 by W. Duncan.

19. MUNC JAC 242 D/PEN/MALAYA. Letter from Sir John Ramsden to Mr. Quintin Hogg, February 9, 1890.

20. Leopold Ainsworth, *The Confessions of a Planter in Malaya: A Chronicle of Life and Adventure in the Jungle* (London: H.F. and G. Witherby, 1933), 47.

21. The last two paragraphs draw on George Netto, 1961, *Indians in Malaya: Historical Facts and Figures* (Singapore: George Netto, 1961), 22–29; Parmer, 16–40; and Jain, 158–182.

22. Ibid., 21 and Akers, 250.

23. On the Khmers' aversion to plantation work, see John Tully, *France on the Mekong: A History of the Protectorate in Cambodia, 1863–1953* (Lanham, MD: University Press of America, 2002), 313–314.

24. Max Weber "Politics as a Vocation," lecture delivered at Munich University in 1918. Available online at http://www.ne.jp/asahi/moriyuki/abukuma/weber/lecture/politics_vocation.html.

25. I am indebted here to the insights of the great English Marxist historian E.P. Thompson. See E.P. Thompson, "Time, Work-Discipline, and Industrial Capitalism," *Past and Present*, No. 38 (December 1967): 56–97.

26. J. Lyng, *Our New Possession (Late German New Guinea)* (Melbourne: Melbourne Publishing, 1919), 163.

27. Parmer, 16.

28. *Daily Telegraph* (Sydney: August 23, 1910).

29. Paul Leroy-Beaulieu, *De la colonisation chez des peuples modernes* (Quatrième ed.) (Paris: Guillaumin, 1891).

30. The question of force is discussed in the next chapter.

31. "Kangani" is an Anglicization of the Tamil word *kankani*, which means foreman, or overseer, or perhaps headman or "coolie of standing."

32. Netto, 15 and 22.

33. Jain, 158.

34. Breman, 23.

35. Ibid., 63.

36. Akers, 277–278.

37. AOM Fonds Ministériels 7 Affeco/25 Main d'ouevre en Indochine. Sur le main d'ouevre en Indochine, 30 novembre 1929.

38. Archives Nationales du Cambodge (ANC), Résidence Supérieure au Cambodge (RSC) M14/M10 File 8218. Rapport sur la situation matérielle et morale des émigrés tonkinois employés sur les plantations de la Cie du Cambodge et du

Syndicat de Mimot, 28 avril 1927, signé Inspecteur du Travail Delamare. The living and working conditions of indentured laborers are discussed in the following chapter.

39. Yeap Joo Kim, *Moon Above Malaya* (Singapore: Graham Brash, 1991), 14. The novelist was never a coolie herself, but the book appears to be based on the life of her immigrant grandfather.

40. The French divided Vietnam into three administrative units: the colony of Cochin-China based on Saigon in the south, the protectorate of Annam in the middle, and the protectorate of Tonkin in the north, centered on the Red River valley and delta. The term "protectorate" was a legal fiction for the colonial reality. The center of government was at Hanoi, the seat of the Governor General, with *Résidents Supérieurs* in the protectorates and a Governor in Cochin-China.

41. "La brûlante question de la main-d'oeuvre," *La Chronique Coloniale* (Paris: Organe de l'Institut Coloniale Français, 30 mai 1929).

42. AOM Fonds Ministériels 7 Affeco/25 Main d'oeuvre et colonisation. Note sur la main d'oueuvre indochinoise, 30 novembre 1929.

43. Tully, 314.

44. MUNC JAC 245 D/PEN/Malaya 2/15, Penang Sugar Estates Co. Letters, (December) 1904 – (June) 1904. John Turner to Percy E.L. Taylor, Secretary in London, March 1, 1907.

45. MUNC JAC 245 D/PEN/MALAYA 1907-1913 2/11A Penang Sugar Estates Quarterly Reports B-R. Quarterly Report Caledonia Estate October 20, 1909. W. Duncan.

46. Jain, 170.

47. Parmer, 20.

48. MUNC JAC 244 Penang Sugar Estates Annual Reports 1910 & 1911. Yearly Report for 1911.

49. Cited in Netto, 45.

50. There were two separate Australian colonial administrations on the island. The first, based in Port Moresby, ruled over the colony of Papua, which Australia inherited from the British in 1906 and the second, based in Rabaul, was a League of Nations mandate over former German New Guinea, which was occupied by Australia in the First World War. The two territories were amalgamated into Papua New Guinea after independence in 1975.

51. "Conditions in Papua," *Daily Telegraph* (Sydney: January 17, 1911).

52. "New Guinea Rubber Planters. Heavy Casualties among Natives. Beaches Strewn with Machines," *Sun* (Sydney: December 3, 1910).

53. "British New Guinea. Native Labour Question," *The Sun* (Sydney: January 17, 1911).

54. "The Policy for New Guinea," *Worker* (Sydney: July 20, 1911). The new capitalist system that was introduced was very different from the traditional economy. As C.A. Gregory has observed, the traditional mode of production "has not even been satisfactorily named, let alone described and analysed." It contained various contradictory elements, Gregory wrote, including primitive communist, primitive capitalist, primitive affluence, stone-age, peasant, gift economy, tribal, and traditional. (C.A. Gregory, *Gifts and Commodities* (London: Academic Press, 1982), 5.)

55. Special correspondent, "Labour in Papua. How Natives Were Exploited. 'Not Lazy but Cautious,'" *Sun* (Sydney: April 27, 1911).

56. *Sun* (Sydney: December 3, 1919).

57. "Papua Labour Problem. Natives Won't Work. Happy in their Own Villages,"
     Sydney Morning Herald (Sydney: May 26, 1911).
58. *Barrier Daily Truth* (Broken Hill: February 20, 1911).
59. *Daily Telegraph* (Sydney: August 23, 1910)
60. "They Have No Troubles," *Daily Telegraph* (Sydney: January 27, 1925).
61. Thomas J. McMahon, "New Guinea Natives and Their Treatment," Part III, *The
     Age* (Melbourne: April 27, 1918).
62. Ibid.
63. A correspondent, 1910, "The Future of Papua. Should the Natives Work?" *The
     Age* (Melbourne: March 18, 1911).
64. McMahon.
65. "Native Labour on Papuan Plantations," *Daily Telegraph* (Sydney: July 3, 1911).
66. Marx, 698.
67. National Archives of Australia (NAA). A1 (A1/5) Item 43419. Employment of
     Indentured Labour for development of Mandated Territories. Letter from J. Bell
     for the New Zealand Prime Minister to the Australian Prime Minister with enclo-
     sure of rpt. by Annual Conference of NZ Methodist Church just concluded in
     Dunedin, May 21, 1923.
68. Ralph Shlomowitz, *The Internal Labour Trade in Papua (1884–1941) and New
     Guinea (1920–1941): An Economic Analysis*, Working Papers in Economic
     History, No. 15 (Adelaide: Flinders University, 1987), 2.
69. Gregory, 4.
70. Hank Nelson, *Taim Bilong Masta: The Australian Involvement with Papua New
     Guinea* (Sydney: Australian Broadcasting Commission, 1982), 78.
71. J. Hubert Murray, "Native Labour in Papua," *The Anti-Slavery Reporter and
     Aborigines' Friend*, Series V, Vol. 18, No. 4 (London: The Anti-Slavery and
     Aborigines' Protection Society, January 1929), 149.
72. NAA. A9816 (A9816/3). Item 245141. External Territories—indentured labour,
     1939–1944. Notes made by Florence Harding.
73. Newbury, 225.

FIFTEEN: THE COOLIES' WORLD

1.   A. Neville J. Whymant, "Chinese Coolie Songs," *Bulletin of the School of Oriental
     Studies*, Vol. 1, No. 4 (London: University of London, 1920), 165.
2.   Cited in Tran Tu Binh (as told to Ha An), *The Red Earth: A Vietnamese Memoir
     of Life on a Colonial Rubber Plantation*, ed. David G. Marr and trans. John
     Spragens Jr. (Athens, OH: Center for International Studies, 1985), 28.
3.   Tran Tu Binh. The claim by Saloth Sar, known to the world under his *nom-de-
     guerre* of Pol Pot, to have been a Cambodian rubber worker is bogus.
4.   Whymant.
5.   See, for instance, Elizabeth J. Perry, "When Peasants Speak: Sources for the Study
     of Chinese Rebellion," *Modern China*, Vol. 6, No. 1 (January 1980): 72–85.
6.   Lily Strickland-Anderson, "Music in Malaya," *The Musical Quarterly*, Vol. 11,
     No. 4 (October 1925): 508.
7.   Ved Prakash Vatuk, "Protest Songs of East Indians in British Guiana," *Journal of
     American Folklore*, Vol. 77, No. 305 (July 1964): 220–235.
8.   Yeap Joo Kim, *Moon Above Malaya* (Singapore: Graham Brash, 1991), 14.
9.   A. Neville Whymant.
10. Tran Tu Binh, 12.

438 NOTES TO PAGES 241–245

11. Madelon H. Lulofs, *Coolie*, trans. G.J. Renier and Irene Clephane (Singapore: Oxford University Press, 1982), 17–19.

12. Vatuk, 224.

13. Persia Crawford Campbell, *Chinese Coolie Emigration to Countries within the British Empire* (London: Frank Cass, 1923), 95–96.

14. George Netto, *Indians in Malaya: Historical Facts and Figures* (Singapore: George Netto, 1961), 29.

15. Tran Tu Binh, 15.

16. Ibid., 16.

17. John McDonald and Ralph Shlomowitz, *Mortality of Indian Labour on Ocean Voyages, 1843–1917*, Flinders University Working Papers on Economic History, No. 28 (Adelaide: 1989), 39. By way of contrast, the mortality rate of British immigrants bound for Australia during the years 1852–1892 was 3.4 percent.

18. Tran Tu Binh, 19–20.

19. Archives d'Outre-Mer, Aix-en-Provence (AOM), Fonds Ministériels 7 Affeco/25 Main d'ouevre en Indochine. Rapport de Mission en Cochinchine de M. l'An-sat BUI-BANG-DOAN et réponse de M. le Gouverneur de la Cochinchine.

20. AOM Fonds Ministériels 7 Affeco/25. Letter from the Governor of Cochinchina to the Governor General at Hanoi, March 30, 1928.

21. Webby Silupya Kalikiti, "Plantation Labour: Rubber Planters and the Colonial State in French Indochina, 1890–1939," unpublished Ph.D. thesis (London: SOAS, University of London, 2000), 26. Kalikiti's claim that Delamare's reports are exaggerated cannot be taken seriously. Kalikiti states that, "My premise is that the trilogy of the state, labour and capital consisted of actors on the colonial scene who were essentially hostile to each other. Labour officers stood accused by both employers and those in support of indigenous labour" (34). If this is the case—and Kalikiti by no means proves it—then one might be justified in thinking that the reports of the labor inspectors were a "golden mean" between the self-serving propaganda of the rubber companies and the claims of radical workers such as Tran Tu Binh. In fact, as the words and deeds of the long-serving and influential colonial official Ernest Outrey indicate, the colonial government and the Colonial Ministry were fervidly pro-capital. Outrey was an apologist for forced labor in the Belgian Congo and an advocate of strong-arm tactics in Indochina. See, for instance, Ernest Outrey, "Le système des cultures obligatoires," *Le Midi-Coloniale* (Paris: 1929). Kalikiti's thesis is further undermined by the sharp repression of striking rubber plantation workers by state forces.

22. Peter Fitzpatrick, "Really Rather Like Slavery," in E.L. Wheelwright and Ken Buckley (eds.), *Essays in the Political Economy of Australian Capitalism*, Vol. 3 (Sydney: Australia and New Zealand Book Company, 1978): 105.

23. Frantz Fanon, *The Wretched of the Earth* (New York: Grove Press, 1963), 31.

24. Cited in Charles Sawai, "Plantation Labour Recruitment in New Guinea in the Period 1922 to 1942," *Yagl-Ambu: PNG Journal of the Social Sciences and Humanities*, Vol. 4, No. 4 (Port Moresby: 1977): 302.

25. "The Native Problem," *The Papuan Times* (Port Moresby: July 15, 1914).

26. Fanon, 31.

27. Colin A. Palmer, *The Worlds of Unfree Labour: From Indentured Servitude to Slavery* (Aldershot: Ashgate Variorum, 1998), iii, xxv. Sepúlveda was Bartolomé de las Casas's opponent in the Valladolid debates over the rights of the indigenous peoples of newly conquered Spanish America.

28.   Robin Blackburn, "Old World Backyard to European Colonial Slavery," cited in Palmer, 85 and 96.

29.   Cited in J. Lyng, *Our New Possession (Late German New Guinea)* (Melbourne: Melbourne Publishing, 1919), 163.

30.   Cited in "The Colour Question," *The Papuan Times* (Port Moresby: July 15, 1914).

31.   University of Akron Archives (UAA). Summit County Historical Society. Box 35. Business. Rubber Companies. Harvey S. Firestone, Jr., "Gathering Rubber in Liberia" in "The Romance and Drama of the Rubber Industry: radio talks delivered by Harvey S. Firestone, Jr., in 'The Voice of Firestone' programs over the nationwide network of National Broadcasting Company, September 1931 to September 1932" (Akron: Firestone Tire & Rubber, 1932), 122.

32.   *Sydney Daily Telegraph* (Sydney: August 23, 1910).

33.   Teed Apha, *By Jungle Track and Paddy Field to Rubber Plantation and Palm Grove* (Liverpool: Henry Young and Sons, 1913), ix.

34.   "'Mary' in the Islands. Servant Trouble Unknown," *Herald* (Melbourne: April 15, 1919).

35.   S. Altson Pearl, "Native Labour: An Account of the Work of a 'Recruiter' Who Supplies Native Workmen for Plantations, Mines and Other Work in New Guinea," *Walkabout*, Vol. 6, No. 9, (Melbourne: July 1, 1940), 12.

36.   "The Native Wuestion," *The Papuan Times* (Port Moresby: July 15, 1914).

37.   A coolie was a hired "native" laborer in colonial Asia. On the etymology of the term, see T. Burrow, Review of R.L. Turner, *A Comparative Dictionary of the Indo-Aryan Languages: Addenda and Corrigenda*, ed. J.C. Wright (1985) in *The Bulletin of the School of Oriental and African Studies*, Vol. 49, No. 3 (London: University of London, 1986), 593. Burrow argues that Turner is wrong to claim that the word is derived from the name of a "primitive"tribe in West India called the Kolis, but that the word is derived from the South Dravidian word *kuli*, which means "a labourer's wage." The Dravidian origin of the word is also supported by *The Concise Oxford Dictionary of English Etymology* (ed. T.F. Hoad), Oxford Reference Online. Available at http://www.oxfordreference.com.

38.   Firestone, "Gathering Rubber in Liberia."

39.   Ladislao (Lázló) Székely, *Tropic Fever: The Adventures of a Planter in Sumatra*, trans. Marion Saunders (New York and London: Harper Bros., 1937), 45.

40.   Hank Nelson, *Taim Bilong Masta: The Australian Involvement with Papua New Guinea* (Sydney: Australian Broadcasting Commission, 1982), 71.

41.   Edward P. Wolfers, "Trusteeship Without Trust: A Short History of Interracial relations and the Law in Papua and New Guinea," in F.S. Stevens (ed.), *Racism: The Australian Experience, A Study of Race Prejudice in Australia*, Vol. 3, *Colonialism* (Sydney: Australia and New Zealand Book Company, 1972), 77.

42.   Székely, 46.

43.   Captain C.A.W. Monckton's book, *Some Experiences of a New Guinea Resident Magistrate*, cited in "New Guinea," *Australasia* (March 5, 1921). Details about this man can be found in the Australian Dictionary of Biography online at http://www.adb.online.anu.edu.au/biogs/A100534b.htm.

44.   MUNC M1347. JAC 246. 2/15 Penang Sugar Estates. Letters [in] 1909 (January–June). Turner to Taylor, January 15, 1909 and Turner to Hamilton, January 19, 1909.

45.   National Archives of Australia (NAA). A1422 (A1422/13) 12/2/40C Item 202663. Commonwealth of Australia. Bureau of Agricultural Economics New Guinea and Papua Rubber Economics Enquiry into the Papuan Rubber Industry 1949.

46.   Jan Breman, *Taming the Coolie Beast: Plantation Society and the Colonial Order in Southeast Asia* (Delhi: Oxford University Press, 1989), 76.

47.   Tran, 26.

48.   Whymant, "Foreign Inventions," 149.

49.   Tran, 23.

50.   John Tully, *France on the Mekong: A History of the Protectorate in Cambodia, 1863–1953* (Lanham, MD: University Press of America, 2002), 319.

51.   Tran, 23.

52.   Archives Nationales du Cambodge (ANC) RSC M17/M12 (1267) File 1108. Incidents de Plantation de Mimot, 1927. Extrait du *Trung-Hoa-Nhat-Bao, journal annamite*, 16 juillet 1927.

53.   ANC RSC M14/M10, File 8218, Part I.

54.   Tully, 319.

55.   Bui-Bang-Doan.

56.   Cited in Breman, 119.

57.   Ibid., 320. My account in *France in the Mekong* is based on Delamare's reports, which can be found in the Archives Nationales du Cambodge in Phnom Penh.

58.   Tran Tu Binh records speaking with Delamare, who was "quite fluent in Vietnamese." Delamare saw the horrors of Phu-Riêng, but after he went back to Saigon, "absolutely nothing out of the ordinary happened," Tran claims. Sadly, Tran was not able to see Delamare's reports, which fully exposed what he had seen, but which were edited and sanitized long before they reached the desks of important officials such as the Governor General and the Colonial Minister. The documents can be found in the Cambodian archives.

59.   AOM. Fonds Ministériels 7 Affeco/25. Main d'ouevre en Indochine. Telegram from Pierre Pasquier to the Minister for Colonies, June 10, 1930.

60.   ANC. RSC D35. File 2799, Box 288. Cited in Tully, 219.

61.   Leopold Ainsworth, *The Confessions of a Planter in Malaya: A Chronicle of Life and Adventure in the Jungle* (London: H.F. and G. Witherby, 1933), 90.

62.   Netto, 35.

63.   Cited in Netto, 38.

64.   MUNC JAC 261 D/PEN/MALAYA 2/18 Penang Sugar Estates. Letters out 1905. Enclosure to Mr. Sargant's letter of November 2, 1905.

65.   MUNC JAC 261 D/PEN/MALAYA 2/18 Penang Sugar Estates Letters out 1905. Mr. Arnold to J. Sargant at Penang, June 16, 1905.

66.   MUNC JAC 245 D/PEN/MALAYA 2/11 Penang Sugar Estates 1907–1913, Quarterly Reports. Caledonia Quarterly Report, October 19, 1910 by W. Duncan.

67.   MUNC. JAC 246 D/PEN/MALAYA 2/15. Letters in January–June 1908. Turner to Taylor.

68.   C.E. Akers, *The Rubber Industry in Brazil and the Orient* (London: Methuen, 1914), 210.

69.   Ralph Shlomowitz and Lance Brennan, *Mortality and Indian Labour in Malaya, 1877–1933*. Working Papers in Economic History, No. 38 (Adelaide: Flinders University, 1990), 9.

70.   British National Archives (BNA). CO 717/74/8 1930. PS Selwyn-Clarke, Principal MO FMS, Kuala Lumpur, May 21, 1930. The figures were for the 1928–1929 financial year.

71.   BNA. CO 717/59/11. Item 52336, Rate of Mortality among Indian Labourers, January 3, 1928.

72.   MUNC. JAC 269 D/PEN/MALAYA 6/3 Straits Sugar Company. Letters from Penang, December 1906–June 1907. D Ritchie Gedong Estate to John Turner, December 31, 1906.
73.   Tran, 23.
74.   Breman, 90.
75.   Lulofs, 78–79.
76.   Vatuk, 225. *Sālā* literally means brother-in-law, but in Hindi slang the implication is that the speaker has had illicit sexual relations with the sister of the person being abused.
77.   Tran, 19.
78.   Ainsworth, 39, 45, 46, 69–70.
79.   D.C. Lewis, *The Plantation Dream: Developing British New Guinea and Papua, 1884–1942* (Canberra: *The Journal of Pacific History*, 1996), 182.
80.   "Natives Thrashed. Law Disregarded. New Guinea Methods. Overseers Condemn Gaol System," *Herald* (Melbourne: July 4, 1923).
81.   *Argus* (Melbourne: November 19, 1925).
82.   Lewis, 271.
83.   NAA. A52. Item 274026. The Parliament of the Commonwealth of Australia. New Guinea, Report of inquiry into allegations of flogging and forced labour of natives by A.S. Canning, printed May 7, 1924.
84.   "Natives flogged. Official Report Challenged. Planter's Statement," *Herald* (Melbourne: October 31, 1923).
85.   *Herald* (Melbourne: October 2, 1924).
86.   Nelson, 81.
87.   "Native problem in New Guinea. Employers Want the Right to Thrash. Boys 'Lazy and Cheeky,'" *Herald* (Melbourne: May 11, 1933). John Decker calculates that between 1932–33 and 1936–37, "an average of twenty-eight employers were tried each year for assaulting native labourers, with an average of twenty-two convictions." See John Alvin Decker, *Labour Problems in the Pacific Mandates* (London: Oxford University Press, 1940), 181, n. 105.
88.   "Crime in New Guinea. Justice Burlesqued. Extraordinary Procedure," *Argus* (Melbourne: January 8, 1925).
89.   MUNC JAC D/PEN/MALAYA 8/9 Rubana Rubber: E.L. Hamilton's Correspondence, 1910–1911. Duncan to Hamilton, re: "the Rubana Incident," August 12, 1910.
90.   MUNC JAC D/PEN/MALAYA 14/6 Taylor to Duncan, May 13, 1910.
91.   According to official French documents, it is likely that Monte was Monteil and Triai was either Triaire, the plantation manager, or else an overseer called Triou.
92.   Tran Tu Binh, 24, 30, 34, 39–40.
93.   ANC RSC M17/M12 (1267). File No. 1108. Incidents de plantation de Mimot, 1927. Rapport sur la manifestation de 330 coolies de plantations de Mimot le 19 août 1927 et sur l'état particulièrement mauvais de la main d'ouevre tonkinoise employée sur ces plantations à cette date. No. 65-C.
94.   Tully, 316–317. This account is based on files in the Archives Nationales du Cambodge.
95.   AOM. Fonds Ministériels. Indochine Nouveau Fonds, Carton 225, Dossier 1839, Incidents sur les plantations Michelin, 1930. (Note: this is mislabeled regarding dates, JT.) "Manifestation sanglante. Comment s'est produit l'incident de la huit de vendredi à samedi à Dau-Tiêng?" also "Note au sujet des incidents qui se sont

produits les 16 et 17 décembre sur la plantation Michelin de Dau-Tiêng (Cochinchine)," Direction de la Sûreté Générale, 6 janvier 1933.

96.   This account is based on Breman, 213–218.

97.   Akers, 253.

98.   H. Van Kol, *Uit onze kolonien: uitvoerig reisverhaal* (Leiden: 1903), 101. (Cited in Breman, 120.)

99.   Decker, 204–205.

100.   "Inferiority of Natives: Study of Psychological Conditions," *The Advertiser* (Adelaide: November 7, 1927).

101.   Whymant, 163.

102.   Ibid., 164.

103.   Ibid,. 156.

SIXTEEN: COOLIE REVOLTS

1.   British National Archives [hereinafter BNA]. CO 717/89/12. 1932 Malay States. E.A. Dickson to the Undersecretary for Colonies, January 12, 1934.

2.   BNA. CO 717/145/12. Item 51514/1. Part I, Malay States 1941 Minute from High Commissioner to British Residents, Advisers and Resident Councillors. May 17, 1941.

3.   Leopold Ainsworth, *The Confessions of a Planter in Malaya: A Chronicle of Life and Adventure in the Jungle* (London: H.F. and G. Witherby, 1933), 56.

4.   D.C. Lewis, *The Plantation Dream: Developing British New Guinea and Papua, 1884–1942* (Canberra: *The Journal of Pacific History*, 1996), 5.

5.   Nguyen Ngoc Phach, *Life in Vietnam: Through a Looking Glass Darkly* (Melbourne: Nguyen Ngoc Phach, 2005), 26. Nguyen uses the term "cudgeons," but this is not a recognized English word, at least not in the sense he intends. *Vè*, as Nguyen points out, is doggerel, "roughly short verse by an anonymous author, often critical of public figures and events" and "satirical but serious in intent and not devoid of artistry" (1).

6.   Hank Nelson, *Taim Bilong Masta: The Australian Involvement with Papua New Guinea* (Sydney: Australian Broadcasting Commission, 1982), 21.

7.   C. E. Akers, *The Rubber Industry in Brazil and the Orient* (London: Methuen, 1914), 253–254.

8.   Pennington of Muncaster (hereinafter MUNC). JAC 265 D/PEN/MALAYA. Duncan to Taylor, September 20, 1912. These are the files of the Ramsden group of companies.

9.   Archives Nationales du Cambodge (ANC), Phnom Penh. Résidence Supérieure au Cambodge, D35 File 2799. Box 288. The most detailed account of the Cambodian plantations is Margaret Slocomb, *Colons and Coolies: The Development of Cambodia's Rubber Plantations* (Bangkok: White Lotus Press, 2007). See also John Tully, *France on the Mekong: A History of the Protectorate in Cambodia, 1863–1953* (Lanham, MD: University Press of America, 2002), Ch. 16.

10.   Tran Tu Binh (as told to Ha An), *The Red Earth: A Vietnamese Memoir of Life on a Colonial Rubber Plantation*, ed. David G. Marr and trans. John Spragens Jr. (Athens, OH: Center for International Studies, 1985), 39.

11.   Archives d'outre-mer, Aix-en-Provence (hereinafter AOM), Fonds Ministèriels, 7 Affeco 26 Main d'ouevre en Indochine. Clipping entitled "Plantations Michelin," *L'Indochine Financière et Economique*, L'Agence Financière d'Indochine, Paris, 29 septembre 1927.

12.   Ibid., telegram from Governor General Varenne to the Colonial Minister, Paris, October 22, 1927.
13.   Ibid., Monguillot, Hanoi to the Colonial Minister, Paris, February 11, 1928.
14.   MUNC JAC 265 D/PEN/MALAYA 3/15 PRE. Sabrang Estate estimates, reports, 1913. A.W. Wilson, Sabrang Estate to General Manager W. Duncan, August 23, 1913.
15.   Breman, ix.
16.   That being said, I do take Peter Linebaugh's point that the English ruling class used capital punishment as a form of social control in a "thanatocracy" during the early stages of the Industrial Revolution. See Peter Linebaugh, *The London Hanged: Crime and Civil Society in the Eighteenth Century* (London: Verso, 2003).
17.   Ravindra K. Jain, "South Indian Labour in Malaya, 1840–1920: Asylum, Stability and Involution," in Kay Saunders (ed.), *Indentured Labour in the British Empire 1834–1920* (London and Canberra: Croom Helm, 1984), 158.
18.   Akers, 207.
19.   MUNC JAC 275 D/PEN/MALAYA Selaba Rubber Estates Correspondence 1910. Harrison, Manager to Harrisons and Crosfields, London, November 17, 1910.
20.   MUNC JAC 265 3/4 D/PEN/MALAYA PRE Quarterly Reports 1913–1917. J. Cruikshank to E.L Taylor, May 11, 1916.
21.   AOM, Fonds Ministériels 7 Affeco/25 Main d'ouevre en Indochine. Rapport de Mission en Cochinchine de M. l'An-sat BUI-BANG-DOAN [capitals in original] et réponse de M. le Gouverneur de la Cochinchine.
22.   AOM Fonds Ministériels, 7 Affeco/25 Main d'ouevre en Indochine. Procès-verbal de la visite de la plantation de Phu-Riêng (Michelin & Cie) 2 mars 1928 – première inspection.
23.   Tran, 28–30 and 43.
24.   Colin Newbury, "The Imperial Workplace: Competition and Coerced Labour Systems in New Zealand, Northern Nigeria, and Australian New Guinea," in Shula Marks and Peter Richardson (eds.), *International Labour Migration: Historical Perspectives* (London: Institute of Commonwealth Studies, 1984), 225.
25.   Charles Gamba, *The Origins of Trade Unionism in Malaya: A Study in Colonial Labour Unrest* (Singapore: Eastern Universities Press, 1962), 10–11.
26.   Breman, 37.
27.   See Pierre Brocheux, "Le prolétariat des plantations des hévéas au Vietnam méridional: aspects sociaux et politiques," *Le Mouvement Social*, No. 90 (January–March, 1975), 55–86.
28.   Police criminal investigation department.
29.   AOM. 7 Affeco/25. Main d'ouevre en Indochine. Traduction d'un tract en Quoc Ngu polycopie trouvé de 25/11/28 dans le boîte aux letters du bureau de poste de Phy Ly.
30.   Tran, 18–19.
31.   Ibid., 34–39.
32.   The piastre, issued by the privately owned Banque de l'Indochine, was worth around five French francs, so the compensation amounted to 25 francs. This was worth around $1.00 in the 1920s .
33.   Tran, 39–42.
34.   Ibid., 65.

35. AOM 7/Affeco/26 Main d'oeuvre en Indochine. Report on strike at Phu-Riêng Michelin plantation, by J.G. Herisson, labor inspector, Saigon, February 28, 1930.
36. Herisson.
37. Tran, 67.
38. AOM 7 Affeco/26. Telegram from Governor Krautheimer to the Governor General at Hanoi, April 10, 1930.
39. AOM. Fonds Ministériels. Indochine Nouveau Fonds. Carton 225, Dossier 1839. Incidents sur les plantations Michelin, 1930. Krautheimer to Pasquier, April 10, 1930.
40. AOM. Fonds Ministériels. Indochine Nouveau Fonds. Carton 225, Dossier 1839. Incidents sur les plantations Michelin, 1930. Telegram from Pasquier to the Colonial Minister, February 7, 1930.
41. Ibid. Letter from Michelin, Thuan Loi Plantation in Bien Hoa province to company headquarters at Clermont-Ferrand, March 31,1930.
42. Ibid. French colonial reports entitled "Manifestation sanglante. Comment s'est produit l'incident de la huit de vendredi à samedi à Dau-Tiêng," "Note au sujet des incidents qui se sont produits les 16 et 17 décembre sur la plantation Michelin de Dau-Tiêng (Cochinchine)." Direction de la Police et le la Sûreté Générale. 6 janvier 1933.
43. Nguyen, 29.
44. David G. Marr, introduction to Tran Tu Binh, *The Red Earth*, x. For a fascinating, in-depth discussion of the importance of prisons in the Vietnamese revolutionary tradition, see Peter Zinoman, *Colonial Bastille: A History of Imprisonment in Vietnam, 1862–1940* (Berkeley: University of California Press, 2001).
45. Gamba, vii.
46. The Kuomintang was the Chinese Nationalist Party, led by Chiang Kai-Shek. Until 1927, it was in alliance with the Chinese Communists but afterwards they were implacable enemies.
47. BNA. CO 717 56/5. 1927 Malay States 29078A. Chinese Labour in British Malaya. Letter from S.S. Govt. to LCMS Avery, Colonial Office, August 31, 1927.
48. A point not lost on the Communist Party of Great Britain. See *British Imperialism in Malaya*, Colonial Series No. 2 (London: CPGB Labour Research Department, 1926) which held that "there is no definite nationalist movement [in Malaya]. The essential struggle is between British capitalists and Chinese and Indian workers; the Malay peasant class, like the peasants of other countries, will never lead the workers in any conflict with capital" (4). Copy of pamphlet in BNA. CO 273/539/12. 1927 Straits Malay States.
49. Gamba, viii, 8, 12, 13.
50. Ibid., 9.
51. Tan Malaka and Alimin were leaders of the PKI, the Communist Party of Indonesia, which did not recognize what it saw as the artificial division of Malaya and the Indies by the colonial powers. One wonders whether Alimin was so definite, given that the PKI and other Indonesian nationalists operated in what became one of the world's most ethnically diverse states, Indonesia, whose national motto is "Unity in Diversity."
52. BNA. CO 273/564/10. Item 72074. 1930 Straits Communist Activities. Report by René Onraet, Director of Criminal Intelligence Dept., S.S. Singapore, April 1, 1930, "A Report showing the connection between Chinese and non-Chinese concerned in Communist Activities in Malaya."

53.   J. Norman Parmer, *Colonial Labor Policy and Administration: A History of Labor in the Rubber Plantation Industry: Malaya, c. 1910–1941* (Locust Valley, NY: J.J. Augustin for the Association for Asian Studies, 1960), 19.

54.   Akers, 217.

55.   Ibid.

56.   MUNC. JAC 246. D/PEN/MALAYA 2/15. Letters [in] 1908 (January–June). Turner to Taylor, January 3, 1908.

57.   BNA. CO 717 56/5. Cipher telegram to Mr. O'Malley, Peking, June 3, 1927.

58.   BNA. CO 717 56/5. Telegram from Officer administering the Government of the S.S. to the Secretary of State for the Colonies, May 17, 1927.

59.   Term ironically applied during the colonial era to Chinese people. China claimed to have been a "celestial" empire.

60.   Workers employed to graft new shoots or stems onto older trees.

61.   M.J. Kennaway, *Some Agricultural Enterprises in Malaya, 1933–1934* (Kuala Lumpur: Department of Agriculture, Straits Settlements and Federated Malay States, 1934), 53.

62.   BNA. CO 717/100/14. Item No. 13422. 1933 Malay States "Labour Report 1932." C.D. Ahearne, Federated Malay States Annual Report of the Labour Department for the Year 1932 (Kuala Lumpur: FMS Govt. Printing Office, 1933).

63.   BNA. CO 272/632/9. 1937 Straits. Labour Disputes in Malaya. Report by Commissioner of Police C.H. Sansom, April 13, 1937.

64.   "Malaya Labour Trouble," *Financial News* (London: April 27, 1937). Copy in BNA. CO 273/632/9. 1937 Straits.

65.   BNA. CO 273/633/1. 1937. "Left Book Club, London. Prohibition of Publications." Thomas also banned a number of publications by Lawrence and Wishart, including "Chess for the Matchplayer," "Women Who Work," and "Hitler and the Empire."

66.   BNA. CO 273/633/2. Straits 1937. "Seditious Literature."

67.   BNA CO 273/632/9 1937 Straits. Labour Disputes in Malaya. Federal Council Minutes.

68.   Ibid. Memo dated August 5, 1937.

69.   Ibid., Sansom's report.

70.   Ibid., Mr S.W. Jones, memo, Kuala Lumpur, April 1937.

71.   Ibid., minute of Lord Dufferin, Colonial Office, August 12, 1937.

72.   BNA. CO 273/666/15. 1941 Malay States Labour Unrest in Malaya. Evidence of Phillip Stewart Gordon, Inspector of Police, Kendang Kerbau police station. Also report by L.A. Thomas, Deputy Inspector of Police (Administration) Straits Settlements.

73.   BNA CO 273/666/15 1941. Malay States Labour Unrest in Malaya. Covering minute by W.B.L. Monson, Colonial Office February 13, 1941 and telegram from High Commissioner Malay States to Colonial Office August 20, 1940.

74.   BNA CO 273/662/10 1940 Straits Malay States Labour Unrest in Malaya Part I. Minutes by Mr. Gent, April 27, 1941.

75.   *Manchester Guardian* (Manchester: February 14, 1940).

76.   BNA CO 273/662/10. 1940 Memo by Director Special Branch Straits Settlements Police in extract from Malaya Combined Intelligence Summary September 30, 1940.

77.   BNA CO 273/662/11 1940 Straits Malay States Labour Unrest in Malaya Part II. The suspicion of Japanese involvement appears to have been unfounded.

78. MUNC JAC 245 D/PEN/MALAYA 1907–1913 2/11A Penang Sugar Estates Quarterly Reports B– R. W. Duncan to Secretary, Quarterly Report Sabran Estate December 6, 1912.
79. BNA 717/72/3 1930 Malay States. "Deportation of Indians."
80. BNA CO 717/145/12 Part I. Malay States 1941. "Labour Conditions—Disturbances on Klang Rubber Estates." High Commissioner, FMS, to Lord Moyne, Colonial Office, July 14, 1941. Report and cover letter.
81. H.E. Wilson, *The Klang Strikes of 1941: Labour and Capital in Colonial Malaya,* Research Notes and Discussion Paper No. 25 (Singapore: Institute of Southeast Asian Studies, 1981), 3. Wilson's account is possibly the only in-depth study of the strike wave. He notes that while the Indian community had "rather a plethora of social clubs, caste associations or societies, most of which enjoyed no more than an ephemeral existence . . . none of . . . [these] represented the interests of the estate labourers."
82. Some accounts claim the Glenmarie Estate.
83. BNA CO 717/145/12 Item 51514/1 Part I Malay States 1941 Labour Conditions – Disturbances on Klang Rubber Estates. Adrian Clark, 13 June 1941. "Chronological note of incidents connected with the Strikes in which I took any action as Legal Advisor or Public Prosecutor," June 13, 1941.
84. Wilson, 12–13.
85. Ibid., 6.
86. BNA CO 717/145/12, Memo by Mr. Gent, Colonial Office, October 14, 1941.
87. Ibid.
88. Ibid. Minutes from High Commissioner to British Residents, Advisers and Resident Councillors. May 17, 1941.
89. Ibid., "Report on the strikes" by E. Bagot, Inspector General of the FMS Police, June 17, 1941.
90. Reported in *The Hindu* (Madras: June 2, 1941) and cited in Wilson, 13.
91. Bagot.
92. Wilson, 5.
93. Old Parliament House, "Menzies," 1941 Diary. Entry for January 29. Available online at http://www.oph.au/menziesonpeople.htm. Original diary kept at the National Library of Australia.
94. BNA CO 717/145/12, Gent.
95. Thomas to Moyne, July 14.
96. BNA CO 717/147/15 1941 Malay States "Indians in Malaya: Commission of Inquiry," October 25, 1941; Sec State Colonial Office to Shenton Thomas.
97. BNA CO 717/145/12, Gent Note, September 1, 1941.
98. Ibid., High Commissioner, FMS, to Sec. State Colonies August 28, 1941.
99. BNA CO 717/147/15 1941. Covering note June 13, 1942. Signature illegible. The repression, perhaps, was a factor in the willingness of Indian POWs to join Subhas Chandra Bose's Indian National Army.
100. As is revealed by a simple Internet search, which will provide websites maintained by former U.S. military personnel who served in the *terres rouges* regions.
101. BNA CO 717/145/12. Extract from Weekly Intelligence Summary No. 9 (undated, c. 1941).

Part Five—Synthetic Rubber, War, and Autarky

SEVENTEEN: THE LONG ROAD TO MONOWITZ

1.   Adolf Hitler's secret memorandum on the Four-Year Plan, August 1936, in Jeremy Noakes and Geoffrey Pridham (eds. and trans.), *Documents on Nazism, 1919-1945* (London: Jonathan Cape, 1974), 406.

2.   Joseph Borkin, *The Crime and Punishment of IG Farben* (New York: The Free Press, 1978), 113.

3.   Ibid.

4.   British National Archives (hereinafter BNA). DEFE 41/8 Dr. Otto Ambros. Min Defence, DSI, Director STIB. Interrogation Report No 112. Dr Ambros. 1951.

5.   Deborah Dwork and Robert Jan van Pelt, *Auschwitz: 1270 to the Present* (New York and London: W.W. Norton, 1996), 203.

6.   Josiah E. Dubois, Jr., and Edward Johnson, *Generals in Grey Suits. The Directors of the International "IG Farben" Cartel, Their Conspiracy and Trial at Nuremberg* (London: The Bodley Head, 1953), 4. The word Buna is a contraction of butadiene and natrium, the two core ingredients of IG Farben's synthetic rubber and was a company trademark.

7.   Dwork and Van Pelt, 197.

8.   DuBois and Johnson, 169-170.

9.   BNA DEFE 41/8 Dr Otto Ambros. STIB Int Report No 112. Report on Interview with Dr. Ambros in Landsberg Prison (WCPL) March 1950.

10.   DuBois and Johnson, 339.

11.   J. Orton Kerbey, *An American Consul in Amazonia* (New York: William Edwin Rudge, 1911), 281.

12.   Howard and Ralph Wolf, *Rubber: A Story of Glory and Greed* (New York: Convici-Friede, 1936), 383.

13.   Ibid., 381-386, and Jean Le Bras, *Introduction to Rubber*, trans. J.H. Goundry (London: MacLaren and Sons, 1965), 16.

14.   Michael Thad Allen, *Hitler's Slave Lords: The Business of Forced Labour in Occupied Europe* (Stroud, Gloucestershire: Tempus, 2004), 24.

15.   Jeffrey Herf, *Reactionary Modernism: Technology, Culture, and Politics in Weimar and the Third Reich* (Cambridge: Cambridge University Press, 1986).

16.   Dwork and van Pelt, 197.

17.   BNA FO 1013/2477. IG Farben. Vol. I. Interessen Gemeinschaft [sic] Farbeninbdustrie AG Frankfurt-on-Main, May 5, 1945. Roughly $8 billion in today's values, although this may be an underestimate.

18.   Ibid. Department of Justice Economic Warfare Section, War Division. Guide for investigation of IG Farbenindustrie AG Frankfurt A/M April 15, 1945. Prepared by Hyman B. Ritchin.

19.   Ibid.

20.   These included the Nobel prize winners Paul Ehrlich, who had developed salvarsan, the first effective drug for the treatment of syphilis; Fritz Haber, famous for his work on the fixation of nitrogen and infamous for his leadership in poison gas warfare. John Cornwell, *Hitler's Scientists: Science, War and the Devil's Pact* (London: Penguin Books, 2004), 61-70; Carl Bosch who had pioneered synthetic saltpeter and petrol; and Gerhard Domagk, who had spearheaded research into new sulfa drugs Borkin, 1-2.

21.   BNA. WO 252/1127. Economic Survey of Germany, Section P, The Rubber Industry, Foreign Affairs and Ministry of Economic Warfare, Economic Advisory Branch, 1944.

22. Howard and Ralph Wolf, 385–393.
23. Ibid., 393; also TR Dawson, "Chronology of Rubber History," in P. Schidrowitz and T.R. Dawson (eds.), *History of the Rubber Industry* (Cambridge: W. Heffer and Sons, 1952).
24. See, for instance, Daniel Guerin's *Fascism and Big Business* (New York: Pathfinder Press, 1938).
25. Committee of Anti-Fascist Resistance Fighters in the German Democratic Republic, *IG Farben, Auschwitz, Mass Murder* (Berlin 1974), 36.
26. Allen, 325.
27. The preceding paragraphs are largely based on Borkin, 54–56.
28. For a discussion of the brutal purge, see Cornwell, 127–141.
29. Myriam Anissimov, *Primo Levi: Tragedy of an Optimist*, trans. Steve Cox (London: Aurum Press, 1998), 106.
30. Office of the Chief of Counsel for War Crimes, Document No N1-11784, cited in Committee of Anti-Fascist Resistance Fighters, 5. See also Anissimov, 106. Farben abandoned the scheme because they considered that the SS could not supply the amount of labor required for a large-scale industrial enterprise at that time.
31. Ibid.
32. Ibid.
33. For instance Susanna Heim, *Autarchie und Ostexpansion. Pflanzenzucht und Agrarforschung im Nazionalsozialismus* (Göttingen: Wallstein Verlag, 2002). This book deals with the Nazis' agricultural research program and its links with the policy of expansion.
34. 1936 Reichsgesetzblatt.
35. Hitler is also said to have revealed his plans for war to the German military top brass on November 5, 1937. The minutes are in the so-called Hossbach Memorandum. See A.J.P. Taylor, *The Origins of the Second World War* (Greenwich, CT: Fawcett 1965), 266–268 and 278–293. There is a debate among historians as to whether Hitler's plans to wage war existed before 1938–39. No doubt Hitler did maneuver within the international political framework, but the evidence suggests that he was bent on war sooner or later.
36. 1936 Reichsgesetzblatt.
37. BNA WO 252/1127. Graph of German Synthetic Rubber Production, 1936–1944.
38. Dwork and Van Pelt, 200.
39. BNA WO 252/1127. Dwork and Van Pelt. 201 claim 115,000 tons by late 1941, but this estimate appears to be too high.
40. Ibid.
41. George Orwell, *1984* (New York: New American Library, 1983), 220.
42. BNA. FO 837/112. Commodities Priority Committee. Sub-committee on Rubber etc., and Tyres, 1940.
43. Ibid.; also see J. Norman Parmer, *Colonial Labor Policy and Administration: A History of Labor in the Rubber Plantation Industry in Malaya, c. 1910–1941* (New York: J.J. Augustin for the Association of Asian Studies, 1960), 9.
44. BNA FO 371/22889 and FO 371/35494.
45. BNA WO 252/1127. Pie Chart, "Relative Size of the World's Rubber Industries."
46. BNA FO/837/112. Calculated at between 30,000 and 40,000 tons by 1940. This incidentally supports the contention that Stalin trusted Hitler and that the Nazi invasion caught him completely by surprise.

47.   BNA 837/112.
48.   BNA FO/Min. Economic Warfare. September 5, 1944. Economic Report on the
        German Synthetic Rubber Plant at Ludwigshafen and Plan for the German
        Synthetic Rubber Industry. Report on visit to IG Farbenindustrie Chemical Plant
        at Ludwigshafen, March 25–27, 1945, by Lt. Col. PD Patterson and US officers,
        Econ. Advisory Branch, FO/MEW.
49.   BNA FO 1078/88. Reports on rubber and synthetic rubber production and uses
        (Germany), 1942–45. Secret. Enemy Markings and Analysis Section General
        Intelligence Unit, EWD. American Embassy.

EIGHTEEN: MONOWITZ: "A BULWARK OF GERMANISM"

1.   Cited in Deborah Dwork and Robert Jan van Pelt, *Auschwitz: 1270 to the Present*
        (New York and London: W.W. Norton, 1996), 209–210.
2.   Ibid., 201.
3.   Michael Thad Allen, *Hitler's Slave Lords: The Business of Forced Labour in
        Occupied Europe* (Stroud, Gloucestershire: Tempus, 2004), 349.
4.   The Polish name is Katowice. Generally I have used the German placenames for
        Silesian towns as these are more recognizable to English-speakers.
5.   Committee of Anti-Fascist Resistance Fighters in the German Democratic
        Republic, *IG Farben, Auschwitz, Mass Murder* (Berlin: 1974), 5. See also Dwork
        and Van Pelt, 204.
6.   Dwork and Van Pelt, 201.
7.   Committee of Anti-Fascist Resistance Fighters in the German Democratic
        Republic, *IG Farben, Auschwitz, Mass Murder* (Berlin 1974), 31.
        British National Archives (BNA) AIR 51/223 Germany, Austria and
        Czechoslovakia: Oświęcim [Auschwitz] June 1944–January 1945. Rpt. on
        Oświęcim [Auschwitz]. Notes from interview British POWs brought from
        Blechhammer camp. Information from Belgian interpreter with *Bauleitung* at IG
        Farben plant.
8.   British National Archives (BNA) AIR 51/223 Germany, Austria and
        Czechoslovakia: Oświęcim [Auschwitz] June 1944–January 1945. Rpt. on
        Oświęcim [Auschwitz]. Notes from interview British POWs brought from
        Blechhammer camp. Information from Belgian interpreter with Bauleitung at IG
        Farben plant.
9.   Walther Dürrfeld, *Leistungkampf der Deutschen Betriebe 1942–1943* (Auschwitz:
        IG Farbenindustrie Aktiengesellschaft Werk Auschwitz OS, 1943), Archives of
        the State Museum of Auschwitz. This is a 64-page bound typed booklet on the
        progress of construction of the IG Farben factory at Auschwitz.
10.   Ibid.
11.   Allen, 173.
12.   John Keats, "The Fall of Hyperion – A Dream." Available online at
        http://www.john-keats.com/gedichte/the_fall_of_hyperion.htm.
13.   Dwork and van Pelt, 202.
14.   IG Farben was not the only corporation to benefit from the SS slave labor force.
        Others included Deutsche Ausüstungs-Werke, Krupps, Weichsel-Union and the
        electrical engineering firm Siemens.
15.   Ibid., 203.
16.   Allen, 325.
17.   Borkin, 112.

18.   Dwork and van Pelt, 211.
19.   Document No N1-1178-4, Office of the Chief of Counsel for War Crimes, Nuremberg. Cited in Committee of Anti-Fascist Resistance Fighters, 5. See also Dwork and van Pelt, 205–207 on discussions between IG Farben and Himmler's staff.
20.   Ibid. (Committee of Anti-Fascists, 134.)
21.   Ibid.
22.   Rudolf Hoess, *Commandant of Auschwitz: The Autobiography of Rudolf Hoess*, trans. Constantine Fitzgibbon (London: Phoenix Press, 1995), 114.
23.   Ibid.
24.   Willi Berler, *Journey through Darkness. Monowitz, Auschwitz, Gross-Rosen, Buchenwald* (Portland, OR: Vallentine Mitchell, 2004), 183.
25.   Committee of Anti-Fascists.
26.   Dwork and van Pelt, 214.
27.   Dürrfeld.
28.   Dürrfeld.
29.   BNA AIR 51/223 Economic Intelligence Note, December 17, 1943 By the end of the war, IG Farben had spent between 700 and 900 million Reichsmarks on the project.
30.   Committee of Anti-Fascists, 31.
31.   BNA AIR 51/223. Economic Intelligence Note, December 17, 1943.
32.   Borkin, 127.
33.   BNA AIR 51/223. Economic Intelligence Note, December 17, 1943.
34.   Allen, 358.
35.   For example Primo Levi, *If This Is a Man*, trans. Stuart Woolf (London: Orion Press, 1960), 136–137. Levi writes that by late 1944, following massive bombing raids, work on the Buna "stopped abruptly." It continued afterwards but "the day on which the production of synthetic rubber should have begun . . . was gradually postponed until the Germans no longer spoke about it."
36.   BNA AIR 51/223 Report on Schkopau and Auschwitz plants, May 11, 1942.
37.   Ibid., 163.

NINETEEN: "THE ONLY WAY OUT IS UP THE CHIMNEY"
1.   Willi Berler, *Journey through Darkness: Monowitz, Auschwitz, Gross-Rosen, Buchenwald* (Portland, OR: Vallentine Mitchell, 2004), 43.
2.   Sim Kessell, *Hanged at Auschwitz*, trans. Melville and Delight Wallace (London: Coronet, 1973), 54.
3.   Cited in Primo Levi, *The Periodic Table*, trans. Raymond Rosenthal (London: Abacus, 1986), 219.
4.   Leon Greenman, *An Englishman in Auschwitz* (London: Vallentine Mitchell, 2001), 55.
5.   Kessell, 93.
6.   Berler, 43.
7.   Myriam Anissimov, *Primo Levi: Tragedy of an Optimist*, trans. Steve Cox (London: Aurum Press, 1998), 195.
8.   Joseph Borkin, *The Crime and Punishment of IG Farben* (New York: The Free Press, 1978), 127.
9.   Gustav Herzog, Statement at Nuremberg. Document N1-12069 Office of Chief of Counsel for War Crimes. Cited in Cited in Committee of Anti-Fascist

Resistance Fighters in the German Democratic Republic, *IG Farben: Auschwitz, Mass Murder* (Berlin, 1974), 18.

10.   Hermann Langbein, *People in Auschwitz*, trans. Harry Zohn (Chapel Hill, NC: University of North Carolina Press, 2004), 454.

11.   Josiah E. Dubois Jr., and Edward Johnson, *Generals in Grey Suits: The Directors of the International "I.G. Farben" Cartel, Their Conspiracy and Trial at Nuremberg* (London: The Bodley Head, 1953), 181.

12.   Berler, 35–37.

13.   Langbein.

14.   Robert J. Lifton, "The Nazi Doctors: Medical Killing and the Psychology of Genocide." Available online at http://www.mazal.org/Lifton/LiftonT147.htm.

15.   Berler, 44–46; Levi, *If This Is a Man*, 21; Greenman, 44.

16.   Berler, 42.

17.   Levi, *If This Is a Man*, 27.

18.   Auschwitz I was the original camp which occupied the old Polish army barracks and Auschwitz II was the extermination camp at nearby Birkenau.

19.   Berler, 182.

20.   Peter Hayes, *Industry and Ideology* (second ed.) (Cambridge: Cambridge University Press, 2001), 354; see also Borkin, 120.

21.   Levi, *If This Is a Man*, 24.

22.   Borkin, 121.

23.   Levi, *If This Is a Man*, 176.

24.   Cited in Dubois and Johnson, 141 and 156.

25.   Cited in Ronald J. Berger, *Constructing a Collective Memory of the Holocaust: A Life History of Two Brothers' Survival* (Niwot: University Press of Colorado, 1995), 71.

26.   Cited in Berler, 184.

27.   Borkin, 125.

28.   Berler, 42–43; Hayes, 354.

29.   Levi *If This Is a Man*, 30.

30.   Ibid., 146–147.

31.   Hayes, 358.

32.   Berler, 52–58.

33.   Levi, *If This Is a Man*, 42.

34.   Berger, 74–75.

35.   Kessell, 63 and 82–83.

36.   Piotr Setkiewicz (chief archivist at the State Museum of Auschwitz), "British POWs at IG Farben" (unpublished manuscript).

37.   Levi, *If This Is a Man*, 202.

38.   British National Archives (hereinafter BNA) AIR 51/223. Germany, Austria and Czechoslovakia: Oświęcim (Auschwitz) June 1944–January 1945. January 12, 1945. Report on Oświęcim (Auschwitz). Notes from an interview with a Belgian interpreter for IG Farben who had visited the Buna.

39.   Colin Rushton, *Spectator in Hell: A British Soldier's Story of Imprisonment at Auschwitz* (Chichester, West Sussex: Summersdale, 2001).

40.   Committee of Anti-Fascist Resistance Fighters in the German Democratic Republic, *IG Farben, Auschwitz, Mass Murder* (Berlin 1974), 26.

41.   Setkiewicz.

42.   State Museum of Auschwitz Archives, HKB-Rajsko. Also BNA WO 208/4661. War Crimes Interrogation Unit. Evidence of Hans Aumeier.

43. Ronald Jones, "Caesar's Cosmic Garden" (Stockholm: Institutionen för Konstoch Musikvetenskap, Lunds Universitet, January 29 to February 20, 2000). Available online at http:www.arthist.lu.se/discontinuities/inscriptions/rj-caesar-eng.htm.

44. W. Gordon Whaley and John S. Bowen, *Russian Dandelion* [Kok-Saghyz]: *An Emergency Source of Natural Rubber* (Washington, D.C.: United States Department of Agriculture, 1947), 11.

45. For a discussion on the relationship between the KWI and the Nazis' expansionist and autarkic goals, see Susanne Heim, "Science Without Scruples," Max Planck Research Project on the History of the Kaiser Wilhelm Institute Under National Socialism (2005). Available online at http://www.mpg.de/english/illustrationsDocumentation/multimedia/mpResearch/2005/heft03/3_05MPR_6 0_65_pdf.pdf. See also Susanne Heim, *Autarchie und Ostexpansion: Pflanzenzucht und Agarfrschung im Nazionalsozialismus* (Gottingen: Wallstein Verlag, 2002).

46. Lukas Straumann, "Nazis: Pflanzenzüchtung für de End-Sieg" (2004). Available online at http://www.onlinereports.ch/2004/. Interest in the possibility of large-scale production of rubber-bearing plants had also led the Nazis to dispatch a large delegation to Casablanca in 1942 to investigate the possibility of growing the Kok-Saghyz on the North African littoral. (BNA FO 922/148. Rubber production. General. 1942.)

47. See, for instance, Peter Staudenmaier, "Fascist Ecology: The 'Green Wing' of the Nazi Party and its Historical Antecedents." Available online at http://www.spunk.orgs/texts/places/Germany/sp001630/peter.html/. See also Anna Bramwell, *Blood and Soil: Richard Walther Darré and Hitler's "Green Party"* (Bourne End, Buckinghamshire: Kensal, 1985).

48. Rudolf Hoess, *Commandant of Auschwitz: The Autobiography of Rudolf Hoess*, trans. Constantine Fitzgibbon (London: Phoenix Press, 1995), 209.

49. Bulletin de la fondation pour le mémoire de la déportation, Mémoire Vivante trimestriel, No. 41, March 2004. Available online at http://www.fmd.asso.fr/updir/37/memoire_vivante41.pdf.

50. Lifton, 308n.

51. State Museum of Auschwitz Archives. HKB-Rajsko.

52. Maria Szaglai—whose name suggests she was a Hungarian Jew—might be one of the millions who perished who have no family left to mourn them. When I read of her fate, I promised I would honor her memory; hence, I have dedicated this book to her and her baby.

53. Hayes, 358.

54. Walther Dürrfeld, *Leistungskampf der Deutschen Betriebe 1942–1943* (Auschwitz: IG Farbenindustrie Aktiengesellschaft Werk Auschwitz OS, 1943), 64.

55. Levin in Johnson and Reuband, 78–79.

56. Levi, *If This Is a Man*, 167.

57. Ibid., 141.

58. Kessell, 83.

59. "Evidence at Nuremberg," cited in Dubois and Johnson, 179.

60. Cited in Deborah Dwork and Robert Jan van Pelt, *Auschwitz: 1270 to the Present* (London and New York: W.W. Norton, 1996), 231–232.

61. Cited in Berler, 187.

62. Améry, 73.

63. Langbein, 451–452.
64. Ibid., 88.
65. Dr. Piotr Setkiewicz, personal conversation with the author, Auschwitz, December 5, 2005.
66. Dürrfeld, 57–58.
67. Ibid., 38–39.
68. Ibid., 55–56.
69. Committee of Anti-Fascist Resistance Fighters, 31.
70. United States Holocaust Memorial Museum, "Auschwitz through the Lens of the SS: Photographs of Nazi Leadership at the Camp." Online at http://www.ushmm.org/museum/exhibit/online/ssalbum/.
71. Langbein, 448–451.
72. Ibid., 452.
73. Cited in Dubois and Johnson, 218–219.
74. Levin in Johnson and Reuband, 81.
75. Berler, 187.
76. Daniel Jonah Goldhagen, *Hitler's Willing Executioners: Ordinary Germans and the Holocaust* (New York: Vintage Books, 1997).
77. Berler, 182.
78. Levi, *If This Is a Man*, 136–137.
79. Borkin, 133.
80. Berger, 84.
81. Primo Levi, *The Truce* (London: New English Library, 1962), 11–12.
82. Anissimov, 209.

TWENTY: THE ALLIED STRUGGLE FOR RUBBER IN THE SECOND WORLD WAR

1. *Congressional Record.* Proceedings and debates of the 78th Congress first session, September 28, 1943.
2. Robert Reiss, "What about Rubber?" in *Philadelphia Record* (Philadelphia: January 15, 1945).
3. Reiss, "Rolling on Ersatz," *Philadelphia Record* (Philadelphia: January 6, 1942).
4. Robert A. Solo, *Synthetic Rubber: A Case Study in Technological Development under Government Direction: Study of the Subcommittee on Patents, Trademarks, and Copyrights of the Committee of the Judiciary* (Washington, D.C.: United States Senate, U.S. Government Printing Office, 1959), 3.
5. UAA. BF Goodrich Files. "Rubber," unpublished typescript. Date of January 3, 1945 is penciled in the margin, but should probably be January 3, 1946.
6. Steven Slivinski, "The Corporate Welfare State: How the Federal Government Subsidizes U.S. Business," *Policy Analysis*, No. 592 (Washington, D.C.: The Cato Institute, May 14, 2007). Available online at http://www.cato.org. The idea is also associated with Noam Chomsky. See for instance "Letter from Noam Chomsky," *Covert Action Quarterly*, online at http://mediafilter.org.
7. British National Archives (BNA) FO 837/112 Commodities Priority Committee. Subcommittee on rubber, etc. and tyres, 1940.
8. BNA WO 252/1127. Pie chart, "Relative Size of the World's Rubber Industries" prior to 1939.
9. BNA FO 371/27860. "U.S. Dependency on Far Eastern Rubber," R. Ashton, Foreign Office minutes July 7, 1941.

10.   Cited in William Ullman, "What about Rubber?" *Westways* (January 1942).

11.   J. Orton Kerbey, *An American Consul in Amazonia* (New York: William Edwin Rudge, 1911), 281.

12.   Frank Robert Chalk, "The United States and the International Struggle for Rubber, 1914–1941," (unpublished Ph.D. History thesis) (Madison: University of Wisconsin, 1970), 238–239, 251.

13.   Jesse J. Hipple, "Revolution in Rubber?" *The Magazine of Wall Street* (New York: June 29, 1940).

14.   BNA FO 371/32593. Allied Rubber Position 1942. A.G. Pawson to FO, December 17, 1941 covering minute.

15.   *Bulletin Financier Suisse* (Lausanne: July 29, 1941). Copy in Archives d'outre-mer (AOM), Aix-en-Provence, FM AGEFORM//200/142.

16.   *Business Week* (1941). Cited in Chalk, 238.

17.   University of Akron Archives (UAA). BF Goodrich Files. BF Goodrich GA2 (Public Relations).

18.   Ibid.

19.   Solo, 7.

20.   Chalk, 252.

21.   Solo, 7.

22.   The lobby advocated the cultivation of guayule rather than building synthetic rubber factories.

23.   UAA. BF Goodrich GA2.

24.   Standard Oil of New Jersey was one of a number of successor companies formed from the Standard Oil Trust after this was broken up by an antitrust court order in 1911. Standard Oil became today's Exxon.

25.   See Ida M. Tarbell (ed. David M. Chalmers), *The History of the Standard Oil Company* (New York: Harper & Row, 1966).

26.   Chalk, 246.

27.   Frank A. Howard, *Buna Rubber: The Birth of an Industry* (New York: D. Van Nostrand, 1947), 35.

28.   Solo, 11.

29.   Standard Oil also supplied the Nazis with aviation fuel and tetraethyl lead after the outbreak of the Second World War. There is also persistent speculation about their involvement in a trust set up by SS boss Heinrich Himmler. U.S. rubber and oil companies—including Firestone—had also supplied Franco with oil, trucks, and tires on credit at the same time as the U.S. government claimed to adhere to the policy of nonintervention in Spain.

30.   Hydrocarbon Chemical and Rubber Co. of Akron.

31.   UAA. JB1-28. BF Goodrich Files. Hycar Information. See also Solo, 14.

32.   UAA. BF Goodrich Files. GA2 (Public Relations).

33.   Solo, 28.

34.   Semon was only shown Farben's "Igelite," which resembled the American "Koroseal," and was kept away from the firm's Buna S rubber.

35.   Steve Love and David Giffels, *Wheels of Fortune: The Story of Rubber in Akron* (Akron: University of Akron Press, 1999), 103.

36.   UAA. JB1-30. BF Goodrich Files. Synthetic Rubber File, 1942.

37.   "Cartels: The Menace of the Worldwide Monopoly," Part Two, *The New Republic* (March 27, 1944).

38.   Chalk, 247.

39.   "Cartels: The Menace of the Worldwide Monopoly."

40.   Joel Bakan, *The Corporation: The Pathological Pursuit of Power* (New York: Free Press, 2004).
41.   Chalk, 242.
42.   Ibid., 271, and W.J.S. Newton, "Synthetic Rubber," in P. Schidrowitz and T.R. Dawson (eds.), *History of the Rubber Industry* (Cambridge: W. Heffer and Sons, 1952), 108.
43.   UAA. BF Goodrich Files. JA1-2. Fragment of article by K.E. Knorr, "Rubber after the War," *India Rubber World*, Part I, 1943.
44.   Todd Wright, *Daily News* (New York: January 11, 1942).
45.   Knorr.
46.   Baruch figured many years earlier in an ill-fated American investment in rubber in Leopold's Congo and had served as chairman of Woodrow Wilson's war industries board in the First World War.
47.   Cited in Chalk, 237.
48.   UAA. NA1-37. BF Goodrich Files. A.C. Brett, "All in the Year's Work: A Story of Wartime Washington," unpublished typescript, 148.
49.   Harold M. Fleming, "Good News on Synthetic Rubber," *Harper's Magazine* (December 1943).
50.   UAA. JB1-35. BF Goodrich Files. Synthetic Rubber File 1946.
51.   BNA. FO 942/63. Statutory Rules and Orders 1944 No. 206. Emergency Powers (Defense) Raw Materials (Rubber).
52.   UAA, Copy in the John L. Collyer Papers. Letter to the Rubber Administrator from Diane Lucille Berntzen, January 25, 1944.
53.   Alfred Lief, *The Firestone Story: A History of the Firestone Tire & Rubber Company* (New York: McGraw-Hill, 1951), 321.
54.   Despite its pro-Axis sympathies, General Vargas's fascist Estado Novo government realized that the Allies would win the war and made a pragmatic decision to back them. See, for instance, Warren Dean, *Brazil and the Struggle for Rubber: A Study in Environmental History* (Cambridge: Cambridge University Press, 1987), 89 and 175.
55.   BNA. FO 371/32593. Allied Rubber Position 1942. Ministry of Economic Warfare to the Foreign Office, May 12, 1942.
56.   "Brazil to Move 100,000 Men, get Rubber for U.S.," *Akron Beacon Journal* (Akron: December 23, 1942).
57.   Michael Goulding, Nigel J.H., Smith, and Dennis J. Maher, *Floods of Fortune: Ecology and Economy along the Amazon* (New York: Columbia University Press, 1996), 35.
58.   Drew Pearson, "Birds, Monkeys Gum up Brazilian Rubber Supply," *Akron Beacon Journal* (Akron: July 18, 1943).
59.   Larry Rohter, "Brazil Forgets Its 'Rubber Soldiers,'" *The Age* (Melbourne: November 25, 2006). See chapter five above.
60.   UAA. JA1-15. BF Goodrich Files. The Conference Board, *Industry Record*, "Rubber and the War," Vol. III, No. 30, March 30, 1944.
61.   BNA. FO 371/28540. Portuguese Guinea Rubber.
62.   BNA. FO 371/42153. French Equatorial Africa: rubber production.
63.   National Archives of Australia (NAA). A518. Item 105016. Australian New Guinea Production Control Board – Rubber Production – Wild Rubber.
64.   Société Haitiano-Americaine de Développment Agricole.
65.   NAA. A518. Item 105019. Haiti in the Second World War; also Russ Simontowne, "Haiti to Begin Producing Cryptostagic Rubber in 1944," *Daily News* (New York, April 2, 1943).

66.   BNA FO 371/38281. Hayti [*sic*]: failure of cryptostegia rubber plantations.
67.   That is, unsustainable rates of extraction that would eventually kill the trees.
68.   NAA. A518. Item 105019. Australian New Guinea Production Control Board "Rubber Production–Slaughter Tapping," August 19, 1943.
69.   Lief, 326.
70.   Brett, 53.
71.   Cited in Lief, 280.
72.   Kyle Crichton, "No Tires Today, Brother!" *Collier's* (July 28, 1945).
73.   Chalk, 273.
74.   UAA. JA1-21. BF Goodrich Files. Synthetic Rubber. Rubber Manufacturers' Association. "Summary of Data on Synthetic Rubber."
75.   UAA. JA1-23. BF Goodrich Files. "Mushroom Rubber."
76.   NAA. A518. Item 105019.
77.   Peter Bruce MacLennan, "The Miracle of the Flying Sieves," *Liberty* (July 1, 1944).
78.   UAA. JA1-2. BF Goodrich Files. Walter E. Burton, "Odd Jobs for Rubber" (October 8, 1941), unpublished typescript.
79.   UAA. Goodyear Files. Goodyear, History, Box 4.
80.   Lief, 257 and 285–303.
81.   James McMillan, *The Dunlop Story: The Life, Death and Re-Birth of a Multinational* (London: Weidenfeld and Nicolson, 1989), 78–79.
82.   "We had to have rubber."
83.   McMillan, 80.
84.   Quoted in "Free Labor Will Win," *Akron Beacon Journal* (September 6, 1942).

TWENTY-ONE: WAR IS GOOD FOR BUSINESS
1.   University of Akron Archives (UAA). Box A1. *The Air Bag* (Akron: United Rubber Workers Local 5 (BF Goodrich), September 13, 1944).
2.   UAA. URW International President Local Unions Box 1-3, letter from C.S. Holmes, organizer, to Sherman Dalrymple, June 17, 1941.
3.   Bertolt Brecht, "Questions from a Worker Who Reads," in John Willett and Ralph Manheim (eds.) with the cooperation of Erich Fried, *Bertolt Brecht Poems 1913–1956* (New York: Eyre Methuen, 1976), 252–253.
4.   "Labor's Right to Organize Is Defended by Dalrymple," *Akron Beacon Journal* (February 28, 1936).
5.   Eric Hobsbawm, *Uncommon People: Resistance, Rebellion and Jazz* (London: Abacus, 1999), viii.
6.   Ibid.
7.   Russ Simontowne, "Giant Buna S Plant Rising on a Typhoon of Heat in Great Texas Oil Field," *Daily News* (New York: May 18, 1943).
8.   *Akron Beacon Journal* (July 12, 1942).
9.   "Akron Hiring 2000 A Week," *Akron Beacon Journal* (October 4, 1942).
10.   Rayy Mitten, "117,000 Work on Akron Jobs," *Akron Beacon Journal* (February 5, 1943).
11.   Cited in "Akron's Speedy Growth Described," *Akron Beacon Journal* (June 28, 1942).
12.   "39 Slump Pictured in Census Figures," *Akron Beacon Journal* (May 12, 1941).
13.   "Labor, Industry Fight over Bill," *Akron Beacon Journal* (February 25, 1943) and "Bricker Signs Bill," *Akron Beacon Journal* (May 16, 1943).

14. Advertisement in *Akron Beacon Journal* (August 15, 1943).
15. "Akron Crowded, Check-Up Shows," *Akron Beacon Journal* (December 26, 1943).
16. Cited in *The Air Bag* (March 1, 1942).
17. Matt Hall, "Shortages May Wipe Out 80 Pct of Restaurants," *Akron Beacon Journal* (March 21, 1943).
18. Alfred Lief, *The Firestone Story: A History of the Firestone Tire & Rubber Company* (New York: McGraw-Hill, 1951), 262.
19. *The Air Bag* (March 15, 1942).
20. "Profits Unlimited!" *United Rubber Worker*, Vol. 10, No. 4 (Akron: URWA, April 1945).
21. James Newton Thurber, *Rubber Workers" History (1935–1955)* (Akron: Public Relations Department, URCLPWA, AFL-CIO, 1956), 24.
22. "Labor Protests Increased Hours," *Akron Beacon Journal* (August 8, 1940).
23. "Article in *Time* Draws Reply," *Akron Beacon Journal* (September 27, 1942).
24. "Six-Hour Day Wiped Out for Akron War Plants," *Akron Beacon Journal* (October 3, 1942).
25. "Plan to Control Unions Shapes Up," *Akron Beacon Journal* (April 20, 1943).
26. "Pole, Father of 3 in Service Can't Work in Defense Plant," *Akron Beacon Journal* (January 4, 1942).
27. "Parley Is Sought on Alien Lay-Offs," *Akron Beacon Journal* (January 5, 1942).
28. "Unions Demand Ruling on Alien Suspensions," *Akron Beacon Journal* (December 31, 1941).
29. Helen Waterhouse, "Guard on Spies Doubled Here," *Akron Beacon Journal* (March 19, 1940).
30. *The Air Bag* (February 1, 1942).
31. Ibid. (August 16, 1942).
32. "WMC Checks Claim Akron Women Meet Discrimination in Search for War Jobs," *Akron Beacon Journal* (September 23, 1942).
33. "Solution Seen in Labor Crisis, *Akron Beacon Journal* (September 30, 1942).
34. Helen Waterhouse, "Girls Accused of Trading Riveting Gun for G-String," *Akron Beacon Journal* (November 19, 1942).
35. Wartime restrictions meant that workers could not leave their jobs without permission.
36. Rayy Mitten, "Day in WMC 'Court' Provides Unusual Study in Industrial Relations," *Akron Beacon Journal* (June 6, 1943).
37. *The Air Bag* (October 18, 1942).
38. "Union Accepts Goodyear Pact," *Akron Beacon Journal* (September 29, 1941).
39. Kathleen L. Endres, *Rosie the Rubber Worker: Women Workers in Akron's Rubber Factories during the Second World War* (Kent, Ohio: Kent State University Press, 2000), passim.
40. Ibid.
41. *The Air Bag* (February 1, 1942).
42. "Dalrymple Denies Trotskyite charge," *Akron Beacon Journal* (March 2, 1939). The article quoted extensively from a piece by B.J. Widick, a former Akron reporter, in the Trotskyist *Socialist Appeal*. Jack Widick was also the first research and educational director of the URW so it is probable that Dalrymple attended meetings he had organized for the union. Widick, who made no efforts to conceal his Marxist politics, was later employed by the UAW in Detroit. Dillard's allegations amount to "guilt by association" and Dalrymple was and remained a Democrat.

43.   "Communist? Dalrymple Steps Back," *Akron Beacon Journal* (October 4, 1944).
44.   "Finds 11,000 Reds in Northeast Ohio," *Akron Beacon Journal* (November 12, 1941).
45.   *The Air Bag* (May 3, 1942).
46.   Ibid. (June 21, 1942).
47.   Thurber, 24.
48.   *The Air Bag* (September 6, 1942).
49.   Ibid. (December 20, 1942).
50.   Ibid. (January 3, 1943).
51.   Ibid. (February 18, 1943).
52.   Ibid. (April 4, 1943).
53.   "If Rubber Workers Wages Go Up What about the Other Fifty Million?" Editorial, *Akron Beacon Journal* (March 30, 1943).
54.   UAA. Goodyear Files. Goodyear History Box 9. P.W. Litchfield, "Current Trends in Industry," address given November 20 in Boston to the New England Council, local business association organized by New England state governors in 1929.
55.   Ed Heinke, "Ask US Quiz after Beating on Trip South," *Akron Beacon Journal* (June 9, 1936).
56.   "Dalrymple Is Mobbed," *The United Rubber Worker*, Vol. 1, No. 3 (Akron: URWA, June 1936).
57.   UAA. URW Box 1–3. URW International President Local Unions. Letter to Rex Murray, URWA International President from R.J. Davidson, Director, National CIO URWA Goodyear Organizing Committee, February 21, 1941.
58.   Charlene Nevada, "The URW Hits 50: An Old Campaigner Looks Back at Those Early, Desperate Years," *Akron Beacon Journal* (September 1, 1985).
59.   "Goodyear's Gadsden Workers Vote URWA," *The United Rubber Worker*, Vol. 8, No. 5 (May 1943).
60.   UAA. URW International President Local Unions Box 1–3. Memo August 11, 1943.
61.   *The Air Bag* (June 27, 1943).
62.   *The United Rubber Worker*, Vol. 8, No. 6 (June 1943); *The Air Bag* (September 5, 1943 and October 21, 1943).
63.   "'They Have Maliciously Violated the Contract," *Akron Beacon Journal* (January 8, 1944).
64.   "Dalrymple Hit by CIO group," *Akron Beacon Journal* (April 15, 1944).
65.   *The Air Bag*, May 7, 1944. See also UAA URW Local 5, Box F2, Minutes of the Special Executive Board Meeting, September 1, 1944.
66.   "Dalrymple Refuses to Intervene," *Akron Beacon Journal* (June 29, 1945).
67.   Bruce M. Meyer, *The Once and Future Union: The Rise and Fall of the United Rubber Workers, 1935–1995* (Akron: University of Akron Press, 2002), 73.
68.   "Dalrymple in Rail Job," *Akron Beacon Journal* (February 23, 1946).
69.   "This is VJ Day, Truman Proclaims. Japs Sign, Allies Take Over," *Akron Beacon Journal* (September 2, 1945).

EPILOGUE: RUBBER IN THE POSTWAR WORLD

1.   Paul Burkett, *Marx and Nature: A Red and Green Perspective* (New York: St. Martin's Press, 1999), 257.
2.   See, for instance, Vere Gordon Childe, *The Bronze Age* (Cheshire, CT: Biblo and Tannen, 1963).

3. For a discussion on one postwar attempt at continuing the tradition, see Staughton Lynd, "A Chapter from History: The United Labor Party, 1946–1952," *Liberation* (December 1973).

4. Eric Hobsbawm, *Age of Extremes: The Short Twentieth Century, 1914–1991* (London: Abacus, 1995).

5. See, for instance, Frederick H. Gareau, "Morgenthau's Plan for Industrial Disarmament in Germany," *The Western Political Quarterly*, Vol. 14, No. 2 (June 1961): 517–534; and Henry Morgenthau, *Germany Is Our Problem: A Plan For Germany* (New York: Harper Bros., 1945).

6. Wolfgang Leonhard, *Child of the Revolution*, trans. C.M. Woodhouse (London: Ink Links, 1979), 343.

7. Christian F. Ostermann and Malcolm Byrne, *Uprising in East Germany* (Budapest: Central European University Press, 2003), 346.

8. A prewar cartel partner with Goodyear.

9. British National Archives (BNA). FO 942/63 Use of rubber – use of in Germany 1944–45. Direction on Control of Natural and Synthetic Rubber and their Products – Article 36(a). No date.

10. Ibid. Economic and Financial Branch. Field Info. Agency, Tech. Control Commission for Germany (BE) BAOR, 21 September 1945. Verbatim report of interrogation of Albert SPEER and KEHRL.

11. Walter Adams, "The Military-Industrial Complex and the New Industrial State," *The American Economic Review*, Vol. 58, No. 2, Papers and Proceedings of the Eightieth Meeting of the American Economic Association (May 1968): 662.

12. Jonathan Galloway, "The Military-Industrial Linkages of U.S.-Based Multinational Corporations," *International Studies Quarterly*, Vol. 16, No. 4 (December 1972): 491–510.

13. Two of the Monowitz camp commandants were, however, captured and punished: Heinrich Schwarz was executed by the French in 1947 at the Natzweiler camp in Alsace, and Vincent Schöttl was hanged by the Americans in 1946. Rudolf Höss, the overall commandant of the Auschwitz death and slave labor complex, was put to death in April 1947 by the Poles on the site of his crimes.

14. Willi Berler, *Journey through Darkness. Monowitz, Auschwitz, Gross-Rosen, Buchenwald* (Portland, OR: Vallentine Mitchell, 2004), 181.

15. Cited in BNA. FO 371/51185. Concentration camps at Oświeçim [Auschwitz] and Birkenau.

16. Josiah E. Dubois, Jr., and Edward Johnson, *Generals in Grey Suits. The Directors of the International "IG Farben" Cartel, their conspiracy and trial at Nuremberg* (London: The Bodley Head, 1953), 339.

17. BNA. DEFE 41/8. Dr. Otto Ambros (1951).

18. At the time of writing it is too soon to say what will be the outcome of the world financial crisis that began in 2008.

19. Nigel Harris, "World Crisis and the System," *International Socialism*, 1st Series, No. 100 (July 1977).

20. Selvakumaran Ramachandran and Bala Shanmugan, "Plight of Plantation Workers in Malaysia: Defeated by Definitions," *Asian Survey*, Vol. 35, No. 4, (April 1995): 394–407.

21. World Rainforest Movement, "Malaysia: Women Plantation Workers' Conditions in Oil Palm Plantations" (2006). Available online at http://www.wrm.org.uy.

22. United Nations, "Human Rights in Liberia's Rubber Plantations: Tapping into the Future" (May 2006). Available online at http://www.stopfirestone.org.

23.   The name Harbel is a contraction of the given names of Harvey and Idabelle Firestone. The couple's Akron mansion, demolished in 1959, was called Harbel Manor.

24.   Ariane Chemin, "Firestone in the Line of Fire," *Guardian Weekly* (London: February 24, 2006).

25.   Shashank Bengali, "Liberia: Firestone's Liberian Base Called a 'Gulag,'" *The Philadelphia Inquirer* (Philadelphia: December 31, 2006).

26.   Firestone Natural Rubber Company website. Available online at http://www.firestonenaturalrubber.com.

27.   See, for instance, Fred Redmond, "USW Helps Empower Workers on Firestone Plantation in Liberia," *The Huffington Post*, September 15, 2008. Available online at http://www.huffingtonpost.com/fred-redmond/usw-helps-empower-workers_b_125171.html.

28.   Li Kei and Yu Shunzang, "Mortality in a Chinese Rubber factory: A Prospective Cohort Study," *Journal of Occupational Health*, Vol. 44, No. 2 (2002): 76–82. Available online at http://joh.med.uoeh-u.ac.jp/e/E/44_2_03.html.

29.   Brice Pedroletti, "Beijing Buys Up Laos Rubber," *Guardian Weekly* (London: October 3, 2008).

30.   See Dan La Botz, *Mask of Democracy: Labor Suppression in Mexico Today* (Boston: South End Press, 1992), 144–146.

31.   Steve Love and David Giffels, *Wheels of Fortune: The Story of Rubber in Akron* (Akron: University of Akron Press, 1999), xiv.

32.   Ibid., xiii.

33.   Katie Byard, "Goodyear Has Tentative Deal to Stay in Akron," *Akron Beacon Journal* (December 5, 2007).

34.   Steven Greenhouse, "As Factory Jobs Disappear, Workers Have Few Options," *The New York Times* (September 13, 2003).

35.   In the mid-1970s, rival firms such as White Tire & Rubber set up non-union plants at places such as Wilson, North Carolina, and Ardmore, Oklahoma. The closure highlighted a long-term decline in which the Akron region's rubber industry was first "decentralized" to other parts of the United States.

36.   Kenneth N. Gilpin, "Rubber Workers' Union Acts to Merge with Steelworkers," *New York Times* (May 13, 1995).

37.   M. J. French, "The emergence of a U.S. Multinational Enterprise: The Goodyear Tire and Rubber Company, 1910–1939," *Economic History Review*, New Series, Vol. 40, No. 1 (February 1987): 69.

38.   Galloway.

39.   Karl Marx, *Capital: A Critique of Political Economy*, Vol. 3, Ch. 27 (London: Penguin, 1981). Cited in Paul M. Sweezy, "Monopoly Capitalism" (1987) in John Eatwell, Murray Milgate, and Peter Newman (eds.), *The New Palgrave Dictionary of Economics* (Basingstoke: Palgrave Macmillan, 1987).

40.   *India Rubber Journal*, Vol. XCII, No. 22 (London: November 28, 1936): 713.

41.   University of Akron Archives (UAA). John D. House papers, 1938-. Box 2. John D. House. URW Education Dept. Labor Scrap Book.

42.   "Goodyear Touts Expansion Plans," *Akron Beacon Journal* (June 27, 2008).

43.   Oyster Band, "Another Quiet Night in England"(Jones and Telfer) on the album *Step Outside*, 1986.

44.   Noam Chomsky, review of Joel Bakan's *The Corporation: The Pathological Pursuit of Power* (New York: Free Press, 2004). Available online at http://www.thecorporation.com/indexcofm?page_id=47.

NOTES TO PAGES 355–360

45. "Rubber Tires Compulsory," *India Rubber World*, Vol. 81, No. 5 (Akron: February 1, 1930), 69.
46. "Rubber," *Tire Review* (September 1937).
47. C. Saurer, "Conquest of the Air," *India Rubber World*, Vol. 81, No. 4 (January 1, 1930): 58.
48. Abdul Aziz bin S.A. Kadir et al (eds.), *Portrait of the Global Rubber Industry: Driving the Wheel of the World Economy* (Kuala Lumpur: International Rubber Research and Development Board, c. 2006), 180–181.
49. "Never Rode Streetcar or Bus since He Came to Akron about 25 Years Ago," *The Wingfoot Clan* (Akron: Goodyear Tire & Rubber, September 15, 1948). Copy in UAA Goodyear Files, Goodyear History Box 7.
50. Cited in Ken Nichols, "Akronites with Good Memories Know Electric Car Nothing New," *Akron Beacon Journal* (November 9, 1979).
51. John Steinbeck, *Travels with Charley: In Search of America* (London: Pan Books, 1965), 66.
52. Garnaut Climate Change Interim Report to the Commonwealth, State and Territory Governments of Australia. Available online at http://www.garnautreview.org.au/CA25734E0016A131/pages/reports-and-papers.
53. In the State of Victoria alone, emissions increased by 2.2 million tonnes in 2008. "Vic. Greenhouse Emissions Rising," ABC News, January 12, 2009. Available online at http://www.abc.net.au/news/stories/2009/01/12/2463405.htm.
54. A fact brought into stark relief by the use of heavily subsidized maize for ethanol production in the United States, which has contributed to the growing food crisis in the Third World.
55. Wade Davis and Alicia Hills Moore, "The Rubber Industry's Biological Nightmare," *Fortune Magazine* (August 4, 1997).
56. See Wade Davis, *One River: Explorations and Discoveries in the Amazon Rain Forests* (New York: Simon and Schuster, 1996).
57. Frederick Engels, *The Part Played by Labour in the Transition from Ape to Man*, in *Dialectics of Nature*, trans. Clemens Dutt (Moscow: Progress Publishers, 1934), 180.
58. See Chico Mendes and Tony Gross, *Fight for the Forest: Chico Mendes in His Own Words* (London: Latin American Bureau, 1989); and Andrew Revkin, *The Burning Season: The Murder of Chico Mendes and the Fight for the Amazon Rain Forest* (London: Collins, 1989).
59. Claudio C. Maretti et al, "From Pre-assumptions to a 'Just World Conserving Nature': The Role of Category VI in Protecting Landscapes," in Jessica Brown, Nora Mitchell, and Michael Beresford (eds.), *The Protected Landscape Approach: Linking Nature, Culture and Community* (Gland, Switzerland: International Union for the Conservation of Nature, 2005), 54.
60. Marx, *Capital*, vol. 1, 43–44.
61. Burkett.
62. Gene L. Howard, *The History of the Rubber Workers in Gadsden, Alabama, 1933–1983* (East Gadsden: URWA Local 12, 1983), 6. See also "Hypocrites Cackle," *United Rubber Worker*, Vol. 1, No. 3 (Akron: URWA, June 1936). That the threat was not merely rhetorical is attested to by the bashing of Sherman Dalrymple and other organizers and rank-and-file unionists in Gadsden.
63. "Lilly Ledbetter Turned Bitter Experience into Fair Pay Reform," *Salt Lake City Tribune* (February 2, 2009).

Index

women: as colonists, 216–18, 221; discrimination against, in Akron,
336–37; at Rajsko facility, 311; as
rubber workers, 150–51; sexual politics and, 218–20; URWA and,
417n10; wage discrimination
against, 359–60; during World War
II, 333
Woodroffe, Joseph, 31, 72, 78
Wooley, Edward Mott, 143
workers in rubber industry: in Amazon,
74; assistants and apprentices,
213–14; blacks, racism directed at,
145–46; Chinese, militancy among,
269–70; colonial employees,
204–13; colonial paternalism
toward, 245–46; in Congo, 109–15;
desertions of, 262–63; exploitation
of, on plantations, 259–60; health
and illnesses among, 248–52; housing provided for, 160; IG Farben's
civilian employees, 311–14; indentured labor for, 231–32; Indian (East
Indians), 228–29, 274–75; interracial marriages among, 217; kangani
system for, 232–33; Kongsi laborers,
242–44; labor systems for, 230–31;
in Liberia, 196, 349–50; May Day
riots of (Malaya; 1940), 272–74;
mental illness and alcoholism
among, 212–13, 215–16; migrations
of, 225–27; music and culture of,
239–41; in nineteenth century,
51–53; occupational safety and
health issues for, 53–59; primitive
protests among, 260–61; Rhemrev
Report on, 255–56; under scientific
management, 152–53; seringueiros,
78–84; slave labor used under Nazis,

299–300; strikes of (see strikes); tax
bondage system for, 234–37; violence against, 252–55; welfare capitalism and, 161; white Southerners
as, 143–47; wildcat strikes by, 341;
women as, 150–51, 216–18; during
World War II, 332; World War II
discrimination against, 335–37; post-
World War II, 351
World War I, 24–25; Germany during,
286–87; rubber embargo during,
193–94
World War II, 25; Allied capture of
Monowitz, 316–17; in Asia, 201–2;
Asian rubber plantations during,
221–22; Auschwitz during, 280,
297–99; Brazilian seringueiros during, 83–84; control over rubber during, 294–95; end of, 341–43; gap
between wages and profits during,
337–38; Hitler's plans for, 292–93;
Monowitz plant during, 300–302;
Nuremberg war crimes trials following, 284–85; rubber industry during,
14–15; rubber used in, 319–20; in
Singapore, 274; U.S. rubber policies
during, 324–30; U.S. rubber production during, 332–35; wildcat strikes
during, 341
Wrottersley, Mr., 213
Wyatt, Carl, 157

Yeap Joo Kim, 232, 240

Zeppelins, 37
Zimet, Susan, 44
Zuber, Rosalie, 311
Zumaeta, Bartolemé, 93
Zumaeta, Pablo, 98